7e

Practicing College Learning Strategies

Carolyn H. Hopper

Middle Tennessee State University

CENGAGE
Learning

Australia • Brazil • Mexico • Singapore • United Kingdom • United States

**Practicing College Learning Strategies,
Seventh Edition**

Carolyn H. Hopper

Senior Product Manager: Shani Fisher

Associate Content Developer: Kayla Gagne

Senior Media Developer: Amy Gibbons

Senior Marketing Manager: Erica Messenger

Senior Content Project Manager: Aimee Bear

Art Director: Linda May

Manufacturing Planner: Sandee Milewski

IP Analyst: Ann Hoffman

IP Project Manager: Farah Fard

Production Service: Integra Software Services Pvt. Ltd.

Compositor: Integra Software Services Pvt. Ltd.

Text Designer: Lisa Buckley

Cover Designer: Lisa Buckley

Cover Image: ©Jag_cz/Shutterstock.com

For product information and technology assistance, contact us at
Cengage Learning Customer & Sales Support, 1-800-354-9706

For permission to use material from this text or product,
submit all requests online at **www.cengage.com/permissions**.
Further permissions questions can be emailed to
permissionrequest@cengage.com.

Library of Congress Control Number: 2014944160

ISBN: 978-1-305-10959-9

Cengage Learning
20 Channel Center Street
Boston, MA 02210
USA

Cengage Learning is a leading provider of customized learning solutions
with office locations around the globe, including Singapore, the United
Kingdom, Australia, Mexico, Brazil, and Japan. Locate your local office at
www.cengage.com/global.

Cengage Learning products are represented in Canada by Nelson
Education, Ltd.

To learn more about Cengage Learning Solutions, visit **www.cengage.com**.
Purchase any of our products at your local college store or at our
preferred online store **www.cengagebrain.com**.

Printed in the United States of America
Print Number: 01   Print Year: 2014

Contents

Preface   xv

1   Making a Smooth Transition to College   1

Where Are We Going?   2
How Do I Make a Smooth Transition?   2
Your Job as a College Student   3
Essential Resources   4
    First Essential Resource: College Catalog   4
PRACTICE 1.1 Using Your College Catalog   5
    General Education, or Core Curriculum, Courses   5
All I Ever Needed to Know I Learned from My Advisor   6
PRACTICE 1.2 Using Your Student Handbook   7
PRACTICE 1.3 Using Your Schedule Book   8
PRACTICE 1.4 Using Your Syllabus   9
For Your Student Survival Kit: Assignment Log   10
    Student Services   10
Frequently Asked Questions: Some FAQs by First-Year College Students or Transfers   10
Higher Education   11
Critical Thinking: About Higher Education   11
    Your Responsibilities?   12
    Modeling the Learning Process: Your Map for Learning How to Learn   12
    Student Power   14
Some Strategies for Success   14
    General Survival Tips to Make Your Transition Smoother   14
    Tips for Taking Notes and Reading Textbooks   15
PRACTICE 1.5 Evaluating Your Classroom Savvy   16
PRACTICE 1.6 Unsavvy Behavior   17
    Your Grade Point Average   17
    How to Calculate Your GPA   18
PRACTICE 1.7 Grade Point Average Practice   18
    E-mail Etiquette   20
    Tips for Online Courses   21
    The BREATHE System: A Tool to Help You Focus   22
    The Big 3: Posture, Neck and Shoulder Muscles, and Breath Support   23
Review—Where did we go?   25
Study Guide 25 • Higher Education Vocabulary Words 27 • Parallel Parking 28 • Evaluating Learning Outcomes 28 • Your Student Tip for This Chapter 28

2 Practicing the Principles of Time Management   29

Where Are We Going?   30

The Importance of Managing Your Time   30

PRACTICE 2.1 Beginning Steps in Time Management   31

Critical Thinking: About Time   31

Scheduling: The Road Map or GPS for Time Management   32

Benefits of Scheduling   32

For Your Student Survival Kit: Principles of Scheduling   33

PRACTICE 2.2 Time Log   35

PRACTICE 2.3 Time Log Analysis   35

Planning a Master Schedule   35

PRACTICE 2.4 Master Schedule Worksheet   36

Putting Your Master Schedule into Practice   37

PRACTICE 2.5 Master Schedule Follow-Up   38

PRACTICE 2.6 Master Schedule   40

Agenda, Large Calendar, To-Do List   41

Critical Thinking: About Prioritizing   42

Career Connections   43

Time Wasters: Side Trips, Road Blocks, and Detours   43

Plan Your Attack on Time Wasters   43

PRACTICE 2.7 My Plan for Time Wasters   44

Review—Where did we go?   45

Modeling the Learning Process 45 • Study Guide 46 • Case Study: What's Your Advice? 47 • Parallel Parking 47 • Evaluating Learning Outcomes 49 • Your Student Tip for This Chapter 49

3 Practicing Critical Thinking   51

Where Are We Going?   52

The Necessity of Critical Thinking   52

The Process of Decision Making   53

For Your Student Survival Kit: Critical Thinking   54

PRACTICE 3.1 The Decision-Making Process   55

PRACTICE 3.2 Decisions About Grades   55

Career Connections   55

PRACTICE 3.3 Thinking About Thinking   56

Fact and Opinion   56

PRACTICE 3.4 Fact or Opinion?   56

Levels of Learning: Bloom's Taxonomy   57

Making Connections   59

PRACTICE 3.5 Levels of Learning   59

PRACTICE 3.6 Asking and Predicting Questions   60

Making Connections   61

Review—Where did we go?   61

Modeling the Learning Process 61 • Study Guide 61 • Case Study: What's Your Advice? 63 • Parallel Parking 64 • Evaluating Learning Outcomes 65 • Your Student Tip for This Chapter 65

4 Setting Goals   67

Where Are We Going?   68

Why Set Goals?   68

PRACTICE 4.1 What Does It Take to Make You Happy?   69

Locus of Control   70

PRACTICE 4.2 Locus of Control   70

PRACTICE 4.3 Why Are You Here?   71

PRACTICE 4.4 Dreaming   71

When Should You Set Goals?   72

Examining Areas of Your Life   72

35-Minute Brainstorming Activity   72

Themes of Goals   74

PRACTICE 4.5 Brainstorm Follow-Up   74

Some Guidelines for Writing Goals   75

Making Dreams Come True   75

Career Connections   75

For Your Student Survival Kit: Writing SMART Goals   76

PRACTICE 4.6 SMART Goal Setting: Let's Think This Through   77

PRACTICE 4.7 Practice Writing an Action Plan   77

PRACTICE 4.8 Writing SMART Goals   78

Tips for Achieving Goals   79

PRACTICE 4.9 Making Your Goals Visible   79

Making Connections   79

Setting Goals for Difficult Classes   79

Critical Thinking: About a Difficult Class   81

Review—Where did we go?   82

Modeling the Learning Process 82 • Study Guide 82 • Case Study: What's Your Advice? 83 • Parallel Parking 84 • Evaluating Learning Outcomes 85 • Your Student Tip for This Chapter 85

5 Learning Principles   87

Where Are We Going?   88

Basic Information About the Brain: Providing Background for Learning Principles   88

Making Connections   91

For Your Student Survival Kit: Learning Principles: Quick Reference Guide   93

Applying the Learning Principles   94

Starting the Connections   94

Interest   94

Intent to Remember   95

Basic Background   96

PRACTICE 5.1 Starting the Connection   97

Controlling the Amount and Form of Information   97

Selectivity   97

Meaningful Organization   98

PRACTICE 5.2 Controlling the Amount and Form of Information Selectivity   99

Strengthening Neural Connections   100

Recitation   101

Visualization   101

Association   102

PRACTICE 5.3 Strengthening Neural Connections   102

Allowing Time to Solidify Pathways   103

Consolidation   104

Distributed Practice   105

PRACTICE 5.4 Consolidation   105

PRACTICE 5.5 Putting Learning Principles to Use   106

Career Connections   107

Making Connections   108

How Memory Works: Putting Principles in Perspective   109

For Your Student Survival Kit: Memory   **110**

Stage One: Getting Information into the Brain—Reception into Short-Term Memory   111

Stage Two: Processing from Short-Term to Long-Term Memory   112

Stage Three: Retrieving from Long-Term Memory   114

PRACTICE 5.6 How Memory Works   116

Critical Thinking: About Retrieval   117

Review—Where did we go?   117

Modeling the Learning Process 117 • *Study Guide 118* • *Case Study: What's Your Advice? 120* • *Parallel Parking 120* • *Evaluating Learning Outcomes 121* • *Your Student Tip for This Chapter 121*

6   Processing Information from Lectures   123

Where Are We Going?   124

Going Beyond Memory: Processing Information   124

Four Essential Functions for Learning   125

Essential Functions of Learning and the Question in the Margin System   126

Relating Information Processing to Learning Principles   127

PRACTICE 6.1 Modeling the Learning Process (Reflecting)   127

Listening Skills   129

PRACTICE 6.2 Obstacles to Listening   130

PRACTICE 6.3 Improving Your Listening   131

Making Connections 132

Taking Notes 133

PRACTICE 6.4 Why Take Notes? 133

Using the Question in the Margin System for Lectures 134

Controlling the Amount and Form of Information in Your Notes 134

Before You Begin 134

Six Steps 135

PRACTICE 6.5 Note Taking 136

Sample Notes—Question in the Margin 140

Critical Thinking: About Taking Notes 140

PRACTICE 6.6 Question in the Margin System 141

For Your Student Survival Kit: Summary Sheet for Question in the Margin: Lecture Notes 142

Career Connections 143

PRACTICE 6.7 Learning Principles Used in the Question in the Margin System 143

Review—Where did we go? 144

Modeling the Learning Process 144 • Study Guide 144 • Case Study: What's Your Advice? 146 • Parallel Parking 146 • Evaluating Learning Outcomes 146 • Your Student Tip for This Chapter 147

7   Processing Information from Textbooks 149

Where Are We Going? 150

PRACTICE 7.1 Differences in Gathering Information from Lectures and from Textbooks 150

For Your Student Survival Kit: Some Basic Reading Strategies 151

For Your Student Survival Kit: Notes about E-texts and Reading on Screens Rather Than Paper 151

Using the Question in the Margin System for Textbooks 152

Starting the Connections 152

Controlling the Amount and Form of Information 152

PRACTICE 7.2 Understanding the Steps of Question in the Margin for Textbooks 154

Making Connections 155

PRACTICE 7.3 Practice Using the Question in the Margin System for Textbooks 155

For Your Student Survival Kit: Summary Sheet for Question in the Margin: Textbooks 156

For Your Student Survival Kit: Summary for Both Lecture and Textbook Question in the Margin 158

PRACTICE 7.4 Do You Understand How the Question in the Margin System Works? 158

Mapping 159

PRACTICE 7.5 Practice with Mapping 162

PRACTICE 7.6 Mapping the Question in the Margin System 164

Career Connections 164

Promoting Concentration   164

    Internal Distractions   164

PRACTICE 7.7 Setting Goals to Promote Concentration   165

    External Distractions   166

PRACTICE 7.8 Identifying External Distractions   166

PRACTICE 7.9 Discovering the Best Place for You to Study   166

For Your Student Survival Kit: Study Habits Analysis   167

Review—Where did we go?   168

Modeling the Learning Process 168 • Study Guide 168 • Case Study: What's Your Advice? 170 • Parallel Parking 170 • Evaluating Learning Outcomes 171 • Your Student Tip for This Chapter 172

8   Learning Styles   173

Where Are We Going?   174

Why Determine Learning Styles?   174

Input Preference: Sensory Modes of Learning   175

PRACTICE 8.1 Sensory Modality Inventory   176

    The Auditory Learner   178

    The Visual Learner   178

    The Kinesthetic Learner   179

PRACTICE 8.2 Sensory Mode Reflection   179

Processing Preference: Analytic or Global   180

Differences Between Analytic (Left) and Global (Right)   180

PRACTICE 8.3 How Does Your Brain Prefer to Process Information?   181

    Linear versus Holistic Processing   183

    Sequential versus Random Processing   183

    Symbolic versus Concrete Processing   184

    Logical versus Intuitive Processing   184

    Verbal versus Nonverbal Processing   184

    Reality-Based versus Fantasy-Oriented Processing   185

    Temporal versus Nontemporal Processing   185

PRACTICE 8.4 Global and Analytic Drivers   186

Response Preference: Multiple Intelligences   186

    Eight Kinds of Intelligence   187

Making Connections   188

PRACTICE 8.5 Multiple Intelligences   189

PRACTICE 8.6 Determining Your Multiple Intelligence Strengths   190

Making Connections   191

Career Connections   191

Critical Thinking: About Multiple Intelligence and Careers   193

Social Learning Preference: Alone or in Groups   194

PRACTICE 8.7 Social Inventory: Study First Alone or in a Group?   195

For Your Student Survival Kit: Your Learning Profile   196

Review—Where did we go? 197

Modeling the Learning Process 197 • *Study Guide* 197 • *Case Study: What's Your Advice?* 199 • *Parallel Parking* 199 • *Evaluating Learning Outcomes* 200 • *Your Student Tip for This Chapter* 200

9 Test-Taking Strategies   201

Where Are We Going?   202

Making Connections   **202**

Types of Tests   204

PRACTICE 9.1 Preparing for Tests   205

Critical Thinking: About Tests   206

PRACTICE 9.2 Self-Analysis: Preparing for Tests   207

Budgeting Your Test-Taking Time   208

    Preview the Test   208

    Budget Your Time   209

PRACTICE 9.3 Budgeting Your Time   209

Following Directions   210

PRACTICE 9.4 Following Directions   210

For Your Student Survival Kit: Survival Tips for Taking Tests   **211**

PRACTICE 9.5 Strategies for Taking Any Test   211

Strategies for Objective Tests   212

    Strategies for True/False Tests   212

PRACTICE 9.6 Practice with Double Negatives   213

For Your Student Survival Kit: Summary of Strategies for True/False Statements   **215**

PRACTICE 9.7 Mapping True/False Strategies   215

PRACTICE 9.8 Practice with True/False Tests   215

For Your Student Survival Kit: Strategies for Multiple-Choice Tests   **217**

PRACTICE 9.9 Practice with Multiple-Choice Questions   218

    Strategies for Fill-in-the-Blank Questions   219

PRACTICE 9.10 Practice with Fill-in-the-Blank Questions   219

    Strategies for Matching Questions   220

PRACTICE 9.11 Practice with Matching Questions   220

Reviewing Returned Tests   220

    A Dozen Reasons to Review a Returned Test   220

Making Connections   **221**

PRACTICE 9.12 Summary for Objective Test Strategies   222

Predicting Test Questions   222

PRACTICE 9.13 Possible Test Questions Dealing with Test-Taking Strategies   223

Strategies for Essay Tests   224

    Basic Strategies for Writing Answers to Essay Tests   224

    For Your Student Survival Kit: Checklist for Essay Tests   **224**

    Direction Words   224

PRACTICE 9.14 Applying the Direction Words   226

PRACTICE 9.15 Practice with Direction Words   227

Making Connections   228

PRACTICE 9.16 Practice with Topic Sentences and Direction Words   228

PRACTICE 9.17 Practice with Evaluating Answers to Essay Questions   230

Critical Thinking: About Preparing for Exams   231

Career Connections   232

Final Exams   232

For Your Student Survival Kit: Final Exam Study Organizer   233

Review—Where did we go?   234

Modeling the Learning Process 234 • Study Guide 234 • Case Study: What's Your Advice? 236 • Parallel Parking 236 • Evaluating Learning Outcomes 237 • Your Student Tip for This Chapter 237

10 Managing Stress   239

Where Are We Going?   240

Stress: What Is It?   240

Analyzing Your Stress   241

Making Connections   242

Critical Thinking: About Stress   242

PRACTICE 10.1 Developing a Plan of Action   243

Coping Strategies for Alleviating Stress Symptoms   243

PRACTICE 10.2 Using the Strategies for Alleviating Stress   246

Lifestyle Habits That Help Reduce Stress: Try a Few!   246

PRACTICE 10.3 Analyzing Lifestyle Habits   247

Making Connections   248

Assertiveness   248

PRACTICE 10.4 Script-Writing Practice   250

Career Connections   250

For Your Student Survival Kit: A Plan for Combatting Stress   251

Review—Where did we go?   252

Modeling the Learning Process 252 • Study Guide 252 • Case Study: What's Your Advice? 253 • Parallel Parking 253 • Evaluating Learning Outcomes 254 • Your Student Tip for This Chapter 254

11 Information Literacy   255

Where Are We Going?   256

What Is Information Literacy?   256

A Systematic Approach to the Research Process   257

　　Step 1: Identifying and Finding Background Information on Your Topic   257

　　Step 2: Using the Library Catalog to Find Books   257

Step 3: Using Indexes and Databases to Find Periodical Articles   258

Step 4: Finding Internet Resources   259

Step 5: Evaluating Your Sources   261

Step 6: Citing Your Sources   261

PRACTICE 11.1 Choosing and Narrowing a Topic   262

PRACTICE 11.2 Finding Books About Your Topic   262

Finding Periodicals   263

PRACTICE 11.3 Finding Articles in Periodicals   264

Finding Articles in Newspapers   264

PRACTICE 11.4 Practice Using Newspaper Sources   265

PRACTICE 11.5 Finding Internet Articles   265

Career Connections   266

PRACTICE 11.6 Practicing What You Have Learned   266

Review—Where did we go?   267

Modeling the Learning Process 267 • Study Guide 267 • Case Study: What's Your Advice? 269 • Parallel Parking 270 • Evaluating Learning Outcomes 270 • Your Student Tip for This Chapter 270

Appendix A: Principles of Studying Math   271

Bibliography   281

Index   283

Preface

Purposes and Goals for This Text

Having taught learning strategies for more than 30 years now, I can honestly say that not a semester has passed that I have not learned from my students. They are innovative, resilient, and want to be successful in college. Many need guidance in the strategies that will help them do their best and efficiently use the time they have. As a professor, writer, and researcher, I have written this text to share what I have learned about learning how to learn and strategies for being a successful student.

Practicing College Learning Strategies models the learning strategies that will give students the foundation for learning how to learn throughout college and becoming lifelong learners. The text and activities in *Practicing College Learning Strategies*, Seventh Edition, are thoughtfully constructed using brain-compatible strategies. Brain-compatible learning is based on how research in neuroscience suggests our brains naturally learn best. This focus encourages students to discover how they learn best, so they can bring that skill of learning to all of their other classes in college and to their life beyond.

By framing the text within the theme of "Being in the Driver's Seat," *Practicing College Learning Strategies* serves as a motivational tool, reminding students that they are in control of their learning. They must be the driver in their life in order to get where they want to go and succeed in college.

In the journey through college, students will discover that learning involves more than getting information. It involves examining new information, making it personal, and determining where it fits into their own experiences. It then requires converting comprehension into a plan or strategy and actively testing the strategy. Learning requires full participation and keeping eyes on the road. The Seventh Edition of *Practicing College Learning Strategies* models this learning process by clearly and concisely presenting the essential information students need to successfully navigate their way through their college education. Structured activities and practices will guide them in the reflection process to make the information personal and useful and provide practice in developing strategies for learning and in testing those strategies.

The straightforward, brief explanations and structured activities modeling the learning process make this text especially useful for first-time college students or returning adults. However, the brain-based academic orientation makes it valuable for anyone who wants to get the most out of his or her college journey.

I'm especially excited about the Seventh Edition's increased focus on skills students need to be successful. This introduction will help students (and instructors) clearly understand that they are not just learning about a topic, but are also discovering how it connects to the other strategies they have learned and will learn later in the text. This interconnectivity shows students the immediate relevance and importance of the strategies in their lives and will help motivate them to continue to learn. The body of each chapter provides practical application and practice of the strategies discussed to demonstrate how students can use them in their everyday lives. Finally, the chapter rounds out with a review section called Where Did We Go? that will help students systematically review and critically think about what they just learned and practiced.

Major Themes

There are two major themes that drive the Seventh Edition. Each theme has been integrated into the text to best help students learn and succeed in college.

Putting Students in the Driver's Seat

Take a minute to consider the following situations. How many of these can you relate to?

- Planning out your route carefully on a map before you get in your car
- Driving in an unfamiliar city with confusing signs
- Getting stuck in traffic on your way to an important meeting
- Unexpected road construction that forces you on a detour
- Carpooling with people you don't know

Now, think about these common issues that college students face:

- Choosing a major and the classes to take next semester
- Navigating around the college campus and finding where classes are
- Managing time in and outside the classroom
- Meeting new people and experiencing new things
- Managing stress and unexpected life events

See any similarities between the above lists? Brain research has found that one of the most powerful ways to learn is by using analogies. The analogy used throughout the Seventh Edition is that college is a journey or road trip and each student must be the driver if the student is to be successful. A passenger may come along for the ride, but the driver is in control and accepts responsibility. The driver does whatever is necessary in order to reach the destination: chooses the route, follows the road signs, steps on the gas and the brakes, fuels up, and asks for directions. The driver fights fatigue and stress and experiences the confusion of driving in an unfamiliar place. But the driver also owns the whole experience of the drive, every curve and bump and every complex intersection. We will use the driver analogy to think critically about student responsibilities in each chapter of the text.

Brain-Compatible Learning

In his book, *Human Brain and Human Learning* (1983), Leslie Hart argues that teaching without an awareness of how the brain learns is like

designing a glove with no sense of what a hand looks like—its shape, how it moves. Brain-compatible, or brain-based, learning is the central focus of the Seventh Edition of *Practicing College Learning Strategies*.

In keeping with the straightforward style of the text, the discussion of learning principles in Chapter 5 includes enough explanation of neurological research on memory to empower students. It provides them with a basic understanding of how to make maximum use of their memory and thereby improve their job performance, school achievement, and personal success. Students' idea of learning has often been limited to memorizing or comprehending a new concept.

The Seventh Edition continues to expand use of what James Zull calls "four essentials of learning." Students gather new information and analyze it, and many students think their learning is complete with the completion of these two steps. However, students must learn to go further and use this new information to form ideas and hypotheses. The learning process is not really complete until these ideas have actually have been tested in action.

Order and Content of Chapters

The order of all chapters in *Practicing College Learning Strategies* has been carefully vetted with reviewers and tested against current students.

The first four chapters of the Seventh Edition help students adjust to the new environment of college. These four chapters, Making A Smooth Transition to College, Practicing the Principles of Time Management, Practicing Critical Thinking, and Setting Goals are designed to get students familiar as quickly as possible with the key skills they'll need in order to succeed in the first few weeks of college.

Chapter 5, Learning Principles, is the core chapter on brain-compatible learning and introduces some basic functions of the brain so students understand not only what they need to do to aid memory, but also why the principles work. The ten learning principles introduced in this chapter act as a guide for students to begin the learning process and as a foundation for developing learning strategies that work.

Chapter 6, Processing Information from Lectures, and Chapter 7, Processing Information from Textbooks, both build on the learning principles in Chapter 5 by demonstrating how students need to use those principles in order to best develop strategies on how to process information from lectures and textbooks. With a focus on note taking and the Question in the Margin System, these two chapters provide students with the knowledge on how to process the information they'll need to succeed in college.

Learning styles are discussed in Chapter 8 to help students determine their preferences for learning. This chapter helps students determine their preferences in how they input, process, and respond to new information, three elements that brain researchers agree are necessary for optimal learning. These elements encourage an approach that helps expand the student's learning styles. The three approaches to learning styles are consistent with the learning process of gathering information and processing it that students learned in the previous two chapters and shows them how to activate that information, which will be useful in the next chapter on test taking.

Chapter 9, Test-Taking Strategies, introduces strategies to help students excel on different kinds of tests, including final exams. Building on the previous strategies that students have learned, this chapter is perfectly poised to show students how the strategies they've learned will help them succeed on their tests.

Although students experience stress and need to know specifics about their higher education environment during the first days of school, the chapters on these subjects are purposely placed toward the end of the text. It has been my experience that students get a bit "antsy" at the beginning of the semester and want to learn skills they can use immediately. Having addressed those skills in Chapters 5–9, they are now seeking ways to practice them and to deal with the stress that higher education presents. Chapter 10 therefore discusses strategies for managing stress and includes a new section on assertiveness training to help students learn to say "no" when they need to. By building upon the previous strategies, including time management, critical thinking, and setting goals, this chapter shows students that the skills they have learned will not only allow them to succeed but will also help them manage their stress.

Finally, a fully revised Chapter 11, Information Literacy, wraps up the text by covering a systematic approach for information literacy and research to help students have the tools they need to be an effective student in the information age. This chapter highlights important critical-thinking strategies for evaluating sources and documenting research.

Appendix A addresses some unique strategies needed for studying math. It is common for students to believe that they are not good at math. The appendix begins with an inventory evaluating students' math study skills, and here many students discover that it may not be math that is the problem; rather it is their approach to studying math that prevents them from being successful. Appendix A walks students back through each textbook topic to discover ways to fine-tune strategies they have already learned and to apply them to the math classroom.

Special Features and Pedagogical Aids

The Seventh Edition includes carefully constructed features that help focus student learning and reinforce the themes of the book.

Learning Outcomes

Clearly defined learning outcomes form a framework for learning by providing instructors and students with standards and expectations for every lesson. Each chapter begins with a list of what students will learn in the chapter. At the end of the chapter, the feature "Evaluating Learning Outcomes" allows students to see exactly what they've learned and accomplished in the text. These learning outcomes should be the basis for selecting content, classroom activities, and assessments such as chapter or unit tests and final projects or exams.

Student Tips

Because students want proof that the strategies really work, each chapter includes tips from students who have actually tried the strategies and who have found unique ways to use them in the college setting. Giving advice about using strategies successfully helps give students ownership of new concepts and confidence to apply them to new situations.

Making Connections

This critical-thinking feature combines the "Making Connections" and "Making It Concrete" features from the Sixth Edition. Making Connections helps students analyze and synthesize what they've learned and apply new concepts or skills to other courses or situations in their life.

Virtual Field Trips

Updated for the Seventh Edition, the "Virtual Field Trip" features provide opportunities to expand textbook information (without adding length) and give students more opportunities to adapt, personalize, and evaluate strategies. Many of the Virtual Field Trips in the Seventh Edition include more activities and videos. These guided Internet activities help students, both on campus and off, to find useful and reliable resources, engage in purposeful Internet searches, and build both confidence and skill in using Internet resources. The Virtual Field Trips also allow students to apply the learning model to student success topics such as campus safety, health issues, and budgeting. In addition, these features allow flexibility to use this text as the core for a student success course and, at the same time, include other important student success issues.

Brain Bytes

"Brain Byte" features appear in the margin throughout the text, providing bite-sized factoids relevant to the chapter material. Updated for the Seventh Edition, these features highlight topics that brain researchers have discovered.

Modeling the Learning Process

In each chapter, students are guided through all four steps of the process with the exercises and activities and debriefed at the end of each chapter with the "Modeling the Learning Process" feature so that they become more aware of the process they just used. They see that the effect is ownership of information, not just memorization. They move from receivers of knowledge to producers of knowledge. By modeling the process repeatedly, students should be able to more easily transfer the learning model to their other classes.

Study Guide

Each chapter includes a "Study Guide" (previously titled "Summary") that students fill out in order to remember content in the chapter and prepare for tests. This study guide is modeled on the Question in the Margin System and helps students learn to develop their own effective study methods using the Question in the Margin System for their other courses.

Parallel Parking

Each chapter in the Seventh Edition ends with a critical-thinking exercise that applies the driving analogy to concepts learned in the chapter. Brain research confirms that using metaphors or analogies is one of the best ways for students to demonstrate that they understand a new concept. We know that the brain needs to know that it knows something. We also know that the only way new learning is processed into long-term memory is to make new connections to connections that are already in the brain. The "Parallel Parking" exercise at the end of each chapter promotes this kind of critical thinking. The analogy that students need to assume the responsibilities of drivers runs throughout the text. The "Parallel Parking" feature is a natural extension of this analogy, which encourages students to think critically about how the strategies used in each chapter and their experience as college students parallel various driving terms.

Case Study: What's Your Advice?

Each chapter summary, with the exception of Chapter 1, is followed by a case study exercise in which students synthesize and evaluate what they have learned in the chapter so that they can provide advice to a fictional fellow student.

New to the Seventh Edition

- **New!** Chapter 10, Managing Stress, has been revised to include a new section on assertiveness training to teach students when and how to say "no," in college and in life.
- **New!** Chapter 11, Information Literacy, includes a new section on how to research job possibilities.
- **New!** Redesigned interior reflects the book's driving motif to remind students that learning is a journey and they must be in the driver's seat, looking for road signs, planning ahead for where they are going, and reflecting on where they went.
- **New!** "Road Map to Success" is a new chapter opener map that provides an easy to follow guide of the chapter's main topics. Clearly listed learning outcomes introduce exactly what the student will learn in each chapter.
- **New!** A new introduction, "Where Are We Going?" facilitates critical thinking by framing every chapter in terms of the other content

in the book so the student understands where and why each strategy fits with the other strategies they are learning.

- **New!** "Career Connections" is a new feature that shows students how the skills they are learning will now apply in the career world.
- **New!** The "For Your Student Survival Kit" feature highlights key strategies within the chapter to encourage students to save the information so they can reference it after class.
- **New!** Exercises have been renamed "Practice" in order to highlight the need to *practice* the strategies in the book, not just memorize them.

Additional Resources

The Seventh Edition offers additional resources to both students and instructors.

For Students

New! MindTap for *Practicing College Learning Strategies* MindTap is a personalized teaching experience with relevant assignments that guide students to analyze, apply, and improve thinking, allowing you to measure skills and outcomes with ease.

- Personalized Teaching: Becomes yours with a Learning Path that is built with key student objectives. Control what students see and when they see it. Use it as-is or match to your syllabus exactly—hide, rearrange, add, and create your own content.
- Guide Students: A unique learning path of relevant readings, multimedia, and activities that move students up the learning taxonomy from basic knowledge and comprehension to analysis and application.

    To assist students with learning course content:

    - Chapter learning objectives
    - Journal-based writing activities
    - "Virtual Field Trip" activities that ask students to research key chapter topics online and report back on their findings

    To assess student learning:

    - Interactive versions of the Practice activities and study guides
    - Additional interactive chapter quizzes
    - Chapter homework assignments powered by Aplia

- Promote Better Outcomes: Empower instructors and motivate students with analytics and reports that provide a snapshot of class progress, time in course, engagement, and completion rates.

College Success Factors Index (CSFI) 2.0 The College Success Factors Index (CSFI) 2.0, developed by Edmond Hallberg and Kaylene Hallberg, is an online survey that students complete to assess their patterns of behavior and attitudes in ten key areas. These areas have been proven by research to affect student outcomes for success in higher education. Accessed online, the CSFI is a useful assessment tool for demonstrating the difference your college success course makes in students' academic success. At the start of the course, the CSFI helps assess incoming students and allows you to tailor your course topics to meet their needs. As a post-test, it provides an opportunity for you (and your students) to measure progress. An Early Alert reporting option identifies students who are most at risk of getting off course in college. This information enables you to intervene at the beginning of the semester to increase students' likelihood of success—and improve retention rates. For more information about CSFI, visit our website at www.cengage.com/success/csfi2.

Study Skills Help Page You and your students may also want to log onto The Study Skills Help Page, the website I developed for the course I teach using this text: http://capone.mtsu.edu/studskl. This website includes Practice Tests, games, and videos to help students study more effectively and more efficiently. Strategies for Success includes tips on being successful in college. A list of Links to Other Useful Sites will help students explore reputable websites that will help them become better students.

For Instructors

The Instructor Companion Site is a comprehensive website that puts teaching tools and resources at your fingertips. By logging in at *CengageBrain.com*, you will find the following valuable instructor resources:

- The complete **Instructor Resource Manual**. Following the structure of the main text, the IRM provides teaching suggestions, additional activities, and exercises by chapter, in addition to the answers to the text's chapter summary questions.
- **MindTap walk-through guide**, which will include strategies for using MindTap in your course.
- **Transition Guide**. The transition guide for the Seventh Edition helps you move from the Sixth Edition to the Seventh Edition.
- **Sample Syllabi** to help you plan out your course.
- **Practice Unit Quizzes** that you can print for your students.
- **Answer Key to the Practice Unit Quizzes** to make grading easier.
- **Links to the Virtual Field Trips** that you can use in class.
- **PowerPoint Presentations** organized by topic and by chapter in order to aid lectures and give you the flexibility to design your course in the way you want.

TeamUP

An additional service available with the text is access to TeamUP, a group of experienced educators who provide an unparalleled suite of services offering you flexible and personalized assistance. Whether online, on the phone, or on campus, TeamUP delivers high-quality support including faculty development events, student success training, and material integration support.

The TeamUP Professional Educators have a wealth of experience teaching and administering the first-year course. They can provide help in establishing or redesigning your student success program. They provide course design assistance, instructor training, teaching strategies, annual conferences, and much more. Learn more about TeamUP today by calling 1-800-528-8323 or visiting http://www.cengage.com/teamup/.

Acknowledgments

I am indebted to many people for the preparation of this book. This text is the result of suggestions from students and faculty involved in the Academic Enrichment courses at Middle Tennessee State University (MTSU), as well as colleagues I have met across the country at workshops and conferences. The success of the learning strategies program at MTSU has been very much a team effort. I have benefited greatly from my association with the talented and caring members of the University College faculty and staff. I give thanks specifically to my colleagues, Angie Kleinau, Andrea Bell, Jeanne Massaquoi, Patsy Davis, and Carla Hatfield, who can be credited with many of the ideas found here, and whose understanding of how crucial it is for students to "learn how to learn" has made the course successful for thousands of students.

And much of the credit for this text goes to the students in the learning strategies classes at MTSU, who continue to keep me fascinated with their development and help me grow in my understanding of how students learn.

Each revision has been student-driven. The longer I teach, the more I learn from my students. Revision has been a direct result of students demonstrating the learning process. They have taken suggestions from the text and processed that information, tried it, adjusted it, and made it work for themselves. Then they have made suggestions to me about how to clarify or adjust the information to perhaps make it easier for other students on the path of learning how to learn. They truly demonstrate that the learning process moves students from being receivers of knowledge to producers of knowledge.

I particularly want to acknowledge the insights given to me these last four years by my granddaughter Chelsey Elliott, who graduated from MTSU this year, and has given me a fresh perspective on the needs of college students entering higher education.

I am particularly indebted to the research of Dr. James Zull at Case Western Reserve University. His book, *The Art of Changing the Brain* (Stylus, 2002), provides concreteness to the complex and validity to what I teach and share with colleagues.

Authors Judy Willis, Eric Jensen and Karen Markowitz, Pierce Howard (*The Owner's Manual for the Brain*), and Eric Chudler (Neuroscience for Kids, http://faculty.washington.edu/chudler/neurok.html) were generous in granting permission to share their findings on what brain research says about learning. A special thanks to Ralph Hillman, the Voice Doc (and friend), for sharing the BREATHE System. The brief introduction included in Chapter 1 in this text does not do justice to this system. I hope you will examine it further at http://thebreathesystem .com/. Ralph Hillman reminds me that no exercise in the text should begin without the Big 3 of the Breathe System: Check your posture, relax your shoulders and neck, and breathe! Thanks to Laurie Witherow and Ginger Corley, who once again granted permission to use their wonderful "All I Ever Needed to Know I Learned from My Advisor."

I can't begin to thank the wonderful staff at Cengage for their vision, suggestions, and persistence. Thanks to Shani Fisher for her continued support and thoughtful input. Rebecca Donahue's perception and creativity made the creation of the Seventh Edition fresh and exciting for me. Special thanks as well to Aimee Bear, Kayla Gagne, Amy Gibbons, Sreejith Govindan, Ann Hoffman, and Erica Messenger for their work on this revision, and to the TeamUP consultants for their continued support.

I would like to extend a special acknowledgment to the following instructors for their reviews of the text and suggestions for the improvement of this edition:

Julia Bensley, SUNY Alfred State College
Hollie Benson, Muskegon Community College
Susannah Chewning, Union County College
Kenneth Christensen, The University of Southern Mississippi
Gary Corona, Florida State University at Jacksonville
Ellen Derwin, Brandman University
Robin Gandy, Lourdes University
Wendy Grace, Holmes Community College
Zach Hudson, Mount Hood Community College
Dara Lawyer, Laramie County Community College
Krista Royal, University of South Florida
Christopher Twiggs, Florida State College at Jacksonville
Timothy Walter, Oakland Community College
Mary Walz-Chojnacki, University of Wisconsin at Milwaukee
Terry Weideman, Oakland Community College
Kessea Weiser, College of DuPage
Kim Winford, Blinn College

Carolyn H. Hopper

Making a Smooth Transition to College

Road Map to Success

- How Do I Make a Smooth Transition?
- Your Job as a College Student
- Essential Resources
- Frequently Asked Questions
- Higher Education
- Some Strategies for Success

In this chapter, you will learn how to

- **Use analogies to explain** what adjustments you will need to make to ensure your transition runs smoother.

- **Explain** what is found in basic resources such as the college catalog, student handbook, schedule book, syllabus, and student services website.

- **Describe** the steps of the learning process.

- **Explain** the responsibilities of a college student and identify behavior that is not acceptable.

- **Calculate** a grade point average.

- **Evaluate** your performance as a student by analyzing the behaviors you exhibit.

- **Demonstrate** how to properly e-mail your instructor.

- **Demonstrate** the BREATHE System.

Where Are We Going?

Brain research says that we may learn best through analogies, comparing something new to things we already know and understand. The primary analogy we will use throughout this text is that your college education is a journey. However, you can't just be a passenger on the journey—you must be the primary driver. You can't hop on a plane, look out at the clouds, read a book, watch a movie, eat and drink a bit, have a casual conversation with your seat mates, catch a nap, and get to your destination. Nor can you get there as a passenger on a bus or train. College education is a rough road trip. You can't take short cuts. You can't get there any other way than by doing it yourself. You must drive, and **you are the driver.** You choose the route, you follow the road signs, you step on the gas and the brakes, you fuel up, and you ask for directions. You fight fatigue and stress. But you also take in the whole experience of the drive, every curve and bump, every complex intersection, and every flat tire or fender bender. This chapter will show you how to be in the driver's seat on your way to reaching your destination. We will make a few stops along the way to help you get familiar with the road to success.

How Do I Make a Smooth Transition?

Driving in an unfamiliar place is difficult, much like trying to transition to an unfamiliar college life. You are definitely out of your comfort zone. You may make a few wrong turns. You may not take the shortest route. Even when you use MapQuest or a GPS, or instructors or other students to help you navigate, driving in a new territory requires concentration. Right now everything is new: the campus, the instructors, the amount of work required, and the speed with which things are covered—the entire college environment with **credit hours, general education requirements**, choice of which classes to take, and what time to take them. It's all pretty overwhelming.

Beginning your college education is a lot like traveling to a foreign country. Your entry into college transports you to a place that is foreign to you. The surroundings, the culture, the customs, and even the language are unfamiliar; you may have difficulty adjusting. Let's carry this analogy a bit further and say that you have just arrived at the airport in a foreign city. Each traveler brings different expectations and experiences. Some of you have visited this place before. You may have some idea of what you want to see again and perhaps you might want to change some things from your last visit. Some of you have carefully planned your trip. You have talked to those who have lived and worked here. You have read the guidebooks and have studied the culture and the language. You have prepared to make the most of the experience. Some travelers have arrived with little idea

of where they are and the opportunities available here. Some of the travelers are here for a visit. Most of you, however, are here to take a job. You will become a resident of this place for a while and so you will want to discover all you can to make your experience meaningful and your job rewarding.

Your approach as you begin college may be the same approach that you would take if you were moving to a foreign city to do a job. You may get irritated because you don't understand the language. You may become frustrated because you are constantly getting lost. You may be confused or unaware that you have offended the local residents. This first chapter can become your travel guide; and although it can't tell you everything you will need to know, it will give you a heads-up on the language, the people, the customs, the expectations, and your responsibilities in your new job. It can also offer some tools to help you make the most of your experience and to make your transition to college smoother. You have chosen to come here. This is your new job. You will be spending a great deal of time, money, and effort trying to be successful in a foreign place. The good news is you can soon be acting like a native.

As you read this chapter, you will find several bold print words. These are words that are frequently used in college; you may not be totally familiar with them. At the end of the chapter in the review section, you will be asked to list at least five of these words and define them as they are used on your campus. When you get to a word, you may want to turn to the end of the chapter and record it as you read.

This is a learning strategies text, a manual with tips to help make your drive smoother, your experience better. This text is about more than how to study. The focus of the text is on *learning how to learn*. The world is changing at an amazing pace. We are able to access more and more information using more and more technology. In fact, the job you will be doing 10 years from now probably doesn't exist now in the form you will be performing it. I honestly believe that the most important thing you will learn in college is *learning how to learn*. You will learn how to maximize your memory, your note taking, your textbook reading, your test-taking, your critical thinking, your time management, and your information literacy. You will be provided with practice so that you can adapt the strategies to your situation. Just as you don't become a good driver (or musician or athlete) without practice, using learning strategies and becoming a successful college student requires practice. The attitude with which you approach this course will make the difference in more than just passing a course. You will be developing skills to make your life better.

Your Job as a College Student

You are a college student. This is your job! Many of you are still working your old job; however, beginning college is the same as beginning a new job. Each semester is a promotion and brings new responsibilities.

Virtual Field Trip
College Budget

Think of your first days on other jobs. In fact, jot down some things you remember about your first few weeks on the job. I'm sure you didn't just choose a place to work and say, "I think I'll work here today." Many of us may have approached college this way, however. For your job, someone interviewed you; when you were hired, someone explained *exactly* what was expected of you, what procedures to use, how to work necessary equipment, and where to go to find out information you did not know, or who to report to. Often this is not the case at the beginning of college. Some of us plunged right in. You should approach college as you would a new job. Don't just wander in and begin work without knowing essential information. This is not your high school, the job you left or currently work, or the world you were immersed in six months ago. Find out as much as you can about this new work environment, both what is expected of you and what resources are available. If you have not already done so, meet with an **academic advisor**. Discover how to register for each term in the most efficient manner and which courses you really need to take. You are spending too much time, effort, and money not to do it right!

Essential Resources

At most colleges and universities, there are some essential resources that will provide you with your "job description" as a student, in addition to explaining how to get "promotions," or better grades.

First Essential Resource: College Catalog

The **first essential resource** you need is the **college catalog**. Because it is changed periodically, the catalog for the year you enroll becomes your contract with the university. Containing the rules, regulations, and procedures you are expected to follow, the catalog corresponds to a company's policy manual.

Most degree or certificate programs require a certain number of **credit hours** to graduate. The catalog will spell out which classes you are required to take. In addition, the catalog lists a detailed description of each course. You need to know what is in the catalog for your college. Similar to how you would use a reference book, you will probably not read the catalog cover to cover. However, it's a good idea to put it in a place where you will look at it often, both to become aware of policies and procedures and to understand your **degree requirements**. If you have declared a **major**, you should also study that section carefully. If you don't have a major yet, the catalog is a good source of information to help you decide on one. What majors are offered? What does each require? What major would you really like to take classes in? When you register for classes, you should consult the catalog for a description of the course you are registering for. These course descriptions may help you determine some possible majors to consider.

PRACTICE 1.1

Using Your College Catalog

Consult your college catalog and find the following information (insert page numbers so you can find this again; you may need to use a separate sheet of paper for some of the questions). You may also find that there is an online version that is easier to use.

Locate the **academic calendar**:

What are the holidays for this semester?

_____

_____

When are your final exams?

_____

_____

How do you **drop or add** a course?

_____

_____

What is the significance of **course numbers**?

_____

_____

What **degrees** are offered at your institution?

_____

_____

What are the requirements for the degree you seek?

_____

_____

Find the course description of one course that you are required to take, and write a brief summary of that course.

_____

_____

What **grade point average (GPA)** do you need to graduate?

_____

_____

General Education, or Core Curriculum, Courses

One of the most important uses of the catalog is determining which courses to take and when to take them. Most colleges and universities have a required **core curriculum**, often called *general education* or *general studies* courses. No matter the major, any student who graduates from that college or university must complete a required number of courses covering a broad area. According to the Association of American Colleges, college graduates should:

> possess the marks of a generally educated person—that is, having such qualities as a broad base of knowledge in history and culture, mathematics and science, the ability to think logically and critically, the capacity to express ideas clearly and cogently, the sensitivities and skills to deal with different kinds of people, sophisticated tastes and interests, and the capability to work independently and collaboratively.[1]

College education should be both specialized (a major) and broad (general education) because we experience the world whole, not in isolated parts such as history or biology. A national survey from CareerBuilder finds that as many as one-half of college graduates work in areas unrelated to their majors. General education provides students with adaptive skills for an uncertain future.

The requirement of general education courses allows students to build a base of general knowledge even before they decide on a major. But here's where you may need to be careful in your choices of classes. Although there are usually many choices in an area of general studies, your major may require a particular class. By seeing an advisor, you can avoid taking and paying for extra courses.

What follows is a copy of a poster loaded with useful things you can learn from your advisor. Students sometimes avoid seeing their advisor, when, in fact, an advisor's services may be one of the biggest bargains included in your tuition. Study "All I Ever Needed to Know I Learned from My Advisor." Circle at least four things you might ask your advisor about.

StudentTIP

"Even though you think you don't need to, check with your advisor to make sure you are on track. If you have been assigned an advisor who is not helpful to you, ask to be assigned another advisor."

©Christophe Testi/Shutterstock.com

All I Ever Needed to Know I Learned from My Advisor

What classes to take this semester, and next semester, and the next semester, and… • *Why I can't take 40 hours if I can work 40 hours* • **That I should study a minimum of two hours outside class for every hour in class** • How many credits I need to graduate • *Information about graduate schools* • **How to get an overload** • Why I must take general studies classes that have nothing to do with my major • *"Mr. Staff" isn't the hardest-working instructor on campus* • **How to withdraw from a class** • An advisor writes a good recommendation letter • *How to change my major* • **What minors might be good for me** • Scholarships offered by my department • *Why I shouldn't take all my classes in a row* • **When and where to file my upper-division and intent-to-graduate forms** • What employers in my field are looking for • *What campus organizations would benefit me* • **Career information** • My advisor cares

—*Laurie B. Witherow and Ginger A. Corely*

---

[1]*Strong Foundations: Twelve Principles for Effective General Education Programs* (Washington, DC: Association of American Colleges, 1994, ii–iii).

A **second resource** you should have is your institution's **student handbook**. Handbooks usually list specific student resources and student organizations, in addition to rules and regulations. Many colleges and universities have the handbook online or incorporated into the college plan book or agenda.

PRACTICE 1.2

Using Your Student Handbook

Consult your student handbook and find the following information. Again, you can probably find an online version by searching your college homepage.

Where do you get a parking permit?

_____

_____

Where can you replace a lost ID?

_____

_____

Name two student organizations you might be interested in joining.

1. _____

2. _____

Where can you go for career counseling?

_____

_____

Name three other things in the handbook, and explain a situation for each that might arise where you would need to know this information.

1. _____

2. _____

3. _____

Virtual Field Trip
Campus Safety

Virtual Field Trip
College Health Issues

A **third resource** that you should keep is the current **schedule** or **registration book**. Some colleges have a printed version of the schedule book, others have a website, and many have both. The schedule book will have the class schedule for that **semester** or **term,** payment instructions, important dates for that semester such as drop-and-add dates, and the **final exam schedule**. Don't think that because you have registered, you are finished with this book. Like the catalog, the schedule book contains information that you are not likely to find elsewhere. Read it carefully, and save it for future reference. Because changes in classes or instructors may be made after the schedule is printed, you should double-check offerings online whenever possible.

There are some basic strategies you should follow when you register for a new semester. Keep the following in mind when choosing classes:

- **Outside Responsibilities.** Consider your responsibilities outside college that may put constraints on your choice of classes. (List things you should consider.)
- **Course Load.** Given these constraints, what is a reasonable course load for you? Will this make a difference in when you can take classes?
- **Options.** Carefully study your options. Read the catalog to see what your logical choices are, both in general education and in requirements for your major. (List the options you have.)
- **Right Mix.** Taking the right mix of classes is also important. You don't want to exclusively take courses that require a great deal of reading. If math is difficult for you, you don't want to take all math-related courses. What classes are you considering for next semester? Is there a mix of types of classes and time required for each course?
- **Other Students.** If possible, talk to other students who have taken the classes you are considering. Many students say this is the best way to get a feel for what the classes will be like. Remember, however, that your learning style preferences and work ethic may be different from the students you ask.
- **Seek the opinion of experts**. Consult with your advisor. Your time and money are too valuable to just take the advice of another student or to guess. (Who is your advisor?) What are some questions you should ask? If you are in doubt about what is involved in a course you are considering, talk with the professor.
- **Time.** The time classes are offered may be important if you are working or have other responsibilities.

PRACTICE 1.3

Using Your Schedule Book

Consult your schedule book for the following (be sure to insert page numbers so you can find them again):

How much does this class cost to take?

_____

_____

When is the final exam for this class?

_____

_____

What are some important things you should consider when choosing classes?

_____

_____

How will you get your grades at the end of the semester?

_____

_____

The fourth resource to keep handy at all times throughout the semester is the **syllabus** for each class. The syllabus gives you a picture of what will be expected of you during the semester. It contains the rules and policies for that particular class. Not all classes will have the same **grading scale, absence policy,** or **make-up policy**. In addition, a syllabus will contain overall course requirements and perhaps class-by-class assignments. The syllabus should contain your instructor's office hours and telephone number. Students forget most of what happens during the first day of class, so it's important to take notes and read your syllabus carefully, both to refresh your memory and to understand policies that perhaps weren't discussed. The syllabus is your contract with your professor. It is a good idea to go through the syllabus of each class and mark assignments and tests. You may also want to list them in your calendar, your plan book, agenda, or mobile devices. This will also help you develop and practice your time-management skills.

PRACTICE 1.4

Using Your Syllabus

Consult the syllabus for this class to determine the following:

What is the absence policy?

_____

_____

How is your grade determined?

_____

_____

Is late homework accepted? Is there a penalty for late work? Can a missed test be made up?

_____

_____

What are your instructor's name, telephone number, and office hours?

_____

_____

For Your Student Survival Kit

Assignment Log

You may find it helpful to keep up with your daily grade in this study skills class by making a chart like this. Record the quiz or assignment requested to be turned in, along with the due date. Check (✓) whether you turned it in or not. When it is returned, record points earned divided by total points possible for your daily average.

Name _____

ASSIGNMENT	DUE DATE	✓	POINTS POSSIBLE	POINTS EARNED

Make sure you know how the grade for each assignment or test is derived. Check your syllabus to see how your final grade is determined.

Virtual Field Trip
Your College Homepage

Student Services

Are you missing out on some valuable resources just because you don't know they exist? Although most colleges try to keep the campus community aware of what they offer, it is difficult to keep up with all options. Take the Virtual Field Trip to identify some of those resources.

Frequently Asked Questions: Some FAQs by First-Year College Students or Transfers

The Student Affairs Office on many campuses offers "one-stop shopping," a place where you can find the answers to most of the questions below. You might also search your college homepage or ask other students, your advisor, or your professors for information.

- I don't own a computer. Where can I use one?
- Can I buy or rent one at a student rate?
- Are there workshops or classes I can take to become more computer literate?
- I don't have any financial aid. Where can I go to see if I qualify?
- What if I get sick? What kinds of health services are available?
- I am having trouble with my math, chemistry, and history. Are there tutoring services available?
- Is there affordable child care available on or near campus?
- I think I may have a learning disability. Is there a place I can get help?

- My professor suggested group study. Are there group study areas available?
- I am having nonacademic problems. Is there help available on campus?
- I need a part-time job. Where can I find out what kinds are available?
- Is tutoring available on campus?
- My professor says the more involved I get on campus, the more sense of belonging I will have. She says that this will contribute to my success as a student. What clubs or activities are available?
- Where can I cash a check or use an ATM?
- Where can I get photocopies made?
- Is public transportation available?
- What is there to do on the weekends?

Higher Education

You have already discovered that there is a great deal of difference in the demands made on you as a high school student or as an employee and those made on you as a college student. Stop and make a list of the differences you have found that affect you. Then examine your list and compare it against what other students have said.

CRITICAL THINKING
About Higher Education

What follows is a list of differences students have noted both between higher education and high school and between higher education and work. Choose at least four of these and comment on how you have learned to handle them. Be specific. If you have not been able to handle these differences yet, set specific goals for improvement.

1. There is more reading to do.
2. The campus is larger. It's hard to know what's available and who to see.
3. College classes are larger, and classmates are more diverse.
4. I have less free time in college.
5. I have more responsibilities in college.
6. College seems more impersonal.
7. I have more financial pressures in college.
8. College professors give fewer tests and are less tolerant of excuses.
9. There are so many courses offered at the college that I don't know what to take or when to take them.
10. Most classes at the college last for only one term (semester or quarter).

What difference *not* noted in the list has been most difficult for you?

Virtual Field Trip

College Life

BRAIN BYTE

In *How People Learn*, John Bransford says that the goal of education today should be "helping students develop the intellectual tools and learning strategies needed to acquire the knowledge that allows people to think productively about history, science and technology, social phenomena, mathematics and the arts." He suggests that fundamental understanding of all subjects, including how to ask questions about many subject areas, is a major factor in understanding the principles of learning that people need to develop in order to become lifelong learners.

Your Responsibilities?

You can't just attend college and expect to be successful. Less than 26 percent of Americans over the age of 25 have earned a college degree. It's not easy. There are certain expectations and responsibilities that go hand in hand with higher education. You are responsible for your learning. You are responsible not only for attending class, but preparing for it by doing the assigned homework and reading. You are responsible for finding a way to understand what goes on in class and working to achieve the learning outcomes set for each class.

You may have already noticed that your idea of learning and your professor's idea of learning are not always the same. Recognizing the difference and adjusting to it may be one of the most difficult (yet important) transitions you make as a first-year student. Your primary job as a college student is to be an information processor. You will process what you hear in lectures and make that information your own. You will process what you read in textbooks or experience in class and process it so that you own that information and can personally use it.

Modeling the Learning Process: Your Map for Learning How to Learn

As you begin your drive toward success as a college student, here is the basic model for learning. In his book *The Art of Changing the Brain*, Dr. James Zull reminds us that first and foremost, learning causes a physical change in the brain and that this change takes time[2]. Dr. Zull says that there are four essentials of learning:

Gathering.
New information enters the brain through the senses. We hear, read, see, or interact with new information. *(Some of us would like to think that listening to a lecture or reading an assignment is enough. It's not.)*

Analyzing.
If we are to use this information in the future, we must understand it and look for relevance and meaning. *(Now, if I understand it, can I stop? Not if you are to own the information.)*

Creating New Ideas.
When we as learners convert comprehension into ideas, hypotheses, plans, and actions, we take control of the information. We have created a meaningful neural network and are free to test our own knowledge.

Acting.
The testing of the knowledge requires action for the learning cycle to be complete. Writing, speaking, drawing, or other action will identify a strategy that works for us and provides a way that we can test the newly learned information.

---

[2]James Zull, *The Art of Changing the Brain* (Sterling, VA: Stylus Publishing, 2002).

We are used to being *receivers* of knowledge, gathering new information and trying to make meaning of it. Learning occurs when we take that knowledge and become *producers* of new knowledge. In the following chapters, as you learn how to be a more successful student, watch for the process of how you take ownership of the knowledge content. In each chapter, we will follow this cycle; at the end of each chapter, we will identify what we have done so that you will be well on your way to understanding what your professors mean by *learning*.

With the learning model in mind, let's look at what professors say they wish their students understood about learning in college.

- I think the biggest adjustment first-year students have to make is understanding and taking responsibility for the amount and quality of work it takes to be successful. Professors are there to lead the class, but you must make the effort to learn.

- Most learning actually takes place outside of the classroom when you are analyzing, creating, and acting on information you gathered in class.

- The connections in your brain are like no one else's. You must take it upon yourself to do whatever it takes (required or not) to learn the material.

- It may seem like an obvious statement, but the work you do will result in the grade you get.

- When you miss a class, whether you are sick; have a family emergency, a court date, a doctor's appointment, or a sick child; are called in to work; or have transportation failure, you are still responsible for what went on in class. Usually turning in a homework assignment is not enough. You should have a partner in each class you can depend on to help you recreate what you missed.

- You are expected to read your e-mail daily.

- You are expected to participate actively in class and ask questions if you don't understand something.

Your professors are human, so they are always forming opinions. You need to be aware that the impression you make can have an effect on your grade. Even how and where you sit communicates something to your professor. The quality of your work is also important. Your assignments and the way you turn them in tell the instructor a great deal about you, how much you care about the course, and how serious you are about being successful in college. Whatever the assignment is, you should make an effort to complete it on time and fully. The more information you can give on an assignment, the higher your professor's opinion of you as a student will be. Getting by is not good enough in college. Not understanding is never an excuse in college, nor is not having enough time.

Try to get to know the professor personally; that way, when you do have a question or an emergency, you are able to relate better. Most of your professors have responsibilities other than teaching your class, just as you have responsibilities outside their class. If you wish to get extra help or clarification on an assignment, you should probably make an appointment during office hours. The professor's office hours are usually included in the syllabus. Check with each professor to see what his or her policy for student appointments is. If you just drop by, you may be disappointed to find another student has scheduled an appointment.

Student Power

You hold more power in the classroom than you may realize. Ask any professor and he or she will tell you that the students in the class significantly affect the delivery of information. By coming prepared, sitting up front, paying attention, taking notes, making eye contact, nodding when you agree or understand, asking questions when you are confused, and actively participating in class activities, you are actually able to affect the professor's enthusiasm and approach to the class. Think about classes that you are taking now. The best professors have the best students. I can't be an exciting professor without your cooperation.

Some Strategies for Success

At the end of each semester, I ask students what they wish they had known at the beginning of their first semester that would have made the journey easier. Below is a list of general survival tips that former students say you should know.

General Survival Tips to Make Your Transition Smoother

If you haven't already registered, try not to schedule back-to-back classes. You'll wear yourself out, besides missing the best times to study—right before and right after class.

- **Begin the first day of class.** Know what's expected of you.
- **Take notes on the first day.** Even if it's routine stuff you think you already know.
- **Take notes in class.** Don't depend on your memory.
- **Read directions carefully** before you begin an assignment. Don't assume you know what to do.
- **Establish a routine time to study for each class.** For every hour you spend in class, you will probably need to study two hours outside class. Study for each subject at the same time and in the same place if possible. Studying includes more than just doing your homework. You will need to go over your notes from class—questioning, editing, and making sure you understand them. Study your syllabus daily to see where you are going and where you have been. Be sure to do reading assignments. (Don't put them off just because there's no written assignment.) Read ahead whenever possible. Prepare for each class as if there will be a pop quiz that day.
- **Establish a place to study.** Your place should have a desk, a comfortable chair, good lighting, all the supplies you need, and so on; and of course, it should be as free of distractions as possible. It should not be a place where you routinely do other things. It should be your study place.
- **Study during the day.** Do as much of your studying in the daytime as you can. What takes you an hour to do during the day may take

you an hour and a half at night. If possible, avoid long blocks of time for studying. Spread out several short study sessions during the day.

- **Stay on top of your work.** Although it may seem obvious, your grades, your preparation for class, and class attendance are directly related to your success as a student. Once you miss a day or an assignment, it is very difficult to ever get caught up.

- **Keep a list of what is due in each class** and try to get as much done ahead of time as you can. You will have major assignments and tests due on the same day.

- **Make use of study resources on campus.** Find out about and use labs, tutors, videos, computer programs, and alternative texts. Sign up for an orientation session in the campus library and computer lab. Get to know your professors and advisors. Ask questions. Remember, not understanding something is never a good excuse. Get involved in school activities in general. And become a part of some group, so that when the unexpected happens (and it will), you have support.

- **Find at least one or two students in each class to study with.** Research shows that students who study with someone routinely make better grades. You will probably find yourself more motivated if you know someone else cares about what you are doing in the class. Teaching a concept or new idea to someone else is a sure way for you to understand it. However, because studying in a group or with a partner can sometimes become too social, it is important to stay focused.

- **Study the hardest subject first.** Work on your hardest subjects when you are fresh. Putting them off until you're tired compounds their difficulty.

- **Be good to yourself.** Studying on four hours of sleep and an empty stomach or a junk-food diet is a waste of time. Avoid food and drink containing caffeine just before or just after studying.

Tips for Taking Notes and Reading Textbooks

It's the first day of class. You need to know that short-term memory can hold only five to seven bits of information at a time. This means that you can understand everything said in class, but will remember very little if you don't take notes. You know you need to take notes, but you're not sure how to record the important information. Examine the illustration titled "Notes That Save Time." The **Question in the Margin System** is a great way to take notes and will be explained in detail later; meanwhile, know that your notes will be more useful if you set your paper up as in the illustration.

- Use the left margin to identify what each section of notes is about by writing a question or label in the margin as soon as you can after class.

- Use the bottoms of pages for reminders such as assignments you need to check.

Student TIP

"When studying in a group I found that you can stay focused and get more done if each person in the group has an assigned task and a list of concepts that are causing them problems. It also helps to set a time limit."

BRAIN BYTE

Dr. Judith Wurtman of M.I.T. says that proper nutrition can boost thinking and learning. The brain's most basic need is oxygen, but ingredients found in protein are critical to the brain. For your mental alertness, make three to four ounces of protein-rich foods a regular part of your daily diet.

Notes That Save Time

Question for key points

Take notes here

Summarize in your words

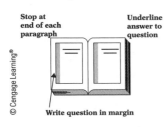

QUESTION IN THE MARGIN SYSTEM

Reading That Saves Time

Stop at end of each paragraph

Underline answer to question

Write question in margin

© Cengage Learning®

- The left margin should be about two and a half inches wide.
- Take your notes on the wide right-hand side.
- Don't write in full sentences. Write only the few words you need to help you remember what was said in class. Use the same techniques you use when you compose text messages: important information in shorthand.

Begin the semester taking notes like this, and when you get to the Question in the Margin System, you will be well on your way to learning how to process important information from lectures into your long-term memory.

Yes, I know that you already have reading assignments, too. You probably remember reading entire chapters and understanding the material as you read it; however, when you finished, you had no idea what you read. Again, the reason is probably that short-term memory holds only five to seven bits of information. This is the amount of information in a well-written paragraph. You read and understand one paragraph. When you begin the next paragraph, short-term memory dumps that information to make room for new information. Begin using the same system that you used for your class notes. As you finish each paragraph, write a question in the left margin that identifies the main ideas and underline the answer in the paragraph before you go to the next paragraph. Furthermore, you will get more out of the assignment if you preview it first. Study the title, headings, bold print, summary, charts, graphs, and tables before you begin reading. Again, *keep up to date with your reading and read ahead whenever you can.*

PRACTICE 1.5

Evaluating Your Classroom Savvy

You have been on the job several class periods by now. Just as when on the job or on the road, you need to meet certain expectations if you are to be successful. At the beginning of your journey, you should be aware of what is expected of you as a college student. How well are you doing? In the following list, put a plus (+) sign beside the behaviors that you already do well and a minus (–) sign beside the ones you need to improve. As you evaluate the behaviors you exhibit, analyze *why* each behavior is important.

_____ 1. Attend every class.

_____ 2. Come to class prepared.

_____ 3. Be alert and attentive in class.

_____ 4. Participate in class discussions.

_____ 5. Show an interest in the subject.

_____ 6. Ask questions when you don't fully understand.

_____ 7. Seek outside sources if you need clarification.

_____ 8. Take advantage of all labs, study sessions, and outside help.

_____ 9. Set up meetings with your professors to discuss your progress.

_____ 10. Go the extra mile with all papers and assignments.

_____ 11. Always be on time for class.

_____ **12.** Take notes.

_____ **13.** When you must miss a class, make sure you find out exactly what you missed, make up the work, and come prepared for the next class.

_____ **14.** Comment on lecture material.

_____ **15.** Get to know your professors.

_____ **16.** Set goals and objectives for your classes.

_____ **17.** Evaluate yourself.

_____ **18.** Be supportive of your classmates.

_____ **19.** Have a positive attitude toward the professor and the class.

PRACTICE 1.6

Unsavvy Behavior

Now let's have a little fun. Your task is to come up with a list of *unsavvy* behaviors you have noticed in the classroom. See if you can list 10 unsavvy things that you have seen happen this semester. You may also want to ask your professors to add to your list. Let's start off with some obvious ones.

1. Coming in late for class.

2. Copying homework or cheating on a test or other assignments.

3. Leaving cell phone on or texting during class.

4. _____

5. _____

6. _____

7. _____

8. _____

9. _____

10. _____

Your Grade Point Average

Your college requires you to have a certain number of credit hours in certain areas in order to graduate. Each course you take is assigned the appropriate number of credit hours. Your college or university also requires that you maintain a certain grade point average (GPA) to stay in school or to qualify for certain programs. Thus, it is important that you know how to calculate your grade point average. The chart on the next page shows how to perform this calculation using a four-point system. Check your college catalog to see by which system your grades are calculated. If a plus or minus system is used, your catalog will explain how to use it to calculate your GPA.

How to Calculate Your GPA

The following is an explanation of how to calculate a GPA. You may want to use the chart to help you calculate the following examples.

1. List each graded course.
2. Enter the letter grade received.
3. Enter the grade point value (A = 4, B = 3, C = 2, D = 1, F = 0).
4. Enter course credit hours.
5. Multiply line items from column 3 by line items in column 4, and put the product in column 5.   = GPA
6. Add column 4 to get total credit hours.
7. Add column 5 to get total quality points.
8. Divide the quality points by the number of credit hours to get your grade point average.

$$\frac{quality\ points}{credit\ hours}$$

Consult your college catalog to find out how your university figures grade point averages.

1	2	3	4	5
NAME OF COURSE	LETTER GRADE	LETTER GRADE VALUE	CREDIT HOURS FOR COURSE	QUALITY POINTS
			×	=
			×	=
			×	=
			×	=
			×	=
			×	=
		Total		

Virtual Field Trip
Check Your GPA

PRACTICE 1.7

Grade Point Average Practice

Calculate John's grade point averages for the fall and spring terms. Carry the averages to hundredths; do not round.

Grade point average for fall term: _____

Grade point average for spring term: _____

Cumulative grade point average: _____

FALL TERM COURSE	HOURS CREDIT	GRADE
Math 1410	3	C
Hper 1070	1	A
Math 1700	3	B
Spee 2200	3	B
UVIV 1010	3	B
Psyc 1110	3	D

Grade point average for fall term: _____

SPRING TERM COURSE	HOURS CREDIT	GRADE
Art 1010	3	A
Math 1000	3	B
Biog 1010	4	D
ROTC	1	C
Eng 1010	3	C

Grade point average for spring term: _____

Now calculate what John's *cumulative* (fall plus spring) grade point average is. The formula is the same:

$$\frac{total\ quality\ points}{total\ credit\ hours}$$

Cumulative grade point average: _____

Add the following courses for the summer term, and compute John's cumulative GPA—his average for all three terms, not just his summer GPA.

COURSE	HOURS CREDIT	GRADE
Phy sci 2000	3	B
Eng 1120	3	C

Cumulative grade point average: _____

E-mail Etiquette

Because the first impression you make on your professors may be by e-mail and because we are in the habit of being very casual with our e-mails, it is important that you be careful to follow proper e-mail etiquette. Remember that your professor is not one of your casual friends; show proper respect in the salutation and in the body of your e-mail. Here are some minimum guidelines:

- **Use the subject line to summarize** the text of your message. With so much spam (junk e-mail), your message will likely be deleted without being read if you don't include a subject.

- **Don't write anything you wouldn't say in public.** Anyone can easily forward your message, even accidentally. This could leave you in an embarrassing position if you divulge personal or confidential information. If you don't want to share something you write, consider using the telephone.

- **Use a spell checker before you send.** This is an option on most e-mail programs. E-mail, like conversation, tends to be sloppier than communication on paper. That's OK; but even with e-mail, you don't want to appear excessively careless. *Read* the e-mail before you send it.

- **Identify yourself.** The message contains your e-mail address (in the header); but many times the header the system uses puts only the e-mail address, and the recipient will not know who the message is from unless you include your name in your e-mail. If you are sending it to your instructor, it's a good idea to identify the class you are in as well. Be sure to address your professor as a professional.

- **Keep your message short and focused.**

- **Don't overuse upper case.** This is viewed as SHOUTING.

- **Check your e-mail at least once a day.** Answer pertinent e-mails as soon as possible.

- **Delete spam.** Even with filters, you will get an excessive amount of junk e-mail. You don't have to open or read it. You can check messages you want to delete and delete without reading.

- **Don't overuse Reply All.** Use Reply All if you really need your message to be seen by each person who received the original message.

- **Don't forward chain letters, jokes, and so on.**

Note the differences in the two e-mails below. Why would you want your e-mail to resemble the first one?

Sample e-mail #1

From: jones3st@mtsu.edu
To: Chopper@mtsu.edu
Subject: Question about homework assignment page 17

Dr. Hopper,
My name is Sam Jones. I am a student in your Student Success 1010 class, Section 11. I am confused about the College Life Virtual Field Trip assignment on page 17. Could I meet with you during your office hours today or tomorrow? I could come before 10 am on either day if you are available.

Thanks,
Sam Jones

Sample e-mail #2

From: jones3st@mtsu.edu
To: Chopper@mtsu.edu
Subject:

Hey,
Don't know wht 2 do with homework. where's ur office?

Tips for Online Courses

- **Familiarize yourself with the course design.** Study the syllabus. Make sure you understand not only what is required but also when it is required and how to complete each requirement.
- **Read the entire course syllabus.** The distance learning course syllabus contains all of the information you need to progress through a distance learning course. This includes information about the course description, objectives, and requirements; course meetings, assignments, and testing; media and technology used; a course calendar or assignment schedule; and support contact information.
- **Be realistic.** You will not have to keep a class attendance schedule, but you will have to do regular academic work. Since you are taking the course online, you should put in at least the minimum of what you would do in a course in the classroom. You should be spending at least three study hours each week for every credit hour you are taking. Depending on the course and your background on the material, it may take more time. You can't "be absent" for several weeks and expect to catch up. So if there is insufficient time in your personal schedule to do the work of the course, you will be frustrated.

- **Set interim goals and deadlines for yourself, and stick to them.** Keep a calendar showing the number of weeks in the semester and mark it off with the amount of work you need to do each week. Mark in the days when you expect to take tests, submit projects, or talk with the instructor. Don't fall behind on your work! Keep reminding yourself that you will always have more to do near the end of a course than you do at the beginning.

- **Organize your goals in a study schedule.** Identify study times when you are fresh and attentive, and stick to those times every week. Think of the study times as reserved times. If you miss too many study times, revise your schedule.

- **Avoid interruptions.** Avoid all interruptions and distractions.

- **Know where to study.** Find a place that is free from distractions. You might consider your workplace—before or after hours and on your lunch hour—a public library, or a separate room in your home.

- **Stay in touch with your instructor.** Contact your instructor regularly, especially when you have questions about course content materials. Instructors are usually available by telephone or e-mail, or you may make an appointment for an on-campus meeting.

- **Prepare for assignments and tests.** In distance learning, course assignments could involve the use of different media: print, video, audio, and the Internet. Remember, you are not just watching or listening. You are learning from the information in these various media. Take notes. When using your study guide, textbook, videos, audiotapes, or Internet course assignments, imagine questions that might be on a test.

The BREATHE System: A Tool to Help You Focus

Let's conclude this chapter with one last tool you may find helpful when dealing with the stress of the first few weeks of college.

Dr. Ralph Hillman has developed a technique he calls the **BREATHE** System, designed to help classroom teachers train their students to reduce anger, control potential violence, and raise test scores. The program has some benefits for college students as well. The **BREATHE** System is a way to deal with low self-esteem, test anxiety, feelings of being overwhelmed, anger, and stress. Like much of what you will learn in this text, the system is relatively simple, but requires discipline. It is probably not something you would automatically think of as a learning strategy; however, when you practice it, you will find that it promotes concentration and clear thinking, as well as relieves stress. The **BREATHE** System involves knowing and consciously forming the habit of using what Dr. Hillman calls the Big 3.[3]

---

[3]From *Delivering Dynamic Presentations: Using Your Voice and Body for Impact* by Ralph E. Hillman (Boston: Allyn and Bacon, 1999). Copyright © 1999. Reprinted by permission of the author.

The Big 3: Posture, Neck and Shoulder Muscles, and Breath Support

1. **Straighten Your Posture.** Good posture allows the organs of your body to operate efficiently and has a positive mental effect on your self-esteem. Moreover, good posture makes you look confident and competent and it supplies your brain with a better supply of oxygen. The six essential components of good posture are listed below:

   A. **Unlock your knees** while standing; if you "snap," or force, the knees back, making your legs rigid, blood flow to your brain is diminished, and the natural curves in your spine are exaggerated.

   B. **Level your pelvis** so that the gentle arch of your lower spine is encouraged. If the pelvis is pulled too far back, the arch is exaggerated, and too much tension is placed on the muscles necessary for efficient breathing.

   C. **Tuck your tummy.** Make a conscious effort to pull your belly button back toward your spine. Leveling your pelvis and elevating your rib cage will make this process easier. Most of us want tight abs, but we are not willing to maintain the constant postural pressure on those muscles to allow them to be in position all the time.

   D. **Elevate your rib cage.** Keeping your ribs slightly elevated frees the thoracic cavity (rib cage) to move freely during inhalation and exhalation.

   E. **Push your shoulders back and down.** If the previous four steps are in place, positioning the shoulders is a lot easier. If you are having trouble getting a "feel" for where the shoulders should be, try this: Put your back up against a wall. For most of us, our buttocks hit the wall first, then the shoulders, and finally the head. Put your hands up at shoulder level with the backs of your hands against the wall or as close to the wall as you can get them. Notice the pull in the muscles of your upper chest. As you are standing against the wall, with your hands by your sides, your thumbs should fall easily along the seams in your slacks or trousers. As your shoulders roll forward, your hands will hang in front of your body and not along the sides.

   F. **Hold your head up** so that there is a straight line from the bottom of your ear to the top of your shoulder, to the top of your hip, and to the center of your foot. Keep your head level, eyes forward. If your body shape is deep through the thoracic cavity, putting your head against the wall may be too far back for you. The goal here is to have your body line up, whether standing or sitting. If the angle of the back of your chair is too far back, then don't lean all the way back. Push your lower back against it, then sit erect. Use good posture as your home position. Use it often, be consistent, and soon it will become your habit.

2. **Relax Your Neck and Shoulder Muscles.** The second part of the Big 3 is to relax your neck and shoulder muscles (remember: shoulders back and down). Most of us are unaware that these muscles are inappropriately tensed much of the time. So relaxing these tensed muscles may be as easy as realizing they are tense. By checking with a mirror, placing your hands on your neck, or using a buddy to check for your visible tension, you can learn to feel when those muscles are tight and tense. Like the home position with posture, this relaxation position should be practiced until it becomes a habit. Once good posture is achieved and awareness of the start of any tension is maintained, we are ready to work on breathing.

3. **Breathe** by taking cleansing breaths. The third part of the Big 3 is **breath support.** For proper breath support, you need to breathe using the muscles of your diaphragm, which "attach at the base of the rib cage and hump up into the chest cavity." Dr. Hillman describes breathing as most efficient when the muscle activity and movement are around the torso, between the navel and the base of the sternum. The ribs should rise slightly and move sideways. You should keep the tummy firm from the navel down, expanding the rib cage sideways.

Dr. Hillman reminds us "to use the upper abdominal muscles without raising the shoulders or puffing out the lower abdominal cavity (our lungs are not down there)." To obtain the most value from diaphragmatic breathing, use a deep, cleansing breath: keep your posture erect and neck and shoulders relaxed (steps one and two of the Big 3).

A. Now, **completely fill your lungs,** allowing the air to enter through your nose, freely and easily expanding the rib cage sideways.

B. Then, **pursing your lips, completely empty your lungs** by blowing the air out, keeping the exhaled air under pressure by using your diaphragm. To determine that you are getting the full benefit of a cleansing breath, place your hands around your abdominal area at the base of the ribs. You should feel this area moving in and out, and expanding sideways.

C. **Concentrate on slowing down your inhales and exhales.** Practice by starting with 5-second inhales and 5-second exhales. Progress to 10-second inhales and 10-second exhales. A cleansing breath will make you both more relaxed and alert.

To help form the breathing habit in the classroom, begin class by taking a few minutes to breathe. You will find that the BREATHE System gives you an edge in practicing other learning strategies. For this reason, it will be suggested as a strategy in several chapters. An overview of Dr. Hillman's BREATHE System is presented later. If you want to know more, read Chapter 7 of his book, *Delivering Dynamic Presentations.* You can also log on to http://thebreathesystem.com for more information.

Review—Where did we go?

Study Guide: Making a Smooth Transition to College

To see if you grasped the major points of the chapter and to make a useful study guide, answer the following questions found in your reading. When you have written your answers, cover them and see if you can say the answer to each question in your own words.

1. We used three analogies at the beginning of this chapter. Explain how each could relate to your college experience.

   1. Student must be the driver. _____

   2. You have landed in a foreign country. _____

   3. You are here to begin a new job. _____

2. List some skills this course should help you maximize.

_____

_____

_____

3. List at least three essential resources found in the college catalog.

_____

_____

_____

4. What are core curriculum or general education courses? Why are they required?

_____

_____

_____

5. List what you consider as three important reasons for consulting with an academic advisor.

   1. _____

   2. _____

   3. _____

6. Explain what is found in your institution's student handbook.

_____

_____

_____

7. What are some important things to consider when choosing classes?

_____

_____

_____

8. Explain what essentials are found in the schedule book for each semester.

_____

9. What is a syllabus? Explain why it is important.

_____

_____

10. Name four student services you will use.

    1. _____

    2. _____

    3. _____

    4. _____

11. Name the four steps of the learning process.

    1. _____

    2. _____

    3. _____

    4. _____

12. List some responsibilities that professors say are necessary for student success.

_____

_____

13. Describe the power you have as student to make your class better or worse.

_____

_____

_____

14. After reviewing the general survival tips to make your journey easier, choose the four tips you consider the most important for you.

    1. _____

    2. _____

    3. _____

    4. _____

15. Briefly explain how to take notes using the Question in the Margin System.

_____

_____

16. Briefly explain how to read your textbook using the Question in the Margin System.

_____

_____

17. What is a GPA?

_____

18. Explain how to calculate your GPA.

_____

_____

19. Examine the list of suggestions for e-mail etiquette. Which three suggestions do you think are most important? Explain why.

1. _____

2. _____

3. _____

_____

_____

20. Explain how you might use the BREATHE System.

_____

_____

_____

Higher Education Vocabulary Words

At the beginning of the chapter, you were asked to list bold print words that might need clarification. List five of these words and define them as they are used on your campus.

VOCABULARY WORD	DEFINITION
1.	
2.	
3.	
4.	
5.	

Parallel Parking

We seem to understand concepts and remember them better when we compare them with something familiar. The running analogy in this text is comparing various strategies you may need to develop to be successful in college with strategies you may need when you are the driver on a road trip. At the end of each chapter, you will be asked to think about what we have discussed so far and compare these discoveries with driving ideas. Let's begin by reflecting on your first few days of college life.

Compare the following driving situations to something you experienced the first few days of college.

The first few days of college were like a **traffic jam** because

The first few days of college were like **getting lost in a new city** because

The first few days of college were like **making a U-turn** because

Evaluating Learning Outcomes

How successful were you in making it to your destination in this chapter?
Analyze what you learned in this chapter. Put a check beside each task you are now able to do. On a separate piece of paper, write a couple of sentences about how you learned each learning outcome and how you plan to continue to use what you learned.

☐ **Use analogies to explain** what adjustments you will need to make to ensure your transition runs smoothly.

☐ **Explain** what is found in basic resources such as the college catalog, student handbook, schedule book, syllabus, and student services website.

☐ **Describe** the steps of the learning process.

☐ **Explain** the responsibilities of a college student, and identify behavior that is not acceptable.

☐ **Calculate** a grade point average.

☐ **Evaluate** your performance as a student by analyzing the behaviors you exhibit.

☐ **Demonstrate** how to properly e-mail your instructor.

☐ **Demonstrate** the BREATHE System.

Your Student Tip for This Chapter

Use the space below to write a tip you would give to other students about what you have learned in this chapter.

_____

_____

_____

_____

Practicing the Principles of Time Management

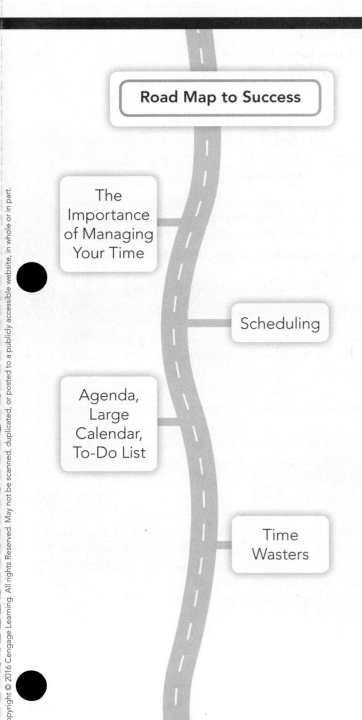

Road Map to Success

The Importance of Managing Your Time

Scheduling

Agenda, Large Calendar, To-Do List

Time Wasters

In this chapter, you will learn how to

- **List** ways you can make use of time previously wasted and do the same task in less time.

- **Demonstrate** time-management strategies, including constructing a master schedule for the semester.

- **Create** an organized to-do list, and show evidence of using a planner.

- **Analyze** a case study, and construct advice for students having difficulty with time management.

- **Explain** the learning process modeled in this chapter.

Where Are We Going?

Now that you have started college, do you feel as though you have been caught in rush-hour traffic or in an extreme traffic jam? Do you wonder where you will find the time to get everything done? Don't professors know you have a life? Time management is a critical issue for college students; how smart students are is less important to their success than how well they manage their time. The demands on your time may be entirely different from anything you have previously experienced, and these demands will force you to make difficult decisions. Strategies for managing your time are the focus of this chapter.

The Importance of Managing Your Time

Obviously, we can't actually manage time. Time keeps moving and we cannot slow it down or speed it up. Time management is your ability to plan and control how you spend the hours in your day to accomplish your goals. Time management puts you in the driver's seat. Before we begin, study the map at the beginning of the chapter. It describes our target destination for the chapter and represents the learning outcomes you should accomplish. It is always a good thing to know where you are going before you begin a journey. Your task is not just to read about time management, but to practice it. This chapter is designed to make you aware of time problems college students often face and help you come up with some viable solutions.

In this chapter, you will learn how to make more time for yourself by identifying time you may be wasting and coming up with ways you can accomplish tasks in less time. You will learn how to construct a trial master schedule to use as your guide for the semester. You will practice using a planner and making organized to-do lists. You will be able to analyze a case study and construct advice for a student having difficulty with time management. This chapter will also guide you through the learning process as you discover that learning is not just memorizing; it involves making new information personal and putting it to use.

How many course hours are you taking? What other responsibilities do you have? What are you willing to give up in order to be a successful college student? There is only so much time. You can't continue to do all the things you used to do and add the job of being a college student without giving up something. Most professors agree that you can count on at least two hours of outside work for every hour you are in class. Many add that those two hours of work may earn you only a C; some classes require even more time.

Obviously, you will never have more than 24 hours in a day. *You can, however, make extra time in two ways: by doing the same task in less time and by making use of time that you previously wasted.* For example: How long do you wait in line for coffee? Five minutes? Ten? That might be long enough to read a couple of pages of your reading or flip through flash cards for your Spanish course. Reading those pages means you're not wasting those 10 minutes in line. Flipping through your flash cards means you're doing the same task in less time, because you won't have to

StudentTIP

"One of the most difficult adjustments I have had to make in college was to allow enough time for outside assignments. In high school I could do most of my work at school. I discovered that in college most of the work, and I guess most of the learning, happens outside of the classroom. This takes organizing my time and making enough effort to do whatever necessary to get it done."

study them later, when you might have other work that needs more attention. Throughout this course, you will be seeking ways to do things not only faster, but also more efficiently. However, few of the learning strategies will work for you if you don't have time to use them.

The cardinal rule of time management is to *always carry pocket work*—something that you can do easily while waiting. Make flash cards of what you need to study for an upcoming test. Make copies of homework assignments. Or just be sure to have a book with you. Those wasted 10, 15, or 20 minutes that you stand in line without studying add up—it's time you'll have to spend studying later. And you will discover later that you usually learn more in short sessions than in longer ones. Program your mind; make it a habit to use waiting time. Use your mobile devices for pocket work. There are apps for flash cards. You can download review sheets, summaries, or exercises. How many times did you hit the snooze button this morning? What could you have done in that 15 minutes of snooze time?

PRACTICE 2.1

Beginning Steps in Time Management

Let's examine what making extra time could mean for you. In the blocks below, list some examples of how you personally could make use of wasted time and ways you can do things in less time. Be as specific as possible. The first thing you will probably want to add are examples of wasted time you could fill with doing pocket work. Fill in things you can think of now, and revisit the chart as you find other ways.

Two Ways to Make More Time

MAKE USE OF WASTED TIME		DO THINGS IN LESS TIME		
Review flash cards, instead of checking Facebook		Get up when alarm rings		

CRITICAL THINKING
About Time

Quarterback Peyton Manning uses a good analogy with money and time that's worth thinking about. Imagine, he says, that someone puts $1,400 into your bank account each day with these stipulations:

1. There can be nothing left at the end of the day.
2. You lose what you fail to invest in worthwhile work.

You have, in fact, been presented with this situation coming to college, except that instead of dollars, you have been given 1,440 minutes each day and those same stipulations apply. You have no minutes left at the end of the day, and those not spent on worthwhile pursuits are lost.

What will you do?

Why is this a good analogy?

How do you determine what is worthwhile?

StudentTIP

"I was sure a schedule would not work for me. But, until I established a routine time to study for each class, I was always behind. Now that I have graduated, I use the habits I formed in college to become successful in my job as an engineer."

StudentTIP

"It didn't take me long to figure out the studying involved more than just getting written assignments."

Scheduling: The Road Map or GPS for Time Management

Scheduling is like using a **GPS** to make sure you don't get lost on each leg of your road trip. Because many of you may never have been in a situation that required scheduling, you may be skeptical about the necessity for doing it. But the truth is, college students are too busy to leave things to chance. There may be other times in your life when you can get by without having a schedule of some sort, but the balancing act most college students are forced to perform makes it difficult to survive without a schedule. Things probably won't ever go exactly as planned, but if you have a basic plan, you can adjust. You may have to take detours or adjust for road conditions, but your schedule is your guide. It will make your journey easier and help you stay on track. In fact, once you get used to being in control of your time, you'll probably never go back to random day-to-day living. For those who are still skeptical about the usefulness of a schedule, what follows is a list of the benefits of scheduling you may not have considered.

Benefits of Scheduling

1. **Avoid Procrastination.** Scheduling helps you avoid one of the great time wasters, procrastination, because it gives you a set time to do each task. It gets you started and helps you avoid putting off doing things that you dislike.

2. **Stay on Top of Things.** Scheduling keeps you up to date and helps you avoid last-minute cramming. By keeping up to date and studying things as you come to them, you will learn much more efficiently.

3. **Balance Life with School.** Scheduling things that you need to do creates time to do things that you want to do. As a college student, you must be careful to keep a balance in your life. You need to have time for things other than studying. Scheduling takes away the guilt because it allows you to know you have a time for play, as well as a time for study.

4. **Stay in Control.** Scheduling keeps you in control. You are the creator of your schedule. You set your priorities and times to do things.

5. **Save Time.** Having a schedule saves time. Yes, it takes time to devise a schedule, but that time is repaid many times over. Your schedule is a guide, telling you what to do next and assuring you that everything will get done. Studying the same subject at the same time and in the same place programs your mind to concentrate on that subject, and you complete your studying more quickly and efficiently. That's what learning strategies are all about. You are seeking ways to study faster and better.

Despite these benefits, many students are still reluctant to use scheduling. Remember, however, that the job of being a college student is like no other job you've ever had. Scheduling may be your only means of survival. At least try scheduling, and choose the aspects of it that help you the most. Remember: one size does not fit all. Keep trying different kinds of schedules until you find something that works for you. Your success is too important to leave it to chance. Let's now examine some basic principles of scheduling so you get the full benefit of this procedure. You may not be able to use all of these this semester. They represent the ideal and will help you save time. If your work schedule leaves you no daylight hours to study or you already have back-to-back classes scheduled, then you may need to add extra study time to the master schedule you will create later in the chapter.

For Your Student Survival Kit

Principles of Scheduling

1. **Make use of daylight hours.** Several studies show that each hour used for study during the day is equal to one and a half hours at night. This means you should try to make use of free hours during the school day. These are the most effective yet most often wasted hours.

2. **Study before a class in which discussion is required or pop quizzes are frequently given.** The material will be fresh in your mind.

3. **Study immediately after lecture classes.** You can enhance your retention and understanding by studying right after class. Use this time to fill in gaps in your notes and to review information you have just learned. When you become more familiar with the Question in the Margin System for taking notes and processing lecture material, you will find that the hours immediately after class are perfect for writing questions in the margin of your notes and that reviewing your notes right after class will save you valuable time as compared to studying later. You will be able to complete your assignments faster and more efficiently because you won't have to refocus your concentration. (Do you see why scheduling back-to-back classes is a mistake?)

4. **Study at the same time every day.** You should have certain hours set aside for study that you treat the same as class. Having the same study time five days a week will soon become a habit and therefore easier to follow. Because the mind is programmed by routine, it will be easier to get started and to concentrate on the task at hand. Studying in the same place also aids concentration. If you have family responsibilities, it's best to schedule your study time while you are on campus if at all possible. There are just too many things at home that could interfere. If you have school-aged children, setting a time for everyone to study is a good idea, but you will accomplish even more if you can schedule study time on campus as if it were a class.

5. **Plan enough time to study.** The rule of thumb that you should study two hours for every hour you are in class is only a guide. Depending on your background or experience or on the difficulty of the class, you may need to allow more. Start out by studying for two hours, but adjust according to your need.

6. **Space your study periods.** A study period of 50 to 90 minutes at a time for each subject is probably most efficient. You should then take a break for 10 to 15 minutes. Studying for longer periods of time often becomes counterproductive.

7. **List activities according to priorities.** What things must get done today? That's where you start. Putting your most important tasks first will save you the stress of always being behind.

8. **Study during your prime time.** We all have daily cycles of alertness and sluggishness. If your work, classes, and circumstances permit, make use of this knowledge. Schedule your hardest subject at your most alert time, and schedule less demanding tasks during the day when you are less productive than you'd like to be.

9. **Leave unscheduled time for flexibility.** Packing your schedule with too many details will almost ensure its failure. Lack of flexibility is the major reason why students don't follow schedules.

10. **Analyze your use of time.** One cause of getting behind in college is not making use of short periods of time. By keeping a time log, you can see where you are currently wasting time. As noted previously, the time between classes and during the school day is the time most often wasted, even though it is the most efficient time to use for studying. Your time log may reveal a waste as simple as not responding to your alarm clock the first time it rings, napping in the afternoon after classes, or spending several hours on Facebook.

Time Log

Name _____

TIME	DAY 1 DAY ___ DATE ___			DAY 2 DAY ___ DATE ___			DAY 3 DAY ___ DATE ___			DAY 4 DAY ___ DATE ___			DAY 5 DAY ___ DATE ___		
	+	0	−	+	0	−	+	0	−	+	0	−	+	0	−
6–7 A.M.															
7–8 A.M.															
8–9 A.M.															
9–10 A.M.															
10–11 A.M.															
11 A.M.–12 P.M.															
12 P.M.–1 P.M.															
1–2 P.M.															
2–3 P.M.															
3–4 P.M.															
4–5 P.M.															
5–6 P.M.															
6–7 P.M.															
7–8 P.M.															
8–9 P.M.															
9–10 P.M.															
10–11 P.M.															
11 P.M.–12 A.M.															

PRACTICE 2.2

Time Log

To use your time most effectively, it is necessary to honestly analyze how you normally use your time. Monitoring your time for a typical week should give you a basis for this analysis.

Carefully fill in the chart on the previous page each day to account for what you did each hour. You do not have to stop each hour to fill it in, but you will probably want to do it several times a day. Don't depend on your memory at the end of the day. In addition to noting what you did, indicate your alertness by using a plus sign (+) for "I really feel sharp," a zero (0) for "I am functioning normally," or a minus sign (–) for "I am sluggish."

At the end of five days, you can take what you discover to help make a schedule that reflects the most efficient use of your time.

PRACTICE 2.3

Time Log Analysis

After keeping the time log (on the next page) for at least five days, answer or do the following:

1. At what times were you really sharp? _____

2. At what times were you the most sluggish? _____

3. What times were virtually wasted? _____

4. Analyze your time log as if you were a stranger. On another sheet of paper, write a short paragraph giving yourself advice.

Planning a Master Schedule

A master schedule should be made every time you have a major change in your use of time—for example, at the beginning of each semester or when you get a new job. *Use the list below and the master schedule worksheet on the next page to plan for this semester.*

1. **First and foremost, note those activities for which *you have no choice about when to do them:* classes, labs, job, picking up children at school, commuting, weekly meetings.**

2. **Count the number of blank spaces. Yes, include Saturday and Sunday. Write this number at the bottom of the master schedule. These are the hours in which *you can choose what you do.*** Note that the master schedule accounts for only the hours between 7 a.m. and midnight. You can create more choices by getting up earlier or accounting for hours after midnight.

3. **Now, note in those blank spaces the activities that *you need to do but have a choice about when to do them.* Assuming that your first priority is school, begin there. For each three-hour class that you are taking, fill in three spaces with study time**

for that particular course. Don't just write *Study*. Write *Study math*. **Make sure that you use what you already know about scheduling to make wise choices.** Use daylight hours. Study right after a lecture class or right before a recitation-type class that may have frequent quizzes or integrate discussions during class. Schedule one hour of study for every hour you are in class. *Treat these times as if they were classes,* as a part of your job! Miss them only for the same reason you might miss class or work. Even if you don't have homework to do, use these times to review or work ahead. For most classes, you will probably need at least two hours of study time. Start out by scheduling one hour of study time per class. As the semester goes on, adjust this length of time.

4. **Note the other things that you need to do: recreation, shopping, meeting with friends, time with family, laundry, cooking, eating, and so on.**

5. **Any remaining blanks are for use in whatever comes up—without guilt!**

PRACTICE 2.4

Master Schedule Worksheet

	SUN	MON	TUE	WED	THU	FRI	SAT
7–8 A.M.							
8–9 A.M.							
9–10 A.M.							
10–11 A.M.							
11 A.M.–12 P.M.							
12–1 P.M.							
1–2 P.M.							
2–3 P.M.							
3–4 P.M.							
4–5 P.M.							
5–6 P.M.							
6–7 P.M.							
7–8 P.M.							
8–9 P.M.							
9–10 P.M.							
10–11 P.M.							
11 P.M.–12 A.M.							

Putting Your Master Schedule into Practice

Now you are ready to make a master schedule for the semester. You will probably need to continue to make a weekly and daily checklist also. Study your master schedule. Did you consider the following things in your planning?

_____ Have you used daylight hours for studying? (For most people, these are more effective than nighttime hours.)

_____ Have you scheduled study time immediately before classes in which there is discussion or a possible pop quiz?

_____ Have you scheduled study time immediately after lecture classes?

_____ Have you scheduled either your most difficult class or your most difficult studying when you are the sharpest?

_____ Have you scheduled either relaxation or exercise when you are the most sluggish?

_____ Have you scheduled enough sleep?

_____ Have you scheduled time for eating well-balanced meals?

_____ Have you considered your work schedule?

_____ Have you considered travel time?

_____ Do you have a regularly scheduled study time for each class (even if you have nothing due for the next class)?

_____ Have you allowed time for family commitments?

What will you do differently when you schedule your classes next semester?

_____

_____

Now it's time to try what you planned to see if it will work. Use your planned master schedule to fill in the time-management log on the following pages. There is a column for what you planned to do and one for what you actually did. Keep the log for a week. Then make adjustments to your master schedule as needed. There is a clean master schedule following the practice sheet if you need to make adjustments. You may also want to put your revised master schedule on any electronic device you usually have with you and use often such as your laptop, your iPad, or your smartphone. Many researchers say that it takes 21 days for something to become habit. Be sure that you purposefully practice your master schedule for that long. Don't abandon it after only a few days.

StudentTIP

"My first semester, I was sure I didn't need anything as complicated as a master schedule. I refused to use it. I was also always behind, late with assignments, and in general not very successful. Second semester, I adjusted my master schedule a bit and used it successfully. What a difference! Don't waste a semester. Make yourself stick to a master schedule."

CRITICAL THINKING
About Prioritizing

Choose *either* John *or* Mary. It is not uncommon to find yourselves in a situation similar to John's or Mary's. Study the things John or Mary needs to do. Prioritize and rank each item in the order you think it should be accomplished. Number the items from 1 to 10. One is the item that should be done first. When you get to class, you may want to compare your rankings with those of your classmates.

John's To-Do List

_____ John's roommate just broke up with his girlfriend—needs comforting.

_____ 500-word English paper due tomorrow afternoon.

_____ Psychology exam tomorrow morning is on the syllabus.

_____ Book report for history due tomorrow. He's read part of the book, but he's not really sure what it's about.

_____ It's his mom's birthday. He promised to go to dinner.

_____ Biology test announced as he left class today.

_____ No clean shirts. He hasn't done laundry in two weeks.

_____ History paper due in two days, but he has tickets to the big basketball game tomorrow.

_____ A date with someone he's been wanting to date all term.

_____ It's not his day to work, but his boss wants him to come in for a couple of hours (probably means all night).

_____ Party tonight with a live band and free food.

Mary's To-Do List

_____ 500-word English paper due tomorrow afternoon.

_____ Psychology exam tomorrow morning is on the syllabus.

_____ Book report for history due tomorrow. She's read part of the book, but she's not really sure what it's about.

_____ Son is having trouble with his math homework.

_____ Tomorrow is gym day, and daughter's gym clothes are dirty.

_____ Biology test announced as she left class today.

_____ Out of milk and stuff for school lunches.

_____ Promised to help desperate friend study for algebra test.

_____ Daughter has spelling test.

_____ Message on voice mail to come in for part-time job interview.

1. What is your rationalization for the order you selected?
2. What are some ways John or Mary could have avoided letting so many things pile up?
3. Suggest a plan for managing upcoming commitments and assignments.

→ CAREER Connections

Managing time is not a skill that is limited to college students. Think of one or two people you admire because they are successful in what they do. Choose one person and list what you know about how he or she manages time.

Person _____

Some time-management skills this person uses:

_____

_____

_____

_____

_____

Which of these could you use as a student?

_____

_____

_____

_____

_____

_____

Time Wasters: Side Trips, Road Blocks, and Detours

Plan Your Attack on Time Wasters

Now that you understand how you waste time, how to do things in less time, how to create a master schedule, and how to use a to-do list and an agenda, let's revisit the idea of wasting time, so you can come up with a plan to be a more efficient learner. Because you are naturally busy as a college student, it is important that you stay in control. This does not mean you can't be flexible, but it does mean you need to have a plan. By analyzing your master schedule and time log, you will get some idea of just how flexible you can be. If you have a job, a family, or other

Virtual Field Trip
Procrastination and
Time Management

responsibilities, you will have less time with which to be flexible. If something unexpected comes up at a time you already have scheduled, try to trade off hours and plan when you can accomplish your originally scheduled task. You want to be careful not to waste time doing something you really don't want or need to do.

Following is a list of frequent time wasters for college students. There is a difference between allowing time to do these things and having them interfere with things you need to accomplish. Plan how you will avoid such time wasters should they occur. Probably the most frequent time waster is visitors dropping in unexpectedly, especially if you study in your dorm room, apartment, or home. One logical solution is to study elsewhere. Can you think of other solutions?

Afternoon naps are another real hazard for college students. Remember, what takes you an hour to do in the daytime may take you an hour and a half at night. Many students use naps as a form of procrastination. Getting enough sleep at night is one solution.

PRACTICE 2.7

My Plan for Time Wasters

Study the list in the first column. Give at least two possible plans in the second column to combat each time waster.

TIME WASTER	PLAN A AND PLAN B WHAT TO DO WHEN THIS OCCURS
Drop-in visitors	Plan A
	Plan B
Phone interruptions	Plan A
	Plan B
TV	Plan A
	Plan B
Afternoon naps	Plan A
	Plan B
Family or friends making demands	Plan A
	Plan B
Checking Facebook	Plan A
	Plan B
Your biggest time waster not mentioned	Plan A
	Plan B

You may have discovered something in this Practice that you want to add to your chart in Practice 2.1, Beginning Steps in Time Management.

Review—Where did we go?

Modeling the Learning Process

As we discussed in Chapter 1, learning is more than memorizing facts. You have modeled the learning cycle in this chapter whether you realized it or not. There were facts about saving time and helping you be more in control of your time, but you went further than gathering facts. You *analyzed* your use of time. You took your personal information and predicted ways for you to save time by creating a master schedule. You then put your plan into action and tried to use your master schedule. For many of you, adjustments were necessary, so you started the cycle over again. As a result, instead of memorizing facts about time management, you learned time-management strategies that you now own. Your plan for dealing with time wasters also fits this model.

Gathering. You learned the benefits and principles of scheduling, how much time to allow for each class, and ways to save time.

Analyzing. You analyzed the use of your time with a log.

Creating New Ideas. You created a master schedule.

Acting. You followed the master schedule.

Your plan for dealing with time wasters also fits this model. Explain what you did at each step.

Gathering

_____

_____

_____

_____

Analyzing

_____

_____

_____

_____

Creating New Ideas

_____

_____

_____

_____

Acting

_____

_____

_____

_____

Study Guide: Practicing the Principles of Time Management

To see if you grasped the major points of the chapter and to make a useful study guide, answer the following questions found in your reading. When you have written your answers, cover them and see if you can say the answer to each question in your own words.

1. According to most professors, how much work outside class will be required?

_____

_____

_____

2. What are two ways to make extra time?

1. _____

2. _____

3. What is the cardinal rule of time management? Give some examples.

_____

_____

_____

4. Explain the significance of the number 1,440 when dealing with time management.

_____

_____

_____

5. What is your road map or GPS for time management?

_____

_____

_____

6. What are five benefits of scheduling?

1. _____

2. _____

3. _____

4. _____

5. _____

7. What are 10 principles of good scheduling?

1. _____

2. _____

3. _____

4. _____

5. _____

6. _____

7. _____

8. _____

9. _____

10. _____

8. **Explain how to create a master schedule.**

_____

_____

_____

9. **What are three tools, in addition to your master schedule, that are necessary in managing your time?**

1. _____

2. _____

3. _____

10. **Name your three biggest time wasters and briefly explain your plan to combat each.**

1. _____

2. _____

3. _____

CASE STUDY
What's Your Advice?

Philip is a junior at a major university. He is 24 years old, not married, and he lives in an apartment near campus with three other students. He does most of his studying there. This semester he is taking 15 credit hours, and he works 20 hours a week. Philip has flexible work hours, and he chose to work on Monday, Wednesday, and Friday and schedule his classes on Tuesday and Thursday. Although he really wants to do well in school, Philip has struggled to make C's in his classes. He says he reads extremely slowly and simply doesn't have time to read everything his instructors assign. What advice would you give Philip?

Write your answer in paragraph form. Address it to Philip, and be specific in your advice.

Parallel Parking

We seem to understand concepts and remember them better when we compare them with something familiar. The running analogy in this text is comparing various strategies you may need to develop to be successful in college with strategies you may need when you are the driver on a road trip.

At the end of each chapter, you will be asked to think about what we have discussed so far and compare these discoveries with driving ideas.

When you fill in your answers, make sure you complete both sides of the analogy by comparing the driving term with a term for being a successful college student. One example is provided. There are no correct or incorrect answers. Choose one or two that you can relate to. This is to get you critically thinking about things you are learning.

Driving

A driver is in charge of where he is going. He chooses the route. He must keep his eyes on the road, know when to fuel up, and know when to ask for directions. He will likely remember where he has been. As a student, you must be in charge of what classes you take, when you must study, when you need a break, and when you need extra help. You must keep your eyes on why you are in college. It's hard work. You can't just sit in class and listen; you must take notes and ask questions.

Defensive Driving

Driving defensively involves _____

As a student, if I want to be successful, I need to: _____

_____

_____

_____

_____

Being a Passenger

_____

_____

_____

Rush-Hour Traffic

_____

_____

_____

_____

License

_____

_____

_____

_____

An additional one you think of

_____

_____

_____

_____

Evaluating Learning Outcomes

How successful were you in making it to your destination in this chapter?
Analyze what you learned in this chapter. Put a check beside each task you are now able to do. On a separate piece of paper, write a couple of sentences about how you learned each learning outcome and how you plan to continue to use what you learned.

☐ **List** ways you can make use of time previously wasted and do the same task in less time.

☐ **Demonstrate** time-management strategies, including constructing a master schedule for the semester.

☐ **Create** an organized to-do list, and show evidence of using a planner.

☐ **Analyze** a case study, and construct advice for students having difficulty with time management.

☐ **Explain** the learning process modeled in this chapter.

Your Student Tip for This Chapter

Use the space below to write a tip you would give to other students about what you have learned in this chapter.

_____

_____

_____

Practicing Critical Thinking

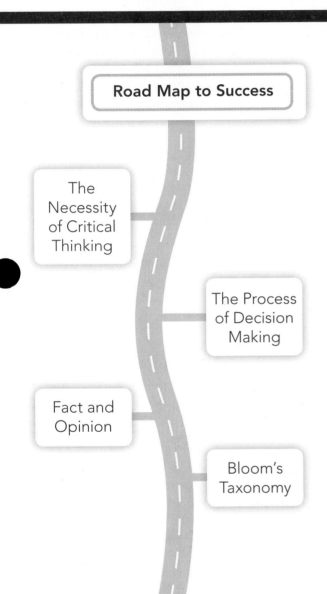

Road Map to Success

The Necessity of Critical Thinking

The Process of Decision Making

Fact and Opinion

Bloom's Taxonomy

In this chapter, you will learn how to

■ **Describe** the importance of the Critical Thinking process and discuss how it is important to your college career.

■ **Solve** a given problem using the decision-making process.

■ **Distinguish** between fact and opinion.

■ **Develop** questions that use lower- and higher-order thinking skills using Bloom's taxonomy as a guide.

■ **Begin** the decision-making process about possible majors and career choices.

■ **Analyze** a case study and construct advice for a student having difficulty with decision making.

■ **Explain** the learning process modeled in the chapter.

Where Are We Going?

By now, you have probably begun your adjustment to college and are starting to find ways to manage your time. So, where are we going in this chapter? What is our destination? When you complete this chapter, you are expected not only to understand some concepts about critical thinking, but to be able to use the decision-making process to solve problems and to distinguish between fact and opinion. You will be able to better predict test questions by developing questions that use both lower- and higher-order thinking skills, using Bloom's taxonomy as a guide. You will be able to analyze a case study and construct advice for a student having difficulty with decision making. You will use the decision-making process to begin to examine what your major might be and possible career choice for you to pursue. Finally, at the end of the chapter you will be able to describe how you used the learning model to become a better critical thinker.

The Necessity of Critical Thinking

Your primary job as a college student, as the driver of your vehicle, is to process information. In order to do your job well, you need to understand how your brain processes information. It will be necessary for you to take control by gathering information from lectures and making that information yours. You want to grasp what you read and process it so that you own it. We will cover these strategies in future chapters. However, a good place to begin learning how to do this is with a brief discussion of *critical thinking*. The thinking demanded of college students goes far beyond the memorization of facts. You will be introduced to some concepts of critical thinking in this chapter and then encounter them again throughout the text. While you are developing basic skills in taking notes, reading textbooks, and taking tests, you will simultaneously be developing critical-thinking skills that form the core of higher education and educated thinking.

There is a great deal of difference between learning the answer to a question and analyzing the implications of the answer, synthesizing and evaluating what you have learned, and applying what you have learned. Problem solving—critically analyzing a situation for the best solution and creatively finding an answer to the problem—is a skill that involves *thinking*. Thinking is a skill and, like other skills, can be learned and improved with practice. In thinking, the focus is not on the final answer, but on the process of getting the answer and going beyond facts. Instead of looking for one correct answer, we need to examine the *what-ifs*? the *whys*? the *what elses*?

Most of the courses you will take in college involve not just learning facts, but also developing thinking skills. In a previous history class you may have learned the dates of the Spanish–American War and the causes of that war. A *thinking* problem might require you to analyze how our country might be different if the war had not occurred. A critical thinker is constantly asking questions, trying to distinguish between fact and opinion. A critical thinker analyzes all sides of an issue to find more in the situation than the obvious. And a critical thinker makes assertions built on sound logic and solid evidence.

It is important to use critical thinking when learning and processing new information, but it is also necessary to use critical thinking in making decisions about when, where, and how to study; managing your time; and setting goals. You will use critical thinking when you take notes in class, read textbooks, and take tests. You will also use critical thinking in determining the validity of an Internet or library source, the best way to complete an assignment, or even how to get along with your professor or classmates. Moreover, you will need to use critical thinking to determine what you believe and what's important to you. And although not a part of this learning strategies text, decisions about partying, drinking, taking drugs, and entering and maintaining relationships are certainly a major factor in your success at college and will benefit from critical thinking.

Students seldom fail because they aren't smart enough; they more often fail because they make poor decisions or fail to seek solutions to problems. The critical-thinking skills you develop will not only make you a better student, but they will also make you a better employee or employer, a better spouse, or a better parent. Critical thinking is a life skill. The important decisions you make in your life will not be based on memorizing the "right answer." Each new situation demands defensive driving: questioning, analyzing, and evaluating. You can use the opportunities this course provides to practice and fine-tune your critical-thinking skills.

BRAIN BYTE

The Nobel laureate Herbert Simon states that the meaning of *knowing* has shifted from being able to remember and repeat information to being able to find and use it.

The Process of Decision Making

By thinking critically, you will find that your decisions are not made randomly. Rather, they follow a pattern. You will **first** determine exactly what the problem is. **Second**, you will gather any information necessary for you to make an informed decision. The **third** step is to determine what your options are. A major decision seldom has one solution. There's always another way. **Fourth**, you will weigh the evidence. Ask all the what-ifs. You will then—**fifth** step—make a choice among your options. The **sixth** step is to take action. Your action will be based on informed critical thinking. After you have taken action, you will review your decision and examine the consequences—the **seventh** step. Many times you may begin the process all over when your decision results in a consequence that requires a decision!

For Your Student Survival Kit

Critical Thinking

Your critical thinking about a decision may look something like this:

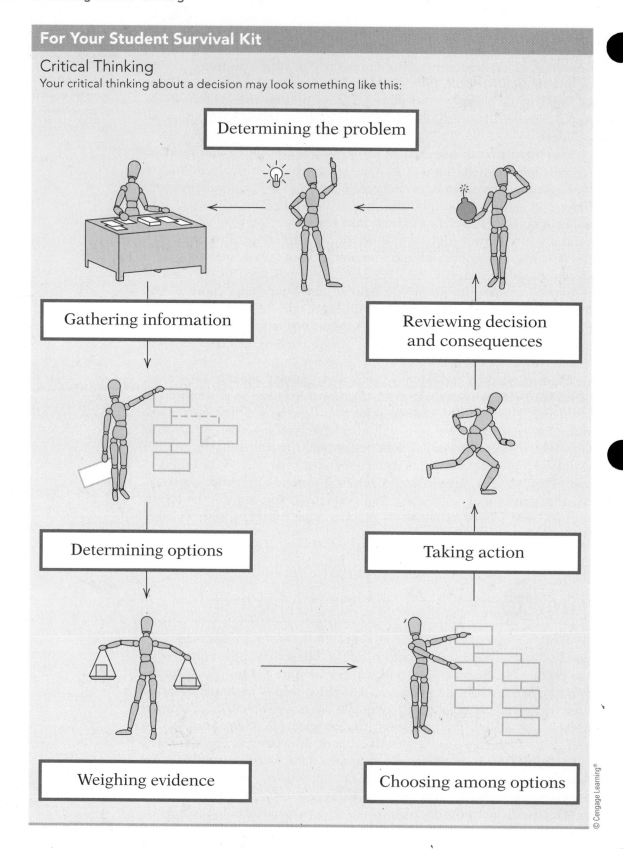

Determining the problem

Gathering information

Reviewing decision and consequences

Determining options

Taking action

Weighing evidence

Choosing among options

PRACTICE 3.1

The Decision-Making Process

Walk yourself through the decision-making process by examining Antwuan's situation. His car has become unreliable. He has missed class twice and missed several appointments lately because of various mechanical problems.

- Clearly state what you think Antwuan's problem is.
- Where can he gather useful information? What types of information does he need to gather?
- What options become apparent?
- What is some of the evidence he should weigh?
- What are some of his options?
- What specific action do you advise he take?
- What might be the consequences of that action?
- So now, what is the problem?

PRACTICE 3.2

Decisions About Grades

You may not have thought About the grade you make in each class as a decision. However, you can use the decision-making process to choose the grade you want.

You may want to earn an A in this class.

Gather the information. List specific things you must do to earn an A.

What are your options?

What evidence is there that they will earn an A?

What options do you choose?

Set goals for those options and take action.

→ **CAREER** Connections

Among the most important decisions you will soon need to make is what your major is and what career you will pursue. These decisions are too important to be taken lightly. Let's begin the decision-making process by determining the problem. It may be something like this, "I must choose a major that will help me get a job that I will be good at and that I enjoy." With critical thinking, the second step is to gather as much information as you can about your interest and abilities. There are many career inventories online. Your campus career planning, counseling, or job placement office may offer one or more of these. You will want to continue the decision-making process as you look for a major and ultimately a career that is a good fit for you.

BRAIN BYTE

Neuroscientist and educator Judy Will says that the most rewarding jobs of the 21st century will be those that cannot be done by computers. The best jobs will go to those who can think critically and communicate clearly.

Virtual Field Trip

Career Planning

Student**TIP**

"I thought steps of the decision-making process were just common sense and I didn't need them. But I found that going through the steps slows me down when I have a decision to make and helps me know that I have looked at all my options."

PRACTICE 3.3

Thinking About Thinking

1. Describe the process of your thinking in both choosing to come to college and choosing this college over other colleges. You may want to include, among other things: What facts did you gather? What opinions did you weigh? What issues were important to you?

2. What is the difference in trying to make an A in a course and trying to determine a way you might learn and use the content of a course?

3. Ben missed the first day of class because he registered late, and then he missed the next two days because he had the flu. Ben didn't notify the instructor. Explain to Ben what critical-thinking skills he should have used and why.

4. Name three specific decisions you will have to make in the next several years that will require the use of critical-thinking skills.

5. Write a short paragraph in which you describe a past situation in which you wish your thinking skills had been better.

Fact and Opinion

A crucial part of critical thinking is distinguishing between fact and opinion. A fact is something that is true no matter what we think about it. A fact can be verified. Opinions, on the other hand, are personal judgments or viewpoints. Opinions should be based on fact and supported by fact, but they themselves are not fact. Let's look at two examples:

Fact   Approximately 18,000 students attend this university.

Opinion   The campus is too crowded.

The school has 18,000 students. That is a fact and is verifiable—that is, you can look it up and make sure it's true. That the campus is too crowded is an opinion. Why? Because it's a personal judgment and someone can disagree with it. Someone coming from a school of 40,000 students may think a campus with 18,000 students is not crowded.

Fact   Teenage pregnancies are at an all-time high.

Opinion   Sex education should begin in elementary school.

PRACTICE 3.4

Fact or Opinion?

Read the following statements. Are they fact or opinion? In the blank to the left mark *F* for fact and *O* for opinion. If the statement is opinion, decide what kinds of facts are needed to support that opinion.

_____ 1. Mickey Mantle was the strongest switch hitter in baseball history.

_____ 2. During his career, Mantle hit 536 home runs.

_____ 3. Grades do not encourage learning.

_____ 4. Human life is not valued in a technological society.

_____ 5. The average car traveling at 57 miles per hour gets only two-thirds the gas mileage of a car moving at 50 miles per hour.

_____ 6. Based on an analysis of census and education statistics, Americans who complete a bachelor's degree have a median income of $50,360 compared with a median of $29,423 for people with only a high-school diploma.

_____ 7. Foregoing sleep by cramming all night reduces your ability to retain information by up to 40 percent.

_____ 8. The attention that the news media gives to criminals contributes to crime.

_____ 9. We should drink less cola.

_____ 10. Eighteen ounces of an average cola drink contain as much caffeine as a cup of coffee.

_____ 11. We should ban smoking in public places.

_____ 12. The amount of nicotine the average pack-a-day smoker inhales a week—400 milligrams—would kill a person instantly if it were taken all at once.

_____ 13. 37 percent of employers use Facebook to pre-screen applicants.

_____ 14. Alcohol is the number one date-rape drug.

_____ 15. There is an overemphasis on sports on college campuses.

A critical thinker, when trying to determine whether something is fact or opinion, asks questions. What was the source of information? Was the source of information an authority? Was the information accurate? Can it be substantiated? Where? Is the information current? Look back over the previous 15 statements. Do any statements that you marked as facts need more evidence? Place a question mark beside any that you think should be verified further. Be sure to explain what verification each needs.

Levels of Learning: Bloom's Taxonomy

When discussing critical thinking, learning experts usually categorize levels of thinking. One of the most influential models for such categorizing is _Bloom's taxonomy of higher thinking_.[1] Bloom's taxonomy says the level, or depth, of your learning will probably depend on several factors. Your interest in learning the material and the urgency of your need to use or master it are two important factors. Bloom asserts that you must master one level before you can move on to the next. You can use Bloom's taxonomy as a road map to see where you are going with your thinking. We learn best by asking questions. Understanding the levels of Bloom's taxonomy will be helpful in formulating questions to ask in class and in determining what questions might be asked on tests and exams. The first three levels of this system deal with lower-order thinking skills

BRAIN BYTE

D. C. Berliner says the better the quality of question asked, the more the brain is challenged to learn. Performance scores of learners improve when they improve the depth of their questioning.

[1]B. S. Bloom et al., eds., _Taxonomy of Educational Objectives: The Classification of Educational Goals. Handbook 1: Cognitive Domain_ (New York: David McKay Company, 1956).

that are essential in laying the foundation for deeper understanding. The last three employ higher-order thinking skills.

1. **First level: Knowledge.** You can remember something without fully understanding it, as you do when you memorize something. Test questions that ask you to *list, define, identify,* or *name who, when, or where* usually require only the knowledge level. Students often fall into the trap of studying for a test at this level and thinking they are prepared, when in fact they will need a higher level of preparation. An example of a knowledge-level question is "Where were the first Olympic games held?"

2. **Second level: Comprehension.** Understanding information means you can explain it in your own words. Test questions that ask you to *summarize, discuss,* or *compare* are likely to be at the comprehension level. An example of a comprehension-level question is "Name and explain the steps necessary for a bill to become law."

3. **Third level: Application.** You use the application level when you apply information you've learned to solve problems. Most of what goes on in a math class is at the application level. You may know a law or understand a formula, but in order to "do your homework," you must apply that law or formula. Test instructions might ask you to *apply, demonstrate, calculate,* or *modify.* An example of an application-level instruction is "Demonstrate that you know how to take notes using the Question in the Margin System."

The next three levels demand a deeper level of thinking. They are sometimes referred to as *higher-order thinking skills (HOTS).*

4. **Fourth level: Analysis.** When you analyze, you break complex ideas into parts and see how the parts work together. You recognize patterns, organize parts, and recognize hidden meanings. An example of an analysis-level question is "What evidence can you present to support the statement that the Confederate Army was unprepared in the Battle of Shiloh?"

5. **Fifth level: Synthesis.** When you synthesize, you make connections with things you already know. You are able to draw conclusions and make predictions. You use old ideas to create new ones, or you relate knowledge from several areas. An example of a synthesis-level question is "What would happen if you combined sulfur and iodine?"

6. **Sixth level: Evaluation.** When you evaluate, you judge something's worth. Did the note taking system work for you in history class, or do you need to make adjustments? This step involves making choices based on reasoned argument, checking, and critiquing. An example of an evaluation-level question is "What were the merits of Hannibal's plan to take Rome?"

In 2001, Anderson and Krathwohl revised Bloom's taxonomy.[2] In the higher-order thinking skills, they list *evaluate* as level 5 and *create* (instead of synthesis) as level 6. For our purposes, learning to ask questions at different levels and preparing for test questions at different levels, the revision is interesting, but the result is really the same. You may want to search the Internet for more about the revised taxonomy and decide which makes more sense for you.

---

[2]L. W. Anderson and D. R. Krathwohl, eds., *A Taxonomy for Learning, Teaching, and Assessing: A Revision of Bloom's Taxonomy of Educational Objectives* (New York: Longman, 2001).

Making **CONNECTIONS**

When trying to learn something new, we get a better understanding if we compare it to something we already know. For example, if I play or watch football, I may know the name of a play; that's *knowledge*. If I can explain that play to someone else, I have moved to the *comprehension* level. When I actually run the play in practice or in a game, that's *application*. If the play isn't successful, I would want to *analyze* it to see why not. The *synthesis* level would be using what I found out in my analysis to determine how I should change the play to make it successful. This would be creating a solution. *Evaluation* would involve determining if it is a good play to run in certain situations or against certain teams.

Now it's your turn to make it concrete. Choose one of the following and explain each level in terms of your selection: (1) making an apple pie, (2) buying a car, (3) planning and taking a vacation, or (4) studying for a test.

Knowledge

Comprehension

Application

Analysis

Synthesis

Evaluation

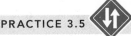 PRACTICE 3.5

Levels of Learning

For a quick check of your understanding of levels of learning, list the level of learning that you think each of the following tasks involves: *knowledge, comprehension, application, analysis, synthesis,* or *evaluation:*

_____ Changing a flat tire

_____ Finding the main idea of a paragraph

_____ Explaining a class lecture to a friend who was absent

_____ Summarizing an article

_____ Finding the lowest common denominator for fractions

_____ Finding the correct answer in a multiple-choice question

_____ Creating a webpage

_____ Appraising the damage on your wrecked car

_____ Listing the states and capitals

_____ Making an apple pie

_____ Comparison shopping for the best buy

_____ Writing an essay for English class

_____ Computing your grade point average

Student**TIP**

"I studied four hours for my first history test. I knew all the facts. However, I made an F on the test. When I examined the test questions, most of them required higher-order thinking skills. I hadn't studied with that in mind. Now when I study, I try to predict questions that include analysis, synthesis, and evaluation."

Virtual Field Trip
Bloom's Taxonomy

Asking and Predicting Questions

We learn best by using the material or asking questions. Bloom's taxonomy provides a framework for identifying things to do or asking questions and for predicting test items. Let's have some fun. Assume you are having a test on "Goldilocks and the Three Bears." Remember the story? Goldilocks goes into the bears' house, eats their porridge, sits in their chairs, and sleeps in their beds. Take a minute to tell the story to students in your group to make sure you all heard the same version and to make sure those who haven't heard the story know what happened. Now let's practice using the material to ask questions at each level. I have provided you with one instruction or question from each level. **Your job is not to do the task or answer that question but to think of another task or question at that level.** Before you begin, you may want to take the preceding Virtual Field Trip to find more about Bloom's taxonomy and the types of tasks or questions to use for each level.

Knowledge (recall specific details)
What are some of the things that Goldilocks did in the bears' house?
Your question: _____

Comprehension (understanding what was read)
Why did Goldilocks like the little bear's chair best?
Your question: _____

Application (converting abstract content to concrete situations)
Draw a picture of what the bears' house looked like.
Your question: _____

Analysis (looking for patterns in the story, maybe even comparing the context to a personal experience)
What parts of the story could not have actually happened?
Your question: _____

Synthesis (making a hypothesis from your analysis)
How might the story have been different if Goldilocks had visited the three fish?
Your question: _____

Evaluation (making judgments)
Do you think Goldilocks was good or bad? Why do you think so?
Your question: _____

Follow-Up
Now select a section from one of your textbooks that you will probably discuss in class and be tested on. Give an instruction or ask a question at each level.

Look over a returned test, and label the level of each instruction or question.

When you first learn something, you can't be expected to jump to the sixth level. In order to master it, first you have to know it, understand it, and apply it. This is why when you wait until the last minute to study for a test, you can do little more than memorize the information, and then you are often caught short when the answer requires more depth.

This chapter is merely an introduction to the critical-thinking skills you'll need to succeed in college. You will continue to look at other aspects of critical thinking when you learn about taking notes, reading textbooks, studying for and taking tests, and doing research both in the library and on the Internet.

Virtual Field Trip
Learning More About
Asking Questions

> ### Making **CONNECTIONS**
>
> Did you notice that *gathering* is similar to the first level of Bloom's taxonomy, knowledge? *Analyzing*, making meaning of the new information, combines comprehension and analysis? *Creating* and *acting* are really a combination of synthesis and evaluation?

 # Review—Where did we go?

Modeling the Learning Process

You have modeled the learning cycle in several ways in this chapter. Let's look at a couple of ways you completed the learning cycle.

Gathering. You got information about the steps of the decision-making process and the levels of Bloom's taxonomy.

Analyzing. You analyzed options in the decision you needed to make. You analyzed and found examples for each level of Bloom's taxonomy to make sure you understood it.

Creating New Ideas. You created a plan for making a decision. You predicted test questions at each level of Bloom's taxonomy.

Acting. You followed your plan for solving your problem. You practiced giving instruction and answering questions you predicted and found actual instructions and questions in tests you had taken.

Study Guide: Practicing Critical Thinking

To see if you grasped the major points of the chapter and to make a useful study guide, answer the following questions found in your reading. When you have written your answers, cover them and see if you can say the answer to each question in your own words.

1. **List three characteristics of a critical thinker.**

    1. _____

    2. _____

    3. _____

2. **List the seven steps of the decision-making process.**

   1. _____

   2. _____

   3. _____

   4. _____

   5. _____

   6. _____

   7. _____

3. **What is the difference between fact and opinion?**

   _____

   _____

4. **What are some important questions you should ask in trying to determine fact or opinion?**

   _____

   _____

5. **List and explain the six levels of Bloom's taxonomy.**

   1. _____

   _____

   _____

   _____

   _____

   _____

   2. _____

   _____

   _____

   _____

   _____

   _____

   3. _____

   _____

   _____

   _____

   _____

   _____

4. _____

_____

_____

_____

_____

_____

5. _____

_____

_____

_____

_____

_____

6. _____

_____

_____

_____

_____

_____

CASE STUDY
What's Your Advice?

Nina is taking her first required history course at her university. She did very well in her history courses in high school and therefore was not worried about the first test. As she read each chapter, she made flash cards of dates, people, terms, and places. She even drew a timeline so that she knew the sequence of events. She prepared a study plan and studied for several days before the test, including the night before. However, when Nina began her test, she found that she didn't know what to do. Instead of asking for dates, people, terms, and places, the test instructions and questions were as follows:

• Compare the ways in which the Market Revolution affected middle-class white women and slave women.

• Describe the role that railroads played in sectional conflicts between 1850 and 1870.

• Trace the changes in Americans' expectations of government that occurred during the Age of Anxiety, and explain what caused those changes.

• Compare the responses of Eisenhower, Kennedy, and Johnson to the civil rights movement.

• In your opinion, what was the true birthday of the United States: 1776, 1789, or 1812? Justify your answer.

What advice can you give to Nina to prepare for her next test?

Parallel Parking

We seem to understand concepts and remember them better when we compare them with something familiar. The running analogy in this text is comparing various strategies you may need to be successful in college with strategies you may need when you are the driver on a road trip. As you did in the parallel parking exercise at the end of Chapter 2, think about what we have discussed so far or what you have discovered about college in your first few weeks and compare these discoveries with driving ideas.

When you fill in your answers, make sure you complete both sides of the analogy by comparing the driving term with a term for being a successful college student.

Side Trips

_____

_____

_____

_____

Refueling

_____

_____

_____

Defensive Driving

_____

_____

_____

_____

Fender Bender

_____

_____

_____

_____

Evaluating Learning Outcomes

How successful were you in making it to your destination in this chapter?
Analyze what you learned in this chapter. Put a check beside each task you are now able to do. On a separate piece of paper, write a couple of sentences about how you learned each learning outcome and how you plan to continue to use what you learned.

- ☐ **Describe** the importance of the critical-thinking process and discuss how it is important to your college career.
- ☐ **Solve** a given problem using the decision-making process.
- ☐ **Distinguish** between fact and opinion.
- ☐ **Develop** questions that use lower- and higher-order thinking skills using Bloom's taxonomy as a guide.
- ☐ **Begin** the decision-making process about possible majors and career choices.
- ☐ **Analyze** a case study and construct advice for a student having difficulty with decision making.
- ☐ **Explain** the learning process modeled in the chapter.

Your Student Tip for This Chapter

Use the space below to write a tip you would give to other students about what you have learned in this chapter.

_____

_____

_____

Setting Goals

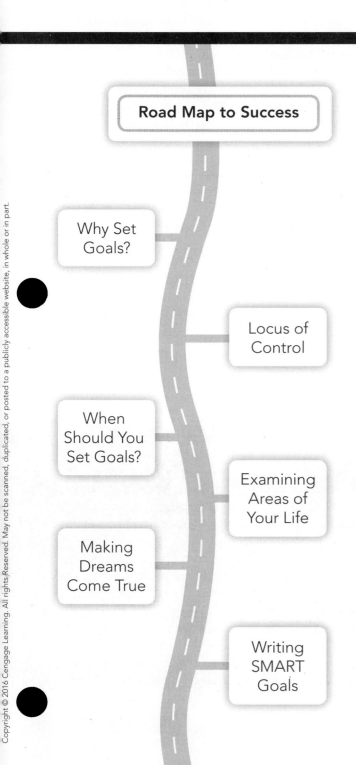

Road Map to Success

Why Set Goals?

Locus of Control

When Should You Set Goals?

Examining Areas of Your Life

Making Dreams Come True

Writing SMART Goals

In this chapter, you will learn how to

- **Identify** your locus of control, and develop a plan for improvement if necessary.

- **Write** goals for various areas of your life that are specific, measurable, have an action plan, are realistic, and have a target time.

- **Develop** an action plan for a personal goal and begin to develop a plan of action for a career goal.

- **Analyze** a case study and construct advice for a student having difficulty coping with goal setting.

- **Explain** the learning process modeled in this chapter.

Where Are We Going?

When you think about the skills you need to be successful in college, you probably think of skills in test-taking, note taking, getting the main idea from textbooks, doing research, writing, enhancing memory, concentrating, managing time, or thinking. However, the driving force behind achieving all these skills is one we seldom think of as a skill at all. It is the skill used to set goals and priorities. We need to know where we want to go and what we need to do to get there. If we are to become proficient at goal setting, we need to look at why we set goals, when we should set goals, and some ways to set useful goals.

Few of us really know specifically what we want out of life. And most of us don't spend time setting goals. We are too busy. We go with the flow and just let things happen to us. The truth is, however, we *can* make things happen. We have choices. The things that we spend our time, money, and emotional energy on are the things we make happen. How would you like to know how to write a goal in such a way that you are actually able to accomplish it? That's the final destination for this chapter. Along the way you will identify your locus of control and develop a plan for improvement if necessary. You will examine various areas of your life and write goals that are specific, measurable, have an action plan, are realistic, and have a target date for completion. You will develop a plan of action for a personal goal and begin to develop a plan of action for a career goal. Using what you learn, you will be able to analyze a case study and construct advice for a student having difficulty setting goals. And finally, at the end of the chapter you will be able to describe how you used the learning model to set achievable goals.

Why Set Goals?

Setting goals may be compared to planning a trip. There is a great deal of difference between going for a drive and just ending up somewhere and planning details to reach a certain destination. There is a great deal of difference between driving a car and being a passenger. You will always arrive at some destination whether you plan for it or not. However, if you carefully plan with a specific destination in mind, if you are in charge of where you are going, you significantly increase your chances for getting where you want to be. You might not always get there, but as the driver of your trip, as the goal-setter, you have a much better chance than someone who remains a passenger.

Like planning a trip, when you set goals, you are essentially organizing a plan to reach a certain destination. Few good things just *happen*; rather, they come with planning and hard work. Not planning leaves us drifting through life and maybe even stalled in a place we'd rather not be.

BRAIN BYTE

Brain research shows that students achieve more when they feel they are in control and have set specific goals for learning. There is a definite connection between being in control and setting goals.

PRACTICE 4.1

What Does It Take to Make You Happy?

List 20 things you love to do.

1. _____
2. _____
3. _____
4. _____
5. _____
6. _____
7. _____
8. _____
9. _____
10. _____
11. _____
12. _____
13. _____
14. _____
15. _____
16. _____
17. _____
18. _____
19. _____
20. _____

Go back down your list and use the following codes for each item:

$ If it costs more than $10

A   For an activity that you prefer to do alone

P   For an activity that you prefer to do with people

AP   For an activity that can be done alone or with people

2   If this would not have been on your list two years ago

10   If you think this will make you happy 10 years from now

M   If you think this might have been on your mother's list when she was your age

F   If you think this might have been on your father's list when he was your age

Personal analysis. Use another sheet of paper and write down what you have discovered about yourself.

Critical analysis. Explain why this practice is relevant in a chapter on goal setting.

Locus of Control

Locus of control refers to how much control people feel they have over their life. Essentially, the way you feel about being able to *make changes* in your life affects your ability to *actually change*. There are two extremes: internal and external.

People with an **internal** locus of control believe they have power over events in their lives. Even if they can't change what happens, they believe they can influence the outcome. In other words, people with an internal locus of control believe in setting goals because they believe they have the power to reach them. And while things beyond their control may affect people with an internal locus of control, they still respond as *creators*; they work to create a solution. People with an internal locus of control are the drivers; they make adjustments for the road conditions.

People who have an **external** locus of control believe that such factors as fate, chance, luck, or powerful others are more important than personal efforts in controlling what they can achieve. Whereas people with an internal locus of control believe they can influence the outcome of things they can't change, people with an external locus of control believe they can't. People with an external locus respond as *victims*. These are the kind of people who believe nothing is their fault. People with the external locus of control are the passengers; they believe they have no control over where the vehicle is going or where it will stop.

PRACTICE 4.2

Locus of Control

Examine the following statements made by students with either a strong internal or external locus of control. Supply an example for each blank. Your answer for internal locus of control should create a solution.

External (victim)	They made me take this learning strategies class.
Internal (creator)	I should be able to gain skills in this class to use in other classes.
External (victim)	That teacher hates me; he'll never give me a good grade.
Internal (creator)	I can meet with my instructor to see how I can do better.
External (victim)	What's the answer to number 5?
Internal (creator)	How do I find the answer to number 5?
External (victim)	The instructor assigns too much reading in history class.
Internal (creator)	_____
External (victim)	My children won't let me study.
Internal (creator)	_____
External (victim)	My boss makes me work too many hours.
Internal (creator)	_____
External (victim)	I have never been good in math.
Internal (creator)	_____
External (victim)	Other people in my class are smarter.
Internal (creator)	_____
External (victim)	I always get the hard questions.
Internal (creator)	_____

External (victim)	Just my luck to be externally motivated. There's nothing I can do.
Internal (creator)	_____

Students who are internally motivated are better adjusted, more independent, more realistic in aspirations, more creative, more flexible, more self-reliant, more open to new learning, more interested in intellectual achievement, and less anxious. They make higher grades than those who are externally motivated. When setting goals, focus on specific short-term goals at first if you've found you have a higher external locus of control. You can still develop an internal locus control of course, and mastering short-term goals is a sure-fire way to beginning to change your locus of control from external to internal.

 PRACTICE 4.3

Why Are You Here?

You have chosen to be a college student, but not everyone in college is here for the same reasons. Why are you here? What are your goals? Stop for a minute and examine your reasons for going to college. Rate the following reasons from 1 (most influential in your decision to go to college) to 16 (least influential in your decision). Please use a different number for each item.

_____ To be exposed to new ideas or experiences
_____ To prepare for a job or profession
_____ To gain problem-solving skills
_____ To gain prestige or status
_____ To prepare for good citizenship
_____ To raise economic status
_____ To gain maturity
_____ To become a productive member of society
_____ To get a degree
_____ To please parents or family members
_____ To assimilate knowledge
_____ To have something to do
_____ To learn how to learn
_____ To find a spouse or mate
_____ To make friends
_____ To have fun

 PRACTICE 4.4

Dreaming

If you already had all the time and money you needed, what would you be doing?
What would you drive?
Where would you live?
What kind of vacations or hobbies would you enjoy?
What kind of education would you provide for your children?
What type of charity or volunteer work would you be involved in?
What would your purpose in life be?

BRAIN BYTE

Dr. Hillman, whose BREATHE System was described earlier, asserts that one benefit of using the BREATHE System is that it helps you feel the confidence you need to be a creator rather than a victim.

Virtual Field Trip
Locus of Control

When Should You Set Goals?

You are constantly setting and reaching small or short-term goals. You need to finish an assignment or see your advisor. You probably should not begin any day without setting some goal to accomplish. This is a relatively simple task; with a little discipline, it can become a habit. However, any time there is a major change in your life, you should take time to reevaluate what you want out of life and possibly set new goals. Some of these times are graduating, starting college, beginning a new job, moving to a new place, getting married, or getting divorced. A birth, a death, a promotion, an illness, or an accident, or another major change may have altered previous goals. Most of us dream of things we would like to do. The major difference between dreams and goals is that goals are written down. However, you need to do more than simply scribble some ideas on a piece of paper. Here's where your critical-thinking skills come in. Your goals need to be complete and focused. A good way to see the big picture is to brainstorm. To guide you in a brainstorming activity, let's examine different areas of your life.

BRAIN BYTE

Professor Martin Ford of George Mason University says the goal-pursuing process will be effective only if learners have (1) enough feedback to make corrections, (2) enough belief in their capabilities to continue in the face of negative feedback, (3) enough actual skill to complete the task, and (4) an environment conducive to success.

Examining Areas of Your Life

Beginning college is a major change for you. It's time to do some goal setting. However, just as it might have been difficult to think of 20 things that make you happy, it could be even more difficult to just sit down and make a list of things you want to do in your life. Some of you clearly know what your goals are, but you may not have examined all areas of your life. Most of us just go from day to day without a great deal of thought about what we ultimately want. Let's direct your focus by examining different areas of your life. To help you think about goals that you might want to set, let's divide your life into different **areas** and think about what you want for that area. (You could just as easily examine your goals by the roles you play: student, son or daughter, father or mother, friend, and so on).

35-Minute Brainstorming Activity

Following is a think sheet containing seven areas of your life: (1) *Family/Home*, (2) *Mental/Educational*, (3) *Financial/Career*, (4) *Social/Cultural*, (5) *Spiritual/Ethical*, (6) *Physical/Health*, and (7) *Fun/ Recreational*. Use this sheet to brainstorm.

Spend five minutes on each area, listing anything you would like to have happen or do in that particular area for the rest of your life. Be as specific as possible. In some areas you will write nonstop for the full five minutes and perhaps need more time. Other areas may be more difficult for you to develop ideas in. You will probably need more room for some areas. Needing more room to write for an area is usually an indication that the area is important to you.

FAMILY/HOME	MENTAL/ EDUCATIONAL	FINANCIAL/CAREER	SOCIAL/CULTURAL	SPIRITUAL/ETHICAL	PHYSICAL/HEALTH	FUN/RECREATIONAL

Themes of Goals

Look back over your brainstorming think sheet. Could you add more to each area with a little more guidance? In order to help you think further about the areas of your life, consider some common themes in each area. You may want to cut back on something, such as eating sweets, or you may want to expand something, such as the amount of time spent on studying. You may want to improve a situation in an area of your life or solve a problem. Sometimes your goals involve maintaining your present situation. And sometimes you want to dream and become innovative.

To help you focus your thinking further, you may want to consider themes that goals might have. At the bottom of each area, list the following themes: (1) *Expansion or Cutting Back*, (2) *Improvement*, (3) *Problem Solving*, (4) *Maintenance*, and (5) *Innovation*.

Continue your brainstorming by thinking of things you need to expand or cut back on having or doing in your family and home. Then think of things that you could improve in your family and home. Is there a problem in your family that you would like to solve? Are there good things about your family or home that you would like to maintain? Or are there things in your family or home you would like to try that are totally different from anything you've ever done? Continue this procedure with each area of your life. When you finish, you will have a wealth of information to help you begin to set some concrete goals. You will probably want to develop goals in all areas of your life; however, you cannot be an expert in all areas. Being an expert usually takes so much time, money, and effort that you have little left for other areas of your life. It is a matter of what you value. You are in control of this journey.

PRACTICE 4.5

Brainstorm Follow-Up

At different times in our lives, one or more of these areas will take priority over the others. After you have completed the brainstorming activity, list the seven areas in order of importance to you at this time.

1. _____

2. _____

3. _____

4. _____

5. _____

6. _____

7. _____

Some Guidelines for Writing Goals

Make sure that the goal you are working for is something that you really want, not just something that sounds good. Be certain it is indeed your goal and not someone else's. Be sure that your goal is positive instead of negative. And be sure that it is something within your control.

Making Dreams Come True

The dreaming practice and the brainstorming should have helped you begin to think about things that are important for you to accomplish in your life. **Long-term goals** are detailed descriptions of what you want for yourself in the future. Your long-term goals may include graduating from college, getting a job you enjoy, owning your home, or being able to travel. Review your brainstorming for specific things that are important to you. What are some things you want to accomplish in your life?

The way to make your long-term dreams come true is to set a series of short-term goals that lead to the accomplishment of what you want. The more specific you can make your long-term goals, the easier it will be to set short-term goals that will help you achieve your dream. You have it in your power to reach your dreams. The first step in making your dreams concrete is to analyze what you must do in order to reach your goal.

Short-term goals are the steps you take to reach your long-term goals. Short-terms goals are plans of action. They are your to-do list for today and tomorrow and the next day. A well-written short-term goal will give you directions for exactly what you need to do and set a deadline for its completion. The first step in your long-term goal to graduate may be completing your math assignment for class today.

BRAIN BYTE

Researchers Edwin Locke and Gary Latham surveyed nearly 400 studies on goals, and the results were definitive. They found that specific, difficult goals lead to better performance than easy, vague ones.

Student**TIP**

"Reaching for a goal is like building with Legos. You have to add one piece at a time until you have a finished product."

CAREER Connections

When setting goals, we can use the same critical-thinking process we used in the decision-making process we discussed earlier in the text. After all, developing a plan is really a decision you make to achieve your goal. This puts you in control of what you accomplish.

With your goal in mind, you first want to gather as much information as you can to help you to determine what your options are for getting closer to your goal.

- What skills do I need to achieve this?
- What information and knowledge do I need?
- What assistance or collaboration do I need?
- What resources do I need?
- What can block my progress?
- Am I making any assumptions?
- Is there a better way of doing things?

Continued

Career Connections continued

If your goal is to declare your major (part of your goal to graduate from college), you want to gather as much information as you can.

What are your options?

- You could visit your academic advisor.
- You could study the college catalog to see what majors are offered.
- You could talk to professors teaching in a field you think you might be interested in.
- You could take a career decision-making inventory.
- You could study references such as *Occupational Outlook Handbook*.
- You could shadow someone in a career that interests you.
- You may, in fact, want to do all of these.

In the decision-making process, we next weigh the evidence— *Do I need to do more than one thing? What needs to be done first?*

Next, you must take some kind of action. Goals are never achieved by just thinking about them. You have to do something. You want to clearly define the plan of action you choose to take.

Your action plan should give you specific directions such as who, what, when, where, why, and how.

"I will schedule an appointment with Dr. Hatfield for February 3 at 3 o'clock to discuss setting career options."

Whether you have declared your major or not, this is a good time to explore some of the options listed above and to set some goals about your career.

BRAIN BYTE

Motivational speaker Zig Ziglar suggests that the day people get the most done is the day before they go on vacation because they have a clear goal and deadline.

For Your Student Survival Kit

Writing SMART Goals

Many coaches and consultants use the **SMART** acronym as a guide to writing useful goals. Read the guide below and then explain how the goal to meet with your advisor meets all of the elements.

With long-term goals, the more of these elements you include, the more likely you are to reach your goal. Short-term goals **should** have all five of the elements, with the emphasis on the action plan or plans.

When writing your goals, make sure each of them includes these five elements:

Specific	Describe what you want to accomplish with as much detail as possible.
Measurable	Describe your goal in terms that can be evaluated clearly.
Action Plan	Your goal should explain what action you will take.
Realistic.	You know you are capable of doing or achieving this goal.
Time Framed	Clearly specify target-completion time, with longer goals broken into shorter pieces.

PRACTICE 4.6

SMART Goal Setting: Let's Think This Through

You did poorly on a test and so you say **that your goal is to study more.** (*Not a SMART goal!*)

Study what? *History*

Exactly what will I do? *Read Chapter 5 and make flash cards for possible test questions as I read it.*

How much? *1 hour 3 times a week*

When? *From 3–4 P.M. Monday, Wednesday, and Friday*

Where? *In the library*

With whom? *By myself*

Why? *I really want to make an A in history.*

What else?

Instead of "I will study more," your goal now reads: **"From 3–4 on this MWF, I will go the library and read Chapter 5 of my history book and make flash cards of possible test questions as I read."**

A separate goal might be **"On Friday at 6 o'clock, I will meet Bob in the library and we will practice flash cards until 7."**

Now, are you going to continue doing this next week with Chapter 6? 7? 8?

How would you rewrite your goal to include that you are setting this study routine as a pattern for the rest of the semester?

PRACTICE 4.7

Practice Writing an Action Plan

Let's say you think that you are overweight. Your long-term goal is to lose weight. You realize that this goal doesn't meet the SMART goal requirements. How much? When and how often will I check my weight loss? What do I need to do to lose weight? Is my goal realistic? What is my deadline? So you revise your goal: **I want to lose 10 pounds in the next three months.** This is specific, measurable, probably realistic, and there is a time frame. However, there is no plan of action—nothing to tell you specifically what to do. You gather your information and determine that you could probably lose 10 pounds in three months by cutting your calories by 300–500 calories a day. Now you are ready to set short-term goals. How can you change your food intake or what exercise could you do to burn 300–500 calories a day?

Let me start the list for you.

1. Each day I can replace drinking one Coke (150 calories) with a bottle of water (0 calories).
   Continue to list things you might do daily to cut 300–500 calories.

2. _____

3. _____

4. _____

Continued

Practice 4.7 continued

Have you given yourself directions that are specific and measurable? Do you have an action to complete? Is your goal realistic? Have you given a time frame?

Looking at these examples, you can see that breaking a goal down to specific steps will help you focus daily on your goal. Remember, your goal needs to be realistic, so you may need to make adjustments to it—not just abandon it.

Setting a long-term goal that you want to be successful or you want a happy life may sound good, but you really have no directions for how to reach your goal. Let's look back at Practice 4.1, What Does It Take to Make You Happy? You listed 20 things that make you happy now. You could develop a plan of action to do some of those things on a regular basis.

List one SMART goal for this week from your What Does It Take to Make You Happy list.

My goal: _____

_____

How do you feel spending this much effort to develop an action plan? Satisfied? Frustrated? Do you feel you don't have time to think through everything? Developing an action plan becomes a matter of setting priorities. If your goal is important to you, you owe it to yourself to make the time. No one else can make that time for you or create an action plan for you.

PRACTICE 4.8

Writing SMART Goals

Look over your brainstorming list. Choose one thing that is important for you to accomplish. List it as your long-term goal. Try to use the SMART guidelines to state your goal.

Next, break it down to three or four short-term goals that you might do to accomplish that goal. Be sure you have included all the SMART elements. Pay particular attention to the action plan.

Long-term goal:

Short-term goal:

Short-term goal:

Short-term goal:

Short-term goal:

Tips for Achieving Goals

1. Make sure the goal you have written is specific, measurable, has a clear plan of action, is realistic, and has a target time for completion.
2. Find someone who has accomplished a similar goal. Ask how this person reached the goal and what obstacles to look out for.
3. Don't drive around aimlessly. Determine what skills, what knowledge, and what information you need to reach your goal.
4. Break your goal into smaller goals that you can readily accomplish.
5. Share your goal with others. They may have valuable information you need, or they may offer the encouragement you need when you get off track.

 **PRACTICE 4.9**

Making Your Goals Visible

Educator Skip Downing suggests that it is useful to draw your goals so you can see them. He suggests framing your picture and putting it where you see it often. Choose three goals that are important to you. Draw or cut and paste a picture you can frame, depicting at least three of your goals.

 Making **CONNECTIONS**

One of my dad's favorite expressions was, "If you don't have directions for where you are going, you may end up somewhere you don't want to be." Write a short paragraph in which you describe a time in your life where setting a specific goal would have resulted in you being in a "different place."

 StudentTIP

"I found making specific goals for each class a real motivation to keep up-to-date. Saying I want to make an A in history is not enough. My goals needed to be what I specifically need to do in a course to make the A on a test or make an A in the course. They involved things like taking notes in each class, making summary sheets when I completed an assignment, and setting aside a specific time to study that course."

Setting Goals for Difficult Classes

As an example of what you can do, examine Gina's most difficult class, American History 221. Here is her brainstorm of what is specifically wrong: "There is too much to read. I am behind three chapters and an outside reading book. The professor goes so fast I can't take notes. I study, but his questions ask more than I know."

You should look at these problems one at a time.

"There is too much to read. I am behind." If Gina is to be successful in the class, she must read all the material. Is there really too much to read so that there is no possible way to read it all within her current time schedule? If so, what can she *give up* in order to make time to read it? Does she need to drop the course until she is able to make time? What elements of time management does Gina need in order to reach her goal? If she chooses to stick with it, here are a couple of smaller goals that will help her.

Gina's Goals I

1. Gina needs to immediately find and set a time to catch up, and set a time for keeping up with her reading—a specific time of day and amount of time—and a place to do it.

2. Gina needs to take notes while reading so that she won't have to reread. ("I will read and take notes on Chapter 3 today at 3 o'clock, Chapters 4 and 5 tomorrow at 10 o'clock.")

"The professor goes so fast, I can't take notes." Of course, you know that if Gina had kept up with her reading, it would be easier to take notes. Where do the notes come from? Do they supplement or follow the reading assignments? Gina needs to analyze her note-taking system. (Taking good notes takes practice.) She needs to check her listening attitude and where she sits in class. She needs to discuss her problem with her professor. Probably, most of all, she needs a partner or group from the class. Immediately after class, her partner or group needs to meet with her and compare notes or non-notes, as the case may be, and maybe even check with the professor to fill in spots.

Gina's Goals II

1. Gina needs to analyze her note-taking system. Is she trying to write too much? Does she give up too easily? What specifically can she do to get more out of the lecture?

2. Gina needs to find a partner or group willing to meet consistently after class and make the effort to get notes. She needs to do it now, not wait until just before a test.

3. Gina needs to make an appointment with the professor. She needs to plan the conference before she goes, tell the professor what efforts she has made, and ask for help with problems she has not yet solved. She needs to be specific in what she asks for. (Just complaining or talking to the professor is not going to take the place of reading assignments and taking notes.) If the professor offers a suggestion, she needs to try it.

"I study, but his questions ask more than I know." One reason Gina has had trouble is that she wasn't keeping up with the assignments. When test time came, she had time to learn only on the first level of Bloom's taxonomy. She recalled facts only. Setting a daily time to study and process information improves the possibility of mastery at deeper levels. When Gina begins to synthesize the information, she can begin to predict what the test questions will be.

Gina's Goals III

1. Gina needs to take time after each class to understand the information presented and to prepare for the next class as if there is going to be a pop quiz on that material.

2. Gina needs to read the assignment and try to predict what questions will come from each section. She needs to write down the questions in the margin.

3. Gina should analyze old tests from the professor.

4. In a study group, she should try to predict what the questions on the test will be.

5. Gina needs to meet with the professor and test the predicted exam questions by asking if she is on the right track with the kinds of questions that will be on the exam.

There is a real difference between saying you want to do well in class and actually giving your best effort. Often students fool themselves into thinking that they can treat the courses they are taking in college like those in high school. You have learned that you can count on at least two hours of outside work for every hour you are in class maybe just to earn a C, depending on the class, and that study involves much more than just doing homework. If you have been out of school for a time, it will take more time in the beginning. It takes time to become a good note taker and an efficient reader. Now, what is your goal? Do you want to master the material in each class or just get through the class? If you are serious about learning, reevaluate your master schedule. Are you sticking with your plan? Practicing time management will also help you accomplish your goals.

CRITICAL THINKING
About a Difficult Class

Brainstorm about your specific problems. Then write at least two goals that address these problems that you will tackle today. (Remember to make your goals SMART—be specific, be measurable, include an action plan, be realistic, and have a target date for completion.)

Class _____

Brainstorm Goal 1

_____

_____

_____

_____

_____

Brainstorm Goal 2

_____

_____

_____

_____

_____

Much of the time in a study session, students fail to have specific goals; they feel they just get homework. Having specific goals for each study session helps you get more from your time.

Review—Where did we go?

Modeling the Learning Process

Again in this chapter, you were modeling the learning process. Remember, the cycle includes gathering, analyzing or finding meaning, creating, and acting.

Gathering. You got information about setting goals: why set goals, elements of a useful goal, and guidelines for setting goals.

Analyzing. You analyzed areas of your life with goal setting in mind. You tried to determine where you really want to be.

Creating New Ideas. You tried to determine what you must do to reach your destination.

Acting. You wrote goals useful for several areas of your life and created a plan by breaking large goals into smaller ones.

You took the first steps in achieving your goals.

You also found that you needed to begin the cycle over by gathering information you need to reach your goals.

Study Guide: Setting Goals

To see if you grasped the major points of the chapter and to make a useful study guide, answer the following questions found in your reading. When you have written your answers, cover them and see if you can say the answer to each question in your own words.

1. Why have goals?

_____

_____

_____

2. Explain locus of control.

_____

_____

_____

3. When is the best time to reevaluate goals?

_____

_____

_____

4. What are seven areas of your life described in the goal-setting practice?

  1. _____

  2. _____

3. _____

4. _____

5. _____

6. _____

7. _____

5. What are five themes of goals examined in the goal-setting practice?

1. _____

2. _____

3. _____

4. _____

5. _____

6. What are the five elements of a SMART goal?

1. _____

2. _____

3. _____

4. _____

5. _____

7. What are two specific goals you have set for your difficult class? (Be sure that your goals contain all elements of a SMART goal.)

1. _____

2. _____

CASE STUDY
What's Your Advice?

Bob has just graduated from high school. He has decided to go to a community college in his hometown because he can continue to work for his dad, live at home, and still take classes. College is not something he's really excited about, because he doesn't know what he wants to do. Bob knows his parents want him to continue his education, so he is really going to college to please them. There is plenty of time to see what comes up. Bob is working on his time management, and most of the time he is able to get everything done at work and at school without having too much free time left. He thinks that it's just his luck that he has instructors who give so much homework and that his dad is always changing his schedule. Given what you have learned about goal setting, what advice would you give Bob?

Parallel Parking

Remember, in college, you are successful only when you are driving, not just going along for the ride. Like the parallel parking practice at the end of the previous chapters, think about what we have discussed so far and compare these ideas to driving concepts. When you fill in your answers, make sure you complete both sides of the analogy by comparing the driving term to a term for being a successful college student.

Knowing Your Destination

_____

_____

_____

_____

_____

Changing Direction

_____

_____

_____

_____

Planning the Trip of a Lifetime

_____

_____

_____

_____

Evaluating Learning Outcomes

How successful were you in making it to your destination in this chapter?

Analyze what you learned in this chapter. Put a check beside each task you are now able to do. On a separate piece of paper, write a couple of sentences about how you learned each learning outcome and how you plan to continue to use what you learned.

☐ **Identify** your locus of control, and develop a plan for improvement if necessary.

☐ **Write** goals for various areas of your life that are specific, measurable, have an action plan, are realistic, and have a target time.

☐ **Develop** an action plan for a personal goal and begin to develop a plan of action for a career goal.

☐ **Analyze** a case study and construct advice for a student having difficulty coping with goal setting.

☐ **Explain** the learning process modeled in this chapter.

Your Student Tip for This Chapter

Use the space below to write a tip you would give to other students about what you learned in this chapter.

_____

_____

_____

Learning Principles

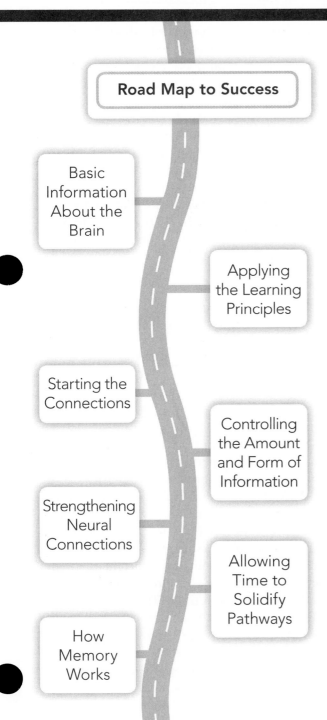

Road Map to Success

- Basic Information About the Brain
- Applying the Learning Principles
- Starting the Connections
- Controlling the Amount and Form of Information
- Strengthening Neural Connections
- Allowing Time to Solidify Pathways
- How Memory Works

In this chapter, you will learn how to

- **Describe** what basic parts of the brain have to do with processing information and learning.

- **Name and explain** ten learning principles.

- **Appraise** examples of students using learning principles and identify which learning principles are being used.

- **Analyze** a learning situation and determine several strategies that would be helpful both in college and in the workplace.

- **Construct** mnemonic devices to help recall information.

- **Reproduce** the flowchart for how the learning principles fit into the way the brain processes information.

- **Discriminate** among the levels of Bloom's taxonomy when applying the learning principles.

- **Demonstrate how** learning principles can be used in studying for a test.

- **Explain** the learning process modeled in this chapter.

Where Are We Going?

Your brain physically grows and changes every time you learn something. With all the changes taking place in your brain, as a college student, you need strategies to make your brain work for you. Intelligence is not fixed at birth; it is forming and developing throughout our lives. The core of academic success is knowing enough about how your brain processes information so that you can successfully develop strategies for learning. This chapter will equip you with some strategies to practice to enhance your learning. The chapter is divided into three sections. The first section deals with some very basic information about how your brain processes information. Yes, you can drive a car without knowing how the engine works, but you are better equipped to troubleshoot if you know the basics. Knowing how your brain works gives you the ability to develop strategies based on how the brain naturally learns best. It gives you the information you need to critically think about your learning strategies. The second section introduces you to ten learning principles based on what we know about the brain. The third section demonstrates how the learning principles work together. To remember what you are studying and to use it on tests and papers (that is, to make it your own) you first have to understand the material. You must also have a desire to learn it. Sometimes you understand the material and truly want to learn it, but just don't know how to process the information in such a way that you are likely to remember it and use it. This chapter will show you how to do this.

Basic Information About the Brain: Providing Background for Learning Principles

It is only in the last decade that scholars from separate disciplines like biology, chemistry, psychology, information science, philosophy, anthropology, and linguistics have come together to discover the information contained in this chapter. Neuroscientists have learned more about the brain in the last decade than in the entire preceding century. Research by neuroscientists has given us the reasons why many strategies used by successful students are so efficient. They are able to see how the brain processes information using neuroimaging devices. With this equipment, neuroscientists are able to determine the chemical and electric reactions taking place in the brain and have mapped exactly what part of the brain is used in various functions. The benefit for you is this: the more you understand how your brain processes information, the more empowered you are to develop techniques to remember relevant material.

Let's begin with a quick look at some basic biology of your brain. Your brain works on electrochemical energy and weighs approximately three pounds. If you make fists with your hands and put your fists together at the knuckles, the two fists give you a fairly accurate picture of the brain's size. Your brain has more than 100 billion brain cells, called **neurons**. However, *it is not the number of neurons that is significant; it is the connections they make with each other that determine learning.*

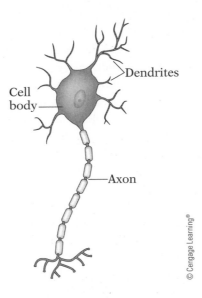

Every neuron is made up of three major regions: (1) a cell body (sometimes called a **soma**), containing a nucleus and other organelles where information is integrated, (2) an **axon**, a long, single fiber that sends information, and (3) **dendrites**, minute twigs, or web-like branches, which receive information.

The action inside the cell is electric, and the action between cells is chemical. Both the axon and dendrites have many connector points, so a neuron receives and sends many messages at a time. The electric activity within cells results in the growth of new dendrites stretching from the neuron. As learning takes place, the branches spread and thicken, making more connections possible. The axon is coated with myelin, an electrical insulation that forms a layer, the myelin sheath, around the axon. The more that path is used, the thicker the myelin becomes and the more efficient the transfer of information becomes. The amount of information stored in a single neuron is so small that it takes hundreds of thousands of neurons connected together to recall something as simple as your own name. No actual contact is made between axons and dendrites; rather, communication occurs through the release of neurotransmitters (chemical molecules) into the space between the axon and dendrite called the **synapse**. There are many types of chemicals that act as neurotransmitter substances. The type of neurotransmitter affects the strength of the connection.

In his article, "A Computer in Your Head?" Dr. Eric Chudler says:

When information is transferred from one neuron to another, molecules of chemicals ("neurotransmitters") are released from the end of one neuron. The neurotransmitters travel across the gap to reach a receiving neuron where they attach to special structures called receptors. This results in a small electrical response within the receiving neuron. However, this small response does not mean that the message will continue. Remember, the receiving neuron may be getting thousands of small signals at many synapses. Only when the total signal from all of these synapses exceeds a certain level will a large signal (an "action potential") be generated and the message continue.[1]

Just as we strengthen our muscles when we exercise, the neural connections are strengthened with use. Likewise, if we don't use connections, neurons are pruned or self-destruct.

In *What You Should Know about the Brain*, neuroscientist and educator Judy Willis summarizes some other important brain facts that will help you understand your brain's role in learning.[2]

- The only way new information enters the brain is through your senses.
- Your brain is exposed to billions of bits of information every second but is not equipped to handle that much. Filters are necessary to control the flow of information to approximately 2,000 bits of information a second.
- New information enters the brain through the senses and is routed either to the **prefrontal cortex (the thinking brain)** where you can consciously process and think about that information or to the **lower automatic brain (the reactive brain)**, which instinctively reacts to information without thinking it through by ignoring it, fighting against it, or avoiding it.
- If information ends up in the reactive brain, you probably won't remember it at all.
- With focus, you can actually control where new information goes and direct it to the prefrontal cortex.
- Three major brain elements that control where new information goes are the **reticular activating system,** the **limbic system**, and the **neurotransmitter dopamine**.
- The first filter that information from your senses passes through is the **reticular activating system (RAS)**. If you focus enough on what is most valuable, relevant, and important, the information goes to your thinking brain. If you are tired, bored, anxious, or overwhelmed, it is sent to the reactive brain.
- When new information gets through the RAS, it must then pass through the **limbic system**, the emotional core of your brain. Here the amygdala and the hippocampus determine where information brought in by the senses goes.
- The amygdala makes routing decisions based on emotions. If you experience negative emotions like fear, anxiety, or even boredom, the amygdala essentially blocks entry to the prefrontal cortex.
- Next to the amygdala in the lymbic system is the hippocampus. It is the hippocampus that links the new sensory input to memories of your past and knowledge that is already stored in your long-term memory to make relational memories.

[1]From "A Computer in Your Head?" by Eric Chudler, as appeared in *Odyssey Magazine*, March 2001.
[2]From the handout created to accompany the article "How to TeachStudents About the Brain," by Judy Willis, Educational Leadership.

- These relational memories are ready for processing in your prefrontal cortex.
- The prefrontal cortex is where executive functions such as judgment, analysis, synthesis, organizing, problem solving, planning, and creativity take place.
- Executive function networks can convert short-term memory into long-term memory. When you are focused and in a positive emotional state, your executive functions organize newly coded information into long-term knowledge.
- All this is done through nerve cells called neurons.
- Memory is not stored in single neurons, but by many neurons communicating with one another.
- When information is recalled, it is instantaneously retrieved from storage areas in many parts of the brain.
- Memory is continually changing and evolving as new information is added to it. (We speak of this as the brain's *plasticity*.)

 Making **CONNECTIONS**

When trying to learn something new, you get a better understanding if you compare it to something you already know. Now that you have read a description of how learning occurs in the brain, try making comparisons of new terms you have learned to some familiar things. I have begun the practice with analogies about a car and driving; you may continue along this line or completely switch to another analogy.

Neurons	are like cars	in that *cars are the bodies containing the parts that provide transportation just as neurons are the bodies that contain the parts to transport information.*
The nucleus	is like *the driver of a car*	in that it
Dendrites	are like	in that they
Axons	are like	in that they
Synapses	are like	in that they
Neurotransmitters	are like	in that they
The connections made	are like	in that they
Learning	is like	in that it

I own a computer and can make it do all sorts of amazing things. I use it to word process, create PowerPoint presentations, use Facebook, Twitter, send e-mail, surf the Internet, and develop webpages. However, it is capable of doing much more than I personally make it do. I could learn how to do more by reading and studying the owner's manual. Your brain, like my computer, can do much more than you make it do. To do your best in college, and later in your career, you need to read your brain's owner's manual!

Owner's manuals begin with a quick look at features. They have a use-and-care guide and chapters detailing specific functions. At the back there is usually a troubleshooting section. I like it best when there is a chart or card that contains a quick reference guide. The learning principles in this chapter are your quick reference guide. As a college student, you have a limited amount of time to learn volumes of information in your classes. The learning principle reference guide will help you get the most out of the time you have to study. The strategies you develop to use the principles become your troubleshooting section. The Brain Bytes scattered throughout the text margins are excerpts from the detailed chapters to help you understand why certain strategies work or act as tips for use and care of your brain.

I know you don't have time to read the entire manual. In fact, you've used your brain for a long time without ever owning a manual. You probably already use many of the learning principles we discuss in this chapter. In the blanks below, list how you remember things that are important to you. Try to list at least five ways.

1._____

2._____

3._____

4._____

5._____

After you have examined the learning principles, come back to your list and see which principles you were already using.

On the next page is a list of ten learning principles and a short explanation of each. Although the learning principles all work together, they are divided into four categories. Each category heading will give you an indication as to how those principles work. After you have read these principles, *make a flash card for each principle* by writing the name of the principle on the front of an index card and the explanation of the principle on the back of the card. You might further your understanding of each principle by drawing an illustration of the principle beside the definition or by including an example. Then carry the cards around with you so that you can study the principles while waiting in line or waiting for class to start or when in between classes, and so on. This will put your time-management skills to work.

For Your Student Survival Kit

Learning Principles: Quick Reference Guide

Starting the Connections

1. **Interest.** The brain prioritizes by meaning, value, and relevance. For something to have meaning, you must understand it. In order to remember it thoroughly, you must be interested in it and think that it has value and relevance in your life.

2. **Intent to remember.** Your attitude has much to do with whether you remember something or not. A key factor in remembering is having a positive attitude, believing that you will get it right the first time. Attention is not the same as learning, but little learning takes place without attention.

3. **Basic background.** Your understanding of new material will depend on how much of it can be connected to knowledge you already have. The more you increase your basic knowledge, the easier it is to build new knowledge on this background.

Controlling the Amount and Form

4. **Selectivity.** You must determine what is most important, and select the main idea before you add the supporting details.

5. **Meaningful organization.** You can learn and remember better if you group ideas into meaningful categories or groups.

Strengthening Neural Connections

6. **Recitation.** Saying ideas aloud in your own words strengthens synaptic connections and gives you immediate feedback. The more feedback you get, the faster and more accurate your learning is.

7. **Visualization.** Visualization is the brain's quickest and probably longest-lasting response to images. By making a mental picture, you use an entirely different part of the brain than you do by reading or listening.

8. **Association.** Memory is increased when facts to be learned are consciously associated with something familiar to you. Memory is formed by making neural connections. Begin by asking: "What is this like that I already know?"

Allowing Time to Solidify Pathways

9. **Consolidation.** Your brain must have time for new information to establish a neuronal pathway. When you make a list or review your notes right after class, you are using the principle of consolidation.

10. **Distributed practice.** A series of shorter study sessions distributed over several days is preferable to fewer but longer study sessions.

As you read a textbook, notice that the author has provided clues and guides as to what is important by dividing the chapter with major headings, using bold print and italics, and providing summaries and questions. Follow these road signs. Finding the important points in a lecture may be more difficult. But there are also road signs here. You can learn to concentrate on both verbal and nonverbal clues such as the numbering of items, the repetition of an idea, or things an instructor writes on the board.

Meaningful Organization

Some scientists estimate that the average brain can hold as many as 1 quadrillion bits (that's a 1 followed by fifteen 0s) in long-term memory. Neuroscientists assure us that our brains, however, are designed to retain meaningful rather than random bits of information. Because memory is stored in web-like fashion throughout the brain, depending on how you process it, it follows that you can improve your memory by learning to encode in a conscious and organized way.

How you organize your memory, much like how you organize your road trips, your office, or your notebooks, will determine how efficient your memory system is. Even though you may know where you are going, you need the names of the highways and interstates in the correct order to get there. Even though information is filed in your memory filing cabinet, your file needs a name to retrieve it. Because the conscious brain can process only five to seven bits of information at a time, you are able to learn and remember better if you group ideas into meaningful categories of fewer than seven items. This is the principle of **meaningful organization.** Note that it combines the principles of interest (making the group meaningful to *you*) and selectivity (cutting the job down to a manageable size) and that it also involves organization. For example, you might break down a list of 25 items into five groups of five (no more than seven) that have some organizational principle in common.

Mnemonic devices are one way of organizing new information. A **mnemonic device** is a means for enhancing memory. Most people think of it as a trick that you use to help memorize something. When you can't find an obvious way to remember something difficult, you can organize it by using a mnemonic device, called a *mnemonic* for short.

BRAIN BYTE

Because of the tremendous volume of information you encounter (millions of bits of random information per minute), it is crucial that you consciously cue into your memory system.

BRAIN BYTE

For you to form a sharp memory of something, the original information must be encoded accurately, maintained and strengthened over time, and triggered by association or cue. When information is poorly encoded, there is no hope for data recovery.

TYPE OF MNEMONIC DEVICE	EXPLANATION	EXAMPLE
Acronym (word mnemonic)	An invented combination of letters, with each letter acting as a cue to an idea you need to remember	**HOMES** to remember the names of the Great Lakes: *Huron, Ontario, Michigan, Erie,* and *Superior*
Acrostic (sentence mnemonic)	An invented sentence in which the first letter of each word is a cue to an idea you need to remember	**K**ing **C**harles **A**dded **A**nd **S**ubtracted **E**quations to remember Bloom's taxonomy: *Knowledge, Comprehension, Application, Analysis, Synthesis,* and *Evaluation*
Poems or jingles	Organizing the information in a catchy rhyme or jingle	*i* before *e* except after *c* or when sounded like *a* as in *neighbor* or *weigh*

[6]Leslie Hart, *Human Brain and Human Learning* (White Plains, NY: Longman, 1983).

PRACTICE 5.2

Controlling the Amount and Form of Information Selectivity

You have been assigned four chapters to read in your psychology course. How will you decide what is important to remember?

_____

_____

_____

Listen to a lecture, and list the verbal and nonverbal clues the lecturer gives to indicate which ideas being conveyed are important.

_____

_____

_____

Meaningful Organization

1. First look at the following list of items and try to remember them: _car keys, a ribbon, a paper clip, a piece of peppermint, a pair of sunglasses, a birthday card, a stapler, a tea bag, a cookie, a windshield wiper blade, a pencil, a flower, a spoon, a pair of scissors, a stamp, a scarf, a ballpoint pen, a computer disk, a Kleenex, a calculator, a pack of gum, an iPod, a dollar bill, a notebook, and flash cards._

2. Study the list for one minute; then cover it and see if you can list all the items.

_____

_____

_____

3. Now group the items into meaningful categories in the space below. Then cover them and see how many you can remember.

Category	Category	Category	Category
_____	_____	_____	_____
List:	List:	List:	List:
_____	_____	_____	_____
_____	_____	_____	_____
_____	_____	_____	_____
_____	_____	_____	_____

4. You are going to the grocery store and have forgotten your list. What are some meaningful ways to organize items you need to buy so that you won't forget what you need?

_____

_____

_____

Continued

Practice 5.2 continued

5. Here's a mnemonic for remembering the seven continents: Eat An Aspirin After A Night-time Snack. Can you list the continents below?

_____

_____

_____

6. List some mnemonic devices you know and use.

_____

_____

_____

Now devise some mnemonic devices of your own.

7. Devise a mnemonic to help you remember the five elements necessary for a useful goal.

_____

_____

8. Make a mnemonic device for a biology class in which you need to learn the seven major taxonomic categories, or taxa, used in classification: (1) kingdom, (2) phylum, (3) class, (4) order, (5) family, (6) genus, and (7) species. Remember, order is important here.

_____

_____

9. Devise a mnemonic (maybe two) to remember the ten learning principles.

_____

_____

_____

In other words, mnemonic devices are a way of using meaningful organization. Although they do not replace other techniques for learning, mnemonics are sometimes the only way to remember something difficult for a short period of time. Mnemonic devices can be rhymes, phrases, or words arranged in a special way to help us remember. Here are some examples.

Strengthening Neural Connections

Once you have manipulated what you wish to learn by selectivity or meaningful organization and have established connections, you need to seek ways to strengthen and maintain those connections. Connections that are not strengthened disappear. As we discussed earlier, learning depends on the *strength of the connection combined with the neurotransmitters*. The more times you have traveled the same road, the more confident you are in your driving and direction.

The next three principles deal with this process. After all, what good is having something in your long-term memory if you can't get it back out or make connections to it?

Recitation

Recitation is probably the most powerful tool you have for transferring information from short-term to long-term memory. Recitation involves saying something out loud in your own words. It is not the same as rereading, just as reading the steps on MapQuest or your GPS is not the same as knowing each turn to take. Recitation works because it triggers the intent-to-remember switch. If you know you're going to recite something, you tend to concentrate and pay more attention.

Recitation gets you involved in the material. It makes you a participant (a driver), not an onlooker (a passenger). Further, recitation gives you immediate feedback. You discover whether you know something well enough to say it in your own words or if you need to go back and study it more. Remember, in addition to making an effort to understand, you are also giving synaptic or neural connections the repetition they need to become strong. You are trying to *own* the material you are learning. This is one reason why flash cards or study index cards are so effective.

You now know that the more senses you use, the stronger the neural trace is. You need repetition and review; particularly, the brain needs feedback in order to judge and correct its course. The more feedback you get, the faster and more accurate your learning is. The neuroscientist Richard Bandler says that you really need to "know that you know" something before learning takes place. Recitation is where the difference in understanding something and knowing something becomes most apparent.

BRAIN BYTE

Seeking feedback is a natural and essential learning tool that helps you minimize false impressions before inaccurate memories are formed.

Visualization

Another very powerful learning principle is **visualization**, which involves making a mental picture of what needs to be remembered. By visualizing, you use an entirely different part of the brain than you use for reading or listening. In addition, you remember pictures for much longer than words. In fact, 90 percent of the brain's sensory input is visual. Researchers have found the brain's quickest response is to color, motion, form, and depth. You have probably found driving directions easier to follow if you have visual landmarks as checkpoints.

Visualization can be a powerful part of preparing for a test. Experiments using brain-imaging equipment show that the same brain patterns occur when people visualize themselves doing something as when they actually engage in the task. Most memory experts say that short-term memory will hold more pictures than words. (Later, when learning styles are discussed, you will see that if you are a visual learner, making a mental video of things you want to remember is a must.) The visualization portion of Practice 5.3 illustrates how powerful the principle of visualization can be for you.

Student**TIP**

"I love to draw. So when I go over my notes, I try to illustrate them. It helps me stop and think about the material, as well as gives me a visual prompt to think of on a test."

BRAIN BYTE

The brain has an attentional bias for high contrast and novelty. The brain has an immediate and primitive response to symbols, icons, and strong, simple images.

BRAIN BYTE

Making associations forms new connections between neurons and encodes new insights, similar to a tree growing new branches.[7]

Association

Another way to strengthen your neural network is to consciously tie new information in with something you already have stored in your long-term memory. This is called the principle of **association**. By recalling something you already know about a subject and placing new information in the same brain file as the old information, you will find that the new information is easier to retrieve and remember. For example, there are certain dates that you are sure of, such as the year Columbus discovered America, the year the Declaration of Independence was signed, your mother's birthday, and the year you graduated from high school.

So, when you need to learn a new date, think of the new date as being, say, five years after or ten years before the one you already know. As scientists observe the working brain with neuroimaging technology, it becomes abundantly apparent that association is central to the process of encoding and retrieval. It is extremely important when you encode new information that you do so consciously. Association is intentionally making a connection to the basic background you have established. Using similes, metaphors, or analogies helps to begin the process of association. For example, we have said being a successful student requires driving, or that building brain connections is like strengthening a muscle.

PRACTICE 5.3

Strengthening Neural Connections

Recitation. List the eight learning principles we have discussed. Then cover them up and recite them until you can name and explain them without looking.

1. _____   5. _____

2. _____   6. _____

3. _____   7. _____

4. _____   8. _____

Visualization. Try the following practice to illustrate how powerful visualization may be for you. It is important that you follow the directions carefully.

Memorize the following pairs of words by repeating the members of each pair several times to yourself. For example, if the pair is CAT–WINDOW, say over and over, "cat–window," "cat–window." Do not use any other memory method.

CUSTARD–LUMBER	MOTHER–IVY
JAIL–CLOWN	LIZARD–PAPER
HAMMER–STAR	BEAR–SCISSORS
APPLE–FRECKLES	CANDLE–SHEEPSKIN
SLIPPER–ENVELOPE	CANDY–MOUNTAIN
BOOK–PAINT	TREE–OCEAN

Now cover the list and try to remember as many pairs of words as you can.

[7]David A. Sousa, *How the Brain Learns: A Classroom Teacher's Guide* (National Association of Secondary School Principals, 1995).

ENVELOPE–_____   JAIL–_____

FRECKLES–_____   IVY–_____

TREE–_____   CANDLE–_____

CANDY–_____   BOOK–_____

SCISSORS–_____   LIZARD–_____

CUSTARD–_____   HAMMER–_____

Now memorize these pairs of words by visualizing a mental picture in which the two objects in each pair are in some kind of vivid interaction. For example, if the pair is CAT–WINDOW, you might picture a cat jumping through a closed window with glass shattering all about. Just make up a picture, and do not use any other memory technique. The more color and action your picture holds, the easier it will be to recall.

SOAP–MERMAID	MIRROR–RABBIT
LAKE–FOOTBALL	HOUSE–DIAMOND
PENCIL–LETTUCE	LAMB–MOON
CAR–HONEY	BREAD–GLASS
CANDLE–DANCER	LIPS–DONKEY
FLEA–DANDELION	DOLLAR–ELEPHANT

Now cover the list and try to remember as many pairs of words as you can.

CANDLE–_____   DOLLAR–_____

FLEA–_____   CAR–_____

BREAD–_____   LIPS–_____

MIRROR–_____   PENCIL–_____

LAMB–_____   SOAP–_____

LAKE–_____   HOUSE–_____

Find something you need to learn for one of your classes. First list or explain exactly what you need to learn. Then explain *specifically* what you could visually do with the material to help yourself remember it.

Association. The Making Connections exercise at the beginning of this chapter is a good illustration of association. What metaphor did you use for learning?

Learning is like _____ in that _____.

BRAIN BYTE

Researcher Eric Jensen reminds us that "optimal learning occurs when the brain's multiple maps work in synchronization or network with each other. The more connected these neural networks are, the greater the meaning derived from learning."[8]

Allowing Time to Solidify Pathways

As you are probably beginning to discover, the learning principles can be used in combination and, in fact, are more powerful that way. For example, as you associate something new with something you already know, you will want to use visualization and perhaps recitation to

[8]Illustration reprinted with permission from Where Memory Resides by Karen Markowitz and Eric Jensen. Copyright © 1999.

strengthen your memory. The last two learning principles are important because, as you learned in regard to short-term memory, the brain can absorb only a certain amount of *new* information and that information needs time for a pathway to solidify—that is, time to soak in, time for connections to form and strengthen.

Consolidation

An important factor to consider in terms of how your brain processes new material is that you are making a biological change in your brain by establishing new neuronal pathways. This is not an easily accomplished task. It takes time for the pathway or connection to become established. Think about the sidewalks on your campus. They are established ways to get from one place to another. However, I'll bet your campus is like mine in that there are paths students' feet have worn where there are no sidewalks. The first time a student cut through that way, the footsteps didn't leave a path; but the more students used that way, the more apparent the new path became. On my campus, eventually the worn paths are made into sidewalks! Compare this to the pathways you are establishing in your brain. (This example is the kind of analogy, simile, or metaphor that you are encouraged to use to connect to your own experience when you process new information.)

Researchers Markowitz and Jensen remind us that the brain is not designed for nonstop learning. As the brain learns new information, new connections are formed. Because learning is a biological process that literally changes the configuration of the brain, "processing time is necessary to build the inner wiring necessary for connectivity and recall."[9] Repetition of information strengthens these new connections just like the repetition of walking creates a worn path. We call this principle **consolidation**. *Consolidation is taking ownership of new information by allowing time for neuronal pathways to be established.*

You are usually bombarded with much more new information than you can remember. You must, therefore, allow time to sort through it, to reflect on it, and to integrate it with old information. As we have discussed, the more ways new information is processed into the brain, the faster and deeper the connections will become. Encoding that is random is at best difficult to retrieve. The brain needs feedback and repetition. John Medina, who you will meet in some Virtual Field Trips, reminds us, "the brain acts like a muscle: the more activity you do, the larger and more complex it can become."[10] You wire and rewire yourself with every activity you choose.

Here are a few ways to consolidate: taking notes in class, asking questions in class, reviewing notes, stopping after each paragraph you read and writing a *Jeopardy!* question, visualizing, reciting, making flash cards, and designing practice tests. Check your smartphone or iPad for

[9]Markowitz and Jensen, p. 7.
[10]Medina, p. 58.

apps that could help you consolidate information. You will notice that many of these activities give you a hard-copy backup of new information, as well as strengthen connections in your brain.

Distributed Practice

If you are going on a long road trip, you are better off not trying to drive it in one stretch. When you get there, you may be too tired to do anything. Similarly, you tend to remember better if you are not overly tired and are able to concentrate; therefore, a series of shorter study sessions (no longer than 50 minutes each) is usually better than hours and hours of straight studying. Using the principle of **distributed practice** is probably the most effective way to study.

Because the connections in your brain are strengthened by the number of times you use them, several short sessions are better than one or a few long ones. The structure of your brain literally changes each time you add new information. When your study sessions are frequent and spread out, there is time for branches to form on dendrites and new chemical and electric responses to occur. Each time you study, the brain will respond more quickly because there are more connections. If you wait until the last minute to cram for an exam, there are fewer dendrites

---

PRACTICE 5.4

Consolidation

List some learning principles that you think are most important in promoting consolidation.

_____

_____

_____

_____

List activities that work for you to promote consolidation.

_____

_____

Check your study schedule. Describe ways you will use distributed practice this week.

_____

_____

_____

_____

and the connections are weaker. You tend to remember things at the beginning and the end, whereas things in the middle often get fuzzy or blurred.

It stands to reason, then, that the more beginnings and endings you experience, the more you will remember. If you remember the first 20 minutes and the last 20 minutes of what you study in a 50-minute study session, you are well on your way to *owning* that material. However, what happens when you study for four hours straight? You remember the first 20 minutes and the last 20 minutes. That amounts to 200 minutes of blur.

PRACTICE 5.5

Putting Learning Principles to Use

Kelley has a textbook assignment for her history class. She uses what she has learned about the learning principles to make sure she knows the material. Circle or highlight all of the learning principles she uses to complete the assignment. (She will probably use more than one in each example.)

1. Before she begins to read, Kelley reviews her notes from the class where the instructor introduced the material.

Interest Intent to Remember Basic Background Selectivity Meaningful Organization Visualization Recitation Association Consolidation Distributed Practice

2. Kelley reads the chapter summary, studies the review questions, and examines pictures and charts before she reads.

Interest Intent to Remember Basic Background Selectivity Meaningful Organization Visualization Recitation Association Consolidation Distributed Practice

3. When she reads, Kelley focuses on the bold print, topic sentences, and italicized words.

Interest Intent to Remember Basic Background Selectivity Meaningful Organization Visualization Recitation Association Consolidation Distributed Practice

4. At the end of each paragraph, Kelley stops and chooses the important information and writes a question in the margin of her book. Kelley then underlines as few words as possible in the text to answer the question.

Interest Intent to Remember Basic Background Selectivity Meaningful Organization Visualization Recitation Association Consolidation Distributed Practice

5. Before she goes to the next paragraph, Kelley covers the text, asks herself the questions in the margin, and says the answer out loud in her own words.

Interest Intent to Remember Basic Background Selectivity Meaningful Organization Visualization Recitation Association Consolidation Distributed Practice

6. In addition, Kelley tries to picture what the people and events she is reading about look like. As Kelley reads, she tries to make connections with things she has already studied.

   Interest Intent to Remember Basic Background Selectivity Meaningful Organization Visualization Recitation Association Consolidation Distributed Practice

7. This chapter is about World War II, and Kelley remembers hearing stories about her grandfather being in the war. Kelley asks her parents exactly what her grandfather did and where he was at that time.

   Interest Intent to Remember Basic Background Selectivity Meaningful Organization Visualization Recitation Association Consolidation Distributed Practice

8. Kelley reads and marks a few pages right after history class, a few more when she has a break between classes, additional pages while she is waiting for her friend Marge, and finishes the chapter before she leaves school. Later that night she reviews the whole chapter.

   Interest Intent to Remember Basic Background Selectivity Meaningful Organization Visualization Recitation Association Consolidation Distributed Practice

9. When Kelley is finished, she makes a chart that lists the roles and major players of each country involved.

   Interest Intent to Remember Basic Background Selectivity Meaningful Organization Visualization Recitation Association Consolidation Distributed Practice

10. Kelley also makes flash cards of terms, people, places, and dates.

    Interest Intent to Remember Basic Background Selectivity Meaningful Organization Visualization Recitation Association Consolidation Distributed Practice

 CAREER Connections

You have been exploring possible careers for you to pursue. Choose one career that interests you. Interview someone who is currently in that occupation. After determining what that person routinely does day-to-day on the job, write a paragraph in which you describe how he or she might use the learning principles in the workplace. Be specific with your examples.

Virtual Field Trip
Learning Principles

Virtual Field Trip
Learning Principles Quiz

 Making **CONNECTIONS**

The learning principles are the core of learning strategies. If you are going to be a successful student, you need to master the principles. Let's review Bloom's taxonomy to show how you are mastering them.

Knowledge. First you memorize the ten learning principles so that you know the name and definition of each principle. You can easily do this without having to use the principles.

Comprehension. Once you are able to list the learning principles, you then explain them to someone. You see that they are more than definitions. You see that the principles explain how you personally can use your brain more efficiently.

Application. You practice using the learning principles—you visualize, you recite, you spread your study time out, and so on. You discover that you can use the learning principles to study faster and better. You are able to process information in less time and retain the information longer.

Analysis. When you analyze, you break complex ideas into parts and see how the parts work together. With the learning principles, you discover relationships among the various principles. You see that there is a time and place to use certain principles, that some principles are best used in combination with other principles, and that some principles work better for you than others. You see that different information and learning situations call for different combinations of learning principles. You can take the learning principles and develop a note-taking or textbook-reading system that uses a combination of learning principles that work for you. You use analysis to determine the best time, place, and way for you to study.

Synthesis. You draw conclusions and make predictions. You are able to take a specific learning situation and use the learning principles to make a plan for learning that is best suited for you and for the information you need to learn. Summarizing a unit or predicting test questions is a form of synthesis. Using a note-taking system built on the learning principles in all of your classes is a way of using synthesis.

Evaluation. When you evaluate, you judge something's worth. Did the note-taking system work for you in history class, or do you need to make adjustments? Did you use the right combination of learning principles to study for your psychology test, or do you need to try a different combination?

How Memory Works: Putting Principles in Perspective

If you use Bloom's taxonomy to measure the depth of learning, you should be competent through three levels in your thinking about the ten learning principles. You have learned the names of the principles (knowledge), you understand how they help you learn new material (comprehension), and you have begun to use them in developing strategies for learning (application). The deeper the level of your thinking, the stronger the neural traces or connections will become.

Let's return to the analogy of the brain owner's manual and expand upon it. You need to understand the relationships among the principles, to see how the principles fit into the overall pattern of information processing and learning, and to determine which combinations of principles work best for you in specific learning situations. When you analyze, synthesize, and evaluate, you have progressed from simply learning something for an exam to using it to become a better student. Neuroscientists may not know exactly how the brain processes information, but they and now you know enough to see how the ten learning principles fit into the overall scheme for learning new material. You know that memory is not an object or file stored in one place in the brain; rather, it is a "collection of complex electrochemical responses activated through multiple sensory channels and stored in unique and elaborate neuronal networks throughout the brain."[11]

We began this chapter by giving a simplistic overview of what happens physically to the brain when learning occurs. We next examined ten learning principles as a quick reference to brain-compatible learning. Now, let's put the two together in a visual representation of where the learning principles fit into the learning process. Again, we are well aware that memory and learning are not linear processes; however, the flowchart on page 108 should help you visualize how the pieces fit together.

Learning can be described as an interactive process that takes place in three stages. First is **reception**, or **encoding**, the gathering of information from your senses. This information enters your short-term memory. In **short-term memory**, information fades away, is intentionally tossed away, or is processed for storage in **long-term memory** as synaptic connections or neuronal pathways, stage two. Stage three is the tricky one. Once information enters long-term memory, there must be a way to retrieve, or activate, the information so that you can use this information when you need it. Without a way to retrieve information from long-term memory, it may as well be lost. Information retrieved from long-term memory is temporarily placed in what we call **active memory**.

---

[11]Markowitz and Jensen, p. 1.

For Your Student Survival Kit

Memory
The process will look something like this.

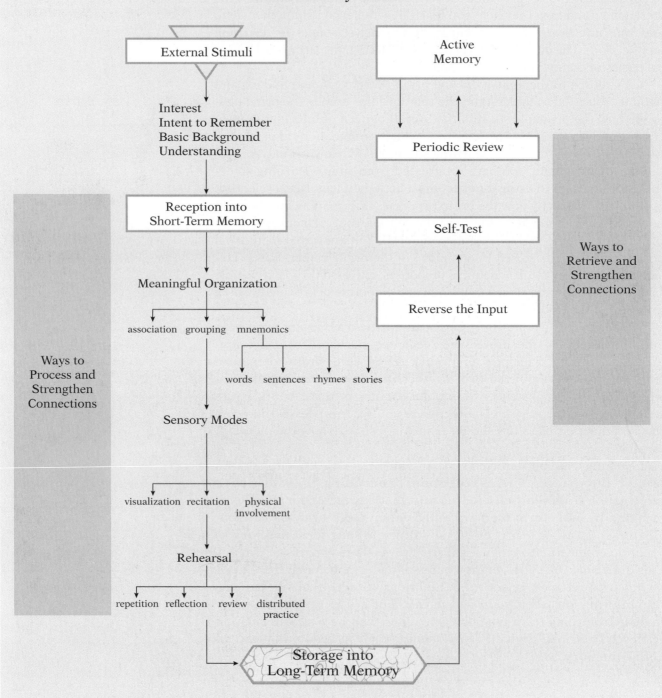

How Memory Works

Stage One: Getting Information into the Brain— Reception into Short-Term Memory

The first stage of the learning process involves information entering the brain. We call this gathering of information, this acquisition of knowledge, **reception**. The brain uses sensory receptors to gather information from things that you see, hear, smell, touch, or taste. Some of these don't make it through the filters—in one ear and out the other, so to speak— whereas others become part of short-term memory.

As we discussed at the beginning of this chapter, everything around you is not important; thus, you do not receive everything. In a classroom lecture, there is more happening in the room than just the lecture. There are other people in the room, each doing his or her own thing. Or there may be something going on outside the window, in the hall, or in your mind. You are feeling, smelling, seeing more than you can take in, but basically you are in control of what you select to receive. Some of the time you may choose to receive nothing at all.

Factors That Influence Reception

As explained earlier in this chapter, when information is received from sensory input, it is encoded in various parts of the brain to form synaptic connections with cell bodies called *neurons*. The axon of the cell reaches out and connects to the newly formed dendrites on other cells, making a network of neuronal pathways. Sometimes, however, you discover that no connections are formed at all or the connections are very weak. There are at least four factors that influence whether the information you need to learn is even received by your brain or whether new connections are formed. Three factors are the learning principles categorized earlier as "Starting the Connection."

The first has to do with your attitude—your **intention to remember**. If you are not listening or reading as if there will be a pop quiz on the material, the information may not even get into your short-term memory. If there is no intent on your part to get it right the first time, you may hear or see the information, but no synaptic connections are made, and no dendrites are grown.

The second is the learning principle of **interest**. If you are not interested, the information probably never makes it into short-term memory to even begin to make connections. Remember that an essential part of the interest learning principle is that you both value and *understand* the new concept. Most of you have heard or seen something in a foreign language that you do not understand. That information simply does not enter the brain as meaningful information to be processed. This is also true of material presented either in lecture or in print that you do not understand. If you do not understand it, it has little chance of being received into short-term memory. So **understanding**, although not one of the three learning principles, also determines if the new information is processed. If the intent and interest are there, information must still be understood in order to be processed. You can probably think of times when you memorized terms for a test without understanding them. In such situations, no real learning or remembering took place.

 BRAIN BYTE

For you to form a sharp memory of something, the original information must be encoded accurately, maintained or strengthened over time, and triggered by an association or cue.

A third learning principle that influences what you allow to go into short-term memory is **basic background**. Everything you see, hear, smell, touch, or taste is affected by that which you already know. If there is no prior knowledge, there is nothing to which new information can be connected. This is why the more you know about something, the easier it is to learn more about it. Your lack of knowledge may make some concepts difficult for you to understand; whereas for some of your classmates, the same concepts seem simple. For example, suppose a classmate builds model airplanes. History lessons about World War II may be easier for her because she has built models of planes used in that war. They may also be easier for the classmate who has heard war stories from his grandfather.

If you are going to encode something in your brain, you must employ the strategies you developed for using the principles of intent to remember, interest, and basic background, in addition to making sure that you understand the information.

Short-Term Memory

The hippocampus acts as a gatekeeper and director of what you experience when information enters the brain through your senses. If you are interested in some information, find it of value, or make a conscious effort to select it, the hippocampus lets that information into short-term memory.

Short-term memory is limited; usually it can hold only five to seven bits of information at a time. When you are presented with more than seven bits, one of two things must happen. The hippocampus gets rid of what's in the short-term bank by letting it escape, that is, you forget it, or it directs the information to an appropriate part of your brain for long-term memory. This is the reason you can understand an entire lecture while you are listening to it but later cannot recall the major points. This becomes an important point in developing strategies for note taking and textbook reading. You need to hold or record information until you can process it into long-term memory.

Yet you must be very careful when you process information for storage into long-term memory, because transferring information to long-term memory is not enough. You must be able to retrieve this information after it is filed. Just as there are several factors influencing whether sensory information gets to short-term memory, there are instructions in your brain's owner's manual for processing information into long-term memory in such a way that you can later retrieve it. Once synaptic connections are made, if they are not strengthened, they may be lost. Remember that path we talked about? It's not enough to walk over it once or twice. You must walk over it multiple times to create an actual worn path.

Stage Two: Processing from Short-Term to Long-Term Memory

There are three broad categories of ways that can aid in transferring from short-term memory to long-term memory, and each has several divisions. The first way makes use of various forms of **organization** and **association**. The second way makes use of various **sensory modes**. The third is **rehearsal**. All three ways overlap and interconnect.

Organization

One method of ensuring that information you want to remember is properly stored is **organization**. If you go into my office, you will usually see my desk cluttered with stacks of papers. If I wanted my desk cleared, I could randomly stack this information and shove it into a desk drawer. However, if I want to be able to find things again, they must be sorted and organized. Your memory is similar to my desk. If you just cram information in, you may not be able to find what you need when you need it. The strategies you developed when using meaningful organization such as color coding and mnemonics help process the information into long-term memory so that retrieval is possible.

You now understand that the brain is a web-like network of neurons that can form memory only by association. Facts are not stored in just one place in the brain; but, rather, when you need to recall something, memory is recreated by the electric and chemical actions in many parts of the brain through synaptic connections. The more associations you make when you process new information, the stronger the connections will be. If associations are not consciously made, connections may be weak and information lost.

Sensory Modes

Another way to ensure that information from short-term memory is properly transferred for storage in long-term memory and that the neural traces are strengthened is to use various **sensory modes**. Most of us have a preferred mode of learning. Some of us are visual learners, others learn best by hearing, and still others learn best by doing. You will want to be sure that you process new information in your preferred mode; however, the more senses you involve, the more neurons are used in the connections and the *more likely you are to remember*.

Visualization and recitation form different connections of the same information. When you physically do something to learn new information, you process that information as procedural knowledge and connect to pathways in different parts of your brain.

Rehearsal

A final way to transfer information from short-term memory to long-term memory is **rehearsal**, or practice. You are familiar with the rehearsal used by actors to learn their lines. Rehearsal does something similar for you. The first form of rehearsal is **repetition**, which is saying or doing things over and over until you are familiar with the information. Repeating something over and over may temporarily transfer information to long-term memory at the knowledge level, but in order to make sure the information is permanent, you need to understand it.

The second form of rehearsal is **reflection**. This involves a deeper level of learning and takes you to at least the comprehension level of Bloom's taxonomy. You quickly lose what you don't understand. One way of promoting a deeper understanding of a concept is reflection, examining information and trying to discover how it relates to what you already know and what meaning it has for you. The more meaning something has for you, the more likely you are to remember it.

The third form of rehearsal is **review**. Once a transfer has been made from short-term memory, review is necessary to make sure you can retrieve the information later. Good times to review are right after class, right before class, and 30 minutes before you go to bed. Reviewing right after class catches material before short-term memory has time to completely dump it and while you still understand certain concepts and can identify concepts you need to ask about. Reviewing before class strengthens your basic background and enables you to more easily store what is presented in class. And reviewing just before you go to bed gets your subconscious working while you sleep.

Note the third form is *review*, not "study for the first time." Neurochemical and biochemical studies using imaging of the brain show that when something new is introduced, a sufficient review of this information *must* take place during the following 24 hours in order for long-term memory to retain the concept. This will be difficult for many students who are extremely pressed for time as it is. However, reviewing within 24 hours will save time later. Your master schedule becomes an essential tool. Remember how you determined a set time to study for each class? Using those times ensures that you have time to review while new information is still fresh.

A fourth important principle of rehearsal is that you tend to remember better with several spaced practices than with one long session. We called this principle **distributed practice**. Forty-five to 50 minute sessions with a 5–10 minute break seems to be about right for most students. Don't fool yourself into thinking you can do it all at once. The more combinations of organization, sensory modes, and rehearsal you use, the more consolidation takes place. And the more powerful the transfer to long-term memory, the more likely you will be able to retrieve the information when you need it

Long-Term Memory

Although short-term memory can hold only a limited amount of information for a very short time, long-term memory acts as storage for larger amounts of information for longer periods of time. Notice that the term is not *permanent* but *long-term*. In actuality, long-term memory is the neural pathways and synaptic connections that have stabilized through repeated use.

Some things do become part of permanent memory through rehearsal, but more things decay with time and interference. It appears that the more frequently we take things in and out of our long-term memory, the more interest we have in the information, and the more understanding we have of the concepts involved, the more stable the connections will be and the longer the information will stay in our long-term memory. Again, long-term memory is not a *place* but a *process* that takes place in many parts of the brain to make connections and reconstruct memory. Think of that path again. It might be worn now, but if you stop using it, weeds will grow back and cover it.

Stage Three: Retrieving from Long-Term Memory

You have cleared your cluttered desk, and your information is either in the trash or in the file cabinet we call long-term memory. Now comes the real challenge, getting the information back out. When test time comes, do you know which drawer to open and how you filed the information? Obviously, the storage and retrieval processes are interactive. The more you use the information—activate connections—the more likely you are to remember where you filed it. There are several things to consider in retrieving information. They involve **reversing the input process, self-testing**, and **periodic review**.

If you were systematic in your filing, to retrieve the information you **reverse the input process**. For example, if you grouped information in categories to remember it, recall those categories to retrieve it. If you used a mnemonic device to file the information, use the same mnemonic device to take the information out of the file. You can use meaningful grouping, association, and mnemonic devices to retrieve information as well as store it. If you stored information using sensory modes, you can use visualization, recitation, or physical involvement to retrieve that information. If you used the rehearsal process to ensure depth of storage, a similar rehearsal can be used to bring the material out of storage.

Remember how we said long-term memory is not necessarily permanent memory? The duration of long-term memory depends on such things as your understanding, your interest, how you stored it, and how often you retrieve it.

One of the best ways to retrieve information is by **self-testing**. Asking yourself questions about the information is important for several reasons. First of all, it simulates test conditions; that is, it gives you practice in taking tests. Self-testing also gives you feedback so that you know whether you remember what you need to know. Brain research shows that an essential part of learning is knowing that you know something. And self-testing is, after all, a form of rehearsal and will strengthen the retrieval process and add to the depth of storage in your memory.

In addition, **periodic review** is necessary because information in long-term memory seems to decay or fade without review. You should review at least once a week for each class you have. All the time you spend reading and studying is wasted if you can't remember what you have read or studied; therefore, the investment of a little extra time spent retrieving and reviewing filed material is worth it. The bottom line is that connections must be strengthened, or they decay.

What Happens When You Retrieve Information From Long-Term Memory?

When you retrieve information from long-term memory, you activate it, or transfer it to **active**, or working, memory. Working memory involves the ability to hold and manipulate information for immediate use. You can compare active memory to your actual desktop or your computer desktop. You bring up information from where it is stored to the desktop. This is the space where you gather the information you need to solve a problem, answer a question, or draw a conclusion. There is a limited amount of work space in active memory; when it becomes cluttered, you must make a decision. Will I need this information in the future? Or do I no longer need this information? Theoretically, when you access information, it is then re-stored into long-term memory, which re-consolidates and strengthens it. However, just as a waiter may remember what each

How Memory Works

Recall what we have discussed and fill in the flowchart describing how memory works.

How Memory Works

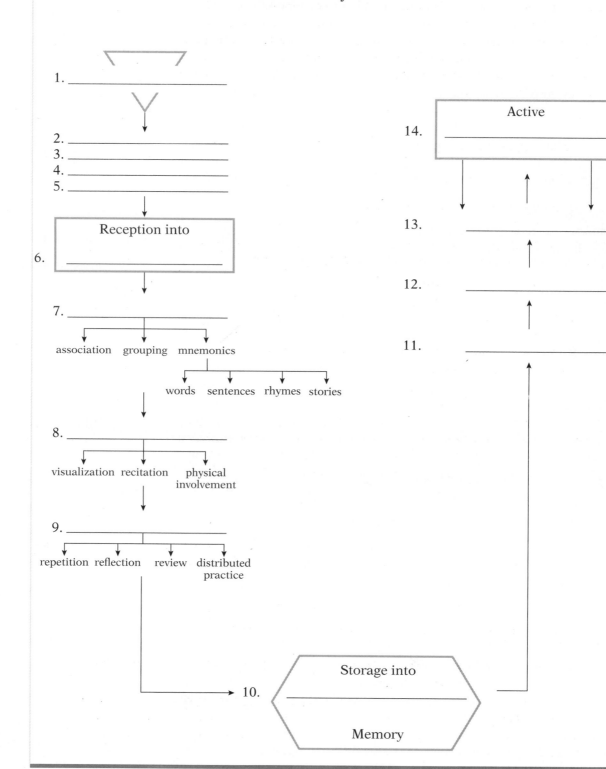

diner ordered, once he delivers the food, he no longer needs that information. Students often do this with information on a test. However, unlike the waiter, the student should go over the test, understand what they missed, correct mistakes, and review important information. That is how you'll succeed in college and life.

The more you activate information—take it out of long-term memory and refile it—the more permanent it becomes. Systematically retrieving and refiling material saves hours and hours of time in the long run. In fact, your aim is to make this filing and refiling a habit. The owner's manual presented here is certainly a simplification of how your brain operates; however, you can now begin to use what you know about the learning principles and how they are used in your brain to devise strategies for processing information.

BRAIN BYTE

Making associations forms new connections between neurons and encodes new insights, similar to a tree growing new branches (Sousa, 1995).

CRITICAL THINKING
About Retrieval

Applying Learning Principles in Retrieval
You studied five hours for your geology test. You remembered most of what you needed to know on the test. On the next test, there were many of the same questions; but you did not remember the answers.

Explain what you think happened.

What could you have done to prevent this from happening?

Virtual Field Trip
Learning More About
the Brain

Review—Where did we go?

Modeling the Learning Process

Although we have also looked at the brain in various ways in this chapter, we have again modeled the learning cycle when we processed the information in each section of the chapter. Let's look at the learning principles section.

Gathering. You gathered information about ten learning principles.

Analyzing. You made sure you understood each learning principle. You could identify which principle was being used.

Creating New Ideas. You created a plan for using learning principles; you predicted which principle might work for a particular learning task.

Acting. You followed your plan by using each of the principles in appropriate ways, such as studying for a test.

Study Guide: Learning Principles

To see if you grasped the major points of the chapter and to make a useful study guide, answer the following questions found in your reading. When you have written your answers, cover them and see if you can say the answer to each question in your own words.

1. **What disciplines came together to discover more about the brain?**

   _____

   _____

   _____

2. **What is brain-compatible (or brain-based) learning?**

   _____

3. **Define the following:**

   • **Neuron**

   _____

   • **Dendrite**

   _____

   • **Axon**

   _____

   • **Synapse**

   _____

   • **Neurotransmitters**

   _____

   _____

4. **Explain the difference between the prefrontal cortex and the lower automatic brain.**

   _____

5. **What does the reticular activating system do?**

   _____

6. **On what basis does the amygdala make routing decisions?**

   _____

7. **Explain one function of the hippocampus.**

   _____

   _____

8. Explain the brain's plasticity.

_____

9. Which three learning principles help you start the connections? Explain each principle.

1. _____

2. _____

3. _____

10. What two learning principles control the amount and form of information to be remembered? Explain and give an example of each.

1. _____

2. _____

11. What is a mnemonic?

_____

_____

12. Name three kinds of mnemonic devices.

1. _____

2. _____

3. _____

13. Which three learning principles strengthen neural connections? Explain and give an example of each.

1. _____

2. _____

3. _____

14. Which two learning principles allow time to solidify pathways? Explain and give an example of each.

1. _____

2. _____

15. What are four factors that influence reception into short-term memory?

1. _____

2. _____

3. _____

4. _____

16. **Organizing is one way to process information into long-term memory. Name three ways of organizing information for transfer to long-term memory.**

1. _____

2. _____

3. _____

17. **Name the three sensory modes used to transfer to long-term memory.**

1. _____

2. _____

3. _____

18. **What are three ways to rehearse?**

1. _____

2. _____

3. _____

19. **Once information is in long-term memory, what are three ways to retrieve it?**

1. _____

2. _____

3. _____

 CASE STUDY
What's Your Advice?

Marlene is a very conscientious and capable 30-year-old student who has quit her job as a reception-ist in a doctor's office to work on her degree in nursing. She attends class every day. Marlene keeps up with her reading assignments and homework and listens carefully in class. She uses a planner to make sure she has plenty of time set aside to study for tests. The night before a test, Marlene rereads the chapters in the text and looks over any review sheet the professor may have given. She repeats definitions and facts she thinks will be on the test over and over. However, Marlene is very frustrated after failing her first history and psychology tests and barely passing her biology test. She is begin-ning to think she may have made a mistake in her decision to attend college. Using what you know about how memory works, what advice can you give Marlene?

Parallel Parking

Remember, in college, you are successful only when you are driving, not just going along for the ride. Like the parallel parking practice at the end of the previous chapters, you are asked to think about what has been discussed so far and compare these ideas to driving terms.

When you fill in your answers, make sure you complete both sides of the analogy by comparing the driving term to a term for being a successful college student using brain-compatible learning and learning principles. Be sure to use a phrase that says both what the driving phrase is like and why it is like it. For example: *Neural pathways and synaptic connections in the brain are similar to the interstate network in that one allows information to flow and the other allows traffic to flow.* You may choose the interstate network as one of the three driving terms to compare if you add other similarities. Choose at least three of the following.

Stopping for Fuel	I've Driven Here Before
Rest Stops	Getting Insurance
Parallel Parking	Finding a Place to Park
Asking for Directions	Finding the Right Exit
Getting Your License	The Interstate Network
Knowing Your Destination	Following the Road Signs

1. _____

2. _____

3. _____

Evaluating Learning Outcomes

How successful were you in making it to your destination in this chapter?
Analyze what you learned in this chapter. Put a check beside each task you are now able to do. On a separate piece of paper, write a couple of sentences about how you learned each learning outcome and how you plan to continue to use what you learned.

☐ **Describe** what basic parts of the brain have to do with processing information and learning.

☐ **Name and explain** ten learning principles.

☐ **Appraise** examples of students using learning principles and identify which learning principles are being used.

☐ **Analyze** a learning situation and determine several strategies that would be helpful both in college and in the workplace.

☐ **Construct** mnemonic devices to help recall information.

☐ **Reproduce** the flowchart for how the learning principles fit into the way the brain processes information.

☐ **Discriminate** among the levels of Bloom's taxonomy when applying the learning principles.

☐ **Demonstrate how** learning principles can be used in studying for a test.

☐ **Explain** the learning process modelled in this chapter.

Your Student Tip for This Chapter

In the space below, write a tip you would give to other students about what you have learned in this chapter.

_____

_____

_____

Processing Information from Lectures

Road Map to Success

- Going Beyond Memory: Processing Information
- Relating Information Processing to Learning Principles
- Listening Skills
- Taking Notes
- Using the Question in the Margin System for Lectures

In this chapter, you will learn how to

- **Demonstrate** the learning model by constructing a plan for taking notes.

- **Use** the ten learning principles to develop strategies for processing information from classroom lectures.

- **Appraise** your listening habits, and construct strategies for improving them.

- **Describe** several reasons for taking notes in class.

- **Demonstrate** the six steps of the Question in the Margin System for taking notes: record, question, recite, reflect, review, and summarize.

- **Explain** how to use the Question in the Margin System to someone who has never used it.

- **Predict** how this note-taking system might be useful in your present or future job.

- **Explain** the learning process modeled in this chapter.

Where Are We Going?

In this chapter we will review some basic learning strategies and then build on them. We have already demonstrated using the learning model of gathering, analyzing, creating new ideas, and acting with each new strategy we learned. In this chapter you will first examine the learning model in more detail and then it will be your turn to demonstrate strategies you have learned by creating a system for taking and processing notes that works for you. Since good notes require good listening, we will take time to analyze your listening skills and devise ways to improve them. Next, you will compare the system you created to the Question in the Margin System explained in this chapter, and eventually you will combine the best of both. You will then practice taking notes using the Question in the Margin System and predict how these skills might be useful beyond the classroom. These steps will prepare you to take control of one of the most essential skills you need as a college student: taking efficient notes. With practice, this skill will put you on the road to success in both college and your career.

Going Beyond Memory: Processing Information

The learning principles are the foundation of memory and learning. However, if you analyze them in light of Bloom's taxonomy, you may conclude that they primarily address lower-level thinking skills. For higher learning to occur, you must go beyond the principles to *own* the information. In other words, the information needs to become your *personal knowledge*, an integral part of your neural network. This process usually involves using the information to make it personal and meaningful and then creating ideas of your own from this information. Higher-order thinking skills involve analysis, synthesis, and evaluation. The proof of your higher learning comes in testing your ideas about what you have learned and finding out that they work. In other words, your goal is to shift your role from passenger to driver—from receiver of knowledge to producer of knowledge. It should become apparent that taking responsibility for your learning is necessary.

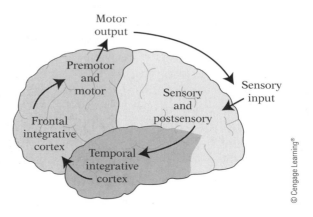

Four Essential Functions for Learning

We used the flowchart, How the Memory Works, to help us put into perspective how learning principles work. Zull's learning model is closer to what actually happens in the brain. The importance of his model is that it takes us beyond memory to higher-level learning.

The four functions Zull outlines become our guidelines for going beyond memory and using what we have discussed. The four functions are gathering, analyzing, creating, and acting. They should sound familiar. We have applied (modeled) the four functions of higher learning in the previous chapters. Now that we have accumulated more basic background about these functions, let's go into a bit more detail.

Gathering

Data enter the brain through the senses. Gathering involves getting information by using many of the learning principles, particularly those that involve Making Connections. Zull says that prior knowledge is the beginning of new knowledge. Prior knowledge is always where all learners start. We have no choice. Part of the learner's job is to find ways to combine the established network with new neural networks—to build new concepts using a mix of the old and the new. Gathering parallels the lower-order thinking skills. In our driving analogy, gathering might include reading the road signs or writing down directions.

Analyzing

Analyzing involves discovering meaning in information by reflection. Zull explains that the back cortex gets information in small bits and reassembles it. In terms of the learning cycle, this integration process is reflective. We examine new information. We try to make it personal. We try to determine where it fits in with our experiences and if it has relevance or meaning for us. We look for connections, and as we find these connections, we make new ones. All this takes time. This process of analyzing also involves most of the learning principles. In terms of Bloom's taxonomy, this is analysis. In our driving analogy, analyzing might involve things like examining alternative routes to adjust for possible traffic and road conditions and investigating what stops we might want to make.

Creating New Ideas

Data enter the brain through concrete experience. The brain organizes and rearranges data through reflection. But it is still just data until the learner begins to work with it. Understanding is not ownership. When we as learners convert comprehension into ideas, hypotheses, plans, and actions, we take control of the information. We have created a meaningful neural network and are free to test our own knowledge. In terms of Bloom's taxonomy, this is synthesis. In our driving analogy, creating new ideas or synthesis is putting together the knowledge we have to predict that if we take a certain route, we may avoid a traffic jam or accident or hypothesizing that although the interstate might be quicker, we would enjoy the scenic route more.

Acting

The testing of the knowledge requires action for the learning cycle to be complete. Writing, speaking, drawing, or other action creates a strategy that may work for us and provides a way that we can test the newly learned information. When this stage, acting, is reached, the learner becomes a producer of knowledge rather than a receiver. Let's look at the bigger picture. We can consider, for example, the choice of your profession. People have previously come up with ideas to improve things within their occupation. Someone created better medicines from this stage of learning. Someone developed the Internet, search engines, a better accounting system, a more efficient engine, and smarter phones and apps for almost everything. Our learning goals move us from receivers to producers of knowledge. Of course, everything learned in a classroom isn't going to be earthshaking. The connections we form, however, multiply the possibilities of creating something better.

Essential Functions of Learning and the Question in the Margin System

If your goal as a learner is to be able to own and use new information, you must reflect and create something of your own beyond the information, then actively test your hypothesis. This chapter provides an opportunity to practice doing this by creating your own system for processing information using what we have discussed in previous chapters. This will become the basis for making the Question in the Margin System work more efficiently for you.

Your primary job as a college student is to process information. You want to take information from lectures and make that information yours. You want to grasp what you read and process it so that you own it. Otherwise, you will spend a great deal of time going to class and even more time reading, yet benefit little in the long run. How, then, do you process information from lectures and textbooks so that you are in control of that information? The system you devise and the Question in the Margin System can help.

Here's the challenge. You want to take what you know about the learning principles, time management, goal setting, critical thinking, and other strategies you may know and analyze this knowledge, then develop your own strategies to help you process information from lectures. You want a way to take what you hear in lectures in the classroom and remember it, understand it, and then take ownership of it by using it. Your task is to devise a system using strategies you have learned so far. The result should be a system that not only processes information faster and better than any you have used before, but also demonstrates that you truly own what you have already studied. Once you have devised your system, you can compare it to the Question in the Margin System explained in this chapter and combine the best features of both.

StudentTIP

"I have found that notes are easier to take if I am prepared for the class by doing the assigned reading and assignments before I come to class."

Relating Information Processing to Learning Principles

In most college classrooms, the primary mode of teaching is the lecture. However, according to Edgar Dale's research, people generally remember only 20 percent of what they hear.[1] Given that short-term memory holds only five to seven bits of information, it is possible to understand everything that the lecturer says, yet remember only a few things.

It is important, then, to use what you know about memory and the functions of the brain to process information from lectures. Try to apply the four brain functions to process information from your classroom lectures. You have already performed the gathering function for the information in the first few chapters of the text. You know strategies for managing time, thinking critically, setting goals, and remembering new information. The reflecting practice that follows will guide you through the other three functions: analyzing, creating, and acting.

PRACTICE 6.1

Modeling the Learning Process (Reflecting)

Keep in mind that your ultimate task here is to come up with step-by-step strategies for taking what you hear in lectures and making it your own. Begin by brainstorming and reflecting. First make a list of what you learned in Chapter 1: Making a Smooth Transition to College that might be useful.

Ideas About Making a Smooth Transition

Now consider what you learned about time management that would be useful in classroom lectures.

Ideas About Time Management to Keep in Mind

Are there things you learned about critical thinking that would be useful in devising your step-by-step system?

Ideas About Critical Thinking to Keep in Mind

Continued

[1]E. Dale, *Audio Visual Methods in Teaching*, 3d ed. (New York: Holt, Rinehart and Winston, 1969).

Practice 6.1 continued

What about things you learned about goal setting that would help you own lecture material?

Ideas About Goal Setting to Keep in Mind

Now consider the learning principles. The four categories of learning principles are listed below to help you brainstorm.

Ideas About Learning Principles to Keep in Mind

Starting the Connections involves *interest, intent to remember,* and *basic background.*

Controlling the amount and form of information involves *selectivity* and *meaningful organization.*

Strengthening memory involves *recitation, mental visualization,* and *association.*

Allowing time for memory to soak in involves *consolidation* and *distributed practice.*

Now that you have this information where you can see it, analyze it, and form a hypothesis—a plan for processing lectures that you think may work for you. Step 1 may involve what you need to do before you come to class. Other steps will involve what to do in class and what to do after class.

You probably won't come up with the perfect system in one try, but you will have accomplished three things in your attempt. You will have begun to take ownership of the material you have already covered in previous chapters, you, will have demonstrated that Zull's model of learning has potential for you and you have a system for taking notes from lectures that you developed yourself.

For each step, explain your reasoning in enough detail that someone could read your explanation and know what to do and when to do it. The following list has fill-in lines for six steps. Your system may have more or fewer steps.

Step 1:_____

_____

_____

_____

Step 2:_____

_____

_____

_____

Step 3:_____

_____

_____

_____

Step 4:_____

_____

_____

_____

Step 5:_____

_____

_____

_____

Step 6:_____

_____

_____

_____

Keep your plan handy. You will use it later in this chapter.

Listening Skills

A quick inventory on college campuses reveals that as much as 80 percent of what you need to learn is delivered through lectures. Sometimes the lectures are exciting and easy to follow. Other times they may be dry, or it may be difficult to grasp the main idea. No matter how entertaining, confusing, or boring the lecture may be, you are responsible for learning and remembering the information presented.

If you are having problems with your note taking, follow the steps of critical thinking and first determine what the problem is. One cause may

 StudentTIP

"When I first started taking notes, I was so bad that I really just wanted to not take notes at all. The more I practiced, the better I got. It really took me several semesters before I was comfortable taking notes. Thank goodness I kept on trying. This semester I took several courses where my grade was totally dependent on my note-taking skills."

be bad listening habits. Use the following practice to check your listening habits. One of the first things you probably will conclude is that intent to remember and interest are triggered by listening carefully.

Obstacles to Listening

From the following list, choose the five obstacles that most often get in the way of your listening in class. In the space following the obstacle, explain in detail how you can overcome this obstacle (not just "I won't do it anymore!").

1. Talking instead of listening

2. Thinking of what you're going to say instead of listening

3. Mentally arguing with the speaker

4. Thinking about something else while the speaker is talking

5. Getting impatient with the speaker

6. Giving in to a poor environment—too noisy, too hot, too hungry

7. Dividing your attention—texting, finishing homework, writing a letter, staring at someone cute

8. Not listening actively—not taking notes, not asking questions, and so on

9. Not being motivated to listen—thinking the subject is boring

10. Being distracted by the speaker's mannerisms, voice, or appearance

Improving Your Listening

Here are some common-sense principles that will help you become a better listener in class. Study the following list and answer the questions that follow each statement.

1. **Come to class** prepared. What does this involve? _____

_____

How will this make you a better listener? _____

_____

What learning principles does this involve? _____

_____

2. **Sit as close to the instructor as possible.** Why?

_____

3. **Come to class as early as possible.** Why? _____

4. **Make eye contact with the instructor.** Why? _____

_____

5. **Listen for verbal clues that something is important.** What are some examples of things the instructor might say to let you know that a point is important?

_____

_____

_____

6. **Watch for nonverbal clues** that a point is important. What are some examples?

_____

_____

_____

_____

7. **Listen with a pen or pencil in your hand.** Why? _____

_____

_____

Continued

Practice 6.3 continued

8. Think of questions as you are listening. Mentally ask questions such as "What is the main idea?" or "What point is she trying to make?" What other questions might you ask? How will this help?

_____

_____

9. Get rid of as many distractions as possible. Name some things that might distract you.

_____

_____

_____

Virtual Field Trip
Improve Your Listening

Making CONNECTIONS

Good listening skills are an essential component of the **intent to remember**, one of the three principles that affect whether new material even gets into your short-term memory. As previously pointed out, attention is not the same as learning, but learning cannot occur without attention.

Review the BREATHE System. Explain how using this system could affect your listening.

_____

_____

_____

_____

_____

_____

_____

_____

_____

_____

_____

_____

Taking Notes

Taking notes in class gives you a record of what was said there so that you can study that information after class. However, taking notes does much more. It helps you learn the material as you write it. In *Brain Rules*, John Medina says that the brain can hold only five to seven bits of information for about 30 seconds. If you don't repeat it within 30 seconds, it disappears.[2] Taking notes is one way of repeating it.

Your notes are not simply a record of what was said in class; they are part of the processes of active listening, mental processing, and manual recording, which employ all ten learning principles. Taking notes in class is the beginning of taking ownership of the lecture material. Remember, you listen better if you understand the lecture. To understand the lecture, you need to drive. You need to be prepared, develop a basic background of the material if you don't already have one, and ask questions. In Practice 6.4, you will study a list of reasons students give for taking notes. Now that you know the learning principles, you can probably add more.

PRACTICE 6.4

Why Take Notes?

Below is a list of reasons students have given for taking notes in class. Read them, decide which is the most important reason to you, and number it 1. Number all the reasons in order of importance to you, with number 1 being the most important and number 8 being the least important. If there are reasons you think of that are not listed, list and rate them.

_____ Taking notes makes me pay attention. It keeps my mind from wandering. I am more likely to stay aware of what is important.

_____ Taking notes helps me concentrate. When I am trying to take good notes, I concentrate more on what the speaker is saying.

_____ Taking notes gives me a record of what was said in class. I know what was said on which days and also what was not covered in class.

_____ Taking notes forces me to select the main ideas. I can't write down everything.

_____ The simple act of writing something down helps me remember it longer.

_____ Taking notes gives me a place to write down assignments so that I will be able to find them later.

_____ Taking notes gives me information to use to study for tests and for class assignments.

_____ Taking notes reminds me of what the teacher has emphasized.

_____

_____

 BRAIN BYTE

Three important findings from studies concerned with note taking:

1. Note taking helps you listen; it does not interfere with listening and comprehension.

2. Students who study their notes on a regular basis remember one and a half times more after six weeks than students who do not review.

3. Students who take no notes or do not study their notes forget approximately 80 percent of the lectures by the end of two weeks.

---

[2]John Medina, *Brain Rules: 12 Principles for Surviving and Thriving at Work, Home, and School* (Seattle, WA: Pear, 2008).

Using the Question in the Margin System for Lectures

A simplified version of the Question in the Margin System was introduced at the beginning of the semester. Now that you understand the learning principles and more about how you learn, you are ready to expand the system and examine why it works. During this discussion, you will want to refer to the steps you devised in Practice 6.1 at the beginning of the chapter. See if you came up with any similar steps.

Controlling the Amount and Form of Information in Your Notes

Although you can't control the amount of information in a lecture or the form in which it is presented, you *can* control what you write down and how you write it down. The Question in the Margin System is the best way I know to control both the amount and the form of your notes. This is more than a system for taking notes. It is a complete system for processing information from lectures that makes use of all the learning principles.

You begin by using the principle of selectivity to choose what's most important to write down in your notes. Then you organize your notes in question-and-answer form, using the principle of meaningful organization.

The Question in the Margin System is based on the note-taking system developed at Cornell University in the 1950s. It is sometimes referred to as the Cornell System. This system may take some getting used to, but in the long run you will find that it saves you energy and time. Because it uses what we know about how our brains work, it provides an extremely efficient way of processing information from lectures. Note taking is a skill, and as with all new skills, it takes practice. The more you use it, the better you become at it!

There are six basic steps in the Question in the Margin System. We will discuss each in turn.

Before You Begin

You will need a loose-leaf notebook with wide-ruled lines. If possible, take your notes in pen instead of pencil; pencil will smudge and fade. You don't want to go to the trouble of taking notes and then not be able to read them later. If you prefer to take notes using your computer or want to type your notes later, you could create your notes page by using a table with 2 columns. In addition, you can find numerous websites that reproduce the Cornell format as a PDF you can print, as well as apps for setting it up on your iPad, tablet, or mobile device.

First, draw a line down your paper about 2 1/2 inches from the left side. Disregard the red vertical line usually used for the margin. (Long lines are more difficult to scan, so by shrinking the area where you take notes, you can review them more quickly.) You will use the wide section on the right to record your notes in class. The section on the left becomes your question (or label) margin, where you will write a question that identifies the main idea (or key words or phrases that will serve as labels for the main idea). The margin at the top of the page is used for indicating the date, class, and page number and for writing assignments or other important information that you don't want to forget. Some students prefer to also leave a space at the bottom for a summary or additional notes or questions.

Six Steps

Step 1. Record what is said. Use a shortened form of writing to *record* what is said. Most of you have already perfected a shortened form of writing for when you send text messages. Be stingy with your words. Never write a whole sentence when a word or two will do. The whole idea behind note taking is to write no more than you need to in order to remember what was said. Use abbreviations whenever possible. Your *basic background* will determine what you write. The more you know, the less you will have to write to remind yourself what was said. One good way to determine what to write down is to pretend that you are texting your friend the important things she should know about class.

Label notes with a question here.	Put name, date, class, and page number here.
	Take text message–like notes here.

For example, if your instructor says:

> *Recitation is the most powerful way of transferring information from short-term memory to long-term memory.*

You might write:

> Recite most pow'ful way to get s-t-mem to l-t-mem

If your instructor says:

> *These are four reasons recitation is so powerful. It makes you pay more attention because you know you are going to recite. It makes you participate in your learning. You must understand in order to explain in your own words. And it gives you feedback as to how much you actually know.*

You might write:

1. Makes pay attent
2. Makes participate
3. Have to understnd
4. Feedbck

Before we go to step 2, let's examine the power of step 1 by determining which learning principles are used just in the process of recording. The more learning principles you use, the more likely you are to remember. Below is a list of the learning principles. Circle any principle you think you use in the record step. Be ready to explain how it was used.

Interest, Intent to Remember, Basic Background, Selectivity, Meaningful Organization, Visualization, Recitation, Association, Distributed Practice, Consolidation

PRACTICE 6.5

Note Taking

Below are parts of lectures your instructors might give and then a space is given for you demonstrate what you might write.

1. Your instructor says:

Because of Switzerland's strict neutrality, Geneva provides an impartial meeting ground for representatives of other nations.[3]

You write:

> Switz neutral so Geneva
> impartial meeting grnd
> for other nations

2. Your instructor says:

The Olympic games were held in ancient times on the plain of Olympia in Greece every four years. It was a time for laying aside political and religious differences, as athletes from all Greek cities and districts competed.[4]
Your turn to try.

You write:

3. Your instructor says:

Obsolescence is a decline in the value of equipment or of a product brought about by an introduction of new technology or by changes in demand.[5]

You write:

Step 2. Question. Recording the information during the lecture is only the first step in using the Question in the Margin System. The next step is to cue yourself as to what each section of your notes is about by writing a question (or key word or phrase) in the 2 1/2-inch margin on the left, and as soon after class as possible. The best way to determine what question to write is to play *Jeopardy!* with the notes you took. What question do your notes answer? If this information appears on a test, how will it be asked? This questioning makes you use your critical-thinking skills. You have gone beyond just the facts you have written down. You understand the information enough to analyze how it might be asked for on a test. As already discussed, learning is enhanced when you ask questions. For example, your questions for the notes on the preceding page might look something like this.

Student TIP

"If you use your laptop or tablet to take notes, there are apps that use the Cornell method format you can use."

---

[3]E. D. Hirsch Jr., J. F. Kett, and J. Trefl, *The Dictionary of Cultural Literacy*, 2d ed. (Boston: Houghton Mifflin, 1993).
[4]Ibid.
[5]Ibid.

PUT A MARGIN QUESTION HERE	PUT NAME, DATE, CLASS, AND PAGE NUMBER HERE. TAKE TEXT MESSAGE–LIKE NOTES HERE
What principle is best in moving from short-term to long-term memory?	Recite most pow'ful way to get s-t-mem transferring to l-t-mem.
What are four reasons why recitation works?	1. Makes pay attent 2. Makes participate 3. Have to understnd 4. Feedbck

Now go back to the other samples you just recorded and write a question in the margin. The *Jeopardy!* question for the first sample might be "Why is Geneva a good place for nations to meet?"

Before we go to step 3, let's examine the power of step 2 by determining which learning principles are used just in the process of questioning. The more learning principles you use, the more likely you are to remember. Below is a list of the learning principles. Circle any principle you think you use in the question step. Be ready to explain how it was used.

Interest, Intent to Remember, Basic Background, Selectivity, Meaningful Organization, Visualization, Recitation, Association, Distributed Practice, Consolidation

Step 3. Recite. The third step in the Question in the Margin System is to test yourself by *reciting* the information. Remember that reciting involves saying out loud in your own words what you have learned. This is part of strengthening your memory, and it begins the process of transferring the information to your long-term memory. Cover up the wide column and use the questions (or key words or phrases) in the left margin to recite the covered material. Repeat this until you are able to recite each section.

Before we go to step 4, let's examine the power of step 3 by determining which learning principles are used just in the process of reciting. The more learning principles you use, the more likely you are to remember. Below is a list of the learning principles. Circle any principle you think you use in the recite step. Be ready to explain how it was used.

Interest, Intent to Remember, Basic Background, Selectivity, Meaningful Organization, Visualization, Recitation, Association, Distributed Practice, Consolidation

Step 4. Reflect. Reflection, step 4, strengthens the memory as it further processes information into long-term memory. To *reflect* is to think about the ideas and how they fit in with other things you know. Try to make them personal—make connections, make them relevant to you. Can you think of examples from your own experience to reinforce the main point? Can you make it concrete by creating an analogy ("This is like …")? Can you visualize the information in some way? Do you agree with the information? How could you use that information?

After reflecting, you will probably want to add comments, illustrations, and questions to your notes. Reflection may be the most important step in the system. This is not only where you process new information, but also where you begin to take ownership of it. You are analyzing new information, integrating it into your experience by relating it to what you already know, and trying to find out if it has relevance and meaning for you. Reflecting takes information that you receive from a lecture and turns it into personal knowledge. This step is, in fact, step 3 of Zull's four pillars of learning, which you worked with in modeling the learning process.

Before we go to step 5, let's examine the power of step 4 by determining which learning principles are used just in the process of reflecting. The more learning principles you use, the more likely you are to remember. Below is a list of the learning principles. Circle any principle you think you use in the reflect step. Be ready to explain how it was used.

Interest, Intent to Remember, Basic Background, Selectivity, Meaningful Organization, Visualization, Recitation, Association, Distributed Practice, Consolidation

Step 5. Review.
Whereas reflection begins the soaking-in, or consolidation, process, reviewing continues it. In step 5, you *review* your notes systematically. If your reviews are regular and routine, you can keep the level of recall high.

In *Use Both Sides of Your Brain*, Tony Buzan makes the following suggestions for reviewing:[6]

1. Use distributed practice to review. You should stop after about an hour of learning and take a 10-minute break. Your **first review** should come after this 10-minute break and should probably last about 10 minutes. This should keep the recall high for approximately one day.
2. The **second review** should take place within one day and should probably not take longer than three or four minutes. This should help you retain the information for about one week.
3. The **third review** should come before the week is up. It should require only a few minutes, because you are reviewing, not relearning, the information.
4. A **fourth review** will probably be required if you have not used the material within a month. This should firmly place the information into long-term memory.

In the first review, you should bring notes up to date by writing your questions in the margin, reciting, reflecting, and so on. In other words, use the Question in the Margin System on the notes you took in class to process the information into your long-term memory.

In the second, third, and fourth reviews, you should make use of any consolidating method that works for you. Do whatever is necessary for the information to soak in. You could use the reciting part of the system again, or you could write down everything you can remember about the question you wrote in the margin. Reviewing might include such things as making and using flash cards, creating mnemonics, making practice tests, and rerunning your mental videos. This activates your memory.

StudentTIP

"My study partners and I found that if we took the time to compare notes after class and write the questions in the margin together, our notes were better because we knew others would see them. Besides, it was more fun and easier, and the result is we know the material better."

StudentTIP

In the reflection step, I like to type or recopy my notes. I find I remember them better if I have put them in a form I can read better. As I rewrite my notes I usually think of more questions and comments.

[6]Tony Buzan, *Use Both Sides of Your Brain* (New York: Penguin Books, 1990).

You are strengthening synaptic connections by taking information *from* your long-term memory. The more you activate information from your long-term memory, the easier it is to find that material when you need it. Make sure you are self-testing, not just mentally mumbling.

The times you set in your master schedule for routine study of a subject should be used for these reviews. Of course, immediately before and immediately after class are good review times. Right before you go to bed is also a good time to review.

One of the most significant aspects of reviewing is the cumulative effect it has on all aspects of learning, thinking, and remembering. You are building basic background. The more you know, the easier it is to learn. People who do not review are, in effect, wasting the efforts they put forth the first time. Your time—and the money you spent on college—is too valuable for that.

Before we go to the final step, let's examine the power of step 5 by determining which learning principles are used just in the process of reviewing. The more learning principles you use, the more likely you are to remember. Below is a list of the learning principles. Circle any principle you think you use in the review step. Be ready to explain how it was used.

Interest, Intent to Remember, Basic Background, Selectivity, Meaningful Organization, Visualization, Recitation, Association, Distributed Practice, Consolidation

Step 6. Summarize. When you summarize, you condense main points in your own words. Either at the bottom of the page or at the end of your lecture notes, you could write a *summary*. You will want to do this immediately after you review. Summarizing is a form of selectivity. If you understand your notes enough to make a concise version of them, you are probably well on your way to owning them. Your summary may be just one sentence, a few sentences, a paragraph, or even a page. Instead of writing a summary in paragraph form, you may find that you prefer to make your summary a list, chart, timeline, or map. Mapping is a good form of summary to use if you rely heavily on visualization to remember (see the illustrations at the beginning of each chapter for examples of mapping).

One of the best strategies I know for summarizing is to pretend that you have been assigned to present to your class the material you need to summarize. Make a PowerPoint presentation for your assignment. Because it is a pretend assignment, you can make pretend PowerPoint slides from index cards. Decide which points you need to include and how you will present them. You should even include the illustrations you will use. You will find that when you finish, not only do you have a great summary, but you also understand the material better and probably already remember most of it.

You've probably started to see all of the connections between the ten learning principles and Question in the Margin System by now.

Circle any principle you think you use in the summary step. Be ready to explain how it was used.

Interest, Intent to Remember, Basic Background, Selectivity, Meaningful Organization, Visualization, Recitation, Association, Distributed Practice, Consolidation

Sample Notes—Question in the Margin

Lecture notes from the information presented about the Question in the Margin System might look something like the following sample:

Why use the Question in the Margin System?	Q-M system based on learn principles Process info into long-term mem
What do I do before class?	Set up w/line 21/2
What is step 1?	Write important info on right—wide—text-like-no more than need 2 rem **RECORD**
What is step 2?	After class asap question infor w/?? here **QUESTION**
What is step 3?	After writing ?, cover notes—ask question & say answer out loud in own wrds **RECITE**
What is step 4?	After basic understanding of info, try to make personal, visualize, make connections **REFLECT**
What is step 5?	B 4 put up notes, go back over all Use difrent techniques like flash cards, practice tests, etc. **REVIEW**
What is step 6?	Condense main points in own words—writ sum at bottom of page or on sep activity **SUMMARIZE**

The Question in the Margin System uses most of the learning principles and consists of six steps—Record, Question, Recite, Reflect, Review, and Summarize.

CRITICAL THINKING
About Taking Notes

Probably the most difficult part of using the Question in the Margin System for many students is breaking the habit of writing too much or writing in complete sentences. Because you will be bringing your notes up to date very soon after class, you can get by with writing less.

While you may use the same form of shortened writing that you use to send text messages, there is a difference in sending a message and deciding what to write down.

Writing margin questions is a skill that you must develop. Most likely, you won't be really good at it for quite some time. If you have ever driven a car with a stick shift, remember when you first began to drive it? You had to really think yourself through it, and sometimes the ride was jerky. Now you shift without even thinking about it. The same is true with taking notes in shortened form. At first you have to really think about what you are going to write. Sometimes it takes more time to think about what you are leaving out than it would to write it! Don't worry. You can think four times faster than most lecturers can talk, so you have time to determine what you will write. With practice, this shortened form of note taking will become natural. You'll do it without much effort. Don't get me wrong. Taking notes is hard work. You have to become involved in class both physically and mentally. At the end of class, you will probably be exhausted. But you don't learn by passively sitting in the passenger seat. You process information only by becoming involved in what you are learning—by driving your education. Don't expect to be an expert immediately. It will take time to develop your skills.

Stop and reflect for a few minutes on how taking notes is like driving a stick-shift automobile. Write down as many comparisons as you can think of. If you've never driven a stick shift before, there are lots of videos online you can review.

Virtual Field Trip
Practice Using the Question in the Margin System
This field trip sends you to several online lectures by John Medina, who will provide you with some practice in taking notes.

PRACTICE 6.6

Question in the Margin System

Study the step-by-step plan you devised in Practice 6.1, "Modeling the Learning Process," at the beginning of the chapter. On the basis of your initial plan, would you make any changes to the Question in the Margin System?

What part of your plan corresponds to the Question in the Margin System? Fill in the chart below with similarities.

Question in the Margin System	Parts of My Learning Model That Correspond
Preparing for the system	
RECORD	
QUESTION	
RECITE	
REFLECT	
REVIEW	
SUMMARIZE	

For Your Student Survival Kit

Summary Sheet for Question in the Margin: Lecture Notes

What You Do	When You Do It	Why You Do It
Input or Gather Information		
Record		
Listen carefully. Write down important information from the lecture in the wide margin of your page. Don't write whole sentences; be *text-like*.	Get out your paper and pen as soon as you come to class. Take notes from beginning to end of class.	Short-term memory will not hold what you hear in class, so you need a record. Use *selectivity* and *write text-like* because you can't write down every-thing. Taking notes also helps you pay *attention*.
Process Information Gathered		
Question		
Read over your notes. *Determine the main ideas* of each section and label them in the form of a possible test question. *Underline*, number, or clean up notes so that they are clear and legible.	Most students think that when they have taken notes in class, their job is over. But forgetting begins immediately; therefore, as soon as possible after class, begin a review of your notes.	Because you forget quickly, if you just take notes and do nothing, you'll end up relearning the material rather than remembering it. Reading over notes begins to *process the information*. *Writing a question* ensures that you *understood* what you wrote and *orga-nizes your notes* in a meaningful way.
Recite		
Cover up your notes. Use the ques-tions as cues. *Say the main ideas out loud in your own words.*	This should be done as soon as you record and label your notes.	*Recitation* is the most powerful means you have of *transferring information from short-term memory to long-term memory.* You have begun to learn the material instead of merely recording it.
Reflect		
Think about the lecture. Make connec-tions with things you already know. How does the lecture connect to the *textbook*? Make it *personal*. *Visualize.* Begin to *organize* your notes.	*As soon as you recite* or while you are reciting, begin to reflect. (You may want to reflect before you recite as well.)	*Reflection* makes the information *real and personal*. Therefore, you process information more deeply into your long-term memory.
Activate		
Review		
Go over your notes. *Recite* by making use of the narrow margin. *Make flash cards, mnemonic devices*, or *practice tests*, or *map* the ideas found in the notes.	Review *10 minutes after you finish going over your notes*, keeping recall fresh for one day. Review again in *one day*, in *one week*, and then once more *before the test*.	Periodic review keeps you from forget-ting what you already know. Before a test, you will just need to review, not relearn, the material.
Summarize		
Condense main points in your own words at the end of each section or each day's notes, write a short sum-mary, or make a summary sheet such as this one.	Summarize *during* one of your *reviews*.	Summarizing allows for *consolidation* and promotes a deeper *understanding* of the material.

CAREER Connections

Let's pause for a minute and think about note taking as not just a skill that could make you more successful in college, but as a life-long skill. Write a short paragraph in which you describe how you could use the note-taking habits you develop in college to make you more successful in your chosen career.

Practice taking notes with this exercise. Go to YouTube and find a clip that explains a career that you might be considering. (For instance, you may ask: "What does a Biomedical Engineer do?") Use the video to practice taking notes.

Virtual Field Trip
Expanding What You
Know About Note Taking

PRACTICE 6.7

Learning Principles Used in the Question in the Margin System

We have said one reason the Question in the Margin System works so well is that it uses all ten learning principles for learning. Review the notes you made while reading the chapter and make a summary chart to explain how each principle is used in the Question in the Margin System. Be sure to consider all steps of the system. I have included a few to get you started. You will need to add to the list.

Learning Principle	How This Principle Is Used in the Question in the Margin System
INTEREST	When I take notes, my brain senses that the information is valuable. Other ways interest is used:
INTENT TO REMEMBER	Knowing that I will have to write a question and recite information later triggers intent to remember.
BASIC BACKGROUND	
SELECTIVITY	
MEANINGFUL ORGANIZATION	
VISUALIZATION	

Continued

Practice 6.7 continued

Learning Principle	How This Principle Is Used in the Question in the Margin System
RECITATION	
ASSOCIATION	
CONSOLIDATION	
DISTRIBUTED PRACTICE	

 # Review—Where did we go?

Modeling the Learning Process

You learned the steps of the Question in the Margin System and created your plan at the beginning of the chapter in Practice 6.1, "Modeling the Learning Process."

Gathering. You took notes in class.

Analyzing. You analyzed your notes, wrote questions in the margin, and looked for connections.

Creating New Ideas. You reflected and reviewed your notes and questions and predicted possible test questions, involving higher-order thinking skills.

Acting. You developed summary sheets, maps, PowerPoint presentations, and practice tests.

Study Guide: Processing Information from Lectures

To see if you grasped the major points of the chapter and to make a useful study guide, answer the following questions found in your reading. When you have written your answers, cover them and see if you can say the answer to each question in your own words.

1. **Name and briefly explain what James Zull outlines as four essential functions for learning.**

    1. _____

    2. _____

    3. _____

    4. _____

2. **What are the five obstacles that keep you from listening well?**

1. _____

2. _____

3. _____

4. _____

5. _____

3. **Name five things you can do to improve your listening.**

1. _____

2. _____

3. _____

4. _____

5. _____

4. **What do you consider the three most important reasons for taking notes during a lecture?**

1. _____

2. _____

3. _____

5. **List and explain the six steps of the Question in the Margin System for processing information from lectures.**

Step 1: _____

_____

Step 2: _____

_____

Step 3: _____

_____

Step 4: _____

_____

Step 5: _____

_____

Step 6: _____

_____

CASE STUDY
What's Your Advice?

Sara is a first-year student taking 12 credit hours in college. She lives in the dorm, and it is her first time away from home. Sara was a very good student in high school and didn't have to study much to get A's and B's. Now she is doing exactly what she did in high school and is struggling even to pass. She listens in class and reads her assignments unless the instructor is going to lecture on them anyway. Then she thinks it isn't necessary to read the assignment. Sara does her homework at night in her room and usually finishes it before visiting her friends or watching TV. Her roommate suggests that Sara needed to take notes in class. Although she never had to take notes in high school, Sara decides it is worth a try. Her history professor talks so fast that when she tries to write down what he says, she can't write fast enough.

Fifteen minutes into the class, Sara is so frustrated that she quits writing. She starts to take notes in her psychology class, but gets so interested in the discussion that she forgets about taking notes. Sara takes notes in biology class but is unable to read what notes she did manage to write when she is ready to study for a test. Although she reads all the assignments her English professor assigns, she has yet to pass the daily reading quiz.

You are sitting at Sara's table at the campus café. She is almost in tears and ready to give up and go home. Using what you have learned in this and previous chapters, can you help her make a list of things she might do? She has not had the benefit of taking this class and needs more instruction than a list. In addition to your list of what to do, you should suggest to her how to do it.

Parallel Parking

List each step of the Question in the Margin System and see if you can create a comparison to driving. For example, you might say that recording important information in class is like putting fuel in your car.

Evaluating Learning Outcomes

How successful were you in making it to your destination in this chapter?
Analyze what you learned in this chapter. Put a check beside each task you are now able to do. On a separate piece of paper, write a couple of sentences about how you learned each learning outcome and how you plan to continue to use what you learned.

- ☐ **Demonstrate** the learning model by constructing a plan for taking notes.
- ☐ **Use** the ten learning principles to develop strategies for processing information from classroom lectures.
- ☐ **Appraise** your listening habits, and construct strategies for improving them.
- ☐ **Describe** several reasons for taking notes in class.
- ☐ **Demonstrate** the six steps of the Question in the Margin System for taking notes: record, question, recite, reflect, review, and summarize.
- ☐ **Explain** how to use the Question in the Margin System to someone who has never used it.
- ☐ **Predict** how this note-taking system might be useful in your present or future job.
- ☐ **Explain** the learning process modeled in this chapter.

Your Student Tip for This Chapter

Use the space below to write a tip you would give to other students about what you have learned in this chapter.

_____

_____

_____

Processing Information from Textbooks

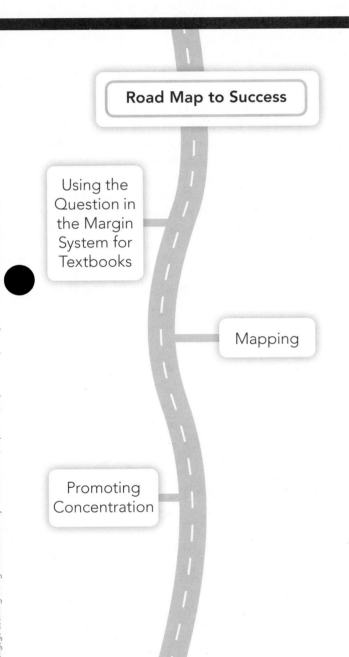

Road Map to Success

Using the Question in the Margin System for Textbooks

Mapping

Promoting Concentration

In this chapter, you will learn how to

- **Demonstrate** how to use the Question in the Margin System for reading textbooks.

- **Explain** how to use the Question in the Margin System to someone who has never used it.

- **Analyze** the Question in the Margin System, and explain how the memory principles are used to complete the system.

- **Explain** the goal of mapping and demonstrate how to map a passage from a text.

- **Illustrate** strategies that promote concentration.

- **Analyze** your study habits and develop a plan to make improvements.

- **Explain** the learning process modeled in this chapter.

Where Are We Going?

One of the biggest adjustments students must make in college is dealing with the amount of reading necessary to be a successful student. I can't do away with those assignments, but we can look at how to make them more manageable. In this chapter, we will first review some basic reading strategies for textbooks and examine some strategies for reading assignments online or in e-books. Then we will build on strategies that we already know will work. Now that you have the basics of the Question in the Margin System for taking notes in class and have discovered how the process uses brain-compatible learning, in this chapter you will learn how the system can work when reading a textbook. You have seen the importance of being the driver, not a passenger, in the classroom. Your role as driver takes on even more importance when doing the reading for your courses. The amount of reading you are responsible for in your college classes presents some real road hazards. There is a temptation to speed, to get to the end of the chapter. However, if you are to own the material in each chapter, you must plan your maneuvers carefully. Later in the chapter you will practice mapping, one of the best ways I know to summarize material I've read. And because reading demands concentration, we will end the chapter with some tips that promote concentration. Finally, you will have an opportunity to stop and take stock by analyzing your study habits.

PRACTICE 7.1

Differences in Gathering Information from Lectures and from Textbooks

We have determined that the first step of gathering information from lectures is to record. Use the following table to brainstorm some specific differences in gathering information from lectures and gathering information from textbooks.

LECTURES	TEXTBOOKS

StudentTIP

"I always thought that most learning occurs in the classroom—teachers taught me what I needed to know. However, since I have been in college, I have discovered just the opposite. Most learning occurs outside the classroom when I have time to reflect and personalize new material."

For Your Student Survival Kit

Some Basic Reading Strategies

Reading Strategy: before you read

- Identify your goal for each study session. What is the purpose of the assignment? How much will you read?
- Set a time and place for reading the assignment.
- Divide the assignment into readable chunks—ten pages or less.
- Survey the chapter or assignment.
- Recall what you already know about the subject.
- Predict what you may be looking for by forming a question in your mind.

Reading Strategy: while you read

- Visualize what the author is saying.
- If it is complicated, read it aloud.
- Look for the answer to the question you predicted.
- Stop and look up any words you don't understand.
- Rephrase the sentence in your own words.
- Try to relate it to something you already know.
- Wait until you finish a paragraph before you mark anything.

Reading Strategy: after you complete a paragraph

- Check to see if your predicted question pertained to the topic of the paragraph.
- Determine the main idea and supporting detail.
- Learn to identify patterns of organization.
- Write a question in the margin that is about the main idea, the most important information in the paragraph.
- After you write your question, mark the answer to your question by highlighting, circling, or numbering the text so you can quickly see the answer to your question. (Come up with a system that works for you.)
- Mark just enough so you don't have to reread the whole chapter, but have a clear idea of the answer to the question you have written.

Reading Strategy: after you mark your text

- Cover the paragraph you have just read and marked. Using the question you wrote in the margin, test yourself.
- Recite the answer aloud.
- Reflect about what you read. Try to connect it to other things that you know. Try to make it personal. Predict what the next paragraph will address and start the process all over again.

Before you put your book away:

- Review the key points of the selection.
- Make a summary or study guide for the selection.
- Create a map or outline to help think about how the information fits together.

For Your Student Survival Kit

Notes about E-texts and Reading on Screens Rather Than Paper

- There is a distinct difference in how our eyes focus on paper and on computer screens that may result in eye strain or other forms of physical fatigue occurring more quickly when you read on a screen.
- Plan your computer reading time so that it is done in chunks rather than a long period of time. (A suggestion we also made when reading on paper.)
- The lighting is extremely important both when reading on screen and reading on paper. When reading on screen make sure you have ambient light from a lamp or ceiling fixture. Don't read from a screen in a dark room.
- Some studies suggest that we read slower and with perhaps less comprehension on the computer; others say we tend to skim more. If you need to own the material, slow down and mark the text just as you would a paper book.

Continued

For Your Student Survival Kit continued

- Most iPads, tablets, or e-textbooks allow the reader to annotate while reading. Annotations include underlining, highlighting, striking-through, and inserting sticky notes.
- Before you start to use an e-text, take time to get familiar with how to annotate. Try out different fonts as well as brightness or contrasts on the screen. You can adjust the size of the font as well as the size of the window.
- Often e-text has embedded interactive definitions, graphics, maps, timelines, animations, and soundtracks. Being able to look up words and references immediately enhances knowledge and fuller understanding; however, it may also get the reader off track.
- Make use of apps that remove banner ads and distractions from online articles.

Using the Question in the Margin System for Textbooks

Starting the Connections

Like listening to lectures, reading textbooks involves starting the connections. The three learning principles in this category are *interest, intent to remember*, and *basic background*. You want to make a conscious effort to use the learning principles before you begin to read. One of the best ways to get familiar with the road you are about to travel is to **survey** the material before you begin, which will help you begin to build interest. Surveying is the first step in using question in the margin in texts. Look at the title, major and minor topics discussed, and bold print; look at the pictures, study the graphs and charts, read the summary, and examine the review questions *before* you do any reading. As you are doing this, try to recall everything you already know about the subject. Surveying often builds interest; but most of all, it gives you a basic background about the material you are going to read. Knowing something about the subject makes it easier to pay attention and easier to remember. By knowing where the reading is going, you can make connections as you read the material for the first time.

Think for a moment about your concentration when you read. If someone gave you a page and said "read this," would you read it in the same way as if she said "read this page to find three ways to process information or five ways to save time"? If you know why you are reading something, you will probably get more out of it. An obvious study strategy to use when reading a textbook, then, is to note the headings or the topic sentence of each paragraph and try to determine what you are looking for as you continue through the paragraph. This **focusing** should be done after you survey and before you begin to read. Focusing—trying to determine what you are looking for—is the second step of the Question in the Margin System and requires no writing.

Controlling the Amount and Form of Information

As you begin to read, you can control the amount and form of the information you gather by not reading more than one paragraph at a time before you process the information contained in each. Remember that

BRAIN BYTE

Multiply the number of pages you have to read by five minutes. Five minutes is the amount of time the average college student needs to read a page. Keep this in mind as you schedule time to do your reading. If you calculate four hours of reading, you might not want to read 7–11 P.M. straight through. I'd recommend getting an hour in before class in the morning or over the lunch break. Spread it out a bit.

your short-term memory can hold only five to seven bits of information at a time. Each paragraph will likely hold about that amount. If you read the entire chapter without processing bits of information into long-term memory, you will probably have to go back and reread most of the chapter in order to process it. Instead, why not use distributed practice by processing information along the way? The next step, then, is to **read one paragraph at a time**.

Once you have read a paragraph, you want to process that information before you go on to the next one. The system works the same here as it did with taking notes. After you read a paragraph, to ensure you have gotten the main idea and selected the important points, write a question in the margin that labels those important points. Aim at writing only one or two broad questions about the main idea rather than many questions about details. Next, underline the answer to your question. Just as you were stingy with what you wrote while taking notes, you want to underline only the main words. You don't want to have to go back and reread the whole paragraph to find your answer. Underlining should be done *after* you read, not *while* you are reading, and the underlined words should answer the question you have written in the margin. This questioning and underlining may seem time-consuming, but you are going to have to process the information at some time before a test, so why not do it the first time? You'll realize that you actually save time in the long run doing it this way.

The result of your efforts is that each paragraph is labeled with a possible test question or two, and you can quickly review the main points without having to reread the chapter. Later, you can use these questions to create a study guide. Know the speed limit. When you are responsible for knowing and using the information, speed-reading is not advisable. Stopping at the end of each paragraph slows you down enough to make sure you make connections and process what you have read. It also gives you an organized way to go back and review without rereading every word.

From here on, the Question in the Margin System works the same as it did for lecture notes. You process the information you read by covering answers underlined in your text and asking yourself the question in the margin. You **recite** the answers until you are sure you have grasped the information. Before going on, **reflect**. Link the information to what you already know, relate it to the previous paragraph, and consider where the author may be going in the next paragraph. Make it personal. How will you use that information? How will you remember it for a test? If possible, make a mental video to help you *see* the information.

Once you are in control of the information in one paragraph, go on to the next and repeat the process. Because this system is demanding, you will probably want to do only several pages at a time. Make use of those minutes you used to waste—in between class, waiting in line, or waiting for someone to arrive. When you have annotated the entire chapter, review the chapter to get the whole picture. If you work on an assignment during the day, when you come to the time that you had set aside to study that assignment, all you will need to do is review and connect the information in the assignment.

The last step in the Question in the Margin System is to **summarize** by bringing together the main ideas in your own words. Some students

StudentTIP

"It was hard to break the habit of underlining as I read. Instead of just mindlessly underlining, now as I read, I am thinking what question I need to write. And I end up with something I can actually use for studying."

find it more useful to study from their notes than from their marked textbook. Making a summary sheet or a study guide to study for each chapter will be helpful. Your summary may be made by making flash cards from the questions you have written in the margin. Some students prefer to write their notes from each chapter on paper or on the computer, as with lecture notes, instead of writing in the textbook or after marking their books. The study guide at the end of each chapter in this text illustrates this. In fact, you have probably already discovered that the questions in each chapter's study guides are the author's Question in the Margin questions moved to the end of the chapter. You can use this process as a model for summarizing chapters in your other textbooks. Writing a summary or creating a study guide with your questions in the margin is a good check to make sure you understand the information enough to condense it in your own words. In addition, if you make this summary or study guide as soon as you finish a reading assignment, you will already have an aid to use to study for a test. This should really cut down on the amount of time needed to study for a test.

Student TIP

"Don't try to mark a whole chapter at one time. It's easier to mark what you need to read throughout the day when you have a few minutes to read and mark a paragraph or two. When you get to your study time where you would have read the assignment, you've already read it and it's ready to study to make sure you understand it."

PRACTICE 7.2

Understanding the Steps of Question in the Margin for Textbooks

In order to gather the information from your assignment, you first **survey** what you need to read.

What does this involve?

The second step of this gathering is to **focus**.

How is this accomplished?

The third step needed in gathering the information is to **read paragraph by paragraph**.

Why read only one paragraph at a time?

Then you **label the margin with a question**. The answer to the question should be the main ideas in the paragraph.

Explain why this is a good method to use.

Next, you **underline the answer to the question in the textbook**.

Explain why you underline after, instead of before, you write the question.

Remember what you learned about reviewing lectures? Now, try to apply that system of note taking to your textbook notes.

1. When should you review? _____

_____

_____

2. Why should you review? _____

_____

_____

3. Name some ways to review. _____

_____

4. List several methods of **summarizing** that are most effective for you.

_____

_____

Virtual Field Trip
Learning More About
Marking Your Textbook

 ### Making CONNECTIONS

Review what you know about using the Question in the Margin System for reading textbooks. Once you understand how the system works for textbooks, go back to the list you made for how each memory principle is used in taking notes. Check your list of learning principles and include your explanations of how the learning principles are used for the textbook model. You may want to use a different color of ink for the textbook items.

 PRACTICE 7.3

Practice Using the Question in the Margin System for Textbooks

On the following pages, you will find a textbook page for you to practice on. You will want to use all of the steps; however, all that you will see is the question step with the question in the margin. The first paragraph has the questions noted for you. You should write questions in the margin for the three remaining paragraphs. Remember to keep your questions broad and focused on the main idea and be sparse in your underlining.

In addition to writing your question in the margin and underlining the answer, you will probably develop other strategies, such as numbering major points, circling important dates, or starring items emphasized in class. You may want to use different colors of highlighters to distinguish answers to different questions. If you are going to take the time to mark your textbooks with questions and answers, it is important that you be able to read it. Use a pen or highlighter, not a pencil, which can smudge or fade.

 BRAIN BYTE

In the *Owner's Manual for the Brain*, Pierce Howard writes that if learning is made too simple in the classroom, it will be more difficult to actually use that information in the "street, home, or workplace." He says we should have to work and dig out our understanding. Isn't this what the Question in the Margin System asks you to do?

Continued

Practice 7.3 continued

Skills for Career Success

There are many types of skills that are valued within the world of work. Careers do not encompass only one skill or even one skill area. Employers want to hire employees who add value, can combine skill areas in unexpected ways, and are eager to build new skills. The need for professional and transferable skills is in high demand in all industries, including those where specific career-related skills are also mandatory.

Types of Skills

Transferable skills. Transferable skills are assets that can be used in a variety of career fields and are portable between various jobs and industries. These include communication, teamwork, creativity, research, organizational, technological, listening, observing, decision making, and many other skills. You can develop transferable skills in everything you do; some examples are coursework, activities, internships, jobs, hobbies, and volunteer activities.

Self-management and professional skills. Self-management and professional skills are used in every career, and can be adapted to meet the needs of your industry. Professionalism in the workplace involves a set of skills that demonstrates that you are ready, willing, and eager to work. Employers want to know that you can manage your time, projects, and relationships in ways that enhance your job performance. These skills are transferable to all fields, and can help you regardless of the setting in which you work.

Career-related or technical skills. Career-related skills involve knowledge that may not be easily transferable, but is useful for specific careers. These skills often involve industry-specific dialogue and terminology that demonstrates experience and familiarity. This may involve technical expertise in one or more areas, such as a fashion designer's ability to do trend research, use Illustrator, create a flat sketch, and source fabrics. Skills in other industries could involve understanding the elements of a legal brief or how to design a landscape for optimal sun exposure. In addition, while basic math knowledge is helpful for all occupations, certain skills are critical for careers in science, technology, engineering, and math fields.[1]

What three characteristics are employers looking for when they hire?

For Your Student Survival Kit

Summary Sheet for Question in the Margin: Textbooks

WHAT YOU DO	WHEN YOU DO IT	WHY YOU DO IT
Input, or Gather, Information		
Survey		
Skim the *title, major headings, bold print*, and *charts*, and read the *summary* and *review questions*.	Don't begin reading with the first page of the chapter. *Survey before you read.*	Surveying helps develop *interest* in what you are about to read. It gives you a *basic background*. Your subconscious begins to work.

---

[1]Francine Fabricant, Jennifer Miller, and Debra J. Stark, *Creating Career Success: A Flexible Plan for the World of Work* (Boston, MA: Wadsworth, Cengage Learning, 2014).

WHAT YOU DO	WHEN YOU DO IT	WHY YOU DO IT
Focus		
Turn each *major heading* into a *general question*, or use some other method of determining what you are looking for in the paragraph.	*Before you begin* reading each paragraph, determine what you will look for when you read.	Looking for the answer to a question rather than just reading promotes better *concentration* and *understanding*. In addition, you use the principle of selectivity.
Read		
Read each section *paragraph by paragraph* to find the answer to the question you have formulated. Look up any unfamiliar words. Read the section out loud if necessary.	*Do not go on to the next paragraph until you understand the one you are reading.* Do not underline or highlight at this time.	Reading paragraph by paragraph puts *small bits of information* into your memory so you need not try to remember the whole chapter at once. It ensures *understanding*.
Process Information Gathered		
Question		
Label the *main idea* by writing a *question* or brief statement *in the margin*. Then *underline* the answer to your question. Be stingy with your underlining.	*After you read* each paragraph, determine the main idea and put a question in the margin. Then *underline* the answers to your questions in the text. Do not underline while reading.	This step ensures that you *understand* the main ideas in each paragraph. *Selectivity* eliminates the need to reread the chapter and organizes it in a way that allows you to *process* it into *long-term memory*.
Recite		
Cover the underlined text and *recite* in your own words the answer to your margin question.	*Recite as soon as you complete the questioning and underlining.* Do not go on to the next paragraph until you can recite the main idea of this paragraph.	*Recitation* promotes consolidation, strengthens neural pathways, and gives you immediate feedback.
Reflect		
Think about what you have read. *Make connections* with things you already know. Make it *personal*. *Visualize.* Begin to *organize* your notes.	*As soon as you recite*, or while you are reciting, begin to reflect.	*Reflection* makes the information *real*, by processing it more deeply into your long-term memory. It is the difference between memorizing something and learning it.
Activate		
Review		
Go over what you have read. *Recite* margin questions. Make *summary sheets, study guides, flash cards, mnemonic devices*, and *practice tests*, or *map* the ideas found in the chapter.	*Review ten minutes after you finish* the whole chapter, keeping recall fresh for one day. Review again in *one day, one week*, and then once more *before the test*.	Periodic review keeps you from forgetting what you already know. Before a test, you will need to just *review, not relearn*, the material.
Summarize		
Condense main ideas in your own words by putting notes on paper, making a summary sheet, map, or timeline.	Do this during one of your reviews.	*Summarizing* promotes the consolidation and understanding needed to use material that you have learned.

For Your Student Survival Kit

Summary for Both Lecture and Textbook Question in the Margin

STAGE	WHEN LISTENING TO LECTURES	WHEN READING TEXTBOOKS
Gather or input.	1. **Listen** carefully. 2. Write down important information in text-message style.	1. **Survey** the title, major headings, pictures, graphs, bold print, and summary. 2. **Focus** your attention on what you will read by turning each major heading into a question. 3. Read each section **paragraph by paragraph**, looking for the answer to the question.
Process information gathered.	1. **Read** over notes and **write a question in the margin**. 2. Cover notes and **recite** them. 3. Make the information personal by **reflecting**.	After completing each paragraph, label what the paragraph is about by writing a question in the margin. **Underline** the answer to the question. (Be stingy with your underlining!) 1. Cover your underlining in the text and **recite**. 2. Make the information **personal** by **reflecting**.
Activate.	1. **Review** ten minutes after going over the entire lecture. Review again in one day, in one week, and before a test. Use other methods such as flash cards, practice tests, and mnemonic devices. 2. **Summarize** at the end of each section of notes.	1. **Review** ten minutes after finishing the chapter. Review again in one day, in one week, and before a test. Use other methods, such as flash cards, practice tests, and mnemonic devices. 2. Make a **summary sheet** or study guide for each chapter.

PRACTICE 7.4

Do You Understand How the Question in the Margin System Works?

Analyze the following situations and label with the correct *source* (classroom lecture or textbook reading), the correct *stage* (input or gather information, process information gathered, or activate), and the actual *step* within the system. The Summary Sheet or Study Guide should be helpful. Pay particular attention to what each student is doing and when they are doing it. Identifying what is being done is not nearly as important as knowing what to do, but this exercise will check your understanding of Questions in the Margin System.

1. When he was finished reading, Julio went back through the entire chapter and tried to recite the answers to the questions he had written in the margin.

   Source _____ Stage _____ Step _____

2. After class, Lakeisha read over her lecture notes and wrote the key words and phrases on the left side of her paper.

   Source _____ Stage _____ Step _____

3. Sally wrote a question beside each paragraph in Chapter 3 of her History 201 textbook and then underlined the answer to each question.

   Source _____ Stage _____ Step _____

4. In order to study for his upcoming exam, Bobby covered up his lecture notes and recited the importance of the questions he had written.

   Source _____ Stage _____ Step _____

5. When the instructor had concluded her lecture series on the different breeds of beef cattle, David wrote a summary at the end of that section in his notes, putting it into his own words.

Source _____ Stage _____ Step _____

6. To make sure he retained the information from the chapters he had read, Yuuki regularly went over the questions he had written in the margin of his textbook.

Source _____ Stage _____ Step _____

7. Jeff made summary sheets and flash cards and used mnemonic devices to refresh, rather than to relearn, the information from his German 210 class.

Source _____ Stage _____ Step _____

8. When class began, Curtis listened carefully to everything that the instructor said.

Source _____ Stage _____ Step _____

9. To begin her Psychology 141 reading assignment, Jane read the title, checked out the bold headings, and surveyed the graphs and the chapter summary.

Source _____ Stage _____ Step _____

10. While reading, Arya turned each major heading into a question, and then read each paragraph to answer the question.

Source _____ Stage _____ Step _____

11. When Beth's instructor said, "There are seven stages in Chickering's student development theory called vectors," Beth wrote "7 stages (vectors)—Chickering s.d. theory."

Source _____ Stage _____ Step _____

12. Mercedes took a few minutes to think about all of the information she had been reciting from Chapter 10 in her Sociology 310 textbook and tried to relate it to things she already knew.

Source _____ Stage _____ Step _____

Questions I need to ask about the Question in the Margin System for textbooks:

_____

_____

Virtual Field Trip
Let's Learn More About
Critical Reading

Virtual Field Trip
Let's Learn More About
Mapping

Mapping

If you find some information particularly difficult, you may want to begin with the learning principle of visualization to start to process it. **Mapping** is useful for students who learn well visually, but other students shouldn't overlook it; the thought process utilized in mapping uses all ten learning principles. Just as a road map gives you a clear picture of the main roads, connections, and possible routes, a concept map is a **visual representation** of important information selected from the text or lecture. It's like a picture outline. A map is usually hierarchical and shows the relationships among pieces of the whole. Once you have

BRAIN BYTE

The human brain is not organized or designed for linear, one-path thought. Many brain researchers confirm that graphic organizers like mapping help learners understand and recall information better. Maps that are revised and color-coded boost learning and retention.

Practice with Mapping

The two-paragraph article below describes things homeowners can do to save energy. Following the article, you will find a student's study **notes** on the first paragraph. The first example is how the information looked in her notes when her instructor was lecturing. The second is her version of the Question in the Margin System from her **textbook**. Then there is an example of a **map** for the first paragraph. Your job is to examine the second paragraph. First, mark it as you would a textbook page using the Question in the Margin System. Next, using your marked text, map it in the space provided under the first paragraph's map. Because the goals of the Question in the Margin System and mapping are the same, the strategies used to process the information into long-term memory will also overlap. When mapping, I find it easier to put my questions in the margin before I map. Remember, you are mapping not to be artistic, but to help you remember the details you might need for a test.

Read the following article. First write your questions in the margin. Then use the space provided under the paragraph to create a map. The first paragraph has been done for you. Your job is to do the 2nd paragraph.

All homeowners can take action if they are serious about saving on energy costs. Those with more than $100 to spend should consider any of the following steps. First, sidewalls and especially the ceiling of a home should be fully insulated. Proper insulation can save 30 percent or more of a heating or cooling bill. Next, storm windows should be installed throughout the house. They provide an insulating area of still air that may reduce energy loss by 10 percent or more. Finally, a homeowner might consider installing a solar hot-water heating system. Four key factors in such a decision are geographical location, the amount of sunlight available, energy costs in the area, and the construction of the house.

Sample Notes if This Had Been a Lecture

What are three actions a homeowner with more than $100 can take to save energy?	Save energy cost > $100
	1. Insulate sidewalls and ceilings, 30% sav
	2. Install storm windows
	3. Solar hot-water heater. Factors to consider: Geo location Amt sunlight avail Energy costs Construction of house

Sample of the Question in the Margin System for Textbooks

What are three actions a homeowner with more than $100 can take to save energy?

All homeowners can take action if they are serious about saving on energy costs. Those with more than $100 to spend should consider any of the following steps. First,[1] sidewalls and especially the ceiling of a home should be fully insulated. Proper insulation can save 30 percent or more of a heating or cooling bill. Next,[2] storm windows should be installed throughout the house. They provide an insulating area of still air that may reduce energy loss by 10 percent or more. Finally,[3] a homeowner might consider installing a solar hot-water heating system. Four key factors in such a decision are geographical location, the amount of sunlight available, energy costs in the area, and the construction of the house.

Sample Mapping

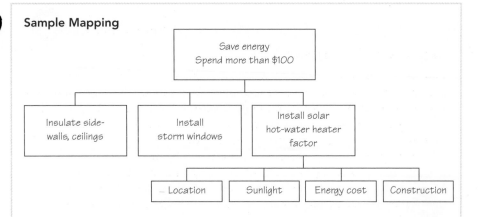

Homeowners with less than $100 to spend can take many energy-saving steps as well. To begin with, two kinds of inexpensive sealers can be used to reduce energy leaks around the house. Caulking will seal cracks around the outside windows, door frames, and at the corners of the house. Weather stripping can be applied to provide a weather-tight seal between the frame and moving parts of doors and windows. Another inexpensive step is to check that a home heating or cooling system is clean. A dirty or clogged filter, for example, can make a furnace or air conditioner work much harder to heat or cool a house. In addition, a "low-flow" shower head can either be purchased separately or a small plastic insert available at the hardware store can be added to a regular head to limit water flow. Blinds and drapes can be used to save energy throughout the year. In winter, they can be closed at night to reduce heat loss. In summer, they can be closed during the day to keep the house cooler. Finally, a ceiling fan can be turned on in the summer to distribute cool air. When the thermostat is set at 78 degrees, the fan will make it seem like 72 degrees. If one reverses the blades to go clockwise in the winter, the fan will force heat down and circulate it throughout the room. A ceiling fan uses no more electricity than a 100-watt light bulb. These and other relatively inexpensive steps can be used to produce large savings.

PRACTICE 7.6

Mapping the Question in the Margin System

In order to study for a test on which you know you will be asked to name and explain the steps of the Question in the Margin System, on a separate sheet of paper construct a map of the Question in the Margin System as a summary sheet.

 CAREER Connections

In order to get a clearer picture of the career options you have been considering and to demonstrate the usefulness of mapping, produce a map of your career decision process. If you are considering more than one career, include all that you are considering. You will want to include interests, abilities, educations required, careers outlook, obstacles, etc.

Promoting Concentration

Have you ever finished a chapter in a book and realized that you had no idea what you just read? Or have you ever sat in class and realized that 15 minutes had passed and, although your body was there, your mind had taken a vacation or dealt with something that was bothering you? These are examples of lapses in *concentration*. In addition to providing enough oxygen to the brain to promote concentration, checking the Big 3 of the BREATHE System reminds you to focus. You already know some strategies for promoting concentration. The learning principles used in the Question in the Margin System provide the basis for strategies that promote concentration. In order to develop the best plan for concentration, you need to determine which kinds of distractions prevent you from concentrating.

Internal Distractions

Many times the causes of your stress are the same things that cause a lack of concentration. These are usually referred to as **internal distractions**. There are so many things going on in your life that the balancing act you are performing may also bring about anxiety and other internal distractions that are detrimental to concentration. Internal distractions come from some source outside—your financial aid check is lost, your mother is ill, your best friend has been in a car wreck, you have lost your cell phone—but you have internalized the problem.

List some things that are going on in your life that might prevent you from concentrating.

_____

_____

_____

_____

_____

You can't always eliminate internal distractions, but you do want to be able to control them when you need to concentrate. Here are a few hints that will help you now:

1. **Keep an attention list.** When you are trying to concentrate and you keep thinking of something else, stop and make a note on your attention list. That way, you won't forget that something needs your attention, even though you have put it aside for the time being.

2. **Check your concentration.** Physically addressing breaks in concentration will help you get back on track. Try using the check mark technique in programming your mind to concentrate. In class or when reading an assignment, have a sheet of paper handy. When you note that you are not paying attention, put a check on the paper and immediately return to your task. The first time you check your concentration, you may fill up an entire sheet. But each subsequent time you use this technique, you will have fewer and fewer checks. (Popping a rubber band on your wrist when your attention strays would have a similar effect, but it's so much more painful!)

3. **Review the time-management and learning principles.** In particular, look for techniques that might be particularly effective for you—taking breaks, visualizing, reciting, and so on.

PRACTICE 7.7

Setting Goals to Promote Concentration

After reviewing what you know about concentration, time management, and learning principles, write three very specific goals that you think will help promote your concentration and that you will try to accomplish this week, each time you are in class and each time you study. (Review the elements of a useful goal before you write them. Give yourself clear directions for what you will do to promote concentration. "I'll try to pay better attention" won't do!)

1. _____

   _____

   _____

2. _____

   _____

   _____

3. _____

   _____

   _____

External Distractions

Often, there are **external**, or physical, **distractions** in your study environment. Our ability to learn is dependent on our ability to take in, filter, select, process, and then apply new information. The choices we make about the time and place we study definitely influence what we learn and how long we remember it. We know that studying every day at the same time and in the same place programs the mind and promotes concentration. Your time-management analysis should have helped you determine the best time for you to study each subject. Now, let's develop a plan for analyzing your place to study.

Your regular place should be one that you use exclusively for studying. If you study in the chair where you normally watch TV or play video games, your mind may automatically want to know what's on TV or how you can get to the next level of your game. If you study at the kitchen table, you will probably get hungry. If you study in bed, even if you weren't sleepy before, you will most likely become sleepy. Your regular study place should have a desk, a comfortable chair, the necessary supplies, good lighting, and so on. Obviously, your senses are involved. Examine each of them to determine the factors that might affect your concentration when you study.

PRACTICE 7.8

Identifying External Distractions

	PROMOTE	HINDER
Sight		
Hearing		
Smell		
Taste		
Touch		

Now, write a short paragraph in which you describe your ideal study place.

PRACTICE 7.9

Discovering the Best Place for You to Study

This week, choose two different times and places to do your regular studying that you think will promote concentration. Use the chart below to analyze each time and place for its effectiveness as a regular study time and place for you.

Time and Place 1

Place	Visual Distractions	Auditory Distractions
Time		

Time and Place 1

Other Distractions	Features That Make This a Good Place to Study

Overall analysis of time and place for use as a regular study place (RSP): _____
_____

Time and Place 2

Place

Visual Distractions	Auditory Distractions

Time

Other Distractions	Features That Make This a Good Place to Study

Overall analysis of time and place for use as a regular study place (RSP): _____

For Your Student Survival Kit

Study Habits Analysis
Are you using all that you've learned so far about studying to learn things faster and better? We are creatures of habit, and often we don't realize that our habits are keeping us from being successful. Choose assignments from two different classes this week and use them to analyze your study habits. One check sheet is provided below. You will need to make copies of the check sheet for the other assignments and several extra copies to use at a later time. Remember to use the time-management and learning principles.

Assignment Check Sheet
Name: _____
Class chosen for assignment: _____

Analysis

1. Describe in detail the assignment you chose.

2. When did you begin working on the assignment in relation to when it was due?

3. Was this a good time to work on the assignment? Why?

Continued

For Your Student Survival Kit continued

4. Where did you work on the assignment?

5. Was this a good place? Why?

6. Did you

_____ take breaks?

_____ take notes even though it was not required?

_____ visualize as you were learning new concepts?

_____ give your full attention to studying?

_____ try to determine when you might be tested on this assignment?

_____ try your best?

Follow-Up

Using what you discovered in your analysis, write a paragraph describing what you discovered about your study habits. Be sure to include both what you found that works for you and a plan of action for those things you could improve.

Virtual Field Trip
Improve Your
Concentration

Review—Where did we go?

Modeling the Learning Process

The steps in the Question in the Margin System used for textbook reading also model the learning process.

Gathering. You surveyed the material you were responsible for and read it paragraph by paragraph.

Analyzing. You analyzed the paragraph, wrote questions in the margin, and looked for connections.

Creating New Ideas. You reflected and reviewed your marked text and questions and predicted possible test questions involving higher-order thinking skills, and you looked for connections with notes you had taken in class.

Acting. You developed summary sheets, maps, PowerPoint presentations, and practice tests.

Study Guide: Processing Information from Textbooks

To see if you grasped the major points of the chapter and to make a useful study guide, answer the following questions found in your reading. When you have written your answers, cover them and see if you can say the answer to each question in your own words.

1. Name and explain four basic reading strategies that you plan to try.

1. _____

2. _____

3. _____

4. _____

2. Name three tips for reading on screens that you plan to try.

1. _____

2. _____

3. _____

3. How does gathering information from lectures differ from gathering information from textbooks?

_____

_____

4. What are the three steps of gathering information from textbooks?

1. _____

2. _____

3. _____

5. How does the question step for reading a textbook differ from the question step for taking lecture notes?

_____

_____

6. Why should you survey before you read a chapter?

_____

_____

7. How do you focus on the paragraph you are reading?

_____

_____

8. Why should you process a paragraph before you go on to the next one?

_____

_____

9. Explain the rest of the Question in the Margin System for textbooks.

Recite

_____

Reflect

_____

Review

_____

Summarize

_____

10. **What is the goal of mapping?**

_____

_____

11. **Explain how to check your concentration.**

_____

_____

12. **How can you eliminate or at least minimize physical or external distractions?**

_____

_____

13. **Describe what components would be included in an ideal study place for you.**

_____

CASE STUDY
What's Your Advice?

This is KaToya's third semester at her university. She has done well, but this semester KaToya is having a difficult time. Four of her classes require a great deal of reading. So far she has managed to get all the reading done, but she rarely remembers what she has read. She has set aside every weeknight from 7:00 to 11:00 P.M. for reading assignments. As she reads, KaToya uses a highlighter and often finds that she has highlighted an entire page. One professor gives pop quizzes based on the reading, so KaToya saves that assignment for last, thinking she'll remember it more easily. She even reads it in bed where it is nice and quiet. She has yet to pass a quiz, and her exam scores are not much better. What advice can you give KaToya?

Parallel Parking

It is important to take responsibility for your reading assignments. Choose two of the driving analogies and compare each to things you know about processing information from reading assignments.

Reading the Map

_____

_____

_____

_____

Going the Speed Limit

_____

_____

_____

_____

Rush-Hour Traffic

_____

_____

_____

_____

Side Trips

_____

_____

_____

_____

Finding a Mechanic

_____

_____

_____

_____

Evaluating Learning Outcomes

How successful were you in making it to your destination in this chapter?
Analyze what you learned in this chapter. Put a check beside each task you are now able to do. On a separate piece of paper, write a couple of sentences about how you learned each learning outcome and how you plan to continue to use what you learned.

☐ **Demonstrate** how to use the Question in the Margin System for reading textbooks.

☐ **Explain** how to use the Question in the Margin System to someone who has never used it.

☐ **Analyze** the Question in the Margin System and explain how the memory principles are used to complete the system.

☐ **Explain** the goal of mapping and demonstrate how to map a passage from a text.

☐ **Illustrate** strategies that promote concentration.

☐ **Analyze** your study habits and develop a plan to make improvements.

☐ **Explain** the learning process modeled in this chapter.

Your Student Tip for This Chapter

Use the space below to write a tip you would give to other students about what you have learned in this chapter.

_____

_____

_____

Learning Styles

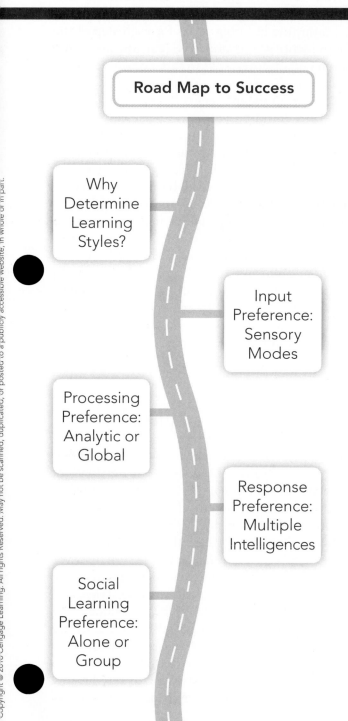

Road Map to Success

- Why Determine Learning Styles?
- Input Preference: Sensory Modes
- Processing Preference: Analytic or Global
- Response Preference: Multiple Intelligences
- Social Learning Preference: Alone or Group

In this chapter, you will learn how to

- **Determine** your preferred learning styles, including sensory mode, styles for processing information, and multiple intelligences.

- **Practice** the strategies presented in the chapter to determine the most efficient strategies for you to process difficult material and reinforce the initial learning.

- **Demonstrate** ways to adapt new learning material to your preferred learning styles.

- **Determine** whether you should first study new material alone or in a group.

- **Construct** guidelines for group study.

- **Generate** a learning profile to describe your learning styles.

- **Illustrate** how your learning styles may influence your choice of career.

- **Analyze** a case study and construct advice for a student having difficulty finding effective study methods.

- **Explain** the learning process modeled in this chapter.

Where Are We Going?

Thus far you have learned a great deal about the brain and learning. You know that you gather new information from your senses. Once that information makes it past your brain's filtering system, you must process that information by analyzing, reflecting, creating hypotheses, and finally, if you are to complete the learning process, you must respond to your analysis with some action. Every brain is unique. The structures, connections, and pathways in your brain are like no one else's brain. In this chapter you will examine various learning styles that correspond to the steps in your learning. By examining learning styles for each step of the learning model, you will both identify your preferred learning style, and perhaps more importantly you will discover ways to expand your learning styles to make a greater and more efficient network in your brain.

Learning styles is a loaded term. It means very different things to different people. There are literally hundreds of ways to measure learning styles. When I did a Google search recently, there were more than 9 million sites about learning styles. You have probably noticed that people prefer different ways of approaching each learning step. Learning styles group common ways that people learn. We all have a mix of styles. Some people find that they have a dominant style and really prefer to use one style. Others find that their learning style is dependent on the circumstances. There is no correct mix. You can develop your less dominant styles. In fact, the efficiency of your brain and the depth of your learning depends on it. In this chapter you will discover your learning preference for gathering new information, your processing preference, and the way you prefer to respond—to act on that information. Then you will practice ways to expand your learning styles. You will also discover if you should first study new information in a group or alone, and examine whether your learning styles could affect your career choices.

Why Determine Learning Styles?

Learning styles are not so much about the style of car you drive; rather, they are about the route you choose to take to get to your destination. When you are driving to specific destinations, there are usually several routes you can take. I have noticed that when driving to my daughter's house, I usually take a different route than my husband takes. Neither route has a particular advantage. Our choices are either from habit or by preference. However, even when going to familiar places, I often discover a new or better route. Traffic conditions or road construction may make that route preferable. With that in mind, let's look at learning styles.

The way each individual processes information is unique. The Question in the Margin System you learned is based on the learning principles and incorporates various learning strategies. Therefore, it works for all learning styles. However, you may have found that you need to modify it slightly to better fit your learning style, or to rely heavily on one aspect of it because of your learning style. No one else processes information in exactly the same way you do.

There are several reasons for determining your learning style preference. First, if you discover how you process information best, you can learn things both more efficiently and in less time. By applying strategies that use your learning style, you can study faster and better. Second now that you understand the cycle involved in the learning process, you can use your preferred learning style to go through the cycle in ways that are comfortable for you. And third you can expand the strategies you use for learning and studying. Just as you discover new or alternative routes when driving, you can customize some of the strategies already discussed in this text. When learning something new or difficult, you naturally tend to use the learning style you prefer. It is good to know what your learning style is so that you can begin to process information in a way that you are comfortable. That way, when material is not presented in the way you prefer, you can use your knowledge of learning styles to adjust and be flexible.

No matter who your instructor is or what the subject matter is, you need to know how to convert what you need to learn to the way you learn best. However, sometimes you need to leave your comfort zones and reinforce learning in as many different ways as possible. Going beyond your comfort zone forces you to drive more carefully and pay more attention. So, although knowing your style preference is good, you also need to expand your ways of learning. Knowing your learning style and being able to recognize and understand the learning styles of others who play a role in your learning—your professors, roommates, significant other, or those in your study group—is useful in getting the most out of any situation.

Input Preference: Sensory Modes of Learning

The most common way of looking at learning styles is for you to consider how you prefer to receive information through your senses, usually referred to as your preferred **sensory modes. Visual** learners find it easier to learn something new if they can see it or picture it. **Auditory** learners want to hear it, and **kinesthetic** learners acquire new information best by experiencing it. Most of us are **mixed-modality** learners. We learn using all of our senses. However, when something is new or difficult, you will probably have a preference as to which of your senses you use to input new information.

The inventory on the next few pages will help you determine the sensory mode that you prefer. You will want to take this inventory before you read about each mode, even though you probably already know which one you prefer. When you are driving to an unfamiliar place, are you more likely to reach your destination with less hassle if you read the directions or follow a map (visual)? Would you prefer to have someone tell you how to get there (auditory)? Or would you be better off studying the directions and drawing a map for yourself or maybe just taking off and feeling your way (kinesthetic)? Consider what you already know about your learning preferences. What things do you automatically do if you want to remember something?

It is extremely important to note that while you probably want to learn new or difficult material within your strongest sensory mode, in order to learn optimally, you need to reinforce that learning mode with other modes. You want to be careful when you determine your preference that you don't ignore other ways of input. If new information is always learned in the same way, the brain will have a limited capacity to use that information in the future. When you acquire information in a variety of ways, multiple areas of the brain will be involved. We have already discussed how you can input new information by visualization, movement, reading, hearing, organizing, and other ways of mental manipulations.

PRACTICE 8.1

Sensory Modality Inventory

There are 12 incomplete sentences and three choices for each. Score the three choices by rating them as follows:

3   The answer most typical of you
2   Your second choice
1   The one least like you

1. When I have to learn something new, I usually:

_____ a. want someone to explain it to me.

_____ b. want to read about it in a book or magazine.

_____ c. want to try it out, take notes, or make a model of it.

2. At a party, most of the time I like to:

_____ a. listen and talk to two or three people at once.

_____ b. see how everyone looks and watch the people.

_____ c. dance, play games, or take part in some activities.

3. If I were helping with a musical show, I would most likely:

_____ a. write the music, sing the songs, or play the accompaniment.

_____ b. design the costumes, paint the scenery, or work the lighting effects.

_____ c. make the costumes, build the sets, or take an acting role.

4. When I am angry, my first reaction is to:

_____ a. tell people off, laugh, joke, or talk it over with someone.

_____ b. blame myself or someone else, daydream about taking revenge, or keep it inside.

_____ c. make a fist or tense my muscles, take it out on something else, or hit or throw things.

5. A happy experience I would like to have is to:

_____ a. hear thunderous applause for my speech or music.

_____ b. photograph the prize-winning picture for a newspaper story.

_____ c. achieve the fame of being first in a physical activity such as dancing, acting, or a sport.

6. I prefer a teacher to:

_____a. use the lecture method with informative explanations and discussions.

_____b. write on the chalkboard, use visual aids, and assign readings.

_____c. require posters, models, in-service practice, and some activities in class.

7. I know that I talk with:

_____a. different tones of voice.

_____b. my eyes and facial expressions.

_____c. my hands and gestures.

8. If I had to remember an event so that I could record it later, I would choose to:

_____a. tell it to someone or hear an audiotape recording or song about it.

_____b. see pictures of it or read a description.

_____c. replay it in some practice rehearsal using movements such as dance, playacting, or drill.

9. When I cook something new, I like to:

_____a. have someone tell me the directions (a friend or TV show).

_____b. read the recipe and judge by how it looks.

_____c. use many pots and dishes, stir often, and taste-test.

10. In my free time, I like to:

_____a. listen to my iPod, talk on the telephone, or attend a musical event.

_____b. go to the movies, watch TV, or read a magazine or book.

_____c. get some practice, go for a walk, play games, or post fun things on Twitter, Tumblr, or Pinterest.

11. If I'm putting together a new bookshelf from IKEA:

_____a. I want someone to tell me how to do it.

_____b. I want to read the directions or watch someone else do it.

_____c. I want to jump right in and do it. I'll figure it out sooner or later.

12. I like the classroom to be arranged:

_____a. in a circle so I can interact with other students.

_____b. in neat rows facing the instructor.

_____c. in random order in case there are activities.

To interpret your sense modality, add your rating for each letter.
Total rating for:

a. _____ Auditory

b. _____ Visual

c. _____ Kinesthetic

If your highest category was:

a, you learn best through listening.

b, you learn best by seeing it in print or other visual modes.

c, you learn best by getting physically involved.

The Auditory Learner

Auditory learners are listeners, but also talkers. They are most comfortable gathering new information if they hear it. If you are an auditory learner, you may need to repeat information verbally in order to get it through your brain's filtering systems. You learn well by discussing ideas and asking questions. You usually like group projects and cooperative learning.

If you learn best by hearing, you should, of course, listen carefully in class. However, just because you learn well by hearing doesn't mean you don't need to take notes; remember the nature of short-term memory? You need to keep a record. You may want to record a difficult class. But be aware that recording a lecture is not a time-saver; you must still take time to process the information.

A better strategy would be to use your iPod, smartphone, or iPad to make audio flash cards after you have taken notes in class. You might also be interested in the smartpens that are now on the market. Pens such as Livescribe allow you to take multimodal notes. An internal flash drive memory captures handwritten notes, audio, and drawings. The user can choose to record audio in addition to the handwritten text. Recorded audio is kept indexed with the handwritten text—tapping on a written word starts playback of the recorded audio from that part of the recording.

The recitation portion of the Question in the Margin System reinforces your auditory learning. It gets you involved, provides feedback, and supplies motivation. This is especially true for the auditory learner. The auditory learner likes discussion and usually learns well in a study group or with a study partner. Auditory learners often need to hear what a difficult passage sounds like or to talk out a difficult concept. As an auditory learner, you should proofread your assignments out loud. Your ears seldom fail you. You may even want to try setting a long or difficult idea to music and singing it. (Remember how you learned the alphabet?) Your recall is best when you teach something to someone. And you will probably learn best by explaining something out loud to someone else.

The Visual Learner

Visual learners much prefer to see something in order to remember it. If you are a visual learner, you want to see the words written down, a picture of something being described, a timeline to remember events in history, or the assignment written on the board. You need to read the material being discussed in class. You also need to study the pictures, charts, maps, or graphs. You should take notes in class in order to see what you are hearing.

Of all the learning principles, visualization works best for you. You need to consistently make mental videos of things you want to understand and remember. You benefit from mapping, clustering, outlining, and using flash cards. You may want to illustrate your flash cards or notes. You should also make use of color as much as possible. Actually, regardless of your preference, you will benefit from this type of learning. The effect of a picture usually lasts longer than words for most of us. You may prefer to gather new information by looking, reading, and watching, but that doesn't mean you need limit your input to the visual. Look for ways to back up that information using as many senses as you can.

The Kinesthetic Learner

Kinesthetic learners prefer the sense of touch and are more comfortable when they interact with what they are studying. Although the mapping strategies explained in the previous chapter are visual, they are also kinesthetic. As a kinesthetic learner, you find that when you are physically involved, you understand and remember. The simple act of doing it helps you understand. The Question in the Margin System will work for you as a kinesthetic learner because it requires physical involvement. You may find that during the recitation step you want to walk around. Making flash cards is a great strategy for kinesthetic learners. You will find that by making and using flash cards, you employ all ten learning principles. No wonder they work so well. And as you learned from time management, flash cards are also easy to carry as pocket work to make use of those bits of time that are normally wasted. In addition to maps, note taking, and flash cards, you may want to make charts, games, or mnemonic devices. As you will discover when we discuss test-taking, making sample tests will help you physically select the main idea, and an added bonus is that taking these tests will cut test anxiety.

Yet learners with kinesthetic preference are not alone in benefiting from learning by doing. All learners seem to benefit. Remember, as Edgar Dale noted, the highest level of remembering comes when you teach someone else. It appears that with all learners, the more actively involved in learning you are, the more you learn. If your instructors do not provide opportunities for active involvement with your learning, you will have to create those opportunities yourself.

PRACTICE 8.2

Sensory Mode Reflection

What specific learning strategies do you already use that involve **auditory** learning?

What are some others that you might try?

What 'specific learning strategies do you already use that involve **visual** learning?

What are some others that you might try?

List some ways you could create hands-on (**kinesthetic**) opportunities in a history class in which your professor always lectures.

Processing Preference: Analytic or Global

A second way of looking at learning styles is to examine the way you prefer to process information. So we have determined that you probably have a preference in the way you input or gather new information. You also probably have a preferred way to process information: how you deal with information once it makes it through the brain's filtering system to the pre-frontal cortex. There are differences of opinion when it comes to describing cognitive styles of processing. A popular way to examine the processing differences is hemispheric dominance theory, or left brain/right brain.

We know that the cerebral cortex is the part of the brain that houses rational functions. It is divided into two hemispheres connected by a thick band of nerve fibers (the corpus callosum), which sends messages back and forth between the hemispheres. Even though we know that the left side of the brain is the seat of language and processes information in a logical and sequential order and the right side is more visual and processes information intuitively, holistically, and randomly, neuroscientists confirm that both sides of the brain are involved in nearly every human activity and consider hemispheric dominance a brain myth that originated in epilepsy research done by Roger Sperry in the early 1980s. Left brain/right brain theory is still popular and often used to describe divergent ways of processing. Because the terms normally used to describe left and right brain differences are familiar, they are good metaphors to use for the categories describing the different ways of processing. However, it would probably be more accurate if we used the more broad terms of **analytic** and **global** to look at ways we prefer to process information. Even that is an oversimplification, though. Remember, we said learning styles group common ways that people learn. These terms give us a way to group ways people process. We will determine that no one is totally global (right) or totally analytic (left). We do have preferences toward one end or the other, especially when information is new and difficult or our lives are stressful. By looking at both ends of the spectrum, you can determine how you prefer to process, how your processing may differ from that of others, and how you can expand the ways you process.

Differences Between Analytic (Left) and Global (Right)

When examining the different processing styles, what you are doing is lengthening your list of strategies for learning how to learn and trying to determine what works best for you. You can develop and use strategies that utilize both ends of the spectrum. Sometimes, driving alternative routes makes us more careful or deliberate, so we actually learn better.

This section will examine some differences between analytic and global processing and will provide a few suggestions for both analytic- and global-dominant students. Be on the lookout for practical strategies that work for you. Following is an inventory to help you determine the balance between analytic and global processing. It might be a good idea to take this inventory before you read the subsequent explanations.

PRACTICE 8.3

How Does Your Brain Prefer to Process Information?

Check the answers that most closely describe your preferences.

1. Are you usually running late for class or other appointments?

_____ a. Yes

_____ b. No

2. When taking a test, you prefer the questions be:

_____ a. objective (true/false, multiple-choice, matching)

_____ b. subjective (discussion or essay questions)

3. When making decisions, you:

_____ a. go with your gut feeling—what you feel is right

_____ b. carefully weigh each option

4. When relating an event, you:

_____ a. go straight to the main point and then fill in details

_____ b. tell many details before telling the conclusion

5. Do you have a place for everything and everything in its place?

_____ a. Yes

_____ b. No

6. When faced with a major change in life, you are:

_____ a. excited

_____ b. terrified

7. Your work style is to:

_____ a. concentrate on one task at a time until it is complete

_____ b. juggle several things at once

8. Can you tell approximately how much time has passed without looking at your watch?

_____ a. Yes

_____ b. No

9. It is easier for you to understand:

_____ a. algebra

_____ b. geometry

10. Is it easier for you to remember people's:

_____ a. names?

_____ b. faces?

11. When learning how to use a new piece of equipment, you:

_____ a. jump in and wing it. (The instruction manual is a last resort)

_____ b. carefully read the instruction manual before beginning

Continued

Social Learning Preference: Alone or in Groups

We have now examined three ways to view your learning style in terms of which sense you prefer, whether you predominantly process information globally or analytically, and the strongest of your multiple intelligences. This knowledge may help you determine how best to initially study new material. The social inventory that follows will give you an indication of whether you should first study in a group or by yourself. Successful students study both alone and with a group; however, your learning style will determine if you need a group to help you learn new information or to reinforce what you already have learned.

Again, you will want to learn new information in your strengths and reinforce your learning with as many other methods as possible. If the following inventory indicates you learn best alone, you will need to make sure you understand the concept that you are striving to learn before you study with others. You need to customize your study environment for minimal distractions. Reciting by writing questions and answers or in the traditional manner of saying it out loud is a good strategy for you to use alone. If the social inventory in Practice 8.7 indicates that you learn best with a group, you want to be careful that your study group or study partner shares your study goals. A few guidelines may be helpful. Notice who the dedicated students in class are. Who takes good notes? Who asks logical questions? Who turns in completed assignments on time? Who makes good grades on tests? Although studying with friends is nice, it can lead to visiting instead of studying. For each class you are taking, find three or four people you think would make up a good study group. Set a time and place to meet.

At the study session, you may want to do the following:

1. Make sure your goals are the same.
2. Determine what the test will cover. Comparing notes is a good way to do this.
3. Divide up your assignments so that each person is responsible for certain material. (Teaching material to others is a very effective way of making sure you know it.)
4. Predict test questions. Come up with a test that is similar to the one you will take.
5. Ask others in the group to help with material that is confusing or difficult for you.
6. Drill out loud on possible test questions.
7. Decide if another session would be profitable, and set a time. Make assignments for the next session. For example, ask each member to create a practice test for the next time.

StudentTIP

"I used to think that it was better to study by myself. I know that I need to self-test and make sure I know the material, but I also discovered it worth the effort to form a group to study. You get different approaches to the same problem and opportunities to teach someone. Someone in my groups always thinks of something I would have forgotten if I had just studied alone."

PRACTICE 8.7

Social Inventory: Study First Alone or in a Group?

Check *a* or *b* in the following questions:

1. When shopping, running errands, or working, I:

_____ a. usually try to go with friends.

_____ b. seldom go with friends.

2. When something is very important to me, I:

_____ a. seek the advice of others.

_____ b. do it myself.

3. For a grade in chemistry class, I would prefer to:

_____ a. work with a lab partner.

_____ b. work alone.

4. When working with groups in class, I would rather:

_____ a. work with the group on the whole task.

_____ b. divide the task up so that each individual does one part.

5. I prefer instructors who:

_____ a. include discussion and group activities as part of the class.

_____ b. allow students to work on their own.

6. When listening to a speaker, I respond more to:

_____ a. the person speaking.

_____ b. the ideas themselves.

7. When faced with difficult personal problems, I:

_____ a. discuss them with others.

_____ b. try to solve them myself.

8. For a summer job, I would prefer:

_____ a. working in a busy office.

_____ b. working alone.

Add the number of *a*'s and of *b*'s. If you checked more *a*'s than *b*'s, you would rather work with someone than alone. If you checked more *b*'s than *a*'s, you would rather work independently.

You now want to use what you have discovered about your learning style to develop more effective ways to study. Don't, however, lock yourself into one way. *Be flexible.*

For Your Student Survival Kit

Your Learning Profile

Beginning with your strongest intelligence, list what you think your multiple intelligences are in order of their strength.

1. _____
2. _____
3. _____
4. _____
5. _____
6. _____
7. _____
8. _____

Do you process information primarily in an analytic or global manner or both? _____

List some characteristics of how you prefer to process.

1. _____
2. _____
3. _____

List the sensory modes you use in order of preference (auditory, visual, and kinesthetic).

1. _____
2. _____
3. _____

Do you prefer to work alone or with others? _____

Given the preceding information, list **specific learning strategies** in the order that you should be using them to process new material.

1. _____
2. _____
3. _____
4. _____
5. _____

Review—Where did we go?

Modeling the Learning Process

The information you learned in this chapter will help in modeling the learning process because you confirmed your learning style preference for each step.

Gathering. When you gather information, you will want to begin with your preferred sensory mode, but you will also want to reinforce it with the other two. The sensory modes include visual, auditory, and kinesthetic. You gathered information about three ways of looking at learning styles.

In analyzing and creating you will begin with your preferred hemisphere and use strategies that are most natural for you. However, you should also try strategies that are not your preference to help you concentrate and to expand ways of learning.

Analyzing. You made the styles more personal by determining what your preferences are.

Creating New Ideas. You predicted strategies that you should start with and those you should add as reinforcement.

Acting. The acting step, your response to your predictions, uses one or more of the multiple intelligences. You created a song, drew a map, constructed a PowerPoint exercise, and so on, using the strategies you developed.

If you haven't already begun, make a conscious effort to recreate the learning process with what you are learning in other classes.

Study Guide: Learning Styles

To see if you grasped the major points of the chapter and to make a useful study guide, answer the following questions found in your reading. When you have written your answers, cover them and see if you can say the answer to each question in your own words.

1. **What does the term "learning styles" refer to?**

_____

2. **Why is it important to determine your learning style?**

_____

3. **Explain some study strategies that a visual learner should use.**

_____

4. **Explain some study strategies that an auditory learner should use.**

_____

5. **Explain some study strategies that a kinesthetic learner should use.**

_____

6. **What are some characteristics of analytic processing?**

_____

7. What are some characteristics of global processing?

_____

8. List and briefly explain the eight kinds of intelligences.

1. _____

_____

2. _____

_____

3. _____

_____

4. _____

_____

5. _____

_____

6. _____

_____

7. _____

_____

8. _____

_____

9. What are good strategies for those students who learn best alone?

_____

10. Name several ways to determine who might potentially be a good member for your study group.

_____

_____

_____

11. Name several guidelines for group study.

_____

_____

_____

CASE STUDY
What's Your Advice?

Jon and Mandy are having a difficult time studying for their psychology test, so they formed a study group with two other classmates. From inventories they had taken in a previous class, Jon discovered that his dominant processing style is analytic. He prefers auditory input and his multiple-intelligence strengths are logical, linguistic, and intrapersonal. Mandy, on the other hand, processes globally, prefers visual and kinesthetic input, and her strengths are interpersonal, musical, and kinesthetic. They had memorized what their learning styles were for the final exam, but really didn't understand what those meant. The preferences and strengths of the two other students (Marc and Amanda) were not known. The upcoming test is about how the brain learns.

1. List some strategies that the group could use to study.
2. Assign specific tasks to each group member to complete before the study session.
3. Make specific suggestions for strategies to use during the session.
4. Make specific suggestions for strategies each should use after the session.

Parallel Parking

We covered different ways of looking at learning styles in this chapter. As a review, let's go back to the driving analogy. Can you compare the parallel parking terms to things you learned about learning styles? Choose at least three. Remember, there is no *right* answer.

Buying a New Car _____

_____

_____

Taking the Scenic Route _____

_____

_____

Asking for Directions _____

_____

_____

Taking the Interstate or Freeway _____

_____

_____

Buying Insurance _____

_____

_____

Making Connections continued

Strategy	Notes about Strategy
Mapping	Mapping uses all ten learning principles and is effective for all learning styles—a must for visual learners. Maps can be made from textbooks or class notes. There is also mapping software available.

Mapping lets you see how everything fits together as a whole. What classes are you taking that you can map in a summary?

Strategy	Notes about Strategy
Timelines, Charts, and Diagrams	Timelines, charts, and diagrams serve to summarize and condense information to a manageable size.

Timelines are important when you need to manage information chronologically. What classes would this be useful for? What classes are you taking that a chart or diagram would help you better understand the material?

Strategy	Notes about Strategy
Making Practice Tests	Making a practice test uses most of the ten learning principles and promotes practice of actual tasks you will be asked to perform on the test. Use previous tests to model your test. This means that if you have an essay question, you practice actually writing your answer. Have each member of your study group make a version.

What classes have you made practice tests for? Did you notice that you had less test anxiety?

Strategy	Notes about Strategy
Making Review Games	Make your own *Jeopardy!*, matching, or *Who Wants to Be a Millionaire?*–type games or check websites and apps that make them for you.

Would playing games with the information get you more interested?

Strategy	Notes about Strategy
PowerPoints	Review PowerPoint slides used in classes or make your own. Have each person in your study group make a PowerPoint and teach something to your group.

Which classes could you make PowerPoints for?

Types of Tests

It is especially important that you be in the driver's seat when taking tests. This chapter addresses some strategies for taking tests. The most important clues for what you will be asked to do on tests are found in the learning outcomes listed in each chapter. Learning outcomes tell you not only what you are expected to learn in a chapter or for a project, but also how those outcomes will be measured. If learning outcomes are not listed in your textbook, your instructor may have them listed on your syllabus.

There are two basic categories of tests. The first is objective. For each item in an objective test, there is one correct answer. This kind of test usually depends on *recognition* to get the answer out of your long-term memory. In other words, there are clues within the question to jog your memory. Objective tests include true/false, multiple-choice, fill-in-the-blank, and matching questions.

The other category of tests is subjective. There is a correct answer for each question on a subjective test but also a range of possible ways to give this answer. Discussion questions, essay questions, and many short-answer questions fall into this category. They depend on *recall*, not just recognition. Recall requires that you bring the information out of your long-term memory and organize it in a way that effectively answers what has been asked.

There is no substitute for having studied thoroughly and knowing the answers. However, certain strategies can be used with each kind of test so that you get the most out of your effort. Just as different road conditions require different driving strategies, different test types require different strategies in both studying for and taking tests.

PRACTICE 9.1

Preparing for Tests

Before you begin practicing specific test-taking strategies, make sure you are effectively preparing for tests. Below is a list of ways that successful students use to prepare for tests. They are strategies you have learned in previous chapters. Be deliberate in your evaluation. You know the strategies, but are you using them? Rate yourself on how well you practice each of them. A *5* means that you almost always do it; *4*, that you usually do it; *3*, that you sometimes do it; *2*, that you rarely do it; and *1*, that you never do it. Be totally honest in your evaluation.

_____ **1.** Keep up to date with assignments.

_____ **2.** Take notes in every class every day. This includes asking questions when you don't understand.

_____ **3.** Process information as you come to it. Learning information is very different from becoming acquainted with it.

_____ **4.** Process information systematically. The Question in the Margin System works well for most people. Adapt it to suit your learning style. Capitalize on the discipline that this system requires, and make it a habit to process information from texts and lectures, not just go over it.

_____ **5.** Have a study place that is free of distractions.

_____ **6.** Have a specific time for the initial study of each subject. You may need more than this time, but having a set time will save you time in the long run.

_____ **7.** Make summary sheets, flash cards, and practice tests.

Continued

Practice 9.1 continued

_____ **8.** Always carry some kind of pocket work so that you can make use of what would otherwise be wasted spare minutes by reciting and thinking about what you are learning.

_____ **9.** Use multisensory ways to learn new information. Reinforce information in as many ways as you can think of.

_____ **10.** Find a study partner or two in each class, and routinely take turns teaching each other the material.

_____ **11.** Prepare for each class as if there will be a pop quiz.

_____ **12.** Study learning outcomes (if your book has them) to predict both what and how material will be asked on a test.

_____ Total your score.

When you have totaled your score, choose the appropriate writing assignment from the list that follows.

Writing Assignment for Practice 9.1

- If your score is from 49 to 60, write a paragraph or two in which you describe the results of using the study strategies listed. Be specific. A comparison of the benefits of your old study habits and your new ones might be one approach.

- If your score is from 38 to 48, write a paragraph or two in which you describe both your good and bad study habits. Discuss reasons for each and goals for incorporating more of the strategies listed above.

- If your score is below 38, write a paragraph or two in which you try to determine why you have not used the strategies listed above to your advantage and which strategies you think you might be able to use effectively. Set some realistic goals and discuss how you might achieve them.

CRITICAL THINKING
About Tests

When we discussed critical thinking, you learned that there are levels, or depths, of thinking and learning. You used Bloom's taxonomy as a model: **knowledge, comprehension, application, analysis, synthesis,** and **evaluation**. You may want to review these concepts. When taking a test, it is important to determine what *level* of learning will be tested. You can study all night memorizing definitions for a test; however, if the test asks for analysis, synthesis, or evaluation of those definitions, you may be sunk!

Identify the level of learning being asked for in the following test questions:

_____ What evidence can you present to support the idea that the Confederate Army was unprepared in the Battle of Shiloh?

_____ Where were the first Olympic Games held?

_____ Name and explain each step of the Question in the Margin System.

_____ What would happen if you combined sulphur with iodine?

_____ Demonstrate that you know how to take notes using the Question in the Margin System.

_____ What were the merits of Hannibal's plan to take Rome?

PRACTICE 9.2

Self-Analysis: Preparing for Tests

Now that you know some strategies that will help you study for tests, let's discuss taking a test. Many students feel that one reason they are not top students is that they are poor test takers. The following diagnostic inventory is designed to help you rate your present test-taking skills and habits. It will also serve as an overview of the topics discussed in this test-taking unit. It is divided into three sections: strategies used to prepare for a test, general test-taking strategies, and strategies for specific types of tests. *Be totally honest. This is not a test!*

Write the number in the column that best describes you.

Strategies Used to Prepare for a Test

	1 NEVER	2 INFREQUENTLY	3 GENERALLY	4 FREQUENTLY	5 ALWAYS
1. Do you find out as much about the test as possible?	_____	_____	_____	_____	_____
2. Do you study the learning outcomes of a chapter to determine what will be on a test and how it may be asked?					
3. As you review material, do you anticipate possible test questions?	_____	_____	_____	_____	_____
4. Do you have notes to review?	_____	_____	_____	_____	_____
5. Do you review your notes systematically?	_____	_____	_____	_____	_____
6. Do you make summary sheets?	_____	_____	_____	_____	_____
7. Do you recite or write down material in your own words?	_____	_____	_____	_____	_____
8. Do you use mnemonic devices and other learning principles for lists, dates, and so on?	_____	_____	_____	_____	_____
9. Do you avoid cramming the night before?	_____	_____	_____	_____	_____
10. Do you get plenty of rest the night before a test?	_____	_____	_____	_____	_____
11. Do you try to do your best on every test you take?	_____	_____	_____	_____	_____
12. Do you take tests without too much anxiety?	_____	_____	_____	_____	_____
13. Do you find other people in your class to study with?	_____	_____	_____	_____	_____
14. Do you arrive early to your classroom the day of the test?	_____	_____	_____	_____	_____

General Test-Taking Strategies

15. Do you preview the test before writing anything?	_____	_____	_____	_____	_____
16. Do you plan test-taking time? (How much time do you allow for each task?)	_____	_____	_____	_____	_____

Continued

Practice 9.2 continued

	1 NEVER	2 INFREQUENTLY	3 GENERALLY	4 FREQUENTLY	5 ALWAYS
17. Do you make sure you are following directions by underlining or circling key words?	____	____	____	____	____
18. Do you answer the easiest questions first?	____	____	____	____	____
19. Do you answer all questions (unless the directions say otherwise or you are penalized for wrong answers)?	____	____	____	____	____
20. Do you check all answers carefully? (This means reworking each question if time permits.)	____	____	____	____	____
21. Do you use all the time allotted for the test?	____	____	____	____	____
22. Do you use specific strategies in taking objective tests such as multiple-choice, true/false, fill-in-the-blank, and matching?	____	____	____	____	____
23. Do you use specific strategies to answer essay questions?	____	____	____	____	____
24. Do you review returned tests to see how you might do better on future tests?	____	____	____	____	____
Subtotals	____	____	____	____	____

Add the numbers you've written in each column to find your subtotals. Add your subtotals to find your final score: ____

HOW TEST WISE ARE YOU?	RATING SCALE	
	32–54	Poor
	55–76	Fair
	77–98	Good
	99–120	Excellent

Personal analysis: On another sheet of paper write a paragraph in which you analyze your strengths and weaknesses in the test-taking strategies specifically covered in the preceding inventory.

Budgeting Your Test-Taking Time

One of the most important strategies for taking any kind of test is budgeting your time. Too often we hear students say that they knew the answers but ran out of time or that they made careless mistakes because they rushed. Taking a test without budgeting your time is like driving to an important appointment without determining how much time it will take to drive there. Because you want to get the most points on a test for the time you spend, you should analyze each test and budget your time accordingly. Stopping to analyze a test before you begin to work on it puts you in control and may have a calming effect.

Preview the Test

1. Determine the types of questions.
2. Calculate the point value of questions.

BRAIN BYTE

The Big 3 of Dr. Hillman's BREATHE System should also improve your test-taking by supplying your brain with sufficient oxygen and giving you a feeling of self-confidence. You've prepared your mind for the test by studying. Now prepare your body: Maintain proper posture, relax neck and shoulder muscles, and take cleansing breaths.

3. Look for questions you need to make notes about; if necessary, use a mnemonic or another review strategy you have learned.

4. Locate easy questions to answer first.

Budget Your Time

1. When calculating the point value of questions, determine the percentage of the total score toward which it counts. (If it counts for 30 points, it's worth 30 percent of a 100-point test.)

2. From the total amount of time allowed for the test, subtract some time for preview and review. (If you have 60 minutes to take a test, you might subtract 5 minutes for previewing the test and 5 minutes for reviewing it. This would leave 50 minutes base time to take the test.)

3. Calculate the percentage of the base time (time remaining after you've subtracted preview and review times) that you should allow for each question or set of questions. If a question counts for 30 percent of the test, multiply 0.30 (percent) × 50 (base time). Allow 15 minutes to answer that question. Use the entire time allotted for the test.

PRACTICE 9.3

Budgeting Your Time

How much time would you allow for the following?

Total Time for Test: 2 Hours

Time allowed for preview _____

Time allowed for review _____

2 essays (20 points each) _____

25 multiple-choice (1 point each) _____

15 matching (1 point each) _____

20 true/false (1 point each) _____

Total Time for Test: 50 Minutes

Time allowed for preview _____

Time allowed for review _____

20 true/false (1 point each) _____

2 essays (10 points each) _____

Matching (30 points) _____

Fill-in-the-blank (10 points) _____

Short answer (20 points) _____

Following Directions

One of the most common reasons for getting lost is not following directions. One of the most common mistakes students make on tests is that they don't follow directions. It is important to follow directions carefully even if the test is timed. Never assume that you know what the directions say. For example, true/false questions may ask you to correct the false ones to make them true. As practice, take the following test.

PRACTICE 9.4

Following Directions

Directions: Read all questions before answering anything. This is a timed test. Your instructor will tell you at the beginning how much time you are allowed. You *must* complete it in the given time.

1. Write your name and section number in the top right corner of this paper.

2. In the top left corner, write today's date in *numbers*.

3. Under today's date, write "Following Directions, Timed Test."

4. If $3 \times 4 \times 2 = 25$, write *green;* if not, write *purple.* _____

5. Count the number of empty desks in this room. _____

6. Draw a house with two chimneys, two windows, and one door.

7. Stand and say in a very loud voice, "I have reached question 9. I am the leader in following directions."

8. Spell the name of your hometown backward. _____

9. Circle one: True or false: Following directions is easy.

10. Underline one: True or false: Following directions is essential.

11. Now that you have read all the questions, do only questions 1, 2, and 3. Then turn your page over and wait for the rest of the class to finish.

For Your Student Survival Kit

Survival Tips for Taking Tests

Below is a list of helpful strategies for you to use when taking tests. The suggestions are common sense, but the strategies will help you establish a routine for taking tests.

Before You Begin

1. Preview the test before you answer anything. This gets you thinking about the material. Make sure to note the point value of each question. This will give you some ideas on budgeting your time.

2. Do a "mind dump." Using what you saw in the preview, make notes of anything you think you might forget. Write down things such as formulas, mnemonics, or lists you used in learning the material that might help you remember it. Outline your answers to discussion questions.

3. Quickly calculate how much time you should allow for each section according to the point value. (You don't want to spend thirty minutes on an essay question that counts for only five points.)

Taking the Test

4. Read the directions. (Can more than one answer be correct? Are you penalized for guessing? And so on.) Never assume that you know what the directions say without reading them.

5. Answer the easy questions first. This will give you the confidence and momentum to get through the rest of the test. You are sure these answers are correct.

6. Go back to the difficult questions. While looking over the test and doing the easy questions, your subconscious mind will have been working on the answers to the harder ones. Also, later items on the test may give you useful or needed information for earlier items.

7. Answer all questions (unless you are penalized for wrong answers or unless the directions say otherwise).

8. Ask the instructor to explain any items that are not clear. Do not ask for the answer, but phrase your question in a way that shows the instructor that you have the information but are not sure how you are expected to present it.

9. Try to answer the questions from the instructor's point of view. Try to remember what the instructor emphasized and felt was important.

10. Use the margin to explain why you chose a particular answer if the question does not seem clear or if the answer seems ambiguous. Express a difficult question in your own words. Rephrasing can make a question clear to you, but be sure you don't change the meaning of the question.

11. Circle key words in difficult questions. This will force you to focus on the central point.

12. Use all of the time allotted for the test. If you have extra time, cover your answers and rework the questions.

PRACTICE 9.5

Strategies for Taking Any Test

Carefully review the survival tips for taking tests above. Then create a summary sheet using the Question in the Margin System. Write the questions below in the margin and put your answers on the notes side. The self-testing employed in the Question in the Margin System simulates a testing situation.

1. Why should you preview your test before answering any questions?

2. What specifically does doing a "mind dump" involve?

3. Why is it important to read directions? Does this step just waste important time?

4. List several reasons why you would want to answer the easy questions first.

5. Why should you skip the harder questions and go back to them later?

6. Name several things you might do if a question is unclear.

7. Why is it important to use the entire test-taking time allotted?

The strategies in your summary sheet can be used for taking any test.

Strategies for Objective Tests

Because you are looking for clues to the best or correct answers when taking objective tests, the strategies you use will differ from those for subjective or essay tests. With that in mind, let's look at strategies for specific kinds of objective tests.

Strategies for True/False Tests

You have a 50/50 chance of guessing the answer to a true/false question even if you don't read the question. So you can be sure that when a test maker writes true/false test questions, there will be some tricky questions. This section will help you build strategies for looking at the way true/false questions are written and help you anticipate possible tricks. **No amount of guessing can replace knowing the answer.** Nevertheless, you should be aware of strategies to use if you are not sure. Although these strategies won't apply every time, they will make you aware of possible tricks that test makers use.

Negatives and Double Negatives

Testing makes most of us somewhat anxious and more prone to making careless errors and errors in reading. If the statement has a negative word in it and you leave it out, your answer will be wrong. Double negatives are a test maker's trick to catch students unaware.

A negative is a word or part of a word, such as *no*, *not*, or *non-*, that indicates negation. Negation, in its most basic sense, changes the truth value of a statement to its opposite. Because insertion of a **negative word** or **prefix** (*not, cannot, un-, dis-, il-, non-, in-*) into a statement reverses the statement's meaning, a good strategy to use is to circle all negatives so that you are sure of what the statement says. Consider the following:

> *A koala bear is a kind of bear.*
> *A koala bear is not a kind of bear.*

The first statement is false, but the addition of *not* in the second makes it true. The effect of negatives is to make the sentence the opposite of what it would be without the negative.

Not is the most commonly used negative. Other negative words include *no, none, nothing, nowhere, neither, nobody, no one, hardly, scarcely,* and *barely*; however, you should also be on the lookout for prefixes that make a word negative. In the following list, fill in the blanks with the negative of the word given:

1. Truthful   Untruthful
2. Alcoholic   _____
3. Direct   _____
4. Saturated   _____
5. Perfect   _____
6. Responsible   _____
7. Agreeable   _____
8. Legal   _____

A **double negative** is the nonstandard use of two negatives in the same sentence so that they cancel each other and create a positive. Sometimes double negatives are used for emphasis, as in "he can't just do nothing." For our consideration, double negatives are often one of those nasty tricks test writers use on tests to confuse or to make sure a student is paying attention.

Because we rarely hear double negatives, our brain processes them much like a foreign language. Therefore, we need to simplify the question by getting rid of *double* negatives. **You can cross out both negatives *without changing the meaning* of the word, phrase, or statement they appear in.** If a question says, "You won't be unprepared," change it to say, "You will be prepared." If a question says, "This is not an imperfect method," change it to say, "This is a perfect method." If a sentence has three negatives, you can cross out two without changing the meaning of the statement.

PRACTICE 9.6

Practice with Double Negatives

Read the following statements. Circle all negatives. If two negatives occur, eliminate both. You won't change the meaning; you will simply clarify the statement. Then read and decide if the statement is true or false.

_____ **1.** Most students are not unwilling to leave class early.

_____ **2.** It is not unusual for students to have math anxiety.

_____ **3.** It is not illegal not to drive on the left side of the road in the United States.

_____ **4.** Most students would not be dissatisfied with an F on an exam.

_____ **5.** The cost of an SUV is usually not inexpensive in comparison to the cost of a sedan.

Qualifiers

Words that limit or change the meaning of a word or sentence are called **qualifiers** and are often used in tricky true/false questions. Understanding the difference between absolute and general qualifiers or modifiers should help you be more confident in your answers.

If you are talking about a child doing chores at home, you can start with the sentence "He does his chores." You can qualify that sentence in several ways.

If you begin with the negative, you can say:

He *never* does his chores.

He did *none* of his chores.   These are *absolute* qualifiers. They mean 100 percent.

He did *no* chores.   The child didn't do *any* chores—not even one.

Then you can move toward the positive.

He *seldom* does his chores.

He did *few* of his chores.

He did *some* of his chores.

He *sometimes* does his chores.   These are *general* qualifiers. They do not include 100 percent.

He *generally* does his chores.

He did *many* of his chores.

He *usually* does his chores.

He did *most* of his chores.

When you get to the other end of the continuum, you get back to absolutes on the positive side.

He *always* does his chores.

He did *all* of his chores.   These are *absolute* qualifiers. They mean 100 percent.

He did *every* chore.   The child did *all* the chores—every one.

We need to understand qualifiers because they make a great deal of difference in answering a true/false question.

No, never, none, nobody, only	*Few, seldom, some, generally, many, usually, most*	*Always, all, every, best*
100%
Absolute	General	100%
Absolute

If **general qualifiers** are present (*generally, probably, usually, many,* or *sometimes*), there is a **good chance that the statement is true.** If **absolute qualifiers** (*all, always, no, never, none, every, everyone, only, best, entirely,* or *invariably*) are used, **the statement is probably false.** Consider these examples.

Honda makes cars. Honda makes *only* cars.

All pit bulls are aggressive.

   Absolutes are words for which there are no exceptions—100 percent words. Learn the absolutes well. Otherwise, you are likely to be confused. When you see absolutes in a true/false statement, you can be sure that 99 percent of the time the statement is false.

Other Educated Guesses

If any part of a statement is false, then the whole statement is false. This is always the case. You should, then, carefully read each statement, looking for any part that may be false. For example, for a true/false test question:

_____ George Washington, Abraham Lincoln, and Benjamin Franklin were U.S. presidents.

While Washington and Lincoln were presidents, Franklin was not a president.

True/false statements that give reasons tend to be false (*because the reason is incorrect or there may be additional reasons*).

_____ Children today get lower grades because they watch too much television.

This may be one reason but not the only reason. Be wary of statements that include words such as *reason, because, due to,* or *since.* They may be indicators of reasons that could very well be false.

Assume statements are true unless you know they are false. (If you absolutely must guess, guess *true.* It is easier to write a true statement than a false one. Unless they make a real effort, test writers will usually have more true than false questions.)

For Your Student Survival Kit

Summary of Strategies for True/False Statements

Negatives	Circle all negatives so that you are sure of what the statement says. Simplify the question by getting rid of *double* negatives.
Qualifiers	If **general qualifiers** are present (*generally, probably, usually, many,* or *sometimes*), there is a **good chance that the statement is true.** If **absolute qualifiers** (*all, always, no, never, none, every, everyone, only, best, entirely,* or *invariably*) are used, **the statement is probably false.**
Guess false	If any part of a statement is false, then the whole statement is false. Carefully check items in a series.
Guess false	True/false statements that give reasons tend to be false. Be on the lookout for phrases introduced by *reason, because, due to,* or *since.*
Guess true	Assume statements are true unless you know they are false (or unless they include the two exceptions above).

PRACTICE 9.7

Mapping True/False Strategies

On a separate piece of paper, use what you learned about mapping to make a map that summarizes the strategies to use for true/false questions.

PRACTICE 9.8

Practice with True/False Tests

Use the methods just discussed to determine whether the following statements are true or false. Write *T* on the lines in front of the true statements and *F* on the lines in front of the false statements. In the blank following each statement, explain the strategy you used to determine if the statement was true or false.

Continued

Practice 9.8 continued

_____ 1. We should eat protein for breakfast because it gets oxygen to the brain.

_____

_____ 2. Most collisions happen within a short distance from home.

_____

_____ 3. As a general rule, one should study two hours for each hour of class time.

_____

_____ 4. July is never a winter month.

_____

_____ 5. A master schedule should never be changed during a semester.

_____

_____ 6. Average drivers commit 2.5 traffic violations every mile they drive!

_____

_____ 7. Short-term memory appears to function in the hippocampus as a clearinghouse that selects chunks of data to remember.

_____

_____ 8. Most students drop out of college because they are not smart enough.

_____

_____ 9. You should always answer the easy questions on a test first because you might forget the answers.

_____

_____ 10. The Question in the Margin System should be used for all reading.

_____

_____ 11. An absolute qualifier will always make a true/false question false.

_____

_____ 12. In taking class notes, students are not unlikely to miss the point if they try to write down everything.

_____

_____ 13. A good study environment should include good lighting, a comfortable seat, quiet music, and plenty of food.

_____

_____ 14. A chunk of information is defined as an unfamiliar array of only seven pieces or bits.

_____

_____ 15. Left-brained students are always smarter than right-brained students.

_____

_____ 16. For most students, getting a good night's sleep is more important than cramming all night.

_____

_____ 17. *Most, few, some, all,* and *rarely* are general qualifiers and usually make a statement true.

_____

For Your Student Survival Kit

Strategies for Multiple-Choice Tests

1. **Realize that there is not always a perfect answer.** You must choose the best answer.
2. **This means you need to read all possible responses.**
3. **Cross out the incorrect answers.** Incorrect answers are called *distracters*. Crossing them out will focus your attention on reasonable options.
4. **Treat** each option as a true/false question. Read the stem and then the first answer. Read the stem again and then the second answer. Read the stem again and then the third answer. And so on. Apply the true/false strategies each time. By doing this, you will keep track of the question in the tangle of answers.
5. **Use educated guesses only as a last resort.** Although there is no substitute for knowing the material, becoming familiar with certain tendencies can be of value when you do not know the answer. Such tendencies are often referred to as test cues or test flaws and require you to use an educated guess. As a general rule, the following types of options tend to be *incorrect* answers:

- **Options with absolutes** (*Can you name ten absolutes?*)
  _____   _____   _____   _____   _____
  _____   _____   _____   _____   _____

- **Options with unfamiliar terms** (*Of course, if you haven't read the assignment or listened in class, all terms may sound unfamiliar!*)

- **Options with jokes and insults or are just plain silly**

- **Options with highest and lowest numbers** (*except on math quizzes*)

And the following types of options tend to be *correct* answers:

- **Options that read "all of the above"** (*especially when you know that two options are correct*)

- **Options with more complete or inclusive answers**

  _____ Where was the American Civil War fought?

  a. Primarily in Tennessee and Virginia

  b. Pennsylvania

  c. Thousands of places: from southern Pennsylvania to Texas; from New Mexico to the Florida coast

  d. South Carolina and Mississippi

  (*Which group includes the most territory?*)

- **One of two similar-looking options**

  _____ In the brain, logical and linguistic functions are processed by

  a. the right hemisphere.

  b. the left hemisphere.

  c. habeas corpus.

  d. the cerebellum.

Practice with Multiple-Choice Questions

Use the strategies just discussed to select the correct answer to the following questions. Write a, b, c, or d on the line in front of the question. Use the line following the question to explain the strategy you used.

_____ 1. Research has found that the ideal length of a nap:
  a. is only 15 minutes.
  b. is as long as your history professor is talking.
  c. is 30 minutes.
  d. One should never take naps.

_____

_____ 2. A sonnet is a:
  a. lyric poem of 14 lines.
  b. love poem with 25 lines.
  c. seven-line rhyme.
  d. flowery hat.

_____

_____ 3. Common driving distractions are:
  a. applying makeup and talking on a cell phone.
  b. adjusting the radio or changing CDs.
  c. dealing with rambunctious or misbehaving kids.
  d. all of the above.

_____

_____ 4. An excise tax is a tax:
  a. imposed on health clubs.
  b. imposed on goods, especially luxuries and cars.
  c. imposed only on diamonds.
  d. added to all incomes over $100,000.

_____

_____ 5. Calvin Coolidge:
  a. was vice president under Warren Harding.
  b. became president in 1923 when Harding died.
  c. was elected president on his own in 1924.
  d. all of the above.

_____

_____ 6. Potassium:
  a. is never found in red meat.
  b. is the only chemical necessary for pH balance.
  c. should never be combined with vitamin C.
  d. is abundant in many fruits and vegetables.

_____

_____ 7. Once a long-term memory has formed, which factor interferes with retrieving it?
  a. clogging at the synapse
  b. deterioration of the neuronal pathways involved
  c. stress
  d. all of the above

_____

_____ 8. During the fifth and sixth centuries, Germanics migrated to England. They were called:
  a. Angles.
  b. Saxons.

     c. Jutes.

     d. Angles, Saxons, and Jutes.

_____ **9.** Henry Clay is classified as:

     a. a great boxer and poet.

     b. a war hawk.

     c. a war hawk and the Great Compromiser.

     d. entirely responsible for the War of 1812 and the Treaty of Ghent.

_____ **10.** The most effective time to study for a lecture class is:

     a. before class.

     b. after class.

     c. right before you go to bed.

     d. irrelevant; it is not necessary to study for a lecture class.

_____ **11.** Prolonged stress produces high levels of cortisol, which can:

     a. cause the hippocampus to shrink.

     b. significantly reduce the production of neurons.

     c. affect memory, mood, and mental functions.

     d. all of the above.

_____ **12.** If you cover 1.47 feet per second for each mile per hour you are driving and if you are driving at 60 miles per hour, every second that elapses, you cover:

     a. 60 feet.

     b. 147 feet.

     c. almost 30 yards.

     d. 1.47 yards.

Strategies for Fill-in-the-Blank Questions

1. Read the question to yourself so that you can hear what is being asked.

2. If more than one answer comes to mind, write both in the margin. Come back later and choose the one you want.

3. Make sure that your choice fits in logically and grammatically.

4. Remember that your answer may require more than one word.

PRACTICE 9.10

Practice with Fill-in-the-Blank Questions

1. One should answer _____ questions, unless you are penalized for wrong answers.

2. _____, _____, and _____ are three kinds of objective tests.

3. Answer the _____ questions first.

4. True/false statements that give a reason tend to be _____.

5. True/false statements with absolutes will almost always be _____.

6. The incorrect choices in a multiple-choice question are called _____.

Strategies for Matching Questions

With true/false questions, you have a 50 percent chance of guessing the correct answer. With multiple-choice questions, you have a 25 percent chance before you begin to eliminate distracters. Although most students think that matching is one of the easier ways to take a test, your chances of guessing the correct answers are very small.

Following are some strategies for matching tests:

1. Preview all of the possibilities before answering anything.
2. Determine whether an answer can be used more than once.
3. Answer the questions you are sure of first.
4. Cross out options as you use them.
5. Use logic to determine what is being asked for. A person? A place? A date?

Virtual Field Trip
Objective Tests

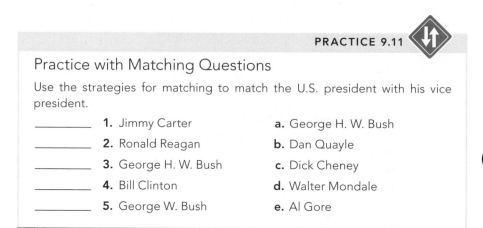

PRACTICE 9.11

Practice with Matching Questions

Use the strategies for matching to match the U.S. president with his vice president.

_____	**1.** Jimmy Carter	**a.** George H. W. Bush
_____	**2.** Ronald Reagan	**b.** Dan Quayle
_____	**3.** George H. W. Bush	**c.** Dick Cheney
_____	**4.** Bill Clinton	**d.** Walter Mondale
_____	**5.** George W. Bush	**e.** Al Gore

Reviewing Returned Tests

A Dozen Reasons to Review a Returned Test

1. Check the point total to make sure it is right. Look for mistakes in grading.
2. Know what questions you missed, what the correct answers are, and why you missed them. The reasons you missed these questions are often as or more important for your performance on the next test as knowing the correct answers.
3. Study the instructor's comments, especially for essay questions, so that you will know what is expected next time.
4. Figure out what kinds of questions (including tricky questions) the instructor likes to use.
5. See if the questions you missed came from the text or the lecture. Concentrate more on that source when you study for the next exam.
6. Correct and understand what you missed. This is information you need to know. It may appear on a later test or the final exam.

7. Determine which type of questions you missed so you can review strategies for that type.

8. Review to get an idea about what kind of test the instructor may give next time.

9. Review to put information back into your long-term memory.

10. Ask questions of your instructor while the test is fresh in your mind.

11. Review how you studied for the exam. Look for better ways to study next time.

12. Reviewing gives you a good reason to talk to your instructor and let her or him know you want to improve.

 Making **CONNECTIONS**

It is important to remember that not all objective test questions fall into the lower-order thinking levels of Bloom's taxonomy. Memorizing definitions, dates, and places will probably not be enough to answer all the questions. Here are some examples of test questions that use the higher-order thinking skills of analysis, synthesis, and evaluation.

_____ 1. You can gain time by:
   a. doing a job in less time than usual.
   b. using blocks of time you usually waste.
   c. obeying your alarm clock.
   d. all of the above.

_____ 2. The most effective time to study for a lecture class is just:
   a. before the class.
   b. after the class.
   c. before the test.
   d. after a party.

_____ 3. Rereading:
   a. is a quick, efficient way to review a chapter.
   b. is better than reciting because you cover more material.
   c. should always be done before major tests.
   d. none of the above.

_____ 4. John was assigned to read a chapter in his psychology textbook. He should begin his assignment by:
   a. turning to the first page of the chapter and reading through from beginning to end.
   b. reading the chapter's introduction, headings, and summary and examining the graphic material in it.
   c. underlining the information that he eventually wants in his notes.
   d. waiting until after the lecture so he will know what's important to the professor.

Continued

Making Connections continued

_____ **5.** Which is the best plan for completing a long reading assignment for your history class?

    a. Find a quiet place and read the assignment in one sitting. Mark it as you read.

    b. Read parts of the assignment throughout the day when you have a few minutes. When you finish a paragraph, write a question in the text's margin and underline the answer. Then review when reading is complete.

    c. Read the summary and mark the text in class as the instructor lectures.

    d. Survey the assignment, then read it in one sitting. Write a question for each paragraph and underline the answers.

PRACTICE 9.12

Summary for Objective Test Strategies

Either add to the map you created for true/false questions or create a new map so that it includes all the strategies you learned about objective tests.

Predicting Test Questions

One of the most important study skills you can develop is predicting what will be on a test. Knowing this with confidence can make your study time more effective, as well as cut down on test anxiety. By using the Question in the Margin System for taking notes from lectures and textbooks, you have already begun to use the essential strategies needed to predict what will be on a test.

Here are some important guidelines to remember in predicting questions that will be on a test.

1. Notice clues to test questions from lecture material.

    a. What an instructor says and how he or she says it (verbal cues)

    b. Ideas that are repeated

    c. Ideas written on the board, in an overhead, or in a handout

    d. "This is important"; "You'll see this again"

    e. Questions the instructor asks

2. Notice clues to test questions from textbook material.

    a. Material in **bold** print

    b. Information in summary section

    c. Problems or questions at the end of chapters

3. Save all tests, quizzes, homework, and so on. Look for patterns.

4. Find out if previous tests are available and analyze the material covered.

Possible Test Questions Dealing with Test-Taking Strategies

Examine the test-taking strategies on the previous pages. Look closely at the strategies described in the diagnostic inventory and strategies for any test: true/false, multiple-choice, fill-in, and matching questions. Now predict 10 true/false questions and 5 multiple-choice questions dealing with these strategies. Use the numbered blanks for your questions.

True/False

_____ 1. _____

_____ 2. _____

_____ 3. _____

_____ 4 _____

_____ 5. _____

_____ 6. _____

_____ 7. _____

_____ 8. _____

_____ 9. _____

_____ 10. _____

Multiple-Choice

_____ 1. _____

a.

b.

c.

d.

_____ 2. _____

a.

b.

c.

d.

_____ 3. _____

a.

b.

c.

d.

_____ 4. _____

a.

b.

c.

d.

Strategies for Essay Tests

Many students dread essay exams and discussion questions. Whereas objective tests require you to choose the correct answer or fill in a specific blank, subjective tests require you to recall and to organize. The main idea is to make sure that the grader knows that you know the answer to the question. Leave nothing to chance.

Basic Strategies for Writing Answers to Essay Tests

The checklist that follows is an important guide for you to use when a test requires you to write a paragraph or essay. You need to understand each point so that when you write an essay for history class or psychology class, you have a guideline to make sure you get the most points for what you know. Use the following as your GPS to guide you in writing the answers and as a checklist after you have written the answers.

For Your Student Survival Kit

Checklist for Essay Tests

_____ **1.** Do I really understand what the question asks me to do?

_____ **2.** Have I done any preliminary planning of my major points?

_____ **3.** From reading the first sentence of my answer, does the reader know both what the question is and how I will develop my answer?

_____ **4.** Do the major points stand out?

_____ **5.** Are the major points supported with examples and facts?

_____ **6.** Are there clear transitions between the major points?

_____ **7.** Would someone who has not taken this class be able to understand the concept discussed in the way I explained it?

_____ **8.** Have I completely covered all major points needed to answer the question?

_____ **9.** Did I stick to the question?

_____ **10.** Have I concluded with a summary statement?

_____ **11.** Did I proofread for misspelled words, sentence fragments, run-on sentences, comma splices, subject–verb or pronoun–antecedent agreement errors, and other errors that might prevent the reader from understanding what I have written?

_____ **12.** Is my handwriting readable, and have I left enough space for comments or additions?

 BRAIN BYTE

Leslie Hart argues that subjective tests are superior to objective tests because learners have to identify patterns and select strategies for using them.

Direction Words

Often students lose points on essay tests, not because they don't know the answer, but because they do not answer the question being asked. The key to what your professor is asking you to do is to understand exactly what the directions ask for. Following is a list of 15 commonly used direction words. Make flash cards to help you remember them. Write a direction word on the front of the card and put the definition and examples on the back or use your flash card app.

DIRECTION WORD	DEFINITION	EXAMPLE
1. Compare	Emphasize similarities but also present differences.	Compare *the strategies used in taking true/false tests with those used in taking multiple-choice tests.*
2. Contrast	Give differences only.	Contrast *the functions of the left brain and the right brain.*
3. Criticize	Give your judgment of good points; then give the limitations with evidence.	Criticize *the Question in the Margin System for taking lecture notes.*
4. Define	Give meaning but no detail.	Define *objective tests.*
5. Describe	State particulars in detail.	Describe *what you found when you took a career inventory.*
6. Discuss	Give reasons pro and con with details.	Discuss *what types of careers best fit your interest and abilities.*
7. Evaluate	Discuss advantages and disadvantages along with your opinion.	Evaluate *the implementation of the online catalog in the library.*
8. Give cause and effect	Describe the steps that lead to an event or situation and the impact of the event or situation.	Give the cause *of our forgetting what we read in textbooks and the effect that the Question in the Margin System has on this forgetting.*
9. Give an example	Give a concrete illustration from your book, notes, or experience.	Give an example *of a reference book that you think will be helpful in other courses.*
10. Illustrate	Give an example.	Illustrate *how the principle of meaningful organization will help transfer information from short-term to long-term memory.*
11. Justify	Prove or give reasons.	*Most students will not use the Question in the Margin System for reading a textbook because it takes too long.* Justify *its use.*
12. Relate	Show how things interconnect.	Relate *the Question in the Margin System for reading textbooks to the Question in the Margin System for taking lecture notes.*
13. Summarize	Organize and bring together main points only.	Summarize *what you have learned in this course.*
14. Support	Back up a statement with facts and proof.	*Researchers say that recitation is the most powerful means for transferring information from short-term to long-term memory.* Support *this statement.*
15. Trace	Give main points from beginning to end of an event.	Trace *ideas from when they first enter the brain to active memory.*

PRACTICE 9.14

Applying the Direction Words

Below are descriptions of what different instructors want you to write on a test. Identify which direction words they are likely to use in their directions.

_____ **1.** In your composition class, the instructor asks you to show how the modes of narration and description are alike and how they are different.

_____ **2.** In a political science class, you are asked to give your judgment on the good points of the electoral college system while acknowledging its limitations.

_____ **3.** Your study skills instructor asks you to point out differences between your study habits now and your study habits at the beginning of the semester.

_____ **4.** In an algebra class, the professor asks you to give the meaning of the term _slope_.

_____ **5.** In a literature class, the professor asks you to depict in detail the setting of the novel _Sula_ by giving particular details.

_____ **6.** An aerospace instructor asks students to give a detailed analysis (both pros and cons) of the reasons NASA was faced with problems during the 1980s.

_____ **7.** Your study skills instructor asks you to discuss the advantages and disadvantages of using the Question in the Margin System for reading textbooks.

_____ **8.** Your political science professor asks you to discuss the steps that led to the resignation of Richard Nixon and what the consequences were for the Republican Party.

_____ **9.** Your nursing professor asks you to give concrete illustrations of the effects of smoking on human health.

_____ **10.** Your physical fitness teacher asks you to give an example showing the link between aerobic conditioning and good health.

_____ **11.** An education professor asks you to prove or give reasons why teachers should use the "whole language" method of teaching reading.

_____ **12.** Your psychology professor asks you to demonstrate how Freud's theories of childhood development interconnect with Jung's theories.

_____ **13.** Your biology professor asks you to organize and bring together the main points regarding the process of photosynthesis.

_____ **14.** Your history professor asks you to use facts to prove that the South was technologically unprepared to win the Civil War.

_____ **15.** Your music history professor asks you to briefly discuss the main composers of the Jazz Age from its beginning to its end.

One reason to know this list of commonly used direction words is to understand exactly what test questions or instructions ask you to do. In addition, being familiar with direction words is also helpful in predicting and preparing for possible questions or instructions about the topics that your tests will cover. Practicing writing questions or instructions using direction words for a topic you think will be on a test helps you be better prepared.

For example, suppose your topic is learning principles. Here are a few possibilities.

Define	Define each of the learning principles.
Discuss	Discuss how the learning principles are used in the Question in the Margin System.
Give an example	Give an example of using visualization.
Evaluate	Evaluate your use of the learning principles.
Compare	Compare association with basic background.

PRACTICE 9.15

Practice with Direction Words

Using defensive driving or distracted driving as your topic, follow the preceding example, choose six of the direction words and write a test question for each about defensive or distracted driving.

DIRECTION WORD	POSSIBLE DISCUSSION QUESTION OR INSTRUCTION

Making CONNECTIONS

Review your notes about Bloom's taxonomy. Remember that each level of learning requires a different level of thinking. First, as a review, list the levels to match the descriptions. Then examine the list of commonly used direction words. In the third column, decide which level of thinking each direction word may require. (Some direction words may fit into more than one level, so you may use them more than once.) Try to place each direction word in an appropriate box.

LEVEL OF BLOOM'S TAXONOMY	DESCRIPTION	POSSIBLE DIRECTION WORDS
	LOWER-ORDER THINKING SKILLS	
	Recall data or information, not necessarily understand it	
	Understand it enough to explain in own words	
	Actually use the information	
	HIGHER-ORDER THINKING SKILLS	
	Subdividing to see how it is put together	
	Put information back together in a unique way	
	Making value judgments	

PRACTICE 9.16

Practice with Topic Sentences and Direction Words

The first sentence of your answer to an essay question is crucial. It should show the grader both that you understand the question and how you will develop your answer. In addition, it becomes your guide as well. It keeps you on track. Pay particular attention to the direction word. You will pay a severe penalty if you know the material but answer the wrong question because you did not pay attention to what the question asked you to do. For each question below, plan what your answer would say, and write a clear topic sentence showing both that you understand the question and how you will develop your answer.

1. *Compare* the role of a defensive driver to the role of a successful college student.

_____

_____

2. *Contrast* the role of student as passenger to that of student as driver.

_____

_____

_____

3. *Evaluate* your computer skills.

_____

_____

_____

4. The cost, time, and effort involved in getting a college education are enormous. *Justify* your decision to enroll in college.

_____

_____

_____

5. *Relate* what you have learned in this course to your other courses.

_____

_____

_____

6. *Summarize* your responsibilities when you miss a class.

_____

_____

_____

7. *Trace* the steps necessary to register for next term.

_____

_____

_____

After planning what should be included in each of these seven answers, choose one and write a complete answer to the question. Use a separate sheet of paper to write your answer.

Virtual Field Trip
Essay Tests

Practice with Evaluating Answers to Essay Questions

One way for you to better understand what the grader is looking for is to examine essay questions from a grader's point of view. Following are four answers to the same question asked on a learning strategies test. The instruction is to discuss how to write an effective answer to an essay question. You are the grader. The question is worth 20 points. Use the checklist we covered earlier in this chapter as your guide for what to look for in the student's answer and which elements the answer should contain (the content). Use the Grade Sheet as a rubric, or guide, in grading the essay answers. For each student answer, give your score, with the highest possible score being 20. Write your comments as to why the student received those points. You will need to make a copy of the rubric for each essay.

Rubric or Grade Sheet for Essay Test

Content	8 points	A point for each item that is actually on the "Checklist for Essay Tests" that you use as a major point in your answer (up to 8 points)
Organization	2 points	If from reading the first sentence of your answer, the reader knows both what the question was and how you will develop your answer
	2 points	If major points stand out and transitions are used
	2 points	If major points are supported with examples, reasons, and facts
	1 point	If there is a concluding statement
Clarity	2 points	If someone who has not taken this class could use this as a guide for writing an effective essay
Grammar, spelling	3 points	
Total score		

Use the back of the rubric to make comments to the student about how she or he could improve her or his answer.

Student 1 Score _____

To write an effective answer to an essay question includes several steps. The first step is to answer by rewriting the question in a complete sentence. The second step is to write your answer in complete sentences. The third step is to support you answer with examples and facts. The fourth step as to conclude with complete sentences. Those are the four steps to answering an essay question. With these steps it lets the reader know how the answers were developed.

Comments:

_____

_____

_____

Student 2 Score _____

In order to write an effective answer to an essay question, you must know the topic. Always answer the question being asked in the first sentence of the answer. Have a strong thesis statement. The thesis statement should be what the paper is about. When you begin the actual essay, you must have proper facts. Detail sentences should support any topics brought up in your paper. Last, you should sum up your paper, not bring up new ideas. This is my idea of how one should write an effective essay.

Comments:

_____

_____

_____

Student 3 Score _____

My instructor says it is important to use the checklist for answering essay questions in order to make sure I get the most points possible for what I know. It's a bunch of stuff to memorize, but after analyzing the list more carefully, I think she may be right. I do need to understand what the question is asking; otherwise I probably won't get any credit even if I know something about the topic. The best way to do this is to plan my answer and then show the grader both that I understand what the question is asking me to do and how I will answer it. The grader knows I know the answer, and it provides a guide for me to follow so I make sure I cover all the points and don't get off the subject. Major points should stand out so that I know I've covered them and the grader can check off points he or she is looking for. If I don't support the major points, I come up with just a list. That's not good. I need to make sure my writing is readable and that I have checked for mistakes. I know, when it's a test situation, I may make more mistakes than usual and not even know I've made them. A concluding statement lets me double-check that I answered the question and reminds the grader again that I know what the answer is. The checklist may be overkill, but if I want to get the most points for what I know, I probably will do better if I do everything on it.

Comments:

_____

_____

_____

Student 4 Score _____

In order for someone to write an effective answer to a discussion question, she must include at least these nine strategies which fall into the categories of developing, supporting and concluding the essay. The first category is to develop and plan your answer. You need to read the question over to see that you fully understand what is being asked of you. Next, you do any preliminary planning that needs to be done in order to organize your answer before you start, and then you make the first sentence of your essay repeat the question and show how you will answer it. The second stage is to support your answer. You need to make sure that you list all your major points and they are supported by examples. You must also make sure that anyone who is not in this class would be able to read your essay and know what the discussion is about. The last and sometimes most important thing to do is conclude your essay. Now this category consists of several items on the checklist. First, did you cover all the major points? Did your completely answer the question? Have you reread your essay and proofed for any spelling or grammar errors? Most importantly you should make sure your handwriting is neat and legible for someone to read and understand, without guessing, what you are saying. If you can include most, if not all, of these strategies in your essay, then you should be able to write an exceptional answer to a discussion question.

Comments:

_____

_____

_____

Virtual Field Trip
Dealing with Test
Anxiety

CRITICAL THINKING
About Preparing for Exams

Suppose your team is going to participate in a championship game a week from Saturday. Your coach calls you together and says, "We have a week to prepare, and I want you to do your best, so we will take it easy and not practice until Friday night. On Friday night, report for practice at midnight. We will practice all night long."

What do you think the results would be for the game on Saturday morning?

Compare how you should prepare for the championship to how you should prepare for your exams. List at least four similarities.

1. _____

_____

2. _____

_____

3. _____

_____

4. _____

_____

◈ **CAREER** Connections

The checklist for writing answers to essay questions can be a useful checklist well beyond the classroom. Many job applications require essays or cover letters. The first item on the checklist says "Do I really understand what the question asks me to do?" This is extremely important when applying for a job or a scholarship. Read the instructions carefully—understand what the directions ask you to do. In fact, no matter what career you choose, you will probably have to answer questions from your supervisor, customers, investors, and so on. In almost any career, you will be writing reports, performance feedback, evaluations, or some type of written communication. The checklist is a good way to assure that you are taken seriously.

Consider the following essay questions that you might be asked to answer on a job application. Choose one and write an essay that you might submit with your job application, using the checklist for answering an essay question as your guide.

1. Describe an obstacle you have faced in your professional or academic life. How did you overcome this obstacle and how did it foster your development?

2. Summarize why you want a career in_____.

3. Discuss your goals for the future.

Final Exams

You should begin preparation for finals the first day of class. Most of us, however, need a bit of organizing to get ready for finals. The following study organizer may be just what you need to use for each of your classes a week or so before finals. List each class you are taking, and fill in the information asked for about each class. *Be very specific*. Make copies so that you will have one sheet for each class.

For Your Student Survival Kit

Final Exam Study Organizer

Class _____　Date and time of exam _____

Instructor _____　Office and telephone number _____

What percentage of the final grade will the final exam comprise? _____

What will be covered on the final exam? (Be specific.)

1. _____
2. _____
3. _____
4. _____
5. _____

What kind of exam will this be (multiple-choice, true/false, essay, and so on)?

_____

_____

What is the best way to study for this exam? (Be specific.)

_____

_____

I need to have flash cards covering

1. _____
2. _____
3. _____

I will use these mnemonics (and why)

1. _____
2. _____
3. _____

Summary sheets will be useful to study (specific concepts)

1. _____
2. _____
3. _____

Name and telephone number of a person in the class with whom I will study for at least an hour

Review—Where did we go?

Modeling the Learning Process

Gathering. You gathered strategies for taking specific tests.

Analyzing. You analyzed examples and took practice tests.

Creating New Ideas. You predicted what questions might be included and planned possible answers.

Acting. You wrote essay answers and a practice test.

Study Guide: Test-Taking Strategies

To see if you grasped the major points of the chapter and to make a useful study guide, answer the following questions found in your reading. When you have written your answers, cover them and see if you can say the answer to each question in your own words.

1. What is the difference between *recognition* and *recall* when answering test questions?

_____

_____

2. Name four specific strategies that you already use to *prepare* for tests.

1. _____

2. _____

3. _____

4. _____

3. Why is it important to budget your time when taking a test?

_____

4. Explain how to budget your time when you take a test.

_____

5. Explain the effect negatives have on true/false statements.

_____

6. What is a double negative?

_____

7. What is the difference between a general qualifier and an absolute qualifier?

_____

8. In true/false statements, why should one carefully check items in a series?

_____

9. What educated guess can you make when a true/false statement gives reasons?

_____

10. Why are there usually more true statements than false ones?

_____

11. What are four basic strategies to use with multiple-choice questions?

  1. _____

  2. _____

  3. _____

  4. _____

12. What options in multiple-choice questions tend to be the incorrect choice?

_____

13. What options in multiple-choice questions tend to be the correct choice?

_____

14. What are basic strategies for fill-in questions?

_____

15. What are basic strategies for matching tests?

_____

16. Name some clues used to predict test questions from lecture material.

_____

17. What clues can you use to predict test questions from textbooks?

_____

18. Why is it important to know the meaning of direction words?

_____

19. Describe what the first sentence of the answer to an essay question should do.

_____

20. List some strategies to use when preparing for final exams.

_____

_____

CASE STUDY
What's Your Advice?

LaNita, Bill, and Charlene have a midterm exam next week in Dr. Watts's philosophy class, one of only two tests in the course for the entire semester. The difficulty of Dr. Watts's exams is legendary on campus, but he is the only instructor who teaches this course, a requirement in their major. Because it is important for them to do well, the three students decide on their first day of class to meet weekly for a study session. The students promise to take notes in class, question them after class, and keep up with reading assignments by writing possible test questions in the margins and underlining the answers in each paragraph.

At their weekly study session, they compare their marked notes and textbooks and take turns answering questions out loud. At the end of each weekly session, LaNita is responsible for making a practice test for next time using that week's material. Bill's responsibility is to come up with as many visual study aids as he can for the material—comparison charts, maps, timelines, and so forth. Charlene's job is to create mnemonics and use her computer program to make flash cards or games involving the information for the week. Because they keep up with weekly sessions, their tasks are relatively simple.

At the class period before the exam, Dr. Watts tells the students that the test will have several discussion questions asking students to compare or just to contrast various philosophies, trace the development of certain philosophies, or discuss how certain philosophers might react to a statement. In addition, there will be a multiple-choice section, a true/false section, and a matching section. They will have 1 hour and 15 minutes for the test.

When the three students meet for a final study session, they agree that they have prepared well but they are worried about taking the test. LaNita says that she usually does great on the objective parts of a test but somehow fails to get full credit on the discussion parts even though she knows the material. For Bill and Charlene, it is just the opposite. They ask for your advice on test-taking strategies they can use. Please make them a guide for taking the test.

Parallel Parking

Choose two of the following and compare the driving term to test-taking strategies:

Going Over a Speed Bump

_____

_____

Planning a Trip Before You Leave Home

_____

_____

Finding a Parking Place

_____

_____

Fueling Up, Checking Tires, Oil, etc.

_____

_____

Missing the Turn You Needed to Make

_____

_____

Taking a Detour

_____

_____

Evaluating Learning Outcomes

How successful were you in making it to your destination in this chapter?

Analyze what you learned in this chapter. Put a check beside each task you are now able to do. On a separate piece of paper, write a couple of sentences about how you learned each learning outcome and how you plan to continue to use what you learned.

☐ **Describe** strategies that you have found effective in preparing for a test.

☐ **Analyze** how you prepare for tests.

☐ **State** strategies to use in taking any kind of test.

☐ **Use** strategies for objective tests: true/false, multiple-choice, fill-in-the-blank, matching.

☐ **Name, explain, and demonstrate** at least eight strategies to employ when writing an answer to an essay question.

☐ **Apply** the checklist for essay questions to a career situation.

☐ **Demonstrate** strategies for dealing with test anxiety.

☐ **Analyze** a case study and construct advice for a student having difficulty with test-taking skills.

☐ **Explain** the learning process modeled in this chapter.

Your Student Tip for This Chapter

Use the space below to write a tip you would give to other students about what you have learned in this chapter.

_____

_____

_____

_____

_____

Use this page to map what you have learned about taking tests.

Managing Stress

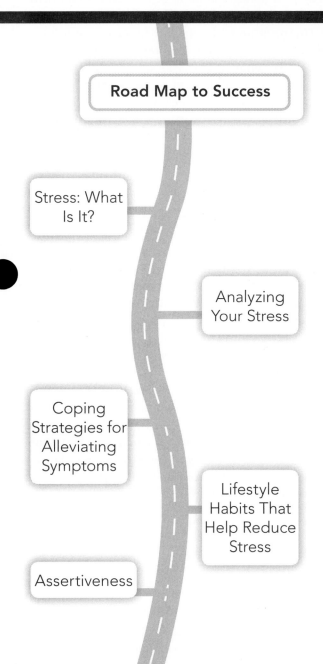

Road Map to Success

- Stress: What Is It?
- Analyzing Your Stress
- Coping Strategies for Alleviating Symptoms
- Lifestyle Habits That Help Reduce Stress
- Assertiveness

In this chapter, you will learn how to

- **Recognize** signs of stress.
- **Analyze** a stressful situation in your life and determine a plan of action.
- **Differentiate** between passive, aggressive, and assertive behaviors.
- **Demonstrate** how to script as practice for assertiveness.
- **Analyze** a case study and construct advice for a student having difficulty coping with the stress.
- **Explain** the learning process used in this chapter.

Where Are We Going?

As a driver you know how to plan your route, schedule your car maintenance, and drive defensively. But one factor that may make your trip almost frightening is the stress caused by being stuck in traffic, lost, late for an appointment, or even having rowdy passengers. As a developing college student, you are learning how to manage your time, process information, and take tests; likewise, there is an additional factor that may determine your success as a college student: How well do you deal with stress? Almost 50 percent of American students who enter college never graduate. Although finances and life circumstances play a role, stress must be considered as a factor. In this chapter you will learn to recognize what stress is, identify what causes you stress, and discover some ways to manage your stress. You will look at some possible lifestyle decisions you may want to make. You will also examine the concept of assertiveness, a life skill that will also help you deal with stressful situations and people in college and beyond.

BRAIN BYTE

Researchers O'Keefe and Nadel have found that positive forms of stress occur when we are challenged to rise to the occasion. Your body releases adrenaline and noradrenaline, which actually heighten perception, increase motivation, and even enhance physical strength.

Stress: What Is It?

If you are not feeling stress at this point in the term, there is something wrong. Stress is completely normal and is our response to our changing environments. Therefore, not *all* stress is bad. There are as many different ideas about stress as there are people who experience it in their lives. **Stress** refers to the way you react physically, emotionally, and mentally to stressors. **Stressors** are physical, psychological, or social forces that put real or perceived demands on the body, emotions, mind, or spirit of an individual. In other words, stressors are anything that causes stress!

You may be going about your daily life and not realize the effect that stress is having on you. But the fact is, stress can make itself known in every aspect of a person's life. When you snap at your roommate, spouse, or children, when you have trouble concentrating, when you feel that you just want to be left alone—all may be symptoms of stress. These symptoms can be reflected in your health, your mental and emotional well-being, and your behavior. Let's look at a list of common symptoms of stress. *Check all those in the following table that apply to you.*

Recognizing Possible Signs of Stress

	HEALTH OR MEDICAL		MENTAL AND EMOTIONAL		BEHAVIORAL
	Migraine or tension headache		Irritability		Sleeping badly
	Upset stomach, diarrhea		Losing sense of humor		Snapping or shouting at those around you
	High blood pressure		Often on the verge of tears		Fiddling with your hair

Continued

Shortness of breath		Crying spells		High-pitched or nervous laughter
Loss of appetite		Feeling that you can't cope		Trembling, shaking, excessive blinking
Frequent or lingering colds		Being suspicious of others		Finding it difficult to talk to people
Acne		Difficulty concentrating		Having trouble completing tasks
Cold sores on mouth		Difficulty making decisions		Overeating
Dizziness		Making poor decisions		Drinking or smoking more than usual
Lack of energy		Not being able to think		Reduced sex drive
Dryness of the throat and mouth		Not being able to stay on task		Grinding the teeth or clenching the jaw

Checking more than four or five of these items suggests you are overly stressed. Throughout this chapter, we will discuss strategies to help manage your stress.

Analyzing Your Stress

As you have learned from critical thinking, if you are going to solve a problem or make a decision, you first need to determine exactly what the problem is. Accordingly, in order to manage stress, it's helpful to know what causes it. At the risk of getting you even more stressed out, let's look at a few of the stressors many college students face.

Financial Stress	Students worry about paying for tuition, as well as other living expenses.
Multi-Tasking Stress	Students must juggle classes, job, family responsibilities, and extracurricular activities.
Peer Pressure	For those who choose not to experiment with drugs, alcohol, sexual activity, or other potentially harmful behaviors, resisting pressure can be stressful. For those who do participate in such behavior, there is both physical and emotional stress.
Independence and Responsibility	Dealing with change and added responsibility, living away from home, or making decisions about one's life and future is stressful.
Academic Pressure	The course work can be demanding and the amount of time required to be successful is stressful, as is the pressure of keeping a scholarship or getting into grad school.
Social Stress	Going to college means creating new social networks. Often it means finding and living with roommates and balancing friends with school work. These types of things are stressful.

StudentTIP

"The classwork is not the hardest part of college. It's dealing with those things that happen outside of the classroom that is the most difficult part of college and sometimes keep you from doing your best in the classroom."

Making **CONNECTIONS**

Remember step 2 of the decision-making process, gathering information? Let's gather information about your stress. Choose two of the categories above, expand on them as necessary, and write a well-developed paragraph in which you describe stress you have experienced this semester.

The study strategies you have developed so far are ways of dealing with situations that are common for college students. Let's review some things you already know about relieving stress:

- You have developed study strategies that use what you know about how the brain processes information in order to process information more efficiently.
- You have developed a system for taking notes and reading textbooks.
- You have developed strategies for studying for and taking tests.
- You have developed a master schedule for help with time management.
- You know how to write goals in order to solve stress-related problems.
- You know how to use the **BREATHE** System to relax and focus.

Are you using these strategies? Remember that if you have a plan or strategy for dealing with stressors, their impact on you will be reduced.

CRITICAL THINKING
About Stress

When you think about stress in your daily life, what images, people, places, and so on, come to mind? List at least five causes of stress in your life.

1. _____

2. _____

3. _____

4. _____

5. _____

Step 3 in critically solving problems is to determine your options. Examine the major causes of stress in your life, and try to determine what your options are for dealing with each. Choose one of the causes you listed, and write down what you think some of your options are. Ask others to help if you are stuck.

● Cause of stress: _____

Possible options I have for dealing with this stress:

1. _____

2. _____

3. _____

4. _____

PRACTICE 10.1

Developing a Plan of Action

Now return to the options you listed for dealing with one of the causes of your stress. Weigh each option carefully and choose one. Using what you know about goal setting, write a plan of action in the form of a useful goal.

Goal for dealing with _____

_____

_____

_____

Coping Strategies for Alleviating Stress Symptoms

When stress is constant and unrelieved, it can become negative and even destructive. But you can break the cycle of negative stress by learning ways to help yourself relax. By taking the time to practice simple relaxation techniques on a regular basis, you can give yourself a chance to unwind and get ready for life's next challenge.

Strategy 1. **Musical background.** Music can be purchased online or in department/music stores. You can also listen to music for free on websites like Pandora and Spotify. Look for relaxing music that includes soothing music or sounds of nature (oceans, thunderstorms, forest wildlife, and so on).

Strategy 2. **BREATHE System.** We learned about the Big 3 of Hillman's BREATHE System earlier. Hopefully, they have become a habit for you. An overview of the system is presented here.

Breathe   Use the Big 3: (1) straighten your posture and elevate your rib cage, (2) relax your neck and shoulder muscles, and (3) breathe by moving your ribs sideways and not raising your shoulders while inhaling to make calming breaths possible. Inhale completely (through your nose) and blow out (through your mouth) as much air as possible with each exhale.

BRAIN BYTE

The body responds to negative stress by releasing the hormone cortisol. Too much cortisol negatively affects the hippocampus, which is very sensitive to this hormone. The result is to weaken the brain's local memory and indexing systems. The hippocampus is the part of the brain that enables the body to fight disease, so the release of cortisol weakens the body's immune system.

Virtual Field Trip
Let's Find Out More
About Managing Stress

Repeat   Take another calming breath, using the Big 3. Focus on the breathing.

Emotion   Become aware of and identify your emotional condition and the emotions of others. Evaluate their effectiveness. Are those emotions working for or against you? Allow your emotional state to reduce in intensity or transform to a more effective emotional state.

Assess   Assess your actions and behaviors and those of others in the situation. Are those behaviors beneficial? Make the choice to change, regain personal control, and redirect your behavior to be more consistent with your goals. Focus on breathing.

Talk   Clarify what the wants, needs, and concerns of others are by asking questions. Be careful how you ask the questions. Use good voice quality and falling inflection, and don't let your voice reflect a negative emotional condition. Is what you are saying, feeling, and doing right now helping you achieve your goals? How might it help you? Focus on breathing.

Hear   Focus on the concepts expressed or implied by the speaker (even if it is you). Look beneath the words to determine what is really being said. Continue to talk and listen as you seek additional options that might resolve this situation. Focus on breathing.

Exit   Seek agreement about how to resolve this situation and return to the learning community, back to a place of security, calmness, and hope. Continue to breathe.[1]

Strategy 3.   Progressive relaxation routine. This is a three-step technique. It can be done while sitting or lying down and takes only 15 minutes or so. It helps if you can practice the technique in a quiet, relaxing place. First, *tighten your hand muscles* and make a fist; then, notice how it feels. Your muscles are taut and strained, and your hand may even be trembling slightly. You may feel tension in your hand, wrist, and lower arm. Hold the tension for a few seconds before relaxing. Now, *release your hand*, relax your fist, and let the tension slip away. You may notice that your hand feels lighter than it did while your muscles were tensed and that your wrist and forearm also feel relieved of pressure. *Notice the difference* between how your hand felt when tensed and how it felt when you released the tension. Does your hand tingle or feel warm when relaxed? Did the throbbing you felt while tensed disappear when you relaxed? It is best to do this exercise on each of the major muscle groups of your body. The basic technique remains the same throughout.

---

[1]From *Delivering Dynamic Presentations: Using Your Voice and Body for Impact* by Ralph E. Hillman.

Tighten the muscle, release the tension, and then notice the difference. You can start with your hands, then progress to other muscles; or you can move from head to toe, tightening and relaxing the muscles in your face, shoulders, arms, hands, chest, back, stomach, legs, and feet.

Strategy 4.   **Visualization.** Visualization can be thought of as a mental vacation, a license to daydream. You can produce feelings of relaxation simply by using your imagination. Visualization allows your imagination to run free. Try to visualize yourself feeling warm, calm, and relaxed. Picture a tranquil setting that has particular appeal for you, and try to imagine all of the details. Are you lying on a warm beach? How does the sun feel on your back? Do you hear waves lapping on the shore? Is there a fragrance in the air? Do you see sailboats on the water? Just by using your imagination, you can give yourself a mental vacation whenever you feel the need to take a moment to relax and enjoy life.

Strategy 5.   **Clearing your mind.** Giving yourself a mental break can help relax your body as well. When you clear your mind, you let your worries slip away. *Reduce distractions*, noise, and interruptions as much as possible as you begin this exercise. Try to set aside five to ten minutes daily to practice clearing your mind. *Sit comfortably*, loosen any tight clothing, kick off your shoes, and relax your body. Then close your eyes and begin to breathe slowly and deeply. *Mentally focus* on one peaceful word, thought, or image. If other thoughts should enter your mind, don't be discouraged; relax, breathe deeply, and try again. *Stretch and exhale* as you complete the exercise. With practice, clearing your mind can help you feel refreshed, energetic, and ready to tackle the next challenge.

Strategy 6.   **Energy-release activities.** Just about anything requiring physical activity will release energy. Get involved in a hobby or sport. Good old-fashioned exercise (jogging, weightlifting, calisthenics, and so on) also works wonders. Aerobic exercise or any exercise that keeps the heart pumping at elevated levels for 12 to 30 minutes is best. But don't fail to exercise just because you can't get in 30 minutes; lesser quantities do have a positive effect on stress. Check out what recreational activities your campus offers.

Strategy 7.   **Talking it out.** Talking with a friend or counselor about a problem will prevent it from becoming bottled up inside, thus giving you a better chance of dealing with it rationally. You will have counseling services on your campus.

Strategy 8.   **Laugh.** Many brain researchers have found that humor and laughter help relieve stress.

PRACTICE 10.2

Using the Strategies for Alleviating Stress

Name three specific situations that occur in your life when you might find it necessary to use one of the strategies for alleviating stress.

1. _____

_____

_____

2. _____

_____

_____

3. _____

_____

_____

Analyze the eight strategies for alleviating stress. List, in order of probability of use, four that you might try.

1. _____

_____

2. _____

_____

3. _____

_____

4. _____

_____

Do you think you may need additional or individual help on stress management?

_____

_____

Lifestyle Habits That Help Reduce Stress: Try a Few!

Stress can cause certain brain functions to literally shut down. Higher-level thinking skills and memory are most affected. Because stress involves both emotional and physical reactions to change, the better you feel in body and mind, the better you'll be able to deal with the stress in your life. When you learn to think positively, exercise, eat well, and rest regularly, you'll be taking care of the most important person you know—you. Just as you can make defensive driving a habit, there are lifestyle habits you can develop to help reduce stress.

PRACTICE 10.3

Virtual Field Trip
What You Need to Know
About Sleep

Analyzing Lifestyle Habits

Read this list carefully. Choose *three* or *four* of the following habits that relate to your lifestyle. On the line below each of those habits, write about a time in your life that you *should have* used that habit.

1. Don't take on more than you can handle. Try to complete one task at a time.

_____

2. Schedule quiet time and time for relaxation and planned exercise.

_____

3. Be assertive and stand up for yourself—or no one else will. Learn to say no.

_____

4. Distinguish between situations you can control and those you cannot.

_____

5. Accept the fact that you can't be perfect and will not always be right.

_____

6. Educate yourself about proper nutrition and how it can affect your mind and body.

_____

7. Use time management to set priorities and allow enough time to complete a task. Eliminate something if too much is happening at once.

_____

8. Don't make too many life changes at once.

_____

9. Analyze your values and accept yourself for who you are.

_____

10. Make efforts to develop close friendships and support systems.

_____

11. Develop a stress-management program and stick to it!

_____

12. Get enough sleep.

_____

13. Seek help with conflict resolution.

_____

Making CONNECTIONS

You have already developed some strategies that will help you deal with stress. Recall the following topics we have studied and briefly describe how each could relate to your handling of stress.

Time management

Goal setting

Memory principles

Question in the Margin System

Your learning style

Test-taking strategies

Assertiveness

Part of the stress you encounter in college is that you are building so many new relationships and coming to terms with and making adjustments to relationships you have already established. You interact with classmates, professors, roommates, and new friends. In addition, old friends or family may not understand your new role as a college student. Many college counselors suggest that assertiveness training may help relieve stress. Assertiveness is being able to honestly express your needs and feelings while respecting the rights and feelings of others. It is speaking up for yourself in a tactful way. Not being able to express your needs or concerns could lead to depression, resentment, frustration, or violence.

People often fall into three primary behavior patterns. The **passive person** does not know how to communicate his feelings to others. He wants to avoid conflict, so he usually just says nothing and usually ends up being a victim. The passive person has a hard time saying "no" and may have a hard time making decisions. The **aggressive person** wants her way regardless of rights and needs of others. Her behavior is based on getting her way no matter what. She may have a tendency to lose her temper, criticize, argue, or bully to get what she wants. Assertiveness, the third behavior pattern, strikes a balance between these two types of people. The **assertive person** clearly expresses his needs. He respects himself, but he also respects the rights and needs of others.

Some people find it easy to be assertive. However, if you are not assertive, you can learn to be. Do you ask for help when you need it? Do you express anger and frustration appropriately? Do you speak up in class? Are you able to say "no" when you don't want to do something? Let's examine some ways that you can practice assertiveness. As we said with note taking, you may not be good at it at first, but the only way to get better is to practice. If a relationship or situation is important to you, learning to be assertive is a win-win situation.

Here are some tips adapted from Revelle College's life skills website. **http://revelle.ucsd.edu/res-life/life-skills/assertiveness.html**

- *Use* **I** *rather than* **you.** *"I really need to finish this history assignment"* instead of *"You are so loud, I can't think."*
- Use facts, not judgments. *"We were supposed to meet at 12:15"* instead of *"Can't you ever be on time?"*
- Express ownership of your thoughts, feelings, and opinions. *"I get upset when he goes out without me"* instead of *"He makes me so mad."*
- Make clear, direct requests. *"Will you please meet me in the library?"* instead of *"Would you mind meeting me in the library?"*
- Keep repeating your point. Don't get coaxed into an argument.
- Learn to say "no" when you need to. Know what you can and cannot do. Do what is best for you.

Make sure that you convey your message with your body language as well as your words. Look the person in the eye. Keep your tone pleasant and polite.

Many assertiveness trainers advise that scripting is a technique that works well in developing assertiveness. They suggest that you actually write out a script and practice it before talking to the person. Your script should include a description of the situation stated as clearly and completely as possible. For example:

> *Sue, when I come home from my classes, I find the den filled with clothes and food you and your friends have left. Also, when I go to the kitchen, I find dirty dishes and food not put up and trash left out. When I leave, I clean up after myself and my friends so things are left clean and organized for both of us.*

Next you should express how you feel about the situation or behavior.

> *This makes me feel used and taken advantage of. I am doing the majority of the cleaning for both of us when we share the apartment.*

You should then state specifically what you would like to happen.

> *If you could put food and trash up, wash and put away your dishes and straighten the den and kitchen, we would have a neat-looking apartment.*

Finally you should describe the consequences both positive and negative.

On Monday nights you like me to cook for both of us. I enjoy doing that. If you cannot work with my request, then I will not want to share my Monday night meal with you.

(Or stronger)—

When I have to clean up after you, it makes me not want to share an apartment with you. I may need to find another roommate.

However, before you decide to act assertively in a given situation, you have to decide if you can live with the consequences. For example, if you say you will have to find a new roommate, you have to first be certain that you are willing to do that.

PRACTICE 10.4

Script-Writing Practice

Here are several situations other students have encountered. Choose one of these or a situation you now have and practice writing a script.

1. Your math professor consistently does not dismiss class on time, making you late to your psychology class, which meets immediately after.

2. Your boss insists that you come in when one of your fellow employees misses work, even though you have classes at that time.

3. On most weekends your roommate throws a party in your apartment. Her friends smoke and drink excessively and pretty much trash your apartment.

4. Your own situation.

 CAREER Connections

Choosing a career that matches your values, interests, and abilities will minimize some stress on the job. But, just as you experience stress as a college student, workplace stress is normal. Too much stress can interfere with your productivity and impact your physical or emotional health. The strategies you learned in this chapter will work well on the job and your life after college.

Consider one or two situations that might occur in your current or potential job and explain some strategies for coping with them. Or imagine the situation where you have too much work to do at work and your boss wants to give you even more.

For Your Student Survival Kit

A Plan for Combatting Stress

Having a plan for how you can combat stress is important in order to succeed in college and beyond. Write a plan on how you will use the strategies in this chapter to combat stress.

_____

_____

_____

_____

_____

_____

_____

_____

_____

_____

_____

_____

_____

_____

_____

_____

_____

_____

_____

_____

_____

_____

_____

_____

_____

For Your Student Survival Kit

Review—Where did we go?

Modeling the Learning Process

Again we modeled the learning process in learning about managing stress.

Gathering. You gathered information both about what causes stress and ways to deal with stress.

Analyzing. You analyzed your situation and strategies you learned in previous chapters and tried to determine how to best manage your personal stress.

Creating New Ideas. You predicted some things that might work for you in preventing and relieving stress.

Acting. You made a plan to deal with your stress and put it into practice to see if it worked.

Study Guide: Managing Stress

To see if you grasped the major points of the chapter and to make a useful study guide, answer the following questions found in your reading. When you have written your answers, cover them and see if you can say the answer to each question in your own words.

1. What is stress?

_____

2. What are stressors?

_____

3. Name some common symptoms of stress.

_____

4. Name three things that cause stress in your life.

    1. _____

    2. _____

    3. _____

5. What is your plan of action for dealing with one of your stressors?

_____

6. This chapter presents eight coping strategies to alleviate stress symptoms. Discuss the four that you think will be most useful to you.

    1. _____

    2. _____

    3. _____

    4. _____

7. Name and explain three behavior patterns.

    1. _____

    2. _____

    3. _____

8. Explain what is meant by scripting.

_____

_____

CASE STUDY
What's Your Advice?

Several students are gathered in the hall before class. It is midterm, and everyone is talking about being stressed out. Most of the class, however, is managing to deal with stress.

Cliff is not sure that's possible for him. He never has time to do his classwork. Besides, he thinks most of it is just busy work. His boss is constantly on his back to work more hours, and his parents are always nagging him about money. Cliff's girlfriend complains that he doesn't spend enough time with her. His roommate is a bore, and there is always something broken in their rented house. If he doesn't pass all his classes, Cliff will lose his financial aid. He has frequent headaches and can't seem to concentrate for more than five minutes at a time. He's smoking up to two packs of cigarettes a day and hasn't really slept well in what seems like months.

Obviously, Cliff needs more help than you can give him, but he would really like some suggestions from you of ways that you deal with *your* stress that might work for him.

Parallel Parking

After reviewing this chapter on managing stress, choose two of the following driving situations and explain specifically how managing stress is similar.

Making Sure Your Car Gets Routine Maintenance

_____

_____

_____

_____

_____

Adjusting to the Road Conditions

_____

_____

_____

_____

Making a Rest Stop

_____

_____

_____

_____

_____

Carefully Planning Your Route So You Are Not Late for Something Important

_____

_____

_____

_____

Evaluating Learning Outcomes

How successful were you in making it to your destination in this chapter?
Analyze what you learned in this chapter. Put a check beside each task you are now able to do. On a separate piece of paper, write a couple of sentences about how you learned each learning outcome and how you plan to continue to use what you learned.

- ☐ **Recognize** signs of stress.
- ☐ **Analyze** a stressful situation in your life and determine a plan of action.
- ☐ **Differentiate** between passive, aggressive, and assertive behaviors.
- ☐ **Demonstrate** how to script as practice for assertiveness.
- ☐ **Analyze** a case study and construct advice for a student having difficulty coping with the stress.
- ☐ **Explain** the learning process used in this chapter.

Your Student Tip for This Chapter

Use the space below to write a tip you would give to other students about what you have learned in this chapter.

_____

_____

_____

Information Literacy

Road Map to Success

What Is Information Literacy?

A Systematic Approach to the Research Process

In this chapter, you will learn how to

- **Explain** the elements involved in information literacy.

- **Explain** a systematic approach to research.

- **Practice** a systematic approach to a research topic by identifying and narrowing the topic; finding books, periodicals, newspapers, and Internet sources; then evaluating each source and listing information that should be cited.

- **Discover** resources for career exploration.

- **Explain** the learning process modeled in this chapter.

Where Are We Going?

One of the most important parts of your college journey is getting familiar with things that make your journey easier. A map does you no good if you can't orient yourself with it, and a GPS is useless if you can't program your destination. As a college student in what is often called the "information age," you will find that you sometimes have too much information to deal with. Because there is so much information available to you, it is necessary to develop a way to efficiently sort through it in order to find what is relevant to your research. This chapter will address some things you need in order to be an effective student in the information age. In this chapter you will explore the concept of information literacy. Then you will practice a systematic approach to a research project so that when you are assigned a project in another class you will know where to begin and how to proceed.

What Is Information Literacy?

Being able to manage and organize information is called **information literacy**. The University of Idaho Library website defines *information literacy* as the ability to (1) identify what information is needed, (2) understand how the information is organized, (3) identify the best sources of information for a given need, (4) locate those sources, (5) evaluate the sources critically, and (6) share that information (University of Idaho Library: http://www.lib.uidaho.edu). Databases in your college library provide valuable resources that will help you with this task. Practice in using these databases should build the confidence and skill you will need for assignments that require research.

Each college library is unique. But there are basic resources in all libraries that you will need to use with proficiency, no matter how large or small or technologically up-to-date your library is. If you have not already done so, take time to learn both what resources are available in your library and how to access them. On some campuses, a library orientation is offered. In addition, handouts and printed instructions are often available, or you can ask the librarians to help you. Do not hesitate to ask. You are certainly not the first or only student who has needed help.

When using the library, you will use many different databases. It is important that you have a concept of what a database is. In *100% Information Literacy*, Gwen Wilson defines a database as "a collection of digitized information organized for simplified, fast searching and retrieval."[1] Your library will have many databases that are regularly updated. The database that tells you what books and periodicals your library has is the library catalog. In the library, you will also use databases for finding articles in journals, magazines, and newspapers or databases for finding information about certain subjects such as education, medicine, or career options.

---

[1]Gwen Wilson, *100% Information Literacy Success* (Boston, MA: Cengage Learning, 2015).

A Systematic Approach to the Research Process

The critical-thinking skills you have developed are crucial when searching for specific information that you need amidst all the information that is available. It is important that you have a systematic, well-thought-out way of finding relevant sources. When you have an assignment that requires research, you want to cover all your bases and get results as quickly and efficiently as possible. There are several steps you can follow to ensure a minimum amount of frustration and results of which you can be proud.

Step 1: Identifying and Finding Background Information on Your Topic

The first step in research is to *identify and develop your topic*. The instructor who gives the assignment is the best source of information for determining your topic. Take time to discuss the assignment before you begin. Make sure you understand exactly what the assignment asks you to do and the scope of the research necessary. You have learned that the more you know about a subject, the easier it will be to gather new information about it. An important first step, then, is to make sure you have enough information about the topic before you leap in.

This usually involves finding background information in one or more sources. The most common background sources are *encyclopedias and dictionaries* from the print and online reference collections. *Class textbooks* also provide background information. Students often go straight to Wikipedia for background. While Wikipedia is generally acceptable to use, make sure you remember that Wikipedia is a general encyclopedia whose authors are unpaid and usually anonymous. There is no way of knowing the author's level of expertise. You should never cite Wikipedia as a source; however, it often provides an overview, a place to start, and perhaps some references.

To make sure that you understand your topic and that you know specifically what you are looking for, it is a good idea to put it in the form of a question. Remember, your brain learns best when you are looking for the answer to a question. For example, if your topic is global warming, you need to determine what it is you need to know about global warming. Some good starting questions may include the following: What causes global warming? What are the impacts of global warming? What solutions are there for global warming? What are some issues involving global warming? You may use what you learned about mapping to brainstorm or draw a clear picture of possible ways to narrow your topic. Choose one of your questions to narrow your topic and the scope of your search.

BRAIN BYTE

The website NoodleTools suggests that instead of limiting your search to one search engine such as Google, various other search engines search in alternate ways and may be more efficient in helping you refine your search by defining your topic, finding quality results, doing research in a specific discipline, finding timely information, or finding opinions and perspectives. It may be worth examining other search engines instead of sticking with what you are comfortable with. http://www.noodletools.com/debbie/literacies/information/5locate/adviceengine.html.

Step 2: Using the Library Catalog to Find Books

There are several types of sources of information in any library. The one we usually think of first is *books*. Depending on its size, your library may have anywhere from several hundred thousand to several million books.

The system used to organize and classify books may also vary. Your library will use either the Library of Congress Classification System or the Dewey Decimal System. Books are usually shelved in stacks in the main collection, the reference section, or special collections.

To find the location and call number for a book, you will use your library catalog. You may find that there are too many books about your topic to use them all. Frequently review the question you developed about your topic to help you analyze the relevance of each source.

When you use a book for research, you want to check the date it was written and the credentials of the author. For example: Is it important that the information in the book be up to date? What is the author's background? What makes him or her an expert on the subject? Also remember that when you use a book in your research, you will need to document it. Be sure to write down the entire title, the author's name, and the date and place of publication, as well as the publisher's name. Note what pages you use as well. Doing so will save you valuable time when you document your research. Some professors suggest making a note card for each source you consider. You will also find that your library catalog lists e-books. An e-book is a digitalized version of a book that you can download onto your computer or other portable electronic reading device. E-books almost always contain the same information as the print book.

Step 3: Using Indexes and Databases to Find Periodical Articles

Periodicals are continuous publications, such as journals, magazines, or newspapers, so called because they come out periodically (weekly, monthly, annually). The advantages of using periodicals over books are that they may be more up to date and more manageable in size. There are three broad types of periodicals. First, *academic* or *scholarly journals* generally have a somewhat academic appearance. Cornell reference librarian Michael Engle says that someone who has done research in the field or is an authority on the subject writes the articles for these journals. The writers in academic journals use discipline-specific language and assume that the reader has the background to understand it. "The main purpose of an academic journal," Engle says, "is to report on original research or experimentation in order to make such information available to the rest of the scholarly world." Writers in academic journals authenticate their work by *always* citing their sources in the form of footnotes or bibliographies.[2]

The second type, *substantive news* or *general interest periodicals,* may have a magazine or newspaper format. Engle describes the content of these as having articles that are "often heavily illustrated, generally with photographs." News and general-interest periodicals sometimes cite sources, though more often they do not. A member of the editorial staff, a scholar, or a freelance writer may write these articles. The language of such publications is geared to any educated audience. There is

[2]See http://www.library.cornell.edu/olinuris/ref/research/skill20.html.

no specialty assumed, only interest and a certain level of intelligence. Commercial enterprises or individuals generally publish them, although some may be published by specific professional organizations. The main purpose of periodicals in this category is to provide information, in a general manner, to a broad audience of concerned citizens.[3]

The third type, *popular periodicals*, comes in many formats, although most often they are somewhat slick and attractive in appearance and contain lots of graphics (photographs, drawings, etc.). Engle says:

> These publications rarely, if ever, cite sources. Information published in such journals is often second or third hand and the original source is sometimes obscure. Articles are usually very short, written in simple language and are designed to meet a minimal education level. There is generally little depth to the content of these articles. The main purpose of popular periodicals is to entertain the reader, to sell products (their own or their advertisers), and/or to promote a viewpoint.[4]

The index or database you choose may vary, depending on the type of periodical article you are looking for. Most college libraries subscribe to an aggregated service that can simultaneously search multiple databases. Examples you may see as you are searching are EBSCO*host*, ProQuest, and Gale.[5] Your library probably subscribes to literally hundreds of databases (such as Academic Search Premier or General OneFile) and thousands of periodicals. Many of the databases found in your college databases will give full text of the article. However, keep in mind the materials in full-text databases usually begin no earlier that the 1980s. Most libraries will have copies going back to the early publication of the periodicals, either physically bound or on microfilm. If you want a historical view of an event, don't forget to research periodicals from the era in question.

Step 4: Finding Internet Resources

The Internet is, of course, a virtual reference desk. You should be able to find up-to-date information on almost any subject. Unless you know the URL of a specific site, you will use a search engine to locate sites that are related to your subjects. You may already be familiar with some search engines, such as Google, Bing, Ask, Yahoo!, or INFOMINE. New search engines appear almost daily. In a recent random check, I located more than 15,000 search engines.

A **search engine** is a type of software that creates indexes of databases or Internet sites on the basis of the titles of files, keywords, or the full text of files. The search engine has an interface that allows you to type what you're looking for into a blank field. It then gives you a list of the results of the search. When you use a search engine on the Web, the

---

[3]See http://www.library.cornell.edu/olinuris/ref/research/skill20.html.
[4]Ibid.
[5]Wilson, *100% Information Literacy Success.*

results are presented to you in hypertext; this means you can click on any item in the list to get the file. Some sites allow you to use more than one search engine at a time. After using various search engines, you will find one or two that you prefer. Although the results will be similar, each search engine will probably identify some hits that are different. If your library subscribes to Google Scholar, you may want to try it. Google Scholar provides a search of scholarly literature across many disciplines and sources, including theses, books, abstracts, and articles.

A very important fact to remember is that a search engine cannot read your mind or identify specific information you need. The search engine simply tries to locate sites that contain your search word, and these sites may or may not be relevant. The search engine Google came up with 68,400,000 hits to my search for *time management*. The engine located anything with the word *time* or *management*. Critical thinking is extremely important in both performing and limiting a search and when evaluating the usefulness of a site on the Internet. It's tempting to just get on the Web and surf. But you can waste a great deal of time if you don't know what you are doing. Before you use any search engine, click on the *search tips* or *help* link for the engine you have chosen. Even if you have frequently used the Internet for research, you will find time-savers and ways to minimize the number of hits you get that are not relevant to your search.

As you search for resources to use, you should keep in mind the value and appropriateness a source adds to your search. The databases you use in the library for books, journals, and other resources have been reviewed, evaluated, and selected by scholars, but what about the sites on the Internet? The fact is that anyone can put virtually anything on the Internet. It doesn't have to be truthful, reliable, or accurate.

It is important, then, that you determine, among other things, where the information came from and the accuracy or bias of the information. Just as the type of information you get from a popular magazine and an academic journal will differ, the type of information you get from Internet sites will also differ. The domain name often gives such clues to the validity of the information on a site. The **domain** is the three-letter code following the "dot." It will tell you the type of organization that sponsors the site. Below is a list of the most commonly used domain names. You want to look for domains that are appropriate for your topic.

DOMAIN NAME	TYPE OF ORGANIZATION
.edu	**U.S. college or university**
	Information here will come from faculty or students at an educational institution. Check the authority of the source.
.com	**Commercial enterprise**
	Companies advertise, sell products, and publish annual reports and other company information on the Web. Many online newspapers or journals also have .com names.
.gov	**Government**
	Federal and state government agencies use the Web to publish legislation, census information, weather data, tax forms, and many other documents.

.org	Nonprofit organizations
	Nonprofit organizations use the Web to promote their causes. These pages may be useful when comparing different sides of an issue.
.net	Internet service providers
	General-purpose domain often used as an alternative to .com
.mil	U.S. military
	U.S. Department of Defense and its subsidiary or affiliated organizations

For most of your research projects, you will use primary resources in the form of books, periodicals, newspapers, and the Internet. It is always a good idea to consult with the professor who assigned the topic or project for suggestions about types of sources he or she wants included and for what bibliographical format to use. Again, be sure to write down all information you will need to document your sources.

Step 5: Evaluating Your Sources

Evaluating the reliability and appropriateness of information and sources is crucial. The questions you ask about books, periodicals, and webpages will be similar. Because so much information is readily available, an important part of information literacy and of research is to make sure the information you find is reliable and appropriate for your topic or argument. Evaluating a source involves a great deal of detective work. Preliminary investigation will save you time by eliminating sources you don't want to use before you waste too much time with them.

Remember this acronym when investigating sources: AAOCC. It stands for accuracy, authority, objectivity, currency, and coverage.

Is the information **accurate**? What clues can you use to tell? Check the author. What are his or her credentials? Is the author an **authority**? Is the information **objective**? Why is the author writing the book or article? What is the domain of a website? Is it fact, opinion, or propaganda? Is it trying to sell you something? Does it appear to be well researched? The next thing to investigate is the **currency**. When was the information published? Do you need the most up-to-date information for the topic you are researching? Is this the most recent edition? An additional thing to investigate is **coverage**. Does it cover the information you need in enough depth to substantiate your research? Later in the chapter, you will be asked to take a virtual field trip to discover more about evaluating sources.

Step 6: Citing Your Sources

It is important that you give proper credit to the source of information. Instructors will usually indicate whether to format the citations using examples from the Modern Language Association (MLA), the American Psychological Association (APA), or the *Chicago Manual of Style* (CMS).

Virtual Field Trip
Evaluating Sites

Follow the format chosen exactly as shown. It is extremely important to record the information you need as you are researching. If you don't write down your source then, you may never find it again when you need it.

PRACTICE 11.1

Choosing and Narrowing a Topic

Examine the following topics and decide which one you would like to research further. You will use this topic in several practice exercises, so choose one you are interested in. Circle the topic.

Distracted Driving	Autism	Natural Disasters
Obesity	Road Rage	Career Options

Identifying and Finding Background Information

Now consider how you can gather some background information about your topic and ways you might narrow your topic. Use an encyclopedia, Internet search, or Wikipedia to find some possible ways to narrow your topic. If you are using the Internet or a library catalog, you can click on Advanced Search to see suggestions about how to narrow your broad topic.

Two Ways You Might Narrow Your Topic

In order to narrow your topic more, write two questions that your research will answer.

1. _____

2. _____

PRACTICE 11.2

Finding Books About Your Topic

Keeping the same topic you chose in Practice 11.1, use your library search engine to find two books about your topic. Once you've found those two books, fill in the following information.

Book 1

Title: _____

Author/Editor: _____

Place of Publication: _____

Date of Publication: _____

Call number: _____

Book 2

Title: _____

Author/Editor: _____

Place of Publication: _____

Date of Publication: _____

Call number: _____

Finding Periodicals

Deciding which index or database to use may depend on the type or date of the periodical you need. Before databases were computerized, researchers used indexes such as the *Readers' Guide to Periodical Literature* to find periodical articles on their subject. The *Readers' Guide* indexes 300 popular magazines in yearly volumes. Other print-version indexes, such as the *Education Index, Humanities Index,* and *Social Sciences Index,* are more subject-specific.

With print versions of periodical databases, you must physically find the periodical in the bound periodical section of the library or on microtext. However, most libraries have an electronic database such as InfoTrac, EBSCO*host,* and ProQuest Direct (all of which are expanded academic indexes such as General OneFile or EBSCO's Academic Search Premier), and many of these databases will have the full text of the article online. Because most electronic databases begin around 1980, you may need to use *Readers' Guide* or other print-version indexes if you are searching for articles before 1980. Or your library may have *Readers' Guide Retrospective,* an electronic version that covers the years 1890 to 1982.

Locate the *Readers' Guide* in your library. Describe where it is and what it looks like.

_____

_____

_____

_____

_____

You will find that the periodical resources available to you in computerized databases are expansive. For example, the *Readers' Guide* indexes 300 popular periodicals; General OneFile, Thomson Gale's electronic resource for access to periodical and news content, includes over 5,000 full-text titles (more than 9,200 titles in all). It contains full indexing of some of the world's greatest newspapers and 89 wire services covering worldwide current events. When you use the *Readers' Guide,* you must look separately at each yearly volume and then locate a hard copy of the periodical. When you use an electronic database, you direct the search to cover the years you want to research. General OneFile's integrated back-file coverage is from 1980 to the present. It is important to remember, then, if you need periodical resources before 1980, you will need to use *Readers' Guide* or *Readers' Guide Retrospective.* Remember that when you read the full text of an article online, you still need to cite the source of the original article. I cannot emphasize enough that writing down that information when you first access it will save you time and grief later.

PRACTICE 11.3

Finding Articles in Periodicals

Use your library database to find two articles in academic journals about the topic you used in Practice 11.1 and Practice 11.2. Fill in the following information about the article you find.

Article 1

Title: _____

Author: _____

Source of Article: _____

　　　Name: _____

　　　Date: _____

　　　Volume/Issue: _____

　　　Page Numbers: _____

Article 2

Title: _____

Author: _____

Source of Article: _____

　　　Name: _____

　　　Date: _____

　　　Volume/Issue: _____

　　　Page Numbers: _____

Finding Articles in Newspapers

An additional source of information you may need to use in your research is newspapers or news periodicals. Most libraries subscribe to several major newspapers and have back copies on microfilm. Your library will probably have several electronic newspaper databases online. National Newspaper Index, ProQuest Newspapers, and LexisNexis are a few.

LexisNexis covers general news and information and legal, business, and medical resources. It gives mostly full-text access to newspapers and magazine articles, state and federal law, company financial information, industry news, and more; it's a good place to start your search for news articles. I like it because full text is given for most articles. If you don't find full text online, you will have to read the article on microtext. Note that your library may have historical newspaper databases that may be useful as well. For example, you might read the actual newspaper account of the assassination of Abraham Lincoln.

PRACTICE 11.4

Practice Using Newspaper Sources

Keep your same narrowed topic you chose in the previous practice exercises and using LexisNexis as your search engine, find two newspaper articles. Find LexisNexis in your library's databases. Limit your search within LexisNexis to News or Newspapers and Wires. Type in your narrowed topic and search. If you get too many hits, you can further narrow your search by using a date or time-range. For example, put in only the previous six months. List two new articles you found.

News Item 1

Headline: _____

Name of Newspaper: _____

Date: _____

Pages/Words: _____

Author (if given): _____

Summary of article: _____

_____

_____

_____

News Item 2

Headline: _____

Name of Newspaper: _____

Date: _____

Pages/Words: _____

Author (if given): _____

Summary of article: _____

_____

_____

_____

PRACTICE 11.5

Finding Internet Articles

As practice using the Internet as a resource, use the same topic you used for the previous practice exercises. Find two websites that will give you information about the topic. For this exercise, limit your sources to URLs that end in .edu, .org, or .gov. Or use *Google Scholar* as your search engine.

Continued

Practice 11.5 continued

Internet Article 1

Search engine used: _____

What did you type to search? _____

URL of website chosen: _____

Describe what information you found and how it was presented: _____

List who is responsible for the material on this site: _____

List the date the information was posted if you can determine it: _____

Internet Article 2

Search engine used: _____

What did you type to search? _____

URL of website chosen: _____

Describe what information you found and how it was presented: _____

List who is responsible for the material on this site: _____

List the date the information was posted if you can determine it: _____

Virtual Field Trip
Careers

CAREER Connections

Your library offers many free resources for exploring your career options. Using your library catalog, begin by searching for books your library has about career exploration.

List four sources that you think will help you in your exploration of career possibilities.

_____

_____

_____

_____

PRACTICE 11.6

Practicing What You Have Learned

Using **learning styles** as your topic, search databases available to you and find information about that topic.

How many books did you find in your database search? _____

Title of one book: _____

Author/Editor of above book: _____

Call number of above book: _____

On what floor in the library will it be found? _____

Is it on the shelf? _____

Periodical Article (*Note:* Do **not** use *New York Times* articles here; the *New York Times* is a newspaper, not a periodical)

Name of one article: _____

Author: _____

Name and date of periodical: _____

Is full text given? _____

Is abstract given? _____

Newspaper Article

Headline of article: _____

Name of newspaper: _____

Date of newspaper: _____

Can you read the article from your computer? _____

Internet Article

Search engine: _____

URL for article: _____

Three facts about your topic found on this site: _____

_____

_____

Virtual Field Trip
Citing Sources

Review—Where did we go?

Modeling the Learning Process

Let's review how you modeled the learning process in this chapter.

Gathering. You learned the steps of the research process.
Analyzing. You analyzed what databases to use.
Creating New Ideas. You projected a limit for your topic and projected which databases to use.
Acting. You planned the parts of a research project. Some of you actually wrote a research paper.

Study Guide: Information Literacy

To see if you grasped the major points of the chapter and to make a useful study guide, answer the following questions found in your reading. When you have written your answers, cover them and see if you can say the answer to each question in your own words.

1. **Name the six elements of information literacy.**

    1. _____

    2. _____

    3. _____

    4. _____

    5. _____

    6. _____

2. **What is a database?**

    _____

3. **Name six steps used to systematically approach a research project.**

    1. _____

    2. _____

    3. _____

    4. _____

    5. _____

    6. _____

4. **What are good sources to use to gather background for your topic?**

    _____

    _____

5. **What system of classification for books does your library use?**

    _____

6. **What advantages may periodicals have over books?**

    _____

    _____

    _____

7. **What are three types of periodicals?**

    1. _____

    2. _____

    3. _____

8. **Give an example of a web browser.**

    _____

9. Define *search engine* and give an example of one.

_____

10. List some frequently used domains.

_____

_____

11. What are some elements you should consider when evaluating sources?

A _____

A _____

O _____

C _____

C _____

12. Name two possible formats for citing sources.

_____

_____

_____

13. Explain how to search for books in your library.

_____

14. Explain how to search for periodicals.

_____

15. Name a database you can use to find articles from newspapers.

_____

16. Choose one search engine and explain how to use it to perform a subject search on the Internet.

_____

_____

_____

CASE STUDY
What's Your Advice?

Nathan is beginning college after working in sales for ten years and enjoying the challenge. In his English class, Nathan has been assigned a research paper. The paper must have at least eight sources, including a minimum of two books, two periodical articles, one newspaper article, and one authoritative Internet source. From his instructor's suggested topics, Nathan has chosen a subject that interests him. However, when he goes to the library, panic sets in. Nathan has not been in a library in ten years and has no idea where to begin.

You find a worried Nathan in the front of the library. Please make Nathan a list of which databases are available in your library for books, periodicals, and newspapers and give him suggestions for using them efficiently. You will also need to suggest a search engine or two he might use to find an Internet article and explain to Nathan how to tell if it's "authoritative."

Parallel Parking

Complete the following driving occurrences with parallels from researching a topic:

Writing Down Directions

_____

Taking an Alternate Route

_____

Programming Your GPS

_____

Stopping for Fuel and Food

_____

Evaluating Learning Outcomes

How successful were you in making it to your destination in this chapter?
Analyze what you learned in this chapter. Put a check beside each task you are now able to do. On a separate piece of paper, write a couple of sentences about how you learned each learning outcome and how you plan to continue to use what you learned.

☐ **Explain** the elements involved in information literacy.
☐ **Explain** a systematic approach to research.
☐ **Practice** a systematic approach to a research topic by identifying and narrowing the topic; finding books, periodicals, newspapers, and Internet sources; then evaluating each source and listing information that should be cited.
☐ **Discover** resources for career exploration.
☐ **Explain** the learning process modeled in this chapter.

Your Student Tip for This Chapter

Use the space below to write a tip you would give other students about what you have learned in this chapter.

_____

_____

_____

_____

APPENDIX **A**

Principles of Studying Math

Your Road to Becoming a Better Math Student

It may be that you are actually better at math than you think. I find that when many students say they are not good at math, it's not because they have no math skills; rather, it's that they have poor study skills when it comes to math, which can be easily remedied with a little effort. If you get lost while driving to a specific destination, it may be that you lost concentration or that your trip preparation was not done carefully in your hurry to get there. Even if the directions were complicated, there were probably things you could have done to avoid confusion in the first place. The same is true of getting to your math destination. The principles of learning we utilized in this textbook are applicable to any subject, but they may need to be adjusted a bit for math. You may need to slow down, drive more carefully, and watch out for speed bumps.

Let's begin by evaluating your math study skills.

Math Study Skills: Diagnostic Inventory

Thoughtfully rate your behavior in regard to the following as **3** for **almost always**, **2** for **sometimes**, **1** for **almost never**, and **0** if you have **never even thought about doing** what the statement says.

Selecting a Math Class

_____ **1.** I schedule my math class at a time when I am mentally sharp.

_____ **2.** When I register for a math class, I choose the best instructor for me.

_____ 3. If I have a choice, I select a math class that meets three or four days a week instead of one or two days.

_____ 4. I schedule my next math class as soon as possible after I have completed my current course.

_____ 5. I make sure that I have signed up for the correct level math course.

During Math Class

_____ 6. I come to class on time and even try to be early.

_____ 7. I sit as close to front and center of the room as possible.

_____ 8. Before class starts, I review my notes.

_____ 9. I never miss class.

_____ 10. If I must miss class, I get clear, accurate notes and homework assignments and try to work on the assignment before the next class.

_____ 11. I make a conscious effort to focus each class period.

_____ 12. My goal for each class is to learn as much as possible.

_____ 13. I try to find a way to connect new concepts to what I already know.

_____ 14. I take good notes in class.

_____ 15. I have a method for taking good notes.

_____ 16. I ask questions when I don't understand.

_____ 17. If I get lost, I identify where I got lost.

_____ 18. I attend additional classes if I need to go through it again.

Time and Place for Studying Math

_____ 19. I study math every day.

_____ 20. I try to do my math homework immediately after math class.

_____ 21. I have a specific time to study math.

_____ 22. I have a specific place with few distractions to study math.

_____ 23. I do my math homework in the lab where I can get help.

_____ 24. I am careful to keep up to date with my math homework.

_____ **25.** I study math at least 8 to 10 hours a week.

_____ **26.** I study in short sessions of 45–50 minutes.

Study Strategies for Math Class

_____ **27.** I read my math textbook before I come to class.

_____ **28.** If I have trouble understanding the textbook, I find an alternative text.

_____ **29.** I take notes in math class.

_____ **30.** I am careful to copy all the steps of math problems in my notes.

_____ **31.** I ask questions when I am confused.

_____ **32.** I go to the instructor or lab when I am confused.

_____ **33.** I try to determine exactly when I got confused and exactly what confused me.

_____ **34.** I review my notes and text before beginning homework.

_____ **35.** I work problems until I understand them, not just until I get the right answer for homework.

_____ **36.** I use flash cards for formulas and vocabulary.

_____ **37.** I develop memory techniques to remember math concepts.

Math Tests

_____ **38.** I preview the test before I begin.

_____ **39.** Before I begin taking the test, I make notes on the test of things such as formulas that I might need or forget.

_____ **40.** I begin with the easy questions first.

_____ **41.** I take the full amount of time allotted for the test.

_____ **42.** I carefully check or rework as many problems as possible before I turn in my test.

_____ **43.** When tests are returned, I correct my errors, and I keep a log of the types of mistakes I made—concept errors, application errors, or careless errors.

_____ **44.** I keep up to date so that I don't have to cram the night before a test.

Anxiety

_____ **45.** I believe that I can succeed in math class.

_____ **46.** I have study partners in my math class.

_____ **47.** I find out as much as possible about each test.

_____ **48.** I take practice tests.

_____ **49.** I know several good relaxation breathing techniques.

_____ **50.** I am comfortable asking for help.

_____ Total score

Scoring

Now that you have evaluated each item from 0 to 3, total your score for all 50 items. Use that total to determine your strengths and things you need to work on.

If your score is 135–150, give yourself an **A**. You are using the study skills you need in order to be successful in math.

If your score is 120–134, give yourself a **B**. You are using good math study skills. Note items with low scores. Choose a few strategies to work on each day, and you will be well on your way to an A. Make a list and set a time frame for incorporating these strategies into your routine study of math.

If your score is 100–119, give yourself a **C**. Your study skills are average. If you want an A, choose one or two strategies in each category to work on until you are using most of the strategies described in the inventory. Make a list of those items you scored low on and write a goal or plan of action to apply toward those strategies. Remember, a goal should be specific, measurable, realistic, and challenging, and have a specific completion date.

If your score is below 100, you are probably having a difficult time in math class. Math may not be your trouble! More than likely, your main problem is the study strategies you are using (or not using). _Make_ yourself do as many of the things listed as you can.

Review this inventory often. It becomes your checklist for improving your math study skills. Highlight those you need to work on first. Now write a goal for raising your score. Remember, a goal should be specific, measurable, realistic, and challenging, and have a specific completion date. Set a specific time to begin each one. The items on the list have nothing to do with how smart you are in math and everything to do with decisions you make about how you will approach math.

Four Reasons Why Math Is Different from Other Subjects

1. Math requires different study processes. In other courses, you learn and understand the material, but you seldom have to *apply* it. You have to apply the material when you do math problems.

2. Math is a linear learning process. What is learned one day is used the next, and so forth. (In history, perhaps you can learn Chapter 2 and not Chapter 3 but still be able to understand Chapter 4. In math, you must understand the material in Chapter 3 before you can go on to Chapter 4.)

3. Math is much like a foreign language. It must be practiced *every day*, and often the *vocabulary* is unfamiliar. Make a list or flash cards of terms you need to remember. Just as the direction words in the test-taking chapter seem to be simple, understanding what each requires makes a difference. Likewise, knowing what each term in math requires you to do could make a real difference in improving your math performance.

4. Math in college is different from math in high school. Instead of going to class every day, in college you go only two or three times a week. What took a year to learn in high school is now covered in only 15 weeks or less. This basically means that the responsibility lies with you to put in as much time as necessary to understand and reinforce what goes on in each class meeting. And it also means that missing class could spell disaster. If you must miss a math class, make every effort to catch up before the next class period.

Applying the Learning Strategies to Math

Your approach should not be just getting through your math course; you should also model the learning process you used and become fully engaged in learning. Let's review some things you've learned and apply them to math.

Time Management

Math is simply going to take more time than you really want to spend on it. Use these strategies to make the most of your time spent on math.

- Set a specific time to study math every day. Use distributed practice. Several shorter sessions are more helpful than a long, tiring, or frustrating one. One session should probably not exceed 45–60 minutes.

- If there is a math lab or math tutoring center, take your homework there as soon as possible after class, before you have a chance to forget. Use an index card and write the location and hours your math lab is open. Use the card to record when you attended and the names of tutors you like after you study with them.
- Even if you have completed the assigned work, work a sample problem each day to see if you still understand how to do it.
- Reread the textbook section. It may not have made sense the first time because you really didn't understand that type of problem. After covering it in class, you have some background to build on.
- Teach a new concept to your study partner.
- If you need help, get it immediately.

Critical Thinking

In the critical-thinking chapter, you learned the steps in the decision-making process. Solving a math problem is not really much different. One reason for learning about math is to develop better problem-solving skills to use in all aspects of life. Many math problems require multiple steps and a systematic approach. Follow these steps.

- Read the full question.
- Analyze and compute.
- Determine what is **given**, what you need to **find**, and what you need to **do** in each question or problem. (It would be nice to have a math GPS to guide you through it, but with critical thinking, you can solve the problem.)
- Draw pictures; they can simplify the problem.
- Use a calculator; do the calculations twice.
- Check your results; do the problem again another way or use methods you've learned to check answers. Make sure that your answer makes sense and that you've used the same terms or units in your answer.

Goal Setting

It is important that you set goals for not just your math class in general, but also that you have a goal for each math class and homework assignment. Review the elements for a SMART goal and apply these elements to math.

Specific	Describe what you want to accomplish with as much detail as possible.
Measurable	Describe your goal in terms that can be evaluated clearly.
Action Plan	Your goal should explain what action you will take.
Realistic	You know you are capable of doing or achieving this goal.
Time Framed	Clearly specify target-completion time—break longer goals into shorter pieces.

Learning Principles and Math

Let's quickly review the learning principles and apply them to math. Here are some basic ideas. Once you get the basics, you can think of other ways to use each principle.

The first group involves **Starting the Connections**.

- Remember, the principle of **interest** says if you are not interested, you won't remember. It may be that you have not always been successful at math and so the learning principle of interest is difficult for you. What do you need to do to get interested in math? It may be as simple as finding a study group or study partner or asking the instructor what real-life situations use this kind of problem. You might compare the steps of a problem to some activity you already know. Chances are that you will use some type of math on your job in the future.

- Second, both in class and when studying, you need to apply the principle of **intent to remember**. What adjustments can you make in your attitude to make sure you really "get it" in class? You might meet with your study partners before class to review and determine questions you may need to ask. Come to class early. Get your material and notes ready. Take notes. Pay attention. Ask questions.

- The third principle will affect just how much effort you must make in order to learn new concepts. Math is linear and your **basic background** is crucial. If you are lost, try to remember the last time you understood and go back and begin there. Your instructor or tutor can help you.

The second group of learning principles deals with **Controlling the Amount and Form of New Information**.

- **Select** the main ideas first. What facts are important and necessary for solving the problem?
- Then **organize** the steps of a new process. Color-code them, draw a flowchart, or make a mnemonic. Make sure the sequence is correct. Always show your work so you can follow the process.

The third group of learning principles is used to **Strengthen the Neural Connections** you have already made.

- Do you self-test by **reciting** the formulas or steps to solving a problem? Try saying the steps out loud as you work a problem.
- Can you **visualize** what you are doing, using real objects? Many times it may be necessary to draw the problem to see if your answer makes sense.

Make an effort to **associate** each new type of problem with something you already know. Determine how it differs from the previous type of problem. Are the steps similar to baking a cake, running a play on the football field or basketball court, or finding a lost object?

The last group of principles is used to **Solidify the Connections** you have made in your brain.

- Your brain must have time for new information to **consolidate**. This requires repetition, reinforcing the concepts in as many different ways as possible. But the key word here is *time*. When you learn a new type of problem in math class, keep a chart of how much time you spend getting that concept secure in your brain. Also note how many different ways you used to reinforce it.

- Quickly doing homework just to get it done won't establish the network you need to build. This brings us back to **distributed practice**. You should work in short sessions **every day** to make sure you understand. The sessions don't have to be the same. You could work the problems on your assignment during one session. Reread the textbook explanation and work a sample problem the next. Compare your class notes with a study partner's the next. Try to teach it to someone the next.

Taking Notes and Reading Math Textbooks

The next strategies you learned used the **Question in the Margin System** to **take notes** in class and to **read** textbooks. You have learned the necessity for taking notes in class. Short-term memory won't hold what you need, even if you understood everything that went on in class. The concepts covered in math class are usually linear (one step builds on another) and complex, so it is especially important to take notes. Use the strategies below for math.

- Your first step is to prepare before you come to class. The more you know, the easier it is to take notes. See if you can make up a problem that parallels the ones you worked in your assignment.
- Review your notes and homework immediately before class. Right before you go to math class, meet a study partner and teach each other the concepts from the previous class.
- Read textbook assignments so you have something to build on. Make note of whether the explanation given in the textbook is different from the one the instructor uses and underline the similarities. Mark rules and procedures and make notes of mistakes that the instructor indicates students often make—having the wrong sign or solving in the wrong order, for example.
- Find the style of note taking that works best for you. I suggest that instead of the two-column system we used in the Question in the Margin System, you may want to modify it to three columns. Keep one column for questions and labels, use the second column for examples, and the third one for explanations. Don't just write down what is on the board; listen carefully for directions—the whys and hows. Use the same text message shorthand to record what you need in order to understand the process. Below is an illustration similar to the three-column note page suggested by Paul Nolting in *Math Study Skill Workbook*.

QUESTIONS/RULE/TERMS	WORK THE PROBLEMS HERE	EXPLANATION OF STEPS AND NOTES FOR WHAT TO CHECK FOR

- Listen actively in class! If you get lost, ask questions. Don't forget to record the answer! Note where you are confused and leave a space to complete later. It is important in math class to review and label your notes as soon as possible after class.
- Compare notes with fellow students. Use the recite and reflect steps of the system and review often. Make summary sheets, maps, and flash cards of each new concept. Time-consuming? Yes, building those connections takes time, especially in math.

Reading a math book is very different from reading a history assignment. Many math students try to depend on the instructor's explanation in class and skip reading the textbook. You will be surprised how much more you understand in class when you read your text before class. Follow the steps below when reading a math textbook.

- You still need to survey and try to determine the main idea before you begin to read. Writers of math books usually are brief and to the point. Make sure you understand each sentence before you go on.
- Pay close attention to diagrams, charts, and problems.
- If you didn't understand, go over it again.
- After class, read the textbook assignment again and use it to clarify or make additions to your notes. As you discovered throughout this text, most learning takes place outside the classroom. You begin the gathering by reading and taking notes in class, but then it is up to you to analyze what you gathered, create situations for using the information, and act by making and working problems.
- Meet with the instructor often. Show her or him your notes. Let her or him help you identify what you did wrong. It is especially important that you state the purpose of the office visit. Not just: "Help, I don't get this stuff," but: "I understand that I must change the numbers to like terms, but I am having trouble understanding how to do it."

Test-Taking Strategies

Use the below strategies when faced with a math test:

- Just as you would in any other test, preview a math test before you begin.
- Write down any formulas or steps you think you might forget.
- Read directions carefully.
- Work the problems you are sure of first.
- Budget your time; if you get stuck, go to another question and come back.
- Show all your work. This helps both you and the instructor see the process.
- When you finish a problem, analyze your answer. Does it make sense? If you finish early, actually rework each problem.
- When your test is returned, make sure you understand why you missed an answer. Did you read the directions wrong? Was it a careless error? Did you really not understand the concept? Did you study the right things?

- If you are consistent in the type of error you make, be sure that before you turn in the next test, you look for that type of error.

Virtual Field Trip Improving Your Math Skills

For additional tips to help in solving all types of math problems and websites to help in dealing with math anxiety, you will want to take the Virtual Field Trip to improve your math skills. Visit the College Success CourseMate.

Managing Stress

Math anxiety is real. But just as you learned to manage other stressors in your life, you can learn to manage the stress caused by math class. Repeated lack of success is the cause of most math anxiety. Let's go back to the beginning of this section to the math study skills inventory and seek the cause of your anxiety.

- Is your lack of time and effort in studying math one of the main factors in your anxiety? As the inventory indicates, improving your approach to studying math can control much of math anxiety.
- You must take positive steps to reduce your anxiety.
- You should learn and practice relaxation skills.
- You should immediately find a study partner or join a study group.
- You should attend all classes and do all homework as assigned and seek extra help when necessary.
- This will probably include seeing the instructor during office hours or scheduling an appointment for assistance.
- You should give math at least the same effort you give to other subjects.
- As a competent adult, you have the responsibility to approach math with an open mind rather than fighting it.

Bibliography

Do you want to know more about how the brain learns?

Brain-Compatible Strategies for Memory and Learning

Arden, John B. *Rewire Your Brain*. Hoboken, NJ: John Wiley & Sons, 2010.

Chudler, Eric. "A Computer in Your Head." *Odyssey*. March 2001.

Ford, Martin. *Motivating Humans*. Newbury Park, CA: Sage Publications, 1992.

Hart, Leslie. *Human Brain and Human Learning*. White Plains, NY: Longman, 1983.

Hillman, Ralph. *Delivering Dynamic Presentations: Using Your Voice and Body for Impact*. Boston: Allyn and Bacon, 1999.

Horstman, Judith. *The Scientific American Day in the Life of Your Brain*. San Francisco: Jossey Bass, 2009.

Howard, Pierce. *The Owner's Manual for the Brain: Everyday Applications from Mind–Brain Research*, 2nd ed. Austin: Bard Press, 2000.

Jensen, Eric. *Brain-Based Learning*. San Diego: The Brain Store, 1995.

Jensen, Eric. *Completing the Puzzle: The Brain-compatible Approach to Learning*. San Diego: The Brain Store, 1997.

Jensen, Eric. *The Learning Brain*. San Diego: The Brain Store, 1995.

Jensen, Eric. *Super Teaching*, 3rd ed. San Diego: The Brain Store, 1998.

Jossey-Bass. *Reader on the Brain and Learning*. San Francisco: Wiley, 2008.

Locke, E. A., and Gary Latham. "Work Motivation and Satisfaction: Light at the End of the Tunnel." *Psychological Science 1* (1990): 240–246.

Markowitz, Karen, and Eric Jensen. *The Great Memory Book*. San Diego: The Brain Store, 1999.

Medina, John. *Brain Rules*. Seattle: Pear Press, 2008.

National Research Council. *How People Learn: Brain, Mind, Experience and School*. Washington, DC: National Academy Press, 1999.

O'Keefe, J., and L. Nadel. *The Hippocampus as a Cognitive Map*. Oxford, UK: Clarendon Press, 1987.

Pink, Daniel H. *A Whole New Mind: Why Right-brainers Will Rule the Future*. New York: Penguin Group, 2005.

Ratey, John. *A User's Guide to the Brain: Perception, Attention, and the Four Theaters of the Brain*. New York: Vintage, 2002; Corwin, 2003.

Smith, Allistair. *The Brain's Behind It*. Norwalk, CT: Crown House Publishing, 2005.

Tate, Marcia L. *Worksheets Don't Grow Dendrites*. Thousand Oaks, CA: Corwin, 2010.

Willis, Judy. "How to Teach Students about the Brain." *Educational Leadership*, 67(4), 2009.

Willis, Judy. *Research-based Strategies to Ignite Student Learning: Insights from a Neurologist and Classroom Teacher*. Alexandria, VA: Association for Supervisions and Curriculum Development, 2006.

Wurtman, Judith. *Managing Your Mind and Mood through Food*. New York: HarperCollins, 1986.

Zull, James. *The Art of Changing the Brain: Enriching Teaching by Exploring the Biology of Learning*. Sterling, VA: Stylus, 2002.

Index

Note: The locators followed by *n* denote note numbers cited in the text.

AAOCC, 261
Absence policy, 9
Absolute qualifiers, 214
Academic advisor, 4, 6, 8
Academic calendar, 5
Academic journals, in research, 258
Academic pressure, 241
Academic Search Premier (database), 259
Accuracy, of research information, 261
Acetylcholine, 95
Acronym, 99
Acrostic, 99
Acting
   Bloom's taxonomy and, 61
   information processing and, 12
   testing knowledge, 126
Action plan, 77–78
Action potential, 90
Active memory, 109
Add a course, 5
Adrenaline, 240
Advisor. *See* Academic advisor
Agenda, time management and, 41–42
Aggressive person, 248–249
American Psychological Association (APA), 261–262
Amygdala, 90, 95
Analogies
   learning through, 2
   time management and, 31–32
Analysis
   Bloom's taxonomy and, 58, 59, 60, 61, 108
   as higher order thinking skill, 58, 124
   learning process and, 12, 125
   reflection and, 125

Analytic (left) processing
   characteristics of, 186
   global (right) difference between, 180–182
   linear *v.* holistic, 183
   logical *v.* intuitive, 184
   sequential *v.* random, 183–184
   symbolic *v.* concrete, 184
   temporal *v.* nontemporal, 185
   verbal *v.* nonverbal, 184–185
Anderson, L. W., 58, 58n2
Anxiety. *See* Stress
Application, Bloom's taxonomy and, 58, 59, 60, 108
Armstrong, Thomas, 187, 187n2
Art of Changing the Brain, The (Zull), 12
Ask (search engine), 259
Assertiveness, stress and, 248–251
Assertive person, 249
Assignment check sheet, 167–168
Assignment log, 10, 22
Assignment(s)
   approach to, 14
   time for outside, 30
Association
   math study and, 277
   neural connections, 93, 102–103, 112, 117
Association of American Colleges, 6
Attention
   concentration and, 165
   dividing, 130
   learning and, 93, 95, 112
   multi-tasking and, 31
   note taking and, 133, 142
   recitation and, 101
   subject knowledge and, 152
Attentional bias, 102

Attention list, 165
Audio recording, 178
Audio Visual Methods in Teaching (Dale), 127n1
Auditory learners
    defined, 175
    as listeners, 178
Authority, research sources and, 261
Axon, brain, 89, 91

Bandler, Richard, 101, 104
Basic background
    brain function and, 96–97, 112
    math and, 277
Berliner, D. C., 57
Bias
    attentional, 102
    in research resources, 261
Bibliography, 261
Bing (search engine), 259
Bloom, B. S., 57n1
Bloom's taxonomy
    critical thinking and, 57–61, 206–207, 228
    learning principles, 108
Bodily–kinesthetic intelligence, 187
Books. *See also* Textbooks
    for research, 257–258
Brain. *See also* Left brain; Right brain
    attentional bias, 102
    cellular connections, 96–97
    emotions and, 95
    getting information into, 111
    information processing, 180–186
    neural connections, 100–103
    optimal learning and, 103
    plasticity, 91
    stimuli and, 95
Brain research
    analogical learning and, 2
    control/goal setting and, 68
    learning and, 88–92
    study breaks, 104
Brain Rules (Medina), 31, 95, 95n3, 133, 133n2
Brainstorming
    follow-up, 74
    goals and, 72–73, 81
    goal themes and, 74
Bransford, John, 12
BREATHE System, 22–24, 96
    confidence and, 71
    listening skills and, 132

    stress relief and, 243
    test taking and, 208
Buzan, Tony, 138, 138n6

Calendar, time management and, 41–42
CareerBuilder, 6
Career-related skills, 156
Careers
    critical thinking and, 55
    goals and, 75–76
    interests, interviews, 107
    job applications, essay questions and, 232
    library research and, 266
    mapping interests, 164
    multiple intelligences and, 191–193
    note taking habits and, 143
    skills for, 156
    stress and, 250
    time management and, 43
Case study
    goal setting, 83
    learning styles, 199
    memory, study and, 120
    Question in the Margin System, note taking and, 146
    Question in the Margin System, reading, and, 170
    research papers, 269–270
    stress and, 253
    test preparation, 63
    tests, study strategy, 236
    time management, 47
Cell body, brain, 89
Cerebral cortex, 180
Chain letters, 20
Charts, study strategy, 204
Chicago Manual of Style (CMS), 261–262
Chudler, Eric (Dr.), 89, 90n1
Classes
    difficult, setting goals for, 79–81
    online, 21–22
Classroom savvy, 16–17
College
    job as student in, 3–4
    making smooth transition to, 2–3
College catalog, 4–5
College resources, 4–10
    catalog, 4–5
    schedule, 7–8
    student handbook, 7
    student services, 10

Comprehension, Bloom's taxonomy and, 58–60, 108
"Computer in Your Head, A" (Chudler), 89, 90n1
Concentration, textbooks and, 164–168
  external distractions, 166–168
  internal distractions, 164–165
Concrete processing, 184
Confidence, BREATHE System and, 71
Connections, brain, 91, 96–97, 100–103
Consolidation
  brain function and, 93, 104–105
  math study and, 277–278
Core curriculum, 5–9
Corely, Ginger A., 6
Cornell University, 134, 258
Cortisol hormone, 243
Course design, 21
Course load, outside responsibilities and, 8
Course numbers, 5
Courses, core curriculum/general education, 5–9
Coverage, research resources and, 261
Creating, Bloom's taxonomy and, 61
Creating Career Success: A Flexible Plan for the World of Work (Fabricant, Miller & Stark), 156n1
Credit hours, 2, 4
  GPA and, 18–19
Critical thinking
  Bloom's taxonomy, 57–61
  careers, multiple intelligences and, 193
  decision making process, 53–56
  difficult classes, 81
  fact and opinion, 56–57
  importance of, 52–53
  math and, 276
  note taking, 140–141
  retrieval, 117
  stress and, 242–243
  tests and, 206–207
  Web searches and, 260
Cues, information, memory and, 99
Cumulative GPA, 18–19
Currency, research sources and, 261

Dale, Edgar, 127, 127n1, 179
Databases, research and, 258–259, 263–264
Decision making process
  critical thinking and, 53–56
  multiple intelligences and, 191
Degree requirements, 4
Delivering Dynamic Presentations: Using Your Voice and Body for Impact (Hillman), 22–24, 22n3, 244n1

Dendrites, 89, 91
Dewey Decimal System, 258
Diagrams, study strategy, 204
Dictionary of Cultural Literacy, The (Hirsch, Kett, & Trefl), 136n3
Dictionaries, as resource, 257
Diet, study and, 15
Directions
  reading carefully, 14
  test, 210. See also Direction words
Direction words, 224–229
Distance learning. See Online courses
Distractions
  external/internal, 164–168
  reducing, 245
Distributed practice
  learning principle, 105–106
  math study and, 278
  rehearsal and, 114
  study and, 93
Domain names (Web), 260–261
Dopamine, 90, 95
Double negatives, test taking and, 212–213
Downing, Skip, 79
Dreams
  goals and, 71
  making them come true, 75
Drop a course, 5

E-books, 258
EBSCOhost (database), 259, 263
Education Index, 263
E-mail etiquette, 20–21
Emotions, learning and, 95
Encoding, brain function and, 104, 109
Encyclopedias, as resource, 257
Engle, Michael, 258, 259
Essay test questions, 224–231
  answers, checklist for writing, 224
  direction words, 224–229
  evaluating answers, 230–231
  job applications and, 232
E-texts, screen v. paper, 151–152
Etiquette, e-mail, 20–21
Evaluation, Bloom's taxonomy and, 58–60, 108
Exam(s). See also Tests
  cramming for, 222
  critical thinking, preparation, 231–232
  final, preparation for, 232–233

Executive function networks, brain, 91
Exercise, stress relief and, 245–246
External distractions, concentration and, 166–168
External locus of control, 70–71

Fabricant, Francine, 156n1
Facebook, 92
Fact and opinion, critical thinking and, 56–57
Fantasy-oriented v. reality-based processing, 185
FAQs, new students and, 10–11
Fatigue, errors and, 104
Feedback
    consolidation and, 104
    as learning tool, 101
Fill-in-the-blank questions, 219
Filters, information, brain function, 90
Final exam schedule, 7. *See also* Exam(s)
Financial stress, 241
First essential resource, college catalog, 4–5
Flash cards, study and, 31, 92, 104, 178, 179, 203
Focusing, 152
Ford, Martin, 72
Frames of Mind: The Theory of Multiple Intelligences
    (Gardner), 186n1
Frontal integrative cortex, 124

Gale (database), 259, 263
Games, for review, 204
Gardner, Howard, 186–187, 186n1
Gathering
    Bloom's taxonomy and, 61
    as learning function, 125
General education
    core curriculum, 5–9
    requirements, 2
General interest periodicals, 258
General OneFile (database), 259, 263
General qualifiers, 214
General studies, 5–9
Global (right) processing
    analytic (left) difference between, 180–182
    characteristics of, 186
    linear v. holistic, 183
    logical v. intuitive, 184
    reality-based v. fantasy-oriented, 185
    sequential v. random, 183–184
    symbolic v. concrete, 184
    temporal v. nontemporal, 185
    verbal v. nonverbal, 184–185
Goals. *See also* SMART goals
    achieving, 79

action plans and, 77–78
advice for, case study, 83
brainstorming and, 72–73
concentration, setting to promote, 165
dreaming and, 71
examining your life, 72–73
guidelines for writing, 75
locus of control and, 70–71
making visible, 79
math, setting, 276
organize, 22
pursuing, process of, 72
setting, 22
short/long-term, dreams and, 75
SMART goals, 76–77
specific, 75
study strategy and, 202
themes of, 74
when should you set?, 72
why are you in college?, 71
why set?, 68–69
Google Scholar (website), 260
Google (search engine), 257, 259
Grade point average (GPA), 5, 17–19
Grading scale, 9
Graphic organizers, mapping and, 159
Group learning, 194–196
Guessing test answers, 214–219

Happiness, 69
Hart, Leslie, 56, 97, 224, 262
Higher Education
    critical thinking about, 11
    student responsibilities, 12
Higher-order thinking, 59, 124
Hillman, Ralph (Dr.), BREATHE System, 22–24, 71, 208,
    244n1
Hippocampus
    cortisol and, 243
    memory and, 112
Hirsch, E. D., 136n3
Holistic v. linear processing, 183
Howard, Pierce, 155
How People Learn (Bransford), 12
How the Brain Learns: A Classroom Teacher's Guide
    (Sousa), 102n7
"How to Teach Students about the Brain" (Willis),
    90n2
Human Brain and Human Learning (Hart), 56, 262
Humanities Index, 263
Humor, 245

Ideas, creating new, 12, 125
Illustrate notes, 101
Indexes, to periodical articles, 258–259
INFOMINE (search engine), 259
Information
    acting on, 12
    analyzing, 12
    controlling amount/form of, 97–100
    cues, memory system and, 99
    gathering, learning process, 12
    ideas, creating new, 12
    lectures v. textbooks, 150
    mapping, organization and, 159
    mental manipulations, 176
    organization and, 113
    rehearsal, 113–114
    review and, 113–114
    selectivity, 100
    sensory modes and, 113
    textbooks, control amount/form of, 152–159
Information age, 256
Information literacy
    defining, 256
    research process, 257–267. See also Research process
Information processing
    analytic/global, brain functions and, 180–186
    beyond memory, 124–128. See also Memory, beyond
    learning principles, relating to, 127
    linear v. holistic, 183
    listening skills and, 129–132
    logical v. intuitive, 184
    multiple intelligences, 186–193. See also Multiple intelligences
    note taking, 133
    Question in the Margin System, lectures and, 134–140. See also Lectures, Question in the Margin System and
    reality-based v. fantasy-oriented, 185
    response preferences, 186–193. See also Multiple intelligences
    sequential v. random, 183–184
    symbolic v. concrete, 184
    temporal v. nontemporal, 185
    verbal v. nonverbal, 184–185
Input preferences, learning, sensory modes of, 175–177
Intelligences, multiple. See Multiple intelligences
Intent to remember
    learning principle, 95–97, 111, 277
    listening skills and, 132

Interest, learning principle, 94–95, 97, 111, 277
Internal distractions, concentration and, 164–165
Internal locus of control, 70–71
Internet resources, research and, 259–261, 265–266
Interpersonal intelligence, 187
Intrapersonal intelligence, 187
Intuitive v. logical processing, 184

Jensen, Eric, 95n4, 96, 97, 103, 103n8, 104, 104n9
Jingles, mnemonic device, 99
Jobs. See Careers, Skills
Jokes, e-mail, 20
Journals, use in research, 258

Kett, J. F., 136n3
Kinesthetic learners
    defined, 175
    interactive learning, 179
Knowledge, Bloom's taxonomy and, 58–60, 108
Krathwohl, D. R., 58, 58n2

Language, discipline-specific, 258
Latham, Gary, 75
Laughter, stress and, 245
Learning
    brain function and, 88–92
    classroom v. outside classroom, 150
    how to learn, 3
    optimal, brain function and, 103
    patterns, 262
Learning, four functions of
    acting, testing knowledge, 126
    analyzing, 125
    gathering, 125
    ideas, creating new, 125
    Question in the Margin System and, 126
Learning principle(s), 92, 93
    applying, 94
    association, 102–103
    basic background, 96–97, 112, 277
    Bloom's taxonomy and, 108
    consolidation, 104–105
    distribution, 105–106
    information processing and, 127
    intent to remember, 95–97, 277
    interest, 94–95, 97, 111, 277
    math and, 275–278
    meaningful organization, 99–100

Learning principle(s) (*continued*)
   memory and, 109–117. *See also* Memory; Long-term memory; Short-term memory
   putting to use, 106–107
   Question in the Margin System and, 143–144
   recitation, 101, 102, 277
   retrieval of, 117
   selectivity, 97–98, 277
   textbooks, Question in the Margin System and, 152
   visualization, 101, 102, 277
Learning process, modeling, 12
   gathering information, 12
   reflecting, 127–129
Learning profile, 196
Learning styles
   analytic/global processing, 180–186. *See also* Analytic processing; Global processing; Information processing
   case study, 199
   social learning, 194–196. *See also* Social learning
   why determine?, 174–175
Lectures, Question in the Margin System and, 134–140
   information, controlling amount in notes, 134
   question, 136–137
   recite, 137
   record what is said, 135
   reflect, 137–138
   review, 138–139
   sample notes, 140
   summarize, 139
   supplies/format for, 134–135
   textbooks and, summaries for, 158
Left brain/right brain theory, 180
LexisNexis, 264
Library catalog, research and, 257–258
Library of Congress Classification System, 258
Lifestyle habits, stress reduction and, 246–248
Limbic system, 90
Linear *v.* holistic processing, 183
Linguistic intelligence, 187
List
   information processing and, 183
   making assignment, 15
Listening skills, auditory learners and, 178
Listening skills, information processing and, 129–132
   BREATHE system, 132
   improve, 131–132
   intent to remember, 132
   obstacles to, 130
Literacy, information. *See* Information literacy

Livescribe, 178
Locke, Edwin, 75
Locus of control, 70–71
Logical–mathematical intelligences, 187
Logical *v.* intuitive processing, 184
Long-term goals, 75
Long-term memory, 95, 109
   retrieving from, 114–115
   what happens during retrieval, 115, 117
Lower automatic brain (reactive brain), 90

Main idea, selecting, 93. *See also* Topic(s)
Major, college catalog and, 4
Make-up policy, 9
Manning, Peyton, 31
Mapping
   Question in the Margin System and, 162–164
   textbooks and, 159–164, 204
   true/false question strategies, 215
MapQuest, 101
Markowitz, Karen, 95n4, 96, 103n8, 104, 104n9
Master schedule
   example, 40
   follow-up, 38–39
   planning, 35–36
   in practice, 37
   prioritizing, 42
   worksheet, 36
Matching questions, test strategy for, 220
Math, studying, 271–280
   critical thinking, 276
   diagnostic inventory, 271–274
   difference from other subjects, 275
   goal setting, 276
   learning principles and, 277–278
   learning strategies and, 275–278
   stress and, 279–280
   test-taking strategies, 279–280
   time-management, 275–276
Math Study Skill Workbook (Nolting), 278
Meaningful organization, learning principle, 99–100
Medina, John, 31, 95, 95n3, 104, 104n10, 133, 133n2
Memory
   brain function and, 91, 93
   cortisol and, 243
   how it works, 116
   information processing and, 184
   intent to remember and, 95–96
   meaningful organization and, 99–100

short/long term, 95, 101
strengthening, 111
study and, case study, 120
Memory, beyond, 124–128
acting, testing knowledge, 126
analyzing by reflection, 125
functions for learning, 125–126
gathering, 125
ideas, creating new, 125
Question in the Margin System and, 126
Memory, functions of, 109–117
long-term memory, 114
organization, 113
reception, factors influencing, 111–112
reception into short-term memory, 111
rehearsal, 113–114
retrieving from long-term memory, 114–115
sensory modes, 113
short-term memory, 112
short-term to long-term, 112–114
Miller, Jennifer, 156n1
Mixed modality learning, 175
Mnemonic device, 99–100
Modern Language Association (MLA), 261–262
Motor output, 124
Multinodal notes, 178
Multiple-choice questions, tests strategies for, 217–219
Multiple intelligences, 186–193
bodily–kinesthetic, 187
critical thinking and, 193
decision-making, careers and, 191–193
determine yours, 190
finding preferred, 188
interpersonal, 187
intrapersonal, 187
linguistic, 187
logical–mathematical, 187
musical, 187
naturalist, 188
spatial, 187
understanding yours, 189–190
Multi-tasking stress, 241
Music, stress relief and, 243
Musical intelligence, 187

Nadel, L., 240
National Newspaper Index, 264
Naturalist intelligence, 188
Negative/double negatives, test taking and, 212–213

Neural connections
recitation and, 101
strengthening, 100–103
Neural networking, 97
Neural pathways, consolidation and, 104
Neurolinguistic programing, 104
Neurons, brain and, 89, 91
Neuroscientists, brain, learning and, 88–92
Neurotransmitters,
acetylcholine, 95
adrenaline, and, 240
brain functions and, 89–91, 95, 240
dopamine, 90
noradrenaline, 240
pleasure and, 95
Newspapers, finding articles in, 264–265
Nolting, Paul, 278
Nontemporal v. temporal processing, 185
NoodleTools (website), 257
Noradrenaline, neurotransmitter, 240
Notes, taking, 14
auditory learners and, 178
case study, 146
class, study strategy and, 203
compare with study partner, 138
critical thinking and, 140–141
illustrate, 101
importance of, 133
information processing and, 133
laptops/tablets and, 136
lectures, 134–140. See also Lectures, Question in the Margin System and
listening skills and, 129–130
mapping and, 162
math, 278–279
practice taking, 129
Question in the Margin System. See Question in the Margin System
reading assignments and, 126
rewrite, 138
social learning and, 194
textbooks, 152–159
time, study and, 31
why take?, 133
Nucleus, brain cells, 91
Nutrition, study and, 15

Objective information, research resources, 261
Objective test, 205
    educated guesses, 214–219
    fill-in-the-blank questions, 219
    matching questions, 220
    qualifiers, 213–214
    strategies, 222
    true/false questions, 212
O'Keefe, J., 240
100% Information Literacy Success (Wilson), 256n1, 259n3
Online courses, tips for, 21–22
Opinion, fact and, 56–57
Optimal learning, 103
Organization
    math study and, 277
    meaningful, 93
    memory and, 112, 113
Outside responsibilities, course load and, 8
Owner's Manual for the Brain (Howard), 155

Paragraph, reading, 153
Passive person, 248
Patterns, perception and, 97
Payment, 7
Peer pressure, 241
Periodicals
    finding, 263–264
    finding articles in, 264
    indexes, databases, 258–259
    popular, research and, 259
Periodic review, 115
Personal knowledge, 124
Physical activity
    brain and, 96
    stress and, 245
Physical distractions, concentration and, 166–168
Plasticity, brain, 91
Pleasure, neurotransmitters and, 95
Pocket work, 31
Poems, mnemonic device, 99
Posture, BREATHE System and, 23–24
PowerPoint presentations, 92, 204
Practice, distributed, 93
Predicting questions, asking, 60
Prefrontal cortex (thinking brain), 90, 91, 95
Prioritizing, 42
Prior knowledge, 112

Professional skills, 156
Professor
    communicate with, 22
    getting to know, 13
ProQuest (database), 259, 263, 264

Qualifiers, in objective tests, 213–214
Quality points, GPA and, 18–19
Question in the Margin System, 15–16
    auditory learners and, 178
    case study, note taking, 146
    kinesthetic learning and, 179
    learning functions and, 126
    learning principles and, 143–144
    learning process, modeling, 141
    lecture notes, 142
    lectures and, 134–140. *See also* Lectures, Question in the Margin System and
    mapping and, 162–164
    math study, 278
    reading and, case study, 170
    sequential *v.* random processing, 183–184
    study and, 33
    test-taking and, 203
    textbooks and, 152–159. *See also* Textbooks, Question in the Margin System and
    understanding, 158–159
Questions
    learn by asking, 60
    note taking and, 136–137
    predicting test, 222–223

Random *v.* sequential processing, 183–184
Reactive brain, 90
Reader's Guide to Periodical Literature, 263
Reader's Guide Retrospective, 263
Reading. *See also* Textbooks, Question in the Margin System and
    math books, 279
    one paragraph at time, 153
    Question in the Margin System, case study, 170
    speed, calculate, 152
    underlining and, 153, 154
Reading assignments, note taking and, 126
Reading strategies, 151
Reality-based *v.* fantasy-oriented processing, 185
Reception, 109, 111–112
Recitation

auditory learners and, 178
math study and, 277
neural connections, 93, 101, 102, 113
Question in the Margin System and, 137
textbooks, Question in the Margin and, 153
Reflection
analyzing information by, 125
modeling learning process, 127–129
Question in the Margin System and, 137–138
rehearsal and, 113
sensory mode, 179
textbooks, Question in the Margin and, 153
Registration book, schedule, 7–8
Rehearsal, memory and, 112, 113–114
Relaxation, BREATHE System and, 23–24, 244–245
Repetition, rehearsal, memory and, 113
Reply All, use of (e-mail), 20
Research process, 257–267
case study, 269–270
citations, 261–262
evaluating sources, 261
indexes, databases, periodicals and, 258–259
Internet resources for, 259–261, 265–266
library card catalog, 257–258
newspapers, 264–265
periodicals, 263–264
topic, identify, 257
Resources, college, 4–10. See also College resources
Reticular activating system (RAS), 90
Retrieval process, memory, 115, 117
Revelle College, life skills website, 249
Reversing the input process, 115
Review
Question in the Margin System and, 138–139
rehearsal and, 113–114
returned tests, 220–222
Right brain theory, 180
Routine, study and, 14

Schedule
benefits of, 32–35
information processing and, 183
master, planning, 35–36
registration book, 7–8
time logs and, 34–35
time management and, 32–35
Scholarly journals, in research, 258
Script-writing practice, 250

Search engines, research and, 259–261
Selectivity
main ideas and, 93
math, 277
principle of, 97–98
Self-management skills, 156
Self-testing, 115
Semester, 7
Sensory modes
inventory of, 176–177
of learning, 175–177
memory and, 112, 113
reactions and, 176
reflection and, 179
Sensory output, 124
Sensory receptors, 111
Sentence mnemonic (acrostic), 99
Sequential v. random processing, 183–184
Seven Kinds of Smart: Identifying and Developing Your Many Intelligences (Armstrong), 187n2
Short-term goals, 75
Short-term memory, 95, 97, 101, 109
factors influencing, 111–112
hippocampus and, 112
into long-term memory, 112–114
math study and, 278
reception into, 111
Simon, Herbert (Nobel laureate), 53
Singing, auditory learning and, 178
Skills
employment, 156
life skills website, Revelle College, 249
multiple intelligences, employment and, 191–193
time-management, 9
transferable skills, 156
Sleep
stress and, 248
study and, 15
SMART goals, 76–77
math and, 276
Smooth transition to college, tips for, 14–15
Social learning, 194–196
Social Sciences Index, 263
Social stress, 241
Solitary learning, 194–196
Soma, brain and, 89
Sources
citing, 261–262
evaluating research, 261

Sousa, David A., 102n7, 117
Spam, deleting, 20
Spatial intelligence, 187
Spell checker, in e-mail, 20
Spelling, sequences and, 183
Sperry, Roger, 180
Stark, Debra J., 156n1
Stress
    analyzing, 241
    assertiveness, 248–251
    BREATHE System and, 22–24, 243
    case study, 253
    cortisol hormone and, 243
    critical thinking about, 242–243
    defining, 240–241
    distractions and, 245
    laughter and, 245
    lifestyle habits for reducing, 246–248
    math class and, 274, 279–280
    music, relaxing, 243
    neurotransmitters and, 240. *See also*
        Neurotransmitters
    physical activity and, 245
    plan for combatting, 251
    relaxation routine, 244–245
    script-writing practice, 250
    signs of, 240–241
    sleep and, 248
    strategies for alleviating, 246
    talking and, 245
    visualization and, 245
Stressors, 240
Strong Foundations: Twelve Principles for Effective General Education Programs (Association of American Colleges), 6n1
Student
    FAQs of new, 10–11
    responsibilities, 12
    your job as, 3–4
Student Affairs Office, 10–11
Student handbook, 7
Student power, 14
Student services, 10
Student survival, 10
    critical thinking, 54
    essay test checklist, 224
    e-texts *v.* paper tests, 151–152
    learning principles, 93
    learning profile, 196
    lecture/textbook Question in the Margin System, 158

    memory, 110
    multiple-choice questions, strategies, 217
    Question in the Margin System, lecture notes, 142
    reading strategies, 151
    scheduling, principles of, 33
    SMART goals, 76–77
    stress, combating, 251
    study organizer, final exam, 233
    test taking tips, 211
    textbooks, Question in the Margin System, 155–156
    true/false statements, strategies for, 214–215
Study
    aids for, 204
    breaks, need for, 104
    campus resources for, 15
    create routine time for, 14
    diet and, 15
    distributed practice, 93
    establish routine time for, 32
    final exam, organizer for, 233
    groups for, 14, 15, 203
    habits analysis, 167–168
    identify best place to, 166–167
    math, 271–280. *See also* Math, studying
    notes, compare with partner's, 138
    place to, 14, 22
    pocket work, 31
    scheduling time for, 35–36
    social learning, alone/groups, 194–196
    times for, 14–15
Study guides, 203
Subjective tests, 205, 224
Substantive news periodicals, 258
Summarize, Question in the Margin System
    lectures and, 139
    textbooks and, 153
Survey, 152
Syllabus, 9, 21
Symbolic *v.* concrete processing, 184
Synapse, brain, 89–91
Synthesis, Bloom's taxonomy and, 58, 59, 60, 108

Talking, stress relief and, 245
Taxonomy for Learning, Teaching, and Assessing: A Revision of Bloom's Taxonomy of Educational Objectives (Anderson & Krathwohl), 58, 58n2
Taxonomy of Educational Objectives: The Classifications of Educational Goals. Handbook 1: Cognitive Domain (Bloom), 57n1
Technical skills, 156

Temporal integrative cortex, 124
Temporal *v.* nontemporal processing, 185
Term, 7
Tests
    critical thinking about, 206–207, 231–232
    directions, follow, 210
    essay, strategies for, 224–231. *See also* Essay questions, strategies for
    exams, final, 232–233
    fill-in-the-blank questions, 219
    guesses, educated, 214–219
    learning styles and, 186
    making practice, 204
    matching questions, strategies, 220
    math, 273
    math, strategies for, 279–280
    multiple-choice questions, 217–219
    negatives/double negatives, 212–213
    objective, 205, 212–221. *See also* Objective tests
    practice, 222
    predicting questions, 59
    preparation, case study, 63
    preparing for, 205–206
    preview, 208–209
    questions, predicting, 222–223
    reviewing returned, 220–222
    self-analysis, preparing for, 207–208
    self-testing, 115
    strategies for taking, 211
    study strategy, case study, 236
    subjective, 205, 224
    time, budget for, 209
    true/false questions, 212, 214–217
    types of, 204–205
    visualization and, 101
Textbooks. *See also* Reading
    concentration, distractions and, 164–168
    mapping and, 159–164. *See also* Mapping, textbooks and
    marked, study strategy, 203
    math, reading, 278–279
    reading, note taking and, 15–16
Textbooks, Question in the Margin System and, 152–159
    information, control amount/form of, 152–159
    lectures and, summary sheet for, 158
    practice using, 156–157
    steps of, 154–155
    summary sheet for, 156–157
    using, 155–156

Thinking, critical, 52–53
Thinking brain, 90
Time
    budget test-taking, 208–209
    establish study, 14
Timelines, study strategy, 204
Time log
    example, 34
    practice, 35
Time-management
    agenda, calendar, to-do list, 41–42
    brain behavior and, 36
    case study, 47
    critical thinking about, 31–32
    importance of, 30–32
    master schedule, planning, 35–36
    math and, 275–276
    practice, 46–47
    prioritizing, 42
    scheduling, benefits of, 32–35
    skills, 9
    steps in, 31
    wasting, 43–44
To-do list, time management and, 41–42
Topic(s)
    choosing, narrowing, researching, 262
    identify/research, 257
    sentences, direction words and, 228–229
Transferable skills, 156
Transition, to college
    general tips for, 14–15
    making smooth, 2–3
Trefl, J., 136n3
True/false questions, strategies for, 212, 214–217
Twitter, 92
Underlining, reading and, 153, 154
Understanding, reception and, 111
University of Idaho Library (website), 256
Upper case use, in e-mail, 20
Use Both Sides of Your Brain (Buzan), 138, 138n6

Verbal *v.* nonverbal processing, 184–185
Visualization
    math study and, 277
    neural connections, 93, 101, 102, 113
    relaxation technique, 245
    visual learners and, 178–179

Visual learners
    defined, 175
    visualization and, 178–179
Visual representation, 159

Wasting time, 43–44
Websites
    CareerBuilder, 6
    Cornell University library, 258n2, 259n3
    domain names, 260–261
    Google Scholar, 260
    Internet resources and, 259–261
    MapQuest, 101
    NoodleTools, 257
    Revelle College, life skills, 249
    University of Idaho, 256
    Wikipedia, 257
    Yahoo!, 259
    YouTube, 143

What You Should Know about the Brain (Willis), 90
Where Memory Resides (Markowitz & Jensen), 95n4, 103n8
Wikipedia, 257
Willis, Judy, 55, 90, 90n2, 95, 176
Wilson, Gwen, 256, 259n3
Witherow, Laurie B., 6
Word mnemonic, acronym, 99
Wurtman, Judith (Dr.), 15

Yahoo! (search engine), 259
YouTube, 143

Ziglar, Zig, 76
Zull, James (Dr.), 12, 125

BRIEF CONTENTS

Introduction—The Choices You Make xvii

CHAPTER 1
Setting the Stage 1
WHAT'S ON YOUR MIND?

CHAPTER 2
Critical Thinking 15
HOW WILL HIGHER-ORDER THINKING SKILLS IMPROVE ACADEMIC SUCCESS?

CHAPTER 3
Goal Setting 35
IF YOU KNOW WHAT YOU WANT TO DO, WHY DO YOU NEED TO READ ABOUT GOAL SETTING?

CHAPTER 4
Organizing Time and Space 57
HOW WILL THESE SKILLS IMPROVE ACADEMIC PERFORMANCE AND REDUCE YOUR STRESS?

CHAPTER 5
Learning Styles 81
HOW WILL KNOWING YOUR LEARNING STYLE HELP WITH YOUR STUDIES?

CHAPTER 6
Class Time 99
HOW CAN YOU BE MORE SUCCESSFUL DURING CLASS TIME?

CHAPTER 7
Note Taking 123
HOW WILL EFFECTIVE NOTES HELP YOU UNDERSTAND CLASS MATERIAL?

CHAPTER 8
Reading 139
YOU HAVE TO READ 1,000 PAGES BY WHEN?

CHAPTER 9
Memory 163
WHY DO YOU FORGET—AND WHAT CAN YOU DO ABOUT IT?

CHAPTER 10
Test Taking 183
HOW CAN YOU IMPROVE YOUR TEST-PREPARATION AND TEST-PERFORMANCE SKILLS?

CHAPTER 11
Information Literacy 205
HOW CAN YOU USE INFORMATION AND TECHNOLOGY FOR YOUR BENEFIT?

CHAPTER 12
Civility 229
HOW CAN WORKING WITH OTHERS AFFECT YOUR ACADEMIC SUCCESS?

CHAPTER 13
The Choices You Make 249
HOW DO YOUR CURRENT DECISIONS AFFECT YOUR FUTURE?

CONTENTS

Introduction—The Choices
You Make   xvii

  THE CHOICES YOU MAKE   xvii

  CRITICAL THINKING   xviii

  REALITY CHECK   xix

  ENERGIZING CHOICES   xx

CHAPTER 1
Setting the Stage   1
WHAT'S ON YOUR MIND?

  SPOTLIGHT ON CLASSROOM SKILLS   1

  PREVIEW   1

  KEY TERMS   1

  CHAPTER INTRODUCTION   2

  WHAT DO YOU THINK OF WHEN YOU HEAR THE
    TERM *STUDY SKILLS?*   2

  I REALLY DO WANT TO LEARN—BUT I JUST
    CAN'T!   2

  WHAT IS ON YOUR MIND?   5

    A quick preview of coming attractions   6

  IS THERE A COMMON THREAD TO THESE
    CHAPTERS?   9

    Locus of control   9

    What will not *happen by using this book?*   10

    What will *happen by using this material?*   10

  CHAPTER SUMMARY   12

  REALITY CHECK: A COVENANT WITH MYSELF   14

CHAPTER 2
Critical Thinking   15
**HOW WILL HIGHER-ORDER THINKING
SKILLS IMPROVE ACADEMIC
SUCCESS?**

  SPOTLIGHT ON CLASSROOM SKILLS   15

  PREVIEW   15

  KEY TERMS   15

  CHAPTER INTRODUCTION   16

  DEFINING CRITICAL THINKING   18

  HIGHER-ORDER THINKING SKILLS   19

  USING HIGHER-ORDER THINKING SKILLS   20

    Critical thinking   20

    Problem solving   22

    Problem-solving models   23

    The problem-solving trap   27

    *Creative thinking: You have to do it differently
      if you want different results*   27

  ADAPTING OLD SKILLS TO NEW SITUATIONS:
    MAKING CHOICES   29

  CHAPTER SUMMARY   31

    Critical thinking expands your confidence   31

  REALITY CHECK: USING YOUR CRITICAL
    THINKING SKILLS TO IMPROVE
    STUDY SKILLS   33

CHAPTER 3
Goal Setting   35
**IF YOU KNOW WHAT YOU WANT TO
DO, WHY DO YOU NEED TO READ
ABOUT GOAL SETTING?**

  SPOTLIGHT ON CLASSROOM SKILLS   35

  PREVIEW   35

  KEY TERMS   35

  CHAPTER INTRODUCTION   36

  MOTIVATION   37

    Where do you find motivation?   38

    Extrinsic and intrinsic motivation   38

    *Characteristics of a motivated learner: Can
      an individual learn to be motivated?*   39

    Overcoming motivational barriers   41

GOAL SETTING   43

    What is a goal?   43

    Why do you need a goal? Converting fantasies to dreams—and dreams to realities   44

    Have you hugged your HOG today?   44

    What does a clearly stated goal look like?   45

    Long-term and short-term goals   48

    Tips on how to develop your action steps   49

    Obstacles, missteps, and detours   49

    Locus of control   51

    WIN: Do you know what's important now?   54

CHAPTER SUMMARY   54

REALITY CHECK: USING YOUR CRITICAL THINKING SKILLS TO IMPROVE YOUR ABILITY TO SET AND ACHIEVE GOALS   56

CHAPTER 4
Organizing Time and Space   57

HOW WILL THESE SKILLS IMPROVE ACADEMIC PERFORMANCE AND REDUCE YOUR STRESS?

SPOTLIGHT ON CLASSROOM SKILLS   57

PREVIEW   57

KEY TERMS   57

CHAPTER INTRODUCTION   58

ORGANIZATION AND TIME   59

    You have a lot to do!   60

    Study time: How much?   60

    How do I establish a study schedule?   60

    Keeping track of your time and commitments   66

    What should you do first? Establishing priorities   69

    Simplify   70

    Backward planning   71

    "I'll do all of this tomorrow!" Dealing with procrastination   71

ORGANIZATION AND SPACE   73

    Home study area   73

    Personal portable storage area   75

    Car   75

ORGANIZATION AND STRESS   76

    Types of stress   76

    Stress signals   76

    Stress-reducing suggestions   77

CHAPTER SUMMARY   78

    Organization: Maximizing time and space while minimizing stress   78

REALITY CHECK: USING YOUR CRITICAL THINKING SKILLS TO IMPROVE YOUR ORGANIZATIONAL SKILLS   80

CHAPTER 5
Learning Styles   81

HOW WILL KNOWING YOUR LEARNING STYLE HELP WITH YOUR STUDIES?

SPOTLIGHT ON CLASSROOM SKILLS   81

PREVIEW   81

KEY TERMS   81

CHAPTER INTRODUCTION   82

ONE SIZE DOES NOT FIT ALL   82

WHY NOW?   82

THINKING: HOW DO YOU PROCESS INFORMATION?   84

    Your brain   84

    Left-brain, right-brain, and whole-brain thinking   84

    Learning styles   85

    How do you learn?   86

    Difficulties in the classroom?   90

    Making learning styles information work for you   93

CHAPTER SUMMARY   94

REALITY CHECK: USING YOUR CRITICAL THINKING SKILLS TO UNDERSTAND AND USE YOUR LEARNING STYLE   96

CHAPTER 6
Class Time   99

HOW CAN YOU BE MORE SUCCESSFUL DURING CLASS TIME?

SPOTLIGHT ON CLASSROOM SKILLS   99

PREVIEW   99

KEY TERMS   99

CHAPTER INTRODUCTION   100

DO I KNOW WHAT THE INSTRUCTOR IS DOING IN FRONT OF THE ROOM?   102

Instructor style and emphasis   102

Identification of instructor style + expectations = classroom success   103

DO I KNOW WHAT I AM DOING IN THE BACK OF THE ROOM?   106

What can you do to maximize classroom success?   106

You really want to pay attention in class. . . but it's not easy   106

How does one "pay attention"?   107

Developing a working and respectful relationship with your instructors   108

A word about being "cool"   109

Active learning   109

You need to be there: Seven steps to classroom success   110

NOTE TAKING AS AN ACTIVE LEARNING STRATEGY   111

Simple abbreviations to increase note-taking speed   114

Managing your studies with a notebook   115

Practice   116

What happens if you don't follow all of the basics?   116

Can you think like the professor?   118

Staying actively engaged as an online student   118

CHAPTER SUMMARY   119

REALITY CHECK: USING YOUR CRITICAL THINKING SKILLS TO IMPROVE YOUR CLASSROOM PERFORMANCE   121

CHAPTER 7
Note Taking   123

HOW WILL EFFECTIVE NOTES HELP YOU UNDERSTAND CLASS MATERIAL?

SPOTLIGHT ON CLASSROOM SKILLS   123

PREVIEW   123

KEY TERMS   123

CHAPTER INTRODUCTION   124

LEARNING *WHILE* TAKING NOTES   124

LEARNING *AFTER* YOU HAVE TAKEN YOUR NOTES: ROI   124

USING YOUR NOTES TO UNDERSTAND THE BIG PICTURE   127

Now that you have your notes, what should you do next? Time for reflection   127

Connections, groups, and chunks   129

Talk to yourself—and then someone else   129

What should you do if you still don't get the big picture?   130

Title/Summary/Details (TSD)   131

TSDs in reverse   132

Exit slips   133

ADDITIONAL OUT-OF-CLASS STRATEGIES TO IMPROVE YOUR NOTES   133

Have you created working relationships with your instructors?   133

Do you need a study partner or group?   135

Using technology   135

CHAPTER SUMMARY   136

REALITY CHECK: USING CRITICAL THINKING SKILLS AND CLASS NOTES TO UNDERSTAND CLASS MATERIAL   138

CHAPTER 8
Reading   139

YOU HAVE TO READ 1,000 PAGES BY WHEN?

SPOTLIGHT ON CLASSROOM SKILLS   139

PREVIEW   139

KEY TERMS   139

CHAPTER INTRODUCTION   140

Brain-based learning: Making sense of the seeming chaos   140

DO YOU KNOW WHY YOU READ AN ASSIGNMENT?   142

I read my assignment. So, why don't I know what I read?   142

Identifying the purpose   143

HOW TO COMPLETE A TEXTBOOK READING ASSIGNMENT   145

How does the instructor expect me to get through this boring textbook?   145

Your current plan for textbook reading   145

A proven process for effective reading: SQ4R   146

Preread   149

Read (finally!)   151

Postread   154

ADDITIONAL STRATEGIES FOR READING SUCCESS   155

Use supplemental sources   155

Vocabulary   155

Using context clues to build your vocabulary   155

Having trouble finding the main idea? Use "mini-SQ4Rs"   156

Understanding and using graphics   156

Now, what do I do with my reading notes?   159

My instructor always falls behind schedule   159

The reading plan is fine for textbooks, but what about novels?   159

CHAPTER SUMMARY   160

REALITY CHECK: USING CRITICAL THINKING SKILLS TO IMPROVE YOUR READING SKILLS   162

CHAPTER 9
Memory   163

WHY DO YOU FORGET—AND WHAT CAN YOU DO ABOUT IT?

SPOTLIGHT ON CLASSROOM SKILLS   163

PREVIEW   163

KEY TERMS   163

CHAPTER INTRODUCTION   164

Three simple steps to improved memory   164

NOTICING THE INFORMATION   167

Why do you forget?   167

Choosing to notice   168

STORING THE INFORMATION YOU HAVE NOTICED   170

Active listening = improved memory   170

Using charts to make connections   171

Mental pictures   173

RECLAIMING THE INFORMATION YOU HAVE STORED   173

Retrieval: Start with what you already know   174

Memory blocks   174

Retrieval failure: What you can do about it   175

Names   177

Mnemonics   178

Practice, practice, and more practice   179

Memory ≠ understanding   179

CHAPTER SUMMARY   179

REALITY CHECK: USING YOUR CRITICAL THINKING SKILLS TO IMPROVE YOUR MEMORY AND RECALL SKILLS   181

CHAPTER 10
Test Taking   183

HOW CAN YOU IMPROVE YOUR TEST-PREPARATION AND TEST-PERFORMANCE SKILLS?

SPOTLIGHT ON CLASSROOM SKILLS   183

PREVIEW   183

KEY TERMS   183

CHAPTER INTRODUCTION   184

WHAT TEST-TAKING SKILLS DO YOU POSSESS?   186

Putting your study skills to work for you: Everything is connected   189

TEST ANXIETY   191

How does test anxiety happen?   192

Test anxiety or inefficient test-taking strategies?   194

Postexam analysis   198

ADDITIONAL TEST-TAKING STRATEGIES   199

General   199

Multiple-choice tests   199

Matching tests   199

Essay tests   200

Emergency studying   200

Test performance and academic integrity   201

CHAPTER SUMMARY   202

REALITY CHECK: USING YOUR CRITICAL THINKING SKILLS TO IMPROVE YOUR TEST-PREPARATION AND TEST-PERFORMANCE SKILLS   203

CHAPTER 11
Information Literacy   *205*
HOW CAN YOU USE INFORMATION AND TECHNOLOGY FOR YOUR BENEFIT?

SPOTLIGHT ON CLASSROOM SKILLS   205

PREVIEW   205

KEY TERMS   205

CHAPTER INTRODUCTION   206
What is information literacy?   *208*
There is more than one type of information   *209*

FOUR STEPS TO COMPLETING AN ASSIGNMENT IN AN INFORMATION-LITERATE MANNER   211
Step 1: Know what information is needed   *212*
Step 2: Access the information   *213*
Step 3: Evaluate information   *221*
Step 4: Use the information   *223*

RESPONSIBILITIES OF THE INFORMATION AGE   223
Academic integrity   *223*
E-mail responsibilities   *224*
Avoiding repetitive strain injuries   *224*

CHAPTER SUMMARY   226

REALITY CHECK: USING YOUR CRITICAL THINKING SKILLS TO IMPROVE YOUR INFORMATION LITERACY SKILLS   228

CHAPTER 12
Civility   *229*
HOW CAN WORKING WITH OTHERS AFFECT YOUR ACADEMIC SUCCESS?

SPOTLIGHT ON CLASSROOM SKILLS   229

PREVIEW   229

KEY TERMS   229

CHAPTER INTRODUCTION   230

EMOTIONAL INTELLIGENCE   231

WORKING WITH PEOPLE   232
The challenges of group work   *232*
Understanding group dynamics   *234*

Forming your own group   *235*
Trust: Building on a shared experience   *236*

INTERPERSONAL RELATIONSHIPS: HOW TO "PLAY NICE" WITH OTHER PEOPLE   237
Who are the "energy vampires" of your life?   *237*
How to guard against energy vampires   *238*
Finding "nutritious people" for your life   *240*

ARE YOU REALLY LISTENING, OR JUST TALKING?   241
The "art" of communication   *241*
Dialogues versus collective monologues   *242*
Active listening   *242*

CONFLICT MANAGEMENT   243
Are you having a disagreement or a conflict?   *243*
Conflict is not always a bad thing   *244*
Ways people deal with conflict   *244*

CHAPTER SUMMARY   246

REALITY CHECK: USING YOUR CRITICAL THINKING SKILLS TO IMPROVE YOUR RELATIONSHIP SKILLS   247

CHAPTER 13
The Choices You Make   *249*
HOW DO YOUR CURRENT DECISIONS AFFECT YOUR FUTURE?

SPOTLIGHT ON CLASSROOM SKILLS   249

PREVIEW   249

KEY TERMS   249

CHAPTER INTRODUCTION   250

THE CHOICES YOU MAKE   250
Returning to the beginning   *250*

WHERE HAVE YOU BEEN—AND WHAT HAVE YOU DONE?   253

CHAPTER SUMMARY   256
A 13-step guide to better study habits   *257*

REALITY CHECK: DREAMS, ACTION, REALITY, AND ENERGY   258

References   261

Problem-Solving Index   265

Subject Index   267

PREFACE

As a classroom instructor, I often greet "second editions" with a raised and cynical eyebrow. Has the content changed so significantly that an entirely new book is warranted?

Now, sitting in front of my computer, I have to confront this question from the author's perspective—and my cynicism has diminished. While the first edition of *Study Skills: Do I Really Need This Stuff?* benefited thousands of students across the country, I have come to understand the power of the review process. With the input of several reviewers, current users, and students, I realize that a revision could indeed be even more powerful and helpful to students.

This edition has two new themes that will connect each chapter. These integrated themes will examine:

- How critical thinking strategies allow students to immediately apply the study skills they are learning in each chapter
- How the choices students have made—or will make–influence what they achieve

This new edition still retains its student-friendly tone and reliance upon reflective activities to help students understand what they can do well—and on what they need to improve.

The outline below highlights the features, changes, and additions of *Study Skills: Do I Really Need This Stuff?*, Second Edition.

FEATURES FOR THE SECOND EDITION

- *Each chapter* starts with *student perspectives* that emphasize what is (probably) on most students' minds concerning the topic of the chapter. The feature also indicates the problems that arise when the chapter skill is not mastered. While this "Spotlight on classroom skills" feature cannot be attributed to any one student, it does reflect a compilation of student thoughts that I have heard from students. The use of the pronoun "I" in the feature is mostly for stylistic purposes.

- *Chapters* start with measurable objectives for the students to master. This feature allows the students to move from fuzzy feel-good words to actual tasks that encourage them to use the chapter skills in a practical and observable manner. For instance:
  - The chapter on class time includes the following measurable objective: *When you have completed this chapter, you will be able to describe one strategy to help develop a working and respectful relationship with your instructors.*
  - The chapter addressing reading strategies includes the following measurable objective: *When you have completed this chapter, you*

will be able to demonstrate how to use the steps of the SQ4R reading process.

- The chapter about civility includes the following measurable objective: *When you have completed this chapter, you will be able to use at least three active listening techniques to improve your communication skills.*

- Each chapter has an *assessment* that allows students to reflect on their experiences and current level of expertise with the chapter topic.

  - *Example:* The chapter 2 activity, *"Reflection on Your Current Level of Critical Thinking Skills,"* allows students to review their experience with lower-level and higher-level thinking skills.

- A *Problem-Solving Index* supplements the typical subject index. The PSI enables students to quickly find answers to study skills questions they may have.

  - *Example:* Rather than just listing *Note-taking* in the index, the PSI will specify a particular problem that students are likely to have: *Note taking: I take notes but still miss the main point. What can I do differently?*

- *Each chapter* provides *Out-of-Classroom Activities* to give students the opportunity to apply the new strategies in different situations, and thus *deepen the sustainability (or permanence) of the strategies.*

  - *Example:* A Chapter 4 activity asks students to move beyond their current class and examine the environment in which they study. This assessment will allow students to more effectively and efficiently organize their study space.

NEW TO THE SECOND EDITION

- The order of the chapters has been modified to reflect the scaffolding of study skills concepts. Each chapter introduces skills that build upon the previous chapters' academic strategies. All chapters will build upon critical thinking skills introduced in Chapter 2.

- The chapter on *organization* goes beyond typical *time* management skills. It also provides tips as to how students can organize personal *space* to enhance growth and decrease *stress.*

- *Active learning* is addressed on two levels: What the student should do *inside* the classroom and *outside* the classroom to maximum the *return on investment* of time. These chapters have been revised.

- An entire *new chapter* is dedicated to the issues of *information literacy.*

- An entire *new chapter* examines various levels of *civility and group dynamics.* It includes how to get the most from study groups and classroom teams and how to build a respectful relationship with the classroom professor.

- The *issue of academic integrity* is addressed.

- *Each chapter* concludes with a comprehension activity titled "Reality Check." This provides students with a *real-life study skills dilemma that they will have to solve by applying skills* from the chapter.

- Over the course of the book, students will collect a portfolio of strategies that they will have developed and tested while internalizing the study skill concepts from each chapter. In this way they will be able to answer the question, "What am I doing to get what I want?"

- A note on terminology: The first edition titled each chapter as a "module." In the second edition all chapters are titled "chapters." The word, module, indicates a sense that something stands alone as independent content. Because the chapters of this book build upon one another, it is more appropriate to call this content "chapters."

- The chapter on writing has been moved to this text's companion website. Recognizing that the most effective writing training will occur in English courses, the companion website module provides a review of simple strategies to help students with the writing process. In addition to activities to help with the general nuts and bolts of crafting papers, strategies will help students conquer writing blocks and self-evaluate (and peer-evaluate) their completed papers before submitting them for teacher review. **New to this edition** is a section on academic integrity and avoiding plagiarism.

OVERVIEW OF THE CHAPTERS: WHAT'S NEW AND REVISED?

Introduction—**The Choices You Make** (new)

- The introduction provides students with an overview of the book's integrated themes:
  - Critical thinking strategies
  - The choices you make

1. **Setting the stage: What's on your mind?** (new)
   - This chapter provides an overview of the major study skill challenges students encounter with college work—and how this book will help them.

2. **Critical thinking:** How will these skills lead to academic success? (new)
   - This chapter examines higher-level thinking skills and how they can be applied to improve study skill strategies and increase confidence. Critical thinkers, problem solvers, and creative thinkers do more than memorize and repeat information. They *reflect* on the information before them, and then they demonstrate understanding by using the knowledge for practical purposes. Seven standards are introduced—and used throughout the book.

3. **Goal setting:** If you know what you want to do, why do you need to read about goal setting? (revised)
   - Many students do not initially see the need to set goals. This chapter goes beyond how to write a goal. It examines common obstacles as well as the connection between locus of control and being able to achieve a goal.

4. **Organizing time and space:** How will these skills improve academic performance and reduce your stress? (**revised**)

   ■ Organizing time *and* space will provide students with strategies to be effective, efficient, and less stressed. Although college does require considerable work, students also have more *unstructured* time than they have ever had before. They will have to organize their schedules to include studies, family responsibilities, recreation, and the like. Additionally, they will have to organize personal study space so it will work efficiently. This chapter also will examine the causes of stress and strategies for dealing with stress.

5. **Learning styles:** How will knowing your learning style help with your studies? (**revised**)

   ■ This chapter explains the connection between whole-brain thinking and learning styles. Practical activities will allow students to apply this knowledge to their academic studies. Students will use the VARK Questionnaire (learning preference inventory).

6. **Class time:** How can you be more successful during class time? (**revised**)

   ■ This chapter describes strategies that will help students become more active and effective *inside* the classroom. Students will build on what they have learned in the previous chapters and on what they learned prior to coming to college. The chapter will include information on how to forge productive working relationships with classmates and instructors.

7. **Note taking:** How will effective notes help you understand class material? (**new**)

   ■ This chapter demonstrates how to remain academically engaged *outside* of the classroom. Specifically, students will examine ways to use classroom notes outside of the classroom to help them understand the "big picture."

8. **Reading:** You have to read 1,000 pages by when? (**revised**)

   ■ The level and quantity of college reading assignments comes as a shock to many students. This chapter examines how to approach a reading assignment in an organized and effective manner. Critical thinking activities will help students connect their homework reading assignments to in-class activities.

9. **Memory:** Why do you forget—and what can you do about it? (**revised**)

   ■ Sound memory strategies help with more than test taking. This chapter will suggest strategies to help you *notice, store,* and *reclaim* information.

10. **Test taking:** How can you improve your test-preparation and test-performance skills? (**revised**)

    ■ Successful test taking is not a one-day event. It requires a plan. This chapter will make connections between test performance and the study skills presented thus far in this book. Students will examine test anxiety—and strategies to combat it.

11. **Information literacy:** How can you use information and technology for your benefit? (**new**)

    ■ Students live in an age that allows them to get information from virtually anywhere in the world with a couple of keystrokes and the push of the Enter button. They have to understand that the explosion of data does not necessarily equate to an explosion of credible knowledge. Consequently, once the information has been found, students need to know how to evaluate what they have found before they decide to use the information.

12. **Civility:** How can working with others affect your academic success? (**new**)

   ■ College work requires more than passively listening to lectures and taking notes. Group work, study teams, debates, lab experiments, oral presentations, and conferences with professors all demand high levels of *civility* and *responsibility*. This chapter will provide strategies for enjoying fulfilling collaborative relationships. Whether the association is a short-term group project or a conference about your grades, respect for yourself and others will help build a meaningful relationship.

13. **The choices you make:** How do your current decisions affect your future? (**new**)

   ■ This chapter reviews the book's integrated themes and how they have affected the choices students made this term. As they near the end of a successful term, it is time to look to the future. What has been learned that will affect the choices they will make next term, next year, and the rest of their lives? Choices change lives, and with these choices come the opportunities to have a rewarding academic experience.

One last note about this second edition: Since the time that I wrote the first edition of *Study Skills: Do I Really Need This Stuff?* I have had the good fortune to write and publish *Rhythms of College Success: A Journey of Discovery, Change, and Mastery* (Pearson Prentice Hall, 2008). Some material from that book has been used in the chapters that follow.*

ACKNOWLEDGEMENTS FOR THE SECOND EDITION

At every step of the writing process, I have been blessed with nurturing friendships, honest critiques, and professional guidance. Trying to thank everyone is impossible—but I would like to mention a few of the people who have added immeasurably to the book you hold in your hands.

An author puts words to paper—but the final product is the work of a larger team. This book benefited from the scrutiny and suggestions from my peers in the field—professionals who helped me shape rough, and at times, confused ideas into reader-friendly chapters. I would like to especially thank Chrissie Chapman, Lewis and Clark Community College; Molly Euken, Alfred State College; Lewis Gray, Middle Tennessee State University; Doriss Hambrick, Baylor University; Patricia Malinowski, Finger Lakes Community College; Terry Miller, South Texas College; and Lisa Taylor-Galizia, Carteret Community College.

If we are fortunate as we move through our professional careers, we get to work with one or two people who *really stand out* and exemplify professionalism, trust, and teamwork. I have been fortunate to have that relationship

---

*Piscitelli, Steve. *Rhythms of College Success: A Journey of Discovery, Change, and Mastery,* 1st edition, © 2008. Electronically reproduced by permission of Pearson Education, Inc., Upper Saddle River, New Jersey.

with Pearson Education. My executive editor, Sande Johnson, and Jenny Gessner, development editor, kept me focused and balanced throughout the process. Sande, thanks for believing in me and supporting my efforts. You are a rare gem. Jenny, thanks for keeping my sentences parallel and my metaphors clear.

I also appreciate the support Jeff Johnston, vice president and executive publisher, has given to this project from beginning to end.

And huge thank you to Lynda Cramer and Kerry Rubadue at Pearson Education, who have never been too busy to answer questions and provide guidance.

It has become a cliché for teachers to say they learn as much from their students as they teach their students. But there is truth in that adage. Many of my past students have passed along ideas about study skills and student success. But I would like to thank, in particular, the following students who contributed their wisdom to the "Spotlight on Classroom Skills" sections found at the beginning of each chapter: Karen McTiernan, Arlysse Bagsic, Jennifer Law, and Laura Camp.

And one more time, my wife, Laurie, has been there every step of the way. From reading all of the initial chapter drafts to giving up weekends and evenings as I wrote, she has been a model of patience. Without her nurturing and love, this book would not have been completed.

I am a lucky man!

Steve Piscitelli
Atlantic Beach, Florida

ABOUT THE AUTHOR

Steve Piscitelli has accumulated more than two decades of teaching and professional development experience. He has taught students of varying abilities and grade levels, from middle school through the university level. He has been recognized for his effective teaching style with awards at the school, county, and international level. Steve is also a seasoned workshop developer and presenter. He brings energy, humor, interaction, live original music, and practicality to his workshops.

Steve received degrees from Jacksonville University, the University of North Florida, and the University of Florida. He is currently a professor of history, education, and student success at Florida Community College in Jacksonville.

In addition to this second edition of *Study Skills: Do I Really Need This Stuff?*, Pearson Prentice Hall published his 2008 book *Rhythms of College Success: A Journey of Discovery, Change, and Mastery*. Steve, also, has authored numerous articles and a history review book for students.

Steve lives with his wife, Laurie, and canine companion, Buddy, in Atlantic Beach, Florida.

INTRODUCTION

THE CHOICES YOU MAKE

After having their planes shot out from under them in 1965, Fred Cherry and Porter Halyburton found themselves in a Vietnamese prisoner of war camp. During their seven years of captivity, they suffered some of the most horrific and brutal conditions any human being could be expected to endure.

But endure they did—with courage, dignity, and a strong sense of purpose.[1] Without trivializing their experiences, or those of their fellow captives, the philosophy enabling these men to survive can be summed up with three words: *dreams, action,* and *reality.* "Your dreams are followed by action, which creates reality."[2]

Those words—*dreams, action, reality*—had a profound impact upon me as I read their stories. Isn't this what success in school and life is really about? Our dreams can never make it to reality if we do not make the choices to put them into action.

Have you ever heard the expression, "One for the money, two for the show, three to get ready, and four to go"? Well, perhaps you have known people who live by the words, "One for the money, two for the show, three to get ready, and three to get ready, and three to get ready, and three to get ready, and. . . ." They never move! They have great dreams that are, in reality, fantasies because they have made the choice not to act: They have never gotten to "go."

I would like to add a fourth word to *dreams, action,* and *reality—energy* (see Figure I.1). Think of the last time you set a goal and reached it. More than likely the accomplishment filled you with excitement. Whether you earned an A on a math test, secured a job promotion, or won a starting spot on an athletic team, you probably experienced a surge of energy from the accomplishment. Perhaps the high you felt gave you a renewed sense of purpose or the extra oomph you needed to move on to the next task.

This book will help you *examine your choices* and how they have made—or will make—your academic dreams a reality. Always present, though perhaps less obvious, is the importance of taking care of your physical and emotional health. In this way, you will have a better chance to achieve your dreams and maintain high levels of energy for continued success.

---

[1]James S. Hirsch, *Two Souls Indivisible.* (Boston: Houghton Mifflin Company, 2004).
[2]Ibid., 195.

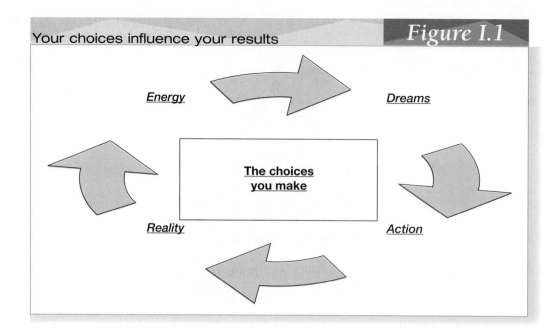

Your choices influence your results

Figure I.1

Energy   *Dreams*

**The choices
you make**

Reality   *Action*

As you work through the activities in the following chapters, you will find that there is nothing particularly magical about study skills. You have used these skills, in one form or another, in your past academic experiences. Still, you may feel a bit intimidated when confronted with new challenges. "Will I be able to do this? I've never done anything like this before. Maybe college wasn't such a great idea for me. I really don't think I can handle failing."

When confronted with such thoughts, *review the choices you have before you and take the steps needed* for academic success. Chapter strategies will help you accomplish this.

Dreams, action, reality, energy. You can—and will—do it.

CRITICAL THINKING

Consider two history classes. One requires students to memorize endless lists of dates, battles, and names. With drooping eyelids and nodding heads, students struggle to get through each class period. The second class has a professor who engages students with thought-provoking questions about why events happened and how yesterday will influence tomorrow. Each class period passes quickly.

In which class do you want to spend your time?

The first class requires little more than lower-level thinking skills—rote memorization. And although sound memory strategies help to build effective study skills, college requires higher-level thinking skills. Such critical thinking skills allow a person to apply, analyze, synthesize, and evaluate information (see Figure I.2). Once you master these skills you can move into the areas of problem solving and creative thinking.

Each chapter of this book will provide opportunities to apply study skill strategies immediately as they are introduced. You will be asked to analyze your current level of skills, connect skills you already know with skills you

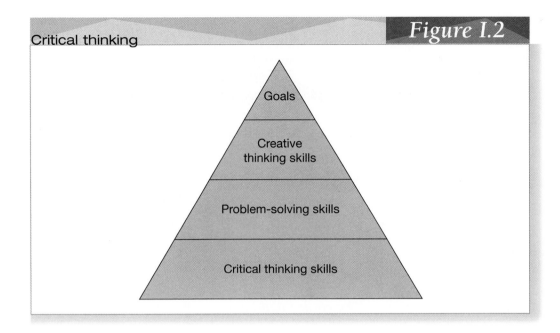

Critical thinking   *Figure I.2*

will learn, and then evaluate your level of competence. In other words, by your engaging in critical thinking activities the study skills strategies on the following pages will come alive with practical applications that will help you achieve your academic goals.

REALITY CHECK

I live on a barrier island in Northeast Florida. Because of its coastal location, it is particularly vulnerable to hurricanes. In order to remind residents to be vigilant and prepared, officials have placed multicolored poles throughout the community with the numbers 1 through 5 on each pole. The numbers indicate how high the ocean's surge tide will rise for categories 1 through 5 hurricanes. Next to the pole is the sign "Reality Check."

Reality check[3]   *Figure I.3*

[3]Photo by Steve Piscitelli.

Academic success, also, requires continual vigilance and preparation. In order to stress this critical point, each chapter of this book will end with a *Reality Check* exercise that will allow you immediately to put into practice the skills introduced in the chapter. So, when you see the reality check image be prepared to apply the knowledge you have just learned. These reality checks will allow you to reflect upon your current level of skills while responsibly adding to your study skill strategies.

ENERGIZING CHOICES

Whatever your level of academic skill might be, this book will allow you to raise your game to a new level. Just as athletes strive to improve from game to game and from season to season, successful students continually look for ways to add to their academic accomplishments.

Dream, action, reality, and *energy.* The strategies in the following chapters will help you put those dreams into action so your academic dreams, they will become reality. *The choice will be yours.* Feel the energy!

Steve Piscitelli
Atlantic Beach, Florida

CHAPTER 1

SETTING THE STAGE

What's on your mind?

SPOTLIGHT ON CLASSROOM SKILLS

When I got to college, I thought I was prepared. After all, I had finished high school without much difficulty and with fairly good grades. So you can imagine that I was a bit "put off" when my adviser told me I had to enroll in a study skills course. "Why do I need that?" was my first thought. "That's a course for students with problems—not me!"

Well, I quickly discovered that I did not know what I did not know! That is, I was unaware that college success would require a new kind of approach to study skills—effective and efficient strategies to learn.

Study skills are necessary for serious students who want to master their academic work. Find a book, find a course, or find a person who can help you evaluate your current level of skills and build a series of success strategies that apply to all of your courses. Improved study skills not only will help you master your course work, but they also will make you feel better about yourself as a student.

Study skills are for all students. They help students develop strategies and techniques to focus their energies on efficient and effective studying. And sound study skills contribute to positive self-esteem. A student who can achieve in the classroom will feel better about his or her capabilities. In other words, competence will foster esteem.

PREVIEW

By the time you finish reading this chapter and completing its activities you will be able to:

- Identify at least two study skill challenges that you have.
- Identify at least two study skill strengths that you have.
- Explain how you might be able to use your study skill strengths to work on one of your study skill challenges.
- List at least five study skill topics covered in this book that you can immediately use.
- Explain how a study skills course can help you experience more success as a student.

KEY TERMS

- Academic challenge
- Academic strength
- Critical thinking
- Locus of control
- Study skills

CHAPTER INTRODUCTION

WHAT DO YOU THINK OF WHEN YOU HEAR THE TERM *STUDY SKILLS?*

Most students approach a study skills course (or book) with little or no enthusiasm. It's not one of the most popular topics in the course catalog. Typical responses include:

- I am too smart for this course!
- Why do I need this course? I do my homework every night. Isn't that studying?
- What makes smart students smart? They must do nothing but home-work—bunch of nerds!
- My adviser made me take this course.
- Sounds like an easy A!

If you break the term *study skills* into its two parts you have:

- *Study:* This is your personal effort to learn something. It could be aca-demic (learn how to speak a foreign language), athletic (learn how to play tennis), occupational (learn how to do a particular job), or emotional (learn how to control anxiety or a temper). You have "studied" your entire life—even before you ever set foot in a school. That is, you have learned how to do certain things. For our purposes, this book will con-centrate on learning within the school setting.

  - *Synonyms* include deep thinking, inspection, analysis, and concentration.

- *Skill:* When someone has a skill he or she can do something with a degree of expertise. A skill is sharpened through practice and experience. Even someone with a natural talent—say in music—will need practice to become expert or "skilled" in his or her area. When you have a skill you are able to do something well. Typically when someone develops a skill it involves a certain amount of studying.

  - *Synonyms* include ability, mastery, competence, and expertise.

For our purposes, *study skills* will refer to your *abilities to learn how to do academic things well.* A look at the table of contents of this book reveals some of the usual study skill topics of organization, note taking, reading, problem solving, active learning, and test taking.

So, whether your school required you to take a study skills course or you decided it would be good for you, recognize that such a course is *not* designed for "problem students," "slow learners," or "struggling students." It remains a course for the committed student who wishes to discover the best ways to learn and excel on campus.

I REALLY DO WANT TO LEARN—BUT I JUST CAN'T!

It is frustrating to have the desire to learn but come up short on result. As you work through the activities in this book, identify obstacles to your learning as well as the strengths that help you learn. What stands in your way of being as successful as you would like? Are these obstacles related to attitude or ability? What strengths have helped you in the past to achieve in the classroom?

Activity 1.1, "Assessment of Strengths and Challenges," will help you focus on some of your academic challenges—as well as your strengths. *All* students bring skills and strategies from academic experiences that will help them be successful in the college classroom.

ASSESSMENT OF STRENGTHS AND CHALLENGES   ACTIVITY 1.1

Before you can work on your challenges, you need to know what they are. That may seem obvious, but sometimes we miss the obvious. So, take a moment and complete the following checklist. At the same time, it will help to remind yourself of your strengths—those things you do well. You may be able to use a strength to minimize or eliminate a challenge. For instance, your ability to critically think may help you determine the best way to address a test-taking challenge.

The challenges you want to concern yourself with at this point are *process* challenges, not *content* challenges. For this activity focus on what you *do,* rather than the material you learn. Concentrate, for instance, on the ways in which you can become a more capable student in math (or English, or history, or science, or Spanish, or some other class).

Below, check your *strengths* when it comes to studying. What do you do well? Check as many or as few as apply. Take your time and think about each choice carefully.

- ◯ Setting goals
- ◯ Completing goals

- ◯ Writing a strong essay thesis statement
- ◯ Supporting an opinion with facts

(continued)

- ○ Establishing priorities
- ○ Completing work on time
- ○ Eliminating distractions
- ☑ Taking notes from class lectures
- ☑ Taking notes from the textbook
- ○ Taking organized notes
- ☑ Getting to class on time
- ☑ Participating in class
- ○ Keeping an organized notebook
- ○ Regularly reviewing and organizing class notes
- ○ Coming to class prepared
- ○ Understanding and using learning style information
- ○ Using critical thinking skills to solve problems
- ☑ Getting the main point from a reading assignment

- ○ Organizing an essay
- ○ Writing and completing an essay
- ○ Establishing relationships and connections
- ○ Remembering important information for exams
- ○ Controlling test anxiety
- ○ Preparing, in plenty of time, for exams
- ○ Completing exams in the time allotted
- ○ Learning from previous exam mistakes
- ○ Taking study breaks
- ○ Studying alone
- ○ Studying with friends
- ○ Locating information for research projects
- ○ Evaluating information for research projects
- ○ Other: _____
  _____

Now, check your *challenges* when it comes to studying. What do you need to improve? Check as many or as few as apply. Take your time and think about each choice carefully.

- ○ Setting goals
- ○ Completing goals
- ○ Establishing priorities
- ○ Completing work on time
- ○ Eliminating distractions
- ○ Taking notes from class lectures
- ○ Taking notes from the textbook
- ○ Taking organized notes
- ○ Getting to class on time
- ○ Participating in class
- ○ Keeping an organized notebook
- ○ Regularly reviewing and organizing class notes
- ○ Coming to class prepared
- ○ Understanding and using learning style information
- ○ Using critical thinking skills to solve problems
- ○ Getting the main point from a reading assignment

- ○ Writing a strong essay thesis statement
- ○ Supporting an opinion with facts
- ○ Organizing an essay
- ○ Writing and completing an essay
- ○ Establishing relationships and connections
- ○ Remembering important information for exams
- ○ Controlling test anxiety
- ○ Preparing, in plenty of time, for exams
- ○ Completing exams in the time allotted
- ○ Learning from previous exam mistakes
- ○ Taking study breaks
- ○ Studying alone
- ○ Studying with friends
- ○ Locating information for research projects
- ○ Evaluating information for research projects
- ○ Other: _____

_____

(continued)

Review your checked boxes in each section above. List below the five *strengths* you consider your biggest assets, ranking them from 1 to 5. Do the same for your *challenges*.

STRENGTHS

1. _____

2. _____

3. _____

4. _____

5. _____

CHALLENGES

1. _____

2. _____

3. _____

4. _____

5. _____

Look at the strengths you listed. In what ways might you be able to use those strengths to help you minimize your challenges? For instance, if one of your weaknesses is "getting the main idea from a reading assignment" and a strength is, "taking organized notes," how can you use that strength to help with your challenges? List the strength you want to discuss here: _____
_____

How can your strength be used to minimize one of your challenges? _____
_____

Based on your rankings above, what can you say about your study skills? Are they strong? How can they be improved? _____
_____
_____

WHAT IS ON YOUR MIND?

Each new term in college presents its own set of challenges. New courses, new instructors, and new demands require students to reevaluate their study and relationship skills in and out of the classroom.

Books such as this present ideas and topics in a rather linear fashion. Each chapter devotes space and activities to a particular topic. After you finish one topic you move to the next—and so on until you finish the book.

The realities of your life, however, do not follow a straight path. You have many things tugging at you on a daily basis. And what may be of importance to the student sitting next to you in class, may not even be on your radar.

For instance, one of the first chapters of this book looks at goal setting. While being able to identify a specific direction is important, you might very well be more concerned *right now* about how to complete—on time—all of the assignments you have.

The purpose of this chapter is to give you a chance to explore what is on your mind about study skills.

A Quick Preview of Coming Attractions

Movie "trailers"—quick advertisements—give previews of coming attractions. With a couple of clips from a movie, viewers have an idea of what the movie has to offer. Effective trailers will draw people to the movie.

Consider, if you would, this book to be the "movie" and the following chapters of this book to be the "scenes." Together they all make up the main feature. This chapter will help you preview the coming attractions—the coming chapters. This will warm you up and prepare you for what is to come. It will also help you locate information that is of immediate interest.

The following twelve activities (1.2 through 1.13) allow you to look at what this book offers and to locate the topics that may be most helpful at this point in your college term.

At first glance you may believe twelve activities (one for each chapter) to be overwhelming. But there is a simple guideline that will help you maximize your time. *Spend no more than five minutes on each activity.* If you desire, you can devote more time but remember that you will have plenty of time to spend on each chapter later in the term. For now, you only have two purposes:

- Concentrate on what is on your mind about effective study skills right now.
- Familiarize yourself with the contents of this textbook.

By time you are done with the activities you will have identified twelve topics of immediate interest to you—and you will have done this in only sixty minutes. What a valuable investment in a short period of time. Wouldn't you say you and your academic success are worth an hour?*

ACTIVITY 1.2   CRITICAL THINKING

Look at the bold-faced headings, tables, and figures of Chapter 2. Choose one item (heading, table, or figure) you can use right now.

○ List the item here. _____

   ○ Briefly, explain your interest in this item. Does it address a strength of yours or a challenge?

   _____

   _____

ACTIVITY 1.3   GOAL SETTING AND MOTIVATION

Look at the bold-faced headings, tables, and figures of Chapter 3. Choose one item (heading, table, or figure) you can use right now.

---

*And you will have practiced a reading strategy known as SQ4R, which will be fully described in Chapter 8.

○ List the item here. _____

   ○ Briefly, explain your interest in this item. Does it address a strength of yours or a challenge?

_____

_____

ORGANIZING TIME AND SPACE   ACTIVITY **1.4**

Look at the bold-faced headings, tables, and figures of Chapter 4. Choose one
item (heading, table, or figure) you can use right now.

○ List the item here. _____

   ○ Briefly, explain your interest in this item. Does it address a strength of yours or a challenge?

_____

_____

LEARNING STYLES   ACTIVITY **1.5**

Look at the bold-faced headings, tables, and figures of Chapter 5. Choose one
item (heading, table, or figure) you can use right now.

○ List the item here. _____

   ○ Briefly, explain your interest in this item. Does it address a strength of yours or a challenge?

_____

_____

CLASS TIME   ACTIVITY **1.6**

Look at the bold-faced headings, tables, and figures of Chapter 6. Choose one
item (heading, table, or figure) you can use right now.

○ List the item here. _____

   ○ Briefly, explain your interest in this item. Does it address a strength of yours or a challenge?

_____

_____

NOTE TAKING   ACTIVITY **1.7**

Look at the bold-faced headings, tables, and figures of Chapter 7. Choose one
item (heading, table, or figure) you can use right now.

○ List the item here. _____

   ○ Briefly, explain your interest in this item Does it address a strength of yours or a challenge?

_____

_____

ACTIVITY 1.8   READING

Look at the bold-faced headings, tables, and figures of Chapter 8. Choose one item (heading, table, or figure) you can use right now.

○ List the item here. _____

  ○ Briefly, explain your interest in this item. Does it address a strength of yours or a challenge?

_____

_____

ACTIVITY 1.9   MEMORY

Look at the bold-faced headings, tables, and figures of Chapter 9. Choose one item (heading, table, or figure) you can use right now.

○ List the item here. _____

  ○ Briefly, explain your interest in this item. Does it address a strength of yours or a challenge?

_____

_____

ACTIVITY 1.10   TEST TAKING

Look at the bold-faced headings, tables, and figures of Chapter 10. Choose one item (heading, table, or figure) you can use right now.

○ List the item here. _____

  ○ Briefly, explain your interest in this item. Does it address a strength of yours or a challenge?

_____

_____

ACTIVITY 1.11   INFORMATION LITERACY

Look at the bold-faced headings, tables, and figures of Chapter 11. Choose one item (heading, table, or figure) you can use right now.

○ List the item here. _____

  ○ Briefly, explain your interest in this item. Does it address a strength of yours or a challenge?

_____

_____

CIVILITY   **ACTIVITY 1.12**

Look at the bold-faced headings, tables, and figures of Chapter 12. Choose one item (heading, table, or figure) you can use right now.

○ List the item here. _____

  ○ Briefly, explain your interest in this item. Does it address a strength of yours or a challenge?

  _____

  _____

IS THERE A COMMON THREAD TO THESE CHAPTERS?

You will find three core study skill principles present throughout this book.

- *Critical thinking.* This requires gathering information, weighing it for accuracy and appropriateness, and then making a rational decision based on the facts that have been gathered. Critical thinkers are active learners who do not stop asking questions about whatever is before them. Each chapter of this book has a common emphasis on problem solving.

- *Organization.* All of the strategies require some level of organization. The successful students have it; those without it struggle. You will learn how to use both your time and space effectively and efficiently to help you enjoy and prosper from your college experience.

- *Practice.* The strategies found in the following chapters are virtually useless unless you take the time to study them, practice them, and apply them. When you find a reflective self-assessment activity in a chapter, set aside some quiet time for yourself and complete it carefully. After all, the time you invest is time you are investing in yourself. What a wonderful investment!

Locus of Control

As you saw in Activity 1.3, Chapter 3 will examine the issue of goal setting and motivation—why you do what you do. You will also read about *locus of control*[1] in that chapter. Generally speaking, this concept describes how people explain what happens to them. Do they accept responsibility for life and make things happen, or do they look for reasons (excuses) why things happen to them?

A student with an *internal* locus of control may explain poor test grades by looking into the mirror, pointing at himself, and saying, "I should have studied more." The student accepts the responsibility for what happens to him. On the other hand, a student who is more apt to blame the teacher exhibits an *external* locus of control. A comment such as "That teacher is not fair" reflects a student looking to assign responsibility elsewhere.

---

[1]Steve Piscitelli, *Rhythms of College Success: A Journey of Discovery, Change, and Mastery.* (Upper Saddle River, NJ: Pearson Prentice Hall, 2008), 39-40.

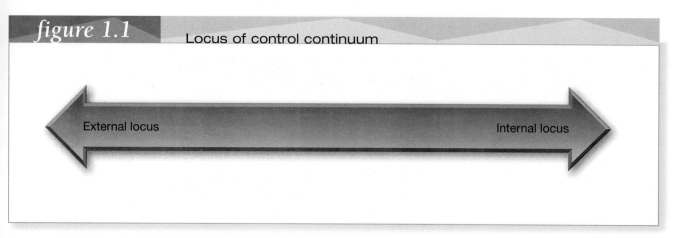

figure 1.1 Locus of control continuum

Refer to Figure 1.1. As with any continuum, few people are found on either extreme. Most of us fall somewhere in between. But upon reflection we will notice that we *tend* to *lean* to one end or the other. As you progress through the semester, think of this continuum. Are you a person who generally takes responsibility for your actions (leaning toward the "internal" end)? Or are you someone who is more apt to blame someone else (leaning toward the "external" end)? Use this information to heighten your awareness.

What Will *Not* Happen By Using This Book?

This book does not offer a way to "beat the system" in order to earn the highest possible grades. No gimmicks, no tricks. To offer such would be like going on a trendy diet to lose weight but never changing the behaviors that resulted in the extra baggage. If it were as simple as just reading a book or watching a video, you, your classmates, and most other students would be happy with high GPAs. Unfortunately, it's not that easy. So if you want a quick-fix approach offering instant gratification, the following chapters will not be for you.

What *Will* Happen By Using This Material?

The material in this book will help you identify and change those behaviors that are keeping you from being the very best student you can be. It will also help you strengthen and maintain the habits that have worked for you in the past.

The following chapters concentrate on practical skills to build academic success as well as a positive self-image. These skills help you make the transition from being a student who simply gets by to being a successful student who is aware, insightful, and confident.

Specifically, if you diligently follow the suggestions in these chapters you will:

- Learn the strategies, use the strategies immediately, and continually practice the strategies.
- Identify your unique learning style and make it work for you.
- Understand that the motivation to do well is within you. External influences may cause a temporary burst of inspiration. However, for the long term,

you must have confidence in your abilities, address your shortcomings, and develop skills that will guide you through school—and through life.

- Find that study skill strategies are also excellent life-management tools. These techniques are easily transferable to everyday life and the workplace.

Interestingly enough, academic success does *not* have to be accompanied by tedious hours of work. Yes, there will be work but what you want are *productive* hours of work. Have you ever studied for a long time only to be baffled by a large red F on an exam? How frustrating. Many students complain, "I sat at that desk for hours last night—and I still bombed!" In situations like this the problem may be your strategy, not the number of hours you have studied. Consider the following:

Given a list of tasks to remember, people will tend to remember best the first thing or group of things and the last thing or group of things on that list. The student who decides to study three hours without a break for an exam more than likely will remember what he or she studied at the very beginning of the study time and at the very end. Retention of the material in the middle will be more questionable. One author has found that "a decline in recall occurs, especially for material studied during the mid-point of the process, if study periods are too lengthy."[2]

An important strategy is to give yourself a break when studying. Be reasonable and moderate in your approach. A related strategy is to give yourself an *appropriate* reward at each brief break. For instance, after one hour of reviewing your reading assignment, you can get a snack, or listen to five minutes of music, or just walk outside for a stretch break. The point is to stay fresh and alert. *More* time is not necessarily *better* time. Examine the following two options.

- *Option 1.* You start studying at 7:00 p.m. and stop at 10:00 p.m. During this time you take no breaks, so you wind up studying for three straight hours. Therefore, there is one beginning point (7:00 p.m.) and one ending point (10:00 p.m.). That means there are *two groups of information* that you will likely remember. And if there is a lot of "information in the middle," you may find that information more difficult to remember.
- *Option 2.* You start studying at 7:00 p.m. and stop at 10:00 p.m. This time you study for one hour and then take a five-minute break. This is followed by another hour of studying, followed by a brief

---

[2]Roger G. Swartz, *Accelerated Learning: How You Learn Determines What You Learn.* (Durant, OK: EMIS, 1991), 61.

break, before resuming your final period of studying. In this example there are three beginnings and three endings during the study period. That means there are *six groups of (potentially) remembered information.*

Which option above do you think will be more effective?

This simple example points out that study strategies do not have to be painful, nor do they have to consume all of your time.

CHAPTER SUMMARY

Before leaving this chapter, keep the following points in mind:

- **Know your purpose** and mission as a student. Make the commitment to focus on success and be a successful student. Chapters 2, 3, 6, and 13 will help you.

- **Organize your time and space.** Successful students take charge of their time. You cannot control others, but you sure can control your own actions. You will find Chapters 4, 7, 8, 10, 11, and 12 of help.

- **Be positive.** Don't hinder yourself with defeatist attitudes. Visualize success and move toward it. Be realistic but also challenge yourself. Chapters 3 and 13 concentrate on helpful strategies.

- **Review, reorganize, and relate.** You will be exposed to a great deal of material in college. Get in the habit of finding connections among your assigned readings, class notes, and discussions. Once you learn how to do this, you will have a better command of the material before you. Chapters 6, 7, 8, 9, 10, and 12 will be of particular help to you.

- **Be an active learner.** Know where your instructors are going with a lesson. Don't just sit there. Follow them—maybe even get there ahead of them. Chapters 6, 7, and 10 will provide helpful strategies.

- **Pick and mix and match the strategies** of this book to suit your personality and learning style. Adapt these strategies to your learning style, practice them faithfully, and apply them to your studies. You will see improvement. Studying is a process. It is not a "get rich" scheme to gain good grades with little effort. Chapters 2 and 5 will be of particular help for you.

CHAPTER 1 MEASURABLE OBJECTIVES   ACTIVITY 1.13

At the beginning of this chapter, five measurable objectives were presented. They have been reprinted below for your convenience. Based on the strategies you have learned in this chapter, fill in the lines beneath each item (or use a separate sheet of paper).

○ Identify at least two study skill challenges that you have.

   ○ List your two challenges here: _____

   _____

   _____

○ Identify at least two study skill strengths that you have.

   ○ List your two strengths here: _____

   _____

   _____

○ Explain how you might be able to use your study skill strengths to work on one of your study skill challenges.

   ○ Write your explanation here. _____

   _____

   _____

○ List at least five study skill topics covered in this book that you can immediately use.

   ○ You may wish to refer to Activities 1.2 through 1.12 before writing your answer._____

   _____

   _____

   _____

○ Explain how a study skills course can help you experience more success as a student.

   ○ Write your answer here. _____

   _____

   _____

   _____

Rivesw surry.edu.

REALITY CHECK *A covenant with myself*

At the end of every chapter in this book, you will be asked to do a "reality check." We all know that it is one thing to read about a topic and quite another to put newfound knowledge into practice. The "reality check" section in each chapter will allow you to do this.

This chapter's reality check will be a bit different from the following chapters'. For this one you are asked to lay a foundation for all future work in this book—and in your college studies. You will be asked to make a commitment to yourself.

Because this academic journey is about you—your desire, your needs, and your success—take a moment and complete the covenant in Figure 1.2. Consider two things about this document:

- This is a *covenant,* not a *contract.* The term *contract* too often has connotations of distrust: "I'm not sure you will do what you say; therefore, I want you to sign this contract." For our purposes, let's use a much more positive approach. A *covenant* implies respect and trust. It is a public proclamation of that respect.

- This covenant is strictly personal. It is an agreement you will make with yourself. If you don't follow through, you don't follow through with yourself. Your signature indicates your desire to improve, your respect for yourself and those around you, and the trust you place in your abilities to do the best you can.

---

figure 1.2   A covenant with myself

- I realize that what I do has an impact on what I want.
- I further recognize that what I do affects those around me.
- Therefore, I pledge to make choices that reflect respect, responsibility, and honesty.

08-25-10
Today's date

My signature

(Keep this covenant in a place where you will see it each day.)

CRITICAL THINKING

How will higher-order thinking skills improve academic success?

SPOTLIGHT ON CLASSROOM SKILLS

When I started college, I was very good at staying inside the box, when it came to learning and studying. I knew how to take notes and I was very good at memorizing and rehearsing facts and figures. I could take information in, whether from reading, writing, or taking notes—and I could give it back to you. But I did not know what it meant to think critically. Formulating opinions and hypotheses on my own was foreign to me. In high school we were not encouraged to challenge or question, just learn. Because of this background, I had severely limited myself.

Perhaps you share a similar background as our student perspective above. The story is repeated each college term. Students arrive on campus used to classroom strategies that rewarded rote memorization—only to be dazed and frustrated when asked to analyze an argument, evaluate a position, or offer their own fact-supported points of view.

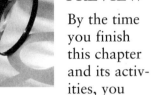

PREVIEW

By the time you finish this chapter and its activities, you will be able to:

- List at least two critical thinking strategies you have used during the past week.
- Describe clearly what critical thinking is by explaining at least four characteristics of critical thinking.
- Apply at least two of the four higher-level thinking skills in order to solve a specific problem.
- Establish a clear and precise plan to minimize (or eliminate) a study skill problem you have.
- Apply specific critical thinking standards when evaluating your study skills.
- Explain one way in which critical thinking skills can help you maintain balance and wellness in your life.

KEY TERMS

- Benjamin Bloom
- Creative thinking
- Critical thinking

College-level work will require you to think critically about issues. Just what that means and how you will do it will be the subject of this chapter.[1]

- Critical thinking standards
- Higher-order thinking skills
- Lower-order thinking skills
- Problem solving
- Problem-solving trap

CHAPTER INTRODUCTION

"But it is my opinion! How can it be wrong?" You probably have heard someone blurt out some such statement. Perhaps the person was trying to buttress an argument with a degree of certainty that would make the point sound reasonable and logical. Unfortunately, such an argument will not meet the test of critical thinking—a skill that your professors will expect you to demonstrate on assignments, tests, and in class discussions.

A critical thinker logically, precisely, and systematically examines an issue from many sides—even if that examination may differ from a deeply held personal belief. College life will expose students to situations that will challenge what they already "know" to be certain. For instance, your opinion may tell you that there is no need to read the textbook assignments or come to class every day. However, as you gain data—such as failed quizzes or exams—you may revisit and then change that mind-set.

This chapter provides strategies to use in each of the succeeding chapters of this book. As you move through each study skill you will critically assess your skill level as it exists at the beginning of each chapter. From there, you will have the opportunity to hone your study skills and build a selection of strategies that will improve your chances for achieving academic success.

ACTIVITY 2.1   REFLECTION ON YOUR CURRENT LEVEL OF CRITICAL THINKING SKILLS

Before you answer the items below, reflect on your school experiences. It might have been last year—or twenty years ago. Can you remember the types of questions your teachers asked you? Not the content of the questions but, rather, the difficulty level of the questions? Were you asked to memorize lists of terms and "spit them back" (known as a lower-order thinking skill) or did you have to understand and "analyze" and "evaluate" terms and concepts (higher-order thinking skills)?

There are no "right" answers for the questions below. It's okay if you cannot recall exactly which type of questions you most often faced; try to remember as best you can. As with all of the reflective activities in this book, write from your heart. This exercise is not meant for you to answer just like your classmates—or to match what you may think the instructor wants to see. Take your time to give a respectful and responsible general accounting of your experiences with critical thinking. A truthful self-assessment now will help you build on skills you possess while developing those you lack.

---

[1]Steve Piscitelli, *Rhythms of College Success: A Journey of Discovery, Change, and Mastery* (Upper Saddle River, NJ: Pearson Prentice Hall, 2008), 102–115.

For the following items circle the number that best describes your *typical* experience with critical thinking. The key for the numbers is:

0 = never, 1 = almost never, 2 = occasionally, 3 = frequently,
4 = almost always, 5 = always

When considering your past course work, how often:

1. Did you have to *memorize* things like terms, dates, and formulas?

   0   1   2   3   4   (5)

2. Were you rewarded (with a good grade) for *spitting back* nearly exact wording from textbooks or lectures?

   0   1   2   3   (4)   5

3. Did you have to *summarize* an explanation in your own words?

   0   1   2   3   4   (5)

4. Were you assigned to read a chapter (or book or essay) and then asked to *evaluate* (judge) what you read according to specific standards or criteria?

   0   1   2   3   (4)   5

5. Did your teachers ask you to *develop* your own theory or explanation for an event?

   0   1   2   3   (4)   5

6. Did your teachers expect you to *use* the knowledge you learned in class to solve a problem you had never seen before?

   0   1   2   3   (4)   5

7. Were you encouraged and rewarded for developing *new* and *unusual* solutions to a problem?

   0   1   2   3   (4)   5

8. Did you have to answer questions simply by searching for the *correct* answer in the textbook or lecture notes?

   0   1   2   3   (4)   5

9 Lower-order thinking skill experience. Add up your scores for items 1, 2, 3, and 8. Divide by 4. Write your answer here: ____4.5_____

10. Using the key explanations for each number (0, 1, 2, 3, 4, 5) for this activity, complete this sentence: When it comes to thinking I _____ used lower-order thinking skills.

11 Higher-order thinking skills experience. Add up your scores for items 4, 5, 6, and 7. Divide by 4. Write your answer here: ____4.5_____

12 Using the key explanations for each number (0, 1, 2, 3, 4, 5) for this activity, complete this sentence: When it comes to thinking I _____ used higher-order thinking skills.

13 Based on your answers, what insights do you have about your experiences with higher-order (critical) thinking skills?_____

_____

_____

© 2005 Stockdisc

DEFINING CRITICAL THINKING

You have read and used the word *critical* many times in your life. You might have heard that someone was injured and in critical condition. Or perhaps in the heat of an argument a friend made a critical comment about you. More than likely, a teacher has asked you to read a particular assignment with a critical eye.

For our purposes—and for most academic purposes—critical thinking has more to do with the third example above than the preceding two. When your instructors ask you to think, read, write, or discuss an issue critically, they generally want you to examine, argue, analyze, or evaluate. Such thinking requires gathering information, weighing it for accuracy and appropriateness, and then making a rational decision based on the facts that have been gathered.

table 2.1   Applying standards of critical thinking to study skills

CRITICAL THINKING STANDARD	APPLICATION TO YOUR STUDY SKILLS	EXAMPLE OF HOW TO USE THE STANDARD
Clarity	Can you clearly state your particular strength or challenge with study skills?	I continually run out of time! Between work, school, and family many things pull at me every day.
Accuracy	How do you know your assessments of your strengths and/or challenges are accurate? Is there any way to gauge the truth of the assessment?	I know I have a time-management problem because I am late everywhere I need to be.
Precision	Can you specifically explain your strengths and challenges with study skills?	Specifically, I do not know how to gauge how much time I will need to complete a given task.
Relevance	Is your assessment of your study skills connected to your actual academic progress?	Since I am always late, my grades have declined in each of my classes.
Depth	When you examine your study skills do you go beyond a superficial explanation and look at all of the complexities involved?	My problem goes beyond just keeping a calendar or day planner. I need to learn how to say "no," prioritize my days—and take control of my life!
Breadth	Have you looked at your study skills strengths or challenges from more than one perspective?	My time problems result from not knowing how to prioritize, taking on too many responsibilities, and forgetting why I am here in college.

(continued)

table 2.1	(Continued)	
CRITICAL THINKING STANDARD	**APPLICATION TO YOUR STUDY SKILLS**	**EXAMPLE OF HOW TO USE THE STANDARD**
Logic	Based on your evidence, does your conclusion about your study skills make sense?	Although I seem to know why I am having time management problems, I need to talk with an objective observer who can help me refocus my energies.

Such thinking requires a person to have command of basic information about an issue. For instance, before making an informed vote in an election, the critical thinker, at the very least, must know the candidates' names and the issues of the election. From there, our would-be voter can compare and contrast candidate proposals.

When it comes to understanding a problem and moving toward a solution, critical thinkers set aside emotion and short cuts and examine the issue on a number of intellectual levels. The table above provides a quick guide using commonly accepted standards and how they might be applied to a particular study skill challenge—in this example, that of time management.[2]

Mark this page with a sticky note or paper clip so that you can easily refer to it. You will draw on the concepts above throughout the book.

HIGHER-ORDER THINKING SKILLS

In 1956, educational pioneer Benjamin Bloom developed a six-tier thinking-skills model:

1. *Knowledge.* Remembering facts, names, events; rote recall
2. *Comprehension.* Putting information into your own words
3. *Application.* Taking learned information and using it in a new situation
4. *Analysis.* Examining or breaking down the parts of information
5. *Synthesis.* Combining pieces of information to create a larger and newer piece of information
6. *Evaluation.* Assessing or judging the worth of information

The first level, *knowledge* or recall information—that is, remembering facts or names—is the lowest order (or level) of thinking. When you memorize a list of vocabulary words and then repeat those words on a classroom quiz, the information has been recalled from your memory. Do not, however, confuse "low level" with "unimportant"; this level is a basic building block in the learning process. Think of it as gathering the fundamental pieces of knowledge. This vital skill helps lay the foundation for the higher-order thinking skills—similar to a football receiver, who cannot be expected to catch a football in a game unless he can first remember the pass pattern he needs to run.

[2]The intellectual standards used here are commonly cited in the literature. Linda Elder and Richard Paul, "Universal Intellectual Standards," *The Critical Thinking Community* www.criticalthinking.org/resources/articles/universal-intellectual-standards.shtml (accessed July 1, 2007) presents the commonly accepted intellectual standards of clarity, accuracy, precision, relevance, depth, breadth, and logic.

The next level up on Bloom's list, *comprehension*, requires an understanding of the information presented. When you can read or hear something and then put it into your own words, there is an increased chance you will remember it. It may be only one step above recalling general knowledge, but comprehension indicates that the information has been interpreted for individual understanding.

The next four levels move your thinking into higher-order thinking skills.

USING HIGHER-ORDER THINKING SKILLS

To make the most appropriate use of the higher-order thinking skills described next, a person must master the smaller details noted in the preceding paragraphs. The effectiveness of critical thinking, problem solving, and creative thinking will be significantly reduced if the basics are not understood.

Critical Thinking

Active learning involves many forms of thinking. You have no doubt been exposed to the terms *critical thinking, problem solving,* and *creative thinking* during your schooling. Some people use the terms interchangeably, freely substituting one term for another.

A more precise view would be to think of each as a distinct thinking process; one leads to the other; one builds on the previous and uses deeper thinking skills.

One author believes that someone who engages in critical thinking "responds with awareness" and leads an "examined life."[3] Critical thinkers take time to reflect on the issue before them. They analyze what has happened and what is needed. Critical thinkers question assumptions; they do not passively accept other people's explanations. But this requires the use of higher-order thinking skills.

Obviously, the facts must be gathered about a particular situation, problem, or question. But knowing the facts is only the first step (lower-order thinking). The information must be seriously examined. For example, during the academic year campuses across the nation hold elections for student government offices. Student candidates place their names on ballots in hopes of winning a spot on the campus decision-making team. A *noncritically thinking* voter may make a decision strictly based on name recognition (a fact): "I know that person from my history class. She seems nice. I'll vote for her." This is an example of a *noncritical review* of the candidate. Factual recall (the name and personality trait) does not mean an understanding of the issues.

The critical thinker will go through a deeper process by seriously examining the issues: "I recognize the name and I also have asked her about the parking problem on campus. She has a four-point plan to provide more space by the end of this term. The plan is reasonable and has a chance to work. I'll vote for her!" This would-be voter has critically analyzed the candidate according to a particular issue, evaluated the proposed solution, and then made a decision based on the analysis and evaluation. The critical thinking process is illustrated in Figure 2.1.

Reviewing Bloom's categories once again, note that the first two categories exhibit *noncritical thinking characteristics,* but the last four levels describe forms of critical thinking. Table 2.2 outlines Bloom's levels of critical thinking

---

[3]Elaine Gray, *Conscious Choices: A Model for Self-Directed Learning* (Upper Saddle River, NJ: Prentice Hall, 2004), 26–34.

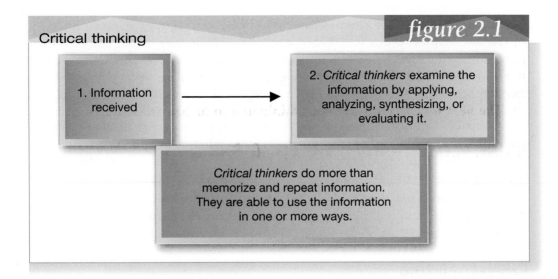

figure 2.1

Critical thinking

1. Information received

2. *Critical thinkers* examine the information by applying, analyzing, synthesizing, or evaluating it.

Critical thinkers do more than memorize and repeat information. They are able to use the information in one or more ways.

and suggests that a critical thinker is actively and deeply involved in processing information.

Also, note that these higher-order thinking skills use the critical thinking standards introduced in Table 2.1. For instance, analyzing an issue requires clarity and precision. Evaluating a position requires depth, breadth, and logic.

table 2.2   Bloom and critical thinking

LEVEL OF THINKING	CHARACTERISTICS	IS IT CRITICAL THINKING? WHY?
Knowledge	Remembering facts, names, events; rote recall	*Noncritical thinking:* Surface learning only
Comprehension	Putting information into your own words	*Noncritical thinking:* Surface learning only
Application	Taking learned information and using it in a new situation	*Critical thinking:* The person understands the information and can use it in a new situation.
Analysis	Examining or breaking down the parts of information	*Critical thinking:* The person understands the information and demonstrates this understanding by separating or splitting the information into its pieces or parts.
Synthesis	Combining pieces of information to create a larger and newer piece of information	*Critical thinking:* The person understands the information and then brings pieces of the information together to form a big picture or new idea.
Evaluation	Assessing or judging the worth of information	*Critical thinking:* The person has the ability to judge or critique the value of the information.

ACTIVITY 2.2   CRITICAL THINKING APPLIED TO STUDY SKILLS

When you consider your study skills, list one of your challenge areas. That is, list one of your own study skills that you know can be stronger. _____ _Taking notes from textbook in my own words._

Using one of the critical thinking skills above (application, analysis, synthesis, evaluation), can you *clearly and precisely* state what your specific problem or challenge is with the study skill you identified? For example, do you have difficulty *applying* your class notes to reading or writing assignments? _____

_____

_____

Problem Solving

The next level of thinking, problem solving, *uses* critical thinking. Not all critical thinking is problem solving, but all problem solving *requires* critical thinking. Problem solving, in short, requires the use of thinking skills to *examine* a dilemma *and* then *propose* a solution. The process is illustrated in Figure 2.2.

For an example, let's look at the issue of campus security. A critical thinker would gather reports on the number of assaults that have taken place on campus during the last twelve months. He would determine at what hours and in what parts of the campus most of the attacks have taken place. The response time of the security personnel might also be considered. All of this requires deep thinking and fact finding. But if our critically thinking student gathers the information, analyzes, and then submits a report *without a solution* then the problem has not been solved.

Whether in an academic setting (as above) or dealing with a personal crisis, the problem solver moves to the next level as he looks at the information *and* then begins to propose alternatives and answers.

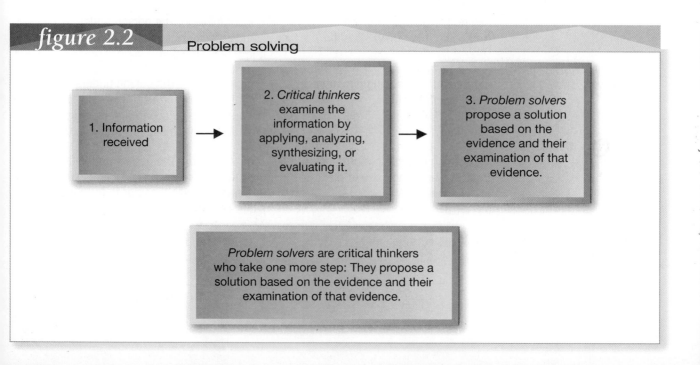

figure 2.2   Problem solving

1. Information received

2. *Critical thinkers* examine the information by applying, analyzing, synthesizing, or evaluating it.

3. *Problem solvers* propose a solution based on the evidence and their examination of that evidence.

Problem solvers are critical thinkers who take one more step: They propose a solution based on the evidence and their examination of that evidence.

Problem-Solving Models

Two main points deserve emphasis:

1. You have confronted and solved problems your entire life.
2. Numerous models for problem solving exist.

While you examine the information below, draw on your real-life experiences as well. Combining the new with the old will expand your collection of effective strategies. Whether you read a study skills book such as this one or look at a book on conflict resolution, you will find they all share the following broad categorical strategies:

- Reflecting on the problem (What happened and why?)

- Brainstorming solutions (What can be done?)

- Choosing and implementing a solution (What steps will be taken?)

- Evaluating the chosen solutions (What happened because of the steps taken?)

To help you reach an appropriate solution, it may help to start with a visual of the problem-solving process.

No matter which model or strategy you choose, Figure 2.3 provides a graphic view of the problem-solving process.[4]

- *Problem identification.* Before you can solve a problem, the actual problem must be identified. Sounds obvious, doesn't it? This is the easiest but most often overlooked step in problem solving. When confronted with a problem, stop and take a breath. How can you solve the problem if you have not clearly identified it?

  Example: "I am scoring As and Bs on all of my math homework assignments. My test grades have not been above a D. My problem: The effort I put into my studies does not match my test grades."

  This simple step allows your body to slow down and ready itself for a more considered opinion. What exactly is the nature of the difficulty? Poor grades? Ineffective studying? A miserable supervisor? Or poor work habits? Apply the critical thinking standards (Table 2.1) for clarity and precision here.

- *Vision.* Once the problem has been pinpointed, identify where you would like to go. Where do you want to end up once you solve the problem?

  Example: "I want my math exam grades to reflect my homework grades. That is, I want to earn As and Bs on my math exams."

[handwritten: Problem Solving]

---

[4]David Straus, *How to Make Collaboration Work* (San Francisco: Berrett-Koehler Publishers, 2002).

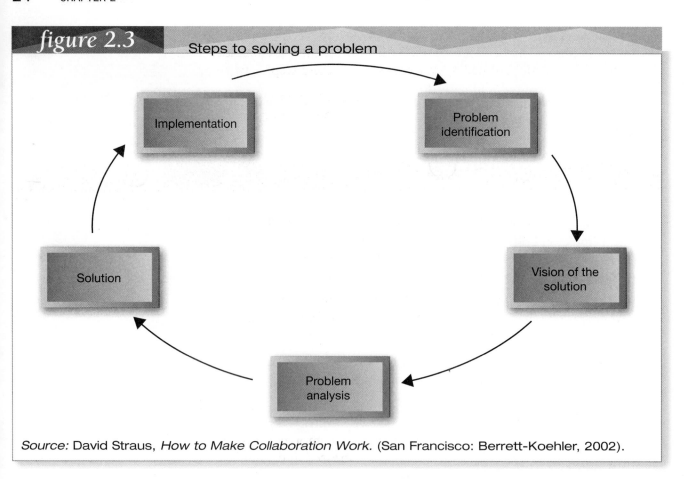

figure 2.3   Steps to solving a problem

Source: David Straus, *How to Make Collaboration Work.* (San Francisco: Berrett-Koehler, 2002).

- *Problem analysis.* Welcome to the *real work* of problem solving. Use your critical thinking standards and try to figure out *why* your problem exists. For instance, why is it that you do not perform as well on your math tests as you do on your math homework assignments? Look at the problem in depth and from as many perspectives as possible.

  Example: "My homework is nonthreatening. I never feel rushed. I start to feel anxious about the math test two or three days before the exam. I stay up late the night before trying to memorize everything in the chapter. When I walk into a math test I am stressed and tired."

- *Solution.* Once you have dissected this problem from various angles, it is time to come up with a solution. Brainstorm (generate) potential avenues on which you can travel to the needed solution. Do not judge; just list possible alternatives. The critical thinking standards of depth and breadth apply here.

  Once you have generated your potential solutions, take a moment and review the consequences for each action. For instance, which of the solutions has the best result? Worst result? Is one riskier than another is? Does each alternative address the problem you identified? Which ones can you tackle right now? Which ones ignore the problem? This step asks you to look logically at the problem and its solutions.

- *Implementation.* It is time to put your plan (goal) into action. It is great to have dreams, but they are only fantasies if you are not breathing life into them. Once you have critically evaluated the merits of each alternative, it is time to make a choice. Pick the best one and then make a plan to put it into action. What is your first step? Second step? Last step?

Consider one last suggestion: Once you have put your plan into action, take time to evaluate what you are doing. Is the plan working? Do you need to make adjustments?

SOLUTION AND IMPLEMENTATION   ACTIVITY 2.3

You will notice in the description above that there are no examples in the Solution and the Implementation sections. Use the space below to identify a solution to the problem presented above and then explain how you would implement that solution. First, here is a review of the problem, the vision, and the analysis.

Problem: "I am scoring As and Bs on all of my math homework assignments. My test grades have not been above a D. My problem: The effort I put in to my studies does not match my test grades."

Vision: "I want my math exam grades to reflect my homework grades. That is, I want to make As and Bs on my math exams."

Problem analysis: "My homework is nonthreatening. I never feel rushed. I start to feel anxious about the math test two or three days before the exam. I stay up late the night before trying to memorize everything in the chapter. When I walk into a math test I am stressed and tired."

Solution space: _____

_____

_____

_____

Implementation space: _____

_____

_____

_____

Now, look at Activity 2.4.

SOLVING ONE OF *YOUR* CURRENT STUDY-SKILL PROBLEMS   ACTIVITY 2.4

To make this process more personal—and more meaningful—complete the items below. Work with a classmate and develop a creative plan.

● *Problem identification.* Think of the study skill problem or a challenge you identified in Activity 2.2. Take a deep breath. Try to be as unemotional as you can about the issue. Close your eyes if you must; do whatever it takes to focus analytically on the issue. What is the problem?

(continued)

Be careful to identify the problem, not the feeling associated with the problem. For instance, you might be failing a math course, and you don't like the instructor because you feel she is inattentive to your needs. Separate the two issues. It might be that you are failing because you are not prepared for the course. Or you might not like the teacher because you are failing the course. Or you are failing because the teacher has not been available to explain important concepts. Make a careful assessment and *determine what problem you need to solve at this time*. Use your critical thinking standards (Table 2.1)

_____

_____

_____

_____

○ *Vision*. Imagine that you have solved your study skill problem. What would the solution look like? That is, because of solving this problem how will your academic performance improve?

_____

_____

_____

○ *Problem analysis*. Now that you have identified what you need to solve, brainstorm some ideas. Look at the problem in depth and from as many perspectives as possible.

_____

_____

_____

_____

○ *Solution*. Problem solving requires a "will and a way" to improve. Effective problem solving involves a plan or a strategy. Brainstorm as many possible solutions to your problem as you can think of at this time. Right now, you want to get possibilities on paper. If you censor yourself at this point, you may end up missing a high-quality solution. You will make an objective and reasoned decision in the next step. Once you have listed your solutions, make a note of the possible consequences for each solution.

_____

_____

_____

_____

(continued)

○ *Implementation.* Now that you have your possible roads to the solution, objectively weigh the merits of each. Which ones appeal to you? Which ones do not? Which option did you settle on? Why? How do you plan to carry this out? What is your first step? Second step? Final step?

_____

_____

_____

_____

_____

○ *One last consideration.* It will be helpful to review the progress of your solution once you put it into action. Set a date at which you will stop and analyze the progress of your solution.

_____

The Problem-Solving Trap

Whether a corporation looks at ways to increase its profit or a community agency examines how to meet the needs of the citizens, a problem must be solved. People in all walks of life and business use various models to tackle problems. But there is a potential trap. Sometimes we can be blinded to *new* alternatives by becoming stuck in routine. Perhaps we continue to look at a particular problem from the same point of view. For example, if you earn poor grades your response may be, "I'll study harder!" Listen to the real communication here: "I'll continue to use the same study methods that have not worked—but I'll do them longer and with more effort." It does not appear practical when viewed from that perspective. It is limited because you have not been particularly creative in determining alternative routes.

Creative Thinking: You Have to Do It Differently If You Want Different Results

Albert Einstein reportedly said, "The definition of insanity is doing the same thing over and over again and expecting different results." The same goes for your studies. If you have difficulties with your math exams, it would seem insane to continue preparing for the exams in the *same* manner you have in the past. Just because you put more effort into your preparation does not mean that you will see better results on the next exam. We use the term *creative thinking* to refer to thinking that develops (creates) a *new* or *different* product. It requires that we look at situations in new ways, from different angles or perspectives (see Figure 2.4).

Look at the example of a campus security concern described earlier in this chapter. Solutions might include hiring more security officers, improving lighting, or installing more emergency phones in high-risk areas.

However, a *new* approach might be to explore the possibility of developing a "citizens watch program" in which student organizations work with security personnel to increase student confidence about campus safety.

By *creatively* tackling a problem, we become more aware of the greater number of possibilities. In fact, we will become better equipped to broaden our thinking and develop new patterns of problem solving.

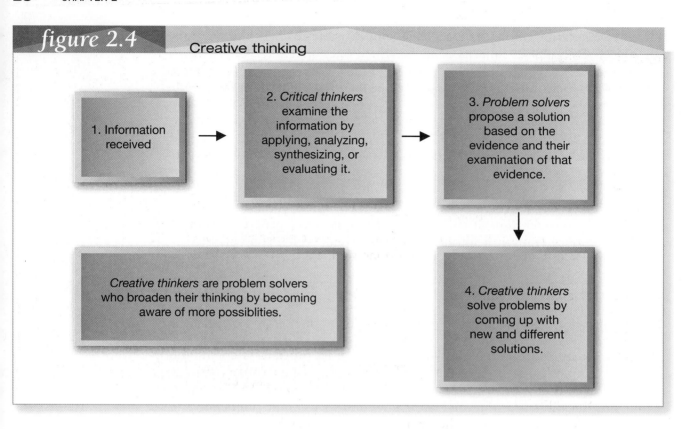

figure 2.4 Creative thinking

For this activity, refer to Activity 2.3 once again. Review your potential solutions. Now try to come up with at least one creative idea to address the challenge. Go ahead; for the purpose of this activity be bold. Even if they seem silly or outlandish, write your ideas here. _____

_____

_____

_____

As you learned above, once you have solutions, you will need to evaluate (a higher-level thinking skill) the potential consequences of each solution. Do that now for your creative ideas. _____

_____

_____

_____

Finally, based on this exercise, which solution do you favor—and why do you think it will successfully address your study skill challenge? _____

_____

_____

_____

ADAPTING OLD SKILLS TO NEW SITUATIONS: MAKING CHOICES

You will continually confront situations in which you must apply the skills you have developed over the years. You learn something in one school year or subject area (for example, how to take notes) and you must apply it in another school year or subject area. Occasionally, a new situation presents itself in which the old skills do not easily work. You must then make some sort of adjustment. In some cases, this may be minor; in others, quite dramatic. Frustration may very likely occur. In such situations you have four broad choices:

1. **Quit** or remove yourself from the situation:
    - The new teacher is requiring things that you have either have not done before, or have tried and not done well. Rather than confront the situation, you drop the class.
    - A similar scenario may be a catalyst for you to quit a job.

2. **Stay** in the new situation without adjusting your skills and suffer a miserable existence.
    - This situation is the same as the first except you cannot drop the class. You dislike the class, but you refuse to modify your skills. Consequently, you are one unhappy student!
    - Do you know someone who cannot adapt to a new boss or manager? Rather than looking for ways to improve the situation, the person suffers a miserable existence in the job.

3. **Modify** your skills to get by in the new situation.
    - You are not particularly happy about the new challenge but you realize you have to make some adjustments. You might not make a dramatic change, but you do enough to get by.
    - The new position at work requires you to develop some new techniques to be successful. You may not like the adjustment but you realize it is necessary in order to stay with a job you otherwise like.

4. **Change** and **adapt** your old skills so that they better fit the new demands.
    - You take the challenge head on. You may stumble a couple of times, but you make the needed changes in your skills to serve you better.
    - You want to thrive in the company and move up the promotion ladder. You search for ways to learn and grow each day.

It is possible for a student to go through all of these choices within a given situation. It can begin with the fear of a particularly challenging instructor at the beginning of the year—bringing on the desire to quit. You are not allowed to quit (perhaps your financial aid requirements will not allow you to withdraw), so you stay in the class, dreading each day. Along the way, the teacher catches your attention, or another student helps you, or you have some inner change and you realize some adjustment must be made. Finally, you know you must completely modify your old skill so it works well with the new situation.

You need to consciously identify and review at which level you are standing. First ask yourself, "Why?" Then ask yourself, "What can I do?" Sometimes, the first option—quit—is the best. You may be "overplaced" in a class (for example, you did not take a prerequisite course that taught the skills needed). Or the job is just not matched to your skills. But don't jump to this choice because it seems like the easy way out. Many times, quitting only postpones the inevitable; you will eventually need the skill in question. Let's examine Activity 2.6 to assess how you adapt old skills to new situations.

ACTIVITY **2.6**   **ASSESSMENT OF BROAD CHOICES: APPLYING YOUR KNOWLEDGE OUTSIDE OF THE CLASSROOM**

For this activity think of a situation outside of this classroom or course. It could be another class or it could involve a relationship with a friend, teammate, or coworker. Using the following questions as guides, complete the items below. The questions in each item are meant to get you thinking. You do not have to answer each question.

1. When was the last time you either quit a situation (class or job, for instance) or seriously considered quitting a situation? What were the circumstances? Were there alternatives, such as seeking assistance or asking for clarification?

   _____

   _____

   _____

   _____

2. When was the last time you stayed in a miserable situation? What were the circumstances? Were there other alternatives? How did you feel?

   _____

   _____

   _____

   _____

3. When was the last time you made some minor adjustments to old skills in order to adjust to a new situation? What were the circumstances? Would you do it differently now?

   _____

   _____

   _____

   _____

4. When was the last time you made a major change to an old skill in order to be successful in a new situation? Would you be able to apply this process of change to another situation in the future?

   _____

   _____

   _____

   _____

CHAPTER SUMMARY

Critical Thinking Expands Your Confidence

In this chapter, you have been asked to think about *how* you should think about *what* you think about. You have examined the importance of taking control of your learning process. As each week on campus passes, you will begin to notice what *is* working for you and what is *not*. You will know where your challenges lie and what strengths you can draw on to meet those challenges. Before moving on to the next chapter, take a moment to reflect on the following points:

- You have been in school before—and you have been successful in school before. Respect the study skills you have and critically think about how you can apply these skills to your new college environment.

- Critical thinking requires reflection and analysis (as well as application, synthesis, or evaluation) of issues or events.

- Problem solving requires the use of critical thinking skills to examine a dilemma and then propose a solution.

- When solving a problem use creative thinking strategies to look at multiple perspectives. This will help you see that problems and issues generally have more than two sides.

- When critically thinking be sure to apply the standards of clarity, accuracy, precision, relevance, depth, breadth, and logic.

    The last activities of this chapter will give you additional opportunities to reflect and apply the chapter concepts in ways that are meaningful to you.

CHAPTER 2 MEASURABLE OBJECTIVES   ACTIVITY 2.7

The beginning of this chapter presented six measurable objectives. They are reprinted below for your convenience. Using the strategies you have learned in this chapter, fill in the lines beneath each item (or use a separate sheet of paper).

- List at least two critical thinking strategies you have used during the past week.

    - List and explain those strategies here: _____

    _____

    _____

    _____

- Describe clearly what critical thinking is by explaining at least four characteristics of critical thinking.

    - List and explain those characteristics here: _____

    _____

    _____

    _____

(continued)

○ Apply at least two of the four higher-level thinking skills in order to solve a specific problem.

　○ Explain how you applied those skills: _____

　_____

　_____

　_____

○ Establish a clear and precise plan to minimize (or eliminate) a study skill problem you currently have.

　○ Briefly explain your plan here: _____

　_____

　_____

　_____

○ Apply specific critical thinking standards when evaluating your study skills.

　○ Briefly explain how you applied at least two of the standards: _____

　_____

　_____

　_____

○ Explain one way in which critical thinking skills can help you maintain balance and wellness in your life.

　○ Briefly explain the connection between critical thinking skills and balance and wellness in your life. _____

　_____

　_____

　_____

REALITY CHECK

Using your critical thinking skills to improve study skills

Situation. Ricky is a first-semester student. His intial excitement about attending college has turned to panic. His first shock hit when he went to the bookstore to get his books. Besides the "sticker shock" of how much the books cost, he was overwhelmed by the sheer number of books he had to buy for each class. Initially, he thought, "There is no way the professors will expect us to read all of these books. I'll wait until the first day of class to see if there has been some sort of mistake."

The first day came—and sure enough there was no mistake. Each instructor plopped a large syllabus and reading assignments page at his seat. He then learned that each instructor required the students to *critically read* each assignment. Ricky's idea of reading had been to skim the chapter for words that might be on a quiz, memorize them, and spit them back when asked. Now, he would have to write or orally explain his readings. He had very little experience with this.

Ricky is considering quitting school. Using at least two strategies from this chapter, help Ricky critically review and solve his problem before he does something drastic (like quit school) because he has not carefully thought the situation through.

A little help to get you started. Because each chapter of this book will end with a "Reality Check," it would be helpful to think about how you can solve the problems posed by these situations. In this case, the following steps may help as you develop a plan for Ricky.

- First, quickly review the main points of the chapter. You can do this by looking back at the bold-faced chapter headings and the figures and tables.* As you do this, you will see the following strategies:

    - Critical thinking standards (Table 2.1). Review the seven critical thinking standards. For instance, is there clarity? (How can Ricky more *clearly* state his problem?) Does Ricky understand the *breadth* of his problem? (Can the problem be viewed from more than one *perspective?*)

    - Bloom's higher-order thinking skills (Table 2.2). Perhaps you can analyze Ricky's concerns. What do you think has *caused* his concerns? Remember to be clear and precise.

    - Problem solving (Figures 2.2 and 2.3). This strategy would walk Ricky through the each of the five steps—from clear problem identification to solution implementation.

    - Visualizing the problem-solving process (Figure 2.3 and Activity 2.4). This provides Ricky with another way to identify and solve his problem.

    - Creative thinking (Figure 2.4 and Activity 2.5). This strategy can help Ricky "step outside the box." That is, he can look at the problem in a new and unique way.

Note: This is reading strategy known as scanning. You will read more about this in Chapter 8.

■ Now, pick and explain two strategies that can help Ricky address his issue. Write your answer below.

_____

_____

_____

_____

_____

_____

_____

CHAPTER 3

GOAL SETTING

If you know what you want to do, why do you need to read about goal setting?

I have always been motivated to attend college. Yes, there were people—like teachers—who encouraged me, but there was something deep down that was pushing me forward. I knew I needed to be here so that I could make a good life for myself. So, now I'm here; I've achieved my dream to go to college.

My adviser and study skills instructor have started to ask me about my long-term goals—and steps to achieve those goals. Honestly, I've never given that much thought. I just focus on a dream and move toward it. If I come to class, pass my exams, and make it to the next term, isn't that good enough? I do not see the need for writing goals. It seems like a complication. Lately, though, it has been more difficult to remain focused. My direction seems to be jumbled and I'm not really sure how to reach those vague goals. I know I have to stay motivated and remember why I am here. But staying motivated and focused on where I am going has become increasingly difficult.

When you establish a goal, you actual put together a strategy to obtain what you desire. Whether or not you achieve the goal depends in great part upon how effectively you plan and carry out your strategy.

PREVIEW

By the time you finish reading this chapter and completing its activities, you will know how to:

- Identify what motivates you to remain in college.
- Identify one intrinsic and one extrinsic motivator you have for doing well in your classes this term.
- Use at least two strategies to overcome a motivational barrier.
- Write a goal that has specific action steps.
- Explain why a particular goal is important to you.
- Evaluate your locus of control.

KEY TERMS

- Action steps
- Goal
- Locus of control
- HOGs
- Motivated learner
- Motivation (extrinsic and intrinsic)
- Motivational barriers

Let's take time to examine the progress you have made so far this term—and what you want to accomplish this week, next month, and next year. This chapter will analyze how to establish specific goals and how to monitor your motivation to achieve your goals.

CHAPTER INTRODUCTION

College has been, and will continue to be, a series of learning experiences. You have had to find your classes, buy books, obtain a parking decal, locate the campus library, fight for a parking space, tackle assignments, and maybe fit in with a new roommate or roommates. At times it might feel like you are moving in a cloud of dust. You might say, "Who has time for strategies? I'm just trying to survive!"[1]

True enough. But a well-developed plan—a strategy to reach a goal—can provide an advantage in the classroom and on the larger campus. As you read this chapter consider the following:

- *What motivates you to achieve a goal?* This question goes to the heart of what you value—and how college can help you put your goals into action.

- *How will you know whether you have chosen the right goal for yourself?* As you move toward your goals it will be helpful to ask yourself, "Is the goal I established still right for me? Is this what I want to do?" Goals should be energizing rather than emotionally draining.

ACTIVITY 3.1 REFLECTION ON YOUR CURRENT LEVEL OF MOTIVATION AND GOAL-SETTING SKILLS

Before you answer the items below, reflect on your current level of motivation and goal-setting skills.

As with all of the reflective activities in this book, answer from your heart. This exercise is not meant for you to answer just like your classmates—or to match what you may think the instructor wants to see. Take your time to give a respectful and responsible general accounting of your experiences with information literacy skills. A truthful self-assessment now will help you build on skills you have while developing those you lack.

For the following items circle the number that best describes your *typical* experience with motivation and goals-setting skills. The key for the numbers is:

0 = never, 1 = almost never, 2 = occasionally, 3 = frequently, 4 = almost always, 5 = always

When considering your past successes and challenges with both motivation and goals setting, how often:

1. Do you establish a specific goal that can be quantifiably measured?

    0   1   2   3   4   5   *(continued)*

---

[1]Steve Piscitelli, *Rhythms of College Success: A Journey of Discovery, Change, and Mastery* (Upper Saddle River, NJ: Pearson Prentice Hall, 2008), 26–41.

2. Do your goals have an established end point—a date for completion?

    0   1   2   3   4   5

3. Do your goals have specific action steps?

    0   1   2   3   4   5

4. Are you motivated to do something just because of the extrinsic reward you will receive?

    0   1   2   3   4   5

5. Are you motivated to do something because of how it makes you feel inside?

    0   1   2   3   4   5

6. Do you expect what you do will have an impact on what happens to you?

    0   1   2   3   4   5

7. Do you establish goals that make you stretch—that are not easy to attain?

    0   1   2   3   4   5

8. Are you able to identify a motivational barrier and then do something to overcome that barrier?

    0   1   2   3   4   5

Add up your scores for items 1, 2, 3, and 7. Divide by 4. Write your answer here: _____

Using the key explanations above for each number (0, 1, 2, 3, 4, 5), complete this sentence: When it comes to goal setting, I _____ establish clearly stated specific goals that make me stretch and grow.

Add up your scores for items 4, 5, 6, and 8. Divide by 4. Write your answer here: _____

Using the key explanations above for each number (0, 1, 2, 3, 4, 5), complete this sentence: When it comes to motivation, I, _____ , am aware of what motivates me and how to take charge of my motivation.

Based on your answers, what insights do you have about your experiences with organization? _____

_____

_____

MOTIVATION

Motivation moves you to act on or toward something. It can come from within you or can be the consequence of some outside force that drives you forward. Actually, you do not need this book or a teacher to tell you what motivation is. Before you ever set foot on this college campus you were driven by desires—and you acted on those desires. For instance, one of those desires was to attend college. You took action to make that happen and here you are, *just like you had the desire to do*. Motivation provided the fuel—the energy—to move toward your goal (go to college).

© 2005 Stockdisc

Where Do You Find Motivation?

Human motivation varies from person to person depending on the opportunities, challenges, tasks, activities, and life experiences we face. An athlete's love for sport may motivate him to get to practice early and remain late. Or perhaps another student did not do as well on a reading quiz as she would have liked, so she pushes herself to improve by 10 points on the next quiz. Maybe you know a single parent who attends school at night, works a full-time job during the day, is the treasurer for her child's school PTA—and awakens early each day to study for her college classes. These are motivated individuals chasing after their goals. But what is it that creates the drive to accomplish these activities? Where does the drive come from?

Extrinsic and Intrinsic Motivation

Motivation either comes from within you (*intrinsic*) or from some source outside of you (*extrinsic*). The single mother who is a student may be moved intrinsically, extrinsically, or both. Table 3.1 provides a glimpse into her motivations. Obviously, this single mother is driven by a variety of factors. Whether they are intrinsic or extrinsic, she gets closer to her goal of college graduation.

Let's make this a little more personal. Think about the beginning of this school term. Your professors outlined course expectations in their syllabi.

table 3.1	Intrinsic and extrinsic motivation	
	WHY? INTRINSIC MOTIVATION	**WHY? EXTRINSIC MOTIVATION**
Attends school at night	She has always wanted to be the first in her family to get a college degree. She has always loved reading and learning—they give meaning to her day.	The only way she can advance in her job and get a pay raise is to have a college diploma.
Works a full-time job	She loves her job and would like to become a supervisor some day.	She has a child to raise and rent to pay each month.
Serves as treasurer for her child's school PTA	She is able to plan activities that will benefit the children of the school. It gratifies her to watch the children laugh and play with new playground equipment that the PTA was able to purchase.	She was told volunteer work would look good on her college application.
Awakens early each morning to study	She loves the classes she is taking and thirsts for as much knowledge as she can retain.	She has to maintain a C average if she wants to keep her financial aid.

Whether or not you adhere to those requirements remains up to you. Will you attend class regularly because you enjoy the lectures, discussions, and classmates (intrinsic motivation), or because you know that attendance counts toward your grade (extrinsic motivation)?

Characteristics of a Motivated Learner: Can an Individual *Learn* to be Motivated?

If you understand what makes up motivation, you can more effectively evaluate your behavior—and begin to make changes as needed. Let's review one model that breaks motivated behavior into five distinct parts.[2]

1. Motivated behavior always involves making a *choice*. Maybe your time in a college classroom means you cannot work as many hours at gainful employment, and, consequently, you will take a pay cut while pursuing your studies. But you still came to college for some reason. In short, you were motivated to make this choice.

2. A motivated person will put forth *effort* to achieve a goal. This person is not waiting for the goal to happen. The motivated individual chooses to make the goal happen.

3. The motivated individual chooses to be *persistent*. Simply put, this student has that trait known as stick-to-itiveness. He can stick with a task until it is completed.

4. Motivated students think—really think—about what they are doing. If they write an essay, they think about the topic, think about the outline, and think about the final product. They *engage* the topic. Like people who are engaged to be married, engaged students choose to be committed to their work.

5. Finally, if the preceding four characteristics—choice, effort, persistence, and engagement—are present, there will be a connection to a high-quality final product. There will be some form of *achievement*—a movement closer to a goal (see Figure 3.1).

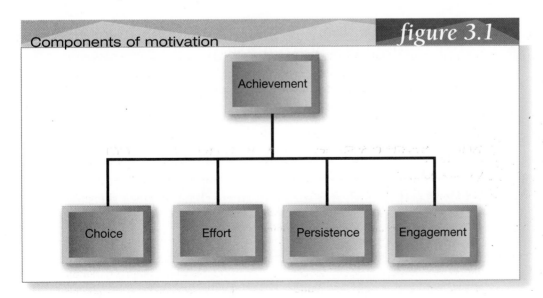

Components of motivation · *figure 3.1*

---

[2]Scott W. VanderStoep and Paul R. Pintrich, *Learning to Learn: The Skill and Will of College Success* (Upper Saddle River, NJ: Prentice Hall, 2003), 40–41.

If your final result is not what you had hoped for, that does not necessarily mean you lacked motivation. It may indicate that it's time to reevaluate your choices and then recommit your efforts. *Flexibility* is important. You cannot control everything that will happen in college (or in life).

ACTIVITY 3.2 SELF-MONITORING CHECK: ARE YOU A MOTIVATED LEARNER?

Reflect on a time when you were committed to something. You may have been an athlete on a sports team, a club member, a student government officer, a recital performer, or involved in some other activity on which you worked diligently.

1. Can you specifically identify *why* you were committed to the task? What characteristics of motivation (choice, effort, persistence, engagement, and/or achievement) were present? *I was comitted to the task because it was something I enjoyed. Effort and achievement were present*

2. Who helped to keep you moving toward your results? Was there someone or something else driving you (*extrinsic motivator*), or did some force within you (*intrinsic motivator*) drive you forward? *intrinsic motivator because I know if I do well it will help me in my college years.*

3. How did you maintain your level of commitment over time? *By doing my work and turning them in on time and studying hard for tests.*

ACTIVITY 3.3 WHO IS RESPONSIBLE FOR YOUR MOTIVATION?

Take a moment to reflect on the following questions:

- *Personal success.* What motivates you to achieve personal success beyond the classroom? *My parents + other family and friends*

  - How has this motivator (or motivators) changed since the same time last year? *They have not changed at all.*

- *Academic success.* What motivates you at this time in the classroom? *Knowing that if I do my best it will pay off later.*

(continued)

○ How has this motivator (or motivators) changed since the last time
you were in a classroom?

It has not changed at all because I want to do my very best and get good grades.

○ What insights (inner flashes of understanding) do you get from your
answers?

I'm not really sure

Overcoming Motivational Barriers

For the moment, consider that you *cannot* control external forces that stand
between you and what you would like to achieve. Whether it's an unfair
instructor, an uncaring employer, or the state of the economy, we'll put those
factors aside for now. Instead, your target for this exercise will be *those things
you can control*—that originate within you.

- *Attitude.*[3] Think of something you have had difficulty staying motivated
  to achieve. Maybe you have not been able to get to the gym as often as
  you would like each week. Or perhaps you have not lost the weight you
  had hoped this year. *Listen to your words*. Consider these statements:

  - "I *hope* to lose weight."
  - "I will *try* to lose weight."
  - "I *think* I will be able to lose weight."

  What do you notice about those words, especially the verbs? Compare
  them with the following statements:

  - "I *will* lose weight."
  - "I *shall* lose weight."
  - "I *pledge* to lose weight."

  This second set of statements present more forceful and more positive
  sentiments. There are no wishy-washy thoughts. Using this "language of
  action" states the point (the goal) in a very definite manner.

  Suggestion: Listen to your words—they might very well reflect your
  commitment level. Are you using the language of commitment, or the
  language of doubt and uncertainty?

- *Mental Paralysis.* Think of a Ping-Pong game. Two contestants paddle a
  small ball back and forth over the table net. One player makes an incredible
  shot, but the opponent makes a masterful return. Back and forth the
  game goes. Eventually, one player will win.

      Sometimes our minds engage in a Ping-Pong game of sorts when we
  try to motivate ourselves to accomplish something. Let's call the two
  opponents *Yes* and *But*. Every time *Yes* presents a reason to move forward

---

[3]Based on William Miller, "Resolutions That Work," *Spirituality and Health* (February 2005), 44–47.

with an action, *But* skillfully returns with a reason why you should stay put. Back and forth the exchange goes. While *Yes* makes good attempts, the exchange can become tiring and nothing is accomplished. *But* has been too persistent and eventually stops the progress. Here is what such a "match" might sound like:

- "*Yes*, I need to study more for my math exam."
- "*But*, I really don't have any more time to devote to that class."
- "*Yes*, I know that time is an issue. Still, I really must devote more time to math class."
- "*But*, I never have been any good at math. The extra time won't help anyway!"
- "*Yes*, I guess I'm just destined to be a poor math student."

In this exchange the person ended up talking himself right out of the commitment. As one professor of psychology has said, "The word *but* functions like an eraser, negating the motivation that went before—and nothing happens."[4]

Suggestion: Erase the word *but* from your motivational vocabulary before it erases your motivation.

- *Commitment.* Sometimes the initial excitement to do something fades away quickly. Maybe it is difficult to maintain motivation because you lack passion for what you are trying to accomplish. For instance, perhaps you committed to play intramural sports with your friends. After two weeks of practice, however, you are not excited about continuing. When you examine the issue, you see that you participated only because you did not want to disappoint the friends who were going to play. You also have noticed that in order to devote time to the sport, you have had to stay up much later each night to complete your homework and have had to give up some hours from your part-time job. After careful analysis, you decide the intramural sport is not where you need—or want—to invest your energies.

Suggestion: Check your commitment as to why you want to do something. If you can honestly say that the "cost" in time, effort, or emotion is more than you are willing to pay, then maybe you should look for another road to follow.

- *Are You in the Way?* There may be times when you create your own obstacles. Sometimes, for example, two motivators might conflict with each other. For instance, perhaps you have pledged that you will earn a 3.5 GPA this term. In addition, you have pledged to work at your part-time job as many hours as you can in order to save money for a car. You are motivated by the high GPA *and* you are motivated by the money to buy a car. But trying to get the one might have a negative effect on the other.

Suggestion: Examine your motivators. If one seems to have a harmful effect on another, you may wish to rethink what you are trying to do. Or look for alternatives. For instance, maybe you could work more hours on the weekends, leaving the nights during the school week for homework. Do not work at cross-purposes with yourself.

---

[4]Miller, "Resolutions That Work," 46.

GOAL SETTING

What Is a Goal?

The first part of this chapter looked at what drives a person to a destination. Now let's turn our attention to that end point—to the goal your motivation moves you toward. Generally, people think of a goal as a place they want to reach. The "place" can be academic ("I want an A in history"), or it can be personal and nonacademic ("I will run and finish a five-mile race"), or it can be community oriented ("I will help paint the community center").

We all have goals of one kind or another. They can be simple short-term goals, like cleaning a room, or more complex long-term destinations, like becoming qualified for a particular career.

CRITICALLY THINKING ABOUT YOUR MOTIVATION AND GOAL-SETTING SKILLS

ACTIVITY 3.4

Let's apply the critical thinking standards from Chapter 2 to your ability to stay motivated to reach your goals. Activities 3.2 and 3.3 may be helpful for this activity.

List a best practice (something you do well in the areas of motivation and goal setting) that you use to stay motivated:_____

CRITICAL THINKING STANDARD	APPLICATION TO YOUR MOTIVATION AND GOAL-SETTING SKILLS	YOUR EXPLANATION HERE OR ON A SEPARATE PIECE OF PAPER
Clarity	*Clearly* state your best practice to remain motivated to reach your goals.	
Accuracy	How do you know this assessment of your practice is *correct*?	
Precision	*Specifically* (give examples) explain your motivation practices.	
Relevance	How is your assessment of motivation *connected* to your academic progress?	
Depth	Examine your motivational best practice beyond a superficial (simplistic) explanation and look at all of the *complexities* involved.	
Breadth	Examine your motivational best practice from more than one *perspective (point of view).*	
Logic	Based on your evidence do your conclusions above *make sense*?	

(continued)

Based on your answers above, what insights have you gained about your motivation? *That if I stay motivated and try my hardest I will accomplish my goal.*

What is the next step you will take to improve your motivation? _____

_____

_____

Why Do You Need a Goal? Converting Fantasies to Dreams—and Dreams to Realities

You already know how to establish goals. Most everything you tried to do in your life—before ever stepping on a college campus—connected directly to goal setting. As you read this chapter, *don't forget what you have learned, but be open-minded to examine and use some new strategies.* In other words, *respect* your past experiences while taking *responsibility* to build new experiences.

Goal setting allows you to focus your sights on something you want to achieve, make a plan, and finally move toward that result. Effective goals, whether long term or short term, address the *why, when,* and *how* of our lives. If your goals lack these components, then your goals turn out to be daydreams or mere fantasies.

Goals provide a challenge. Some may affect more than one aspect of your life. Quitting your job, for instance, so that you can attend school full time will have a far-reaching impact on your life. Whether the goal is large and long term or small and short term, it should set forth a challenge.

Have You Hugged Your HOG Today?

In their book *Built to Last*, Jim Collins and Jerry I. Porras describe what they refer to as BHAGs.[5] In their research of successful companies they found that companies that set *big, hairy, audacious goals* left their competition in the dust. In other words, these companies did not settle for making goals that would be easily reached—they set goals that required effort to attain.

The same holds true for your personal goals. If you continually set goals that you can easily reach, you may never know the joy and exhilaration of stretching yourself to new heights. You may not reach the potential of which you are really capable.

So, when setting your goals, think of the acronym* HOG—set a *huge outrageous goal.* This does not mean to establish a goal that is impossible to reach. Think of it more as a reminder to not settle for something that will not allow you to take advantage of your best efforts. If you aim high and take appropriate action steps, you will move further than you may have thought possible. Yes, you may stumble; you may even fail to achieve a particular goal. But if you aim low (the easy way), you will hit your mark every time—and more than likely never achieve your potential.

Yet, while it is good to have ambition and potential, without initiative, your ambition and potential may never be realized. Stretch—grab on to a huge outrageous goal—and move toward the potential you have.

---

[5]Jim Collins and Jerry I. Porras, *Built to Last: Successful Habits of Visionary Companies* (New York: Harper Business Essentials, 2002), 93–94+.

*A memory technique that creates a word from the letters of other words. See Chapter 9.

UNDERSTANDING YOUR GOALS   ACTIVITY 3.5

Reflect on one of your current goals. It can relate to one of your classes, a campus club of which you are a member, your current job, or some other part of your life.

1. State the goal: _To graduate from SECHS and transfer to NC State to become a vet._

2. Why do you have this goal? Why is it something you want to do? _Because I want a good education_

3. When do you wish to accomplish this goal? (What is the date for completion?) _When I graduate from NC State and start my own animal clinic_

4. How will you accomplish this goal? That is, what resources will you need to achieve your goal? _By doing my very best in high school and college, and get good grades_

5. How will you know when you accomplish your goal? What will have specifically happened? _When I start my own animal clinic_

6. Is this a huge outrageous goal (HOG)? Explain your answer. _Yes because it is my big dream to become a vet and take care of animals my whole life._

7. Finally, here is a question that many times is ignored: How do you know that this is the correct goal for you to pursue now? Does the goal move you toward an emotionally satisfying result? _Because I have grew up with animals my whole life and that is what I want to accomplish in life_

What Does a Clearly Stated Goal Look Like?

The questions in Activity 3.5 provide a glimpse into the parts of a goal.[6] A useful goal—as opposed to mere fantasy—must provide the means to help you reach your desired destination (see Figure 3.2).

The first step to reach your challenge involves developing a clear *goal statement*—a concrete step to make your dreams become reality. A clearly stated goal has the following six properties:

1. *A clear goal is <u>written</u>.* This is the step in which you state precisely *what* you want to achieve. Once in writing, it becomes an affirmation of intent. Put it where you will see it every day. Some people find the process of actually *writing* a goal awkward and a waste of time. Nevertheless, this is a valuable exercise as you develop the habit of establishing long-range plans.

---

[6]For a more detailed discussion, refer to Susan B. Wilson, *Goal Setting* (New York: American Management Association, 1994), 4–9.

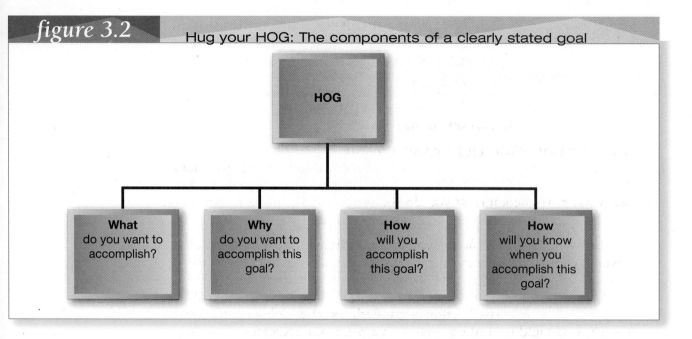

figure 3.2   Hug your HOG: The components of a clearly stated goal

2. *A clear goal must be <u>specific and measurable</u>.* Exactly what will be accomplished? Saying "I want to have a better English grade" is admirable, but it is incomplete. How do you define "better"? If your current grade is a D, would you be satisfied with a D+ (which, after all, is "better" than a D)? By *how much* do you wish to raise your grade? By *when?* How will you know when you have achieved the goal? Write in concrete terms so that you clearly know when you have achieved the goal: "I want to get a B in my English class by the end of the semester" is a much clearer statement. There is no doubt as to what you want to accomplish. You have also identified the time frame in which the goal will be accomplished.

3. *A clear goal has to be <u>realistic</u>.* It should be challenging, yet attainable. Saying you will raise your English grade from an F to an A by the end of the week is not realistic. Challenge yourself, but do not frustrate yourself. Many students have tried to turn around an abysmal term, only to become discouraged because they set their sights unrealistically high—and waited too long to begin moving toward the goal. Refer to the discussion above about HOGs.

4. *A clear goal must have a practical <u>road map</u>.* Know where you are going, how you are going to get there, and when you plan on arriving. Aimlessly wandering toward a goal will waste your valuable time. Simplify the goal into manageable, bite-size action steps. In other words, once you have a long-range goal, establish short-range action steps to achieve that goal. *Do not skip this important step.* You want to motivate, not overwhelm yourself. Here is an example of a road map:

Long-term:	To attain an A in math by the end of the semester.
Short-term:	Carefully read the instructor's course description, assignment page, and any other handout.
	Complete all assigned homework.
	Correct and rework any problems marked as incorrect on homework or tests.

See the instructor at least once a week for extra help—for a second explanation or a chance to work additional problems.

Find a study group.

Participate in class.

Get As on all the tests.

5. *A clear goal <u>anticipates</u> potential problems or obstacles.* Your goals will not be immune to twists and turns of the road. Don't become paranoid or obsessive about potential problems, but do try to anticipate some of the problems you may encounter. If you do so, obstacles will not be a surprise— and they will not be as demoralizing.

6. *A clear goal has built-in <u>incentives.</u>* Even though you want to reach a point where your goals are intrinsically motivating, it is a good idea to recognize (and enjoy) your achievements. Provide appropriate rewards for yourself as you make progress. In fact, establish a schedule of incentives (rewards) that coincide with your "bite-size" action steps. Perhaps, after doing all of your homework, you could reward yourself with a pizza or a recreational activity. When you get that hard-earned A, treat yourself to a movie with friends. It really does not make any difference what that reward is so long as it provides you with a little fuel (motivation) to keep plugging away at your goal.

In any study skills book you will find suggested steps to follow in goal setting. And incorporated into these plans you will usually find all (or most) of the forgoing six properties of a clearly stated goal. One model, for instance, uses the acronym *SMART*[7] that is, goals need to be *specific, measurable, attainable, realistic,* and *tangible.*

Whatever works for you, use it.

IDENTIFYING CLEARLY STATED GOALS   ACTIVITY 3.6

Your best friend has asked you to review the following list of personal goals. Put a check (✓) in the circle next to the items you think clearly state a goal and an X in the circle next to the items you think are not very clear.

○ I will do better in school next term.

○ I will raise my math average by at least one letter grade.

○ I will write something worthwhile in English class.

○ I need to remember more stuff.

○ I want my instructors to like me.

○ I will be able to write a clear thesis statement for every essay I am assigned.

○ I will study more effectively by appropriately rewarding myself each time I move closer to my goals.

○ I will be nicer to my family.

○ I will become a better friend.

○ I will become healthier by doing at least 30 minutes of aerobic exercise four days per week.   *(continued)*

---

[7]Paul Meyer, "Creating S.M.A.R.T. Goals," 2004, Top Achievement, www.topachievement.com/smart.html (accessed on July 1, 2007).

Take a moment and write what is wrong and what is right with the goals you just reviewed. Pick one of the poorly written goals and make it better. Now, assume this is your goal. How are you going to be successful at achieving this goal? Briefly write your action steps below.

_____

_____

_____

Long-Term and Short-Term Goals

Goals go beyond the classroom. In fact, goals address many issues in life. Figure 3.3 gives a broad overview of categories of goals.

The four main categories of goals, in the middle tier of Figure 3.3, can be classified as *long-term goals*—larger goals that will be accomplished in the future. These goals will not be reached in a day or two. In the case of career goals, years will be required.

You may have heard a classmate say, "My long-term goal is to be rich—and my short-term goal is to get an A in my math class." While getting rich may definitely be a long ways down the road, there is a lot of ground to cover between getting an A in math and amassing riches for life. For our purposes here, let's consider an A in math as the long-term goal for this term—and that may move you a step closer to your dream of being rich.

Move toward your goal with specific, measurable, and responsible *short-term goals*. For one, the short-term goals focus on small, incremental steps toward a larger goal. Rather than tackling too much at once, short-term goals establish manageable and action-oriented steps. For many people, a bite-size move forward is not as overwhelming as a more complex and long-range goal. These action steps get a person moving in the right direction.

Secondly, specific short-term goals will help you mark your progress, step by step, toward your ultimate goal. If one of your academic goals is to get an A in your English class by the end of the term, a short-term goal may be to find a study group, or to attend tutoring sessions, or to visit the professor once per week with specific questions.

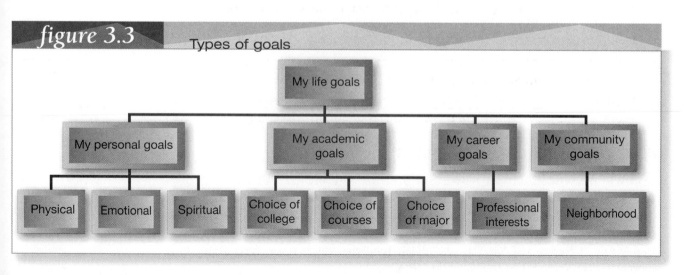

figure 3.3   Types of goals

Tips on How to Develop Your Action Steps

- Once you have identified a goal, identify the most important step you can take to reach it.
- Make a commitment to take an important step as soon as possible. Can you do it tonight? Tomorrow?
- Be diligent, but be flexible. That is, treat your goals and their action steps with respect, but understand that you may need to make adjustments. As the Dalai Lama has said, "Remember that not getting what you want is sometimes a wonderful stroke of luck"—as you will be forced to look in a new direction.
- Be willing to ask for help. The 3 Fs—friends, family, and faculty—can be wonderful resources.

ESTABLISHING SHORT-TERM GOALS TO REACH YOUR LONG-TERM GOALS

ACTIVITY 3.7

For this exercise, determine a long-term personal goal *and* a long-term academic goal for one of your courses. Then, for each of these long-term goals, identify two short-term goals (specific action steps) that will take you closer to the bigger goal. As the term implies, these will be *action-oriented* movements toward your destination.

Remember to keep the goals measurable—state them in terms that will enable you to know when you have achieved them.

- Personal goal: _To do well in high school_

  - Short-term goals (or action steps) to reach the personal goal:

    A. _Study and do all my work_

    B. _Pay attention in class, pass all exams and test by studying_

  - What incentive or reward will there be for you to reach this goal?

    To get in a good college and become a vet when I graduate college.

- Academic goal: _____

  - Short-term goals (or action steps) to reach the academic goal:

    A. _____

    B. _____

  - What incentive or reward will there be for you to reach this goal?

    _____

Obstacles, Missteps, and Detours[8]

Think about your favorite movie or novel for a moment. Can you remember the hero or heroine? That person started at a certain point in his life and ended

---

[8]For a more in-depth discussion of this analogy see Martha Beck, *Finding Your Own North Star: Claiming the Life You Were Meant to Have* (New York: Three Rivers Press, 2001). Pay particular attention to her discussion of the change cycle.

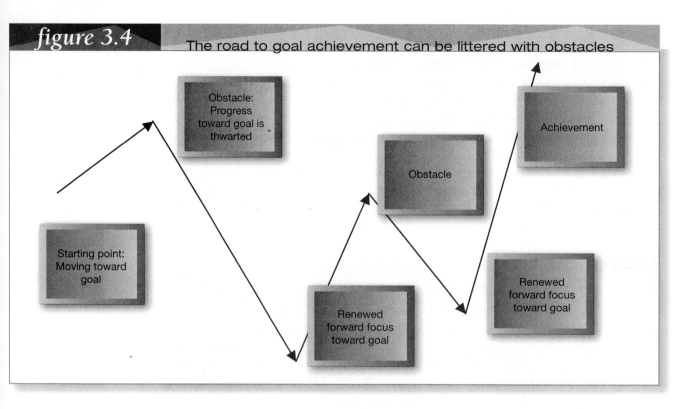

figure 3.4   The road to goal achievement can be littered with obstacles

at another at the conclusion of the story. The final scene usually represented some type of success or progress for the main character. However, that achievement did not occur without twists and turns of the plot. Those adventures—or misadventures—kept you turning the pages of the book or sitting in your seat watching the screen. As the hero made his way toward a particular goal, an obstacle presented itself and the hero detoured from his goal. He had to gather his thoughts, refocus, and then move back up the road toward the goal. This continues until he reaches the final scene. Plotting the journey of the lead character would look more like the up-and-down path you see in Figure 3.4 rather than a straight line.

Just like the hero and heroine, you, too, will probably have missteps along the way. Goals are set in the *real world*. Problems, unforeseen circumstances, and "bad luck" are also part of the *real world*. Expect them, plan for them, and keep moving toward the desired result.

Here are some common obstacles to achieving goals.[9]

- *Not expecting mistakes.* If you expect to move along without any glitches, and then one occurs, you may become so dejected that you will give up. For instance, when planning the steps to finish a term paper, leave flexibility and "breathing room" for an unexpected detour like a computer malfunction. Being prepared for missteps and wrong turns, you will be able to handle them better. They won't be pleasant, but you will be able to remain focused.

- *Blaming obstacles for your lack of abilities.* Sometimes an obstacle is beyond your control; sometimes it happens because you never tried to reach this type of goal before. You might become frustrated with a particular instructor's teaching style. Or the content may stretch you beyond

---

[9]For a more in-depth discussion, see VanderStoep and Pintrich, *Learning to Learn*, 32–35.

your previous experiences. It can become too easy to say "I'm stupid" or "I don't *do* history!" Abilities can change. Each time you enter a classroom you bring your *old skills* to a *new situation*.

- *Not changing your environment.* If you want to increase your biology grade by one letter grade by the end of the term, you may need to change your study environment. Or maybe the study group you work with is not working for you. Take stock of where, when, and how you are doing things and then make a well-planned move. It may mean you have to make choices regarding when and where to meet with your friends. Learn to say no, if saying yes to a particular situation would compromise your goals. Refer to the sections titled *"Commitment"* and *"Are You in the Way?"* earlier in the chapter.

Locus of Control

There is one more potential obstacle, one that springs from how you see yourself in the world. Do you believe that your actions can influence the way things turn out? Do things just "happen" to you—or do you cause things to happen? How you answer questions like these reflects your locus of control, a concept attributed to psychologist Julian Rotter[10] that refers to how much you believe your actions can affect your future. In short, do you *expect* your actions to affect your life—or do you wait for someone or something to happen to you?

A simplified description of locus of control is the *focus of one's power.* Do you believe the power to control events resides within you—or do you believe events are controlled by outside forces?

Generally speaking, a person's locus of control can be either internal or external. A student with an *internal* locus of control, for example, explains a poor test grade by looking into the mirror, pointing at himself, and saying, "I should have studied more" or "Before the next exam I will be sure to visit my professor in his office." The responsibility is placed squarely on that student's shoulders *by that student.* On the other hand, a student who is more apt to blame the teacher exhibits an *external* locus of control. Statements such as "That teacher is not fair" or "How could I possibly do well when the teacher covers so much material each class period?" characterize a student looking to assign responsibility elsewhere.

IDENTIFYING LOCUS OF CONTROL   **ACTIVITY 3.8**

Read the following scenario and then identify and support whether the person exhibits an external or internal locus of control.

Natasha has missed a number of math classes lately due to child care difficulties. She recently missed two quizzes—and the instructor does not allow makeup quizzes. She fears that her grade may be severely reduced as a result.

(continued)

---

[10]See, for example, Jack Mearns, "The Social Learning Theory of Julian B. Rotter," Department of Psychology, California State University—Fullerton, psych.fullerton.edu/jmearns/rotter.htm (accessed on July 1, 2007). In 1966 Rotter developed a locus of control personality test. Variations of the Rotter test can be found at www.dushkin.com/connectext/psy/ch11/survey11.mhtml and www.prenhall.com/rolls_demo/sal_demo/wam/q3.html (both sites accessed on July 1, 2007).

Yesterday morning, Natasha went to the instructor's office. "I know it is my responsibility to get to class and take the quizzes on time," she said. "But my babysitter is no longer available. I think I have a new person lined up. Is there any extra credit I can do to make up for the lost points on those two quizzes?"

1. Did Natasha exhibit an internal or external locus of control? Briefly explain your answer.

   Internal locus

2. How can this knowledge benefit you?

   It will help me when I am in college

Refer to Figure 3.5. As with any continuum, few people are found on either extreme. Most of us fall somewhere in between. But upon reflection we will notice that we *tend* to *lean* to one end or the other. Are you a person who generally takes responsibility for your actions? Or are you someone who is more apt to blame someone else? Use this information to heighten your awareness.

Recognize that there are times we all face when *other people* (external) will have significant influence or control over what we will or will not do. For instance, the college or university sets the final exam schedule; the students must adjust their own schedules to meet those dates. The point is to understand what *you* (internal) can have an impact on—and what you may be avoiding because it is easier to do so.

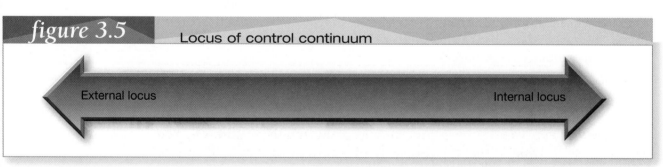

figure 3.5   Locus of control continuum

External locus   Internal locus

ACTIVITY 3.9   FIX WHAT?

Let's say you wish to do better in your English class. What's the first thing you have to do? You must first understand why you are not doing well. That is, before you can fix the problem, you have to know what you are fixing. (A review of critical thinking and problem solving in Chapter 2 might prove helpful.)

(continued)

For this activity, pick a class (or something in your life outside of school that needs fixing/changing). Write this on the line below:

I need to fix/change _do better in school_.

Now briefly explain why you need to change this: _____

_____

_____

_____

Here comes the tricky part. From the following list, choose the items that may have a connection to this problem. Check as many as apply, and at the end briefly explain why.

- ◉ Teacher
- ◉ Parent
- ◉ Student
- ◉ Friend
- ◉ School administration
- ○ Government
- ○ Boss
- ◉ Society
- ○ Other (specify)
- ○ Some combination (specify)_____

Finally, look at what you have checked. What is *your* connection to each? Can you, in fact, make an immediate impact on each one you checked? Or are some more long-term and therefore not of help right now? For instance, you may believe you are doing poorly in English because the college or university system requires all students to take so much English in order to move through school. Well, that may be the case. But you probably aren't going to change an entire system by the time the semester ends! Write your thoughts here.

_____

_____

_____

_____

The point: Pick what you can have an impact on, and then address it. You must be able to make realistic assessments of what is within your ability to change—and what is not. Too often, we attempt to fix what we cannot, should not, or will not. First, identify the *what* and the *why*. Make a realistic assessment of *where* to go and *what* steps to take. Here are four simple questions to ask yourself:

- *What* happened?
- *Why* did it happen?
- *Where* do I go from here? (Think of this as your goal.)
- *What* is my first step? My second step? (Think of these as your action steps.)

WIN: Do You Know What's Important Now?

Successful athletic coaches motivate their student athletes. When their players confront a difficult choice, coaches oftentimes instruct them to follow the principle of WIN—What's Important Now. So, every day, no matter how small or seemingly insignificant, take some step toward your goal. Ask yourself, "What's important now for me to achieve my goal?" Once you have identified the step, act on it. If you do not make progress toward your goal, no one else will.

CHAPTER SUMMARY

This college term will pass quickly—and another will approach just as rapidly. The weeks ahead will require completion of academic work, focused planning, a strong knowledge of yourself, and strategies to take responsibility for your time and behavior (*an internal locus of control*). In the end it will be up to you to stay motivated, set goals, and set your course for success. You control your fate. Keep the following points in mind as you move with determination through your semester:

- Motivation is the driving force moving you toward your goals.
- Goals provide purpose and meaning to life. They can help energize you to reach the destination by keeping the end in focus.
- Short-term goals—the action steps to reaching one's dreams—need to be specific, measurable, and responsible.
- Goals are set in the real world. Problems, unforeseen circumstances, and bad luck are also part of the real world. Expect them and plan for them.
- Effective goals are written, specific, measurable, realistic, and have an end point—a date for which to strive.
- Locus of control influences whether you believe life will *just happen to you*, or that you will be able to *influence what happens*.

ACTIVITY 3.10 | CHAPTER 3 MEASURABLE OBJECTIVES

At the beginning of this chapter, six measurable objectives were presented. They are reprinted below for your convenience. Using the strategies you have learned in this chapter, fill in the lines beneath each item (or use a separate sheet of paper).

- Identify what motivates you to remain in college.

  - Identify two of your motivators:

    1. _____

       _____

(continued)

2. _____

_____

○ Identify one intrinsic and one extrinsic motivator you have for doing well in your classes this term.

○ Intrinsic: _____

_____

○ Extrinsic: _____

_____

○ Use at least two strategies to overcome a motivational barrier.

○ List the strategies:

1. _____

_____

2. _____

_____

○ Write a goal that has specific action steps.

○ Write a goal for the remainder of the semester:

1. _____

_____

○ Write at last three action steps: _____

_____

○ Explain why a particular goal is important to you.

○ Explanation: _____

_____

_____

○ Evaluate your locus of control.

○ Generally speaking, do you have an internal or external locus of control? Provide two pieces of evidence to support your evaluation.

_____

_____

_____

_____

REALITY CHECK

Using your critical thinking skills to improve your ability to set and achieve goals.

Situation. Reflect on what you need to accomplish between now and the end of this semester. Your list could contain one, some, or all of the following: study for final exams, complete a term project for one of your classes, register for next term's classes, secure financial aid, find a part-time job, run for a student government office, or patch up a difference of opinion with a friend. From your list, pick what you consider to be the most important item. Below (or on a separate piece of paper) write a goal for that item. Include the action steps, incentives, and possible motivational barriers you might encounter.

- Goal: _____

  _____

- Action steps (with incentives): _____

  _____

  _____

- Possible motivational barriers—and strategies to overcome the barriers:

  _____

  _____

  _____

ORGANIZING TIME AND SPACE

How will these skills improve academic performance and reduce stress?

SPOTLIGHT ON CLASSROOM SKILLS

Time management was a big problem for me at first. I would spend too much time focusing on one subject and forget to study for other subjects. I got so far behind due to my lack of time-management skills I was forced to drop classes. I was spending too much time working and not enough time studying or going to class. It took dropping classes to finally wake me up and make me realize that I had to focus and discipline myself in order for me to be successful.

Students around the nation can share stories similar to the account above. College life offers a great deal of personal freedom and flexibility. Class schedules are not as regimented as a high school day or a forty-hour-per-week job. But college, as described in our student perspective above, requires students to develop a level of organizational skills with which most students have little experience.

PREVIEW

By the time you finish reading this chapter and completing its activities you will be able to:

- Identify at least three types of procrastination and a strategy to deal with each.
- Develop a written schedule that reflects at least two hours of study time for every hour scheduled in the classroom.
- Use and evaluate one time-management tool (calendar or planner) for at least one week.
- Develop a weekly to-do list that ranks your tasks in order of importance.
- Draw (or describe) your home study area.
- Describe how organizational skills can help you balance your life's demands.

KEY TERMS

- Anticipation
- Calendars
- Personal storage area
- Personal study area

This chapter will explain how to organize time and space to improve efficiency and effectiveness while minimizing stress.[1]

- Priorities
- Procrastination
- Stress
- Study time

CHAPTER INTRODUCTION

Time management challenges even the best students during their first term in college. The flexible time schedule of college classes represents new territory. A typical college student may only have two or three hours of class on a particular day. The increased amount of *unstructured* time can be troublesome for some college students. For other students, returning to school can create a new set of challenges as they try to juggle family, work, and school.

But time is only one resource you have to organize. You also need to consider space: Where will you study, how will you file your papers, and where will you keep your supplies? Whether you live on campus, in an off-campus apartment, or at home with your family, you will benefit by designating a place for your out-of-class study time.

Organization will not only improve your study habits and grades, but it will also allow you to feel in control of your life.

ACTIVITY 4.1 — REFLECTION ON YOUR CURRENT LEVEL OF ORGANIZATIONAL SKILLS

Before you answer the items below, reflect on your current level of organizational skills. Think of how well (or poorly) you have organized your time and workspace.

There are no "right" answers for the questions below. As with all of the reflective activities in this book, write from your heart. This exercise is not meant for you to answer just like your classmates—or to match what you may think the instructor wants to see. Take your time to give a respectful and responsible general accounting of your experiences with organization. A truthful self-assessment now will help you build on skills you have while developing those you lack.

For the following items circle the number that best describes your *typical* experience with organizational skills. The key for the numbers is:

0 = never, 1 = almost never, 2 = occasionally, 3 = frequently,
  4 = almost always, 5 = always

When considering your past successes and challenges with organization, how often:

1. Were you able to find an item (a paper, a book, your keys) after you put it somewhere?

   0   1   2   3   (4)   5

(continued)

---

[1]Steve Piscitelli, *Rhythms of College Success: A Journey of Discovery, Change, and Mastery* (Upper Saddle River, NJ: Pearson Prentice Hall, 2008), 70–91.

2. Did you arrive punctually for class or other appointments?

    0   1   2   3   (4)   5

3. Did you turn homework assignments in on time?

    0   1   2   (3)   4   5

4. Did you work in a study space dedicated specifically for you?

    (0)   1   2   3   4   5

5. Did you not overwhelm and stress yourself by limiting your workload?

    0   1   (2)   (3)   4   5

6. Were you able to handle your stress in an effective and healthy manner?

    0   (1)   (2)   3   4   5

7. Did you seek advice from a classmate, adviser, or professor about ways to better organize your class work and reduce stress?

    (0)   1   2   3   4   5

8. Did you organize your class notes and materials with an effective notebook?

    0   (1)   (2)   3   4   5

Add up your scores for items 2, 3, and 5. Divide by 3. Write your answer here: $3\frac{1}{3}$.

Using the key explanations above for each number (0, 1, 2, 3, 4, 5), complete this sentence: When it comes to organizing time, I _relativly_ organize my time effectively.

Add up your scores for items 1, 4, and 8. Divide by 3. Write your answer here: _2_.

Using the key explanations above for each number (0, 1, 2, 3, 4, 5), complete this sentence: When it comes to organizing space, I _hardly_ organize my space effectively.

Add up your scores for items 5, 6, and 7. Divide by 3. Write your answer here: $3\frac{2}{3}$.

Using the key explanations above for each number (0, 1, 2, 3, 4, 5) for this activity, complete this sentence: When it comes to organization in general, I _don't can_ organize space and time so as to minimize stress.

Based on your answers, what insights do you have about your experiences with organization? _I'm not very organized, but I can easily deal with stress._

ORGANIZATION AND TIME

No one can give you a foolproof/crisis-proof time-management system, but *successful* students can adapt to changes and unforeseen events. Be prepared; no matter what you have planned, try to give yourself some breathing room. This is one reason *not* to wait until the night before to complete an assignment. What if the power goes out? You won't be able to use the computer or study for an exam. Anticipation will help to reduce pressure on you and avoid crisis.

You Have a Lot to Do!

Between course work, homework, after-school activities, family responsibilities, and personal activities, there are many demands on your time. A partial list may look like this:

- Finding personal free time
- Finding time to do activities with friends
- Finding recreation time
- Finding quality family time
- Finding the time to study
- Juggling work hours, school hours, and study hours
- Getting enough good sleep
- Juggling family responsibilities with school expectations

The clock keeps ticking—no matter what you do. You cannot control time. You cannot create time. However, you *can* effectively use time for your benefit. The strategies discussed here will help you juggle all the obligations that look you in the face each day.

Study Time: How Much?

This is nearly an impossible question to answer. If you are taking a full load of classes, then your homework and class time could very well add up to a forty-hour workweek—based on the long-referenced formula of spending two or three hours a week *out* of class for every hour you spend *in* class. In this way, if you were spending twelve hours in class each week, you would need to devote another twenty-four to thirty-six hours to study time—reading, writing, researching, meeting with study groups, completing assignments, and preparing for tests outside of class.

That is a lot of time.

Keep in mind that the type of work you do will also dictate how much time is necessary. For instance, if you are reviewing elementary concepts in an introductory math course, your amount of homework time may be less than for someone tackling higher-level calculus for the first time.

How Do I Establish a Study Schedule?

Let's ask the "how much study time" question in a different way. How much time do *you have available* for homework and study purposes?

Complete Activity 4.2 and then examine Table 4.1.

ACTIVITY 4.2   WHERE DOES YOUR WEEK GO?

There are 168 hours in every week. Whether you are a first-year student or a graduating senior, the number of hours remains constant. We cannot create or eliminate any of them.

In the first column of the table that follows, list all of the things you do in a week. You will find some common categories already entered for you.

(continued)

Add as many as apply to your week's schedule. Once you have completed that, go back and estimate the number of hours *per week* that you devote to each category, and enter these numbers in the next column. (Recognizing that it is difficult to be exact with this type of exercise, estimate as best you can.) The third column asks you to rate how necessary the activity is to you. That is, was this something you had to do?[2]

WHAT I DO EACH WEEK	NUMBER OF HOURS I SPEND DOING IT	HOW NECESSARY IS THIS TO MY LIFE? 1 = NOT VERY NECESSARY 5 = EXTREMELY NECESSARY
Sleep		
Eat meals		
Hygiene (showers, haircuts, general grooming)		
Time in class		
Time at employment		
Practice (sports, music, theater)		
Travel (time I spend on the road each week)		
Child care		
Religious or spiritual activities		
Recreation		
Chores and errands		
Other family obligations		
Club activities		
Other		
Total time spent on all of the above activities		
Time remaining from my 168-hour week. This is the amount of time I could use for homework and study purposes.		

(continued)

[2]For a more in-depth discussion of evaluating how your time is spent see Edward M. Hallowell, *Crazy Busy: Overstretched, Overbooked, and About to Snap!* (New York: Ballantine Books, 2007), 148–161.

CRITICAL THINKING STANDARD	APPLICATION TO YOUR STUDY SKILLS	YOUR EXPLANATION HERE OR ON A SEPARATE PIECE OF PAPER
Clarity	*Clearly* state this particular organizational challenge.	
Accuracy	How do you know this assessment of your challenge is *correct*?	
Precision	*Specifically* explain this organizational challenge.	
Relevance	How is your assessment of your organizational challenge *connected* to your academic progress?	
Depth	Examine your identified organizational challenge beyond a superficial (simplistic) explanation and look at all of the *complexities* involved.	
Breadth	Examine your organizational challenge from more than one *perspective (point of view)*.	
Logic	Based on your evidence does your conclusion about your organizational challenge *make sense*?	

Based on your answers above, what insights have you gained about your time-management challenge? _____

_____

What is the next step you will take to eliminate this challenge? _____

_____

_____

Keeping Track of Your Time and Commitments

Once you understand how much time you must devote to school and studies, you'll need a way to manage that time. Whatever strategy you choose, make sure it is something you will *use*. A calendar—or even a simple piece of paper—can work wonders *if* it helps you manage your time. Like your note-taking style (discussed in Chapters 6 and 7), whatever you decide to go with, make sure it works for you—and use it consistently. Three common tools for keeping track of priorities and managing time are the monthly calendar, the weekly calendar, and the daily to-do list. This can be either in paper/book format or in the form of a digital calendar on your computer or handheld device.

Monthly calendar

figure 4.1

Monday	Tuesday	Wednesday	Thursday	Friday	Sat/Sun
March 1	2	3	4	5	6
					7
8	9	10	11	12	13
					14
15	16	17	18	19	20
					21
22	23	24	25	26	27
					28
29	30	31	April 1	2	3
					4

Monthly Calendar. This format allows you to see up to four weeks at a time. You can easily spot conflicts, tests, personal commitments, and the like (see Figure 4.1).

Weekly Calendar. Although a weekly calendar won't show the entire month at a glance, it will allow you to enter more details for each day (see Figure 4.2). Some weekly calendars will even provide space to schedule specific appointment times (say, a study group meeting).

Daily To-Do List. You can be very detailed with a daily calendar. A variation of this format is the tried and true "to-do" list (see Figure 4.3). This can be a simple piece of notebook paper. Write the date across the top. Down one side, list and number the items you need to do today. As you finish an item, cross it off. A daily to-do list has two advantages:

1. You have a concrete record of what you actually accomplished.
2. You have immediate proof (gratification) of task completion.

If you don't finish an item today, transfer it to tomorrow's list. You probably will not check off every item every day. There is nothing wrong with that. Simply progress toward your goals one task at a time.

figure 4.2   Weekly calendar

ACTIVITY 4.6   USING YOUR CALENDAR TO KEEP TRACK OF ASSIGNMENT PROGRESS

For this activity you will need to have all of your class syllabi in front of you as well as your planner (either in paper or digital format). Every time you see an assignment and due date listed in a syllabus, enter that information on your calendar. Do this for all assignments in each of your classes. Specific items to look for include exams, term projects, reading assignments, quizzes, service learning projects, and lab visits.

How do you believe doing this will help you be successful? _____

_____

_____

| Daily calendar | *figure 4.3* |

| Monday, May 15 |
| 7:00 a.m. |
| 8:00 |
| 9:00 |
| 10:00 |
| 11:00 |
| 12:00 p.m. |
| 1:00 |
| 2:00 |
| 3:00 |
| 4:00 |
| 5:00 |
| 6:00 |
| 7:00 |
| 8:00 |
| 9:00 |

What Should You Do First? Establishing Priorities

OK, let's recap. You have an idea of where your time goes each week. You know how many hours are available for homework and studying. You even adopted a method for keeping track of your commitments. Now, you must determine what to do first, second, and so on. Then, once you have established your list of things to do, you are ready to address the most important aspect of time management—prioritization.

Without establishing priorities (an order of importance) you can easily end up spending time on minor tasks while ignoring the major projects that require immediate attention. Let's consider a few basic tips. After you have your list of things to do, make the following determinations:

- *Which items must be addressed immediately?* Studying for a quiz that will be given at 8:00 a.m. tomorrow has more immediacy than typing a research paper that is due two months from today.

- *Which items represent a crisis?* You are scheduled to meet with your chemistry study group at noon today. But you just got word that the financial aid counselor wants to discuss your scholarship, also at noon today. Both are immediate. But the scholarship is critical to your continuing in college.

■ *Can you plan ahead?* Using your syllabi and assignment pages, map out your entire semester. As you did in Activity 4.6, record on your calendar when each exam, quiz, and assignment is due. Then you will be able to see the big picture—and there will be fewer surprises.

Simplify

A major strategy for managing time is to look at the big picture, and then break down the overall task into smaller steps. Although the big picture is necessary in order to find your direction, it might be a bit overwhelming. It might help you to break the bigger task or project into smaller, less intimidating steps. Then take one step at a time to complete the task. Activity 4.7 will help you apply this strategy to a classroom assignment.

ACTIVITY 4.7   COMPLETING A CLASS PROJECT

For the purpose of this activity, let's assume your assignment is to research and to write about the importance of the video gaming industry to education. The assignment is due in three weeks. Briefly jot down the steps you would take to complete the assignment—in other words, how you would manage your time in tackling this project. Days 1–3 and days 4–6 have been filled in to help get you started.

Days 1–3: Carefully read the assignment and make sure I know exactly what I need to do for this paper. Note any special requirements and due dates the professor has listed. Look through the textbook to narrow down a list of possible topics. Conduct an initial search of Internet sites (Chapter 11 will provide more information about this). Perhaps there is a professor I can talk to and help focus my thoughts.

Days 4–6: Go to the campus library with my list of topics. Ask a reference librarian to help guide me. Check out books and/or copy articles that may be of help. Start reading and taking notes.

Days 7–9:

_____

_____

Days 10–12:

_____

_____

Days 13–15:

_____

_____

(continued)

Days 16–18:

_____

_____

Days 19–21:

_____

_____

Backward Planning

Another time management strategy is to plan *backward*. Suppose you have a test scheduled in one week. Start with the end product—walking into class prepared for the exam. Now work backward: How will you get to this point? Table 4.2 provides one option.

"I'll Do All of This Tomorrow!" Dealing with Procrastination

All the tips, strategies, calendars, and campus resources to help you with classroom success will do absolutely nothing if you don't take the first step toward putting them into action. Procrastination—avoiding and postponing what should be taken care of now—can rob your time and derail your best intentions.

Procrastinators may have various reasons for their behavior, but regardless of the motivation, the habit is usually self-defeating. Procrastination is not synonymous with laziness. In fact, suggests one psychologist, procrastinators have energy to spare—it just is not focused in the appropriate direction. And there is usually an excuse attached to why an assignment or task is not completed. Thus, the first step in dealing with your procrastination is to "listen" to your excuses and then develop a plan to refocus your efforts. Table 4.3 provides a

Backward planning goal: To receive an A on the next biology exam	*table 4.2*

DAY	TASK
Thursday	Successfully take the biology exam (the result).
Wednesday	Briefly review major topics—no cramming necessary (☺).
Tuesday	Review vocabulary and potential exam questions.
Monday	Review your class notes again (reread).
Sunday	Review chapter questions in textbook; try to identify potential exam questions.
Saturday	Review class notes; review vocabulary and study guide sheets.
Friday	Review class notes; reorganize; write a brief summary of your notes; provide a descriptive title for your notes.
Thursday (the day you started)	Make sure all textbook readings are complete.

table 4.3 — Strategies to deal with procrastination

TYPE OF PROCRASTINATOR	DESCRIPTION	WHAT CAN YOU DO?
Perfectionist	You don't want to let yourself or others down. Everything you do has to be "just right." You end up postponing completion by doing more work on the task than is needed.	Change your thinking from everything *must* be perfect to everything will be as good as possible. Know the difference between *practical* and *ideal*. (This does not mean you have to settle for inferior work. It simply means you should allow yourself some leeway. Don't unduly pressure yourself.)
Dreamer	Big plans and big ideas—but you never put them into action. You hope someone else will take care of the details for you.	Replace your dreams with *plans*. Develop *action steps* (see Chapter 3)— and then follow them one at a time.
Worrier	You fear taking a risk. So rather than do something different or challenging that may be risky, you avoid commitment and/or following through as long as possible.	Speak confidently about your abilities. Associate with people who are positive and will help you see your talents. Each week take a little calculated risk (nothing foolish) in order to get used to stretching your abilities.
Crisis maker	You live for adrenaline rushes! You wait until the last minute to study or complete a paper. The more pressure involved with a project, the better. You may even secretly like the attention that this type of behavior brings. Unfortunately, as more projects stack up, you are not able to complete the tasks satisfactorily.	Write assignment goals (see Chapter 3) that include specific due dates that come *before* a course deadline— maybe two or three days before the due date. Use sports or some other activity to satisfy your adrenaline needs.
Defier	Ever the maverick or rebel, you don't see why your time should be affected by other people's demands (like class attendance or completing a written assignment).	Refocus. "What can *I* do?" and "What do *I* need to do?" should be asked, rather than "Why do I have to do what *they* want me to do?" *You* made the choice to come to school and *you* (probably) made the choice to take the particular class.
Overdoer	You do not know how to say no. You do not want to disappoint people so you take on too much, run out of time, and turn in a half-done or unsatisfactory project. You can do certain tasks very well but you eventually run out of energy and crash. Ironically, you then *do* disappoint the very people you were	Learn that the healthiest word in the English language can very well be *no*. Reevaluate your goals (see Chapter 3). Before taking on too much to do, make sure your goals are being advanced. Obviously, there is a fine line between being self-centered and willing to help others. But if you are an overdoer, you

(continued)

		table 4.3

(Continued)

TYPE OF PROCRASTINATOR	DESCRIPTION	WHAT CAN YOU DO?
	trying to please, as well as yourself.	probably have long ago crossed this line and have failed to take proper care of your needs.

Source: From Linda Sapadin with Jack Maguire, *Beat Procrastination and Make the Grade: The Six Styles of Procrastination and How Students Can Overcome Them* (New York: Penguin Books, 1999), 15–20.

brief overview of six styles of procrastination, along with suggestions on how to fight these time-wasting behaviors.[4]

ORGANIZATION AND SPACE

Once you have organized your time, examine your space. For the purposes of this section, *space* refers to those areas around you that relate to your studies outside of the classroom: your home study area, your book bag or purse, and, if you have one, your car. The time that you spend searching your space for a book, notes, or a syllabus is time taken from the priorities you established on your calendar or to-do list.

Home Study Area

Whether you have a separate room dedicated to studying or just a small corner of a larger room, there are ways to organize your space so it works for you.

© 2000 Corbis Corporation

Workspace. The first thing to do is to mark an area that will be yours for schoolwork—a personal study area. Do whatever you can to clearly "mark your territory." Make sure others in your residence know this area is for your studies—not for stacks of laundry, not for someone else's personal items, and not for trash

[4]See Linda Sapadin with Jack Maguire. *Beat Procrastination and Make the Grade: The Six Styles of Procrastination and How Students Can Overcome Them* (New York: Penguin Books, 1999) for an in-depth review of the types of procrastination. See pages 10–20 for a quick overview.

ORGANIZATION AND STRESS

Disorganization—whether in the way you manage your time or the way you keep your work and storage areas—can create stress. Because stress is emotionally and physically draining, it makes sense to develop strategies that will help limit the stressors in your life.

Types of Stress

Stress can compromise the integrity of your body. When we refer to *stress*, we typically describe how our bodies react to external and internal pressures. Physiologically, stress represents a time of extreme arousal in the body. Blood pressure can rise, the heart and pulse beat more rapidly, the body can perspire, and clear thinking may become more difficult. Psychologists generally recognize two types of stress: distress and eustress.

Distress is what we usually refer to when using the word *stress*. It is considered "bad" stress or pressure. For instance: A student just received a letter from the financial aid office saying she was in danger of losing her aid because her grade point average has fallen below the criterion. Without financial assistance she will not be able to remain in school. Her heart begins to beat quickly; she feels flushed and sick to her stomach.

Eustress is positive, or "good," stress or pressure. For example: It is graduation day. This is what you have worked so hard to achieve. Your family and friends are in the audience. As your name is called to cross the stage and get your diploma, your heart is racing—but your chest is full of pride!

Stress can move us to action. But continual exposure to stress can lead to physical ailments or emotional trauma—both of which will compromise the integrity of your body.

Stress Signals

Stressors differ from person to person. Pay attention to your body; it will give clues when something is wrong. Some of the more common signals include those on the list in Activity 4.9.[5]

ACTIVITY 4.9 STRESS SIGNALS

Place a check mark next to stress signals you experience.

- ○ Shallow or rapid breathing
- ○ Sweating

(continued)

---

[5]This list is not meant to be diagnostic. Seek professional assistance as needed. For additional information see the St. Vincent Catholic Medical Center Web site, www.svcmc.org/body.cfm?xyzpdqabc=0&id=841&action=detail&AEProductID=HW%5FCatholic&AEArticleID=rlxsk&AEArticleType=Brain%20and%20nerves (accessed on July 1, 2007).

- ○ Increased heart rate
- ○ Headache
- ○ Muscle tension
- ○ Grinding teeth
- ○ Hunched shoulders
- ○ Eye strain
- ○ Hives or similar rash
- ○ Change in appetite (loss or gain)
- ○ Anxiety or depression
- ○ Short temper
- ○ Anger
- ○ Change in sleep patterns

Stress-Reducing Suggestions

As with stress signals, stress-reducing strategies are individualistic. What works for one person may not work for another. The following list provides a few of the more common healthful and legal suggestions:[6]

- Limit intake of caffeine (a stimulant).
- Exercise regularly.
- Get a good night's sleep.
- Take a break and relax.
- Maintain realistic expectations.
- Reinterpret situations in a positive light (reframing).
- Examine your belief systems.
- Develop a support network.
- Maintain a sense of humor.
- Take breaks for peak performance.
- Learn to say "no" if saying "yes" will overwhelm you.
- Engage in healthy recreation.
- Concentrate on your breath—slower, deeper and longer.
- Practice guided imagery.
- Meditate or pray.
- Talk with a trusted friend or mentor.

---

[6]David B. Posen, "Stress Management for Patient and Physician," *Canadian Journal of Continuing Medical Education*, April 1995, www.mentalhealth.com/mag1/p51-str.html# Head_1 (accessed August 10, 2006). Also see St. Vincent Catholic Medical Centers, www.svcmc.org/ body.cfm?xyzpdqabc=0&id=841&action=detail&AEProductID=HW%5FCatholic&AEArticleID= rlxsk&AEArticleType=Brain%20and%20nerves (accessed on July 1, 2007).

Some other strategies, while they may reduce stress in the short run, have long-term unhealthy consequences:

- Drinking alcohol to excess
- Abusing drugs
- Promiscuous sexual activity
- Smoking
- Binge eating

ACTIVITY 4.10   HOW DO YOU HANDLE STRESS?

1. List the *healthy* strategies you have used in the past to deal with stress.

   _____

   _____

2. Which strategy or strategies do you tend to use the most—and why?

   _____

   _____

3. If you have engaged in any *unhealthy* stress-reducing strategies, what can you do to replace those choices with *healthier* choices?

   _____

   _____

CHAPTER SUMMARY

Organization: Maximizing time and space while minimizing stress

Organized people respect their time. They know it is a precious resource and they refuse to waste it. An organized workspace will have a positive impact on personal time. Organization, also, will help create a calmer more manageable environment. This in turn will reduce stressors.

As you apply the tools for managing your time and space outlined in this chapter, remember that life can have organization but still be adventuresome. Planning does not translate into rigidity. You can be efficient and effective—and still be spontaneous.

Before leaving this chapter, keep the following points in mind:

- You cannot control time. You cannot create time. *However,* you *can* effectively use time for your benefit.
- The more classes you take means more demand on your time. That sounds simplistic, but many students fail to look at the big picture when planning a semester.

- Without establishing priorities (an order of importance) you can easily end up spending time on minor tasks while ignoring the major projects that require immediate attention.
- Procrastination can rob you of your time and derail your best intentions.
- Organize your personal and portable spaces outside of the classroom.
- Organizing time and space will help to limit the chaos and stress in your life.

CHAPTER 4 MEASURABLE OBJECTIVES   ACTIVITY 4.11

At the beginning of this chapter, six measurable objectives were presented. They are reprinted below for your convenience. Using the strategies you have learned in this chapter, fill in the lines beneath each item (or use a separate sheet of paper).

○ Identify at least three types of procrastination and a strategy to deal with each.

   ○ Write the strategies here:_____

   _____

   _____

   _____

○ Develop a written schedule that reflects at least two hours of study time for every hour scheduled in the classroom. For example, English: 3 hours in class; 1 hour writing an essay; 2 hours studying for the unit test; 3 hours reading the assigned novel.

   ○ Write your schedule here:_____

   _____

   _____

   _____

○ Use and evaluate one time-management tool (calendar or planner) for at least one week.

   ○ Write an evaluation of the tool you used during the past week. How did it (or didn't it) help your organization? _____

   _____

   _____

   _____

○ Develop a weekly to-do list that ranks your tasks in order of importance.

   ○ Write your list here: _____

   _____

   _____

   _____

(continued)

○ Draw (or describe) your home study area highlighting its strengths and weaknesses.

　○ Place your drawing or description here: _____

　_____

　_____

　_____

○ Describe how organizational skills can help you balance your life's demands.

　○ Briefly explain one way in which your organizational skills have helped you bring more balance to your life. _____

　_____

　_____

　_____

REALITY CHECK
Using your critical thinking skills to improve your organizational skills

Situation. Marie is a single mother with one child. She has four on-campus classes and one online class. She receives financial aid. In addition, she works thirty hours per week at a store in the mall. It is now the fourth week of the term and she is feeling overwhelmed by all of the projects, tests, and reading assignments she must complete for her classes. Her class averages are not impressive—one C and three Ds. She has not had a good night's sleep in more than two weeks and the stress of everything is beginning to show. She has been late to most of her classes; not by much, but she is *never* on time. And her homework is always late. Things constantly "slip her mind." She moves in what appears to be a constant cloud of dust.

Using at least three strategies from this chapter, help Marie critically review and solve her problem.

_____

_____

_____

_____

_____

_____

CHAPTER 5

LEARNING STYLES

How will knowing your learning style help with your studies?

SPOTLIGHT ON CLASSROOM SKILLS

Students must handle a great deal if they want to be successful in college. Developing sound reading habits, taking effective class notes, and avoiding procrastination rank high on the list for student success. But it, also, helps to recognize your learning style.

Once you understand what helps you learn you will be able to "get" the information your teachers and textbooks present to you. You need to pay attention to the lighting, chair, desk, and room temperature that work best for you. If you need quiet, for instance, avoid noisy places when you try to read. Once you understand your learning style you will stop working against yourself—and begin working for yourself.

This book has provided—and will continue to provide—many study skill suggestions. You will benefit the most when you concentrate on those that fit your learning style best. Whether you prefer absolute quiet or light background noise, structure or flexibility, solitude or group interaction, hearing a lecture or seeing a video, if you understand what works best for you then your chances of success greatly improve.

PREVIEW

By the time you finish reading this chapter and completing its activities you will know how to:

- Identify the preferences of your learning style.
- Develop practical ways to use your learning style to help you in class.
- Develop practical ways to use your learning style to help in your life outside of class.
- Connect your knowledge of learning styles with your knowledge of study skills.
- Use environmental factors to your benefit when studying.

KEY TERMS

- Auditory
- Environmental factors (affecting learning)
- Kinesthetic
- Learning styles
- Left-brain
- Preferences
- Right-brain
- Visual
- Whole-brain

CHAPTER INTRODUCTION

ONE SIZE DOES NOT FIT ALL

Imagine this: You walk into a doctor's office and announce, "Doc, I don't feel well. Fix me." Any reasonable doctor would first need to know some specifics: What are your symptoms? What medications are you taking? To what drugs are you allergic? In other words, the doctor has to recognize you as an individual patient with distinct and separate characteristics from other patients in the waiting room. The same goes for study skills.

You are a unique student with experiences, skills, and challenges. A prescribed study skill for a classmate might not be appropriate for you. Your style of receiving and using information will not necessarily be like that of the person sitting next to you in math class. This chapter's main goal is for you to become more mindful of your style.

WHY NOW?

You may wonder, "If knowing my learning style is so important for classroom success, why did the author wait until now to cover it?" Many books introduce learning styles in the first or second chapter. In fact, in the first edition of *Study Skills: Do I Really Need This Stuff?* students read about learning styles in the second chapter.

Its placement here does not diminish its importance but rather gives a nod to the importance and—in many cases—the pressing nature of the previous chapter topics. For example, organizing time and space—the preceding chapter—generally rank high on the list of things to master as soon as possible.

Now it is time to turn inward and examine how you actually learn. With this knowledge you can continue to modify the study skills you have learned and make them fit your rhythms as a student. You, at the least, have a general idea of what works for you and what does not. This chapter will allow you to dig deeper and discover complementary strategies to move to even higher levels of student success.

ACTIVITY 5.1 | REFLECTING ON YOUR LEARNING STYLE

As with all of the reflective activities in this book, answer from your heart. This exercise is not meant for you to answer just like your classmates—or to match what you may think the instructor wants to see. Take your time to give a respectful and responsible general accounting of your experiences with your study environment and how you prefer to learn (verbally, visually, movement). A truthful self-assessment now will help you build on the insights you already have while developing those you lack.

For the following items circle the number that best describes your *typical* experience. The key for the numbers is:

0 = never, 1 = almost never, 2 = occasionally, 3 = frequently,
4 = almost always, 5 = always

(continued)

When considering your past successes and challenges with learning, how often:

1. Did you notice that a classroom lecture, when it was accompanied with photos, slides, transparencies, or a PowerPoint presentation, either positively or negatively affected your ability to understand the material?

   0   1   2   3   4   5

2. Did you notice that directions when they were given verbally, without any visuals, affected your ability to understand the message?

   0   1   2   3   4   5

3. Did you notice that when you were allowed to do something physically with material, like create a picture or model of it, had an impact on your learning?

   0   1   2   3   4   5

4. Did you notice that the amount of lighting in a room either positively or negatively affected your ability to study or pay attention?

   0   1   2   3   4   5

5. Were you aware of how the temperature of a classroom or study space had an impact on how well you focused on the topic at hand?

   0   1   2   3   4   5

6. Did you perform better when instructors clearly mapped the exact steps you had to follow to complete a task?

   0   1   2   3   4   5

7. Did you notice the effect eating or not eating a meal before an exam had on your performance?

   0   1   2   3   4   5

8. Did you notice how background noise helped or hindered your concentration?

   0   1   2   3   4   5

Add up your scores for items 1, 2, 3, and 6. Divide by 4. Write your answer here: _____.

Using the key explanations above for each number (0, 1, 2, 3, 4, 5), complete this sentence: When it comes to how I receive and understand information, I _____ am aware of my learning preference.

Add up your scores for items 4, 5, 7, and 8. Divide by 4. Write your answer here: _____.

Using the key explanations above for each number (0, 1, 2, 3, 4, 5), complete this sentence: When it comes to how environmental factors affect my learning, I _____ am aware of these factors.

Based on your answers, what insights do you have about your experiences with identifying and using your learning style?_____

_____

_____

THINKING: HOW DO YOU PROCESS INFORMATION?[1]

Your Brain

Enclosed in your skull is a wrinkled three-pound lump of tissue and nerve impulses that never sees the light of day—yet it interprets all you experience. Long lists of words attempt to describe what the brain does. These tend to be action words such as *analyze, argue, compare, contrast, describe, deliberate, evaluate, fantasize, guess, solve,* and *understand.*[2]

Exploring in depth how the brain operates creates a set of challenges that are beyond the scope of this book. But we will examine how to acquire knowledge (*learning*), how to remember that information (*memory*), and how to manipulate that information (*thinking*).[3]

Left-Brain, Right-Brain, and Whole-Brain Thinking

Each side of the brain has a different function (see Figure 5.1). In the most general terms, the left side of the brain has been associated with logical, analytical, linear, and sequential (step-by-step) thought processes. Studies have shown a "specialization of the left hemisphere for language."[4] It is the organized and fact-loving side of the brain. Methodically working through a math problem requires the sequential skills of the left side of the brain.

Whereas the left hemisphere is associated with verbal abilities, the right hemisphere is considered to be the home for nonverbal thinking processes and

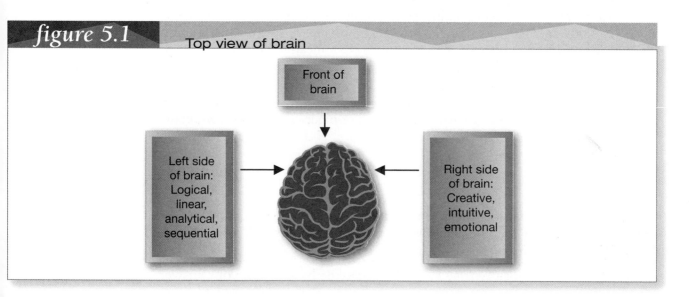

figure 5.1

Top view of brain

Front of brain

Left side of brain: Logical, linear, analytical, sequential

Right side of brain: Creative, intuitive, emotional

[1]Information for this section has been adapted from Steve Piscitelli, *Rhythms of College Success: A Journey of Discovery, Change, and Mastery.* (Upper Saddle River, NJ: Pearson Prentice Hall, 2008), 96–99.

[2]See Frank Smith, *To Think.* (New York: Teachers College Press, 1990), Chapter 1, for Smith's list titled "Thinking in Seventy-seven Words."

[3]Smith, *To Think,* 12.

[4]Arthur W. Toga and Paul M. Thompson, "Mapping Brain Asymmetry," *Nature Reviews: Neuroscience 4* (January 2003): 37.

pattern recognition. From here the traits of creativity, intuition, and emotion spring into action. Molding a statue from a ball of clay relies on the right side of the brain.

There is also the argument that rather than discuss right-brain/left-brain, we should consider the "whole-brain" model to understand the thinking process.[5] This model continues to recognize the distinct traits and abilities of the sides of the brain, but it maintains that the two must eventually work together. For instance, the right side of the brain might help a student arrive at a creative solution to a problem or see the "big picture" of a particular issue—but then the sequential, organized, and detailed-oriented left brain will put the creative solution into action. Have you ever known a creative person who had marvelous ideas yet never seemed able to apply them to the real world? His creative ideas needed a left-brained rational driver to carry them to reality.

Do you tend to be a methodical and organized learner? Have you done better with teachers who clearly map the exact steps you must take to complete a task? Or have you been more comfortable with teachers who allowed you a great deal of flexibility in completing a project? Are you comfortable thinking about abstract ideas, or do you need concrete instructions and explanations? In short, what helps you understand your course material and assignments?

Learning Styles

When students are engaged—taking an active part—in their course work, the chances for success increase significantly. One way to become an engaged student is to know as much as possible about the way you learn—and then apply that knowledge to your academic tasks.

Learning style is a multidimensional model that examines the factors that influence how we process information. Although the material in this section just scratches the surface of a large body of research, it will provide an opportunity to deepen your understanding of your preference for processing information.[6]

---

[5]See Ned Herrmann, "Is it true that creativity resides in the right hemisphere of the brain?" *Scientific American,* January 26, 1998, www.sciam.com/askexpert_question.cfm?articleID= 00049843-7DBA-1C71-9EB7809EC588F2D7&modsrc=related_links (accessed on July 1, 2007); M. Alan Kazley, "Ned Herrmann's Whole Brain Model," kheper.net, www.kheper. net/topics/intelligence/Herrmann.htm (accessed July 1, 2007). Also see John McCrone, "Right Brain or Left Brain—Myth or Reality?" *New Scientist* 163 (July 3, 1999): 26ff.

[6]A great deal has been written about learning styles. My intent here is to provide a brief overview. This chapter uses the VARK instrument to help you examine your preference for using information (part of a learning style). You may also wish to examine Nancy Lightfoot Matte and Susan Hillary Henderson, *Success, Your Style: Right- and Left-Brain Techniques for Learning* (Belmont, CA: Wadsworth, 1995); Rita Dunn and Kenneth Dunn, *Teaching Students Through Their Individual Learning Styles: A Practical Approach* (Reston, VA: Reston, 1978); Roger G. Swartz, *Accelerated Learning: How You Learn Determines What You Learn* (Durant, OK: EMIS, 1991); James Keefe, *Learning Style Handbook: II. Accommodating Perceptual, Study and Instructional Preferences* (Reston, VA: National Association of Secondary School Principals, n.d.).

© 2005 Stockdisc

Various factors—from the classroom setting to the manner of presentation by the instructor—will affect people differently. These factors include:

- *Environmental* (the impact of the physical surroundings on learning)
- *Auditory* (the impact of hearing on learning)
- *Visual* (the impact of seeing on learning)
- *Kinesthetic* (the impact of doing, touching, and moving on learning)

Environmental influences include such factors as food and drink (what we put into our bodies), light (how the room is illuminated), sound (how much silence or noise surrounds us), and temperature (how cool or hot the room is). Other environmental factors are comfort of furniture (how soft, hard, or firm the chair is), structure of time and/or task (how much time we have), ability to move about (how much movement we can have while working), and peer interaction (who we work best with or without when completing a task).

When it comes to teacher presentation, individual students typically have a particular preference that helps them best understand the material being presented. For instance, some can *listen* to a verbal explanation of a task and then carry out the assignment. These students receive *auditory* (oral) directions and translate them into a product.

Other students must *see* something before processing it effectively. For example, if such students had to assemble the components of a desktop computer, it would be very helpful to have diagrammed instructions on what to do. *Visual* aids enhance their ability to learn; if they received only oral instructions, the process would be more difficult for them to complete. Similarly, some people must be able to *read* and *write* about a task in order to understand it.

Other people work best by *handling* or *manipulating* objects. A student who is better able to understand a biological principle by physically performing a laboratory experiment learns in a *kinesthetic* (or body movement) manner.

How Do *You* Learn?

Activity 5.2 gives you the chance to use a learning preference inventory—the VARK questionnaire. VARK measures four preferences for taking in and putting out information: *visual, auditory, read-write,* and *kinesthetic.*[7] Some people have a strong preference for one of these modalities of learning; others prefer more than one. There is no right or wrong preference—there is *your* preference.

---

[7]Neil Fleming, "Is VARK a learning style?" VARK. 2001–2006. http://vark-learn.com/english/page.asp?p=faq (accessed May 14, 2007).

THE VARK QUESTIONNAIRE (VERSION 7.0): *
HOW DO I LEARN BEST?

Choose the answer which best explains your preference and circle the letter(s) next to it. **Please circle more than one if** a single answer does not match your perception. Leave blank any question that does not apply.

1. You are helping someone who wants to go to your airport, town center, or railway station. You would:
   A. go with her.
   B. tell her the directions.
   C. write down the directions (without a map).
   D. draw, or give her a map.

2. You are not sure whether a word should be spelled "dependent" or "dependant." You would:
   A. see the words in your mind and choose by the way they look.
   B. think about how each word sounds and choose one.
   C. find it in a dictionary.
   D. write both words on paper and choose one.

3. You are planning a holiday for a group. You want some feedback from them about the plan. You would:
   A. describe some of the highlights.
   B. use a map or Web site to show them the places.
   C. give them a copy of the printed itinerary.
   D. phone, text, or e-mail them.

4. You are going to cook something as a special treat for your family. You would:
   A. cook something you know without the need for instructions.
   B. ask friends for suggestions.
   C. look through the cookbook for ideas from the pictures.
   D. use a cookbook where you know there is a good recipe.

5. A group of tourists want to learn about the parks or wildlife reserves in your area. You would:
   A. talk about, or arrange a talk for them about parks or wildlife reserves.
   B. show them Internet pictures, photographs or picture books.
   C. take them to a park or wildlife reserve and walk with them.
   D. give them a book or pamphlets about the parks or wildlife reserves.

6. You are about to purchase a digital camera or cell phone. Other than price, what would most influence your decision?
   A. Trying or testing it.
   B. Reading the details about its features.
   C. It is a modern design and looks good.
   D. The salesperson telling me about its features.

(continued)

7. Remember a time when you learned how to do something new. Try to avoid choosing a physical skill, such as riding a bike. You learned best by:

    A. watching a demonstration.

    B. listening to somebody explaining it and asking questions.

    C. diagrams and charts—visual clues.

    D. written instructions—like a manual or textbook.

8. You have a problem with your knee. You would prefer that the doctor:

    A. gave you a Web address or something to read about it.

    B. used a plastic model of a knee to show what was wrong.

    C. described what was wrong.

    D. showed you a diagram of what was wrong.

9. You want to learn a new program, skill, or game on a computer. You would:

    A. read the written instructions that came with the program.

    B. talk with people who know about the program.

    C. use the controls or keyboard.

    D. follow the diagrams in the book that came with it.

10. You like Web sites that have:

    A. things you can click on, shift, or try.

    B. interesting design and visual features.

    C. interesting written descriptions, lists, and explanations.

    D. audio channels where you can hear music, radio programs, or interviews.

11. Other than price, what would most influence your decision to buy a new nonfiction book?

    A. The way it looks is appealing.

    B. Quickly reading parts of it.

    C. A friend talks about it and recommends it.

    D. It has real-life stories, experiences and examples.

12. You are using a book, CD, or Web site to learn how to take photos with your new digital camera. You would like to have:

    A. a chance to ask questions and talk about the camera and its features.

    B. clear written instructions with lists and bullet points about what to do.

    C. diagrams showing the camera and what each part does.

    D. many examples of good and poor photos and how to improve them.

13. Do you prefer a teacher or a presenter who uses:

    A. demonstrations, models, or practical sessions.

    B. question and answer, talk, group discussion, or guest speakers.

    C. handouts, books, or readings.

    D. diagrams, charts, or graphs.

(continued)

14. You have finished a competition or test and would like some feedback. You would like to have feedback:

    A. using examples from what you have done.

    B. using a written description of your results.

    C. from somebody who talks it through with you.

    D. using graphs showing what you had achieved.

15. You are going to choose food at a restaurant or cafe. You would:

    A. choose something that you have had there before.

    B. listen to the waiter or ask friends to recommend choices.

    C. choose from the descriptions in the menu.

    D. look at what others are eating or look at pictures of each dish.

16. You have to make an important speech at a conference or special occasion. You would:

    A. make diagrams or get graphs to help explain things.

    B. write a few key words and practice saying your speech over and over.

    C. write out your speech and learn from reading it over several times.

    D. gather many examples and stories to make the talk real and practical.

The VARK Questionnaire Scoring Chart

Use the following scoring chart to find the VARK category that each of your answers corresponds to. Circle the letters that correspond to your answers. For example, if you answered b and c for question 3, circle V and R in the question 3 row.

QUESTION	A CATEGORY	B CATEGORY	C CATEGORY	D CATEGORY
3	K	V	R	A

Scoring chart

QUESTION	A CATEGORY	B CATEGORY	C CATEGORY	D CATEGORY
1	K	A	R	V
2	V	A	R	K
3	K	V	R	A
4	K	A	V	R
5	A	V	K	R

(continued)

QUESTION	A CATEGORY	B CATEGORY	C CATEGORY	D CATEGORY
6	K	R	V	A
7	K	A	V	R
8	R	K	A	V
9	R	A	K	V
10	K	V	R	A
11	V	R	A	K
12	A	R	V	K
13	K	A	R	V
14	K	R	A	V
15	K	A	R	V
16	V	A	R	K

To calculate your scores

Count the number of each of the VARK letters you have circled to write your score for each VARK category.

Total number of Vs circled = ___2___

Total number of As circled = ___6___

Total number of Rs circled = ___4___

Total number of Ks circled = ___5___

Calculating your preferences

Once you have determined your preferences, visit the VARK Web site (www. vark-learn.com) and study the "Helpsheets" for learning strategies for each of the preferences. Finally, reflect for a moment on the helpsheet for your preference. How will you use this information today? _____

_____

_____

_____

Difficulties in the Classroom?

Questionnaires like VARK can provide important insights. For instance, if you have difficulties in the classroom, they may not be due to a lack of effort on your part. The problem might be related to whether or not you handle information in the most effective manner *for you*. If you are a visual learner but never play to that strength, you might be making things harder for yourself.

Let's assume, for example, you have to study for a quiz on the branches and functions of the nervous system. If your preferred method for learning is auditory, you could recite the information aloud to yourself in an attempt to hear and "burn" the concepts into your memory.

If, however, you learn best visually, by seeing the material, you could read your class textbook and review your class notes.

However, you could just as well draw up a diagram of the nervous system and physically label it as a warm-up activity for your in-class quiz. Such a study approach encourages the whole-brain model described earlier. Drawing a diagram (creativity) and then labeling the particular parts (organization) engages more of the brain than just staring at a piece of notebook paper with terms written on it. It also allows you to work kinesthetically (drawing and physically labeling the diagram) and visually (looking at the diagram and the labels).

So, for the remainder of this chapter, this book, and this term refer to your VARK preferences. Use them to help you process, organize, understand the vast amounts of information you will receive.

CRITICALLY THINKING ABOUT YOUR LEARNING STYLES   ACTIVITY 5.3

This activity has a different emphasis than that of previous chapter critical thinking activities. Rather than concentrating on a challenge, concentrate on how you can use the preference information you identified for yourself in the VARK Questionnaire (Activity 5.2). Apply the critical thinking standards from Chapter 2 to examine this information.

CRITICAL THINKING STANDARD	APPLICATION TO YOUR STUDY SKILLS	YOUR EXPLANATION HERE OR ON A SEPARATE PIECE OF PAPER
Clarity	*Clearly* state what your particular learning preference is according to the VARK.	
Accuracy	Based on your experiences, how do you know VARK has *accurately* identified your preference?	
Precision	*Specifically* (give examples) explain how this preference has shown itself in school experiences.	
Relevance	How do you believe the VARK assessment of your learning preference is *connected* to your academic progress?	
Depth	Examine your identified learning preference beyond a superficial (simplistic) explanation. What are the *various pieces* of this preference?	

(continued)

CRITICAL THINKING STANDARD	APPLICATION TO YOUR STUDY SKILLS	YOUR EXPLANATION HERE OR ON A SEPARATE PIECE OF PAPER
Breadth	Examine your learning preference from more than one *perspective (point of view)*. That is, how can this help in school and in your world outside of school?	
Logic	Based on the evidence before you, does your conclusion about your learning preference *make sense*?	

Based on your answers above, what insights have you gained about your learning style preference?

_____

_____

What is the next step you will take to use your learning preferences for your benefit?

_____

_____

ACTIVITY 5.4   HOW DO YOU LEARN BEST?

Reflect on the various ways you process information. Then answer the following questions.

1. *Auditory:* Describe a recent class situation in which you understood the material by *hearing* the explanation. You really "got it"! Rate how often this happens on a scale of 1 (almost never) to 5 (almost always). Explain why you think you got it or why you think you did *not* get it.

   Rating: _____

   Explanation: _____

   _____

2. *Visual:* Describe a recent class situation in which you understood the material by *seeing* the explanation. Maybe the instructor used pictures or a model. Whatever she used, you really "got it"! Rate how often this happens on a scale of 1 (almost never) to 5 (almost always). Explain why you think you got it or why you think you did *not* get it.

   Rating: _____

   Explanation: _____

   _____

(continued)

3. *Kinesthetic:* Describe a recent class situation in which you understood the material by *physically doing something.* Maybe it was a science lab or maybe you constructed a model. Whatever happened, you really "got it"! Rate how often this happens on a scale of 1 (almost never) to 5 (almost always). Explain why you think you got it or why you think you did *not* get it.

Rating: _____

Explanation: _____

_____

4. *Environment:* Describe the environment (climate, lighting, ventilation, sound) that helps you learn the best.

_____

_____

Making Learning Styles Information Work for You

It is one thing to *know* how you learn best but it is quite another to *use* the knowledge. When we actively learn we listen, view or manipulate information, *and* then we process that information. That is, we *use* it in some way.

Table 5.1 provides questions and suggestions to apply learning style information to your academic success.

table 5.1	Make your learning style work for you	
IF YOU SHOW A PREFERENCE FOR . . .	**THEN ASK YOURSELF . . .**	**A FEW SUGGESTIONS INCLUDE . . .**
Auditory learning	How can I use verbal cues to help me understand my class work?	• Sit as close to the instructor as possible to make sure you hear all that is said. • Tape record lessons. • Tape record yourself as you describe your notes–then play the tape back and listen. • Join a study group. • If available, use the audio notes of the textbook located on the textbook's companion Web site.
Visual learning	How can I use visual aids to help me understand my class work?	• If available, use the visual aids on the textbook's companion Web site. • Perhaps your instructors have posted PowerPoint presentations or outlines on their Web sites; if so print them. • Change your note-taking strategy by using more diagrams and flowcharts.

(continued)

table 5.1	(Continued)	
IF YOU SHOW A PREFERENCE FOR . . .	**THEN ASK YOURSELF . . .**	**A FEW SUGGESTIONS INCLUDE . . .**
Kinesthetic learning	How can I use movement to help me understand my class work?	• If possible, construct a model of your class material. • Perform a skit, role play, or debate that uses the main ideas from the lesson. • If you need to move, walk or pace while you try to learn new concepts.
Structure and clear explanation	How can I more formally structure my assignments?	• If your instructor's instructions sound vague, stop by his office and seek clarification. • Join a study group to help you organize your thoughts. • Ask a classmate for her interpretation of the assignment instructions.
A quiet study environment	How can I minimize noise so that I can concentrate more on my studies?	• Close the door to your room and post a "Do not disturb" sign. • If you live with someone else, request that they respect certain hours as study hours. • If you do not have a quiet space at your residence, block regular time on your calendar to work in the campus library.
A brightly lighted study area	How can I have the best lighting for my studies?	• Be mindful of eye strain, which can be caused by certain types of lighting. • Buy a small inexpensive desk light for your study area. • When possible, you might read outdoors in sunlight.

CHAPTER SUMMARY

In this chapter you have been asked to think about *how* you should think about *what* you think about. You have examined the importance of taking control of your learning process. As each week on campus passes, you will begin to notice what *is* working for you and what is *not*. You will know where your challenges lie and what strengths you can draw on to meet those challenges. Before moving on to the next chapter, take a moment to reflect on the following points:

- Your style of receiving and using information will not necessarily be like the style of the person sitting next to you in class.
- The whole-brain model recognizes that that the left-brain and right-brain must work together to provide the best learning.
- Learning style is a multidimensional model that examines the factors that influence how we process information.

- When students are engaged—taking an active part—in their course work, the chances for success increase significantly.
- Various factors—from the classroom setting to the manner of presentation by the teacher—will affect people differently.
- According to VARK, there are four preferences for taking in and putting out information: *visual, auditory, read-write,* and *kinesthetic.*

CHAPTER 5 MEASURABLE OBJECTIVES   ACTIVITY 5.5

At the beginning of this chapter, five measurable objectives were presented. They are reprinted below for your convenience. Using the strategies you learned in this chapter, fill in the lines beneath each item (or use a separate sheet of paper).

○ Identify the preferences of your learning style.

   ○ List four preferences associated with your learning style. Include environmental factors as well as how you prefer to receive information.

   _____

   _____

   _____

   _____

○ Develop practical ways to use your learning style to help you in class.

   ○ Describe one practical way in which your knowledge of learning styles has helped you in class.

   _____

   _____

   _____

○ Develop practical ways to use your learning style to help in your life outside of class.

   ○ Describe one practical way in which your knowledge of learning styles has helped you outside of class. Maybe it helped you in a campus club or a job interview.

   _____

   _____

   _____

(continued)

○ Connect your knowledge of learning styles with your knowledge of study skills.

　　○ Choose one of the following study skills and describe how knowing your learning style will help you further develop that skill. For instance, a student with an auditory learning style may wish to supplement her textbook reading with a book on tape or CD.

　　　○ Critical thinking

　　　○ Organizing time and space

　　　○ Class time

　　　○ Note taking

　　　○ Reading

　　　_____

　　　_____

　　　_____

　　　_____

○ Use environmental factors to your benefit when studying.

　　○ In what ways have you been able to use environmental factors to enhance your academic success?

　　　_____

　　　_____

　　　_____

　　　_____

REALITY CHECK

Using your critical thinking skills to understand and use your learning style

Situation. Allen is a happy and well-adjusted first-year college student. He reads his assignments, attends class, participates in all discussions, and studies for all of his exams. Unfortunately, his grades are not what he would like them to be. On the suggestion from an adviser, he recently took a learning styles assessment. Although he did not learn anything new, the information reinforced that he was a visual learner and that he preferred a quiet and well-lit study area. His problem is that all of his professors lecture with very few visual aids. Most do not even use PowerPoint. His home **study area is anything but quiet; noise comes from both inside and outside his home.**

Using the information you learned in this chapter, describe four specific strategies that may help Allen use his learning style preferences.

_____

_____

_____

_____

_____

_____

_____

CHAPTER 6

CLASS TIME

How can you be more successful during class time?

SPOTLIGHT ON CLASSROOM SKILLS

When I started college I was able to skim and scan my reading for important points. I also had decent problem-solving skills. But I had trouble with note-taking. I knew how to take notes but I had difficulty identifying the important things from the professor's lesson that I needed to remember. Consequently, I would waste time trying to write all of the notes I could without considering how much I would actually need. After taking a student success class, I quickly mastered my note-taking skills. This in turn helped me to study more effectively.

Student success results from what you do inside and outside of your classroom. This chapter will examine what you can do to get the most from your hours inside your classrooms. This chapter will propose strategies to help you focus your attention, find the main points of a lesson, and then record those ideas in an organized and usable format.[1]

---

[1]Steve Piscitelli, *Rhythms of College Success: A Journey of Discovery, Change, and Mastery* (Upper Saddle River, NJ: Pearson Prentice Hall, 2008), 118–133.

PREVIEW

By the time you finish reading this chapter and completing its activities you will be able to:

- Identify at least three classroom distractions and a strategy to deal with each.
- Explain how instructor style affects your classroom success.
- Describe one strategy to help develop a working and respectful relationship with your instructors.
- Use and evaluate one note-taking style for at least one week.
- Critically evaluate at least one of your classroom challenges.
- Identify at least two tips to help you pay attention in class.

KEY TERMS

- Active learning
- Attention
- Classroom success
- Distractions
- Instructor expectations
- Note-taking styles
- Office hours
- Online classes

CHAPTER INTRODUCTION

Students are expected to listen, remember, comprehend, and apply a great deal of information. In some cases, the information is quite complex. If you passively sit in class acting as a receptacle for your instructor's notes or, worse yet, if you *simply sit there* and *not take notes*, you will have completed, at best, only one piece of the learning process—the listening part. Students engaged in active learning accomplish two tasks:

1. Taking in information
2. Manipulating or using the information

This chapter describes strategies that will help you become more active and effective *inside* your classroom. Later chapters will examine the issue of active engagement *outside* the classroom, helping you build on class lectures, discussions, and student group work once you leave the classroom.

ACTIVITY 6.1   **REFLECTION ON YOUR CURRENT LEVEL OF CLASSROOM PERFORMANCE SKILLS**

Before you answer the items below, reflect on your current level of classroom success skills. Think of how well (or poorly) you have performed in past classes.

As with all of the reflective activities in this book, answer from your heart. This exercise is not meant for you to answer just like your classmates— or to match what you may think the instructor wants to see. Take your time to give a respectful and responsible general accounting of your experiences with classroom success. A truthful self-assessment now will help you build on skills you have while developing those you lack.

For the following items circle the number that best describes your *typical* experience with classroom success skills. The key for the numbers is:

0 = never, 1 = almost never, 2 = occasionally, 3 = frequently,
    4 = almost always, 5 = always

When considering your past successes and challenges in the classroom, how often:

1. Were you able to figure out what most of your instructors expected you to do in order to receive good grades?

    0   1   2   3   4   5

2. Did you adjust successfully to your instructors' teaching styles?

    0   1   2   3   4   5

3. Did you develop a respectful and civil relationship with your instructors?

    0   1   2   3   4   5

4. Were you able to fight off distractions and pay attention during class?

    0   1   2   3   4   5

5. Did you take notes on the lesson during class time?

    0   1   2   3   4   5

(continued)

6. Were you able to pick out the most important ideas from your instructor's lectures?

   0   1   2   3   4   5

7. Did you use a consistent note-taking format during class?

   0   1   2   3   4   5

8. Did you maintain an organized notebook of your classroom notes and paper?

   0   1   2   3   4   5

Add up your scores for items 1, 2, 3, and 4. Divide by 4. Write your answer here: _____.

Using the key explanations above for each number (0, 1, 2, 3, 4, 5), complete this sentence: When it comes to class, I _____ am able to develop a positive and focused working relationship with my instructors.

Add up your scores for items 5, 6, 7, and 8. Divide by 4. Write your answer here: _____.

Using the key explanations above for each number (0, 1, 2, 3, 4, 5), complete this sentence: When it comes to note-taking skills, I _____ take and organize my notes effectively.

Based on your answers, what insights do you have about your experiences with successful classroom strategies? _____

_____

_____

WHAT HAS SURPRISED YOU?   ACTIVITY 6.2

Take a moment and reflect on a few of the major surprises you have encountered with your classes this term. For instance, were you surprised by the amount of work required, the size of your classes, or the manner in which professors interacted with students? Or maybe the first test result was not what you expected, or your study group did not prove to be very productive. You may not know when your professors hold office hours; you might not even know where their offices are located. Write your response below. Be as specific as you can.

1. What has surprised you about your courses this term?

   _____

   _____

2. What changes have you made (or do you plan to make) to address the above reflections?

   _____

   _____

You may find after reflection that you need to make a few changes to enhance your potential for success. Whether the adjustments involve your relationship with instructors or the manner in which you take notes, this is a good time to build on the skills you have and accept the responsibility to make corrections that will benefit you.

DO I KNOW WHAT THE INSTRUCTOR IS DOING IN FRONT OF THE ROOM?

This section will look at the front of the room: what the teacher is doing and what the teacher's expectations are. In the next section we will look at the back of the room: what you are doing in class. Specifically, we will review strategies that if practiced will enable you to become a more successful student.

Instructor Style and Emphasis

When it comes to teaching styles, instructors come in all shapes and sizes. Think of the teachers you have had. Their styles may have ranged from lecture, to question and answer, to group work, to lab work, to discussion, to seat work. Regardless of the method of presentation, each instructor has a set of expectations for student performance. Activity 6.3 will help you to determine just what your instructors expect from you.

ACTIVITY 6.3   **IDENTIFYING HOW YOUR INSTRUCTORS CONDUCT CLASS**

Below is a sampling of instructor styles. Write the names of your instructors across the top of the chart. Down the left side of the chart you will find descriptions of styles and methods. Check the ones that apply to the instructors.

INSTRUCTOR NAME / INSTRUCTOR STYLE	#1	#2	#3	#4	#5
Primarily lectures the entire class					
Uses lots of question and answer discussions					
Uses lots of group work activities					
Uses lots of in-class seat work					
Concentrates on details like dates, formulas, and classifications					
Pays close attention to grammar and writing skills					
Very seldom assigns a writing assignment					
Is very serious and does not allow for any joking in class					
Is very serious but does allow lighthearted moments					
Never accepts an assignment late					
Accepts assignments late but with a penalty					
Accepts assignments late with no penalty					
Takes attendance each class					
Expects punctual attendance in class					
Seems to always go off on a tangent (stray from the topic)					
Stays on target, seldom straying from the topic at hand					

How can this information help you be successful in each of your classes?

_____

_____

Identification of Instructor Style + Expectations = Classroom Success

Instructors, like students, have personal teaching styles and professional expectations in the classroom. Activity 6.4 will allow you to examine more closely the styles and expectations (often found in the syllabus) of your instructors. Being aware of these will help you prepare for and participate in class. You may wish to make a copy of the chart and complete it for each instructor you have this term. Check all that apply. Place the completed chart someplace (like your notebook) where you will be reminded of these important expectations.

WHAT DOES MY INSTRUCTOR EXPECT FROM ME?

Course name: _____

Instructor's name: _____

MY INSTRUCTOR REQUIRES THAT I:

○ Maintain a notebook
○ Complete mostly reading homework
○ Complete mostly writing homework
○ Complete reading and writing homework
○ Participate in class
○ Do group work
○ Other

MY INSTRUCTOR WILL GRADE ME WITH:

○ Reading quizzes
○ Homework assignments
○ Class participation
○ Exams
○ Projects and/or research papers
○ Group work
○ Other

MY INSTRUCTOR USES A LOT OF:

○ Group work
○ Lecture
○ Class discussion
○ Worksheets
○ In-class problems or writing assignments
○ Material from the textbook
○ Other

MY INSTRUCTOR'S TESTS FOR THIS COURSE ARE PRIMARILY:

○ Multiple choice
○ Matching
○ Completion/fill in the blank
○ True/false
○ Short answer
○ Essay
○ Some combination of the above
○ Other

IN THIS CLASS MY BIGGEST CHALLENGE WILL BE:

○ Taking notes
○ Understanding the teacher
○ Dealing with distractions
○ Staying focused
○ Completing my homework on time
○ Following instructions
○ Answering questions orally
○ Working with groups
○ Getting ready for tests
○ Dealing with the volume of homework
○ Being a procrastinator
○ Managing my time
○ Getting to class on time
○ Having excessive absences
○ Having a negative attitude
○ Feeling sleepy
○ Other

STEPS I CAN TAKE TO DO BETTER IN THIS CLASS:

○ Seek tutoring from the teacher
○ Seek tutoring from a classmate
○ Follow through on my assignments
○ Reevaluate how I budget my time
○ Ask for a seat change
○ Review my notes more regularly than I already do
○ Prepare earlier for exams
○ Break big projects into smaller, easier-to-manage steps
○ Be on time for class
○ Be absent less often
○ Ask the teacher for assistance
○ Seek computer-assisted instruction where available
○ Read the textbook more carefully
○ Review class notes regularly
○ Devote more time to high-quality studying
○ Other

CRITICALLY THINKING ABOUT CLASSROOM CHALLENGES

Let's apply the critical thinking standards from Chapter 2 to examine one of the challenges you identified for yourself in Activity 6.4.

List your challenge here: _____

CRITICAL THINKING STANDARD	APPLICATION TO YOUR STUDY SKILLS	YOUR EXPLANATION HERE OR ON A SEPARATE PIECE OF PAPER
Clarity	*Clearly* state this particular classroom challenge.	
Accuracy	How do you know this assessment of your challenge is *correct*?	
Precision	*Specifically* (give examples) explain this classroom challenge.	
Relevance	How is your assessment of your classroom challenge *connected* to your academic progress?	
Depth	Examine your identified classroom challenge beyond a superficial (simplistic) explanation and look at all of the *complexities* involved.	
Breadth	Examine your classroom challenge from more than one *perspective (point of view)*.	
Logic	Based on your evidence, does your conclusion about your classroom challenge *make sense*?	

Based on your answers above, what insights have you gained about your classroom challenge?

_____

_____

What is the next step you will take to eliminate this challenge? _____

_____

_____

DO I KNOW WHAT I AM DOING IN THE BACK OF THE ROOM?

What Can You Do to Maximize Classroom Success?

Rarely does a problem fall totally in the lap of one person. For example, if there is a personality clash with a particular instructor, sit back and evaluate the situation. Have you contributed to the problem? What can you do to change the predicament? Is the instructor a difficult grader, or is it simply that you lack some basic process skills? Be honest. *Just because you got an A in a previous course does not mean you were challenged.* The following sections will provide strategies to help you succeed now and in the future.

You Really Want to Pay Attention in Class . . . But It's Not Easy

The class has just started. You're in your seat, the teacher starts the lesson, and you start to "drift away." You really want to pay attention, but it is so difficult.

ACTIVITY 6.6   **WHAT CAN YOU DO TO FIGHT DISTRACTIONS?**

First, let's identify some reasons that you might start to daydream or become restless.

- ○ The student next to you is making noise.
- ○ The teacher or the lesson is boring.
- ○ There is noise outside the classroom window or in the hall.
- ○ You are hungry.
- ○ You stayed up late last night to watch a movie.
- ○ You are reading a note from your friend.
- ○ You are writing a note to your friend.
- ○ You do not understand the lesson.
- ○ You have left your class material (pencils, pens, paper, or book) at home or in the car.
- ○ You are thinking about the argument you had with a friend.
- ○ You do not know the answer to any of the questions the teacher is asking the class.
- ○ You are attracted to another student in the room.
- ○ A great sporting event is scheduled later this week.
- ○ It is your last class of the day.
- ○ List any other distractions you have encountered in class.

_____

Now that you have identified the distractions, what can be done to control them? With a classmate, brainstorm your methods to overcome these distractions.

_____

_____

_____

_____

How Does One "Pay Attention"?

As a college student you will receive, and be expected to process, a great deal of information. While Chapter 9 will present specific strategies for remembering more information, for our purposes here let's examine the first step of improved memory.

Before you can remember a name, a process, a date, or a telephone number, you must first notice it. This requires attention. But how does one "pay attention"?

Attention requires listening to and observing your surroundings but more specifically it requires that you sort through the vast amount of information that comes your way; you have to make sense of what is before you. One researcher describes paying attention as "processing a limited amount of information from the enormous amount of information available."[2] In other words, when you pay attention you have to sift through all the stimuli bombarding you—and then decide to focus on a particular pertinent piece of information.

TIPS TO PAY ATTENTION   **ACTIVITY 6.7**

The following list provides ideas that may improve your attention.[3]

○ In class you can:

  ○ Listen for verbal clues from the teacher.

  ○ Stay involved in the class discussion.

  ○ Move your seat away from distractions.

  ○ Listen to what classmates say and ask.

  ○ Take notes and review them (more in Chapter 7).

  ○ Come to class prepared; read your assignments (more in Chapter 8).

○ Outside of class you can:

  ○ Get appropriate sleep each night.

  ○ Eat well and avoid foods that make you sleepy.

  ○ Exercise regularly.

  ○ Eliminate distractions as best you can.

  ○ Enjoy what you do.

  ○ Avoid monotony.

  ○ Recognize that your attention has to be renewed; it is not an unending source.

  ○ Avoid substance abuse.   *(continued)*

---

[2]Janet N. Zadina, "The mystery of attention." Presentation at the National Association for Developmental Education annual conference, Nashville, TN, March 22, 2007.

[3]Edward M. Hallowell, *Crazy Busy: Overstretched, Overbooked, and About to Snap!* (New York: Ballantine Books, 2007), 178–185.

○ Laugh.

○ Try mental exercises or calisthenics (more in Chapter 9).

○ With a classmate, brainstorm additional tips that have helped you in the past.

_____

_____

_____

You can also allow yourself the luxury of "accepting" a distraction. Distracting thoughts can be merciless, continually nagging and interrupting. Try this: Once the distracting thought intrudes, welcome it in. If possible, jot it down on a piece of paper: "Call Joe tonight"; "What time is the party on Friday?"; "Gee, I'm bored with school!" Now, let go. You have mentally told yourself that you will address the issue later.

Developing a Working and Respectful Relationship with Your Instructors

The relationship you have with your instructors should be positive, not distracting. Perhaps you have heard the expression, "Do unto others as you would have them do unto you." When dealing with your professors, treat them as you want to be treated yourself. Paying tuition does not entitle a student to treat *any* college employee (or classmate) in a rude, disrespectful, or demanding manner. Nor does college enrollment entitle students to immediate and around-the-clock access to their instructors. Whether you are in the

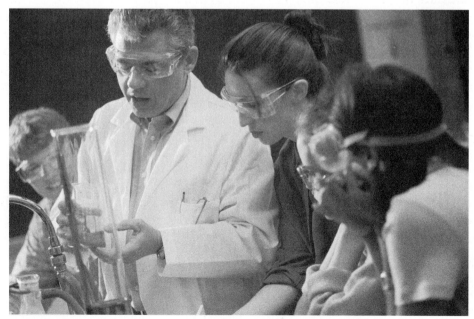

classroom, visiting your instructor during office hours, or corresponding by e-mail, remember two things:

1. You are interacting with a fellow human being. Be courteous and respectful.
2. Your professors have the authority and professional obligation to require you to do work and have it in by a certain time. You can expect first-class teaching and appropriate feedback, but professors are not there to respond to your every demand.

It is not uncommon for some students to be intimidated by the idea of a visit to a professor's office—and that is understandable. If you can concentrate on behavior that will build a strong foundation of support, encouragement, and respect you will find the instructor-student relationship one of the most important you will develop in college. Take advantage of the opportunity to talk with and learn from your instructors.

A Word About Being "Cool"[4]

Visualize yourself as a teacher. You are in your classroom looking at a room full of students. And every student *behaves just as you do* as a student in class. Each student responds, acts, and writes as you do. Are you pleased with this picture?

Students who respectfully respond to instructors with on-task comments and questions help build a positive classroom atmosphere. When a student responds to a professor's request with rude and inappropriate comments, he telegraphs the following to the teacher and class:

- I have no respect for the teacher.
- I am so insecure about my knowledge in this class that I have to act this way to protect myself.
- I am not a successful student.
- I am *not* cool!*

You see, if you are *cool* you don't have to make a point of showing it. Those who try to *show* they are cool just aren't. And they also have placed themselves in a terrible position with the instructor. Instructors are individuals with feelings and emotions just like students. If you continually try to make them look bad or try to disrupt the class with inappropriate comments and actions, you will have a difficult time building a positive relationship with the very person who is in the classroom to assist you and evaluate your performance. Trust me on this one.

Active Learning[5]

Another key to success inside the classroom is *participation*. If you can discuss a concept, you have a much better chance of understanding it. If your instructor's style does not lend itself to class discussion, you can still be actively involved by anticipating her lecture (based on reading assignments *outside* of

---

[4]Piscitelli, 120.
*In this context, "cool" means great, excellent, clever, self-confident, and neat. One might even say a cool person is "groovy"! ☺
[5]Piscitelli, 122.

the classroom and past class sessions), asking questions of yourself, and so forth. Do what you can to maintain focus. If you understand your instructor's style and expectations (Activities 6.3 and 6.4), you will be better able to identify the important class material. Understanding the major points of a lesson makes note taking easier; you will not need to write down every word spoken by the instructor. Let's break this down into practical steps.

You Need to Be There: Seven Steps to Classroom Success[6]

You probably have heard instructors explain the importance of attendance. "You need to be here," they will say, "in order to learn and understand the material." The reality is that your physical presence, while important, is only part of the success equation.

Not only do *you need to be there* in class, *you need to be there* in class. That is, your attention, your thoughts, and your head, need to be focused on the class lesson. Your physical presence is important as it allows you to hear explanations, ask questions, and add to the class discussions. You know the importance of being in class—that is not new information. But every so often we all can find wisdom in reminders of past lessons. Think of the following checklist as providing basic strategies that will move you toward a more active and successful term.[7]

1. *Do you come to class?* Be serious about your education. It is difficult to meet instructor expectations if you are sitting in the student lounge during class time or asleep in your bed.

2. *Do you bring all you need for class?* This is not the time to be without paper, pen, or textbook. A baseball player would not take the field without a glove. You, too, need to have your proper tools of the trade.

3. *Do you arrive on time?* Punctuality is important. Many instructors orchestrate each moment of class. There may be a review of the last class at the very beginning of the current class. Perhaps the instructor will announce a new test date—you most definitely do not want to miss that important nugget of information. And remember that latecomers are almost always a distraction to the instructor and to the class. If you do arrive late, enter quietly (hold the door) and quickly find a seat. And turn off your cell phone, please.

4. *Do you sit where you will benefit the most?* To minimize distractions, you may wish to sit close to where the instructor is standing. To see the PowerPoint presentation well, jockey for a good seat close to the screen. Remember basic civility. This is not the time to text message and, for goodness sake, don't put your head down for a quick nap. (The snoring will annoy the student next to you.)

5. *Do you carry your passion with you?* Be excited! That can be difficult for some classes, but it is something that will pay dividends. Practice your active listening skills. Listen intently; ask questions; be involved.

---

[6]Piscitelli, 124–126.

[7]Even though this list provides fairly basic and common points, I would like to thank Joseph B. Cuseo, professor of psychology and director of Freshman Seminar at Marymount College, for helping focus these thoughts. He facilitated a session at the 2004 Conference on the First Year Experience (Dallas, Texas) that addressed many of these issues.

6. *Do you remain actively engaged?* The class period has a recognized starting and ending time. Just as it is important to be punctual, plan on remaining for the entire period. Think of a movie. If you come in late or leave early you will miss critical scenes that will hinder your understanding of the entire film. Help yourself and avoid the temptation to pack up your books before the end of class.

7. *Do you review your class notes as soon as possible?* If you have the time, complete this review before you leave the room. Remain in your seat for a few moments and quickly determine whether you have any questions or confusion about the day's material. If the instructor has already left the room, this may be a perfect opportunity to visit his or her office. Of course, many times you will need to leave the room quickly for another class or appointment. In those cases, find a quiet place as soon as possible to complete your review (see Chapter 7).

NOTE-TAKING AS AN ACTIVE LEARNING STRATEGY

Successful students have learned how to take notes on important material in the classroom and outside of the classroom (reading assignments, for example). Note taking is a very personal activity; do not feel that you must copy any of the following note-taking styles exactly as shown. If you have a style that works for you, great! If what you currently do is not working or if you do not have a consistent note-taking style, find one that works for you and use it consistently. The styles described below provide very basic approaches. If you are not satisfied with your current note-taking system, consider tying one of these. Or, maybe you could use parts of each style to develop your own. However you decide to take class notes, keep the following points in mind:

- Be consistent.
- Try it for a period of time before abandoning it.
- Periodically review your style to make sure it works for you.

Even if a class is easy and you feel notes are not needed, take them anyway. *Organized class notes will help you focus* on teacher expectations and emphasis—and minimize distractions.

If you learn best by using very structured and orderly models, the format in Figure 6.1 may be for you. Note that this outline is organized with Roman numerals, capital letters, and Arabic numerals (lowercase letters would be used for a fourth classification). Each indentation represents a smaller classification (or information of lesser importance).

Perhaps you cannot easily use this note-taking strategy. You are not too sure where the instructor is moving with the lecture, and it is extremely difficult to determine what a subcategory of a larger category is. In other words, you need a model that allows more flexibility.

The model in Figure 6.2 has the same basic information as the traditional outline. If pictures (visuals) help you learn, why not put your notes in a picturelike (or graphlike) structure? It is also very easy to add information when using this model; a simple arrow or line can be used.

figure 6.1   Traditional outline

The Traditional Outline

I. Main topic #1
   A. Subtopic
      1. important detail
      2. important detail
   B. Subtopic
      1. important detail
      2. important detail

II. Main topic #2
   A. Subtopic
      1. important detail
      2. important detail

   B. Subtopic
      1. important detail
      2. important detail

III. Main topic #3
   A. Subtopic
      1. important detail
      2. important detail
   B. Subtopic
      1. important detail
      2. important detail

The format in Figure 6.3 is an adaptation of the Cornell Note-Taking System.[8] Note that there is an expanded margin on the left side of the page for student questions or other organizing comments to use as a study guide. This model is more linear in fashion than the flowchart model (Figure 6.2), but not quite as structured as the first model.

Figure 6.4 offers one more model for you to consider. This format allows you to arrange the *intricate parts* around the body of an *issue*.[9] This format

figure 6.2   Flowchart outline

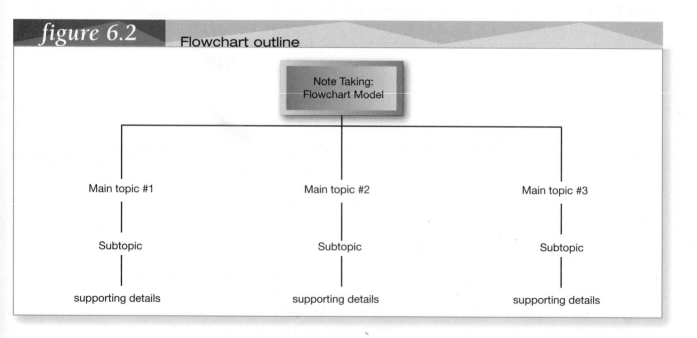

[8]Walter Pauk, *How to Study in College,* 5th ed. (Boston: Houghton Mifflin, 1993), 110–114. Also see Nancy Lightfoot Matte and Susan Hillary Henderson, *Success, Your Style: Right- and Left-Brain Techniques for Learning* (Belmont, CA: Wadsworth, 1995), 78–82.

[9]Some people refer to this type of overview as spidergrams while others call it clustering. For an example of this method, see Matte and Henderson, 84.

figure 6.3

Notes with a study guide

PERSONAL STUDY GUIDE	CLASS NOTES	DATE OF THE CLASS

Write a question you might have about topic #1 or any of its subtopics.
    Comment on an important detail the instructor emphasized.
	I. Main topic #1
	    A. Subtopic
	        1. important detail
	        2. important detail	

Write a question you might have about topic #2 or any of its subtopics.
    Comment on an important detail the instructor emphasized.
	II. Main topic #2
	    A. Subtopic
	        1. important detail
	        2. important detail	

Write a question you might have about topic #3 or any of its subtopics.
    Comment on an important detail the instructor emphasized.
	III. Main topic #3
	    A. Subtopic
	        1. important detail
	        2. important detail	

figure 6.4

Spidergram

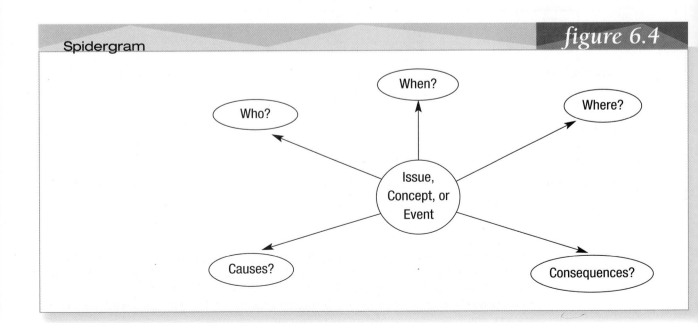

allows quick organization. It can be helpful in reorganizing your notes prior to a test, as well as in putting your thoughts together for an essay. This type of model might be what you need to jog your memory. The idea is to generate ideas, relationships, and analysis.

Once again, the note-taking style you choose is really a personal thing. No one can tell you which one to use. Pick one with which you feel comfortable and consistently use it.

Simple Abbreviations to Increase Note-Taking Speed[10]

Your class notes are an important aid in learning and remembering the course concepts. But regardless of your note-taking technique, consider using short phrases rather than full sentences; by using this type of shorthand, there will be less chance of your getting lost while trying to write the points presented by the professor. Be sure to write any key phrases or words the instructor emphasizes. And try to write legibly; eventually you will need to review this material for a quiz or exam.

Avoid taking notes word for word. That is, do not try to write every word the professor says or every word that is on a PowerPoint slide. Look for key words—those that have been emphasized and repeated by the instructor; or those that are underlined or written in italic or boldface type. Once you have determined what to write, abbreviate your words to increase your speed. If you text message on your cell phone, you already know how to do that. Here are some very basic suggestions. Can you add to the list in Table 6.1?

table 6.1	Abbreviations for your notes
IF THE WORD IS:	**CONSIDER USING:**
plus	+
without	w/o
Florida	FL
United States of America	US
information	info
because	bc
greater than	>
less than	<
as a consequence	→

[10]CC Consulting Limited, "Office Survival" www.crazycolour.com/os/notetaking_01.shtml (accessed April 15, 2007).

PRACTICE YOUR NOTE-TAKING SKILLS

Read the paragraphs below about healthy living and then, on a separate piece of paper, outline the reading selection using one of the outline formats described above.[11] Once you have completed your outline, compare it with a classmate's.

HEALTHY LIVING

Health is one of those topics where words do not necessarily match actions. People talk about following a regular exercise program, or reducing their intake of junk food, or getting more sleep. But the challenge comes when the talk must be put into regular action. Quite a gap exists for most people.

How many times have you heard the following (or something close)?

- On your way to class one day, your friend complains about being out of shape and says he is determined to do something about it. As he is telling you this, he pushes the elevator button so he does not have to walk up a flight of stairs.

- Your roommate says she looks fat in last year's bathing suit. She vows to start watching her diet—after she finishes the bag of potato chips cradled in her arms.

- Sam has not been getting much sleep lately, and his performance on the baseball team has suffered. He planned on getting a good night's sleep tonight, but his friends just called and told him about a party. He went— and promised to start better habits tomorrow.

Living a healthy lifestyle requires the development of healthy habits. When you have a habit, *it is something you cannot help but do. It has become second nature. If you have started every morning of the last five years drinking a can of caffeinated soda or a cup of coffee with your breakfast, it has become a habit. You feel as though you cannot function without that drink in your hands. The same goes for tobacco users. They wake up and reach for a smoke. Or perhaps each time you go to a movie, you just have to have a tub of buttered popcorn. After all, what is a movie without popcorn and a soda!*

Managing Your Studies with a Notebook

Well-organized notes will help you study for final course tests, national certification exams, or future courses. Great notes are useless, however, if you cannot find them once you get *outside* the classroom. Consider using a class notebook to organize and store your notes. A notebook will allow you to quickly find past notes and handouts that may prove helpful during a class discussion or group activity.

Perhaps you already use a notebook for your classes. The key to an effective notebook, however, is found in one word—*organization*. Think twice about using those "stuff-it-in-the-pocket" folders. They may have a

---

[11]Piscitelli, 242.

ACTIVITY 6.9   CHAPTER 6 MEASURABLE OBJECTIVES

At the beginning of this chapter, six measurable objectives were presented. They are reprinted below for your convenience. Using the strategies you have learned in this chapter, fill in the lines beneath each item (or use a separate sheet of paper).

○ Identify at least three classroom distractions and a strategy to deal with each.

   ○ Write the distractions and strategies here._____

   _____

   _____

   _____

   _____

○ Explain how instructor style affects your classroom success.

   ○ Write your explanation here._____

   _____

   _____

   _____

   _____

   _____

○ Describe one strategy to help develop a working and respectful relationship with your instructors.

   ○ Write the strategy here. _____

   _____

   _____

   _____

   _____

○ Use and evaluate one of the note-taking styles for at least one week.

   ○ Write your evaluation here. How did the note-taking style help you? Did you have to modify it for your personal tastes? Will you continue to use it? _____

   _____

   _____

   _____

   _____

(continued)

○ Critically evaluate at least one of your classroom challenges.

   ○ Write your evaluation of the challenge here. _____

_____

_____

_____

_____

_____

○ Identify at least two tips to help you pay attention in class.

   ○ Write the tips here. _____

_____

_____

_____

_____

REALITY CHECK

Using your critical thinking skills to improve your classroom performance

Situation. Myron enjoys college life. He likes his instructors, his courses, and his classmates. Generally speaking, he is positive and excited about being on campus. However, he just got back his first round of exams for the term; they were not what he had hoped for. In one class he received a D+; all the other grades were in the C range. "I don't understand," he said to himself. "I write everything that comes out of the instructor's mouth. How come I am not performing well on the exams?" Myron tried to analyze why he was not performing better. He found that although he liked the course material, he was having a difficult time paying attention in class. When he pulled his notepaper from the bottom of his book bag, he noticed large gaps in what he had written—and there was a good bit of doodling in the margins. He has come to you for assistance.

Using at least three strategies from this chapter, help Myron critically review and solve his problem.

_____

_____

_____

_____

_____

_____

_____

CHAPTER 7

NOTE TAKING

How will effective notes help you understand class material?

SPOTLIGHT ON CLASSROOM SKILLS

My notes may not be the best in the world, but I know I get the main points from each lesson. Most of my professors use PowerPoint presentations. I copy every word that is up on that screen. Some professors actually post notes on their Web sites. I print those out and then put them in my notebook. This gives me a record of every word the professor has used. My thought has always been if the professor believes it's important enough to put on the screen, a Web site, or on the board, then it should go into my notebook.

With all of this writing, though, I have a problem! I have so much material to study that I end up getting lost in the details. The night before a test I'm elbow deep in papers, notes, PowerPoint copies. I stay up all night trying to understand my notes—and I am doing poorly on my tests. I thought all I had to do was take the notes in class—and the good grades would follow.

If you followed the strategies proposed in the last chapter you too may have a notebook full of class notes. But just having the notes is not enough. The next step is knowing what to do with the

PREVIEW

By the time you finish reading this chapter and completing its activities you will be able to:

- Establish a schedule for immediate review of each day's class notes.
- Find and explain at least one connection between recent class notes and your previous knowledge.
- Develop and write at least one TSD for your class notes from the past week.
- Develop and write at least one Exit Slip for your class notes from the past week.
- Visit each of your professors at least one time to discuss material from class.
- Understand why (or why not) you should consider working with a study partner.

KEY TERMS

- Connections
- Exit slip strategy
- Professors' office hours
- ROI

notes—and when to do it. This chapter provides quick and easy suggestions to help you make sense of your notes.

- Review, relate, reorganize strategy
- Study partner
- TSD strategy

CHAPTER INTRODUCTION

While building relationships with classmates and instructors will help students persist and succeed in their studies, there is another type of relationship building that is every bit as vital to school success.

Research has shown that learning has a better chance of occurring when students establish connections—build relationships—between what they know from their experiences and what they read in textbooks and hear from their professors. Note taking provides the chance to build these connections. In fact, opportunities for learning will occur at two levels: while taking the notes and while reviewing the notes.[1]

LEARNING *WHILE* TAKING NOTES

You can learn while taking notes in class, attending a guest lecture in the campus auditorium, or while reading your textbook. At this point in note taking, however, you will not have much time to build connections as you will more than likely be concentrating on writing the main points in your notebook. Perhaps you use one of the note-taking styles explained in Chapter 6. You may even be able to write rather quickly using abbreviations (also introduced in Chapter 6). But the chance of building lasting connections with this new information while taking notes will be difficult. You will be focused on trying to determine what is important and what you need to write, not on how the new information supports or refutes what you already know.

Deeper learning will increase when you take the time to review your notes.[2]

LEARNING *AFTER* YOU HAVE TAKEN YOUR NOTES: ROI

Business people invest money and time when they believe an opportunity exists to earn a profit. Return on investment (ROI) many times will drive a business decision. Why invest resources if there is not a return, a profit?

---

[1]Bonnie B. Armbruster in Rona F. Flippo and David Caverly, *Handbook of College Reading and Study Strategy Research* (Mahwah, NJ: Lawrence Erlbaum Associates, 2000), 176.

[2]Armbruster, 178.

The same analogy can be applied to your investment in class. Beyond tuition and the cost of books, every day you enter class you invest your time and your attention in the subject of the day. Let's assume you take picture-perfect notes; every piece of important information has been legibly recorded. As you learned in Chapter 6, this is an excellent step to classroom success. So far, so good.

But, at this point, what is the return on your investment? You might have been able to see connections between the classroom discussions with your textbook. Possibly as you wrote down the instructor's remarks you had an insight about the material. But you might not know the true return on your investment of time until you take the unit exam. Then you will have an idea of how much of the material you have retained and learned.

The second part of note taking—reviewing—allows you to make deeper connections between what you know and what you are learning. This chapter will focus on these strategies.

REFLECTION ON HOW YOUR NOTES HELP YOU UNDERSTAND CLASS MATERIAL

ACTIVITY 7.1

Before you answer the items below, reflect on your current skill level of using your notes to help you study for quizzes and exams. Think of how well (or poorly) you have been able to use your notes from past classes.

As with all of the reflective activities in this book, answer from your heart. This exercise is not meant for you to answer just like your classmates—or to match what you may think the instructor wants to see. Take your time to give a respectful and responsible general accounting of your experiences with your notes. A truthful self-assessment now will help you build on skills you have while developing those you lack.

For the following items circle the number that best describes your typical experience when it comes to using your notes to study. The key for the numbers is:

0 = never, 1 = almost never, 2 = occasionally, 3 = frequently,
    4 = almost always, 5 = always

When considering your past successes and challenges when using your notes, how often:

1. Did you review your notes within the first 24 hours of taking those notes in class?

    0   1   2   3   4   5

2. Did you review your notes *at any time* before the next class?

    0   1   2   3   4   5

3. Did notes (the words, sentences, phrases) you wrote during class make sense to you once you reviewed them after class?

    0   1   2   3   4   5

4. Were your notes legible and easy to read?

    0   1   2   3   4   5

(continued)

5. Did your notes capture the main points from the instructor's lesson?

      0   1   2   3   4   5

6. Did your notes reflect you putting the instructor's words into your words—rather than an almost word for word copying of the instructor's PowerPoint slides or notes on the board?

      0   1   2   3   4   5

7. Did you develop study guides from your notes?

      0   1   2   3   4   5

8. Did you review your notes and relate them to your textbook reading or the previous lesson's notes?

      0   1   2   3   4   5

Add up your scores for items 3, 4, 5, and 6. Divide by 4. Write your answer here: _____.

Using the key explanations above for each number (0, 1, 2, 3, 4, 5) complete this sentence: When it comes to the *quality* of my notes, I _____ write *legible* notes that are in *my words* and that reflect the *main points* of the lesson.

Add up your scores for items 1, 2, 7, and 8. Divide by 4. Write your answer here: _____.

Using the key explanations above for each number (0, 1, 2, 3, 4, 5) complete this sentence: When it comes to *actively using my notes after* class, I _____ review and reorganize my notes to prepare for quizzes and exams regularly prior to exams and quizzes.

Based on your answers, what insights do you have about your experiences with organization? _____

_____

_____

ACTIVITY 7.2   CRITICALLY THINKING ABOUT HOW TO USE YOUR NOTES

Let's apply the critical thinking standards from Chapter 2 to examine one of the challenges you identified for yourself in Activity 7.1.

List your note-taking challenges here: _____

CRITICAL THINKING STANDARD	APPLICATION TO YOUR STUDY SKILLS	YOUR EXPLANATION HERE OR ON A SEPARATE PIECE OF PAPER
Clarity	*Clearly* state this particular note-taking challenge.	Not understanding a lesson Information over load
Accuracy	How do you know this assessment of your challenge is *correct*?	

(continued)

CRITICAL THINKING STANDARD	APPLICATION TO YOUR STUDY SKILLS	YOUR EXPLANATION HERE OR ON A SEPARATE PIECE OF PAPER
Precision	*Specifically* (give examples) explain this note-taking challenge.	Talking to fast: Can't Comprend
Relevance	How is your assessment of your note-taking challenge *connected* to your academic progress?	When my teacher teaches and I don't understand a lesson I can't do well on homew
Depth	Examine your identified note-taking challenge beyond a superficial (simplistic) explanation and look at all of the *complexities* involved.	
Breadth	Examine your note-taking challenge from more than one *perspective (point of view).*	
Logic	Based on your evidence does your conclusion about your note-taking challenge *make sense*?	

Based on your answers above, what insights have you gained about your note-taking challenge?

_____

_____

What is the next step you will take to eliminate this challenge?

_____

_____

_____

USING YOUR NOTES TO UNDERSTAND THE BIG PICTURE[3]

Now That You Have Your Notes, What Should You Do Next? Time for Reflection

Taking clear notes in class moves you another step closer to becoming a successful student—but more needs to be done. *Studying* truly begins the next time you look at those notes. The "Seven Steps to Classroom Success" (see Chapter 6) recommend reviewing your notes as soon as possible after the class. For this review to truly be active and engaging, you want to do more than passively read the notes. A simple three-step strategy—*review, relate,* and *reorganize*–will help you understand the class material, cut

---

[3]Steve Piscitelli, *Rhythms of College Success: A Journey of Discovery, Change, and Mastery* (Upper Saddle River, NJ: Pearson Prentice Hall, 2008), 141–143.

down on last-minute test preparation, and be ready for your next test-day performance.

Review.   As soon as possible after class, look at the day's class notes. Read them and highlight what you consider to be the important information. Make sure all words have been legibly written—and neatly correct any words that may be difficult to read. Is there anything that is not clear? Do you understand all principles, generalizations, and theories?

If you have questions, put an asterisk or question mark in the margin of your notes. This should be your first question at the beginning of the next class meeting—or when you visit the instructor during office hours. If you wait until the night before the unit exam, it becomes rather difficult to get a clarification from the instructor. In addition, by asking the question in class, you are actively participating—which is, coincidentally, another success strategy. Doing a nightly review of your class notes will help focus your attention on what you know and what you need to clarify.

Relate.   Too many times, students attempt to memorize isolated pieces of information. This is a daunting and boring task. As an alternative, look at the previous day's notes and reading assignments and ask yourself the following questions:

- What connections exist between my new notes and the previous material?
- What patterns, or repetitions, are developing?
- Does the new material help me or am I confused and need clarification?
- What textbook information could help me fill in my notes?

Once you start seeing this big picture, the material will make sense and will be easier to remember.

Reorganize.   As you look over your notes, try to see if there is a clearer way in which to understand the message of the lesson. Sometimes an instructor will present material out of order or go off on tangents. Shuffle your notes so they make sense *to you*. You may wish to write a brief outline in the margin of the notes. Perhaps highlighting important concepts and facts with different-colored pens may help you focus on the key points.

ACTIVITY 7.3   REVIEW, RELATE, AND REORGANIZE

Flip back to Activity 6.8 in the last chapter. You read a piece titled "Healthy Living" and took notes on the ideas presented. For this activity, first *review* those notes you took in Activity 6.8 (just like you would when studying for a test). Then *relate* the information to what you already know about the topic of healthy living. Finally, based on your connections between your previous knowledge and what you read in the article, can you *reorganize* your notes in any way? Do you have any questions about the material?

Connections, Groups, and Chunks

Sometimes in the heat of a classroom lecture or the excitement of group discussion, your notes—despite your best efforts—may look like a long list of confusing and disjointed words, names, details, or dates. This is where a nightly review can prove most beneficial.

As stated in this chapter's introduction, there is a better chance to understand a classroom lesson if you can connect new material with either a textbook reading or your own previous knowledge. As you review your notes, look for logical groupings and connections. Attempt to establish categories of information. For instance, if you are given a list of twenty-five items to remember, "chunk" the terms into three or four major categories. In a history class, it might be helpful to group philosophers, scientists, and political leaders. From a literature discussion, you may have information about setting, plot, characters, or theme. This strategy can even work for vocabulary lists. For instance, the following French vocabulary list may seem daunting to manage and learn.

aimer mieux (v)	lorsque (adv)
l'anorak (n)	le peuple (n)
le bateau (n)	porter (v)
bientôt (adv)	prochain (adj)
célébrer (v)	puissant (adj)
le danger (n)	le roi (n)
la devise (n)	tricolore (adj)
entouré (adj)	

Rearranged according to parts of speech, the list of fifteen words looks like this:

NOUNS	VERBS	ADJECTIVES	ADVERBS
l'anorak	aimer mieux	entouré	bientôt
le bateau	célébrer	prochain	lorsque
le danger	porter	puissant	
la devise		tricolore	
le peuple			
le roi			

Now, instead of learning fifteen isolated items, you have "chunked" the material into a more bite-sized four categories of fewer words, each category with no more than six words.

Talk to Yourself—and Then Someone Else

"I've tried all this stuff, but I still don't understand the new math formula," you say. In this case, try to "talk" your math problem through step by step. Try to fully explain each step as best you can. Go as far in the process as possible. You

may make it through four or five steps—or might not be able to get past the first step.

Once you have done this, ask a classmate to listen to your explanation. Perhaps she can help you get past the spot that is befuddling you. If you are still confused, now might be a good time to visit your professor. You will be able to tell her exactly what you know and exactly where you get stuck. In this way, the professor will understand where she needs to start working with you. This will make for a more effective and efficient office visit.

ACTIVITY 7.4   ONE MORE TIME: REVIEW, RELATE, AND REORGANIZE

Choose the notes from one of your classes this term. They could come from this class, your history class, psychology class, math class, science class, computer class, or foreign language class. It might be best to pick the class where you are having the most difficulty. In your notebook (or in a computer document file) practice the review, relate, and reorganize note-review strategy.

○ *Review.* Read your notes; highlight important words; make sure all words are legible.
○ *Relate.* As best you can, make connections between the class notes and what you have been talking about in earlier classes. Look at how the textbook can help you clarify your notes. Write your thoughts here. _____

_____

_____

○ *Reorganize.* Do you need to reorganize your notes in any way? This can be as simple as writing some clarifying comments in the margins or as involved as either rewriting your notes or typing and saving them in a computer document folder. One last time, ask yourself whether any part of the notes is confusing to you. Perhaps you need to ask the instructor about this for further clarification.

What Should You Do If You Still Don't Get the Big Picture?

Even the best note taker can be overwhelmed by a mountain of information and miss the overall meaning of a lesson. Two strategies that you can use in conjunction with the *review, relate, reorganize* strategy are TSDs and exit slips.

Title/Summary/Details (TSD)

You will have a better chance of understanding class notes if you put the material into your own words. Copying word for word from the board, overhead transparencies, or PowerPoint presentations will not be useful if you cannot explain the material in language that makes sense to you.

Try the TSD strategy, an *active* review strategy that consists of three simple steps:

- *T:* Start by giving the notes a *title*. What is the big picture? Try to come up with your own title that effectively captures the day's notes.
- *S:* Write a one- or two-sentence *summary*. How would you summarize the notes, in your words, in a sentence or two? What was the central theme or main point? If you can do this, you understand the overall thrust of the instructor's lesson. Be careful: Do not quote the instructor's words; *use your words*.
- *D:* List three *details* that support your summary. What do you see as the major details in the lecture? What questions might the instructor pose on the exam?

Once written (or typed and saved in a computer file), the review could be no more than about a quarter of a page in length. Quick, easy, and efficient.

Continue to review, relate, and reorganize each night in this manner. Keep your TSDs at the beginning of your unit material (or in a computer document file). Add to them each day. By test time, you will have several pages of review notes to serve as a practical study guide. *You have developed an ongoing study guide based on your class notes.* No more cramming for the exam.

PRACTICING A TSD   **ACTIVITY 7.5**

Return to the notes you used for Activity 6.8 in the last chapter and complete a TSD for that article. Remember to use *your own words*.

Title: _____

Summary: _____

_____

Details:

1. _____

2. _____

3. _____

TSDs in Reverse

The TSD strategy asks you to first see the big picture (topic and summary) and then look at the details that support that larger view.

Perhaps you are the type of student who focuses on details first before you can see the big picture. If so, you can still use the strategy but do it in reverse; work backward. First list the main details. Then, based on the details you have listed, write a summary that shows the connection of the details. Finally, write the topic that captures the idea of the entire class or reading assignment.

ACTIVITY 7.6   **ONE MORE TIME: DEVELOPING A TSD**

The following information on maintaining a healthy weight comes from the Centers for Disease Control and Prevention Web site.[4] As you read the article, circle, underline or highlight the major details. After you complete the reading, write three main details the article stressed. Then, write a statement that effectively summarizes the connection of the details you identified. Finally, create your own brief title that describes the topic of the piece.

HEALTHY WEIGHT

Whether you want to lose weight or maintain a healthy weight, it's important to understand the connection between the energy your body takes in (through the foods you eat and the beverages you drink) and the energy your body uses (through the activities you do). To lose weight, you need to use more calories than you take in. To maintain a healthy weight, you need to balance the calories you use with those you take in. . . .

There is a right number of calories for you to eat each day. This number depends on your age, activity level, and whether you are trying to gain, maintain, or lose weight. You could use up the entire amount on a few high-calorie foods, but chances are, you won't get the full range of vitamins and nutrients your body needs to be healthy. Choose the most nutritionally rich foods you can from each food group each day—those packed with vitamins, minerals, fiber, and other nutrients, but lower in calories. Pick foods like fruits, vegetables, whole grains, and fat-free or low-fat milk and milk products more often. . . .

Becoming a healthier you isn't just about eating healthy—it's also about physical activity. Regular physical activity is important for your overall health and fitness. It also helps you control body weight by balancing the calories you take in as food with the calories you expend each day. . . .

Whether you want to lose weight or maintain a healthy weight, it's important to understand the connection between the energy your body takes in (through the foods you eat and the beverages you drink) and the energy your body uses (through the activities you do).

---

[4]Department of Health and Human Services, Centers for Disease Control and Prevention, "Healthy Weight," www.cdc.gov/nccdphp/dnpa/nutrition/nutrition_for_everyone/healthy_weight/index.htm (accessed July 1, 2007).

Details: Write the main details of this lesson here:

1. _____

2. _____

3. _____

Summary: Based on the details you identified, what statement will summarize this piece accurately? _____

_____

_____

Title: In a couple of words, state the topic of the piece you just read. _____

_____

Exit Slips

Another review strategy is the *exit slip* concept used by some classroom instructors. Before students exit the class at the end of the class period, they write a sentence or two about what they learned from the lesson. A variation asks the students to write about the most confusing point in the lesson. You can do the same thing to determine your level of understanding of the day's notes, as follows:

- After reviewing your notes, write (or highlight) *three new* things you learned in the lesson.
- Then write *two* items from the lesson that you found to be the most *interesting*.
- Finally, what is the *one* thing you found the most *confusing*?

You can adjust these steps to fit the particular class. For instance, in a computer class you may find it helpful to list two new strategies that you can apply immediately to help organize your computer files.

ADDITIONAL OUT-OF-CLASS STRATEGIES TO IMPROVE YOUR NOTES

Have You Created Working Relationships with Your Instructors?

If, after a careful review of your notes and use of the forgoing strategies, you are still confused, consider a visit to your instructor's office. Instructors typically post the office hours they are available to students. You can find this information in the syllabus, on the instructor's office door, or in the department office. If you still cannot locate the office hours, you can send a quick e-mail to the instructor. Whatever it takes, find the office, know the office hours, and make it a goal to visit your instructors this term.

Use these hours as the valuable resource they are. When you enter your professor's office, you can:

- Obtain clarification on class notes.
- Seek assistance on a particularly troubling lesson.

- Ask to review the last exam or quiz to learn from any mistakes you may have made.
- Obtain clarification on future assignments.
- Start to develop a face-name relationship, as your instructor will likely remember you as a student who has taken the time to seek help and clarification of course material.
- Discuss challenges you are experiencing in the class.
- Seek advice about future courses.

ACTIVITY 7.7   FINDING YOUR INSTRUCTORS

On the chart that follows, write the name of each instructor you have this term. Next to the name, write the professor's office hours and where the office is located. Make a note of the last time you visited this instructor and when you will visit the instructor next. Finally, what classroom issues or questions will you bring to the office visit? If you know what you need to discuss with your professor before you walk in the door, chances for a positive meeting (and relationship) will increase dramatically.

Hint: When you visit an instructor with a problem, be as specific as you possibly can. Starting your visit with "I'm lost" or "I don't understand this book" or "I don't do math" does not give the instructor much to work with. You may, in fact, be lost—but start your conversation by telling the instructor what *you do know.* For instance, you may start a math office visit with, "I can get up to the point where I try to find a reciprocal fraction—and then I'm totally flummoxed." Now, at least there is a place to start.* (By the way, "flummoxed" is a way of saying "I'm really confused!")

INSTRUCTOR'S NAME	OFFICE HOURS	OFFICE LOCATION	LAST VISITED	WHEN WILL YOU VISIT NEXT?	WHAT TOPIC OR QUESTION WILL YOU BRING TO THE OFFICE VISIT? THAT IS, WHAT WILL BE THE PURPOSE OF YOUR VISIT?
1.					
2.					
3.					
4.					
5.					

*Before going to your professor's office, review the section of this chapter titled "Talk to yourself—and then someone else."

Do You Need a Study Partner or Group?[5]

An old saying is that misery loves company. A more positive approach holds that success loves good company!

The importance of a strong support network to help you develop your intellectual skills cannot be overemphasized. Students who feel connected to their classes and their campus have a better chance to experience success. This support system can be as simple as a compatible roommate, as socially dynamic as a study group, or as effective as a good mentor.

A peer study partner (or a study group) can help you with the following:

- Making sense of those crazy scribblings you call notes
- Understanding lengthy and confusing reading assignments
- Seeing different perspectives (interpretations) of the course material
- Choosing a topic for the term research paper
- Preparing for an upcoming exam
- Understanding a difficult concept
- Coping with classroom failures
- Celebrating classroom successes

A study partner may be one of the most important people you will meet. He or she can be the beginning of a larger support group. A major reason students leave college (especially within their first year) is because they do not feel a part of the college community. As one professor noted:

> Support is a condition for student learning. . . . Least [sic] we forget the first year is a period of becoming, a period of transition. . . . Without academic and social support some students are unable to make that transition.[6]

Your study partner is a small step toward building a much larger network of support.

Sometimes, however, working with study partners or study groups can seem like a nightmare that never ends. If you function better without a group, you may wish to pursue another course of action. Your campus may have peer tutors or other types of academic support services that can provide valuable resources as needed.

There will be times, however, when your instructors assign group work. For instance, an in-class activity might require a group product. Generally, you will not have much control in choosing these groups, although sometimes you will be able to select your own partners. (Chapter 12 provides suggestions to make any group experience a positive one.)

Using Technology

Examine the following ideas and then commit time to try each one at least once over the next week:

- Tune in to a TV channel or a streaming video computer presentation and take notes on the presentation. Ideally, you could look at an educational

---

[5]Piscitelli, 119–120.

[6]Vincent Tinto, "Taking Student Learning Seriously," keynote address to the Southwest Regional Learning Communities Conference, Tempe, AZ, February 28–March 1, 2002, www.mcli.dist.maricopa.edu/events/lcc02/presents/tinto.html (accessed July 1, 2007).

presentation like those on the History Channel or a public television station. Or you could watch a program about solving crimes. Perhaps there you can find a podcast of interest to you. Have a friend do the same thing and then compare notes.

- If you would rather work alone, tape the same presentation. Take notes at the same time you are taping the presentation. Then replay the presentation and compare your notes to the taped material. Did you miss anything?

- You could also tape record a teacher lecture, take notes, and replay the tape later. Students with documented learning disabilities have used this strategy. It may work for you whether or not you have a disability. But use this strategy with caution. Students can end up taping each lesson but fail to take notes at the same time. This type of taping ignores the real issue—improving note taking. Practice is necessary. If you tape a lesson, ask yourself, "When will I have the time to listen to this tape and take notes?" Perhaps a more direct question is, "After sitting in class for an hour, do I want to listen to the same information for an *additional* hour of my own time?" Consider taping as a stopgap measure until you are more comfortable with your note-taking skills. (Make sure you ask your instructor's permission before taping a presentation.)

After using one of these strategies, look at the notes you wrote—and critically evaluate them. Are they *clear, accurate, precise,* and *logical*? Were the notes you wrote in sufficient *depth* to help you at a later time—like if you had to review them for an exam?

CHAPTER SUMMARY

In order to be successful, students need to become involved and engaged in active learning outside the classroom. Before leaving this chapter, keep the following points in mind:

- As soon as possible after class review your class notes.
- Research has shown that learning has a better chance of occurring when students establish connections between class material and what they already know.
- Once you start seeing this big picture, the material will make sense and will be easier to remember.
- You will have a better chance of understanding class notes if you put the material into your own words.
- Whatever it takes, find your instructors' offices, know the office hours, and make it a goal to visit your instructors this term.
- A peer study partner (or a study group) can help you understand class material and review your notes.

ACTIVITY 7.8   CHAPTER 7 MEASURABLE OBJECTIVES

At the beginning of this chapter, six measurable objectives were presented. They are reprinted below for your convenience. Based on the strategies you have learned in this chapter, fill in the lines beneath each item (or use a separate sheet of paper).

○ Establish a schedule for immediate review of each day's class notes.

   ○ Have you reviewed your notes immediately after class, nightly, or at some other time? Write your schedule here. _____

     _____

     _____

○ Find and explain at least one connection between recent class notes and your previous knowledge.

   ○ Choose your notes from one class this week. Write one connection or relationship between this material and either your previous knowledge or something you have read in your textbook. _____

     _____

     _____

○ Develop and write at least one TSD for your class notes from the past week.

   ○ Write the TSD here.

     T: _____

     S: _____

     D: 1. _____

        2. _____

        3. _____

○ Develop and write at least one exit slip for your class notes from the past week.

   ○ Write the exit slip here.

     ○ Write *three* new things you learned in the lesson. _____

        _____

        _____

     ○ Write *two* things from the lesson that you found to be the most interesting. _____

        _____

        _____

     ○ Finally, what is the *one* thing you found the most *confusing* about this material? _____

        _____

        _____

○ Visit each of your professors at least one time to discuss material from class.

   ○ What topics did you discuss with your professors during the past week? Write the topics and the professors' names here: _____

_____

_____

_____

_____

○ Understand why (or why not) you should consider working with a study partner.

   ○ What are the benefits—or drawbacks—for you working with a study partner? _____

_____

_____

_____

REALITY CHECK

Using your critical thinking skills and class notes to understand class material

Situation. Tina is a quiet student. Although she seldom misses a class, she very seldom participates in her classes. She is doing mostly C work in her classes—except biology. Science has never been her strongest subject area, but in the past she has been able to read her textbook and do well. She has found that her biology professor's exams rely heavily on classroom lectures, group discussions, and demonstrations.

Tina sits in the front of the room so that she can hear everything her professor says. She copies all of the PowerPoint presentations word for word. Her notebook is complete with classroom notes and handouts, all filed in precise order. In fact, her classmates are in awe about how thick her class notebook has become. Still, she struggles to pass her biology exams. She is tired of pulling all-night cram sessions prior to the exams. Worst of all, Tina has become discouraged.

Using at least three strategies from this chapter, help Tina critically review and solve her problem.

_____

_____

_____

_____

_____

_____

CHAPTER 8

READING

You have to read 1,000 pages by when?

SPOTLIGHT ON CLASSROOM SKILLS

When I started college I had a true desire to learn the material but my reading comprehension was a little rusty. I was a slow reader—and I never did any kind of prereading. You know, I did not use the study questions in the back of textbooks or on the textbook Web sites. Sometimes I tired quickly when reading and then pushed the assignment to the side. The problem with that "strategy" was that it became much too easy to not complete the reading.

Now, I find it easier to look at the title of a chapter and know what it is basically about. I've learned how to pick out what I need to get from a reading. I might not be a speed reader but I am a better reader than I was four months ago. If you make a commitment to yourself to read something each day you will improve as a reader.

Reading involves more than your eyes seeing words on a page. Effective and skilled readers know that reading is a process. That is, if you systematically follow a few basic steps you can tackle assignments effortlessly. Once you master the techniques in this chapter you, too, can be an effective reader.

PREVIEW

By the time you finish reading this chapter and completing its activities you will know how to:

- Identify the main idea of a paragraph.
- Identify the purpose of a reading assignment.
- Demonstrate how to use the steps of the SQ4R reading process.
- Use reading notes for improved classroom success.
- Use graphics to help you understand a reading assignment.
- Demonstrate how to make connections between a reading assignment and prior knowledge.

KEY TERMS

- Active reading
- Brain-based learning
- Comprehension
- Context
- Graphics
- Main idea
- Purpose
- Reading notes
- Scan
- Skim
- SQ4R
- Vocabulary

CHAPTER INTRODUCTION

In our society of instant Internet access as well as on-demand video and music downloading, one may wonder whether reading has become a lost art. "Why read a book when I can *listen* to a book or *see* a movie on my own personal hand-held portable digital device?"

While the medium may have changed—become more digitized—reading remains a crucial skill. As you progress through your college program of study the amount of required reading will increase in volume, difficulty, and complexity. Besides traditional textbooks, you will have library databases, indexes, and e-books at your disposal for research purposes. Whether you read electronic material (Internet articles and blogs), a literature novel, or a chemistry textbook you will want to find an effective and efficient way to complete your reading requirements in a manner that respects your precious time while preparing you for discussions, quizzes, and exams.

To do this you need to take an active part in the reading process. Active reading, like active learning requires you to *do* something rather than passively seeing the words on the page. Regardless of your current comprehension level, all students share at least one commonality: You have read books before. This is not new territory for you. Respect the reading skills you currently have and build on those experiences. Activity 8.1 will give you the chance to reflect on your current reading skills—and think about how you can make immediate improvements.

Brain-Based Learning: Making Sense of the Seeming Chaos

Research indicates that the brain seeks out meaning. It looks for connections as it tries to establish patterns that will help it make sense of the world. In this way, these brain-based learning studies suggest we can take raw facts and make them mean something. And, after all, isn't that what you want to do with all of the details thrown at you during the course of a college term? You want to make sense out of what, at times, can seem like chaos.

In order for learning to take place, three steps have to be taken:[1]

- You have to sense or notice the material.
- You have to integrate or combine it with what you already know.
- You have to act on or use the information.

The same principles hold for reading. If you want to understand and remember more of what you read, you have to:

- *Notice* what you read—the words, the headings, the bold-faced type, the graphics, the questions, and the key terms.

---

[1]Elayne Shapiro, "Brain-based Learning Meets PowerPoint." *Teaching Professor 20*, no. 5, May 5, 2006. vnweb.hwwilsonweb.com/hww/shared/shared_main.jhtml?_requestid=8439 (accessed July 1, 2007).

- *Connect* what you already know to the topic about which you are reading.
- *Use* the information as soon as possible to strengthen learning and retention.

REFLECTING ON YOUR CURRENT LEVEL OF READING SKILLS   ACTIVITY **8.1**

Before you answer the items below, reflect on your current level of reading skills. Think of how well (or poorly) you have performed in past classes.

As with all of the reflective activities in this book, answer from your heart. This exercise is not meant for you to answer just like your classmates—or to match what you may think the instructor wants to see. Take your time to give a respectful and responsible general accounting of your experiences with reading. A truthful self-assessment now will help you build on skills you have while developing those you lack.

For the following items circle the number that best describes your *typical* experience with reading skills. The key for the numbers is:

0 = never, 1 = almost never, 2 = occasionally, 3 = frequently,
    4 = almost always, 5 = always

When considering your past successes and challenges with reading, how often:

1. Did you skim your reading assignment for main points *before* jumping right into the reading?

    0   1   2   3   4   5

2. Did you take effective notes from your reading?

    0   1   2   3   4   5

3. Did you use your reading notes to help you with class discussions?

    0   1   2   3   4   5

4. Were you able to read an assignment and understand the main idea of the assignment?

    0   1   2   3   4   5

5. Could you figure out the meaning of a word from the words surrounding it?

    0   1   2   3   4   5

6. Were you able to remember what you read?

    0   1   2   3   4   5

7. Did you review your reading notes immediately after completing your reading assignment?

    0   1   2   3   4   5

8. Was your vocabulary strong enough so that you could understand the meaning of a textbook assignment?

    0   1   2   3   4   5   *(continued)*

Add up your scores for items 1, 4, and 6. Divide by 3. Write your answer here: _____.

Using the key explanations above for each number (0, 1, 2, 3, 4, 5) complete this sentence: When it comes to identifying the main points of a reading, I _____ do this effectively.

Add up your scores for items 2, 3, and 7. Divide by 3. Write your answer here: _____.

Using the key explanations above for each number (0, 1, 2, 3, 4, 5) complete this sentence: When it comes to reading notes, I _____ take and use reading notes effectively.

Add up your scores for items 5 and 8. Divide by 2. Write your answer here: _____.

Using the key explanations above for each number (0, 1, 2, 3, 4, 5) complete this sentence: When it comes to vocabulary, I _____ understand the vocabulary in my reading assignments.

Based on your answers, what insights do you have about your reading skills?

_____

_____

_____

DO YOU KNOW WHY YOU READ AN ASSIGNMENT?

At first glance, the question "Do you know why you read an assignment?" appears simplistic and obvious. "Of course I know why I read my assignment. Because the instructor said it would be on the test."

OK. That might explain the motivation that gets you to open the book. But once you have the assigned chapter in front of you, *why* are you reading? Or even more to the point, *do you know what you are looking for in the chapter*?

I Read My Assignment. So, Why Don't I Know What I Read?

If you were asked to clean the garage (or the student government office, or your room, or the athletic workout room), would you just start working anyplace, moving anything? Probably not. You most likely would want to know exactly what should be moved, thrown away, put away, or cleaned. In other words, you would want to know what the *purpose or result* of your work should be. The same holds true for reading.

ACTIVITY 8.2   WHY DO YOU FORGET WHAT YOU READ?

Have you ever completed an assigned reading but you could not remember what you had just read? Or you didn't know what material was most important to remember? So, you tried to remember everything, got overwhelmed, and felt like you wasted your time. This type of frustration happens to students at some point in their education.

(continued)

For this exercise, think of your general experiences with school reading assignments. Whether it was this term or last year, do any of the following sound familiar? Check as many reasons (below) for forgetting what you have read as apply to you.

- ○ You did not understand the material.
- ○ You did not learn earlier background material.
- ○ You did not know what to remember.
- ○ You did not have the right attitude when reading.
- ○ You got bored.
- ○ You read inefficiently.
- ○ You could not establish relationships.
- ○ You got distracted.
- ○ You did not have an adequate vocabulary to understand the material.
- ○ Other. _____

_____

Briefly, what strategies have you used to address any of the issues above? _____

_____

_____

_____

Identifying the Purpose

The key to increased reading comprehension is to know what the result should be. There are various purposes or reasons for reading.[2] Sometimes we read to do one or more of the following:

- To answer specific questions (like at the end of a chapter)
- To apply (use it in new situations) the reading material (to solve a problem)
- To find details (to support an argument or to answer questions)
- To get a message (such as from a political candidate's statement)
- To evaluate (judge) the reading material (to help you make a decision)
- To entertain (like when you read a novel, a blog, or song lyrics)

If you can identify the purpose of a reading assignment *before* you start reading, there is less of a chance of slamming the book closed in frustration.

But how do you determine what the purpose of a reading assignment is? The following list provides some quick tips to get you moving in the right direction:

- Pay attention in class. The teacher most always gives clues.

- Review your class notes. Perhaps you will find a clue as to what has been emphasized over the past few lessons.

_____

[2]Ron Fry, *Improve Your Reading* (Hawthorne, NJ: The Career Press, 1991), 18. The six purposes listed here can be phrased in a number of ways. One source lists the purposes as assessing, learning, and doing. See Julie Zeleznik and Mary Purugganan, "BIOS 305 Writing and Visual Design in the Biosciences," Rice University. 209.85.165.104/search?q=cache:TRbQuRno00MJ :www.owlnet.rice.edu/~bios305/Abstracts_Lecture_2003.ppt+%22purposes+for+reading% 22&hl=en&ct=clnk&cd=56&gl=us (accessed July 1, 2007).

- Ask a classmate for advice.
- Ask your instructor for advice.
- Learn to skim and scan.
- Use the textbook features that give clues as to what is important. Look for key terms, a chapter introduction, and a chapter summary.

ACTIVITY 8.3   CRITICALLY THINKING ABOUT HOW YOU READ YOUR ASSIGNMENTS

Let's apply the critical thinking standards from Chapter 2 to examine one of the reading challenges you identified for yourself in Activity 8.2.

List one of those challenges here: _____

CRITICAL THINKING STANDARD	APPLICATION TO YOUR READING SKILLS	YOUR EXPLANATION HERE OR ON A SEPARATE PIECE OF PAPER
Clarity	*Clearly* state this particular reading challenge.	
Accuracy	How do you know your assessment of your reading challenge is *correct*?	
Precision	*Specifically* (give examples) explain this reading challenge.	
Relevance	How is your assessment of your reading challenge *connected* to your academic progress?	
Depth	Examine your identified reading challenge beyond a superficial (simplistic) explanation and look at all of the *complexities* involved.	
Breadth	Examine your reading challenge from more than one *perspective (point of view)*.	
Logic	Based on your evidence does your conclusion about your reading challenge *make sense*?	

Based on your answers above, what insights have you gained about your reading challenge? _____

_____

(continued)

What is the next step you will take to eliminate this challenge?_____

_____

_____

HOW TO COMPLETE A TEXTBOOK READING ASSIGNMENT

How Does the Instructor Expect Me to Get Through This Boring Textbook?

If you are like most students, you probably have asked this question many times during your school years. Unfortunately, students find most textbooks dry and sleep inducing. One would think authors get a bonus for writing boring and encyclopedic volumes. Like it or not, your instructors *will* expect you to read the assignments.

The following plan will not only help you get through the dullest of textbooks, but you will also retain more than you ever thought possible. Moreover, if this works for boring books, think of the results with exciting works you want to read.

Your Current Plan for Textbook Reading

First, let's review what you currently do to complete a reading assignment.

MY PLAN FOR COMPLETING A READING ASSIGNMENT   ·   **ACTIVITY 8.4**

Date: _____

Class: _____   Assigned pages: _____

Select one of your textbooks in which you currently have a reading assignment. Below write the steps you normally would take to complete the assignment. When you finish, compare your answers with a classmate.

While completing this reading assignment, I will follow these steps:

Step 1: _____

_____

_____

Step 2: _____

_____

_____

Step 3: _____

_____

_____

(continued)

Step 4: _____

_____

_____

Step 5: _____

_____

_____

Step 6: _____

_____

_____

Step 7: _____

_____

_____

Step 8: _____

_____

_____

A Proven Process for Effective Reading: SQ4R

Probably the most common approach to tackling a reading assignment is the SQ4R method.[3] Activity 8.5 provides a quick overview of this strategy. It also gives you a chance to rate how often you do each of the steps.

ACTIVITY 8.5 **SQ4R: WHAT YOU NEED TO KNOW RIGHT NOW TO IMPROVE YOUR READING**

This introduction to SQ4R will allow you to rate how you currently use each skill. A more detailed description of this process will follow later in the chapter.

○ *Survey.* Quickly look over the reading assignment for clues as to what you will be reading. Look at the headings, captions, bold-faced terms, and any other features the assigned pages might include. Engage your curiosity.

    ○ Circle the number that corresponds to your answer to the question *How often do you survey a reading assignment?*

        0 = never, 1 = almost never, 2 = occasionally, 3 = frequently, 4 = almost always, 5 = always

---

[3]Franklin Pleasant Robinson developed the now-famous SQ3R method during World War II. The first edition of his book *Effective Study* was published in 1946. SQ4R has added to Robinson's pioneering work. Numerous sources reference this process. Once such site is "SQ4R: A classic method for studying texts." University of Guelph (The Learning Commons). 2007. www.learningcommons.uoguelph.ca/LearningServices/Fastfacts-SQ4R.html (accessed July 1, 2007). Some variations of the SQ4R model substitute "relate" for "record". For instance, see "SQ4R Reading Method." West Virginia University at Parkersburg. www.wvup.edu/Academics/learning_center/sq4r_reading_method.htm (accessed July 1, 2007).

○ *Question.* Ask yourself questions about what you think the assignment will address. Also, while reading, continue to ask yourself questions about what you have just read.

   ○ Circle the number that corresponds to your answer to the question *How often do you ask yourself questions about a reading assignment?*

      0 = never, 1 = almost never, 2 = occasionally, 3 = frequently, 4 = almost always, 5 = always

○ *Read.* In this step you actually read your assignment.

   ○ Circle the number that corresponds to your answer to the question *How often do you actually read a reading assignment?*

      0 = never, 1 = almost never, 2 = occasionally, 3 = frequently, 4 = almost always, 5 = always

○ *Recite.* Periodically, stop reading and try to put into your own words what you have just read. Consider this a self-quiz on your comprehension of the material.

   ○ Circle the number that corresponds to your answer to the question *How often do you try to summarize, in your own words, a reading assignment?*

      0 = never, 1 = almost never, 2 = occasionally, 3 = frequently, 4 = almost always, 5 = always

○ *Record.* Physically mark your book or write the important words you are reading. You could highlight, underline, write in the book, or jot down notes on a separate piece of paper.

   ○ Circle the number that corresponds to your answer to the question *How often do you highlight or take notes on a reading assignment?*

      0 = never, 1 = almost never, 2 = occasionally, 3 = frequently, 4 = almost always, 5 = always

○ *Review.* Once you have completed your assignment, but before closing the book for the day, review what you have just read to make sure you understand the material. If you find the material confusing, make a note of the troubling passages and ask a classmate or the instructor for assistance.

   ○ Circle the number that corresponds to your answer to the question *How often do you review a reading assignment as soon as you complete the assignment?*

      0 = never, 1 = almost never, 2 = occasionally, 3 = frequently, 4 = almost always, 5 = always

Based on your answers above, what insights do you have about how you approach a reading assignment? _____
_____

The SQ4R method is graphically summarized in Figure 8.1.

Most study skills books have some variation of SQ4R. Call it what you will, there are essentially three stages to the plan: preread, read, and postread.

---

figure 8.1   SQ4R

Warm up!

- *Survey* the material you are about to read. Stretch your reading muscles and move to the starting line.

Get set!

- Ask yourself *questions* about the reading assignment. Before you start reading, give yourself a purpose for reading.

GO!

- *Read* the assignment. Quiz yourself along the way by *reciting* what you have read to that point. *Record* important information.

Finish!

- Before you close your book, *review* your notes.

Preread

This part of the process involves the *survey* and *question* steps introduced above. Consider this the warm-up phase of reading. Before beginning practice or entering an actual game situation, athletes perform stretching exercises to limber up their muscles. Reading should be no different. If you just open your book to the assigned page and start reading, you have started running without warming up. Anticipate (try to guess) what is to come in the reading.

Two simple questions will help you focus during this warm-up stage: *What do I already know about this material? What would I like to know about this material?*

- *Warm up your intellectual muscles and establish a purpose.* Actively prepare to read. If you don't know what to look for, the reading can seem like torture. Refer to the purposes for reading listed on page 143.* Ask some basic questions.
  - What is this instructor concentrating on in class?
  - What kind of test questions might come from this reading?
  - What past knowledge do you have about the reading assignment?
- *Skim and scan.* If you were asked to find the phone number for Dominic Jones would you pick up the phone book and start reading from the As? Probably not; that would be a waste of your time. You would search for the Js, then scan for his last name and finally for his full name until you found it. Try to make your reading as efficient as possible. So, still warming up, quickly flip through the pages of the assignment. Skimming provides a quick feel for what the big picture is. What you want is a general sense of the assignment. Read the introduction and the summary of the chapter. If you have to accomplish a certain outcome by the end of your reading—say, answer teacher-provided questions—then scan the material with this particular purpose in mind.

This strategy, though it adds a little time to the front end of your reading, will aid comprehension and actually trim time from the overall reading assignment. Once you finish this prereading activity, you will have a better idea what you need to read.

| PRACTICE: SKIMMING AND SCANNING | ACTIVITY **8.6** |

Before you move to the next section, practice your skimming and scanning skills. Use this textbook chapter that you are reading right now. Do the following:

○ Read the chapter introduction and the chapter summary.

(continued)

---

*Telling yourself "I gotta read because my teacher told me to" is *not* the purpose to focus on at this point.

◎ Based on the introduction and the summary, write a couple of sentences that explain what you will learn in this chapter. *Hint*: Be more specific than "This chapter will teach me how to read better." _____

_____

_____

_____

◎ Look at the key terms at the beginning of the chapter.

   ◎ As you skim the chapter, ask yourself, *Why have these words been labeled "key terms"?* _____

   _____

   _____

   _____

◎ Read the chapter's headings/subheadings and form questions based on them. These questions will give you a *purpose* for reading. You will be actively looking for information (answers to your questions). For instance, one section is titled "Identifying the purpose." The question you could form may be *Why do I need to identify the purpose?*

   ◎ Write a couple of the questions you formed: _____

   _____

   _____

   _____

◎ Look at all pictures, graphics, and captions. They have a purpose for being in the text.

   ◎ What types of graphics have you found in this chapter? Why do you think they have been included? _____

   _____

   _____

   _____

◎ Look at bold-faced, italicized, and underlined terms.

   ◎ Why do you think these particular terms have been highlighted? ____

   _____

   _____

   _____

Any new skill is awkward at first. It takes practice for it to become habit. Your reading comprehension should increase with more effective reading strategies. But it takes practice. Take a few minutes now to complete Activity 8.7.

MORE PRACTICE: DEVELOPING YOUR OWN QUESTIONS FROM CHAPTER HEADINGS

Below you will find some of the headings from this chapter. For each heading, develop a question that will help you find the purpose of the section. Be an investigative reporter and ask the *Who? What? When? Why? Where?* and *How?* questions. The first one has been completed as an example.

○ *Do you know why you read an assignment?* <u>My question about the heading: Why is it important that I know why I am reading an assignment? OR How can I find out why I am reading an assignment?</u>

○ *Brain-based learning: Making sense of the seeming chaos*

_____

_____

○ *Identifying the purpose*

_____

_____

○ *A proven process for effective reading: SQ4R*

_____

_____

○ *Using context clues to build your vocabulary*

_____

_____

Read (Finally!)

Once you have warmed up, you are ready to *read, recite,* and *record.*

- This is the time to satisfy your curiosity and look for answers to the questions you posed in Activity 8.7. As you read, ask more questions.

- Look for the main idea of the reading selection. What is the main reason the author wrote the paragraph, chapter, or book you are reading? Don't forget your English training. Whether you found them in a textbook or on a Web site, paragraphs have topic sentences—the sentence that explains the main idea of the paragraph. While many times this can be found in the first sentence, sometimes it will appear later in the paragraph. As you develop stronger reading talents, you will find the topic easily—and have a better understanding of the entire passage you have read.

- Pay particular attention to the words that give you trouble. These words may be the very ones the author is using for a significant reason. This sound advice comes from Mortimer J. Adler and Charles Van Doren in their classic work *How to Read a Book*. They state, "From your point of view as a reader, therefore, the most important words are *those that give you trouble*" (cited author's emphasis).[4]

- In other words, if a word appears awkward, unusual, or strange within the context, there is a good likelihood that it's an important term. This is not foolproof, but if you pay attention to the context of the paragraph, you will have a better chance of determining the main point. More on this later in this chapter.

- Textbooks of different disciplines are *not* meant to be read in the same manner.[5] Once you realize that all texts are *not* created equally, it will be easier to find the main point. A science book with lots of facts and a strange vocabulary is not read like your history text or a novel. Recognize the differences and make adjustments. For instance:

  - When reading a *history* text, look for cause and effect, important people, impact of events on people, turning points, and hints of bias or prejudice by the author.

  - A *science* book may be more likely to focus on classifications, experimental steps, hypotheses, and unexplained phenomena.

  - That *English* novel you have been struggling with is bound to have symbolism, character thresholds, a hero, tragic flaws, and a developing message.

  - And, yes, even *math* books have their particular characteristics. You may need to know which variables, functions, theorems, and axioms are the building blocks of the chapter.

ACTIVITY 8.8   PRACTICE: IDENTIFYING THE MAIN IDEA

Read the passage below and then write what you think to be the main idea.[6] Then, share your answer with a classmate.

If you find yourself considering changing your major course of study, do not do it lightly. Think carefully about the situation. Is changing your major the only answer? Perhaps a discussion with a professor or advisor might clear up some concerns you have—concerns that may seem large and forbidding if you have not gathered correct information. Understand what you can "fix" with a change of major—and what you cannot.

For instance, you may be able to "fix" the problem of content comprehension by moving from a math-oriented major to one that focuses on literature. But if you are experiencing difficulties with your major because you are homesick, you can change your major monthly but the real problem—homesickness—will not have been addressed. You have to know what to address

(continued)

---

[4]Mortimer Adler and Charles Van Doren, *How to Read a Book*. (New York: Simon & Schuster, 1972), 102.

[5]Ibid., Chapters 13 and 19, passim.

[6]Steve Piscitelli, *Rhythms of College Success: A Journey of Discovery, Change, and Mastery*. (Upper Saddle River, NJ: Pearson Prentice Hall, 2008), 277.

What do you think the main idea of the passage on the previous page is? ____

_____

_____

■ *Record.* The importance of this step is to make the words you are reading "your own" words. The better able you are to put the author's words into your words, the more likely you will remember the material (more in Chapter 9). There are a couple of ways to execute the recording part of SQ4R.

  ■ *Highlighting.* Use a pen, pencil, or brightly colored marker to underline, circle, or box important information. A word of caution about highlighting: You want to highlight the *major* points. Too many students highlight almost every word. This is useless. Look for key words.

  ■ *Margin notes.* As you read, make notes in the margins of your book. Maybe you have a question about the paragraph you just completed reading. If so, write it in the margin. Or as you highlight part of a sentence or passage, write the main point—in your words—in the margins. Learn to "use" your book—read it, write in it, consume it!

  ■ *Notes.* Using the strategies introduced in Chapter 5, actually write notes in your notebook. You may find this more effective than highlighting because it forces you to encode the material, to put the material into your own words. If you can do this, you *understand* it. Concentrate on main points, themes, and questions you might have.

PRACTICE: RECORDING IN YOUR OWN WORDS   ACTIVITY **8.9**

Read the passage below.[7] Highlight, underline, and/or circle the important words, details, and points raised in the passage. Based on the words you noted, can you write a summary in your own words? Once you have completed the activity, share your answer with a classmate.

One key to successful communication is to speak with an air of confidence. A self-assured person will capture attention better than someone stammering for the correct words. Self-confidence will lead to an assertive *communication style. To say that one communicates with assertiveness means that the person can stand up for herself. The person can face demands and can also make requests in a nonaggressive manner.*

Aggressive behavior, *on the other hand, represents a harsher attitude. It can border on hostility or a bully-like approach to other people. Bullies take advantage of* passive *individuals—people who will submit to verbal and, in some cases, nonverbal attacks without resistance. A fine line can separate passive behavior from assertive behavior, or assertive behavior from aggressive behavior. Although every situation presents unique circumstances, generally speaking, assertive behavior is seen as the favored road to travel.*

(continued)

_____
[7]Piscitelli, 223.

Write your summary here. _____

_____

_____

_____

Postread

Once you have completed your reading assignment, do not immediately close the book. It's time to *review*. Even if your review is brief, the repetition will help you strengthen connections and deepen your learning.[8] The question to ask yourself at this point is *"What did I just read?"*

Immediately take five or ten minutes to study the notes you just wrote or the words you highlighted. Organize and reorganize your notes according to categories, theories, trends, or some other grouping. It may help to ask yourself:

- What is the big picture?
- Can I connect this new knowledge to previously learned material?
- Can I see any relationships emerging?

This step keeps you focused, while also preparing for the next class as well as the coming exam. If you are confused about the reading, bring your question(s) to the next class.

ACTIVITY 8.10 **PRACTICE: WHAT HAVE YOU JUST READ?**

Before you go to the next section, briefly ask yourself—and answer—what you have read thus far in this chapter. Write your answers here:

○ _____

○ _____

○ _____

○ _____

○ _____

Well, there you have it. Nothing is guaranteed, but this is an achievable plan. The benefits are many. The notes you develop while reading, for instance, will serve as an excellent guide for your classroom notes. With your reading complete and organized, you are then armed and ready for the teacher's presentation. You can participate; you can actively learn; you can earn better grades; and you will be able to use your precious time more effectively.

---

[8] Eric Jensen, "Brain-based Learning: A Reality Check." *Educational Leadership*. April 2000, 78. Jensen says, "The brain strengthens learning through repetition. Repetition is bad only when it becomes boring."

ADDITIONAL STRATEGIES FOR READING SUCCESS

Use Supplemental Sources

If you have a difficult time understanding your textbook, look for other sources. For instance, most bookstores sell short versions of American history. Such books concentrate on the major points of historical periods. The same holds true for books in other disciplines. The *Cliffs Notes* series presents the major points for novels and plays. *Supplemental* books provide an outline of major points. These sources *should not be a substitute*, but they may be able to help you understand the main points.

Vocabulary

One author estimates that the average eighteen-year-old student has a 60,000-word vocabulary. By the end of a college career, the typical student will add another 20,000 words to her vocabulary.[9] Here are two ways in which you can help to increase your vocabulary.

© Jaimie Duplass—Fotolia.com.

- *Build your vocabulary (part I).* Use a dictionary to clarify meanings. Look up new words, correct misspellings on exams and homework, and become familiar with synonyms and antonyms. Consider purchasing an inexpensive pocket-sized dictionary and thesaurus.

- *Build your vocabulary (part II).* Take about fifteen minutes in the morning to work on the daily crossword puzzle in the newspaper. This has two benefits: (1) it builds your vocabulary, and (2) it limbers up your "mental muscles" for the coming academic day.

Using Context Clues to Build Your Vocabulary

Reality being what it is, few students stop, reach for a dictionary, leaf through the pages, and read the definition of a troublesome word. And, in some cases like exams, using a dictionary is not practical or possible.

In such instances you will want to rely on context clues. *Context* here refers to the words that surround the word you are trying to understand. Using the knowledge of words you do understand, you make an educated guess about the meaning of the words you do not know.

PRACTICE: USING CONTEXT CLUES   ACTIVITY **8.11**

For each sentence, write the meaning of the **underlined** word *and* briefly explain how the context (surrounding words) helps define the word.

○ *Rather than* <u>accelerate</u>, *Jeremy tapped his brakes as he entered the intersection.*

  ○ The meaning of <u>accelerate</u>: _____

(continued)

---

[9]D. J. Henry, *The Effective Reader* (updated edition). (New York: Pearson Longman, 2004), 46.

○ How does the context help you understand the underlined word? ____

_____

○ *Successful leaders know when to <u>delegate</u>, or assign, work to other people.*

  ○ The meaning of <u>delegate</u>: _____

  ○ How does the context help you understand the underlined word? ____

_____

○ *The customer showed his <u>integrity</u> when he came back to the store to return the extra money the cashier had given him in error.*

  ○ The meaning of <u>integrity</u>: _____

  ○ How does the context help you understand the underlined word?

_____

○ *Joe <u>overhauled</u> his old car with new tires, a sparkling paint job, and an engine tune-up.*

  ○ The meaning of <u>overhauled</u>: _____

  ○ How does the context help you understand the underlined word? ____

_____

Having Trouble Finding the Main Idea? Use "Mini-SQ4Rs"

One author maintains, "The most important reading skill you can develop as a college student is the ability to determine the author's main idea. The main idea of a paragraph is the most important point the author makes about the topic."[10] Therefore, if you have difficulty determining the main idea you may wish to break your reading task into smaller pieces.

Try reading one paragraph at a time—and use the SQ4R strategy that you now know. Skim the paragraph, ask yourself a question or two about the paragraph, jot down a few notes, then review what you have read. Once you find that you can understand one paragraph, expand your reading to two, three, or more paragraphs at a time. If you get to a point where you do not comprehend the main idea, back up and read fewer paragraphs. While this will take more time at first, think of the time you will have wasted if you read an entire chapter and do not understand most or all of what you have read.

Understanding and Using Graphics[11]

Authors use graphics to simplify their message. Using fewer words than paragraphs, graphics can help the reader make connections between concepts, understand the main point of a paragraph, and show support for a particular opinion. They also are important guides to help you *survey* your reading (the first step of the SQ4R). Some of the more common graphics include those shown in Table 8.1.

---

[10] D. J. Henry, *The Skilled Reader* (updated edition). (New York: Pearson Longman, 2004), 108.

[11] For a clear review of various types of graphics, see Brenda D. Smith, *Bridging the Gap: College Reading*, 9th *ed.* (New York: Pearson Longman, 2008), 534–547.

table 8.1   Types of graphics

GRAPHIC LABEL	WHAT YOU SEE
Bar graph	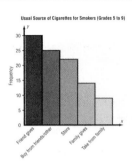
Chart	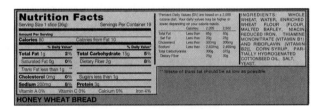
Diagram	
Flowchart	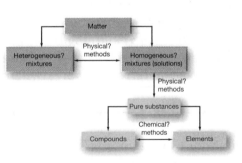
Map	

(continued)

○ Your example. Stretch your awareness of smell by describing the smell of a damp room or old running shoes. _____

_____

_____

STORING THE INFORMATION YOU HAVE NOTICED

Once you notice the information, you need to file it away for future use. Remember, just because you have *heard* or *seen* or *touched* or *tasted* or *smelled* something does not mean you have paid attention to it. In order to move information (textbook reading, a lecture, song lyrics, or statistics about a sports team) from your short-term memory to long-term memory, you have to learn how to encode it into a meaningful form for yourself. This section will suggest strategies that, if practiced (rehearsed), can decrease the times you freeze or go blank when trying to remember something of importance.

Active Listening = Improved Memory

Active listeners are engaged in what they hear. They try to make meaning of what is said. The following tips will help you become a more active listener— and effectively store more information:

- *Focus.* Practice courtesy and you will retain more. Pay attention to the speaker. Put aside other distractions. Focus on the words and meanings. Take notes if need be.

- *Find relevance.* Face it: Not every speaker will be a living, breathing dynamo. Find something in the presentation and focus on it. Find a relationship to something you already know.

- *Listen.* Do it with your ears—not your mouth. If you mentally begin phrasing your response while the speaker is still speaking, you may very well miss an important point. It can be difficult to understand the speaker if you are just waiting to jump in and give your opinion. If you "listen" in this manner, you are creating your own distraction.

- *Participate.* Once the speaker has finished, rephrase what was said. If you can explain, in your own words, what has just been presented, you will have a better chance of retention. By paraphrasing you are, in effect, rehearsing the new material, which leads to understanding.

- *Ask questions.* This is also part of the participation strategy. Ask for clarification, relationships, or the significance of the topic at hand. Not only are you repeating the information, but you are also doing it in the context of the big picture of the presentation. This will help in the development of memory hooks (discussed later).

- *Offer another explanation or another application.* This is a particularly effective strategy in classes that follow a discussion or seminar format. As you process the new information, try to present another side of the issue. This can be done in a noncombative manner as an attempt to understand other aspects of the topic. This allows for analysis and, consequently, better understanding.

By becoming actively involved, you will be more apt to retain the information.

PRACTICE: ACTIVE LISTENING

Pick one of the strategies described above and try it later today when you have a conversation with a classmate, friend, or family member. Afterward, write your observations below.

○ Which strategy did you try? _____

○ What did you find easy about the strategy? _____

○ What was difficult about the strategy? _____

_____

○ In what ways do you think this can help you with your academic success?

_____

_____

Using Charts to Make Connections

Another helpful technique to organize information is the data retrieval chart (DRC). Used for many years in education, this model allows for easy categorization, comparison, and contrast of information.

As you can see in Figure 9.2, a DRC can be used to show how one event leads to another. In this case, it allows students to see the connection between the actions and responses of two groups. This simplified view of cause and effect demonstrates how England found itself in a war with its colonies.

Figure 9.3 shows how a data retrieval chart can be used to compare and contrast. In this case, different empires are the focus of study.

Sexually transmitted infections (STIs) receive attention in Figure 9.4. In this case, a student can quickly grasp the nature of the infection (or disease) and its consequences.

Figure 9.5 shows how the data retrieval chart can be used with novels as well as textbooks.

As you can see after studying Figures 9.2 through 9.5, the DRC can be used to compare authors, scientific findings, historical developments, artistic

---

American War for Independence: Cause and Effect — *figure 9.2*

ENGLAND'S STRICTER NEW COLONIAL SYSTEM

PRIME MINISTER	EXAMPLE OF BRITISH ACTION	EXAMPLE OF COLONIAL RESPONSE
Grenville	Stamp Act passed to collect taxes	Colonists upset, Stamp Act Congress convened
Townshend (Pitt)	More taxes placed on the colonists	Colonists upset, boycott English goods
North	Tea Act passed	Boston Tea Party dumps tea into Boston Harbor

figure 9.3 The Middle Ages

HEIRS OF THE ROMAN EMPIRE

	BYZANTINE EMPIRE	ISLAMIC EMPIRE	GERMANIC KINGDOMS (EARLY)	GERMANIC KINGDOMS (LATE)
Administration				
Contributions				
Events of significance				
Challenges				

relationships, and the like. Each cell allows for easy comparison with another cell. Relationships and connections, which are vital to improving memory, can be easily established.

Don't wait for the teacher to provide a DRC. Make up your own when reviewing and reorganizing your notes. This becomes a great one-page study guide—efficient, effective, and practical.

figure 9.4 Sexually transmitted infections

NAME OF THE INFECTION OR DISEASE	BRIEF DESCRIPTION	CONSEQUENCES
Chlamydia		
Genital herpes		
Gonorrhea		
Human papillomavirus (HPV)		
HIV/AIDS		
Syphilis		
Vaginitis		

figure 9.5

Comparing and contrasting characters in a novel.

Of Mice and Men
John Steinbeck introduces a variety of characters in this classic novel. Use this chart to analyze the significance of each character to the overall story line.

CHARACTER	WHEN INTRODUCED	SYMBOLISM	SIGNIFICANCE
George			
Lennie			
Slim			
Candy			
Crooks			
Carlson			
Curley			
Curley's Wife			
Old dog			

Mental Pictures

Albert Einstein is reported to have said, "If I can't picture it, I can't understand it." This leads us to another suggested way to improve memory—think in pictures. Pictures give you more than word concepts on which to hold. For instance, refer to the DRC on "American War for Independence" in Figure 9.2. Visualize the British in their red coats. See the Boston Tea Party in your mind. Imagine the first shots at Lexington and Concord. This sort of creativity uses much more of the brain than if you just attempted to memorize the words without a clear conception of what was actually transpiring. By bringing the creative right side of the brain together with the orderly nature of the left brain, you use the whole brain to help you make connections—and increase your chances of being able to recall the information. (You may wish to refer to the information on learning styles in Chapter 5.)

RECLAIMING THE INFORMATION YOU HAVE STORED

The third step of memory, *reclaiming* (retrieving) the information you have stored, typically refers to what we have remembered or forgotten. In the storage process you placed the information in "files"; now you have to flip through the file cabinet and locate the "folder." At this step you reach back into your brain's file drawers and pull out the information you need to use. Whether it is a phone number, directions to a party, or information for a test, this step requires that you effectively have noticed and stored the material.

Retrieval: Start with What You Already Know

Before we examine some new strategies, pause for a moment and reflect upon what you have read so far in this book. Topics from the preceding chapters can be used to improve your memory. For instance, if your retrieval problem (failure to remember something when you need to know it) stems from poor labeling, review the SQ4R reading strategies presented in Chapter 8. Skimming, scanning, questioning, outlining, and anticipating make information processing more efficient. The more you review (study), the more likely you will be able to retain and retrieve.

"What about my class notes?" you may ask. "I can't seem to make any lasting sense of these scribblings." There are a couple of strategies you can employ here. First, think of the links between Chapters 6 (class time), 7 (note taking), and 8 (reading). Ask yourself, "What are the connections between my homework readings and the instructor's presentations?"

For instance, perhaps your economics instructor has been describing how the economic concepts of supply and demand set the price of a product. Later that day in your textbook assignment, you read about the rising cost of gas prices in our nation. Looking at your notes from class, try to draw a connection (a relationship) between your instructor's lecture and what you just read: How do the concepts of supply and demand affect the price you pay for gas?

With a little practice, you will be able to determine these relationships more easily. Once you establish them you will have an increased ability to retain, understand, and retrieve. This moves beyond shear memorization. The material starts to take on a life of its own. It makes sense; you understand it.

Memory Blocks

It has happened to most students at one time or another. They know the material, but they freeze on the exam or during the presentation. Something seems to "block" the information from emerging out of the recesses of the mind to the here and now. Let's examine a few reasons why this occurs.

- *Emotional memory blocks.* Perhaps, you have struggled in your math classes for years. No matter what you seem to do, your grades are less than satisfactory. As you prepare for the next math exam of the current term, you do not expect to do any better. Whether it is a fear of failure, the memory of a distressing prior experience, or some other traumatic issue, some students fear the challenges that wait inside the classroom door. The emotion effectively blocks any attempt to reclaim the information.

- *Physical memory blocks.* Our physical well-being can affect how clearly we think and remember. For instance, staying up until the wee hours of the morning studying for tomorrow's psychology exam will create some difficulties. Even if you review everything that the instructor could possibly ask, you may become so tired you will not think straight. By the time you get to class all the information stored in your brain will be a jumbled mess. So much for your hours of studying.

- *Mechanical blocks.* You put a lot of time into your studies but you can't seem to recall the data during the exam. You feel at ease and you are well rested. But you still can't get the information you studied "out of your brain." This is usually an indication of some retrieval difficulty. This is typically due to a problem with the second step of memory—you did not store the information in a clear and recognizable location in your brain's filing cabinet. If you just throw the information into the drawers without labeling, so to speak, you will have difficulty retrieving, or finding, it.

Retrieval Failure: What You Can Do About It

As stated earlier in the chapter, you have a short-term and a long-term memory. The short term can last anywhere from thirty seconds to a couple of days. If the information is not used, it is virtually lost to you.

The long-term memory consists of those items that have not been "lost." For whatever reason—practice, concentration, or desire—you have retained this information.

"But," you reasonably may ask, "why do I still forget things when it comes to test time? I've practiced. I have desire. But my test grades sure don't reflect this!" Let's examine a few reasons why this may be. Following each point you will find a strategy or two to combat the retrieval challenge.

- *Poor labeling.* What would happen if you just threw pieces of paper into a file cabinet drawer without any order whatsoever? Obviously you would have a difficult time finding material. Just as you would store valuable documents carefully, do the same with the facts, concepts, and generalizations with which you come into contact.

  - *Strategy.* Remember the suggestion to review your notes nightly (Chapter 7)? Reviewing, relating, and reorganizing will help you develop connections, which are the best way to fight against improper filing.

- *Disuse (or decay).* Just like with your muscles, if you don't use information, you will, more than likely, lose it. Ever have difficulty remembering some course material after a prolonged vacation or absence from school? The reason is simple—you have not used the information in some time. Once you start using the information again, your memory usually returns (assuming you have labeled the information correctly).

  - *Strategy.* Once you have stored the material, find ways to use it as soon and as often as possible. Consider this practice, or rehearsal, for when you will need to use the information "for real." For instance, if you learn a vocabulary word in class but do not review and use it soon after, you increase your chances of forgetting the word.

  - *Strategy.* If you find practicing information tedious and boring, perhaps you could reframe the way you view the information (or a course) that does not hold interest for you. Make a short-term commitment to yourself to find in the instructor's lesson at least two items of interest each day you go to class. Perhaps you could go a step further and search for a connection between the course and your passion (or eventual major). If that proves difficult or impossible to do, use that as a reason to visit your instructor's office. For instance: "I love science and do very well in those courses. Could you help me find a connection between your United States History course and science? Do they have anything in common?" Such questions let the instructor know of your passion and your interest to do well in the course—and they help build or maintain an important relationship.

■ *Strategy for class notes.* Set aside time each day to review your class notes. Use the TSD strategy (see Chapter 7).

■ *Strategy for reading material.* Use the SQ4R process described in Chapter 8. The final R asks you to review what you have read immediately after you have finished reading. Additionally, as soon as possible *before* class, review your reading notes or your highlighting. This will prepare you for the day's class.

■ *Extinction.* Our schools are based on a series of rewards. These incentives vary, ranging from grades to awards for high GPA (like making the dean's list). Many students have been conditioned by these extrinsic rewards—that is, those given to us by someone else (see Chapter 3). The grade, for instance, becomes the overriding reason for performance. Once the reward (grade) is removed, the incentive to continue to work with the material is removed. No reward, no effort, no retention.

■ *Strategy.* Can you find an internal (intrinsic) reward to help motivate you? If the reading is related to your major, you might be moved because you have a passion for the content. Maybe success with the material will satisfy a personal goal of yours. However, the reality remains that for most students many of the required courses hold little interest. Someone with a deep passion for literature may find it difficult to stay focused in a history course. Perhaps the best advice is to remember that these prerequisites serve as "gatekeepers." You must pass through them in order to move into the course work that really interests you. Once you navigate these early courses, you will be able to concentrate on those subject areas that hold intrinsic motivation for you.

■ *Response competition (interference).* Visualize this scenario: You have studied for a science unit exam. Your science class, however, follows right after your math class in which the instructor has introduced a new process complete with formulas and equations. Your brain feels like it is going to burst! Or perhaps earlier that morning you had an argument with a friend; in your mind you are still running through what he said. By the time you get to the science exam your mind moves in three or four directions—and none of them seems related to the exam in front of you. The new information interferes with what you studied for the exam.

■ *Strategy.* This is where an efficient filing system in your brain's attic will pay off. If you develop connections, rehearse (practice) the material, and develop a feeling of confidence, you have a better chance of the material becoming "second nature"—almost automatic. While you may not be able to stop the competing signals, you will have a better chance to find and recall the information needed.

- *Strategy.* This strategy looks to the future. When scheduling classes for your next term, try to leave an hour or two between classes so that you will have time to sit somewhere quiet and refocus before going into the test situation. The same goes for work schedules. Leave yourself some breathing room rather than rushing from work to the parking lot to the classroom.

- *Situational variation.* Let's call this stage fright. Consider these scenarios: You practiced a guitar lead for months. You never missed a lick. The first time you perform it in public—you guessed it—your fingers turn to jelly. Or you never flubbed a line during drama rehearsal. Opening night has arrived, and you can't remember your name! Why? The situation—the setting—has changed. You practiced in one environment but had to perform in quite a different situation.

  - *Strategy.* Practice the material in various situations to help eliminate this distraction. Perhaps you can sit in the classroom where you will take the real exam. If you can, try to do practice exercises within the same time frame as you will have on test day. If your instructor will allow only fifty minutes for the test, practice in fifty-minute blocks of time. Prepare for the content as well as for the timed situation. Maybe your study group (if you choose to be part of one) can meet one day in the actual classroom in which you will sit for the exam. Does your textbook have a companion Web site (most do) that provides practice questions? If it does, use it regularly. Maybe the instructor has an old exam for you to practice. Do as many practice tests as you can in a test-like environment. Depending on how much of a concern this is for you, you may give thought to actually doing a practice test, in the classroom, for the specified time.

WHAT STRATEGIES HAVE YOU USED?   ACTIVITY 9.5

Pick one of the following challenges that you have encountered. What have you done (or tried to do) to either eliminate or minimize your memory challenge?

- ○ Memory blocks
- ○ Extinction
- ○ Poor labeling
- ○ Response competition
- ○ Situational variation

_____
_____
_____

Names

Remembering names does not have to be difficult. A few simple techniques will avoid embarrassment and may even impress people.

- *Decide you want to remember the name.* Make a conscious effort. Say to yourself, "I want to remember this person's name."

- *Listen and repeat.* Carefully listen to the name of the individual. Repeat it. Ask for a spelling of the name. Use the name immediately. An exchange might go something like this:

"Steve, I would like you to meet my friend Jenny."

"Jenny, I'm pleased to meet you. Jenny, is your name short for Jennifer, Or is that the full name? Well, it was nice meeting you, Jenny. I look forward to talking with you later."

In a matter of about 15 seconds, the new name was used multiple times. Practice makes permanent.

- *Look at the face.* Lock the name to the face.
- *Notice physical features.* Does this person possess any unique features? Very short, very tall, long hair, big nose, beautiful eyes, or lots of jewelry? Exaggerate this feature. Have fun with this!

Mnemonics

This strange-looking word (ni-mon-icks) is a strategy that allows you to get creative. Let's look at four examples.

- *Acronyms.* An *acronym* is a word formed from the letters (usually the first letters) of other words. Do you wish to remember the names of the Great Lakes? Just remember *HOMES*. This stands for Huron, Ontario, Michigan, Erie, and Superior.
- *Acrostics.* An *acrostic* uses the first letter of each word to create a sequential message. Having trouble with the order of mathematical operations? Then remember: *Please Excuse My Dear Aunt Sally.* Now you will forever remember to first do the operation in parentheses, followed by exponents, multiplication, division, addition, and subtraction. Want to remember the notes assigned to the lines of a musical staff which are *EGBDF? (Every Good Boy Does Fine)*. How about the taxonomic levels in biology? *King Philip Came Over For Green Stamps (Kingdom, Phylum, Class, Order, Family, Genus, Specie)*.
- *The hook, number, linking, location, or peg system.* A peg is something you can hang an item on. A mental peg (or hook) allows you to attach a concept, a word, an item, or something else. You "locate" what you want to remember by connecting it with an object. For instance, you may tend to forget where you put your keys after using them. The next time you toss them on to the table think of the table spinning or maybe even lighting up. Creating a vivid and outrageous picture of the peg (movement, light) *and* the concept engages your brain and creates a better chance to reclaim what you want to remember. If you have to remember the steps of a mathematical formula, you can try to visualize the rooms in your house. Each room of the house can hold one of the steps of the formula. As you move from one room to the other you find the next step until you finally complete the formula process. The associations do not have to be logical. All you are trying to do is create a picture of the item or items you need to remember. This system can work with lists, such as vocabulary words, bones of the body, and parts of speech.

Practice, Practice, and More Practice

When trying to learn new material, it helps to do three things: practice, practice, and practice some more. To learn a new skill perform activities that stretch your mind. Just like an athlete does stretches, calisthenics, and wind sprints to get in shape, it will help you to do mental gymnastics. Consider your mental warm-ups as mind exercises. Use them and you will expand your capabilities.

PRACTICE: ACRONYMS, ACROSTICS, PEG SYSTEMS   ACTIVITY 9.6

With a classmate, write an example of each of the following memory strategies. You can either describe one you have learned in another class or you can make one up.

○ Acronym. _____

_____

○ Acrostic. _____

_____

○ Peg system. _____

_____

Memory ≠ Understanding

While an effective memory may be impressive, and it may even help you get by on tests, it does not indicate that you understand the material. In fact, a "good memory" might end up being one of your (unknown) weaknesses. For instance, some students spend many hours in school *memorizing* lists of vocabulary words and spelling words. Their exams and quizzes reflect high scores. But, in reality, the students could be missing out on the important rules that guide spelling exceptions. This, in turn, can cause embarrassment in later years when they have to learn basic spelling rules they should have *understood* in elementary school.

True learning will usually cause some frustration. After all, learning indicates a change in behavior. Learning anything new can be challenging to some of us. So, too, with memory strategies. As you look back on the ideas from this chapter, keep two points in mind. First, if you are not used to them, they may seem awkward. Don't give up for that reason alone. Second, not every technique is for you. Pick and choose—but find something that works for you—and then use it regularly.

CHAPTER SUMMARY

To cope with the vast quantities of information vying for your attention, develop observational and listening skills. This requires discipline and concentration. You must have a desire to notice and store information. No desire, no understanding, no memory. Finally, memory is the process of finding information in the brain. Developing an efficient system for filing and retrieving information will enhance your memory. If you have been following the organizational strategies in these chapters, you are well on your way to establishing effective recall strategies.

In order to be successful, students need to become involved and engaged in active learning to build their memory. Before leaving this chapter, keep the following points in mind:

- There are three steps to remembering information: noticing, storing, and reclaiming. You must see something, put it someplace, and then go find it.

- There is a difference between memory and understanding. Memory requires retention *and* retrieval of material. Understanding takes you to a higher level.

- The key to comprehension is the creation of relationships.

- Understand why your memory might be blocked–and then apply a strategy to remove that block.

- Develop an efficient and effective filing system in your brain.

- Use of organizing models (DRC, mnemonics, mental imaging).

- Practice active listening everyday.

- Whatever you learn, use the new knowledge as soon, and as often, as possible.

ACTIVITY 9.7   CHAPTER 9 MEASURABLE OBJECTIVES

At the beginning of this chapter, five measurable objectives were presented. They are reprinted below for your convenience. Using the strategies you have learned in this chapter, fill in the lines beneath each item (or use a separate sheet of paper).

○ Identify and use two strategies to improve your skill of noticing what you need to remember.

   ○ Explain the two strategies you used this past week. _____

   _____

   _____

   _____

   _____

○ Identify two reasons why you have forgotten information for a test.

   ○ What two reasons most often cause you to forget? _____

   _____

   _____

   _____

   _____

(continued)

○ Identify and use two strategies to help you improve how you store information.

　　○ Identify the two strategies and briefly explain how they helped you during the past week. _____

　　_____

　　_____

　　_____

　　_____

○ Demonstrate active listening skills.

　　○ How did you use an active listening skill during the past week? _____

　　_____

　　_____

　　_____

　　_____

○ Identify and use at least two organizational models to help you reclaim information.

　　○ Identify the two organizational models you used—and how you used them—during the past week. _____

　　_____

　　_____

　　_____

　　_____

REALITY CHECK

Using your critical thinking skills to improve your memory and recall skills

Situation. Dominic's biology professor told Dominic today that he was in serious danger of failing for the semester. Dominic knows he can do better. He told you that his biggest problem is with memory. "I take notes. I study the notes. I still do poorly on the exams."

Pulling from strategies introduced in this chapter and in previous chapters, develop at least three specific suggestions for Dominic. In particular, suggest to Dominic how he might be able to use the following to help improve his memory skills.

- Organizing his priorities (Chapter 4).
- The VARK learning style questionnaire (Chapter 5).
- TSD strategy (Chapter 7).
- SQ4R (Chapter 8).
- Memory blocks (Chapter 9).

Write your suggestions here or on a separate piece of paper. _____

_____

_____

_____

_____

_____

_____

CHAPTER 10

TEST TAKING

How can you improve your test-preparation and test-performance skills?

SPOT LIGHT ON CLASSROOM SKILLS

It seems to be the same tired story. Even though I have taken hundreds and hundreds of tests over the years, I still get nervous every time an exam is placed in front of me. I'll admit there have been times when I went into a test situation unprepared, but most times I have at least done a little studying to get ready. Still, no matter whether I am prepared or not, as soon as the test starts I get jittery, my mind goes blank, and eventually I run out of time.

A couple of weeks ago the campus testing center offered a workshop on test-taking skills. I heard a lot of things I already knew: Prepare early, review all notes and readings, do the easy test items first. But there were some strategies I had not thought about before. For instance, I never thought of asking instructors for old exams to use for practice. Nor was I aware that my textbook had an online site that provided practice tests. The most important strategy was also the simplest: It is really up to me to block out time for test preparation. I already know how to take notes, read a textbook, and critically think. If I use those skills I will improve my test performance.

PREVIEW

By the time you finish reading this chapter and completing its activities you will know how to:

- Identify at least two successful test-preparation strategies you have used in the past (within the last two months) and continue to use them for your benefit.

- Identify at least two reasons why you either *do* have test anxiety or do *not* have test anxiety.

- Explain how to apply at least one study skill strategy (introduced earlier in this book) to improve your test-taking skills.

- Explain at least two clues an instructor can give about potential test items.

- Apply the postexam analysis strategy to at least one of your most recent exams.

KEY TERMS

- Academic integrity
- Emergency studying
- Inefficient test-taking strategies

As you study this chapter, remember that you have been confronted with tests, in one form or another, your entire life. While the tests described in this chapter are of the academic nature, don't lose sight of the fact that you have taken these types of tests often in your career as a student. Whether your transcript reflects a test-savvy student or a person who freezes at the thought of an examination, one commonality remains: You have been down this road many times before. The content and the courses may have changed, but you already have test-taking strategies. Remember them, learn from them; and move to a higher level of competence and success.[1]

- Postexam analysis
- Test anxiety
- Test clues
- Test-performance skills
- Test-preparation skills
- Trigger words
- Types of exams

CHAPTER INTRODUCTION

Tests. While they may strike fear into the hearts of many, tests are nothing new. Whether you are a student right out of high school or returning after a twenty-year break, you have confronted—and mastered—tests all your life.

This chapter will look at your test performance skills from three perspectives:

- *What skills do you already have that will help you with test preparation and performance?* You will be asked to draw on those experiences. Keep the good practices, modify the questionable practices, and get rid of those practices that have been hindering you. In keeping with the themes of this book, reflect on your experiences, respect the skills you have, and take responsibility for the changes you need to make.

- *What causes test anxiety—and what can you do about it?* Anyone who has taken an exam has experienced, at one time or another, some form of apprehension. As you will see in this chapter, sometimes test anxiety can actually be beneficial. It can keep you alert and ready to perform. At the same time, test anxiety can be paralyzing. Even if you do not experience test anxiety, a general review of strategies will help to maintain a healthy level of confidence prior to an exam.

- *What do you need to do in order to improve your test-taking skills?* Effective note-taking, time management, and memory techniques are a few of the factors that influence test performance. So, too, will your physical conditioning and your emotional well-being. A tired, sick, or stressed student will have greater difficulty successfully completing an exam than a rested, alert, and calm student.

ACTIVITY 10.1 | **REFLECTION ON YOUR CURRENT LEVEL OF TEST-PREPARATION AND TEST-TAKING SKILLS**

Before you answer the items below, reflect on your current level of test-preparation and test-performance skills. Think of how well (or poorly) you have performed on tests in past classes.

As with all of the reflective activities in this book, answer from your heart. This exercise is not meant for you to answer just like your classmates—

(continued)

[1]Steve Piscitelli, *Rhythms of College Success: A Journey of Discovery, Change, and Mastery.* (Upper Saddle River, NJ: Pearson Prentice Hall, 2004), 164, 171–172.

or to match what you may think the instructor wants to see. Take your time to give a respectful and responsible general accounting of your experiences with test preparation and test performance. A truthful self-assessment now will help you build on skills you have while developing those you lack.

For the following items circle the number that best describes your *typical* experience with test-preparation and test-performance skills. The key for the numbers is:

0 = never, 1 = almost never, 2 = occasionally, 3 = frequently,
   4 = almost always, 5 = always

When considering your experience with test-preparation and test-performance skills how often:

1. Did you prepare for an exam earlier than the night before the exam?

    0   1   2   3   4   5

2. Did you prepare for an exam a week or more before the exam date?

    0   1   2   3   4   5

3. Did you review your graded exam for more than your grade? That is, how often did you seek clarification about missed questions so that you could learn from your mistakes?

    0   1   2   3   4   5

4. Did you review your test-preparation strategies for effectiveness or ineffectiveness?

    0   1   2   3   4   5

5. Did you ask your instructor (or read the syllabus) about the test format before exam day?

    0   1   2   3   4   5

6. Could you complete a test without your mind going blank or freezing up?

    0   1   2   3   4   5

7. Did you, before you started your test, read all the directions and quickly survey the exam for its content and format?

    0   1   2   3   4   5

8. During an exam did you complete all of the easy items before you attempted the more difficult items?

    0   1   2   3   4   5

Add up your scores for items 1, 2, 3, 4, and 5. Divide by 5. Write your answer here: _____ .

Using the key explanations above for each number (0, 1, 2, 3, 4, 5), complete this sentence: When it comes to test-preparation skills, I _____ prepare for tests effectively.

Add up your scores for items 6, 7, and 8. Divide by 3. Write your answer here: _____.

(continued)

Using the key explanations above for each number (0, 1, 2, 3, 4, 5), complete this sentence: When it comes to test-performance skills, I _____ perform on tests effectively.

Based on your answers, what insights do you have about your experiences with test-taking?_____

_____

_____

WHAT TEST-TAKING SKILLS DO YOU POSSESS?

If you were to add together all of the tests you have ever taken, you would be surprised to see you have been in hundreds and hundreds of exam situations. Whatever your background or age, you bring positive experiences and, perhaps, a few challenges to your college exams.

Activity 10.2 gives you the opportunity to build on Activity 10.1. Take a moment to think about your testing experiences. Specifically, examine how you prepared, when you prepared, what worked, and what did not work. This allows you to identify practices you may want to continue in college—and those it is time to eliminate.

ACTIVITY 10.2   WHAT TEST-TAKING SKILLS DO YOU HAVE RIGHT NOW?

Reflect on your test-taking experiences. Try to think about the "big picture." That is, don't just concentrate on an exam you completed last week. Try not to concentrate on only the good experiences or only the poor grades. Rather, think about your testing experiences in general as you complete this activity.

1. *Preparation.* What have you done to prepare for exams? Check any of the following items that apply to you:

    _____ I used instructor study guides when provided.

    _____ I reviewed my notes nightly.

    _____ I participated in a study group.

    _____ I asked the instructor if there were old tests I might be able to use for practice.

    _____ When available, I used the textbook publisher's companion Web site to review chapter objectives and take practice quizzes and tests.

    _____ I used a tutor.

    _____ I visited my instructor's office for content clarification.

(continued)

_____ I very seldom did any preparation for a test.

_____ Other methods of test preparation I tried included these:

_____

_____

2. *Timing.* Generally speaking, when did you start preparing for an exam? Check any of the following items that apply to you:

_____ At the beginning of a new unit of material, I would study my class notes nightly.

_____ I would start reviewing my notes and readings at least three or four days prior to the examination.

_____ I waited until the night before the exam.

_____ I only looked over my notes the morning of the exam.

_____ Generally speaking, I never did study for exams.

_____ Is there any other way to describe when you started to prepare for exams?

_____

_____

3. *Good results.* What test-preparation strategies have *worked well* for you in the past? Describe them below.

Study and taking notes, Study Guide

4. *Poor results.* What test-preparation strategies *did not work well* for you in the past? Describe them below.

not studying the few days before

5. *Best practice.* Based on your past test-taking success, which strategies do you believe will continue to work for you in school? Explain how you know this is a beneficial strategy.

Studying and taking notes before the test

6. *Questionable practice.* Based on your past test-taking success, which strategy or strategies will you need to *discontinue*? Explain how you know this is *not* a beneficial test-taking strategy.

Not studying, and not paying attention in class

ACTIVITY 10.3   CRITICALLY THINKING ABOUT YOUR TEST-PREPARATION SKILLS

Let's apply the critical thinking standards from Chapter 2 to examine *either* one of the best practices *or* one of the questionable practices you identified in Activity 10.2.

List the best or questionable practice here: ——————————————————

CRITICAL THINKING STANDARD	APPLICATION TO YOUR TESTING SKILLS	YOUR EXPLANATION HERE OR ON A SEPARATE PIECE OF PAPER
Clarity	*Clearly* state this particular testing practice.	
Accuracy	How do you know this assessment of your testing practice is *correct*?	
Precision	*Specifically* (give examples) explain this testing practice.	
Relevance	How is your assessment of this testing practice *connected* to your academic progress?	
Depth	Examine your identified testing practice beyond a superficial (simplistic) explanation and look at all of the *complexities* involved.	
Breadth	Examine your testing practice from more than one *perspective (point of view).*	
Logic	Based on your evidence does your conclusion about your testing practice *make sense?*	

Based on your answers above, what insights have you gained about your testing practice?

There not so bad, when you pay attention in class and study notes

What is the next step you will take to improve your testing skills?

Be prepared for the test

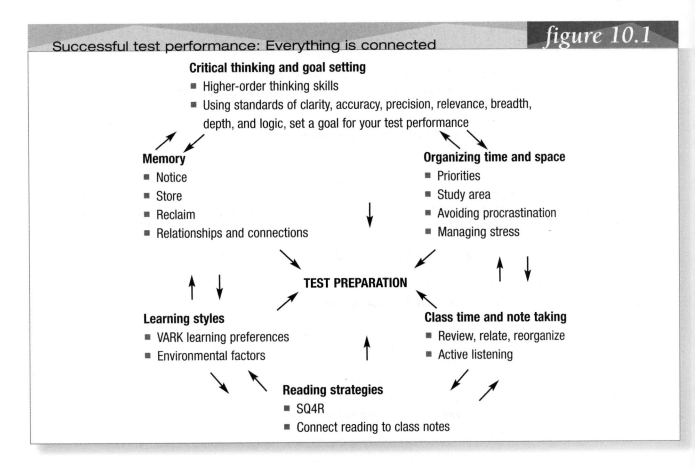

figure 10.1

Successful test performance: Everything is connected

Critical thinking and goal setting
- Higher-order thinking skills
- Using standards of clarity, accuracy, precision, relevance, breadth, depth, and logic, set a goal for your test performance

Memory
- Notice
- Store
- Reclaim
- Relationships and connections

Organizing time and space
- Priorities
- Study area
- Avoiding procrastination
- Managing stress

TEST PREPARATION

Learning styles
- VARK learning preferences
- Environmental factors

Class time and note taking
- Review, relate, reorganize
- Active listening

Reading strategies
- SQ4R
- Connect reading to class notes

Putting Your Study Skills to Work for You: Everything Is Connected

The chapters in this book emphasize the need to relate information. If you have diligently reviewed and practiced the study skill strategies found in these chapters, you probably have noticed that each step along the way prepares for the exam. The arrows in Figure 10.1 indicate the continuous and flowing nature of these strategies.

Let's examine how the study skills strategies you have learned are related—and how they connect to test preparation.*

Using these interconnected strategies will lead to test-taking success. If you can consciously tie all of the material together, you will see that test preparation is not a one-time event. Table 10.1 further explains and organizes the connections as it takes a closer look at how a few of the main points from previous chapters can be highlighted and connected to test-performance strategies.†

After reading the table, see whether you can identify any other strategies.

---

*We will be talking about test preparation for the classroom and teacher-made exams. Test preparation for exams such as the PSAT, SAT, ACT, or GRE involve other strategies that are not addressed here.

†You will note that the table is in the form of a data retrieval chart—a strategy introduced in the memory chapter (9).

table 10.1	Test-performance strategies: Building on previous skills and strategies

STUDY SKILL STRATEGY	APPLICATION TO SUCCESSFUL TEST-PERFORMANCE STRATEGIES
Critical thinking (Chapter 2)	Take time to analyze any test-taking difficulties you may have. Go beyond a superficial explanation; move into a deeper examination of the factors that have an impact on your test performance. ■ Use the standards of critical thinking to solve test-taking problems.
Problem solving (Chapter 2)	Using your critical thinking skills, can you propose a solution to improve your test performance? Review the following examples and examine Figure 10.2: ■ Using the information received from your review of previous exams, your instructor's input, and a tutor's opinion, you decide that you will begin a new studying program that will set aside time to visit your professor once a week with specific questions about new material covered in class. ■ You will consider working with a study group. ■ At the very least, you decide to write a TSD for each day's notes (refer to Chapter 7). This ten-minute exercise will be the beginning of a nightly review of your notes.
Creative thinking (Chapter 2)	Sometimes desperate measures require desperate actions. Maybe you feel that you have tried absolutely everything to turn around your test performance—but nothing seems to work. The frustration mounts. It's time for creative—outside-the-box, outside-the-lines, novel—thinking. For instance: ■ You recognize that you have not been exercising as you once did. You feel sluggish most of the time. Combining physical activity with intellectual stimulation, you decide to engage in a yoga class once a week. You believe yoga's meditative emphasis will help calm and focus your mind.
Attitude (Chapter 3)	When you examine why you have difficulty with tests (in general or in a particular course), do you use self-defeating words or positive words? ■ Self-defeating: *What should I expect? I never have done well on math exams. There is no reason to expect that will change this term. I'll hope for the best.* ■ Positive: *My experience with math has been a troubled one at best. I might not earn an A in this course, but I do know that by using the campus resources available to me I will do better this term than I have ever done before.*
Intrinsic and extrinsic motivators (Chapter 3)	Find a motivator that will help to move you through the test challenge you have been experiencing. Whether intrinsic or extrinsic, look for incentives that will prove motivating enough for you to meet and defeat your challenge. ■ Intrinsic: *I know what I need to do in order to achieve favorable test results. I've worked hard and owe it to myself to do the very best I can.* ■ Extrinsic: *Regardless of what I have done in the past, my financial aid depends on passing all my courses. Doing well on tests will not only prepare me for other course work but it will allow me to continue receiving the funding I need for school.*

(continued)

table 10.1 (Continued)

STUDY SKILL STRATEGY	APPLICATION TO SUCCESSFUL TEST-PERFORMANCE STRATEGIES
Review the review: Knowing the topic, summary, and details (TSDs) (Chapter 7)	The TSD strategy allows for nightly reflection on class work through a brief writing activity. Try the following: ■ Maintain an ongoing file of your TSDs. Perhaps creating a computer folder labeled "TSDs" will make it easier to organize and keep up with your daily reviews. Over the course of a unit's material, you will build a comprehensive study guide. Reviewing your TSDs will help prepare you for the coming exam.
Reading (Chapter 8)	Use the SQ4R strategy (survey, questions, read, recite, record, review) to make sense of your reading assignments—and to remember more of what you read. Remember: ■ Before reading, understand the purpose of the assignment—why you are reading it. ■ Take reading notes, review them, and use them with your class notes. ■ Build your vocabulary.
Learning styles (Chapter 5)	We all have unique ways to process information. Make sure you understand your learning preferences—and practice strategies to make your learning preferences work for you. ■ Review your VARK Questionnaire preferences. Use this information to prepare for exams. ■ Understand how you take in information effectively. ■ As best as you are able, create a study environment that complements your learning preference.
Memory (Chapter 9)	Remember the three components to an improved memory: Notice the material, store the material, and reclaim the material. Consider the following: ■ Use review time and organizational charts to help you make connections. ■ Understand why you forget and then review strategies to help you more effectively retrieve information.

TEST ANXIETY[2]

Anxiety is a general feeling of unease, uncertainty, anticipation, and even fear about an event. The resulting stress may be positive, helping you stay on your toes and perform well, or it may be so debilitating that it causes you to freeze up. As you read in Chapter 4, stress exists in two forms: positive stress and negative stress. Both physically arouse the body. Positive stress helps a person remain focused and move toward a goal. This may be similar to having "butterflies in your stomach," but your heightened sense of awareness allows you to perform at a higher level of competence. Negative stress goes beyond a few butterflies; you may actually feel as though a boulder is crushing your chest and breathing becomes difficult. The fight-or-flight response may be triggered.

---

[2]Piscitelli, 164–169.

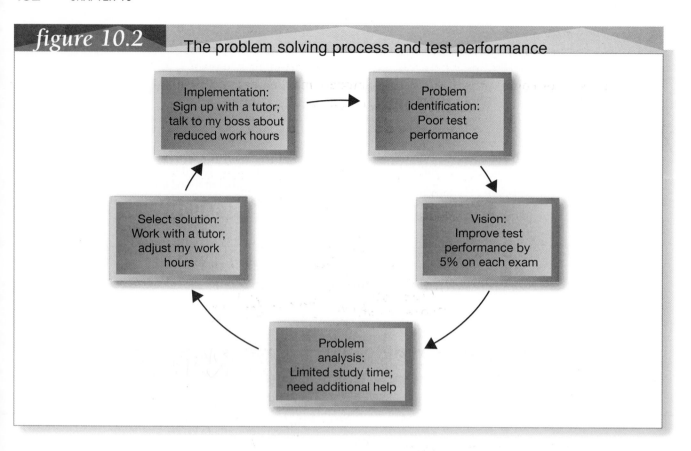

figure 10.2   The problem solving process and test performance

The same kinds of feelings can occur on test day, resulting in test anxiety. A reasonable amount of uncertainty is bound to be present in most students. They wish to perform well, score high, maintain a respectable GPA, and feel good about their efforts. Even when well prepared, there may still be nagging doubts: "Did I study the correct material?" "Maybe I should have looked at my notes one more time." "I wonder if a study group or a visit to the professor's office would have been helpful." "Maybe the instructor will be ill and the test canceled!" Whatever may have caused the anxiety, these students make their way to the class, complete the test successfully, and move on to the next unit of material.

Other students can become so paralyzed by thoughts of an examination that they make themselves ill with worry. One unsuccessful testing experience leads to another, which leads to another, and a self-fulfilling prophecy is born: "I never do well on tests!"

How Does Test Anxiety Happen?

One source maintains that "20 percent of U.S. college students experience symptoms of test anxiety and most athletes and artists experience performance anxiety at some point in their careers."[3] But why does this happen? Among the reasons are fear, feelings of inadequacy, and lack of preparation.

---

[3]From "Test and Performance Anxieties," Campus Blues, 2002–2004, www.campusblues.com/test.asp (accessed July 1, 2007). This article provides a breakdown of physical, emotional, behavioral, cognitive indicators of test anxiety.

- *Fear.* The consequences of the test or performance may be so great as to cause an unhealthy physical or emotional response. For instance, if one test result would determine whether you get into a particualr program (say, nursing or engineering), your level of anxiety may increase due to the fear of losing your dream. This form of high-stakes testing heightens your physical and emotional arousal.

- *Feelings of inadequacy.* You believe that no matter what you do, your lack of ability (perceived or real) will be the reason you cannot perform to an acceptable standard. This may be the case, for instance, when a student auditions for a play with a number of talented actors.

- *Lack of preparation.* The final exam is in one hour—and you have not read the assigned readings, not looked at your notes, nor reviewed the instructor-provided study guide. No wonder your blood pressure is elevated, your hands are sweating, and your mouth is a little dry!

Take a moment to complete Activities 10.4 and 10.5.

WHAT IS YOUR LEVEL OF TEST ANXIETY?   ACTIVITY **10.4**

How often do you experience test anxiety? For each of the following items, rate yourself on a scale from 0 (not at all) to 5 (all the time). Circle the numbers that most closely apply to you.

1. When you look back on your test performance this term (or over a number of years if you so desire), how often do you experience the following?

SYMPTOM	FREQUENCY (0 = NOT AT ALL, 5 = ALL THE TIME)
Headaches	0–1–2–3–4–5
Nausea	0–1–2–3–4–5
Vomiting	0–1–2–3–4–5
Diarrhea	0–1–2–3–4–5
Sweating	0–1–2–3–4–5
Increased heartbeat	0–1–2–3–4–5
Shortness of breath	0–1–2–3–4–5
Dizziness	0–1–2–3–4–5
Crying	0–1–2–3–4–5
My mind "goes blank"	0–1–2–3–4–5

2. Add your ratings and divide by 10. On a scale from 0 to 5, you have rated your level of test anxiety to be —————. (A score of 4 or higher indicates that testing situations create high levels of apprehension for you.)

(continued)

3. Reflect on your score in item 2. Why do you think you have come to respond to tests in the manner you do? What insights can you draw from this exercise?

I respond really well to tests if I
am prepared and ready

Identifying stressors is the first step in learning to overcome them. What are *your* sources of test anxiety?

1. Do you tend to be anxious about exams due to any of the following? Check all that apply to you.

    _____ Lack of appropriate effort on my part

    ___✓___ Lack of ability (course material beyond my capabilities)

    _____ Negative self-talk (convinced myself I would do poorly)

    ___✓___ Not studying

    ___✓___ Fear of how others may judge me

    ___✓___ Listening to classmates complain about the difficulty of exams

    ___✓___ Poor previous testing experiences

    _____ Panic brought on by timed situations

    ___✓___ Focusing on the effect the test grade would have on my GPA

    ___✓___ Comparing my performance to other students

    ___✓___ Pressuring myself to get nothing but an A

    _____ Other sources:

    _____

    _____

    _____

2. Share your answers with a classmate. Brainstorm ideas to lessen your test anxiety. Write your answers here.

    Be prepared and don't worry about
    anything except what concerns yourself

Test Anxiety or Inefficient Test-Taking Strategies?

Some students are not anxious about exams. They are prepared and comfortable on test day. But they still perform at a less than satisfactory level. One reason may be time—they usually run out of it. Effective test preparation can be hampered by inefficient behaviors during the test. If this is your problem, try the following test-taking strategies:

■ *Review the entire exam.* Before you begin writing your exam answers, review all items. Get a "feel" for the test. How long will you need to do page 1? Page 2? In other words, establish a pace for yourself. Use your SQ4R (Chapter 8) strategy here.

■ *Keep track of time.* Wear a watch.

■ *Do the easy items first.* If you do run out of time, you don't want to have missed the easy points. "Easy" in this case refers to content as well as item type. Obviously, make sure you answer all the questions you *know.* You may wish to do the types of questions you are most comfortable with before you tackle the more challenging ones. If matching is easy for you, do it first.

■ *Watch for trigger words.* Don't get an item wrong because you failed to see a trigger (important) word. Underline, circle and/or box key words. (See page 200 for examples of trigger words.)

■ *Block your test paper.* If your eyes tend to drift from one item to another during an exam, a blocking technique will help you focus. Using two blank pieces of paper cover the item above the problem you are working on with one piece and cover the succeeding item with the other. For example, if you are working on problem 3, "block out" problems 2 and 4. You force your eyes to focus on only one item.

■ *Remove yourself from distraction.* If possible, sit as far away from any distractions as you can. Get away from windows, open doors, noisy students, and the like. In large lecture halls this may be difficult, but your instructor may be able to suggest some alternatives.

■ *Become familiar with format.* Ask the instructor whether he or she has past exams to review. By becoming familiar with the teacher's particular format, you are also mastering the content.

■ *Consider tutoring.* If you have been diligent with your studies but still have difficulties with the subject matter, you may wish to seek help from the instructor or a student-tutor. Your academic adviser should have information on peer tutors.

■ *Know your material.* The more comfortable you become with the course content, the more confident you will be on the exam. Timely and organized studying (see Chapters 4, 6, and 7) will help you become comfortable, confident, and successful. Activity 10.6 will help you to look for instructor clues about important material.

■ *Find out whether "props" are allowed.* If you have a math test requiring many formulas, can you write the formulas on an index card and use it during the exam? How about your notes? Will the instructor allow their use during the exam?

■ *Ask your instructor about an alternative testing environment.* If distractions are really a problem, perhaps the instructor will allow you to complete the exam in the campus testing and assessment center. If you have a documented disability, the student services office may be able to assist with specific accommodations.

ACTIVITY 10.6   SEARCHING FOR TEST CLUES

Select one of your courses for this term, and complete this activity to help you determine potential exam questions.

Course Title: _____

Instructor: _____

1. *What kind of tests will your instructor use during this term?* Your instructor may present you with multiple-choice questions, fill-in-the-blank items, matching exercises, true-false statements, short-answer definitions, or lengthy essay exams. Some tests use a combination of these formats. What will your teacher use this term?

    All of these

2. *What does the instructor do in class to emphasize key points?* Does she write on the board, provide PowerPoint slides, or emphasize points with her voice?

    Yes

3. *Did the instructor provide a study guide?* Perhaps there is a study guide in your syllabus or maybe one was distributed at a study session.

    No

4. *Does your school provide supplemental instruction?** If so, where and when is it held?

    Yes

5. *Finally, you and a classmate may be able to find other clues to help you prepare for exams.* Keep searching; the clues are there—and they will help you be successful on your exam.

*More and more colleges provide some form of supplemental instruction (SI). It typically takes the form of an additional session per week in which the participating students use their notes and class discussions to better understand the course content and prepare for exams. See your instructor or learning resource center to find out whether such a program is available on your campus.

ACTIVITY 10.7   TEST-PREPARATION CHECKLIST (✓)

Select one of the courses you are taking this term, and complete the following checklist to evaluate your preparation for the next exam.

Class: English 101

Instructor: Mrs. Badgett

Test date, location, and time: whenever she tells us

(continued)

1. Type of exam:
   - ◉ Multiple-choice
   - ○ True-false
   - ○ Matching
   - ◉ Completion
   - ○ Identification
   - ◉ Essay
   - ○ Lab work
   - ◉ Problems
   - ○ Other _____

2. What I need when I study:
   - ◉ Textbook
   - ◉ Notes
   - ◉ Teacher's study guide
   - ◉ Worksheets
   - ○ Past exams (these can be very helpful)
   - ○ Supplemental readings
   - ○ Calculator
   - ◉ Pens, pencils, paper
   - ○ Other _____

3. Will I study alone or with a study group? ☑ Alone ❏ Study group

   (To get the most from a study group you may wish to set an agenda before the meeting.)

4. Will the teacher lead any study sessions before or after class? ☑ Yes ❏ No

   If "yes," when? _____

5. When will I study? Make a plan—and stick to it.

   Date/time: _____

   Date/time: _____

   Date/time: _____

   (Put these dates on your calendar.)

6. Prioritization: What topics will the exam cover?

TOPIC	I REALLY KNOW THIS STUFF	I AM NOT TOO SURE ABOUT THIS STUFF	I HAVE NO CLUE ABOUT THIS STUFF	TOPIC REVIEWED AT LEAST ONCE
1.	Commas			
2.	How to write a essay			
3.	Semi-Colons			
4.				

7. Predict some test questions. (Review Activity 10.6.)

(continued)

8. Things I need for test day:

- ◉ Pens, pencils, paper, bluebook
- ○ Calculator
- ◉ Notes (if I can use my notes during the test)
- ○ Textbook (if the test is open-book)
- ◉ Ruler
- ○ Wristwatch
- ○ Other _____

Test preparation does *not* end when you hand in your test. Start preparing for your next exam by doing a postexam analysis:

9. I was *most prepared* for ___Commas_____

10. I was *not well prepared* for ___Linker_____

   Why?_____

11. The biggest help was:

- ○ My notes
- ○ My homework
- ○ Tutoring sessions
- ○ My study schedule
- ○ My study group
- ○ My study environment
- ○ Meeting with my instructor outside of class
- ○ Other _____

12. My major weakness(es):

- ○ Ran out of time during the test
- ○ Did not expect this type of test
- ○ Studied the wrong material
- ○ Did not start studying early enough
- ○ Other _____

13. Grade I *realistically* expect to receive: _____ Grade I received: _____

14. My *realistic* plan to improve for the next exam:

_____

_____

Postexam Analysis

A common reaction by many students after an exam is to forget it and concentrate on the next opportunity. Although this is an understandable reaction, the successful student needs to pause, even if momentarily, and reflect on the exam.

Look at the checklist in Activity 10.7 once again. Notice that the last portion is a postexam analysis. This type of activity accomplishes a couple of things. While the material is still fresh in your mind, content review is critical. There is a good chance you will see some of this information again on a midterm or final examination. Make sure you have it correct now. Don't get it wrong again! It is important to understand what did and did not work for you. Use this time to identify your challenges and strengths. Set a goal for the next exam.

ADDITIONAL TEST-TAKING STRATEGIES

There are several types of exams—multiple-choice, true-false, matching, essay, and so forth—but no matter what type of test you are taking, some general suggestions apply.

General

- Get a good night's sleep prior to the exam. Do not study right up until bedtime. Give your brain a rest and do something nonacademic before going to bed. Otherwise, you might wake up feeling like you have not had a break. You want to be as sharp as possible going into the test.
- Depending on the time of the exam, eat a good breakfast or lunch, but don't overeat—this might leave you groggy. Some students do not ordinarily eat breakfast or lunch, and that works for them. Use strategies that fit your lifestyle, body requirements, and personality.
- Have all your tools with you (see Activity 10.7).
- Wear a watch or, at the very least, have the class clock in your sight. It is your responsibility, not the teacher's, to keep track of time. Be aware, though, that school-issued room clocks are notorious for being slow, fast, or broken.
- Read *all* instructions carefully. Do *not* start until you know what you are expected to do.
- Know your material. Don't just memorize it. More than likely, the wording on the exam will be different from what you found in your book or what the teacher said in class. That is why it is important to *know* your material. Review the strategies in Chapters 6, 7, 8, and 9.

Multiple-Choice Tests

- Read carefully. Look for words such as *not, except, which is incorrect, best, all, always, never, none.*
- Block all the answer choices before you look at them. Treat the item like a fill-in-the-blank question. Come up with an answer before you look at the choices. This might keep you from being swayed by a "close" answer.
- If you are not sure of an answer, use the process of elimination to arrive at the correct answer. At least you can narrow your options and make an educated guess.
- Answer the easy questions first; save the tough ones for the end.
- <u>Underline</u> key words.
- If you are using an answer sheet, make sure you transfer your answers to the correct number on the sheet.

Matching Tests

- Read all the answer choices first.
- Cross out the items you pick. (Some instructors do not want writing on the exam packet. If this is the case for an exam you are taking, make

cross-out marks lightly with your pencil so that you can erase them before you turn in your exam.)

- Find out whether you are allowed to use an answer more than once.
- Answer the easy items first; save the tough ones for the end.

Essay Tests

- Know what your task is. At the very least, know these key trigger words:

  analyze: to divide a topic or issue into its parts; to show the relation of one part to another

  apply: to use your knowledge in a new or different situation

  assess: to judge the merits of some issue; to evaluate

  classify: to put things into categories

  compare: to provide similarities, differences, consequences (see *analyze*)

  contrast: to provide differences

  criticize: to judge critically

  defend: to argue for a particular issue

  describe: to explain an event, issue, topic; to explain the main characteristics

  discuss: to explain in detail; to go beyond mere description

  evaluate: to judge, criticize, establish standards

  identify: to show how something is unique or individual

  illustrate: to provide examples

  interpret: to describe the meaning of an issue

  motivations: what caused something to happen

  relative importance: how two or more factors compare with one another

  summarize: to restate briefly

  trace: to provide an order or sequence of events

- Know what the essay topic is.
- Develop a main idea and follow it.
- Support your thesis with substantial facts; don't insult the teacher with "fluff."
- Pay attention to grammar and sentence structure.
- Never leave an essay item blank. Put something down—you might get credit.
- If you tend to get writer's block, practice the strategies introduced on the Companion Web site module for this book.

Finally, as you prepare for the exam, be kind to yourself. Don't say you are going to fail.

Emergency Studying

"Okay," you say. "Organization is great, but what do I do if I have not kept up? What do I do to survive a test when I'm down to the night before, and I'm not ready?" Here are some pointers for emergency studying. Please remember that this is not desirable, but if it's all you have, then let's get the most from it.

- *Do not . . .*

  - Be tempted to read quickly everything you have not read yet. If you read large quantities of knowledge too fast, you will have poor recall.
  - Panic. Okay, so you didn't study as you wish you had. Test day is no time to panic.
  - Give up—especially on essay exams. Never leave the item blank. Think. You surely can come up with something to write. You just may get credit.

- *Do . . .*

  - Accept the fact you will not be able to study everything.
  - Relax as best you can.
  - Start by anticipating your teacher. What type of questions will the teacher ask? What types of content and/or skills will be tested? Recall? Relationships? (This will be much easier if you have been practicing the 3Rs from Chapter 7.)
  - Go to your notes and text to find the most important material. Clues to guide you: chapter titles and subtitles, major emphasis in class discussions, and lectures, relationships with past material, chapter summaries. Use your SQ4R strategy (Chapter 8).
  - Follow these steps when you find important information:
    - Read it.
    - Ask yourself a question for which the information is an answer.
    - Say the information to yourself.
    - Check to see whether you were correct.
    - Do it until you get it correct twice.
    - Try to find and study some important information from every chapter that was assigned.

  Next time, plan ahead and establish a study schedule.

Test Performance and Academic Integrity[4]

Behaving with *integrity* means to conduct oneself in an honest, responsible, and respectful manner. When it comes to testing situations, this means doing and submitting your own work without any unauthorized assistance. Any violation on exams is broadly classified as cheating and will be punished according to specific guidelines laid out by the school. Unless approved by the instructor prior to the exam, the following examples can be considered violations of academic integrity during an exam:

- Copying from a classmate's paper
- Using "cheat sheets"
- Using class notes and/or the textbook and/or any other supplemental source

---

[4]Piscitelli, 178.

- Receiving assistance from or giving assistance to another student
- Accessing text messaging from a cell phone
- Listening to recorded material
- Using a laptop computer to access information
- Looking at or otherwise using stolen copies of exams

Colleges and universities publish academic integrity policies and consequences for violations of those policies. Schools expect that students be responsible for completing their work in an honest manner that is respectful of their fellow students and instructors.

CHAPTER SUMMARY

Effective test preparation starts at the completion of the most recent exam. Before leaving this chapter, keep the following points in mind:

- Whatever your background, you bring positive experiences and, perhaps, a few challenges to the table. Recognize and build upon these experiences.
- Test anxiety is common. Even when well prepared, you may still have doubts. Recognize them but don't let them paralyze you.
- Strategies introduced earlier in this book can be applied to address test performance challenges.
- Take time to analyze the reasons why you have difficulty with tests. Go beyond a superficial explanation; move into a deeper examination of the factors that have an impact on your test performance. Use the critical thinking standards introduced in Chapter 2.
- Effective test preparation can be hampered by inefficient actions during the test.

ACTIVITY 10.8   CHAPTER 10 MEASURABLE OBJECTIVES

At the beginning of this chapter, five measurable objectives were presented. They are reprinted below for your convenience. Based on the strategies you have learned in this chapter, fill in the lines beneath each item (or use a separate sheet of paper).

○ Identify at least two successful test-preparation strategies you have used within the last two months and continue to use them for your benefit.

    ○ List the strategies here:

      1. _____

      _____

      2. _____

      _____

○ Identify at least two reasons why you either *do* have test anxiety or do *not* have test anxiety.

    ○ List the two reasons here:

    1. _Nervos about what's on the test, don't Know what's on the test_

    2. _Didn't study the night before_

○ Explain how to apply at least one study skill strategy (introduced earlier in this book) to improve your test-taking skills.

    ○ Identify and explain the strategy here. _Studying_

○ Explain at least two clues an instructor can give about potential test items.

    ○ Explain the two clues here. _Study guide, chapter quizzes_

○ Apply the postexam analysis strategy to at least one of your most recent exams.

    ○ What insights did you get from using the postexam analysis strategy? _You feel more prepared for class_

REALITY CHECK

Using your critical thinking skills to improve your test-preparation and test-performance skills

Situation. You have been asked by the dean to be a guest speaker at the new student orientation for your college. The dean has heard good things about your academic performance and wants you to share your best practices with the first-year class. In particular, he would like for you to provide your best test-taking practices. He wants you to concentrate on three topics: test anxiety, test-preparation practices, and test-performance strategies.

Below, or on a separate piece of paper, explain what you consider to be the most important strategy for each topic. Briefly explain (perhaps with a personal example) how you have used the strategy to your benefit.

- Test anxiety—best practice for avoiding it and how you used it: _____

  Studying for the test or exam,
  Being prepared for the test

  _____

  _____

  _____

- Test preparation—best practice and how you used it: _____

  _____

  _____

  _____

  _____

- Test performance—best practice and how you used it: _____

  _____

  _____

  _____

  _____

  _____

CHAPTER 11

INFORMATION LITERACY

How can you use information and technology for your benefit?

SPOTLIGHT ON CLASSROOM SKILLS

Today's students are technologically savvy, especially the younger students who have grown up with computers, cell phones, the Internet, blogs, YouTube, and MySpace. Even older "nontraditional" students have become more at ease with technology. Whether because of work requirements or their own children, older adults have themselves stepped into the cybergeneration.

But college has put a few new twists and turns on the information highway. While I may know my way around a chat room, I need more for my classes. Professors throw around terms like databases, indexes, accuracy, bias, and online courses. I have a lot to learn!

Welcome to the information age. It can be daunting—but it can be exhilarating to have the world at your fingertips. This chapter will explore strategies that will help you efficiently and effectively locate, evaluate, and use this vast storehouse of information.

PREVIEW

By the time you finish reading this chapter and completing its activities, you will know how to:

- Explain the difference between databases, media, and visuals.
- Begin and complete a keyword search to find information.
- Use a search engine to locate information.
- Request a book through your college's interlibrary loan procedure.
- Explain how a Web site URL (address) can provide a clue about the nature of the site.
- Critically evaluate a source of information for accuracy, authority, objectivity, currency, and scope.

KEY TERMS

- Academic integrity
- Authority
- Ergonomics
- Information literacy
- Interlibrary loans
- Keyword search
- Reference librarian
- Repetitive stress injuries (RSI)
- Search engines
- Surfing the Web
- World Wide Web

CHAPTER INTRODUCTION[1]

Have you ever considered how much information is produced *worldwide* in one year? One study discovered the following intriguing facts:[2]

- "A half a million new libraries the size of the Library of Congress print collections" would be needed to hold *just* the new information produced in 2002. And the amount of information continues to increase each year.

- There is enough new information produced annually to create a thirty-foot-high pile of books for *each person* in the world.

- Ninety-two percent of this information is not in print form. Most of it can be found on hard disks. Paper only accounts for 0.01 percent of the new information.

- Even though paper accounts for a minimal amount of the stored information, it takes 786 million trees to produce the paper the world needs in *one year*. In the United States, that equates to almost twelve thousand sheets per person per year—or about thirty-two sheets of paper per person per day.

- The amount of information stored on disks, film, and paper *doubled* from 1999 to 2002. In less time than it would take a student to master course material for one undergraduate degree, the amount of available information worldwide increased by 100 percent!

Because there does not appear to be any slowdown in this phenomenal explosion of information, a number of challenges present themselves. For instance, just because information is increasing in *volume* does not mean that it is increasing in *quality*. How can you separate the credible from the absurd? Sometimes having too much information can be overwhelming. What should be done when you find hundreds—or thousands—of possible sources? How will you know which have the best information? Or, more practically, what is the most effective way to trim the vast numbers of sources to a workable few?

This chapter will explore strategies that will help you efficiently and effectively locate, evaluate, and use this vast storehouse of information.

© 2005 Stockdisc

---

[1]Most of the material in this chapter was previously published in Steve Piscitelli, *Rhythms of College Success: A Journey of Discovery, Change, and Mastery.* (Upper Saddle River, NJ: Pearson Prentice Hall, 2008.)

[2]Peter Lyman and Hal R. Varian (senior researchers), "How Much Information? 2003," School of Information and Management, University of California at Berkeley, 2003, 1–12.

REFLECTION ON YOUR CURRENT LEVEL OF INFORMATION LITERACY SKILLS

Before you answer the items below, reflect on your current level of information literacy skills. Think of how well (or poorly) you have used these skills in the past.

As with all of the reflective activities in this book, answer from your heart. This exercise is not meant for you to answer just like your classmates—or to match what you may think the instructor wants to see. Take your time to give a respectful and responsible general accounting of your experiences with information literacy skills. A truthful self-assessment now will help you build on skills you have while developing those you lack.

For the following items, circle the number that best describes your *typical* experience with information literacy skills. The key for the numbers is:

0 = never, 1 = almost never, 2 = occasionally, 3 = frequently,
    4 = almost always, 5 = always

When considering your past successes and challenges with information literacy, how often:

1. Did you understand what information you needed to locate to complete a project?

    0   1   2   3   4   5

2. Did you know where to look for information to complete your project?

    0   1   2   3   4   5

3. Did you evaluate information you found for accuracy?

    0   1   2   3   4   5

4. Were you able to find enough appropriate information to complete a project?

    0   1   2   3   4   5

5. Were you able to determine whether the information you found presented only one side of an issue?

    0   1   2   3   4   5

6. Were your projects completed responsibly and honestly—according to the standards of academic integrity?

    0   1   2   3   4   5

7. Did you protect (and not give out) your personal information on Web chat rooms or in blogs?

    0   1   2   3   4   5

8. Did you maintain your integrity or dignity in an e-mail?

    0   1   2   3   4   5

Add up your scores for items 1 through 8. Divide by 8. Write your answer here: _____

(continued)

Using the key explanations above for each number (0, 1, 2, 3, 4, 5) complete this sentence: When it comes to information literacy, I _____ use information and technology in an effective manner.

Based on your answers, what insights do you have about your experiences with information literacy? _____

_____

_____

What Is Information Literacy?

As noted in the chapter introduction, the amount of available information has exploded—and all indications point to the explosion continuing well into the future. Not only is there an abundance of information, but there are a variety of locations in which to find the information. Libraries, blogs, commercial Web sites, government publications, service organizations, political action committees, and professional organizations are but a few of the disseminators of information.

This complex informational system creates challenges. If you were looking for information and did not care about its quality but only wanted to find something *fast*, a dizzying array of information is quickly available with a few clicks of a computer mouse. But ease does not always equate with quality. The key is to know not just *where* to look for information, but also *how* to separate the good from the bad, the informative from the misleading. An information literate person can "recognize when information is needed and [has] the ability to locate, evaluate, and use effectively the needed information."[3] These four facets

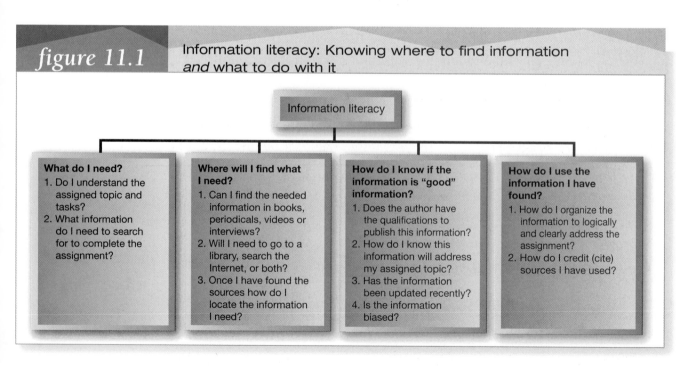

figure 11.1   Information literacy: Knowing where to find information *and* what to do with it

Information literacy

What do I need?
1. Do I understand the assigned topic and tasks?
2. What information do I need to search for to complete the assignment?

Where will I find what I need?
1. Can I find the needed information in books, periodicals, videos or interviews?
2. Will I need to go to a library, search the Internet, or both?
3. Once I have found the sources how do I locate the information I need?

How do I know if the information is "good" information?
1. Does the author have the qualifications to publish this information?
2. How do I know this information will address my assigned topic?
3. Has the information been updated recently?
4. Is the information biased?

How do I use the information I have found?
1. How do I organize the information to logically and clearly address the assignment?
2. How do I credit (cite) sources I have used?

[3]Association of College and Research Libraries (a division of the American Library Association), "Information Literacy Competency Standards for Higher Education," 2006, www.ala.org/ala/acrl/acrlstandards/informationliteracycompetency.htm#ildef (accessed July 1, 2007).

of information literacy—knowing what information you need, where to find it, how to evaluate it, and how to use it properly—are discussed in Figure 11.1.

While the thought of information literacy may be intimidating at first glance, consider that you have been doing this sort of thing for years. When you sought information about a computer or a car, when you prepared a report for a class or your boss, and when you analyzed information about a political issue, you were using information literacy skills. Activity 11.2 asks you to use the information literacy skills you currently have.

BUILDING ON YOUR INFORMATION LITERACY SKILLS   **ACTIVITY 11.2**

Think of a time when you bought a piece of technology. It might have been a cell phone, a television, a laptop computer, or perhaps a personal portable digital audio player. For the purposes of this exercise, let's assume you want to purchase a cell phone. You would like one that provides reliable service for a reasonable price, but you are confused as to which phone represents the best purchase. Applying the four basic facets of information literacy, answer the following questions:

1. What information do you need to know before you can buy a cell phone?

   _____

   _____

2. How will you find the information you need?

   _____

   _____

3. How will you evaluate the information you found? That is, how will you know a "reliable and reasonably priced product" when you see it?

   _____

   _____

4. Once you have evaluated all of the literature about cell phones, how will you use the information?

   _____

   _____

There Is More Than One Type of Information

Whether you are searching for a new cell phone or researching a term paper, you will be able to unearth a variety of pertinent sources. Information formats include visuals, print or electronic media, and databases.[4]

- *Visuals.* These are photos and illustrations including graphs, charts, tables, and maps (see Chapter 8). Visuals will not only help you understand the

---

[4]From Michael B. Eisenberg, Carrie A. Lowe, and Kathleen L. Spitzer, *Information Literacy: Essential Skills for the Information Age*, 2nd ed. (Westport, CT: Libraries Unlimited, 2004), 7–11.

material but may also suggest a way for you to effectively present your information in a term paper. Visuals can be found in books, periodicals, advertisement brochures, or on Internet sites.

- *Example:* Maps comparing nationwide cell phone coverage may provide information that is the deciding factor determining which phone to purchase.

- *Media.* Electronic media include video clips (on tape or DVD) and CD recordings, which present information in visual and/or oral format. Print media that can provide information about the topic you are researching include books, magazines, journal articles, and newspapers.

  - *Example:* An article in a magazine such as *Consumer Reports* will provide lab-tested reliability results. You might even find an article that compares cost of cell phones and cost of phone service.

  - *Example:* If one of the requirements for a term paper is to use a non-print source, the library's video collection may hold the film or documentary that you need.

- *Databases.* These hold a great deal of information in computer-based indexes. You can find periodicals (newspapers, journals, magazines, research abstracts) in databases. Because some may require a password to enter, ask the reference librarian for assistance. The wealth of information found in a database has typically been professionally reviewed. Whether evaluated by an editor or a professional reviewer, these articles carry more credibility than information simply posted to the Internet by individuals without a review process. If your professor has required that you use an Internet source, make sure that a database will meet that requirement.

  - *Example:* Perhaps an English assignment requires you to find and compare literary reviews of a novel. Your library's collection of *Book Review Digest* will provide that information. Depending on the library, this resource could be found in book-bound form or in an electronic database.

ACTIVITY 11.3 CRITICALLY THINKING ABOUT YOUR INFORMATION LITERACY SKILLS

Let's apply the critical thinking standards from Chapter 2 to your ability to find, evaluate and use information. Pick one area of information literacy that is a challenge for you. Activities 11.1 and 11.2 may be helpful for this activity.

List your information literacy challenge here: _____

Based on your answers, what insights have you gained about your information literacy challenge?_____

_____

What is the next step you will take to improve your information literacy skills? _____

_____

_____

(continued)

CRITICAL THINKING STANDARD	APPLICATION TO YOUR INFORMATION LITERACY SKILLS	YOUR EXPLANATION HERE OR ON A SEPARATE PIECE OF PAPER
Clarity	*Clearly* state your challenge with information literacy.	
Accuracy	How do you know this assessment of your information literacy skills is *correct*?	
Precision	*Specifically* (give examples) explain your information literacy challenge.	
Relevance	How is your assessment of this information literacy challenge *connected* to your academic progress?	
Depth	Examine your information literacy challenge beyond a superficial (simplistic) explanation and look at all of the *complexities* involved.	
Breadth	Examine your information literacy from more than one *perspective (point of view)*.	
Logic	Based on your evidence do your conclusions above *make sense*?	

FOUR STEPS TO COMPLETING AN ASSIGNMENT IN AN INFORMATION-LITERATE MANNER

In its simplest form, information literacy involves four steps, as mentioned earlier in this chapter:

1. *Knowing what information is needed.* This requires reflection before starting your search.
2. *Accessing the needed information.* This requires time to responsibly seek out pertinent information.
3. *Evaluating the information that is located.* This requires responsible action to judge the effectiveness of the information found.
4. *Using the information that has been found and evaluated.* This requires time to reflect on the appropriate use of the information retrieved.

Each step builds upon the previous step. Miss one step, and the information gathered can be seriously flawed.

Step 1: Know What Information Is Needed

Knowing what information is needed is a basic but often rushed step. Before digging through the library or surfing the Internet, be sure you understand what to look for. Take, for example, the following assignment, which could be found in a history class:

> One of the requirements is to write a ten-page paper identifying and explaining five major consequences of World War II. The sources you use must include at least five books, three periodicals and two nonprint sources. The paper is due two weeks before the final exam. The paper will be worth 25 percent of the final course grade.

By asking yourself a few simple questions, the nature of the assignment becomes clearer:

- What do I need to do?
  - *Write a 10-page paper*
- What is the topic?
  - *Identify and explain five consequences of World War II*
- What types of source material must be used?
  - *At least five books*
  - *At least three periodicals*
  - *At least two nonprint sources*
- When is the paper due?
  - *Two weeks before the end of the term* (You can enter this on your calendar; see Chapter 4.)
- How much is this assignment worth?
  - *25 percent of the final course grade* (In other words, this is a *major* part of your grade for the entire term.)

ACTIVITY 11.4   PRACTICAL APPLICATION: WHAT'S THE ASSIGNMENT?

Using an assignment from another class, answer the following questions. These initial steps require a relatively small investment of time and energy and will help maximize your efforts to efficiently find appropriate source material.

1. What is the *exact* wording of the instructor's assignment? Write that here and then highlight the key words in the assignment.

   _____

   _____

2. What task(s) do you have to complete? Is there a required length and format specified?

   _____

   _____

(continued)

3. What is the exact topic? Can you state specifically what you need to write or speak about? This is *critical,* as it will guide you in the step of finding the needed information.

   _____

   _____

4. What types of sources are specifically called for? Are you required to use class notes, the textbook, databases, the Internet, or other sources?

   _____

   _____

5. When is the paper due? How much time do you have to complete this assignment? (Put it on your personal planning calendar.) _____

6. How much is the assignment worth? Is this a major portion of your grade for the course? _____

Step 2: Access the Information

Once you know what topic you will research, the time has arrived to find pertinent information. One question guides this part of the process: Where can you locate the source material?

- *Taking a trip to the library: The traditional human-touch method.* Ease and accessibility make the Internet a remarkable tool. It can be accessed from virtually anywhere, and it connects to millions of sites. There may be times, however, when you need to or wish to do it the traditional and time-tested way—by walking into a library and using the reference material there. Once you enter your campus (or community) library, you will find the following:
  - *Online catalogs.* The card catalog is a thing of the past. Most libraries now have electronic catalogs of their holdings—often called OPAC (online public access catalog) or WebPAC. These can be accessed in much the same manner as when you use a search engine; Boolean searches will work here. (Boolean logic will be covered more fully a little later in the chapter, in the discussion of keyword searches.) Once you find the call numbers you can physically examine the books, photos, charts, and videos on the library shelves.
  - *Reserve.* This material is usually held on a shelf behind the circulation desk. This is where an instructor might place a copy of an article he wants the class to read.
  - *Reference librarian.* Sometimes nothing can replace real human contact. The reference librarian will help you navigate the library's holdings. If you are having a difficult time getting started—knowing what keywords to use, for instance—this person will be ready to introduce you to various search strategies and direct you to the most appropriate databases.
  - *Interlibrary loans.* Perhaps you have found a book that would be a perfect source for your term paper—but it is in a university library on the other side of the state or nation. Librarians can arrange for the

© Elisam—Fotolia.com

book to be sent to your campus library. Once your request is received by the library, the interlibrary loan will arrive on your campus within a matter of days.

- *Databases, indexes, and e-books.* Databases hold a large amount of material. Libraries typically subscribe to a number of these. Usually, a password is required to access a library's database. Once again, the reference librarian will prove invaluable by helping you obtain the password and also recommending the best databases to use based on your topic.

- *Taking a trip on the World Wide Web: The modern high-tech method.* Perhaps you are a bibliophobe* and the thought of searching through endless stacks of books brings perspiration to your brow. Twenty years ago you would have been out of luck. Either you used the library or you depended on your personal collection of books. If all you had was an ancient encyclopedia set and you did not wish to go to the library, you were doomed! Today you have the option of being able to search a collection that is far more immense than any single library. The World Wide Web provides an entry point to a vast array of books, articles, nonprint sources, and personal communications that until recently were considered out of the reach of the common person. When accessed effectively, this information brings power to the hands of the users; unfocused use of this vast storehouse, however, results in a huge waste of time.

  - *Knowing how and why to use the Internet.* Some have labeled the Internet as "the most important technology innovation of our generation."[5] Once connected to the Internet, your computer can access the

---

*One who fears books.

[5]"Internet," NetLingo the Internet Dictionary, www.netlingo.com/lookup.cfm?term=Internet (accessed July 1, 2007).

World Wide Web (the *www.* found in most Internet addresses is the accepted abbreviation). The amount of information is virtually endless. You could "surf the Web" for hours, days, or even months and not exhaust the information available. Therein lays a potential calamity for the uninformed or unfocused user.

"Surfing the Web", in its popular usage, has come to describe an aimless ride through cyberspace, following one link to another without much thought or direction. Although this can be entertaining, it does not help a college student who has four or five classes and a like number of research papers to complete in a short time. Time becomes a critical resource that must be managed carefully. Step 1—knowing what information is needed—helps limit wasted time. You can then effectively use the Internet rather than drifting from link to link.

Not all information on the Internet is created equally. Some Web sites provide expert and scholarly analysis, while others post inflammatory personal opinions with little substance. Other sites promote particular products, services, or causes. In short, the casual user will encounter various types of Web sites.[6] At the very least, be aware of what the sites represent and how their information will affect your research. (Step 3 will provide more on evaluating information.)

A Web site address (also called a *URL,* the acronym for "uniform resource locator") will usually end with *.com, .net, .gov, .org,* or *.edu.* This suffix can indicate whether the site is trying to peddle a product or service (*.com* or *.net*), advance the cause of an organization (*.org*), provide information from government agencies (*.gov*), or present information from an educational institution (*.edu*). While this description is an oversimplification, paying attention to the end of the address will provide a clue about the objectivity of a site.

WEB ADDRESSES   ACTIVITY **11.5**

Using a search engine (Google, for instance), type in the following address suffixes one at a time and hit the Enter key.

1. Type *.com.* Explore a few of the links that appear. Do you find any similarities between sites that end with *.com?*

_____

_____

_____

2. Type *.net.* Explore a few of the links that appear. Do you find any similarities between sites that end with *.net?*

_____

_____

(continued)

[6]See Ann Marlow Riedling, *Learning to Learn: A Guide to Becoming Information Literate* (New York: Neal-Schuman, 2002), 72.

3. Type *.org*. Explore a few of the links that appear. Do you find any similarities between sites that end with *.org?*

_____

_____

_____

4. Type *.edu*. Explore a few of the links that appear. Do you find any similarities between sites that end with *.edu?*

_____

_____

_____

In recent years, the Web has seen an explosion of Web log sites known as *blogs*. In some cases, these sites may be used internally by an organization to distribute information and generate discussion. More often, a blog will contain personal opinions by anyone who wishes to have his or her opinion on the Web.[7] Approach the information on such sites with a "user beware" mind-set. Traditional publishing (especially scholarly journals, books, and textbooks) requires that other professionals in the field review a manuscript for credibility and accuracy. There is no such requirement for a blog. A blogger can immediately post any material that he or she wishes.

■ *Using search engines.* Literally billions of pages of information can be found using the Internet. How can you sift through that much information? How can anyone find anything in such a cyber pile of material? Without a method or effective strategy to help your search, this could take the better part of your college career to complete.

Search engines provide that strategy. They may be used for on-campus collections found in the library, or they can be found on the Internet to assist in gathering pertinent information from the many databases on the World Wide Web. Search engines speed the search process by allowing you to instantaneously find material that is related to the area of your research.

The Internet offers a variety of search engines. You possibly have already used some of the following:

www.google.com
www.yahoo.com
www.altavista.com
www.dogpile.com
www.lycos.com
www.ask.com

Once you arrive at the home page of a search engine, it will be beneficial to look for a "Help" link that will explain how to navigate the site.

---

[7]See "Global Availability of MSN Messenger and MSN Spaces Connects People Around the World," Microsoft PressPass, www.microsoft.com/presspass/press/2005/apr05/04-07Global MessengerSpacesPR.mspx (accessed July 1, 2007).

table 11.1	Locating help with a search engine
SEARCH ENGINE NAME	**INFORMATION ABOUT THE ENGINE'S "HELP" FEATURE***
www.google.com	On the home page click "About Google." The next page will provide links with information about different search features for this engine.
www.yahoo.com	Click "Help" on the home page (look toward the bottom of the page). The next page provides a list of more specific links to help with searching this engine.
www.altavista.com	On the home page click "Help." On the next page click "Search." The next page will provide links on how to search as well as information about the features of this engine.
www.dogpile.com	On the home page click on "Tools and Tips." The next page will have a list of links to help you search effectively.
www.lycos.com	A "Help" link is located at the bottom of the home page.
www.ask.com	Click "About" on the home page. On the next page you will find information on how to conduct a search.

*All sites accessed on May 29, 2007.

Each search engine has its benefits and liabilities—and each will have its own quirks and operating features. Table 11.1 indicates where you will find the "Help" link on each of the sites.

Just like people, search engines have their unique appearances. Some open with a page full of columns, colors, and information. Others prefer a more minimalist approach, showing a few basic links on the home page. Which is best will depend on your personal preferences. Do you like a site that looks clean and neat but requires you to dig down a few "layers" by clicking through one, two, or three pages to get what you want? Or would you prefer a site that provides a lot of information with a variety of links right on the home page? Some sites you will find very easy to navigate; others will appear to be a maze of sensory overload. Besides the look of the site, you will come to prefer a site based on the good fortune you experience each time you search for information.

One cautionary note: While these search engines provide a wonderfully useful resource, remember that using databases (discussed above) may actually save you time. Once you find information through a search engine, you have to determine accuracy. Databases tend to control for accuracy with peer reviews and the like.

- *Conducting keyword searches.* You may turn to your campus library or conduct an Internet search from your personal computer to find information. One of two things usually happens: Either you find very few sources, or you quickly turn up hundreds—if not thousands. In the first instance you may be frustrated by the lack of pertinent material. The other scenario provides so much information that you become overwhelmed by the sheer volume.

Exploring the holdings of your campus library or the Internet can be maximized with a keyword search, using a word or phrase to help you find material on your topic. It can uncover books, periodicals, and nonprint materials. (*Note:* Capitalization is not required for such a search.)

For example, let's say you type in *consequences of world war II* for a keyword search—and your search turns up *zero* possible sources. At this point you might narrow your search by typing in *cold war.* This time your search of the campus library catalog turns up sixty-nine "hits," which include information in all formats.[8] This means that this particular library collection holds sixty-nine sources in either print or nonprint format. The point is that with a more refined search (more precise wording) the number of hits you get may increase.

A few simple strategies will allow you to narrow or broaden your computer searches. These will work on a campus library system or on the World Wide Web.

One such strategy is known as *Boolean logic,* by which you can either broaden or narrow your search using one of three words: *AND, OR,* or *NOT.*[9] (Some search engines or databases require that these connector words be typed in uppercase letters.) Using *OR* will expand your search to turn up as many hits as possible. On the other hand, the connector words *NOT* and *AND* will limit the number of hits received on a topic; they are valuable to use if your initial keyword search turned up more sources than you wanted.

- *Example:* Going back to our example, typing *cold war AND united states* will reduce the sixty-nine sources to forty-five. Only those sources that contain all of the keywords will be listed.

- *Example:* Typing *cold war NOT soviet union* will help you locate source material that has "cold war" in the title but not "soviet union." This tool could help eliminate material you will not need for your paper. (*Note:* Some search systems may use the symbols "+" or "−" to do the same as *AND* or *NOT.*)

The use of quotation marks (" ") is another strategy that may help limit your search to just those words and just in that order.

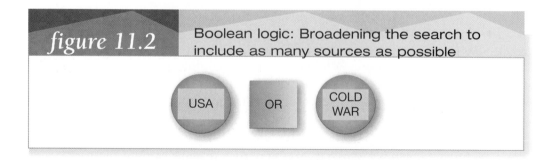

figure 11.2   Boolean logic: Broadening the search to include as many sources as possible

USA   OR   COLD WAR

---

[8]This example used the Florida Community College at Jacksonville library catalog (LINCC), www.fccj.org/library/ (accessed December 4, 2005).

[9]Riedling, *Learning to Learn,* 28–32.

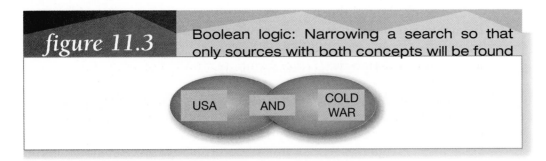

figure 11.3 Boolean logic: Narrowing a search so that only sources with both concepts will be found

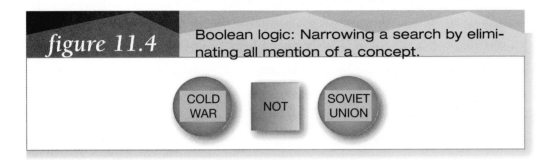

figure 11.4 Boolean logic: Narrowing a search by eliminating all mention of a concept.

For instance, if you conducted a keyword search using *consequences of world war II,* your hit list would include all source material that contains any of those words. But if you were to place quotation marks around the words ("*consequences of World War II*"), your search will uncover only sources with those words in that exact order.

- *Example:* Typing *consequences of World War II* into one Internet search engine yielded more than two *million* hits. Placing quotation marks around the words limited the results to less than sixteen *thousand.* Now, that is still a considerable number (and would need to be further limited), but it does graphically show the value of limiting a search with the use of quotation marks.

  There is a downside, however, to any keyword search: If your keywords are not broad enough, you may miss a significant portion of information. To compensate, you may wish to look for additional subject headings. (These can be found in the library's online catalog.) For instance, other subject headings that may relate to the topic of the Cold War include *nuclear weapons, foreign relations—Soviet Union, world politics—1945 to 1989, Cuban Missile Crisis,* or *diplomatic history.* Be aware of your many options. Your reference librarian can help.

  Keywords also can help you locate images and photos online with a click of your mouse. For instance, when you arrive on the Google home page,[10] click on the "Images" link. Then type in the term or name you wish to search for.

---

[10]For an interesting article providing ten search tricks on Google, see Peter Grad, "Rev Up Your Engine," NorthJersey.com, December 3, 2005. www.mtsu.edu/~studskl/pcguy.pdf (accessed July 1, 2007).

- *Example:* Go to the Google image search page and type in *cold war* (including the quotation marks). How many images are available?

- *A second example:* Type in a name—yours, a friend's, a family member's, or a celebrity's. What do you locate?

ACTIVITY 11.6   KEYWORDS AND SEARCH ENGINES

In Activity 11.4 you performed step 1 of information literacy, determining what information you need to find. This activity gives you practice in step 2, accessing that information.

1. Return to Activity 11.4. List five keywords that might help you find information about the topic of your assignment.

   _____

   _____

   _____

   _____

   _____

2. Choose two of the search engines mentioned in Table 11.1. Once you reach the home page for each, type in a keyword. Answer the questions below for each search engine used.

   a. Name of search engine: _____

       Once you typed in the search phrase, how many "hits" appeared?_____

       How easy or difficult was it to navigate this search engine? _____

       _____

       What kind of information did the initial hits page provide to you *and* how helpful would this information be in guiding your search? _____

       _____

       _____

   b. Name of search engine: _____

       Once you typed in the search phrase, how many hits appeared? _____

       How easy or difficult was it to navigate this search engine? _____

       _____

       What kind of information did the initial hits page provide to you *and* how helpful would this information be in guiding your search? _____

       _____

       _____

3. Finally, of the two search engines used, which one did you find to be the more beneficial? Why?

   _____

   _____

Step 3: Evaluate the Information

Once you locate information on the Internet, a natural tendency is to use it immediately. After all, wasn't that the purpose of the search in the first place? Yes, it was—but another step remains: evaluating the information. How do you know if the information is credible? On the Internet, there is no guarantee of a "consistent and reliable" peer review process.[11]

When evaluating information, consider these four criteria:[12]

1. *Accuracy and authority.* Is the site precise and expert? What experience (credentials) does the author have? Is there a sponsoring site or organization?

2. *Objectivity.* Is the site evenhanded and impartial? Is the material factual, unbiased, and in-depth? Is the coverage balanced? Is the site one of advertisements, or is it scholarly?

3. *Currency.* Is the site up to date and current? Is there a copyright date? (This indicates *ownership*; it does not indicate credibility or accuracy.) Are there references (bibliography and footnotes if appropriate)? Has the site been recently updated, or is the information old?

4. *Scope.* Is the range of coverage small or vast? What is the "breadth and depth" of the site? That is, does it provide an in-depth review of the topic, or is it a superficial overview with broad, general statements?

EVALUATING A WEB SITE: INTERNET CAREER SITE REPORT   ACTIVITY 11.7

The Internet provides a wealth of great information. But some sites are not very accurate or credible. This short activity will help you review the Internet with a critical eye, incorporating the four criteria of accuracy, objectivity, currency, and scope. Please find an Internet site that addresses a career area that interests you and then answer the following questions:

1. What is the common name of the site? (This is usually found on the home page of the site.)

   _____

2. What is the *exact* URL? This is the address (location) of the site. It will typically begin with *http://* or *http://www.* (*Note:* When entering a URL be sure to type it *exactly.* If only one character is incorrect, the site cannot be located.)

   _____

3. What is the career that the site addresses? List three things the site presents about this career.

   _____

   _____

   _____

(continued)

---

[11]Riedling, *Learning to Learn,* 61.

[12]Riedling, *Learning to Learn,* 62. These are basic criteria that most information literacy resources list.

4. *Accuracy and authority:* Can you rely on the information you find on this site?

   a. Who is the author of the site?

   _____

   b. What evidence exists that the author is qualified to publish this material?

   _____

   _____

   c. What are the credentials of the author? Include any affiliations (e.g., university professor, government agency). If none are listed, state that.

   _____

   _____

   d. What is your opinion of the credentials of this author? Why do you, or don't you, trust this site?

   _____

   _____

   _____

5. *Currency:* Is the site current? When was it last updated?_____

6. *Scope:* Explore some of the links of this site. A link takes you immediately to another page (or another place on the same page) when you click your mouse on it. What types of links exist?

   _____

   _____

   _____

7. *Objectivity:* Specifically discuss one of these links. Is the information biased or slanted in any way?

   _____

   _____

   _____

   _____

8. Would you recommend this site to other students with the same career interest? Why or why not?

   _____

   _____

9. Briefly summarize what you learned from this site. Are you still interested in this career? Why or why not?

   _____

   _____

   _____

   _____

(continued)

10. What other questions do you still have about this career? Who could help
    you with these questions?

_____

_____

_____

Step 4: Use the Information

Information is power. As with any form of power, though, information must
be used responsibly—and it must be conveyed in a clear and convincing manner. Whether you deliver a classroom presentation, write an analysis of a
current event, or describe the features of a new video game, what and how you
communicate the information will have an impact on how it is received.

Consider the history term paper described earlier in the chapter. Let's
assume you completed that paper as an actual assignment. You put in a number of hours figuring out exactly what you were going to research; you found
appropriate information in the library, on the Internet, or both; and then you
determined what information was suitable for your final product. At this point,
keep one question in mind: Do you want to waste all of that hard and worthwhile work with a hastily crafted paper that looks like it was thrown together
in the wee hours of the morning?

The presentation—how you use your information—is critical. No matter
how much you may know, if it is not clearly and thoroughly presented its impact
will be minimal. Let's review some basic steps for organizing and presenting your
hard work. (See the textbook's Companion Web site for more detail.)

- Provide the final product in the form required by the assignment: length
  of the paper, cover page, illustrations, bibliography, and so forth.

- Ask someone you respect to critically review your paper, evaluating
  the organization of the presentation as well as grammar and
  mechanics.

- Before you turn in your final product, be sure that what you have written
  reflects what was asked for by the instructor.

RESPONSIBILITIES OF THE INFORMATION AGE

Academic Integrity

When students or professors exhibit academic integrity, they have completed
their research and writing in a respectful, responsible, and honest fashion.
Violations of academic integrity are not new. Ever since there have been
schools, there have been students looking for shortcuts to complete assignments or exams. Plagiarizing papers, cheating on exams, and copying
homework were not created by today's students. If anything is "new" it is,
perhaps, the technological methods that make plagiarizing easier. Whether it
is copying material from a Web site and directly pasting it into a student paper
(without proper citation), or buying a paper from any of the various "dot-com
paper mills" on the Internet, cheating has moved to cyberspace. (See the textbook's Companion Web site for more information.)

And more colleges and universities are rising to the challenge. At the very least, violations of academic integrity typically result in a failure for the particular assignment. But the punishments can, and do, become more severe. Students can fail a course, be suspended for a term, or be expelled from school. Some schools have created a new grade that reflects failure due to violation of academic integrity.

ACTIVITY 11.8   YOUR SCHOOL'S ACADEMIC INTEGRITY POLICY

1. Locate and read your school's academic integrity policy. What are the possible punishments a student can receive for violating the academic integrity policy?

   _____

   _____

   _____

E-Mail Responsibilities

E-mail has revolutionized communication. As long as there is an Internet connection, one person can instantaneously contact another on any continent. Information can be rapidly accessed and just as quickly passed along to another location. E-mail communication is quick, paperless, and free.[†] It is also faceless and open to abuse. Therefore, remember to observe e-mail *netiquette* (the rules of behavior for using the Internet). Table 11.2 provides a brief list of e-mail do's and don'ts that the information literate person observes.

Avoiding Repetitive Strain Injuries

In addition to being responsible for the academic integrity of your work, take time to be responsible for the health and condition of your body. Although hours sitting at the computer workstation may not appear to be demanding, they can have a debilitating effect on your body.

Repetitive strain injuries (RSI)—also called *repetitive stress injuries*—commonly occur to people who spend long hours typing at a keyboard and staring into a computer monitor. As the name implies, the injury results from repetitive (continual) motions or actions. Typing at a keyboard for a prolonged period, for instance, has been cited as a cause for carpal tunnel syndrome (CTS). The repeated keystroke activity can lead to a swelling of the thumbs and wrists if care is not taken. Various sources provide a checklist of activities that can be

---

[†]At the writing of this book, e-mails can still be sent without having to pay postage or some type of access fee (not counting the cost of an Internet service provider). There have been limited conversations about the possibility of charging for e-mails, mainly in conjunction with ideas on how to limit *spam* (unwanted e-mail solicitations and correspondence).

table 11.2	Cyberspace do's and don'ts

CYBERSPACE DO'S	CYBERSPACE DON'TS
Do adhere to rules of grammar, punctuation, and capitalization in all e-mails. An e-mail represents you in cyberspace.	Don't type in all capital letters (the equivalent of SHOUTING!).
Do be courteous.	Don't send inflammatory notes.
Do respect the privacy of your e-mail recipients. If you use a distribution list, put the names in the "blind copy" (bcc) space when composing your e-mail. Everyone will receive the e-mail but no one's e-mail address will be displayed for others to see and use.	Don't abuse distribution lists and don't send spam. You may think the latest joke or inspirational story is great, but the fifty people in your address book may not have the same taste. You could also be sending someone a computer virus.
Do protect your own privacy. The Internet is a wonderful tool but it also attracts its share of predators. Be ever vigilant.	Don't give out private information in cyber chat rooms or on cyber bulletin boards. This includes address, phone, photos, and other identifying characteristics.
Do maintain the highest level of academic integrity.	Don't compromise your dignity or integrity (part 1).
Do choose an e-mail address or screen name that portrays a respectful self-image. What you think is a cute e-mail or screen name may be perceived in a negative way: "foxylady," "spoiledrotten," "studpuppy," and "Uwannabeme" may sound creative and adorable, but they do not impart the image of a serious student—or potential employee.	Don't compromise your dignity or integrity (part 2).
Do use clear language. Judiciously use emoticons* to indicate the emotion behind a statement if the wording is not clear. (Better still, if the wording is not clear, rewrite or eliminate the passage altogether.)	Don't be sarcastic. Because the facial expressions behind the e-mail cannot be seen, your words must speak for themselves.

*An *emoticon* uses the computer keyboard characters to represent an emotion. For instance, a smiley face can be depicted as :>) by using the colon, caret, and close parenthesis keys.

followed to minimize the risk of RSI.[13] Perhaps your school has such information available. Ergonomic‡ workshops may be offered on your campus. Such instruction typically addresses proper positioning of your monitor, keyboard, and chair to reduce eyestrain and muscle fatigue (see Figure 11.5). Remember to take appropriate stretch breaks and eye breaks. Simply standing up and walking away from the computer screen for a couple of minutes can reduce fatigue.

[13]For one example of such a list, see Paul Marxhausen, "Computer Related Repetitive Strain Injury," 2005, University of Nebraska-Lincoln Electronics Shop RSI Web Page, eeshop.unl.edu/rsi.html (accessed January 1, 2006).

‡Dictionary.com defines *ergonomics* as "The applied science of equipment design, as for the workplace, intended to maximize productivity by reducing operator fatigue and discomfort." See dictionary.reference.com/search?q=ergonomics (accessed July 1, 2007).

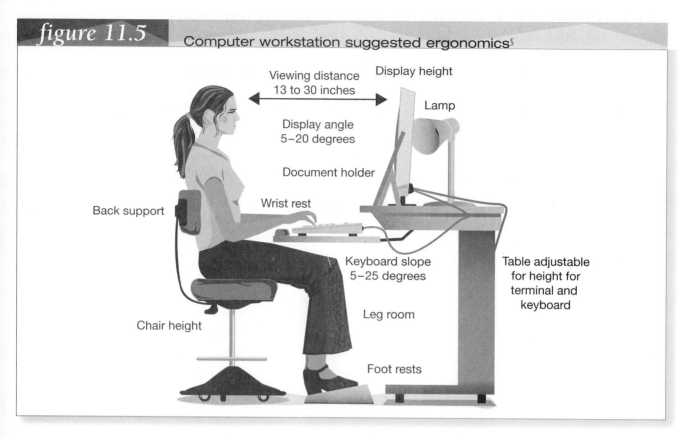

figure 11.5 Computer workstation suggested ergonomics[§]

Source: Library of Congress (Integrated Support Services, Workforce Ergonomics Program), "Ergonomics and VDT Use," *Computers in Libraries 13* (May 1993). From a flyer prepared by the Library of Congress Collections Services VDT Ergonomics Committee, 1991–1992.

CHAPTER SUMMARY

Before you leave this chapter, keep the following points in mind:

- The information explosion has not only increased the availability of information, but it has also increased the types and locations of the information.
- Information literacy requires a person to know *what* information to look for, *how to find* that information, *how to judge* the information's credibility and quality once it has been found, and *how to effectively use* the information once it has been found and evaluated.
- Locate and use school resources that will sharpen your information literacy skills.
- Academic integrity demands a strict code of conduct (moral expectation) that governs the manner in which students and professors do research and behave in class.
- E-mails represent you in cyber space.

[§]Library of Congress (Integrated Support Services, Workforce Ergonomics Program), "Ergonomics and VDT Use." *Computers in Libraries, 13,* no. 5. (May 1993).

CHAPTER 11 MEASURABLE OBJECTIVES   ACTIVITY 11.9

At the beginning of this chapter, six measurable objectives were presented. They are reprinted below for your convenience. Using the strategies you have learned in this chapter, fill in the lines beneath each item (or use a separate sheet of paper).

○ Explain the difference between databases, media, and visuals.

   ○ Write a definition and an example for each of the following:

      Databases. _____

      _____

      Media. _____

      _____

      Visuals. _____

      _____

○ Begin a keyword search to find information.

   ○ Using a chapter title from this book, write five keywords that you could use to find more information about the topic. _____

   _____

○ Use a search engine to locate needed information.

   ○ Use one of the search engines introduced in this chapter to locate information on the five keywords above. Briefly explain which engine you used and how successful your search was using the search engine. _____

   _____

   _____

○ Request a book through your college's interlibrary loan procedure.

   ○ Briefly explain your campus library procedure for an interlibrary loan.

   _____

   _____

   _____

○ Explain how a Web site URL (address) can provide a clue about the nature of the site.

   ○ Write your explanation here. _____

   _____

(continued)

○ Critically evaluate a source of information for accuracy, authority, objectivity, currency, and scope.

  ○ Partner with a classmate and conduct this evaluation for this chapter you just read. Write your findings here. _____

_____

_____

REALITY CHECK

Using your critical thinking skills to improve your information literacy skills

Situation. You have been assigned to write a research paper on the topic of "Civility in America: Have we forgotten how to be nice to one another?" Please do the following:

- Rewrite the topic in your words to make sure you understand what you must address. _____

  _____

- List at least three *keywords* you could use to search for information on the topic. _____

  _____

- Choose any *search engine* and type in your keywords. How many hits (potential sites) do you find for each key word? _____

  _____

- Choose one of the sites that you found on the keyword search above. For that site address the following:

  - **Authority.** What credentials indicate the site is credible and accurate?

    _____

  - **Objectivity.** What indicates the site is either impartial or biased? _____

    _____

  - **Currency.** When was the site last updated or revised? Based on this date, do you believe the site has the most recent information available?

    _____

    _____

  - **Scope.** Is the site narrowly focused, or does it cover a broad range of ideas?

    _____

CHAPTER 12

CIVILITY

How can working with others affect your academic success?

SPOT LIGHT ON CLASSROOM SKILLS

"Class, please form a group with three other people and complete the assignment by the end of the hour." How many of us have heard something similar from one or more of our instructors? Group work—or collaborative learning, as some professors like to call it—has to be one of the most challenging experiences for students. I don't know about you, but I always end up with people who will not work. I have to do most of the work and then everyone gets the same grade.

Instructors will tell us that real life—careers, relationships, and the like—require that we learn how to interact with all types of people. That may be true but here in the classroom, where my GPA is at stake, I'd just as soon be responsible for my own work and not have to depend on the guy in the back of the room who is either late or sleeping through the lecture!

Unless you plan on living the life of a hermit, dealing with people will be a reality for the rest of your life. You will have intimate relationships, you will have casual relationships, and you will eventually become involved in important professional associations.

PREVIEW

By the time you finish reading this chapter and completing its activities you will know how to:

- Identify the stage of group development that is typically the most difficult for you—and develop a strategy to cope with this challenge.
- Explain at least two considerations when forming your own group.
- Identify a person on campus you trust—and explain why you trust the person.
- Identify at least one healthy way to minimize the negative impact of energy vampires.
- Use at least three active listening techniques to improve your communication skills.
- Explain how to use at least two conflict management strategies.

KEY TERMS

- Active listening
- Assertiveness
- Collective monologue

229

Learning how to communicate a message of confidence and competence will affect how people perceive you. Maximizing relationships does not equate to "using" people or "taking advantage" of their good graces. It refers to ways that you and the people you interact with can enjoy a rewarding experience. Whether the association is a short-term group project or one of enduring intimacy, respect for yourself and others will help you make meaningful connections.

But not all of those relationships will be harmonious. If you interact with people long enough, conflict will present itself. It is part of the human drama—but it can be a positive force in your life. The key to dealing with conflict successfully is first to recognize when and why it is happening, and then to have a healthy plan for managing and resolving the conflict. This requires practice, patience, and persistence. This chapter will help you learn to confront and resolve the conflicts in your life.

- Conflict
- Elephant in the corner
- Emotional intelligence
- Energy vampires
- Interpersonal skills
- Nutritious people
- Trust

CHAPTER INTRODUCTION[1]

More than likely, when you were a young child you were told by parents, grandparents, uncles, or teachers to "play nice" with the other children. That simple piece of advice holds true as an adult—probably even more so. For that reason, this chapter will address the concepts of civility, healthy interpersonal relationships, effective communication, and conflict management.

Students choose their classes but, for the most part, they do not decide who else will register and sit in the same classroom. Thus, all sorts of personalities converge each day in campus classrooms. This will create challenges as the quiet person tries to deal with the loud student, the obnoxious student offends the quiet student in the corner, a rude e-mail insults a professor, or a demanding instructor intimidates an anxious student. Civility—polite and courteous behavior—will make the classroom and college experience more enjoyable for everyone. Interpersonal skills—your strengths and challenges when interacting with other people—play as important a role in your school years as do your academic studies.

---

[1]Steve Piscitelli, *Rhythms of College Success: A Journey of Discovery, Change, and Mastery.* (Upper Saddle River, NJ: Pearson Prentice Hall, 2008), 214–223, 227–228.

EMOTIONAL INTELLIGENCE

We have all heard stories of intelligent people who never seem to be able to "make it." While they may have high IQs,* their potential is never realized. How can this be?

Daniel Goleman, in his book *Emotional Intelligence*, states that "at best, IQ contributes about 20 percent to the factors that determine life success, which leaves 80 percent to other factors."[2] He and other psychologists† believe a person needs more than a high score on an IQ test to be successful. Emotional intelligence, says Goleman, is a more accurate predictor of success in life. In particular, the emotionally intelligent person:

- Is aware of his emotions as they occur
- Can soothe himself appropriately and "shake off rampant anxiety, gloom, or irritability"
- Delays gratification and controls impulses
- Has the ability to "tune in" to the emotions of others
- Is skilled at helping others manage their emotions[3]

As you work with people, be mindful of how you manage your emotions and impulses, the manner in which you respond to disappointments, and the effectiveness with which you work with others. The emotionally intelligent person practices civility even when circumstances are not what he would like them to be. "Book smarts" must be complemented with "people smarts" in order to achieve success.

REFLECTION ON YOUR CURRENT LEVEL OF COLLABORATIVE SKILLS

ACTIVITY 12.1

Before you answer the items below, reflect on your current level of interpersonal skills. Think of how well (or poorly) you have related to classmates and instructors in past classes.

As with all of the reflective activities in this book, answer from your heart. This exercise is not meant for you to answer just like your classmates—or to match what you may think the instructor wants to see. Take your time to give a respectful and responsible general accounting of your experiences with interpersonal relations. A truthful self-assessment now will help you build on skills you have while developing those you lack.

For the following items circle the number that best describes your *typical* experience when relating to other people. The key for the numbers is:

0 = never, 1 = almost never, 2 = occasionally, 3 = frequently,
    4 = almost always, 5 = always

(continued)

---

*Intelligence quotient (IQ) is a single measure, determined by a test score, used to indicate one's intelligence.

[2]Daniel Goleman, *Emotional Intelligence* (New York: Bantam Books, 1997), 34.

†Robert Sternberg (*Successful Intelligence*) speaks of three types of intelligence: analytical, creative, and practical. Howard Gardner's theory of multiple intelligences maintains that *interpersonal intelligence* recognizes what motivates others and how best to work with other people.

[3]Goleman, 43.

When considering your past strengths and challenges with interpersonal skills, how often:

1. Have you been able to identify and appropriately deal with the feelings of a group member?

   0   1   2   3   4   5

2. Have you been able to soothe and calm yourself appropriately when you have become angry?

   0   1   2   3   4   5

3. Were you able to work effectively with a group on a class project?

   0   1   2   3   4   5

4. Have you been able to distance yourself from people who continually drain your energy?

   0   1   2   3   4   5

5. Are you able to associate with people who energize and excite you?

   0   1   2   3   4   5

6. Do you let a speaker know, either by body language or verbal response, that you are truly listening?

   0   1   2   3   4   5

7. Have you asked questions of the person speaking to you?

   0   1   2   3   4   5

8. Have you been an energizing force for another person?

   0   1   2   3   4   5

Add up your scores for items 1 through 8. Divide by 8. Write your answer here: _____.

Using the key explanations above for each number (0, 1, 2, 3, 4, 5) complete this sentence: When it comes to relating to other people, I _____ effectively relate to other people.

Based on your answers, what insights do you have about your experiences with interpersonal skills? _____

_____

_____

WORKING WITH PEOPLE

The Challenges of Group Work

By the time you find your way to college, you have already been involved in group work on various levels. Whether working on a community project or a school assignment, group work is a common experience for all students. Some groups last for a very brief time. For instance, teachers commonly assign students to groups for in-class activities. These groups typically wrestle with a question or problem and then present a response before the end of class. Other class groups may exist longer. Perhaps the class has been split into two groups that will debate the pros and cons of a current political issue. Each side is responsible for preparation and a presentation. Such an activity would no doubt involve research, planning sessions, and rehearsals.

Groups also help the participants develop communication, collaboration, and conflict resolution skills. They prepare members to handle situations in which a group member fails to live up to his or her part of the group assignment. Most everyone can share one tale of a "nightmare group" that presented one problem after another.

CRITICALLY THINKING ABOUT YOUR INTERPERSONAL SKILLS   ACTIVITY 12.2

Let's apply the critical thinking standards from Chapter 2 to your ability to relate to and work with others in a civil manner. Activity 12.1 above may be helpful for this activity.

List either your interpersonal strength or challenge here: _____

_____

CRITICAL THINKING STANDARD	APPLICATION TO YOUR INTERPERSONAL SKILLS	YOUR EXPLANATION HERE OR ON A SEPARATE PIECE OF PAPER
Clarity	*Clearly* state your strength or challenge with relationship skills.	
Accuracy	How do you know this assessment of your inter-personal skills is *correct?*	
Precision	*Specifically* (give examples) explain your strength or challenge with relationship skills.	
Relevance	How is your assessment of your strength or challenge with relationship skills *connected* to your academic progress?	
Depth	Examine your strength or challenge with relationship skills beyond a superficial (simplistic) explanation and look at all of the *complexities* involved.	
Breadth	Examine your strength or challenge with relationship skills from more than one *perspective (point of view).*	
Logic	Based on your evidence do your conclusions above *make sense?*	

(continued)

1. When talking with people, do you continually "replay" your same stories over and over?

   ❑ Yes   ❑ No

2. Do you hold a conversation with people, or do you engage in a self-centered monologue about your life?

   ❑ Yes   ❑ No

3. When someone speaks with you, do you avoid asking meaningful and substantive questions? Do you lack interest in the other person's "stories"?

   ❑ Yes   ❑ No

4. When describing events that have occurred, do you typically describe things as being devastating and particular only to you? That is, do you believe no one could ever experience the hardships that you do?

   ❑ Yes   ❑ No

5. Do you start most of your conversations with "You are never going to believe what happened to me!" (or something similar)?*

   ❑ Yes   ❑ No

6. When in a group, do you always have to be center stage?

   ❑ Yes   ❑ No

7. Do you find your conversation peppered with insults, anger, and attempts to make others look bad?

   ❑ Yes   ❑ No

8. Any *Yes* answers may indicate that you have a tendency to drain energy from others. Think of the mental list you made of people who drained your energy. Do you think *your* name would appear on anyone's list of energy vampires?

   ❑ Yes   ❑ No

9. Based on your answers, what do you plan to do to make sure you do not drain energy from those around you? _____

   _____

   _____

---

*Orloff labels these types of people "drama queens"(*Positive Energy,* 299). And of course you will also find "drama kings."

Finding "Nutritious People" for Your Life

One way to protect your energy and sanity is to associate with nutritious people.[9] These people help to ward off the poison spewed by the energy vampires. A nutritious person has three main characteristics that stand out:

---

[9]For a clear review of this concept, see Richard Leider and David Shapiro, *Repacking Your Bags: Lighten Your Load for the Rest of Your Life* (San Francisco: Barrett-Koehler, 1995), Chapter 7; and Richard Leider, *The Power of Purpose* (New York: MJF Books, 1997), 64.

As you read the following characteristics of an active listener, conduct a mental checklist of how you measure up:

- *An active listener has to be quiet and focus on the speaker.* It becomes increasingly difficult to listen to another person if you are talking yourself. Quiet your mouth. An old saying reminds us that we have two ears and one mouth, so we should listen twice as much as we talk.

- *The active listener needs to quiet her mind.* If she attends to the chatter in her own mind, she will miss what the speaker is saying.

- *An active listener pays attention to what is said.* In a face-to-face conversation, the active listener maintains eye contact, does not interrupt, and tries to understand what the speaker wants to convey.

- *The active listener lets the speaker know that he is listening.* He nods his head, says "I see" or in some other way indicates that he hears what is being said. The key is to be sincere. Nodding and saying "I understand" while really thinking about what you will be doing tonight is not actively listening—it is preparation for a collective monologue.

- *Active listeners not only hear the words, but "listen" to the body language.* Are there clues in the body position that would help understand the message being delivered?

- *The active listener often asks questions about what the speaker has just said.* The questioning is not meant to be confrontational; rather, it is an attempt to make sure the message has not been misunderstood. Such questions indicate interest in the other person's comments.

- *Finally, the active listener will attempt to repeat what she has just heard to make sure the message is understood.* In this way the speaker feels affirmed. The listener does not have to agree with the speaker; she only conveys that she has correctly understood what was said.

CONFLICT MANAGEMENT

Conflict describes a state of disharmony where one set of ideas or values contradicts another. It can range from the fairly minor—a roommate who rises for morning jogs and disturbs your sleep—to the serious—two group members getting into a shouting and shoving match about the group's work. There will be times when you will have to confront conflicts of various degrees of severity.

Are You Having a Disagreement or a Conflict?

Conflict is not the same as a disagreement. For our purposes, an argument about which college football team should be the national champion does not constitute a conflict. It is a difference of opinion to be sure, but this disagreement does not pit one belief system against another.

Conflict, on the other hand, rears its head when two or more deeply held ideas, values, or perspectives are contradictory.[10] The conflict can be between two or more people—or it can be an internal conflict between your values and

[10]Carter McNamara, "Basics of Conflict Management," 1999, www.managementhelp.org/intrpsnl/basics.htm (accessed December 30, 2005).

your own actions. Suppose a young man has been reared with a deeply held value that having sexual relations before marriage constitutes a violation of personal integrity. If he finds himself in a situation that now challenges his deeply held beliefs, he will experience a period of conflict as he tries to reconcile the contradictory signals.

Conflict Is Not Always a Bad Thing

Earlier in this chapter you read about the dynamics of group formation. *Storming* is a real and necessary stage that groups and teams will encounter. Conflict about the exact purpose for the team, who has the best talents to be the leader, and what tasks should be assigned to whom can expose contradictory values and perspectives. One of the *dysfunctions* of teams occurs when passionate debate does *not* take place.[11] So, whereas an absence of conflict may seem to be heavenly, it is an unrealistic goal in most human relationships—and it may even be unhealthy. The required ingredient is a mechanism to discuss why the conflict exists and how it can be managed and resolved.

Whenever two or more people come together for any length of time, the risk for conflict presents itself. You do not need to enter every relationship with the dread of impending conflict. But it may be healthy to understand that when it does occur, the conflict itself can produce a positive outcome for you and the other person or people involved.

Ways People Deal with Conflict

Just as with problem solving (see Chapter 2), there are many ways to deal with conflict. If five people are involved in a conflict, there will be probably *at least* five solutions presented. If ten people are present, there is a good chance you will find at least ten ideas. For this reason, any listing of strategies to manage conflict will be necessarily incomplete. As you read the following strategies and examples, think about how you might handle each situation.[12]

- *Ignore the issue.* Some people will do anything to avoid a confrontation. They believe that peace at all costs is better than arguments and loud voices. This could lead to a lose-lose situation in which the initial flame of conflict gets worse because it has not been addressed. Eventually the conflict consumes all parties in an inferno of controversy. This can result in ill feelings and resentment.

    - *Example:* One member of your group always complains about the project at hand. He drags down your energy each time you are around him. Rather than saying anything to him, your group quietly goes

---

[11]See Lencioni, *The Five Dysfunctions of a Team.*

[12]See McNamara, "Basics of Conflict Management."

about its work, many times taking on tasks that he was to do. You all hope this person will change his ways or leave the group, but nothing is said or done.

- *Refusing to see another side.* In this scenario, everyone knows a problem exists but no one willingly changes position. In fact, as the conflict increases people may become more entrenched in their views. Depending on the severity of the disagreement, this lose-lose situation can bring a relationship or team to a grinding halt.

  - *Example:* There are four members in your group. Each believes his or her direction for the group is the best. No one is willing to concede on anything. No work gets done—and the deadline for the group product gets closer.

- *Give in to the "Demands."* In the interest of peace, once again, one person decides to do whatever the other person wants. This win-lose situation may leave the underlying issue of the conflict unresolved.

  - *Example:* Your roommate likes to party late into the night. Unfortunately, her late hours have been interfering with your sleep patterns. Each day you awaken tired. When you talk to your roommate about this, she begins to whine about how you do not appreciate what she does around the apartment. Your early morning routines, she says, have bothered her. She threatens to move out and leave you to pay the entire monthly rent. You give in—and buy some earplugs.

- *Compromise.* You give a little, the other person gives a little, and the conflict is minimized if not totally resolved. This creates a modified win-win situation, as each person has not been able to achieve all that he or she had hoped for. But for the sake of harmony, a middle course has been agreed upon. Because all situations do not reach the synergy level (see the next strategy), sometimes compromise represents a very positive resolution.

  - *Example:* Your late-night roommate has agreed to enter the apartment quietly and not turn the television on when she returns after midnight. You agree to be quieter when you arise early for your 8:00 a.m. class.

- *Synergy.* When two or more people hit upon a solution that actually is better than any of the previous ideas, a synergistic solution has been reached. A win-win situation results. Although highly desirable, this outcome requires considerable effort to achieve.

  - *Example:* You and your late-night roommate have discovered that two of your good friends are having the same problem—one is an early riser and one is a night owl. The four of you decide to switch roommates. The two early risers will now live together and the two night owls will room together. All friendships have been maintained; all four are happier than they had been prior to the new arrangement; and you are now able to get a great night's sleep.

ACTIVITY 12.8   CAN YOU THINK OF ANY OTHER APPROACHES TO CONFLICT MANAGEMENT?

1. Once you have read the five ways people address conflict, as presented in this chapter, reflect for a moment and then add any alternative strategies you have used.

_____

_____

_____

_____

_____

_____

CHAPTER SUMMARY

Before leaving this chapter, keep the following points in mind:

- While groups present an opportunity for people to share talents and develop a better product than one person could produce they can be unpredictable and create challenges.
- Beware of people who constantly drain energy from you—the energy vampires.
- Seek out nutritious people, who will help energize you.
- Effective communication is an art form that has no room for collective monologues.
- If you want to be considered a nutritious person, then pay attention to how you work with other people.
- Conflict can be positive when appropriately managed.

ACTIVITY 12.9   CHAPTER 12 MEASURABLE OBJECTIVES

At the beginning of this chapter, six measurable objectives were presented. They are reprinted below for your convenience. Based on the strategies you have learned in this chapter, fill in the lines beneath each item (or use a separate sheet of paper).

○ Identify, for yourself, which stage of group development is typically the most difficult for you—and develop a strategy to cope with this challenge.

  ○ Which stage is most difficult for you? _____

  ○ What is your strategy to cope with this challenge? _____

  _____

  _____

(continued)

○ Explain at least two effective considerations when forming your own group.

   ○ List and briefly explain your considerations here: _____

   _____

   _____

   _____

○ Identify a person on campus you trust—and explain why you trust the person.

   ○ Who is the person? _____

   ○ What led you to trust this person? _____

   _____

   _____

○ Identify at least one healthy way to minimize the negative impact of energy vampires.

   ○ Identify your strategy here. _____

   _____

   _____

○ Use at least three active listening techniques to improve your communication skills.

   ○ List the techniques that you have used in the last week. _____

   _____

   _____

   _____

○ Explain how to use at least two conflict management strategies.

   ○ Write your answer here. _____

   _____

   _____

   _____

REALITY CHECK

Using your critical thinking skills to improve your relationship skills

Situation. You and four other students in your psychology class have been assigned to a group. Your group's assignment is to choose one psychological disorder that you studied in class this term. Once you agree on the choice, you have to develop a fifteen-minute presentation (complete with PowerPoint slides) to describe the topic and introduce what you consider to be the best treatment for the disorder.

Using the following information, identify which stage of development the group is in—and what strategies can be used to help the group succeed.

- The instructor has passed out one sheet of instructions for each group. No one grabs for the instructions, so you pick up the paper and read them to the group. There are a number of tasks that the group will have to complete by the end of this four-week assignment. Each member will be responsible for taking on at least one of the tasks. After you read the instructions and assignment description, stony silence confronts the group; no one volunteers to do anything! "This is why I hate groups," you say to yourself. You ask whether anyone wants to be the group leader. Jamesha looks at the floor; Rhonda points at John; Tony has his head on the desk. John reluctantly agrees to take charge. He quickly breaks down the assignment into bite-sized tasks. Before you leave class for the day, you all agree to meet in the campus cafeteria thirty minutes before the next class to discuss the project further. Each person is to think about which part of the assignment he or she wants to tackle.

Write your response here or on a separate piece of paper.

Stage: _____

Strategies: _____

_____

_____

_____

_____

_____

_____

CHAPTER 13

THE CHOICES YOU MAKE

How do your current decisions affect your future?

SPOTLIGHT ON CLASSROOM SKILLS

Whew! The school term has come and gone. Overall, I feel pretty good about what I accomplished. Yes, I could have done a little better in a few of my courses, but for the most part I'm satisfied.

One of my teachers asked the class today whether we had any advice for new students coming to college next term. Just about every student had something to say. Generally, they spoke about staying on top of things—not procrastinating. More specifically, they suggested that students:

- *Check their syllabus daily.*
- *Ask questions in class.*
- *Contact someone for help if they fall behind.*
- *Plan ahead.*
- *Come to class regularly.*
- *Not take too many courses.*
- *Take class seriously—don't waste their money and time.*
- *Believe in themselves and in their goals.*

I guess we have all learned a few things over the last few months. We are better students—and ready to take on the next semester.

PREVIEW

By the time you finish reading this chapter and completing its activities you will be able to:

- Evaluate the progress you have made this term toward minimizing or eliminating your study skill challenges.
- Explain at least two strategies that have most significantly enabled your academic success this term.
- Describe one study skill challenge that you still have to work on for next term.
- Write a goal with action steps that will address your study skills challenge for the coming term.

KEY TERMS

- Ambition
- Choices
- Initiative
- Potential

End-of-the-book chapters like this one run the risk of becoming cliché driven. Phrases like "preparing for the end," "a new beginning," "the next step," and "where do you go from here?" often appear as chapter titles. In reality, all reflect excellent sentiments and accurate thoughts. They let the student know that while the work is finishing for this term, more work and decisions are still to come.

This chapter will discuss those issues within the context of choices. In particular, you will be asked to do the following:

- Reflect on the choices—specifically study skill choices—you have made since the beginning of this school term.
- Consider the consequences your choices have had for yourself this term.
- Think about the academic choices that lie ahead of you.

CHAPTER INTRODUCTION[1]

You have covered a lot of ground since you first opened this book. In the first chapter you read the following words: *Study skills are for all students. They help students develop strategies and techniques to focus their energies on efficient and effective studying.* Since then you have worked through more than 120 activities to develop those strategies and that focus. Only you (and perhaps your instructor) know how well you have internalized this material.

Before you close this book one final time, take one more accounting of what you have accomplished—and what you still would like to work on in the future. As you complete the activities in this chapter keep this question in mind: *Are you satisfied with the choices you have made this term?*

THE CHOICES YOU MAKE

You probably have heard someone say that this person or that person "has so much *potential.*" Or perhaps someone observed, "I know she will go far. She has so much *ambition.*" While ambition (a desire to reach a goal) and potential (the possibility of becoming something greater than you are) are important characteristics, they are useless without *initiative.* Responsible decision making and follow-through are needed to put potential and ambition into action. Ambition is *the desire*; potential *the ability*; initiative is *the doing.*

- Throughout this school term you have had to make decisions—choices—every day so you could put your ambition and potential into action.

Returning to the Beginning

This chapter will give you a chance to reflect on what you have *done* and how far you have progressed since the first day of the term. To do that, you will be asked to once again complete the

[1]Steve Piscitelli, *Rhythms of College Success: A Journey of Discovery, Change, and Mastery.* (Upper Saddle River, NJ: Pearson Prentice Hall, 2008), 285–286, 300–301.

activities you tackled in the first chapter of the book. This will allow you to gauge your progress—and make plans for the future.

ASSESSMENT OF STRENGTHS AND CHALLENGES   ACTIVITY **13.1**

In Chapter 1 you completed this assessment of study skill strengths and challenges. Take a moment and complete the following checklist once again. At the end of the checklist you will have the opportunity to reflect on your progress.

For this activity, focus on what you *do*, rather than the material you learn. Concentrate, for instance, on the ways in which you can become a more capable math student (or English, or history, or science, or Spanish, or some other class).

Below, check your STRENGTHS when it comes to studying. What do you do well? Check as many or as few as apply. Take your time and think about each choice carefully.

- ○ Setting goals
- ○ Completing goals
- ○ Establishing priorities
- ○ Completing work on time
- ○ Eliminating distractions
- ○ Taking notes from class lectures
- ○ Taking notes from the textbook
- ○ Taking organized notes
- ○ Getting to class on time
- ○ Participating in class
- ○ Keeping an organized notebook
- ○ Regularly reviewing and organizing class notes
- ○ Coming to class prepared
- ○ Understanding and using learning style information
- ○ Using critical thinking skills to solve problems
- ○ Getting the main point from a reading assignment

- ○ Writing a strong essay thesis statement
- ○ Supporting an opinion with facts
- ○ Organizing an essay
- ○ Writing and completing an essay
- ○ Establishing relationships and connections
- ○ Remembering important information for exams
- ○ Controlling test anxiety
- ○ Preparing, in plenty of time, for exams
- ○ Completing exams in the time allotted
- ○ Learning from previous exam mistakes
- ○ Taking study breaks
- ○ Studying alone
- ○ Studying with friends
- ○ Locating information for research projects
- ○ Evaluating information for research projects
- ○ Other: _____

_____

Now, check your CHALLENGES when it comes to studying. What do you need to improve? Check as many or as few as apply. Take your time and think about each choice carefully.

- ○ Setting goals
- ○ Completing goals
- ○ Establishing priorities
- ○ Completing work on time
- ○ Eliminating distractions
- ○ Taking notes from class lectures

- ○ Writing a strong essay thesis statement
- ○ Supporting an opinion with facts
- ○ Organizing an essay
- ○ Writing and completing an essay
- ○ Establishing relationships and connections
- ○ Remembering important information for exams

(continued)

○ Taking notes from the textbook

○ Taking organized notes

○ Getting to class on time

○ Participating in class

○ Keeping an organized notebook

○ Regularly reviewing and organizing class notes

○ Coming to class prepared

○ Understanding and using learning style information

○ Using critical thinking skills to solve problems

○ Getting the main point from a reading assignment

○ Controlling test anxiety

○ Preparing, in plenty of time, for exams

○ Completing exams in the time allotted

○ Learning from previous exam mistakes

○ Taking study breaks

○ Studying alone

○ Studying with friends

○ Locating information for research projects

○ Evaluating information for research projects

○ Other: _____

_____

Review your checked boxes in each section above. List below the five STRENGTHS you consider your biggest assets, ranking them from 1 to 5. Do the same for your CHALLENGES.

STRENGTHS

1. _____

2. _____

3. _____

4. _____

5. _____

CHALLENGES

1. _____

2. _____

3. _____

4. _____

5. _____

Compare your assessment above with your answers in Activity 1.1. What differences do you see? Have your challenges been minimized? Have you discovered any new challenges that you did not have at the beginning of the term?

_____

_____

_____

Consider your study skill strengths. How have they gotten stronger? How have they made you a better student? _____

_____

_____

(continued)

Finally, what choices have you made this term that have helped you improve your study skills? _____

_____

_____

_____

_____

WHERE HAVE YOU BEEN—AND WHAT HAVE YOU DONE?

In Chapter 1 you were asked to quickly review the chapters of this book. Your purpose was twofold:

- Concentrate on what was on your mind about effective study skills at that point in time.
- Familiarize yourself with the contents of this textbook.

It is time to revisit those activities. Now, however, you will be asked to review what you have learned about study skills—and asked to identify one strategy from each chapter that you think you can use in the coming months and years.

Just as in Chapter 1, there is a simple guideline that will help you maximize your time. *Spend no more than five minutes on each activity*.

By the time you are done with the activities you will have reviewed and identified twelve study skill strategies—and you will have done this in only 60 minutes. And, just like in Chapter 1, what a valuable investment in a short period. Wouldn't you say you and your academic success are worth an hour?

CRITICAL THINKING   **ACTIVITY 13.2**

Look at the activities, bold-faced headings, tables, and figures of Chapter 2. Choose one item (activity, heading, table, or figure) you can use to either sustain or improve your academic success.

- List the item here. _____

  - Briefly explain how you think this item will help you be a more successful student.

  _____

  _____

GOAL SETTING AND MOTIVATION   **ACTIVITY 13.3**

Look at the activities, bold-faced headings, tables, and figures of Chapter 3. Choose one item (activity, heading, table, or figure) you can use to either sustain or improve your academic success.

(continued)

○ List the item here. _____

    ○ Briefly explain how you think this item will help you be a more successful student.

_____

_____

ACTIVITY 13.4   ORGANIZING TIME AND SPACE

Look at the activities, bold-faced headings, tables, and figures of Chapter 4. Choose one item (activity, heading, table, or figure) you can use to either sustain or improve your academic success.

○ List the item here. _____

    ○ Briefly explain how you think this item will help you be a more successful student.

_____

_____

ACTIVITY 13.5   LEARNING STYLES

Look at the activities, bold-faced headings, tables, and figures of Chapter 5. Choose one item (activity, heading, table, or figure) you can use to either sustain or improve your academic success.

○ List the item here. _____

    ○ Briefly explain how you think this item will help you be a more successful student.

_____

_____

ACTIVITY 13.6   CLASS TIME

Look at the activities, bold-faced headings, tables, and figures of Chapter 6. Choose one item (activity, heading, table, or figure) you can use to either sustain or improve your academic success.

○ List the item here. _____

    ○ Briefly explain how you think this item will help you be a more successful student.

_____

_____

NOTE TAKING   ACTIVITY **13.7**

Look at the activities, bold-faced headings, tables, and figures of Chapter 7. Choose one item (activity, heading, table, or figure) you can use to either sustain or improve your academic success.

○ List the item here. _____

  ○ Briefly explain how you think this item will help you be a more successful student.

  _____

  _____

READING   ACTIVITY **13.8**

Look at the activities, bold-faced headings, tables, and figures of Chapter 8. Choose one item (activity, heading, table, or figure) you can use to either sustain or improve your academic success.

○ List the item here. _____

  ○ Briefly explain how you think this item will help you be a more successful student.

  _____

  _____

MEMORY   ACTIVITY **13.9**

Look at the activities, bold-faced headings, tables, and figures of Chapter 9. Choose one item (activity, heading, table, or figure) you can use to either sustain or improve your academic success.

○ List the item here. _____

  ○ Briefly explain how you think this item will help you be a more successful student.

  _____

  _____

TEST TAKING   ACTIVITY **13.10**

Look at the activities, bold-faced headings, tables, and figures of Chapter 10. Choose one item (activity, heading, table, or figure) you can use to either sustain or improve your academic success.

(continued)

ACTIVITY 13.13   **CHAPTER 13 MEASURABLE OBJECTIVES**

At the beginning of this chapter, four measurable objectives were presented. They are reprinted below for your convenience. Based on the insights you have gained from this book, fill in the lines beneath each item (or use a separate sheet of paper).

○ Evaluate the progress you have made this term toward minimizing or eliminating your study skill challenges.

   ○ Compare Activity 13.1 with Activity 1.1. How would you judge the progress you made on improving your study skills? Provide at least one specific example of your progress.

     _____

     _____

     _____

○ Explain at least two strategies that have had the most significant impact upon your academic success this term.

   ○ Strategy #1: _____

     _____

   ○ Strategy #2: _____

     _____

○ Describe one study skill challenge that you still have to work on for next term.

   ○ Describe the challenge here. _____

     _____

     _____

○ Write a goal with action steps that will address your study skills challenge for the coming term.

   ○ Your goal with action steps: _____

     _____

     _____

REALITY CHECK

Dreams, action, reality, and energy

In the introduction to this book you read the following:

Whatever your level of academic skill might be, this book will allow you to raise your "game" to a new level. Just like athletes strive to improve from game to game and season to season, successful students continually look for ways to add to their academic accomplishments. . . . The strategies in the following chapters will help you put those *dreams* into *action* so your academic dreams will become *reality*. The choice will be yours. Feel the *energy!*

For this final reality check of the book, reflect on the choices you have made this term—especially those concerning your academic progress. In the first chapter you signed a "Covenant with Myself" in which you "pledged to make choices that reflect respect, responsibility, and honesty."

■ Write how your choices have (or have not) reflected respect, responsibility, and honesty. _____

_____

_____

_____

_____

_____

_____

_____

_____

_____

■ How have these choices led you closer to realizing your academic dreams? _____

_____

_____

_____

_____

_____

_____

_____

_____

_____

_____

REFERENCES

Adler, Mortimer and Charles Van Doren. *How to Read a Book*. New York: Simon & Schuster, 1972.

Armbruster, Bonnie B. in Rona F. Flippo and David Caverly, *Handbook of College Reading and Study Strategy Research*. (Mahwah, NJ: Lawrence Erlbaum Associates, 2000.

Beck, Martha. *Finding Your Own North Star: Claiming the Life You Were Meant to Have*. New York: Three Rivers Press, 2001.

Carter, Carol, Joyce Bishop, and Sarah Lyman Kravits. *Keys to Success*, 5th ed. Upper Saddle River, NJ: Prentice Hall, 2006.

CC Consulting Limited. "Office Survival." www.crazy colour.com/os/notetaking_01.shtml (accessed July 1, 2007).

Collins, Jim and Jerry I. Porras. *Built to Last: Successful Habits of Visionary Companies*. New York: HarperBusiness Essentials, 2002.

Department of Health and Human Services, Centers for Disease Control and Prevention. "Healthy Weight." www.cdc.gov/nccdphp/dnpa/nutrition/ nutrition_for_everyone/healthy_weight/index.htm (accessed July 1, 2007).

Dunn, Rita and Kenneth Dunn. *Teaching Students Through Their Individual Learning Styles: A Practical Approach*. Reston, VA: Reston, 1978.

Eisenberg, Michael B., Carrie A. Lowe, and Kathleen L. Spitzer. *Information Literacy: Essential Skills for the Information Age*, 2nd ed. Westport, CT: Libraries Unlimited, 2004.

Elder, Linda and Richard Paul. "Universal Intellectual Standards," *The Critical Thinking Community*. www.criticalthinking.org/resources/articles/universal-intellectual-standards.shtml (accessed July 1, 2007).

Fleming, Neil, D. Christchurch, and Charles C. Bonwell. VARK (version 7.0). New Zealand and Green Mountain Falls, CO, 2006.

Fleming, Neil. "Is VARK a Learning Style?" VARK. 2001–2006.vark-learn.com/english/page.asp?p=faq (accessed May 14, 2007).

Fry, Ron. *Improve Your Reading*. Hawthorne, NJ: The Career Press, 1991.

"Global Availability of MSN Messenger and MSN Spaces Connects People Around the World," Microsoft PressPass.www.microsoft.com/presspass/ press/2005/apr05/04-07GlobalMessengerSpacesPR .mspx (accessed July 1, 2007).

Goldberg, Bruce. "Energy Vampires." www.drbrucegold berg.com/EnergyVampires.htm (accessed July 1, 2007).

Goleman, Daniel. *Emotional Intelligence*. New York: Bantam Books, 1997.

Grad, Peter. "Rev Up Your Engine," NorthJersey.com, December 3, 2005. www.mtsu.edu/~studskl/pcguy .pdf (accessed July 1, 2007).

Gray, Elaine. *Conscious Choices: A Model for Self-Directed Learning*. Upper Saddle River, NJ: Prentice Hall, 2004.

Hallowell, Edward M. *Crazy Busy: Overstretched, Overbooked, and About to Snap!* New York: Ballentine Books, 2007.

"Health Information." Saint Vincent Catholic Medical Centers. www.svcmc.org/body.cfm?xyzpdqabc=0 &id=841&action=detail&AEProductID=HW%5F Catholic&AEArticleID=rlxsk&AEArticleType=Brain %20and%20nerves (accessed July 1, 2007).

Henry, D. J. *The Effective Reader* (updated edition). New York: Pearson Longman, 2004.

Henry, D. J. *The Skilled Reader* (updated edition). New York: Pearson Longman, 2004.

Herrmann, Ned. "Is It True That Creativity Resides in the Right Hemisphere of the Brain?" *Scientific American*, January 26, 1998. www.sciam.com/ askexpert_question.cfm?articleID=00049843-7DBA-1C71-9EB7809EC588F2D7&modsrc=related_links (accessed July 1, 2007).

"Information Literacy Competency Standards for Higher Education." Association of College and Research Libraries (a division of the American Library Association), 2006. www.ala.org/ala/acrl/acrlstan dards/informationliteracycompetency.htm#ildef (accessed July 1, 2007).

"Internet." NetLingo the Internet Dictionary. www.netlingo.com/lookup.cfm?term=Internet (accessed July 1, 2007).

Jensen, Eric. "Brain-Based Learning: A Reality Check." *Educational Leadership*. April 2000.

Katzenbach, John R. and Douglas K. Smith. *The Wisdom of Teams: Creating the High-Performance Organization.* New York: HarperBusiness Essentials, 2003.

Kazley, M. Alan. "Ned Herrmann's Whole Brain Model," Kheper.net. www.kheper.net/topics/intelligence/Herrmann.htm (accessed July 1, 2007).

Keefe, James. *Learning Style Handbook: II. Accommodating Perceptual, Study and Instructional Preferences.* Reston, VA: National Association of Secondary School Principals, n.d.

Leider, Richard and David Shapiro. *Repacking Your Bags: Lighten Your Load for the Rest of Your Life.* San Francisco: Barrett-Koehler, 1995.

Leider, Richard. *The Power of Purpose.* New York: MJF Books, 1997.

Lencioni, Patrick. *The Five Dysfunctions of a Team.* San Francisco: Jossey-Bass, 2002.

Marxhausen, Paul. "Computer Related Repetitive Strain Injury," 2005. University of Nebraska–Lincoln Electronics Shop RSI Web Page. eeshop.unl.edu/rsi.html (accessed July 1, 2007).

Matte, Nancy Lightfoot and Susan Hillary Henderson. *Success, Your Style: Righ- and Left-Brain Techniques for Learning.* Belmont, CA: Wadsworth, 1995.

McCrone, John. "Right Brain or Left Brain—Myth or Reality?" *New Scientist 163* (July 3, 1999), 26ff.

McNamara, Carter. "Basics of Conflict Management," 1999. www.managementhelp.org/intrpsnl/basics.htm (accessed July 1, 2007).

Mearns, Jack. "The Social Learning Theory of Julian B. Rotter," Department of Psychology, California State University–Fullerton. psych.fullerton.edu/jmearns/rotter.htm (accessed July 1, 2007).

Meyer, Paul. "Creating S.M.A.R.T. Goals," 2004, Top Achievement. www.topachievement.com/smart.html (accessed July 1, 2007).

Miller, William. "Resolutions That Work," *Spirituality and Health* (February 2005), 44–47.

Minninger, Joan and Eleanor Dugan. *Rapid Memory in 7 Days: The Quick-and-Easy Guide to Better Remembering.* New York: Berkeley, 1994.

Orloff, Judith. *Positive Energy.* New York: Harmony Books, 2004.

Pastor, Marc. "Short-Term Memory." San Diego State University, College of Education. coe.sdsu.edu/eet/articles/stmemory/start.htm (accessed July 1, 2007).

Pauk, Walter. *How to Study in College,* 5th ed. Boston: Houghton Mifflin, 1993.

Peter, Lyman and Hal R. Varian (senior researchers). "How Much Information? 2003," School of Information and Management, University of California at Berkeley, 2003.

Piscitelli, Steve. *Rhythms of College Success: A Journey of Discovery, Change, and Mastery.* Upper Saddle River, NJ: Pearson Prentice Hall, 2008.

Posen, David B. "Stress Management for Patient and Physician," *Canadian Journal of Continuing Medical Education,* April 1995. www.mentalhealth.com/mag1/p51-str.html#Head_1 (accessed July 1, 2007).

Procter, Margaret. "How Not to Plagiarize," 2006. Writing at the University of Toronto. www.utoronto.ca/writing/plagsep.html (accessed July 1, 2007).

Riedling, Ann Marlow. *Learning to Learn: A Guide to Becoming Information Literate.* New York: Neal-Schuman, 2002.

Sapadin, Linda with Jack Maguire. *Beat Procrastination and Make the Grade: The Six Styles of Procrastination and How Students Can Overcome Them.* New York: Penguin Books, 1999.

Shapiro, Elayne. "Brain-Based Learning Meets PowerPoint." *Teaching Professor 20,* no. 5, May 5, 2006. vnweb.hwwilsonweb.com/hww/shared/shared_main.jhtml?_requestid=8439(accessed July 1, 2007).

Smith, Brenda D. *Bridging the Gap: College Reading,* 9th ed. New York: Pearson Longman, 2008.

Smith, Frank. *To Think.* New York: Teachers College Press, 1990.

Smith, Mark K. "Bruce W. Tuckman—Forming, Storming, Norming, and Performing in Groups," 2005. *Infed: The Encyclopaedia of Informal Education.* www.infed.org/thinkers/tuckman.htm (accessed July 1, 2007).

"SQ4R Reading Method." West Virginia University at Parkersburg. www.wvup.edu/Academics/learning_center/sq4r_reading_method.htm (accessed July 1, 2007).

"SQ4R: A Classic Method for Studying Texts." University of Guelph (The Learning Commons). www.learningcommons.uoguelph.ca/LearningServices/Fastfacts-SQ4R.html (accessed July 1, 2007).

Stevens, Jose. *The Power Path: The Shaman's Way to Success in Business and Life.* Novato, CA: New World Library, 2002.

Straus, David. *How to Make Collaboration Work.* San Francisco: Barrett-Koehler, 2002.

Swartz, Roger G. *Accelerated Learning: How You Learn Determines What You Learn.* Durant, OK: EMIS.

Taylor, Bill. "Integrity: Academic and Political. A Letter to My Students." No date, 1. www.academicintegrity .org/pdf/Letter_To_My_Students.pdf (accessed July 1, 2007).

"Test and Performance Anxieties." Campus Blues, 2002–2004, www.campusblues.com/test.asp (accessed July 1, 2007).

"The Stages of Group Development." University of California, Santa Barbara, Office of Student Life, www.sa.ucsb.edu/osl/LeadershipDevelopment/ LeadershipResources/pdf/StagesOfGroup Development.pdf (accessed July 1, 2007).

Tinto, Vincent. "Taking Student Learning Seriously," keynote address to the Southwest Regional Learning Communities Conference, Tempe, AZ, February 28–March 1, 2002, www.mcli.dist.maricopa.edu/ events/lcc02/presents/tinto.html (accessed July 1, 2007).

Toga, Arthur W. and Paul M. Thompson. "Mapping Brain Asymmetry," *Nature Reviews: Neuroscience 4* (January 2003).

VanderStoep, Scott W. and Paul R. Pintrich. *Learning to Learn: The Skill and Will of College Success.* Upper Saddle River, NJ: Prentice Hall, 2003.

Wilson, Susan B. *Goal Setting.* New York: American Management Association, 1994.

Winstead, Elizabeth. "Mastering Time Management." Jacksonville, FL: Jacksonville University, no date, presentation.

Zadina, Janet N. "The Mystery of Attention." Presentation at the National Association for Developmental Education annual conference, Nashville, TN, March 22, 2007.

Zeleznik, Julie and Mary Purugganan. "BIOS 305 Writing and Visual Design in the Biosciences," Rice University. 209.85.165.104/search?q=cache:TRb QuRno00MJ:www.owlnet.rice.edu/~bios305/ Abstracts_Lecture_2003.ppt+%22purposes+for+ reading% 22&hl=en&ct=clnk&cd=56&gl=us (accessed July 1, 2007).

Procrastination: I suffer from procrastination. Is there a cure? . . . 71–73

Professors: I have no idea what to say to my professors, so why should I go to their offices? . . . 108–109

Punctuality: The lecture hall is so large, the professor will never know if I come late or leave early. Why worry about it? . . . 110–111

Reading: How can I remember more of what I read? . . . 142–144, 146–152

Reading: I am a slow reader with poor comprehension. What can I do about that? . . . 155–159

Registering for classes: How many classes are considered to be too many classes for a term? . . . 62–63

Research skills: How do I find information in the library or on the Internet? . . . 213–220

Return on investment (ROI): Besides tuition, what investment do students make in class? . . . 124–125

Rude people: Why do some people seem so rude when talking? . . . 231, 238, 241–243

Stress: I'm so stressed. What can I do about it? . . . 76–78

Study area: I live with other people and do not have my own area to study. What can I do? . . . 73–75

Study groups: Why should I get into one of these? It always seems like I do all of the work! . . . 135

Study skills: What are these? . . . 1–2, 6–9

Study time: How much time do I need for homework each day? . . . 60–62

Test performance: How can I perform better during tests? . . . 189–191, 196–198

Test performance: It's the night before an exam; I haven't kept up with the work. Is there anything I can do? . . . 200–201

Test preparation: What is the most effective way to prepare for an exam? . . . 71

Time: I never seem to have enough time. What can I do? . . . 60–70

SUBJECT INDEX

Abbreviations, for note-taking, 114
Ability, 250
Academic goals, 48, 49
Academic integrity, 201–202, 223–224
Academic strengths and challenges, assessment of, 3–5, 251–253
Academic success
  classroom performance skills and, 103–105, 106, 110–111
  motivation and, 40–41
  study strategies for, 10–12
  See also Classroom performance skills; Study skills
Accommodations, for test taking, 195
Accountability, 236
Accuracy, 18
  classroom performance skills, 105
  collaborative skills, 233
  goal setting, 43
  information literacy skills, 211
  Internet information, 221, 222
  learning styles, 91
  memory skills, 167
  note-taking, 126, 136
  organizational skills, 66
  reading, 144
  test-taking skills, 188
Achievement
  goal setting and, 50
  motivation and, 39
Acronyms, 178, 179
Acrostics, 178, 179
Action, 258–259
Action-oriented goal setting, 49
Action steps, 49
Action words, 84
Active engagement, 111, 117, 118–119
Active learning, 109–110. *See also* Note-taking
Active listening, 170–171, 242–243
Adaptation, 29, 30
Adjourning stage of groups, 235
Adjustments, 29, 30

Adler, Mortimer J., 152
Alternative testing environments, 195
Ambition, 250
Analysis, 19, 21
Analytical thinking, 84. *See also* Critical thinking
Anxiety. *See* Test anxiety
Application, 19, 21, 22
Armbruster, Bonnie B., 124
Assessment, of academic strengths and challenges, 3–5, 251–253
Assignments
  information literacy skills and, 211–223
  reading, 142–145
  textbook, 145–154
Association of College and Research Libraries, 206
Attainability, of goals, 46–47
Attendance, 110, 117
Attention, 64, 106–108
Attitude, 41, 190
Auditory learning, 86, 92, 93
Authority, 221, 222
Autos, as storage areas, 75
Backward planning, 71
Bags, for storage, 75
Balance, 64
Bar graphs, 157, 158
Beck, Martha, 49
Big picture, note-taking and, 127–133
Bishop, Joyce, 235
Blocking techniques, 195
Blogs, 216
Bloom, Benjamin, 19, 20–21. *See also* Higher-order thinking skills
Body language, 243
Bold-faced terms, 150
Boolean logic, 218–219
Brain, 84
Brain-based learning, 140–141
Brain hemispheres, 84–85
Brainstorming, 23, 24, 26

Breadth, 18, 21
  classroom performance skills, 105
  collaborative skills, 233
  goal setting, 43
  information literacy skills, 211
  memory skills, 167
  note-taking, 127
  organizational skills, 66
  reading, 144
  test-taking skills, 188
Built to Last (Collins and Porras), 44
Calendar, 67
Career goals, 48
Carpal tunnel syndrome (CTS), 224
Cars, as storage areas, 75
Carter, Carol, 235
Catalogs, online, 213
Caverly, David, 124
CC Consulting Limited, 114
Centers for Disease Control and Prevention, 132
Challenges
  assessment of, 3–5, 251–253
  group work, 232–233
Change, 29, 30
Chapter headings and subheadings, 150, 151
Chapters, of novels, 160–161
Charactergram, 160
Charts, 157, 158, 171–173
Cheating, 201–202, 223
Choices. *See* Decision making
Chunks, 129
Civility. *See* Collaborative skills
Clarity, 18, 22
  classroom performance skills, 105
  collaborative skills, 233
  goal setting, 43, 45–48
  information literacy skills, 211
  learning styles, 91, 94
  memory skills, 167
  note-taking, 126, 136
  organizational skills, 66
  reading, 144
  test-taking skills, 188

Class notes, reviewing, 111, 117. *See also* Note-taking

Class projects, time management for, 70–71

Class time activity, 7

Classroom atmosphere, 109

Classroom difficulties, learning styles and, 90–91

Classroom materials, 110

Classroom participation, 109–110, 117. *See also* Note-taking

Classroom performance skills, 99–100
  active engagement, 111
  active learning, 109–110, 111–119
  attendance, 110
  attention, 106–108
  class notes, reviewing, 111
  classroom atmosphere and, 109
  classroom materials, 110
  classroom seating, 110
  classroom success and, 106, 110–111
  coolness and, 109
  critical thinking, 105, 121
  decision making, 254
  expectations and, 103–105
  instructor relationships, 108–109
  instructor style and emphasis, 102–105
  note-taking, 111–119
  objectives, 119–120
  passion and, 110
  punctuality, 110
  reflection on, 100–101
  study habits and, 257
  summary, 119
  surprises, 101–102
  test taking and, 189

Classroom seating, 110

Classroom success, classroom performance skills and, 103–105, 106, 110–111

Cliffs Notes series, 155

Collaborative skills, 229–230
  active listening, 242–243
  communication, art of, 241–242
  conflict management, 243–246
  critical thinking, 233–234, 247–248
  decision making, 256
  dialogues versus collective monologues, 242
  emotional intelligence, 231

"energy vampires," 237–240
  group dynamics, 234–235
  group formation, 235–236
  group work challenges, 232–233
  "nutritious people," 240–241
  objectives, 246–247
  reflection on, 231–232
  study habits and, 257
  summary, 246
  trust, 236–237

Collaborative skills activity, 9

Collective monologues, 242

College schedules, adjusting to, 65–66

Collins, Jim, 44

Commitment, 42, 66–68

Communication
  art of, 241–242
  dialogues versus collective monologues, 242
  time management and, 63
  See also Listening

Community goals, 48

Comprehension, 19, 20, 21

Compromise, 245

Computers. *See* Online classes

Confidence, 31

Conflict, 243–244

Conflict management, 243–246

Connections
  charts for, 171–173
  note-taking and, 129

Context clues, 155–156

Contracts, 13–14

Coolness, 109

Cornell Note-Taking System, 112, 113

Covenant, 13–14

Cramming, 200–201

Creative thinking, 20, 27–28
  right-brain thinking and, 84, 85
  test taking and, 190

Crisis maker procrastinator, 72

Crisis management, 69. *See also* Organizational skills; Stress management; Time management

Critical thinking, 9
  Bloom, Benjamin, 20–22
  classroom performance skills and, 105, 121
  collaborative skills and, 233–234, 247–248
  creative thinking and, 27–28

decision making and, 29–30, 253
  defining, 17–19
  goal setting and, 43–44, 56
  information literacy skills and, 210–211, 228
  learning styles and, 91–92, 96–97
  memory skills and, 166–167, 181–182
  note-taking and, 126–127, 136, 138
  objectives, 31–32
  organizational skills and, 80
  preview, 15–16
  problem solving and, 22–27
  reading and, 144, 162
  reflection on, 16–17
  study habits and, 257
  study skills and, 32–33
  summary, 31
  test-taking skills and, 188, 189, 190, 203–204
  See also Higher-order thinking skills

Critical thinking activity, 6

Currency, 221, 222

Cuseo, Joseph B., 110

Daily calendar, 67, 69

Data retrieval chart, 171–173

Databases, 210, 214

Decision making, 249–251
  class performance skills and, 254
  collaborative skills and, 256
  critical thinking and, 29–30, 253
  dreams, action, reality, and energy, 258–259
  goal setting and motivation, 253–254
  information literacy and, 256
  learning styles and, 254
  memory skills and, 255
  motivation and, 39
  note-taking and, 255
  objectives, 257–258
  reading and, 255
  strengths and challenges, 251–253
  study habits and, 257
  summary, 256–257
  test taking and, 255–256
  time management and spatial organization, 254

Defier procrastinator, 72

Depth, 18, 21
   classroom performance skills, 105
   collaborative skills, 233
   goal setting, 43
   information literacy skills, 211
   learning styles, 91
   memory skills, 167
   note-taking, 127, 136
   organizational skills, 66
   reading, 144
   test-taking skills, 188
Details. *See* TSD
Detours, in goal setting, 49–51
Diagrams, 157, 158
Dialogues, 242
Dictionary. com, 225
Disagreements, 243–244
Distractions, 106, 108, 195
Distress, 76
Disuse/decay, of information,
   175–176
"Drama queens," 240
Dreamer procrastinator, 72
Dreams, 44, 258–259
Dugan, Eleanor, 164
Dunn, Kenneth, 85
Dunn, Rita, 85
Dysfunctions, of teams, 244
Eating habits, 199
E-books, 214
Effort, 39
Einstein, Albert, 27, 173
Eisenberg, Michael B., 209
Elder, Linda, 19
Electronic media, 210
Email, 118, 224, 225
Emergency studying, 200–201
Emotion, 84, 85, 184
Emotional Intelligence (Goleman),
   231
Emotional intelligence, 231
Emotional memory blocks, 174
Energy, 258–259
"Energy vampires," 237–240
Engagement, 39. *See also* Active
   engagement
Environment
   classroom atmosphere, 109
   classroom seating, 110
   goal setting and, 51
   leaning styles and, 93, 94
   spatial organization, 73–75, 189,
      254, 257

test-taking, 195
   time management and, 64
Ergonomics, 225, 226
Essay tests, 200
Eustress, 76
Evaluation
   critical thinking, 19, 21
   home study area, 74–75
   Internet information, 221–223
Exit slips, 133
Expectations, 64, 103–105
Experiences, shared, 236–237
External locus of control, 9–10,
   51, 52
Extinction, of incentives, 176
Extrinsic motivation, 38–39, 40,
   176, 190
Family, time management for, 64
Fear, 193
File folders, 74
Filing methods, 74
Fleming, Neil D., 86, 87
Flippo, Rona F., 124
Flowchart outlines, 111, 112
Flowcharts, 157, 158
Focus, 117, 170
Forgetfulness, 167–168
Formats, of tests, 195
Forming stage of groups, 234
Fry, Ron, 143
Gardner, Howard, 231
Goals
   backward planning, 71
   defining, 43
   HOG (huge outrageous goal), 44,
      46
   long-term, 46, 48, 49
   short-term, 46–47, 48, 49
   types of, 48, 49
   understanding, 45
Goal setting, 35–36
   action steps, 49
   critical thinking and, 43–44, 56
   decision making and, 253–254
   goal statements, 45–48
   HOG (huge outrageous goal),
      44, 46
   locus of control, 51–53
   long-term goals, 48, 49
   motivation and, 37–42
   objectives, 54–55
   obstacles, missteps, and detours,
      49–51

reasons for, 44
   reflection on, 36–37
   short-term goals, 48, 49
   study habits and, 257
   summary, 54
   WIN (What's Important
      Now), 54
Goal setting activity, 6–7
Goal statements, 45–48
Goldberg, Bruce, 237
Goleman, Daniel, 231
Grad, Peter, 219
Graphics, 150, 156–159
Graphs, 157, 158
Gray, Elaine, 20
Groups
   challenge of, 232–233
   dynamics of, 234–235
   dysfunctions of, 244
   formation of, 235–236, 244
   note-taking, 129, 135
Hallowell, Edward M., 58, 107
Headings, 150, 151
Hearing. *See* Listening
Henderson, Susan Hillary,
   85, 112
Henry, D. J., 155, 156
Herrmann, Ned, 85
Higher-order thinking skills, 17,
   19–20
   creative thinking, 27–28
   critical thinking, 20–22
   problem solving, 22–27
   See also Critical thinking
Highlighting, 153
History textbooks, 152
HOG (huge outrageous goal),
   44, 46
Home study area, 73–75
Identification, for storage, 75
Implementation, 23, 24–25,
   26–27, 192
Inadequacy, feelings of, 193
Incentives, 47, 176
Indexes, 214
Information
   amount of, 206
   necessary, 211, 212–213
   noticing, 164, 167–170
   types of, 209–210
Information access, 211, 213–220
Information age, 223–226
Information literacy activity, 8

Information literacy skills, 205–206
  assignments and, 211–223
  building on, 209
  critical thinking and, 210–211, 228
  decision making and, 256
  defining, 208–209
  information age and, 223–226
  information types and, 209–210
  objectives, 227
  reflection on, 207–208
  study habits and, 257
  summary, 226
Information processing. *See* Learning
  styles
Information retrieval, 164, 173–179
Information retrieval failure,
  175–177
Information storage, 164, 170–173
Initiative, 250
Instructors
  classroom performance skills and,
    108–109
  note-taking and, 133–134
  reading schedules and, 159
  style and emphasis, 102–105
  test-taking environment and, 195
  textbook reading assignments
    and, 145
  thinking like, 118
Intelligence quotient (IQ), 231
Interference, in memory retrieval,
  176–177
Interlibrary loans, 213–214
Internal locus of control, 9–10, 51, 52
Internet, 214–223. *See also* Online
  classes
Interpersonal intelligence, 231
Interpersonal skills. *See*
  Collaborative skills
Interruptions, 63
Intrinsic motivation, 38–39, 40, 190
Intuition, 84, 85
Italicized terms, 150
Jensen, Eric, 154
Katzenbach, John R., 235
Kazley, M. Alan, 85
Keefe, James, 85
Keyword searches, 217–220
Kinesthetic learning, 86, 89–90, 93,
  94
Knowledge, 19, 21
Kravits, Sarah Lyman, 235
Labeling, 175

Learning
  brain-based, 140–141
  difficulties with, 2–3
  motivation, 39–40
  note-taking and, 124–125
Learning styles, 81–82
  brain, 84
  brain hemispheres and whole-brain
    thinking, 84–85
  classroom difficulties, 90–91
  critical thinking and, 91–92,
    96–97
  decision making and, 254
  factors affecting, 85–86
  importance of, 82
  objectives, 95–96
  reflection on, 82–83
  study habits and, 257
  summary, 94–95
  test taking and, 189, 191
  VARK, 86–94
Learning styles activity, 7
Left-brain thinking, 84–85
Leider, Richard, 240
Lencioni, Patrick, 234, 244
Libraries, 213
Linear thinking, 84
Listening
  active, 170–171, 242–243
  dialogues versus collective mono-
    logues, 242
  memory skills and, 168, 169,
    170, 178
Lists, to-do, 67
Literacy. *See* Information literacy skills
Locus of control, 9–10, 51–53
Logic, 19, 21
  classroom performance skills, 105
  collaborative skills, 233
  goal setting, 43
  information literacy skills, 211
  left-brain thinking and, 84
  memory skills, 167
  note-taking, 127, 136
  organizational skills, 66
  reading, 144
  test-taking skills, 188
Long-term goals, 46, 48, 49
Lowe, Carrie A., 209
Lower-order thinking skills, 17,
  19–20
Lyman, Peter, 206
Maguire, Jack, 73

Main ideas, 151, 152–153, 156
Maps, 157, 158
Margin notes, 153
Marxhausen, Paul, 225
Mass communication, 241–242
Matching tests, 199–200
Materials, classroom, 110
Math textbooks, 152
Matte, Nancy Lightfoot, 85, 112
McCrone, John, 85
McNamara, Carter, 243, 244
Mearns, Jack, 51
Measurable goals, 46, 47
Mechanical memory blocks,
  174–175
Media information, 210
Memorization, 179
Memory blocks, 174–175
Memory skills, 163–164
  active listening, 170–171
  charts for connections, 171–173
  critical thinking and, 166–167,
    181–182
  decision making and, 255
  forgetfulness, 167–168
  improving, 164–165
  information retrieval, 173–179
  information retrieval failure,
    175–177
  information, noticing, 167–170
  information storage, 170–173
  memory blocks, 174–175
  mental pictures, 173
  mnemonics, 178, 179
  names, 177–178
  objectives, 180–181
  practice, 179
  reading and, 142–143
  reflection on, 165–166
  senses and, 168–170
  short-term memory, 168
  study habits and, 257
  summary, 179–180
  test taking and, 184, 189, 191
  understanding and, 179
Memory skills activity, 8
Mental paralysis, 41–42
Mental pictures, 173
Message center, 74
Meyer, Paul, 47
Microsoft PressPass, 216
Miller, George, 168
Miller, William, 41, 42

Miller's Magic Number, 168
Mini-SQ4Rs, 156
Minninger, Joan, 164
Mistakes, in goal setting, 49–51
Mnemonics, 178
Modifications, 29, 30
Monologues, collective, 242
Monthly calendar, 67
Motivation, 37
    decision making and, 253–254
    drive for, 38
    goal setting and, 35, 36
    intrinsic and extrinsic, 38–39, 40
    learning, 39–40
    objectives, 54–55
    reflection on, 36–37
    responsibility for, 40–41
    self-monitoring, 40
    summary, 54
    test taking and, 190
Motivation activity, 6–7
Motivational barriers, overcoming,
        41–42
Multiple-choice tests, 199
Multiple intelligences, 231
Names, 177–178
Netiquette, 119, 224, 225
NetLingo the Internet Dictionary, 214
Noncritical review, 20
Noncritical thinking characteristics, 20
Nonverbal communication, 243
Norming stage of groups, 234
Notebooks, 115–116, 117
Notes
    margin, 153
    reading, 159
    reviewing, 111, 117
    textbook reading assignments, 153
Note-taking skills, 111–114,
        123–124
    abbreviations for, 114
    big picture, 127–133
    connections, groups, and
        chunks, 129
    Cornell Note-Taking System, 112,
        113
    critical thinking and, 126–127,
        138
    decision making and, 255
    exit slips, 133
    instructors, thinking like, 118
    learning through, 124–125
    notebooks, 115–116

novels and, 161
    objectives, 120, 136–138
    online, 118–119
    outlines, 111, 112
    out-of-class strategies, 133–136
    practice, 115, 116
    reflection on, 125–126, 127–128
    reviewing, relating, and reorganiz-
        ing, 128, 130
    self-talk and talking with others,
        129–130
    spidergram, 113
    strategies for, 116–117
    study guides and, 112, 113
    study habits and, 257
    summary, 136
    test taking and, 184, 189
    textbook reading assignments,
        124–125, 126, 128, 129–130,
        137, 138
    TSD (title/summary/details),
        131–133
Note-taking skills activity, 7
Novels, 152, 159–160, 173
"Nutritious people," 240–241
Objectives, 54–55
    classroom performance skills,
        119–120
    collaborative skills, 246–247
    critical thinking, 31–32
    decision making, 257–258
    information literacy skills, 227
    learning styles, 95–96
    memory skills, 180–181
    note-taking, 120, 136–138
    organizational skills, 79–80
    reading, 161–162
    study skills, 12–13
    test-taking skills, 202–203
Objectivity, 221, 222
Obstacles, in goal setting, 47, 49–51
Online catalogs, 213
Online classes, note-taking for,
        118–119
Open-mindedness, 44
Organization, 9
Organizational skills, 57–58
    critical thinking and, 80
    decision making and, 254
    objectives, 79–80
    reflection on, 58–59
    spatial organization, 73–75
    stress management, 76–78

study habits and, 257
    summary, 78–79
    time management, 59–73
Organizational skills activity, 7
Orloff, Judith, 237, 238, 240
Outlines, 111, 112
Out-of-class note-taking strategies,
        133–136
Overdoer procrastinator, 72
Participation, 109–110, 117, 170.
        See also Note-taking
Passion, 110
Pastor, Marc, 168
Pauk, Walter, 112
Paul, Richard, 19
Peg systems, 178, 179
Perfectionist procrastinator, 72
Performance skills. *See* Classroom
        performance skills
Performing stage of groups, 235
Persistence, 39
Personal goals, 48, 49
Personal portable storage area, 75
Personal success, motivation for, 40
Perspective. *See* Breadth
Physical fitness, test taking and, 184
Physical memory blocks, 174
Pie graphs, 158
Pintrich, Paul R., 39, 50
Piscitelli, Steve
    class performance skills, 99, 109,
        110, 115, 118
    collaborative skills, 230
    critical thinking, 16
    decision making, 250
    information literacy skills, 206
    learning styles, 84
    motivation, 36
    note-taking, 127, 135
    organizational skills, 58, 62
    reading, 152, 153
    study skills, 9
    test-taking skills, 184, 191, 201
Plagiarism, 223
Planning
    backward, 71
    textbook reading assignments,
        145–146
    See also Organizational skills;
        Time management
Point of view. *See* Breadth
Porras, Jerry I., 44
Portable storage area, 75

Posen, David B., 77
Positive Energy (Orloff), 237, 238
Postexam analysis, 198
Postreading, 154
Potential, 250
Practice, 9
    memory skills, 179
    note-taking, 115, 116
    test taking and, 187
Precision, 18, 22
    classroom performance skills, 105
    collaborative skills, 233
    goal setting, 43
    information literacy skills, 211
    learning styles, 91
    memory skills, 167
    note-taking, 127, 136
    organizational skills, 66
    reading, 144
    test-taking skills, 188
Predictable unpredictability, 235
Preparation. *See* Test preparation
Prereading, 149–151
Presentation, of information, 223
Priorities, 68–70
Problem analysis, 24, 25, 26, 192
Problem identification, 23, 24,
    25–26, 192
Problem solving, 20, 22–27, 190, 192
Problem-solving models, 23–25
Problem-solving trap, 27
Process challenges, assessment of, 3–5
Procrastination, 71–73
Props, 195
Psychic parasitism, 237
Punctuality, 110, 117
Purpose, of reading, 143–144,
    149, 150
Purugganan, Mary, 143
Questioning, 147, 148, 150,
    170, 243
Quitting, 29, 30
Reading, 139–140
    assignments, 142–145
    brain-based learning, 140–141
    context clues, 155–156
    critical thinking and, 162
    decision making and, 255
    graphics and, 156–159
    instructors and schedules, 159
    main ideas, 156
    notes, 159
    novels, 159–160

objectives, 161–162
reflection on, 141–142
SQ4R, 146–154
study habits and, 257
summary, 160–161
supplemental sources, 155
test taking and, 189, 191
textbook assignments, 145–154
vocabulary, 155–156
Reading activity, 8
Reading purpose, 143–144, 149, 150
Reading schedules, 159
Read-write learning, 86, 89–90
Realistic goals, 46
Reality, 258–259
Recall. *See* Memory skills
Recitation, 147, 148
Reclamation. *See* Information
    retrieval
Recording, 147, 148, 153
Recreation, time management for, 64
Reference librarian, 213
Reflection, 23, 127–128
Relating, with notes, 128, 130
Relationship skills. *See* Collaborative
    skills
Relevance, 18
    classroom performance skills, 105
    collaborative skills, 233
    goal setting, 43
    information literacy skills, 211
    learning styles, 91
    memory skills, 167, 170
    note-taking, 127
    organizational skills, 66
    reading, 144
    test-taking skills, 188
Reorganization, of notes, 128, 130
Repetition, 178
Repetitive strain injuries, 224–226
Reserve, 213
Respect, for instructors, 108–109
Response competition, 176–177
Responsibilities
    information age, 223–226
    motivation, 40–41
Results, test taking and, 187
Return on investment (ROI),
    124–125
Review
    class notes, 111, 117
    noncritical, 20
    note-taking, 128, 130

SQ4R, 147, 148, 154
    storage areas, 75
    test taking, 191, 195
Rewards, memory skills and, 176
Riedling, Ann Marlow, 215, 218, 221
Right-brain thinking, 84–85
Road map, for goals, 46–47
Robinson, Franklin Pleasant, 146
Rotter, Julian B., 51
St. Vincent Catholic Medical Center
    Web site, 76
Sapadin, Linda, 73
Scanning, 149–150
Schedules, reading, 159. *See also*
    Organizational skills; Study
    schedule; Time management
Science textbooks, 152
Scope, 221, 222
Search engines, 216–220
Seating, classroom, 110
Self-monitoring, of motivation, 40
Self-talk and talking with others,
    129–130
Senses, memory skills and, 168–170
Sequential thinking, 84, 85
Shapiro, David, 240
Shapiro, Elaine, 140
Shared experiences, 236–237
Short-term goals, 46–47, 48, 49
Short-term memory, 168
Sight, 168–169
Simplification, 70–71
Situational variation, 177
Skills, 2
Skimming, 149–150
Sleep, 199
SMART (specific, measurable, attain-
    able, realistic, and tangible), 47
Smell, 169–170
Smith, Brenda D., 156
Smith, Douglas K., 235
Smith, Frank, 84
Smith, Mark K., 234
Solutions, 23, 24, 25, 26, 192
Spatial organization, 73–75
    decision making and, 254
    objectives, 80
    study habits and, 257
    summary, 78–79
    test taking and, 189
Spatial organization activity, 7
Specificity. *See* Precision
Spidergram, 113

Spitzer, Kathleen L., 209
SQ3R, 146
SQ4R, 146–154, 174, 176, 191
Stage fright, 177
Staying, in bad situation, 29, 30
Sternberg, Robert, 231
Stevens, Jose, 235
Storage areas, 74
Storming stage of groups, 234, 244
Strengths, assessment of, 3–5,
        251–253
Stress, types of, 76
Stress management, 64, 76–78
Stress-reducing strategies, 77–78
Stress signals, 76–77
Structure, 94
Study areas, 73–75, 94
Study groups
        challenge of, 232–233
        dynamics of, 234–235
        dysfunctions of, 244
        formation of, 235–236, 244
        note-taking, 129, 135
Study guides, 112, 113
Study habits, 257
Studying, 2
        emergency, 200–201
        rewards for, 11
Study partners and groups, 135
Study schedule, 60–66
Study skills, 1, 2
        activities related to, 6–9
        creative thinking and, 28
        critical thinking and, 18, 22, 32–33
        problem solving and, 25–26
        test taking and, 189–191, 192
        See also specific skills
Study strategies, 10–12
Study time, 60
Subheadings, 150, 151
Suggestion, 41
Summary. *See* TSD
Supplemental sources, 155
Surprises, 101–102
Survey, 146–147, 148
Swartz, Roger G., 11, 85
Symbols, in novels, 161
Synergy, 245
Synonyms, 2
Synthesis, 19, 21
Tables, 158, 159
Talking with others, about notes,
        129–130

Tangibility, of goals, 47
Taping, for note-taking, 136
Taste, 169
Teams. *See* Groups
Technology
        information literacy skills and,
                210, 213, 214–223
        note-taking, 135–136
        online classes and note-taking,
                118–119
        storage, 74
Test anxiety, 184, 191–194
Test clues, 196
Test formats, 195
Test preparation, 186–187, 193,
        196–198
Test-taking skills, 183–184
        critical thinking and, 188,
                203–204
        decision making and, 255–256
        inefficient strategies, 194–195
        objectives, 202–203
        postexam analysis, 198
        reflection on, 184–186
        strategies, 199–202
        study habits and, 257
        study skills and, 189–191, 192
        summary, 202
        test anxiety, 191–194
        test clues, 196
        test-preparation checklist,
                196–198
        types of, 186–188
Test-taking skills activity, 8
Test types, 199–200
Textbook graphics, 156–159
Textbook reading assignments,
        145–154
Thinking skills. *See* Critical thinking;
        Higher-order thinking skills;
        Lower-order thinking skills
Thompson, Paul M., 84
Time management, 59–60
        backward planning, 71
        commitments and, 66–68
        decision making and, 254
        objectives, 79
        online classes and, 119
        priorities, 68–70
        procrastination, 71–73
        simplification, 70–71
        study habits and, 257
        study schedule, 60–66

        study time, 60
        summary, 78–79
        test taking and, 184, 187, 189,
                195
Time management activity, 7
Tinto, Vincent, 135
Title. *See* TSD
To-do lists, 67
Toga, Arthur W., 84
Touch, 169
Traditional outlines, 111, 112
Trigger words, 195
Trust, 236–237
TSD (title/summary/details),
        131–133, 191
Tuckman, Bruce W., 234
Tutoring, 195
Underlined terms, 150, 155–156
Understanding, memory skills
        and, 179
U. S. Department of Health and
        Human Services, 132
Unpredictability, 235
VanderStoep, Scott W., 39, 50
Van Doren, Charles, 152
Varian, Hal R., 206
VARK, 86–94
Vision, 23, 24, 25, 26, 192
Visual aids, 86. *See also* Graphics
Visual information, 209–210
Visualization, 173
Visual learning, 86, 89–90, 92, 93
Vocabulary, 155–156
Web addresses, 215–216
Weekly calendar, 67, 68
Whole-brain thinking, 84–85
Wilson, Susan B., 45
WIN (What's Important Now), 54
Winstead, Elizabeth, 63
Words
        action, 84
        difficult, 151–152
        trigger, 195
Workspace, 73–74
Workstation ergonomics, 225, 226
World Wide Web (WWW),
        214–223
Worrier procrastinator, 72
Writing skills, 257. *See also* Read-
        write learning
Written goals, 45
Zadina, Janet N., 107
Zeleznik, Julie, 143